Frommer's®

Norway

4th Edition

W9-AHE-941

by Darwin Porter & Danforth Prince

Here's what the critics say about Frommer's:

"Amazingly easy to use. Very portable, very complete."
—BOOKLIST

"Detailed, accurate, and easy-to-read information for all price ranges."
—GLAMOUR MAGAZINE

"Hotel information is close to encyclopedic."
—DES MOINES SUNDAY REGISTER

"Frommer's Guides have a way of giving you a real feel for a place."
—KNIGHT RIDDER NEWSPAPERS

WILEY
Wiley Publishing, Inc.

Published by:
WILEY PUBLISHING, INC.
111 River St.
Hoboken, NJ 07030-5774

Copyright © 2009 Wiley Publishing, Inc., Hoboken, New Jersey. All rights reserved. No part of this publication may be reproduced, stored in a retrieval system or transmitted in any form or by any means, electronic, mechanical, photocopying, recording, scanning or otherwise, except as permitted under Sections 107 or 108 of the 1976 United States Copyright Act, without either the prior written permission of the Publisher, or authorization through payment of the appropriate per-copy fee to the Copyright Clearance Center, 222 Rosewood Drive, Danvers, MA 01923, 978/750-8400, fax 978/646-8600. Requests to the Publisher for permission should be addressed to the Permissions Department, John Wiley & Sons, Inc., 111 River Street, Hoboken, NJ 07030, 201/748-6011, fax 201/748-6008, or online at http://www.wiley.com/go/permissions.

Wiley and the Wiley Publishing logo are trademarks or registered trademarks of John Wiley & Sons, Inc. and/or its affiliates. Frommer's is a trademark or registered trademark of Arthur Frommer. Used under license. All other trademarks are the property of their respective owners. Wiley Publishing, Inc. is not associated with any product or vendor mentioned in this book.

ISBN 978-0-470-43213-6

Editor: Michael Kelly
Production Editor: Jana M. Stefanciosa
Cartographer: Guy Ruggiero
Photo Editor: Richard Fox
Production by Wiley Indianapolis Composition Services

Front cover photo: Wooden shops lining the fjord in the Bryggen area of Bergen
Back cover photo: Kayaking on the Nærøyfjord, off the small village of Undredal

For information on our other products and services or to obtain technical support, please contact our Customer Care Department within the U.S. at 877/762-2974, outside the U.S. at 317/572-3993 or fax 317/572-4002.

Wiley also publishes its books in a variety of electronic formats. Some content that appears in print may not be available in electronic

5 4 3 2 1

CONTENTS

4 SUGGESTED NORWAY ITINERARIES 77

5 SETTLING INTO OSLO 90

6 EXPLORING OSLO 127

7 SIDE TRIPS FROM OSLO 170

8 LILLEHAMMER & THE PEER GYNT ROAD 188

9 SOUTHERN NORWAY 219

10 STAVANGER 239

11 BERGEN 258

12 THE WEST COAST FJORD COUNTRY 298

13 TRONDHEIM 346

14 TROMSØ 378

15 THE ROUTE TO THE NORTH CAPE 396

APPENDIX A: FAST FACTS, TOLL-FREE NUMBERS & WEBSITES 441

APPENDIX B: USEFUL TERMS & PHRASES 449

INDEX 453

LIST OF MAPS

AN INVITATION TO THE READER

In researching this book, we discovered many wonderful places—hotels, restaurants, shops, and more. We're sure you'll find others. Please tell us about them, so we can share the information with your fellow travelers in upcoming editions. If you were disappointed with a recommendation, we'd love to know that, too. Please write to:

Frommer's Norway, 4th Edition
Wiley Publishing, Inc. • 111 River St. • Hoboken, NJ 07030-5774

AN ADDITIONAL NOTE

Please be advised that travel information is subject to change at any time—and this is especially true of prices. We therefore suggest that you write or call ahead for confirmation when making your travel plans. The authors, editors, and publisher cannot be held responsible for the experiences of readers while traveling. Your safety is important to us, however, so we encourage you to stay alert and be aware of your surroundings. Keep a close eye on cameras, purses, and wallets, all favorite targets of thieves and pickpockets.

ABOUT THE AUTHORS

As a team of veteran travel writers, **Darwin Porter** and **Danforth Prince** have produced titles for Frommer's including guides to Italy, France, the Caribbean, England, and Germany. A film critic, columnist, and broadcaster, Porter is also a Hollywood biographer. His recent releases include *Brando Unzipped,* documenting the private life of Marlon Brando, and *Jacko: His Rise and Fall,* the first complete biography ever written on the tumultuous life of Michael Jackson. Prince was formerly employed by the Paris bureau of *The New York Times* and is today the president of Blood Moon Productions. Porter and Prince's latest non-travel-related venture, jointly co-authored and published in 2008 by Blood Moon, is *Hollywood Babylon—It's Back!,* which one critic described as "the hottest compilation of intergenerational scandal in the history of Hollywood."

Other Great Guides for Your Trip:

Frommer's Denmark
Frommer's Sweden
Frommer's Scandinavia
Frommer's Europe

FROMMER'S STAR RATINGS, ICONS & ABBREVIATIONS

Every hotel, restaurant, and attraction listing in this guide has been ranked for quality, value, service, amenities, and special features using a **star-rating system.** In country, state, and regional guides, we also rate towns and regions to help you narrow down your choices and budget your time accordingly. Hotels and restaurants are rated on a scale of zero (recommended) to three stars (exceptional). Attractions, shopping, nightlife, towns, and regions are rated according to the following scale: zero stars (recommended), one star (highly recommended), two stars (very highly recommended), and three stars (must-see).

In addition to the star-rating system, we also use seven feature icons that point you to the great deals, in-the-know advice, and unique experiences that separate travelers from tourists. Throughout the book, look for:

Finds	Special finds—those places only insiders know about
Fun Facts	Fun facts—details that make travelers more informed and their trips more fun
Kids	Best bets for kids, and advice for the whole family
Moments	Special moments—those experiences that memories are made of
Overrated	Places or experiences not worth your time or money
Tips	Insider tips—great ways to save time and money
Value	Great values—where to get the best deals

The following **abbreviations** are used for credit cards:

AE	American Express	DISC	Discover	V	Visa
DC	Diners Club	MC	MasterCard		

FROMMERS.COM

Now that you have this guidebook to help you plan a great trip, visit our website at **www.frommers.com** for additional travel information on more than 4,000 destinations. We update features regularly to give you instant access to the most current trip-planning information available. At Frommers.com, you'll find scoops on the best airfares, lodging rates, and car rental bargains. You can even book your travel online through our reliable travel booking partners. Other popular features include:

- Online updates to our most popular guidebooks
- Vacation sweepstakes and contest giveaways
- Newsletter highlighting the hottest travel trends
- Podcasts, interactive maps, and up-to-the-minute events listings
- Opinionated blog entries by Arthur Frommer himself
- Online travel message boards with featured travel discussions

What's New in Norway

In an overpopulated world, Norway remains one of the most sparsely inhabited nations. Yet despite its relatively low profile, Norway has entered the post-millennium world with more glitter and polish than ever. Its cities, especially Oslo, are taking on a new look, with daringly avant-garde office buildings and hotels. Foreigners continue to pour in at a rapid rate, waking up the sleepy taste buds of old Norway with spicy fare that relies heavily on Mediterranean foods. And Oslo, Bergen, and other cities no longer shut down at 9 in the evening; young Norway flocks to bars and clubs until the early hours.

Here are some new developments for you to consider while you plan your Norwegian itinerary.

OSLO HOTELS **Thon Hotel Gyldenløve** ("The Golden Lion" in English), Bogstadveien 20 (✆ **23-33-23-03**), has emerged from a dowdy little second-rate hotel into a bright, well-run, and desirable address, lying only 10 minutes from the Royal Palace on a tree-lined street in the West End. Nordic designs and light Scandinavian pastels prevail.

OSLO RESTAURANTS Not only do you get good food at **Ekeberg,** Kongsveien 15 (✆ **23-24-23-00**), but also a panoramic view of the Oslofjord. The view from here is said to have inspired Edvard Munch to create his masterpiece, *The Scream.* A finely honed Norwegian and international cuisine is served here, including such dishes as marinated venison with a juniper berry sorbet.

In the trendy Grünerløkka district, **Südøst,** 5 Trondheimsveien (✆ **23-35-30-70**), has become a casual chic place where young Oslovians like to dine on its fusion Norwegian and international cuisine. In summer, its terrace is one of the most popular in town, great for people-watching. Market-fresh ingredients are used in such dishes as grilled swordfish with risotto.

In the vanguard of Norwegian cuisine, **Madserud Gård,** 34 Madserud Allé (✆ **22-54-54-22**), lies on the western fringe of Oslo. The cuisine is inventive, and the chefs turn out such delights as sautéed scallops with fresh Norwegian caviar on a champagne sabayon.

For more reviews of accommodations and dining options in Oslo, see chapter 5.

LILLEHAMMER In the major ski resort of Norway, locals and visitors are flocking to the **Big Buffalo,** in the Quality Hotel Astoria (✆ **62-70-70-00**), for the tastiest and most tender steaks in this part of the country. Some of the fare is Tex-Mex, including a pepper steak with three kinds of pepper. The interior is decorated with dark woods and scenic photos of Old Mexico.

More details about Lillehammer can be found in chapter 8.

STAVANGER The newly reorganized airline, **SAS Scandinavia Airlines Norge** (formerly known as Braathens), flies to Stavanger from Oslo, Bergen, and Kristiansand S.

The hot new dining choice in Stavanger is **Setra,** Eiganesveien 8 (✆ **51-52-86-26**), serving first-rate Norwegian and international cuisine. The cuisine is also called "New Nordic," using such Mediterranean ingredients as olive oil, foie gras, sun-dried tomatoes, and garlic. Excellent foodstuff is rounded up from the surrounding Rogaland region, and other products are flown in from the North Atlantic, including king crab.

See chapter 10 for more coverage of Stavanger.

BERGEN HOTELS Operated by the management of the Bergen Congress Center, **Scandi Hotel Bergen City,** Hakonsgate 2–7 (✆ **55-30-90-80**), is stylish and inviting, with midsize and well-furnished bedrooms. It's a convenient stopover for those interested in the Bergen cultural scene, as it lies near Den National Theater and Grieghallen.

A reasonably priced choice in high-priced Bergen, **Rica Travel Hotel,** Christiesgate 5–7 (✆ **55-36-29-00**), has emerged, attracting vacationers and business travelers alike. Bedrooms are only standard, yet they are comfortable and well maintained. The hotel is more for those seeking a good bed for the night; it's not a place to hang out, because there are few facilities.

BERGEN RESTAURANTS **Bølgen & Moi,** Rasmus Meyers Allé 9 (✆ **55-59-77-00**), has opened in the Bergen Art Museum, making a great place for lunch. Its food is good and affordable and gets even better if you want to return for a more formal dinner, including such dishes as braised pork belly with an apple marmalade.

Catering to the influx of Swedes who have moved to Bergen in recent years, **Naboen,** Neumannsgate 20 (✆ **55-90-02-90**), serves the cuisine of Norway's neighbor, Sweden. In addition to such Swedish specialties as ping-pong sized meatballs, the chefs here prepare many classic Scandinavian dishes, even some based on recipes from Norway itself.

Another new restaurant to appear on the scene is **Mago,** Neumannsgate 5 (✆ **55-96-29-80**), featuring a Norwegian and Mediterranean cuisine. The chefs successfully blend different flavors and textures to create a fine-tasting array of meat, poultry, and lamb dishes. The best item on the menu is the homemade ice cream, available in many flavors.

For our complete take on Bergen, see chapter 11.

WEST COAST FJORD COUNTRY It's now possible to enjoy the fjord country's most elegant B&B at Norway's only barony, **Baroniet Rosendal** at Rosendal (✆ **53-48-29-99**). The castle, bequeathed to the University of Oslo, is surrounded by a rose garden and some of western Norway's most dramatic scenery. Summer concerts are presented here, and it's also possible to arrange for an elegant lunch, with some of the produce coming from the estate gardens.

South of Åndalsnes, you can visit **Norsk Tindemuseum** (Norwegian Mountain Museum) along Hwy. E139 (✆ **71-22-12-74**). The museum honors Arne Randers Heen (1905–91), one of Norway's most famous mountaineers.

Chapter 12 has more information about this region of Norway.

TRONDHEIM In the center of the city, **Comfort Hotel Park,** Prinsensgate 4A (✆ **73-83-39-00**), stands near Nidaros Cathedral and the river. This well-run, red-brick chain hotel offers sleek, streamlined, and midsize bedrooms. On the top floor, a special feature is a sauna and an outdoor hot tub.

You can find more about Trondheim in chapter 13.

TROMSØ In this city in the far north of Norway, there has been a big shake-up at one of the town's leading hotels, the

Radisson SAS Hotel Tromsø, Sjøgata 7 (© **77-60-00-00**). The hotel was not only expanded to 269 accommodations, but also all existing rooms were massively renovated. Today you can ask for rooms in two distinct styles—"Arctic" or "Chili." The Arctic rooms come in soothing white, orange, and green tones; the Chili units are imbued with hot colors such as Mexican red.

As part of the renovation, the Radisson's upscale restaurant is now the **Aurora.** It's become one of the most preferred places to dine in the area. The chefs specialize in classic dishes of the Arctic, and we're talking reindeer and coldwater fish. Other market-fresh ingredients of the far north of Norway and its chilly waters are also featured.

For more about Tromsø, see chapter 14.

NORTH NORWAY A lot of management changes in hotels occurred in 2008. Expect improvements in some properties during the life of this edition. For example, in Hammerfest, a city in the far north, the Quality chain has moved on, making way for the **Thon Hotel Hammerfest,** Strandgt 2–4 (© **78-42-96-00**), which stands right in the heart of town, at Town Hall Square. The hotel remains the same good choice it always was, but expect some rejuvenation.

We have much more detail about North Norway in chapter 15.

1

The Best of Norway

The "Land of the Midnight Sun" offers a truly unique experience. Norwegians view their scrub-covered islands, snow-crested peaks, and glacier-born fjords as symbols of a wilderness culture. The majestic scenery inspired the symphonies of Grieg, the plays of Ibsen, and the paintings of Munch. The landscape has also shaped the Norwegians' view of themselves as pastoral dwellers in one of the world's most splendid countrysides.

The name *Norway* (in Norwegian, *Norge* or *Noreg*) is derived from *Norvegr,* meaning "the way to the north." The Vikings used the term more than 1,000 years ago to describe the shipping route along the west coast of Norway. Norwegians have been seafarers since the dawn of history, so it seems natural for the country to have a nautical name.

To the ancients, Norway was a mythical land. A journey held unspeakable perils. Writers called the mythical land "Ultima Thule" and feared that strange, barbaric, even fabulous creatures inhabited it. In the 4th century B.C., the Greek writer Pytheas thought the laws of nature did not apply there and said that everything—water and earth included—floated in midair. In what may have been an attempt to describe a snowstorm, Herodotus claimed that in Norway, feathers covered everything and constantly blew into one's face.

Norway is a land of tradition, exemplified by its rustic stave churches and its folk dances. But Norway is also modern. This technologically advanced nation is rich in petroleum and hydroelectric energy. Norwegians also enjoy a well-developed national social insurance system that provides pensions, health insurance, unemployment insurance, and rehabilitation assistance. The system is financed by contributions from the insured, which makes Norway one of the most heavily taxed nations on earth.

One of the last great natural frontiers of the world, Norway invites exploration, with its steep and jagged fjords, salmon-filled rivers, glaciers, mountains, and meadows. In the winter, the shimmering aurora borealis (Northern Lights) are the lure, before giving way to the midnight sun of summer.

So you won't have to exhaust yourself making difficult decisions, we've compiled the best deals and once-in-a-lifetime experiences in this chapter. What follows is the best of the best.

1 THE BEST TRAVEL EXPERIENCES

- **Enjoying Nature:** Norway is one of the last major countries of the world where you can experience a close encounter with nature in one of the last partially unspoiled wildernesses in the world. The country extends 1,770km (1,097 miles) from south to north (approximately the distance from New York to Miami). Norway is riddled with 20,000km (12,400 miles) of fjords, narrows, and straits. It's a land of contrasts, with soaring mountains, panoramic fjords, ice-blue glaciers, deep-green forests, fertile valleys, and rich pastures. The glowing red midnight sun and the Northern Lights have fired the imaginations of artists and craftspeople for centuries (see below).

- **Experiencing "Norway in a Nutshell":** One of Europe's great train rides, this 12-hour excursion is Norway's most exciting. The route encompasses two arms of the Sognefjord, and the section from Myrdal to Flåm—a drop of 600m (1,968 ft.)—takes you past seemingly endless waterfalls. Tours leave from the Bergen train station. If you have limited time but want to see the country's most dramatic scenery, take this spectacular train trip. See section 8, "Flåm: Stopover on Europe's Most Scenic Train Ride," in chapter 12.
- **Visiting the North Cape:** For many, a trip to one of the northernmost inhabited areas of the world will be the journey of a lifetime. Accessible by ship, car, or air, the North Cape fascinates travelers in a way that outweighs its bleakness. Ship tours started in 1879 and, except in wartime, have gone to the Cape ever since. Hammerfest, the world's northernmost town of significant size, is an important port of call for North Cape steamers. See chapter 15.
- **Exploring the Fjord Country:** Stunningly serene and majestic, Norway's fjords are some of the world's most awe-inspiring sights. The fjords are reason enough for a trip to Norway. Bergen can be your gateway; two of the country's most famous fjords, the Hardangerfjord and the Sognefjord, can easily be explored from here. If you have time for only one, our vote goes to the Sognefjord for its sheer, lofty walls rising to more than 1,000m (3,280 ft.) along its towering cliffs. Sheer cliff faces and cascading waterfalls create a kind of fantasy landscape. As Norway's longest fjord, the Sognefjord can be crossed by express steamer to Gudvangen. You can go on your own or take an organized tour, which will probably include the dramatic Folgefonn Glacier. See p. 316.
- **Seeing the Midnight Sun at the Arctic Circle:** This is one of the major reasons visitors go to Norway. The Arctic Circle marks the boundary of the midnight sun of the Arctic summer and the sunless winters of the north. The midnight sun can be seen from the middle of May until the end of July. The Arctic Circle cuts across Norway south of Bodø. Bus excursions from that city visit the circle. The adventurous few who arrive in the winter miss the midnight sun but are treated to a spectacular display of the aurora borealis, the flaming spectacle of the Arctic winter sky. In ancient times, when the aurora could be seen farther south, people thought it was an omen of disaster. See chapter 15.

2 THE BEST SCENIC TOWNS & VILLAGES

- **Fredrikstad:** Founded in 1567 at the mouth of the River Glomma, Fredrikstad preserved its Old Town, which had become a fortress by 1667. Today Fredrikstad (97km/60 miles south of Oslo) offers a glimpse of what a Norwegian town looked like several hundred years ago. The old buildings in the historic district have been converted into studios for craftspeople and artisans, while maintaining their architectural integrity. After a visit here, you can drive along Oldtidsveien (the "highway of the ancients"), the most concentrated collection of archaeological monuments in Norway. See section 1, "Fredrikstad: Norway's Oldest Fortified Town," in chapter 7.
- **Tønsberg:** On the western bank of the Oslofjord is Norway's oldest town. It was founded in 872, a year before King Harald Fairhair united parts of Norway and the Viking town became a royal

coronation site. Its hill fortress is sometimes called "the Acropolis of Norway." Its ancient district, Nordbyen, is filled with well-preserved houses, and the folk museum houses a treasure trove of Viking-era artifacts. See section 3, "Tønsberg: The First Settlement," in chapter 7.

- **Bergen:** The gateway to Norway's fjord country, this town is even more scenic than the capital, Oslo. It was the capital of Norway for 6 centuries and a major outpost of the medieval Hanseatic merchants. The town's biggest tourist event is the Bergen International Music Festival, but there are also many year-round attractions. Many visitors come to explore Bergen's museums (including Edvard Grieg's former home) as well as its varied environs—especially fjords, mountains, and waterfalls. See chapter 11.
- **Trondheim:** Norway's third-largest city traces its history from 997, when the Vikings flourished. Norway's kings are crowned at the ancient Nidaros Cathedral. Scandinavia's largest medieval building, the cathedral was erected over the grave of St. Olaf (also spelled Olav), the Viking king. Trondheim is the popular stopover for travelers from Oslo to destinations north of the Arctic Circle. See chapter 13.
- **Bodø:** Lying 1,305km (809 miles) north of Oslo, this far-northern seaport, the terminus of the Nordland railway, is the gateway to the Arctic Circle, which lies just south of this breezy town. Another excellent place to observe the midnight sun from June 1 to July 13, Bodø is the capital of Nordland. From the center, you can also explore the environs, filled with glaciers and "bird islands." Bodø is also a gateway to the remote Lofoten Islands. See section 2, "Bodø: Gateway to the North," in chapter 15.

3 THE BEST FESTIVALS & SPECIAL EVENTS

For more details on these events, see "Norway Calendar of Events" in chapter 3.

- **Bergen International Festival:** This European cultural highlight, which takes place in late May and early June, ranks in importance with the Edinburgh and Salzburg festivals. Major artists from all over the world descend on the small city to perform music, drama, opera, ballet, folkloric presentations, and more. The works of Bergen native Edvard Grieg dominate the festival, and daily concerts are held at his former home, Troldhaugen. Contemporary plays are also performed, but the major focus is on the works of Ibsen. See p. 41.
- **Molde International Jazz Festival:** In this "City of Roses," Norway's oldest jazz festival is held every summer, usually around mid-July. Some of the best jazz artists in the world wing in for this event. People stay up most of the night listening to music and drinking beer. Sometimes the best concerts are the impromptu jam sessions in smoky little clubs. See "Molde: City of Roses" (p. 340).
- **Holmenkollen Ski Festival:** This large ski festival takes place in March at the Holmenkollen Ski Jump, on the outskirts of Oslo. The agenda is packed with everything from international ski-jumping competitions to Norway's largest cross-country race for amateurs. See p. 41.

4 THE BEST ACTIVE VACATIONS

- **Fishing:** The cold, clear waters of Norway's freshwater streams are renowned for their salmon and trout, and the storm-tossed seas off the coast have traditionally provided enough cod and mackerel to satisfy most of the nation's population. Serious anglers sometimes end up losing themselves in the majesty of the scenery. Tips on fishing in and around the Norwegian fjords are provided by the **Bergen Sportsfiskere (Bergen Angling Association),** Damsgaardveien 106, Bergen (✆ **55-34-18-08**), and the tourist information offices in Oslo and Bergen. Rural hotels throughout the nation can also give pointers on good spots. For a truly unusual fishing experience, **Borton Overseas** (✆ **800/843-0602;** www.bortonoverseas.com) can arrange treks and accommodations in old-fashioned fishermen's cottages in the isolated Lofoten Islands. The rustic-looking, fully renovated cottages are adjacent to the sea. Rentals are for 3 days and include bed linens, maid service, boat rentals, and fishing equipment. For our favorite fishing-hole recommendations, refer to "The Best Fishing," below.
- **Hiking:** The woods *(Marka)* around Oslo boast thousands of kilometers of trails, hundreds of which are lit for nighttime use. If you don't want to leave the city, Frogner Park also has many paths. Any Norwegian regional tourist bureau can advise you about hiking. In Bergen, for example, refer to the **Bergen Touring Club** (p. 291), whose members have spent years hiking through the western fjord country and can advise about the best trails. For our favorite hikes, refer to "The Best Hikes," below.
- **Skiing:** This is the undisputed top winter sport in Norway, attracting top-notch skiers and neophytes from around the world. Norway is a pioneer in promoting skiing as a sport for persons with disabilities. Modern facilities, comparable to those in Europe's alpine regions, dot the landscape. If you're a serious skier, consider the best winter resorts, in Voss, Geilo, and Lillehammer (site of the 1994 Winter Olympics). See section 2, "Lillehammer of Olympic Glory," in chapter 8; section 6, "Voss: A Winter Playground," in chapter 12; and section 9, "Geilo: A Winter Wonderland," in chapter 12. For our choices for the best downhill skiing and the best cross-country skiing, see section 6, below.
- **Mountain Climbing:** Local tourist offices can offer advice. What we like best are guided hikes to the archaeological digs of the 8,000-year-old Stone Age settlements near the Hardangerjøkulen (Hardanger Glacier). The digs are about an hour's drive north of the mountain resort of Geilo. For information, contact the **Geilo Tourist Office** (✆ **32-09-59-00;** www.geilo.no). See section 9, "Geilo: A Winter Wonderland," in chapter 12.

5 THE BEST HIKES

- **Besseggen Ridge:** In the Jotunheimen Nasjonal Park, Norway's greatest park, you'll find a landscape of glaciers, mountains, lakes, and waterfalls, crowned by two towering peaks: Glittertind, at 2,452m (8,043 ft.), and Galdhøpiggen, at 2,469m (8,098 ft.), the highest peak in northern Europe.

This park also boasts the country's most justifiably popular hike across Besseggen Ridge, towering over one of the country's most beautiful lakes, Gjende, which earned the praise of Henrik Ibsen, among others. The trail along the ridge links the remote mountain lodges of Memurubo and Gjendesheim. See p. 209.

- **Preikestolen:** Outside the city of Stavanger, on the western coast of Norway, you can take one of the most memorable hikes in this part of the world, through scenic fjord country with mountain landscapes as a backdrop. The ultimate goal is Pulpit Rock (its English name), with a vertical drop of 609m (1,998 ft.) over the stunningly blue Lysefjord. You can drive to a rock car park to begin a hike of 4km (2$^1/_2$ miles). The hike has a height difference of 350m (1,148 ft.); it begins steeply, climbing past rocky, even boggy sections before the final ascent. The cliffs are exposed and extremely windy, but all this is part of the Norwegian experience. Despite an alarming crack in the rock, making it look as if you're about to plunge to your death in the fjord below, geologists claim it will take thousands of years for the rock to break apart. Once on the rock, looking down at the 42km (26-mile) fjord, you'll perhaps understand why poets have praised its "ethereal light." See p. 256.
- **Lofoten Fishing Villages:** The best hikes in Norway don't always have to be up steep mountains. In the remote Lofotens in the north of Norway, while based on the glaciated island of **Moskenesøy,** we like to hike along a seascape of little fishing villages stacked up one after the other like a string of pearls. The mountain peak of Hermannsdalstind, rising to 1,029m (3,375 ft.), offers a scenic backdrop. Begin in the north, at the little fishing village of Hamnøy, and then hike southward to other quaint settlements at Sakrisøy, Reine, Moskenes, Sørvägen, and the curiously named Å. To extend the hike at Sørvägen for another 2 hours, you can hike inland along a signposted rambler's trail to get acquainted with the interior of a Lofoten island. See section 4, "The Lofoten Islands: The Soul of Norway," in chapter 15.

6 THE BEST DOWNHILL SKIING

- **Lillehammer:** It may not be Switzerland, but Norway has its own alpine skiing, a lot of it centered at Lillehammer. The skiing at Lillehammer, Norway's oldest ski resort, is so superb that the 1994 Olympic committee chose the resort as the site of its winter games. **Hafjell Alpine Center** lies 9.3km (5$^3/_4$ miles) north of the center and was the main venue for the Olympic alpine competitions, offering seven lifts and 20km (12 miles) of alpine slopes. The longest slope at Hafjell is 7km (4$^1/_4$ miles) long, and there's a wide range of alpine slopes for different levels of skiing proficiency. The Lillehammer mountains lie 850m (2,788 ft.) above sea level. See section 2, "Lillehammer of Olympic Glory," in chapter 8.
- **Geilo:** Superior to Voss but not an Olympic ski spectacle like Lillehammer, Geilo features five different ski centers. The best is the Geilo Skiheiser, with 24km (15 miles) of slopes, many as exciting as those in Gstaad, Switzerland. The area is also equipped with 18 lifts and a "ski-board" tunnel. Cable cars will take you to the top of the resort at 1,060m (3,477 ft.) above sea level. From that point, marked trails

split off in many directions. See section 9, "Geilo: A Winter Wonderland," in chapter 12.

- **Voss:** This winter resort is a virtual ski circus with eight chairlifts and an aerial cableway carrying passengers up to a peak of 788m (2,625 ft.). In all, there are 40km (25 miles) of alpine slopes that have been compared favorably to those in western Austria. One ski lift climbs 900m (2,952 ft.) from Traastolen to the top of the mountain of Slettafjell, with a wide and varied choice of downhill runs. See section 6, "Voss: A Winter Playground," in chapter 12.

7 THE BEST CROSS-COUNTRY SKIING

- **Lillehammer:** The Olympic resort in central Norway boasts 402km (249 miles) of prepared cross-country tracks, 6km (3$^{3}/_{4}$ miles) of which are illuminated. From mid-December, cross-country skiers arrive from all over Europe, and sometimes America, to test out the well-groomed trails. The landscape is even more beautiful than that found in Geilo (see below), though it may be gauche to some to compare one scenic landscape with another. However, Lillehammer is set in an area of Norway that contains its highest mountains and its best-known national parks, making it a cross-country-skiing paradise as you glide across the dramatic Hardanggervidda Plateau. See section 2, "Lillehammer of Olympic Glory," in chapter 8.
- **Peer Gynt Ski Area:** Consistently, Norwegian skiers rate this beautiful countryside as one of the best venues for cross-country skiing. Because it's a part of the same region, the landscape encountered cross-country is virtually the same as for Lillehammer. This vast ski region in central Norway is most suitable for those skiers who'd like to combine cross-country skiing with alpinelike slopes. For cross-country skiers, there are 460km (285 miles) of well-prepared trails; in winter, floodlit trails in Espedalen and in Gålå make it possible to go cross-country skiing at night. A ski bus links all the main resorts, such as Espedalen, Fefor, and Gålå. See p. 204.
- **Geilo:** For more than a century, Geilo, in a central location in southern Norway, has excelled as a ski resort. At 800m (2,624 ft.) above sea level, it lies halfway between Bergen and Oslo, and is even more dramatically situated than Voss, its major competitor. The Hallingskarvet Mountain—frosted with several small glaciers—is its "backbone," and it stands on the largest mountain plateau. Cross-country skiers will find a total of 220km (136 miles) of well-groomed and well-marked trails through forests, hills, and moors. You'll traverse the Hardangervidda National Park, which is 3,430 sq. km (1,334 sq. miles) in area. This is some of the most beautiful and protected tundra in Norway and home of Norway's largest herds of wild reindeer, called caribou. See section 9, "Geilo: A Winter Wonderland," in chapter 12.

8 THE BEST FISHING

- **Alta:** In the north of Norway, 1,989km (1,233 miles) north of Oslo, this frontier outpost is known for having the best salmon-fishing waters in the world. Hook up with **AKU,** Storengveien 26 (✆ **78-43-48-40;** www.aku-finnmark.no), which leads salmon-fishing trips. It also offers deep-sea fishing and can arrange outings for fishing below glaciers, along with boat rentals and fishing tackle. See section 5, "Alta: City of Northern Lights," in chapter 15.

- **Suldalslågen:** Lying to the north of the western port city of Stavanger, this is the longest salmon river in the west. No license is required if you're angling for saltwater fish. Founded more than a century ago, **Lindum** (✆ **52-79-91-61;** www.lakseslottet.no) is the best fishing lodge in Norway. The salmon season here lasts from July to September. See p. 249.
- **Fjord Fishing:** Bergen and its environs lay claim to the best fjord fishing in the west. The area is known for its catches of haddock, coalfish, cod, and mackerel. You can fish in the sea without a permit, though fishing in freshwater streams and ponds requires a permit arranged through the **Bergen Angling Association** (p. 291).

9 THE MOST SCENIC BOAT TRIPS

- **Sognefjord:** If you take only one fjord trip in your life, make it that panoramic marvel known as Sognefjord in western Norway. Excursions leave from the harbor at Bergen (p. 297). As you sail along, it's like a fantasy look at Norway, with the deep blue fjord waters broken by many waterfalls. Sognefjord is the longest fjord in Norway, stretching for a distance of 205km (127 miles), until it reaches the mountains of the Jotunheimen National Park. But most fjord excursions end long before that happens. Along the banks of this fjord—best explored in the late spring and summer—are farms, 19th-century villages, and lush landscapes. In springtime plum, pear, apple, and cherry trees grow in profusion.
- **Oslofjord:** A web of cays, skerries, sandbars, and towering rocky banks parades before you when you take one of the Båtservice sightseeing boats that make summer trips from Oslo along this historic old fjord, the former stamping grounds of the Vikings. You'll sail aboard one of a trio of sloops with 19th-century rigging, one dating from 1892. Included in the cost are large buckets of Norwegian shrimp served buffet style. See p. 154.
- **Telemark Canal:** Norway's answer to the Panama Canal, the 1892 Telemark Canal carrics boats from its gateway, the southern city of Skien. As you sail along, you'll penetrate deep into the panoramic countryside of Norway, with its lakes, rivers, and dark forests that you just know are inhabited by trolls. You can also see some of the marvelous feats of engineering that made such a boat ride possible. See p. 228.
- **Coastal Steamer to the North Cape:** One of the sea voyages of a lifetime, the route along the west coast of Norway from Bergen to the remote northern frontier town of Kirkenes is plied by elegantly comfortable coastal steamers. Passengers and cargo are carried to 34 ports. Along the way, ships sail through some of the lesser known but most beautiful fjords in the country. Passengers are allowed to make excursions into the mountains and across glacier country. The highlight of the sea voyage—with the most evocative scenery—is a visit to Nordkapp (North Cape), at the top of Europe. See p. 396 and 436.

10 THE MOST UNFORGETTABLE LANDSCAPES/DRIVES

- **Overland Route Oslo/Bergen:** The mountainous drive from Oslo to Bergen is one of the grand scenic trips of Europe. You'll go through mountain passes and even make a ferry crossing here and there. Along the way, you'll pass fjords and snowcapped mountains, along with waterfalls, fjord villages, and even an ancient stave church. The most memorable stopover is at the town of Flåm, which lies on the Aurlandsfjord, a tip of the Sognefjord, the most scenic fjord in Norway (p. 297). If time allows, we recommend that you allow at least 2 days for this memorable motor tour. Faced with a choice of the northern or southern route, we prefer the southern. See section 8, "Flåm: Stopover on Europe's Most Scenic Train Ride," in chapter 12, for specific directions.
- **Electric Train from Myrdal to Flåm:** In our view, there is no more scenic train ride in Europe—even in Switzerland—than from Myrdal to the village of Flåm. There's no railway line of this adhesion type anywhere in the world steeper than this railway; the train and track were designed so that they would lock into each other with greater adhesion than smooth tracks. The trip is 19km (12 miles) long and takes 50 minutes. During that time you'll travel 883m (2,896 ft.) up a steep mountain gorge and down again. Picture 20 tunnels and spectacular waterfalls in what we rate as the most beautiful and lushest mountain scenery in Norway. See p. 317.
- **The Route to the North Cape:** If you're up for it—and we know our readers are hardy people—you can leave Bergen and drive to the Arctic Circle in a relatively relaxed 3 days. To push on, you can even drive from Bergen to the North Cape in 5 days. Locals call the northern route the Arctic Highway. The road, which is well maintained, allows you to experience the majestic beauty of the far north of Norway as you move toward polar-bear country. Those who've driven in the far north of Alaska will roughly know what to expect. Fertile fields in the south in the fjord country give way to lakes and dark forests. In summer, you'll be driving into the land of the midnight sun. The Arctic Highway is faster, but the Kystriksveien Coast Route allows the most dramatic views of the landscape and seascape. As for what to see and where to stop over along the route, see chapter 15 for suggestions.
- **Hardangerfjord:** For the best motoring along a fjord, we suggest the Hardangerfjord, centered in the town of Loftus, former retreat of composer Edvard Grieg and other well-known artists. You can take in the scenery of this fjord by either a boat ride or a motor trip along its shores. The fjord stretches a total distance of 179km (111 miles), and there are panoramic waterfalls on each of its banks. Along the way, you can take in views of the Folgefonna, Norway's third-largest glacier, stretching for 37km (23 miles). See p. 302.

11 THE BEST WILDLIFE VIEWING

- **Dovrefjell National Park:** In central Norway, Dovrefjell (p. 211) is one of Norway's great national parks. You can see reindeer in the park, and it's also a habitat for the wolverine and the arctic fox, but don't count on seeing these elusive creatures. Many visitors come here just for a glimpse of the musk ox. While this unusual species almost vanished during World War II, careful breeding has brought it back in very limited herds. To see the rare animal, which may not make it through the century, you need to go on one of the safaris conducted by **Moskus Safari Dovrefjell.** See p. 213.

- **Rondane Nasjonalpark:** Entered through the little town of Jeska, this national park was the first ever to open in Norway, having been created in 1962. Peppered with little lakes and rivers, the park is famous throughout Norway for being inhabited by more than two dozen types of animals, including reindeer. Rondane is also home to some 125 different species of birds, making it a regular birder's Valhalla. See p. 212.
- **The Puffins of Vaerøy:** In the remote Lofoten Islands in the north of Norway is one of Europe's great bird-watching retreats. The thinly populated island is the nesting place for more than 1.5 million seabirds, including sea eagles, auks, guillemots, kittiwakes, cormorants, the arctic tern, petrels, gulls, and other species, which breed from May to August. Many birders come here just to see the famous puffins at the seabird rookeries. See p. 426.

12 THE BEST HOTELS

- **Grand Hotel** (Oslo; ✆ **800/223-5652** in the U.S., or 23-21-20-00; www.grand.no): This is Norway's premier hotel, the last of Oslo's classic old-world palaces. It opened in 1874 and is still going strong. Ibsen and Munch were regular visitors. Constant renovations keep the hotel up-to-date and in great shape. The opulent suites house the Nobel Peace Prize winner every year. See p. 100.
- **Hotel Bristol** (Oslo; ✆ **22-82-60-00;** www.bristol.no): Inspired by Edwardian-era British taste, the interior design is the most lavish and ornate in Oslo. You'll enter a world of rich paneling, leather chairs, glittering chandeliers, and carved pillars. The most inviting area is the bar off the lobby, decorated in a library motif. The guest rooms boast painted classic furnishings and rich fabrics. See p. 104.
- **Skagen Brygge Hotell** (Stavanger; ✆ **51-85-00-00;** www.skagenbryggehotell.no): Southwestern Norway's most architecturally impressive hotel at the harborfront duplicates the look of a string of antique warehouses that used to stand here. Some of the preferred bedrooms are in the original 19th-century core. Accommodations in the newer section contain large windows and more modern furnishings. See p. 242.
- **Radisson SAS Hotel Norge** (Bergen; ✆ **800/333-3333** in the U.S., or 55-57-30-00; www.radissonsas.com): This grand hotel on Norway's west coast is sleek, modern, and cosmopolitan. The center of Bergen's major social events, the hotel is both traditional and handsomely up-to-date. It's also equipped with all the amenities guests expect in a deluxe hotel, and highly professional service. See p. 266.
- **Solstrand Hotel & Bad** (Os, outside Bergen; ✆ **56-57-11-00;** www.solstrand.com): This is the finest hotel in the fjord district around the city of Bergen. Dating back to 1896, the hotel evokes the nostalgia of the Belle Epoque era, and you'll be coddled in comfort in cheerfully decorated bedrooms. Come here for a vacation retreat instead of an overnight stopover. See p. 271.

- **Dr. Holms Hotel** (Geilo; ✆ **32-09-57-00;** www.drholms.com): One of Norway's most famous resort hotels, this establishment was opened by Dr. Holms in 1909. It still stands for elegance, comfort, and tradition, all of which are especially evident during the winter ski season. The hotel offers beautifully furnished rooms with classic styling and two new wings with a swimming complex. Famed musical artists often perform here. See p. 321.
- **Clarion Collection Hotel Grand Olav** (Trondheim; ✆ **73-80-80-80;** www.choicehotels.no): This is the most stylish hotel in Norway's medieval capital, a tasteful enclave of comfort and good living. Located next to the city's concert house, the property is modern, filled with amenities, and imaginatively decorated. See p. 352.
- **Rica Ishavshotel** (Tromsø; ✆ **77-66-64-00;** www.rica.no): Although chain-owned and operated, this is the best hotel in the chilly north of Norway. From its dramatic perch, the hotel provides views in all directions. Looking like a space-age yacht, it nicely houses guests near the pier where the coastal steamers stop. See p. 381.

13 THE MOST CHARMING INNS & RESORTS

- **Dalen Hotel** (Dalen I Telemark; ✆ **35-07-70-00;** www.dalenhotel.no): At the terminus of the Telemark Canal, the Dalen Hotel's architecture is studded with dragon heads and Viking-inspired gingerbread. Built in 1894 and still going strong, it has kept abreast of the times. It's the kind of nostalgic and evocative Norway that we like, filled with comforting but also whimsical architecture—including towers, turrets, and wide verandas. You'll be wined and dined royally here—after all, the King of Siam once was a guest. See p. 228.
- **Hotel Ullensvang** (Loftus i Harganger; ✆**53 67 00 00;** www.hotel-ullensvang.no): Our favorite inn within the fjord country, the Ullensvang, from 1846, lies on the bank of the Hardangerfjord. Once it was the retreat of the composer Edvard Grieg, whose piano is still in a cottage on the grounds. Expanded over the years, the hotel has been run by the same family for four generations. These family members extend a hearty Norwegian welcome to their guests, whom they feed and house most comfortably. See p. 303.
- **Fretheim Hotel** (Flåm; ✆ **57-63-63-00;** www.fretheim-hotel.no): Set in the midst of an impressive scene of mountains and waterfalls, this 1866 hotel opens onto a panoramic vista of fjord waters. Long renowned for its hospitality and now equipped with a modern annex, it houses you comfortably in attractive and well-maintained bedrooms. Salmon is the chef's specialty in the hotel's first-class restaurant. See p. 318.
- **Union Hotel** (Geiranger; ✆ **70-26-83-00;** www.union-hotel.no): Located at one of the most majestic fjords in Norway, the Geirangerfjord, this is a celebrated 1891 family-style hotel. Kings, queens, and kaisers have found lodgings here in the beautifully furnished bedrooms, many with private balconies opening onto the water. The hotel's restaurant is one of the best and most traditional in the area, featuring a classic Norwegian buffet of the groaning-table variety. See p. 333.
- **Hotel Mundal** (Fjaerland; ✆ **57-69-31-01**): On the banks of the Fjaerlandsfjord, a scenic branch of the greater Sognefjord, this hotel has been run by

the same family since it opened its doors back in 1891. With its peaked roofs, wooden scrollwork, round tower, and cavernous dining room, it is one of Norway's most classic hotel examples of Victorian architecture. Modern improvements have ensured that it's still a wonderful choice to base yourself in one of the most scenic parts of the western fjord country. See p. 325.

14 THE BEST RESTAURANTS

- **Bagatelle** (Oslo; ✆ **22-44-63-97**): Owner-chef Eyvind Hellstrøm has made a grand cuisine a great cuisine with his expertise in market-fresh ingredients. He still focuses on seafood, insisting on the best and freshest catch of the day. Anticipate a light, modern French and Continental cuisine, served with flair. See p. 120.
- **Oro** (Oslo; ✆ **23-01-02-40**): A hyper-stylish restaurant, Oro is as good as it gets in Norway's capital, ranking right up there with anything else Norway has to offer. The Continental cuisine at this first-class dining citadel evokes the best of Paris's restaurants. See p. 111.
- **Statholderens Krostue** (Oslo; ✆ **22-41-88-00**): Gourmets from all over Norway have flocked here to sample Chef Bent Stiansen's interpretation of modern Norwegian cooking. Stiansen is almost fanatically tuned to what's best in any season, and he serves some of the capital's finest dishes. He uses great imagination and widely varied ingredients—everything from arctic char to a rare vanilla bean imported from Thailand. See p. 118.
- **Restaurant Julius Fritzner** (Oslo; ✆ **23-21-20-00**): One of the most impressive dining establishments to make its debut in Norway in the mid-1990s, this restaurant in the Grand Hotel is still getting rave reviews. The chef uses only the finest Scandinavian ingredients in contemporary and traditional dishes; the emphasis is on enhancing and balancing flavors rather than creating surprises. See p. 111.
- **Bilbao** (Stavanger; ✆ **51-53-33-00**): A fine international and Spanish cuisine lures the oil barons of this rich city to this converted 1860 building. A product of a Norwegian and Basque partnership, the downstairs is an informal bodega, like a tavern in the Pyrenees, and upstairs is the more formal dining venue, featuring a cuisine that is both upscale and savory. See p. 245.
- **Finnegaardstuene** (Bergen; ✆ **55-55-03-00**): In a converted Hanseatic League warehouse, this Norwegian-French restaurant is one of the finest in western Norway. The cuisine revolves around only the freshest ingredients, especially fish. The kitchen uses classical French preparation methods to create such delectable items as lime-marinated turbot in caviar sauce or breast of duck in lime-and-fig sauce. See p. 272.
- **Lucullus** (Bergen; ✆ **55-30-68-00**): Quiet luxury and refinement mark this deluxe gourmet choice, serving an artful Continental cuisine in the Neptun Hotel. Dishes are prepared with such top-quality ingredients and with such flair that we wouldn't dream of criticizing them. Savor the latest offerings, including the namesake filet of beef Lucullus, our favorite. See p. 271.
- **Emma's Drømmekjøkken** (Tromsø; ✆ **77-63-77-30**): Anne Brit, called "Emma," operates this dream kitchen and is the best-known culinary personality in the north of Norway. Although she uses mainly ingredients from the north, often fish from Arctic waters, she wanders the globe for her flavors, which might include everything from chili to wasabi. See p. 384.

15 THE BEST MUSEUMS

- **Viking Ship Museum** (Oslo): Three stunning burial vessels from the Viking era were excavated on the shores of the Oslofjord and are now displayed in Bygdøy, Oslo's "museum island." The most spectacular is the *Oseberg*, from the 9th century, a 20m (66-ft.) dragon ship with a wealth of ornaments. See p. 134.
- **Edvard Munch Museum** (Oslo): Here you'll find the most significant collection of the work of Edvard Munch (1863–1944), Scandinavia's most noted artist. The museum, his gift to the city, contains a staggering treasure trove: 1,100 paintings, 4,500 drawings, and about 18,000 prints. See p. 130.
- **Norwegian Folk Museum** (Oslo): Some 140 original buildings from all over Norway were shipped here and reassembled on 14 hectares (35 acres) at Bygdøy. Although Scandinavia is known for such open-air museums, this one is the best. The buildings range from a rare stave church, constructed around 1200, to one of the oldest wooden buildings still standing in Norway. Old-time Norwegian life is captured here like nowhere else. See p. 132.
- **Vigelandsparken** (Oslo): This stunning park in western Oslo displays the lifetime work of Gustav Vigeland, the country's greatest sculptor. In 30-hectare (74-acre) Frogner Park, you can see more than 200 sculptures in granite, bronze, and iron, including *Angry Boy*, his most celebrated work. See p. 133.
- **Det Hanseatiske Museum** (Bergen): Depicting commercial life on the wharf in the early 18th century, this museum is housed in one of the city's best-preserved wooden buildings. German Hanseatic merchants lived in similar medieval houses near the harbor. See p. 281.

16 THE BEST BUYS

Most of the products mentioned below are available at better shops in Oslo and Bergen; see "Shopping" in chapters 6 and 11.

- **Ceramics:** In the 1960s and 1970s, Norway earned a reputation among potters and stoneware enthusiasts for its chunky, utilitarian pottery. The trend today is to emulate the fragile, more decorative designs popular in France, England, and Germany, so Norwegian ceramists are producing thinner, more delicate, and more ornate forms. The best selection is found at **Tibords Interiør Bergen Storsenter** (© **55-55-33-41**) in Bergen. See p. 292.
- **Costumes:** Norway boasts more than 450 regional costumes, especially in the coastal communities. The original fishermen's sweater was knit of naturally colored wool (beige, brown, black, or off-white) in a deliberately large size and then washed in hot water so that it shrank. The tightly woven sweater could then resist water. Modern versions of these sweaters are known for their nubby texture, sophisticated patterns, and varying shades of single colors. The best purveyor of Norwegian costumes and folk dress from both north and south is **Heimen Husflid** in Oslo (© **23-21-42-00**). See p. 159.
- **Crystal:** In Norway you can buy flawless crystal that's as clear as a Nordic iceberg. Norwegian tastes lean toward the clean, uncluttered look, stressing line, form, and harmony. Crystal is sold

at many stores, especially in Bergen and Oslo, but we've consistently been impressed with the selection on display at the prestigious **Norway Designs** (✆ **23-11-45-10**) in Oslo. See p. 157.

- **Knitwear:** Many visitors eagerly seek Norwegian knitwear. Among the best buys are hand-knit or "half-handmade" garments. The latter, knit on electric looms, are so personalized and made in such small quantities that only an expert can tell that they aren't completely handmade. The tradition of women hand-knitting sweaters while rocking a cradle or tending a fire thrives in rural Norway, especially during the long winter. Beautifully made Norwegian knitwear is on sale at **Norway Designs** (✆ **23-11-45-10**; p. 157) in Oslo, and there's an especially large selection at the **Oslo Sweater Shop** (✆ **22-42-42-25**; p. 161), also in Oslo.

17 THE BEST WEBSITES

- **Norwegian Tourist Board, www.visitnorway.com**: This is the official travel guide to Norway, welcoming you to this far-northern outpost with lots of tips on attractions and special interests, accommodations, dining, and entertainment, along with maps and notes on the weather.
- **Norway.com, www.norway.com**: This is a good website for Norway, covering all the major cities, not just Oslo and Bergen, but Ålesund, Tønsberg, Hamar, Kristiansand S, and Lillehammer, among others. Travel-planning data is highlighted, as are the best travel deals.
- **Explore Fjord Norway, www.fjordnorway.com**: This site focuses on one of Scandinavia's most visited attractions, the fjord country of western Norway. It provides information on fjord trips and cruises, with details for the active vacationer on climbing, walking, and cycling, plus information about fjord culture.
- **Cruise Norway, www.cruisenorway.com**: This site previews the best itineraries for those who'd like to cruise the fjords of Norway or take various Scandinavian cruises in general. Independent vacation packages are highlighted.
- **Skiing Norway and Lillehammer, www.lillehammer.com**: This site is loaded with details about Norway's oldest sports resort and a venue for the 1994 Winter Olympics. The skiing terrain is previewed, along with tips on activities, accommodations, and attractions.
- **Official Site Oslo Tourist Office, www.visitoslo.com**: This site promises "everything else you need to know about Oslo." That is a bit of an exaggeration, but the site explores the city in detail, with tips on attractions, restaurants, activities, accommodations, and shopping.
- **Official Internet Site for Trondheim, www.trondheim.com/engelsk**: The first capital of Norway—today a modern university city—is explored in this databank, with pictures, useful information, a city map, and details about accommodations and attractions.
- **Bergen Guide, www.bergen-guide.com**: Norway's second city is explored in some detail on this site, with a comprehensive database on maps, restaurants, shops, sports, sightseeing, transportation, accommodations, and other useful information.
- **Visit Flåm, www.visitflam.com**: This site offers information about charming Flåm in the heart of the Sognefjord district. It's a major stop on the Flåm

Railway, the world's most spectacular and panoramic line.

- **European Travel & Tourism Bureau, www.alltravelnorway.com/Norway/Destination_Guides/cities/Stavanger.htm**: This site explores Norway's oil capital of Stavanger, with tips on accommodations, attractions, bars, cafes, sights, and restaurants.
- **European Travel & Tourism Bureau, www.alltravelnorway.com/Norway/Destination_Guides/cities/Tromso.htm**: Like the site on Stavanger (see above), this site takes you to Norway's small but spirited capital of the far north: the city of Tromsø.

2

Norway in Depth

Imagine a headless sea horse hanging over Denmark, with an elongated tail curving northward along the Swedish border—beyond the Arctic Circle—the tip of its tail brushing against Russian Lapland. This is the shape of Norway, a land that features porcupine ridges of mountain, broken in spots by unladylike fingers—fjords—that gouge into the rocky surfaces of the earth.

Norway is a land of waterfalls and rapids, majestic mountains and glaciers, green islands, crystal lakes, pine and spruce forests, steep-sloped farmsteads, secluded valleys, craggy cliffs, peaceful fjords, and fishing villages.

In the north the coastline is dotted with brightly painted houses, their sparkling colors contrasting with the somber grandeur of fjords and mountains. The northern slice of Norway—Finnmark, or Lapland—is low and hilly, bleak and forlorn, peopled in part by nomadic Sami with reindeer herds.

Norway is an ancient land of myth and legend, mountains, and nature. It also has a strong folklore tradition. As children, Norwegians grow up on stories of huldres (see "A Long-Tailed Seducer," below) and trolls. Trolls—who can be both good and evil and who come in all shapes and sizes—have become part of the folklore of the country. And in their secret hearts, many Norwegians still believe in them.

Trolls have very long noses—but often only one eye per family. To compensate for this lack of vision, some trolls possess as many as 12 heads. In case a Norwegian farmer should chop off one of the troll's heads, three more will grow back in its place. Mrs. Troll has a bigger nose than her husband. She uses it for everything from stirring porridge to whipping the children. Trolls never come out in sunlight. If they should happen to make a sudden appearance during the day, they burst and are petrified as mountains. That's why Norway has so many mountains—or so the legend goes.

But not only mountains. Norway also has fjords and waterfalls unlike any found elsewhere in Europe.

Go to Norway for an experience not only with folklore but also with the great outdoors. Spain and Italy overflow with legendary, treasure-filled cities. Norway has nothing to equal them. England has preserved the crooked old architecture from the days of Samuel Johnson. Norway's wooden villages have burned to the ground, for the most part. Many of Norway's towns along the coast—such as Bodø—were destroyed during World War II. But in sheer scenic beauty, Norway is about the greatest thing this side of Valhalla.

Norway is a blend of the ancient and the modern. How curious but how common it is to see a Sami grandmother—attired in a brightly colored braided costume, bonnet, and deer-hide moccasins with turned-up toes—waiting to board an airplane at the Tromsø airport.

Search long and hard enough, and you might turn up a sod-roofed house, where old Grandfather Per—wearing high trousers—sits in a tub-chair in the corner downing his curds-and-whey. On the other hand, his grandson, clad in swimming trunks, will probably be sunning himself on a rock, listening to American music.

Fun Facts A Long-Tailed Seducer

At a cafe in Oslo, the wife of our host picked up a fork, leaned over the table, and tapped her husband on the knuckles, "Keep your eyes off the huldre, darling."

The "huldre" was a tall blonde in pants at least three sizes too small.

In Norwegian folklore, a huldre is supposed to be a most beautiful woman—but she has a cow's tail tucked under her skirt, perhaps tied around her waist. And this bovine appendage is always dropping out at the most inopportune times. For her tail to drop off completely, she has to marry a man in a church.

The huldre makes a clever housewife and is resented—for that and other reasons—by Norwegian women. The Anna, Noram, or Birgit who wants to hang on to her husband is not averse to warning him against accepting an invitation to go home with a huldre for the night. The huldre has the power of stretching that night out for 7 years. At least, that's what many an errant Olav has claimed when he finally stumbles back to his older spouse.

(Frankly, the tall blonde singled out probably wasn't a real huldre. It was impossible for her to conceal a caudal appendage under those pants. But that didn't matter. The wife knew her to be a huldre—and that was that.)

1 NORWAY TODAY

This long, narrow country stretches some 1,770km (1,097 miles) north to south, but rarely more than 96km (60 miles) east to west. Norway is a land of raw nature. It occupies the western and extreme northern portion of the Scandinavia peninsula, bordering Finland, Sweden, and Russia. In the west, its 21,342km (13,232 miles) of coastline confront the often-turbulent North Atlantic Ocean. For more details about the Norwegian coastline, see the box "Norway Just Grows & Grows," below.

There's plenty of breathing room for everybody. When you factor in the Arctic desolation of the north, Norway averages about 20 people per square mile. Most of the four million inhabitants are concentrated in the swag-bellied south, where the weather is less severe. Even so, the population of Oslo, the capital, is less than half a million. Aside from Oslo, there are no really big cities; the populations of Bergen and Trondheim are 210,000 and 135,000, respectively.

Norway does not want to be a melting pot, and immigration is strictly controlled. The largest minority group is the Sami, who live in the far north; they have broad powers of self-government, including their own parliament. Although many people have emigrated from Norway—about one million to America alone—immigration to Norway from other countries has been limited. About 3.2% of the population originally came from Great Britain, Denmark, and Sweden.

Norway is a constitutional monarchy. Though without political power, Norway's royal family enjoys the subjects' unwavering support. The real power is in the Storting, or parliament. Women play a major role in government. Some 40% of all elected officials are women, and women head several government ministries. Many

Fun Facts Norway Just Grows & Grows

Without conquering other nations, it's almost impossible for a country to expand its coastline by 25,600km (15,872 miles), but Norway has done just that without invading its neighbors, as the Vikings did in days of yore. Today the conqueror is a computer.

Norwegian mapmakers in 2002 announced that new computer programs are able to measure thousands of tiny inlets and islands in Norway, something that was virtually impossible 3 decades ago. The old figures gave Norway a coastline of 56,928km (35,295 miles), of which 21,342km (13,232 miles) were on the mainland, 35,586km (22,063 miles) around islands. The new figures suggest that Norway is actually 3,968km (2,460 miles) longer than previously believed and that the distance around islands is 21,872km (13,561 miles) greater.

"We are still the same," Tore Hegheim, a resident of Tromsø, said over the state radio network, NRK, "only our country got much bigger."

industries—especially energy—are fully or partially state controlled. Oil from the North Sea is a vital resource; the government has a Ministry of Oil and Energy. The government grants large subsidies to agriculture and fisheries.

As a result of their natural surroundings, Norwegians are among the most athletic people in Europe. Nearly every Norwegian child learns to ski as readily as he learns to walk. They are also among the best-educated people in the world. Norway's educational standard has risen considerably since World War II, and some 90% of Norwegian young people take a 3-year course in academic or vocational school after completing their compulsory education.

About 90% of the population belongs to the national Lutheran church, of which the king is the titular head. Freedom of worship is guaranteed to all.

Because the economy depends significantly on foreign trade, most business is conducted in English. Norway has two official languages, Riksmal and Landsmal, both of Danish origin. The Sami, the indigenous people of the north, have their own language.

Cultural activities are important in Norway. The government subsidizes book publishing, guaranteeing sales of 1,000 copies of each book published for distribution to public libraries. Encouraging Norwegian writers helps preserve the language. Movie production, limited by population and language, fares poorly, however. Opera is fairly new to the country, and Norway didn't acquire a professional ballet ensemble until 1948. Folk music, however, has roots going back to Norse times and is still very much alive. Norway encourages the arts by providing a guaranteed income to active artists whose work has achieved and maintained a high standard over a period of years.

2 LOOKING BACK AT NORWAY

Norway has been inhabited since the end of the Ice Age. The earliest Scandinavian settlers hunted reindeer and other game in these northern lands. Some 5,000 to 6,000 years ago, the inhabitants turned to agriculture, especially around the Oslofjord.

Fun Facts A 40% Quota for Women on Boards

In 2002, the Norwegian government informed public companies that it will now be mandatory that boardrooms consist of 40% women. There are 650 public companies in Norway that must comply with this demand. Since then, the European Union continues to study the proposal. Would other countries ever consider such a requirement? Would America? Stay tuned.

Artifacts show that in the Roman era, Norway had associations with areas to the south.

THE AGE OF THE VIKINGS Prehistory ended during the Viking era, roughly A.D. 800 to 1050. Much of what is known about this era wasn't written down, but has been conveyed through sagas passed by word of mouth or revealed by archaeological finds. Some scholars consider the looting of the Lindisfarne monastery in northern England in 793 the beginning of the "age of the Vikings."

"The Vikings are coming!" became a dreadful cry along the coasts of Europe. The victims expected fire and sword. Scandinavian historians are usually kinder to the Vikings, citing the fact they often went abroad to trade and colonize. From Norway, the Vikings branched out to settle in the Orkney and Shetland Islands (now part of Scotland). They also settled in the Scottish Hebrides and on the Isle of Man. Viking settlements were established on Greenland and Iceland, which had previously been uninhabited. The Norse communities on Greenland eventually died out. The sagas claim that in 1001, Leif Eriksson discovered "wineland of the good," a reference to the American continent. Many scholars, however, claim that the Vikings' long ships reached America long before Leif Eriksson.

The road to unification of Norway was rough. In 872, Harald Fairhair, after winning a battle near Stavanger, conquered many of the provinces; but other battles for unification took decades. Harald was followed by his son, Eric I "Bloody Axe," to his enemies. Eric began his reign by assassinating two of his eight brothers and later killed five other brothers. His one surviving brother, Haakon, succeeded him as king in 954. Haakon tried unsuccessfully to convert Norway to Christianity. After he died in the Battle of Fitjar (960),

DATELINE

- **800–1050** The age of the Vikings, when Norsemen terrorized the coasts of Europe.
- **872** Harald Fairhair conquers many small provinces and reigns as first king.
- **1001** Leif Eriksson discovers America (or so the sagas claim).
- **1030** Christianity is firmly established; Olaf II is declared a saint.
- **1066** The Viking Age ends with the defeat of Harald III in England.
- **1350** The Black Death wipes out much of the population.
- **1397** Margaret becomes queen of Norway, Denmark, and Sweden at the Union of Kalmar.
- **1439** Danish rule is imposed on Norway.
- **1814** Norway breaks from Denmark and adopts a constitution, but comes under Swedish rule.
- **1905** The Norwegian parliament breaks from Sweden and declares independence.
- **1914** Norway declares its neutrality in World War I.
- **1920** Norway joins the League of Nations, ending its isolation.
- **1940** Nazi troops invade Norway; the king and government flee.

continues

Harald II Graafell, one of Eric's sons, became king of Norway. Cruel and oppressive, he died in battle in 970.

Haakon, son of Sigurd of Lade, became the next king of Norway. He resisted Danish attacks and ruled for about 25 years, but died in a peasant riot in 995. After the Battle of Swold in 1000, Norway was divided between Denmark and the Jarl of Lade.

Impressions

I would not enter Norway again for all the firs in Scandinavia. The blight of temperance has settled on the place.

—Archer Grant of Stroud, Gloucestershire, 1912

Olaf II Haraldsson was a Viking until 1015, when he became king of Norway. Although oppressive and often cruel, he continued to spread Christianity. Canute of Denmark invaded Norway in 1028, sending Olaf fleeing to England. Canute's son, Sweyn, ruled Norway from 1028 to 1035. Sweyn was forced out when Olaf II was proclaimed a saint and his son, Magnus I, was made king. Magnus was also king of Denmark, a position he lost when Canute's nephew led a revolt against him and he was killed. Olaf's sainthood firmly established Christianity in Norway.

Harald Sigurdsson (known as Harald III) ruled Norway from 1046 until his death in 1066. His death marks the end of the Viking Age.

THE MIDDLE AGES Wars with Denmark continued, and civil wars raged from 1130 to 1227. Norwegian towns and the church continued to grow. Under Haakon V in the 13th century, Oslo became the capital of Norway. The Black Death reached Norway in 1350 and wiped out much of the population.

From 1362 to 1364, Norway and Sweden had a joint monarch, Haakon VI (1340–80), son of the Swedish king, Magnus Eriksson. Haakon married Margaret, daughter of the Danish king Valdemar Atterdag. Their son, Olaf, was chosen to be the Danish king upon Valdemar's death in 1375. He inherited the throne of Norway after his father died in 1380, bringing Norway into a union with Denmark. The union lasted until 1814.

UNION WITH DENMARK When Olaf died at the age of 17, Margaret became regent of Norway, Denmark, and Sweden. She ruled through her nephew, Eric of Pomerania, who had become king of Norway in 1389. He was recognized as a joint ruler at Kalmar. Margaret was actually the

- **1945** Norway regains independence and executes its Nazi puppet ruler, Quisling.
- **1960s** An oil boom hits Norway.
- **1986** The Labor Party installs first female prime minister, Gro Harlem Brundtland.
- **1989** A center-right coalition regains power.
- **1990** Brundtland becomes prime minister again.
- **1991** Harald V becomes king.
- **1994** Lillehammer plays host to XVII Olympic Winter Games.
- **1995** Norway wins Eurovision Song Contest, an annual cultural event observed by 600 million viewers.
- **1996** Eurovision Song Contest is held in Oslo; Norway takes second place.
- **1998** Oil prices fall, but Norway plunges ahead with costly engineering projects.
- **2001** U.N. group votes Norway most desirable place to live in the world.
- **2004** A future queen is born—perhaps.
- **2005** New bridge links Sweden and Norway.
- **2008** Norway turns to the Barents Sea in its search for oil fields.

Impressions

I have saved the world from a mediocre painter and given the world a literary genius.

—Henrik Ibsen's wife, Susanna

Only when you see the provincialism of Oslo do you appreciate the wonderfulness of Ibsen.

—Arnold Bennett, Journal, 1929

power behind the throne until her death in 1412. Eric of Pomerania tried to rule the three countries, but Sweden and Norway rebelled. Eric fled in 1439 and Christopher III of Bavaria became the ruler, imposing Danish rule.

Denmark led Norway into the Seven Years' War of the North in 1563 and took unfair advantage of its position in trade, in the military, and even in surrendering Norwegian land to Sweden.

During the Napoleonic Wars (1807–14), Denmark and Norway were allied with France, although it created much economic hardship. Famine was widespread. In 1814, Frederik VI of Denmark surrendered to Napoleon's opponents and handed Norway over to Sweden. That officially ended 434 years of Danish rule over Norway.

SECESSION FROM SWEDEN On May 17, 1814, an assembly adopted a constitution and chose Christian Frederik as the Norwegian king. May 17 is celebrated as Norwegian National Day. The Swedes objected and launched a military campaign, eventually subduing Norway. The Swedes accepted the Norwegian constitution, but only within a union of the two kingdoms. Christian Frederik fled.

Soon thereafter, Norway suffered through one of its greatest economic depressions. Norway's parliamentary assembly, the Storting (Stortinget), engaged in repeated conflicts with the Swedish monarchs. Bernadotte ruled over both Norway and Sweden as Charles XIV from 1818 to 1844.

By the 1830s, the economy of Norway had improved. The first railway line was laid in 1854. Its merchant fleet grew significantly between 1850 and 1880.

From the 1880s on, the Liberals in the Storting brought much-needed reform to the country. But by the end of the century, the conflict with Sweden was growing as more and more Norwegians demanded independence.

In August 1905, the Storting decided to dissolve the union with Sweden. Sweden agreed to let Norway rule itself. In October 1905, Norway held an election, and the son of Denmark's king was proclaimed king of Norway. He chose the name Haakon VII.

AN INDEPENDENT NORWAY Free at last, Norway enjoyed peace and prosperity until the beginning of World War II. Even though the economy was satisfactory, thousands of Norwegians emigrated to the United States around the turn of the 20th century. In 1914, Norway joined Sweden and Denmark in declaring a policy of neutrality. Despite the declaration, around 2,000 Norwegian seamen lost their lives in the war because of submarine attacks and underwater mines.

In 1920, Norway joined the League of Nations, ending its policy of isolation. At the outbreak of World War II, Norway again declared its neutrality. Nonetheless, Allied forces mined Norway's waters in 1940, and the Nazis attacked on April 9, 1940. Great Britain and France provided some military assistance, but Norway fell after a 2-month struggle. The government and the royal family fled into exile in

England, taking 1,000 ships of the Norwegian merchant fleet. In spite of the resistance movement, Nazis occupied Norway until the end of the war in 1945. Vidkun Quisling, the Norwegian minister of defense in the 1930s, served the Nazis as leader of the puppet government.

Impressions

Norway is a hard country: hard to know, hard to shoot over, and hard—very hard—to fall down on: but hard to forsake and harder to forget.
—J. A. Lees, in *Peaks and Pines,* 1899

Quisling was executed following the Nazi retreat from Norway. On June 7, 1945, the government-in-exile returned from Britain. The retreating Nazis had followed a scorched-earth policy in Finnmark, destroying almost everything of value. In the late 1940s, Norway began to rebuild its shattered economy.

After an abortive attempt to form a Nordic defense alliance, Norway and Denmark joined NATO in 1949. The Communist Party tried to secure recognition in Norway but failed.

By the 1960s, oil prospecting in the North Sea had yielded rich finds, which led to a profound restructuring of Norwegian trade and industry. In 1972, Norway voted not to enter the Common Market, following a bitter political dispute.

Norway had a non-Socialist government from 1981 to 1986. In 1986, Labor Party leader Gro Harlem Brundtland headed a minority government as Norway's first female prime minister. She introduced seven women into her 18-member cabinet. Soon, however, tumbling oil prices and subsequent unemployment led to a recession. The Labour government lost the 1989 elections. A center-right coalition assumed control of government. In November 1990, Brundtland returned to office as prime minister, this time with nine women in her 19-member cabinet. In 1991, Olav V died and was succeeded by his son, Harald V.

Today the Norwegian government faces many of the same problems that confront other nations: violent crime, drugs, immigration control, unemployment, acid rain, and pollution. Concern about acid rain and pollution, much of which comes from Great Britain, was so great that riots erupted when Margaret Thatcher visited Norway in 1987.

Although some Conservatives objected, Norway applied for membership in the European Union (E.U.) in 1993. The country also began to assert itself more on the international scene. Thorvald Stoltenberg, the minister of foreign affairs, was named peace negotiator for ravaged Bosnia-Herzegovina and, in clandestine meetings held outside Oslo, helped effect a rapprochement between the PLO and Israel. All these history-making events were eclipsed by the XVII Olympic Winter Games, held in Lillehammer in February 1994. In November 1994, Norwegians rejected a nonbinding referendum on E.U. membership. Following that, everyone waited for the Norwegian parliament to vote on whether the country would join. The parliament deliberately avoided the issue and did not vote on the matter. The referendum, though nonbinding, remains in force, and Norway is still not a member of the E.U. But that does not mean the country has no economic links with the rest of Europe. In 1994, Norway reinforced its commitments to membership in the EEAA (European Economic Area Agreement), an association initiated in 1992 to ensure its access to the E.U.'s single market. It includes cooperation in a variety of cultural and economic areas.

In 1995, Norway won the Eurovision Song Contest for best songs evocative of a country, repeating its sweep of a decade earlier and ensuring that the event would

A Sifter of Viking Secrets

The world press gave scant attention to the death, in 1997, of Norwegian archaeologist Anne-Stine Ingstad, but she was a pioneer, sifting through the sandy soil above a Newfoundland beach to uncover the remains of a Viking outpost.

She was the wife of Helge Ingstad, whose discovery of the site in 1961 produced the first conclusive evidence that Vikings had made a North American beachhead 500 years before Columbus. Vikings sailed from a colony in Greenland to reach the North American continent (today's Canada). Icelandic sagas had described the voyages in detail, and few scholars doubted that Leif Eriksson and other Vikings had made such voyages and explorations. But until the Ingstads made their startling discoveries, no hard evidence of a Viking presence existed—only a spate of spurious artifacts.

The initial discovery was met with skepticism. But once Anne-Stine Ingstad started to dig, most doubts evaporated. Her husband had used vivid geographic descriptions in Icelandic sagas to find the camp described by Eriksson and others. Once the site was discovered, she carried out excavations over several months. In time, she uncovered the foundations of eight buildings, including a large house almost identical to Eriksson's great hall in Greenland.

In 1964, she unearthed a tiny stone spinning wheel, suggesting that female Vikings had used the camp. In 1980, UNESCO designated the settlement, L'Anse aux Meadows, a World Heritage Site, along with the Pyramids of Egypt and the Grand Canyon.

be held there in 1996. As the host country, Norway captured second place.

By 1998, Norway was having its share of troubles, as oil prices plunged to their lowest levels in a decade. Turmoil in financial markets knocked the krone lower and prompted the central bank to double interest rates to 10%. The popular prime minister Kjell Magne Bondevik, who took over the office in 1997, stunned the country by taking a temporary leave from office. His doctors said he was having a "depressive reaction" to too much work and stress. In late 1998, Bondevik came back to his job—and is now running the country.

Today Norway continues pushing forward with major engineering projects. The country is connecting its sparsely inhabited outcroppings and linking its interior fjord-side villages in an effort to stem the flow of people to larger towns and villages. At Hitra, a largely barren island off the west coast, a new 5.5km (3½-mile) tunnel (the world's deepest and second longest) has been built at a cost of $41 million. It links mainland Norway to a hamlet with some 4,100 residents. On the North Cape, at Norway's Arctic tip, a $140-million bridge and tunnel was constructed to Mager Island, home to only 3,600 people (and more than that many reindeer). An additional $135 million went into the earth in the mountains east of Bergen to link the towns of Aurland (pop. 1,900) and Laerdal (pop. 2,250). Its 24km (15-mile) tunnel casts the previous world record holder, the 16km (10-mile) St. Gotthard tunnel in Switzerland, into a distant second place.

A more artistic bridge opened in December of 2001. The designer? None other than Leonardo da Vinci, in 1502. The 99m (325-ft.) laminated timber bridge links Norway and Sweden over a highway at the town of Aas, 26km (16 miles) south of Oslo.

In 2001, Norway ranked first (with the U.S. in sixth place) as the best country in the world in which to live. The judge? The United Nations Human Development Report. Australia followed Norway in second place, with both countries moving narrowly ahead of Canada. The annual survey is based on statistical profiles of what people can expect in life beyond economic growth.

The year 2001 also was witness to the marriage of Crown Prince Haakon and Mette-Mari Tjessem Hoiby, a single mom who lived with the royal before marrying him. The couple's marriage raised some astonishment among Norway's more conservative factions, because the father of Hoiby's child is a convicted cocaine supplier and she had been well known on Oslo's "dance-and-drugs house party scene," as one newspaper commentator put it. Some Norwegians wonder if the modern-minded heir to the throne, Prince Haakon, a direct descendant of Queen Victoria, even plans to maintain the monarchy.

The crown prince and princess became parents to a daughter on January 21, 2004. Ingrid Alexandra may be the first reigning queen of Norway since 1412.

In 2005, the world's largest single-arched bridge was opened between Sweden and Norway and inaugurated by King Harald V of Norway and King Carl XVI Gustaf of Sweden. The Svinesund Bridge spans a fjord south of Oslo, stretching for 2,300 feet. The occasion also marked Norway's celebration of 100 years of independence from Sweden, which dominated a union between the two countries until 1905.

Norway, in 2008, was the third biggest exporter of oil in the world, after Saudi Arabia and Russia. Its future looks good as an oil-producing nation. Faced with exhaustion of resources in the North Sea, oil and gas companies have turned to the vast Barents Sea, where large reserves are believed to exist. For example, major oil and gas deposits off the northern tip of Norway, in a previously unexploited area of the Barents Sea, are being "harvested." The oilmen, predictably, are engaged in fights with environmental groups, who want to protect the fragile environment and its major fishing waters.

This oil-fueled economy has made Norway a magnet for young Swedes, because their own economy has lagged far beyond. Long a poor cousin of Scandinavia, Norway has forged ahead, and thousands of Swedes are now flocking here to work, many in menial jobs. The number of Swedes living and working in Norway doubled between 1990 and 2008.

3 ART & ARCHITECTURE

From the Age of the Vikings, Norway has given the world art and architecture, ranging from its famous wooden stave churches to the paintings of Edvard Munch, Scandinavia's most celebrated artist.

ART

Just before the Viking period, carved stones bearing runic inscriptions began appearing in Norway from the 3rd century A.D. on.

The Vikings may not have been the insensitive barbarians their reputation has it, as they showed a high artistic skill as reflected by the decorations on the Oseberg burial ship at the Vikingskiphuset (Viking Ship Museum) in Oslo (p. 134). The ship has a carved likeness of a ferocious beast, a traditional feature of Viking boats. The Vikings seemed to have been inspired by Carolingian art, which stemmed from Byzantine traditions.

Not much is left of Christian art in Norway. The country converted to Christianity in the 10th century. In early art, human figures were not often represented, the early Norwegians preferring to stick to the dragonlike heads as seen on the prows of Viking ships that terrified Western Europe.

It took a long time before art firmly established itself in Norway. Cut off from the cultural life of Europe, Norwegian art experienced a long slumber from the 15th to the 18th centuries. The coming of the plague and the loss of political independence are blamed for this decline.

Local painters showed little originality, preferring to copy more famous examples established by artists in the south or central Europe.

As a decorative motif, the painted rose swept the country in the mid-1700s, introducing a striking use of color for the first time in Norwegian art. Later, the rose was combined with the acanthus leaf as a motif. The trend was toward abstract design in most Norwegian popular art.

Even as late as the beginning of the 1800s, there was little noteworthy art. The most original artist was Johan Christian Clausen Dahl (1788–1857), a major landscape painter who drew his inspiration from the North German Romantic School. His cloud studies are still viewed as brilliant art today.

French influence in painting made itself known in the works of the painter Christian Krohg (1852–1925). But with the birth of Edvard Munch (1863–1944), Norway was to experience an artist who became the most celebrated painter in Scandinavia. His works can be seen, among other places, at the Munch Museet (Edvard Munch Museum) in Oslo (p. 130).

Munch became the leading force in the creation of the Expressionist style. His *Scream* (1895) remains one of the most reproduced paintings on earth. In this masterpiece, he used form and color (reds and yellows) to convey his deep personal vision of the horror of existence. In his works Munch explored the themes of life, love, fear, melancholy, and death. He portrayed women either as frail, innocent sufferers or the reason for jealousy and despair.

The Nazis labeled Munch's works "degenerate art," but that was only a temporary setback for him. He wrote: "From my rotting body, flowers shall grow and I am in them and that is eternity." And so it came to be.

Other notable artists that you'll see in the museums of Norway include Christian Skredsvig (1854–1924), whose most famous work is the neo-romantic *The Sallow Flute* (1889), and Adolph Tidemand (1814–1876), who became known for his paintings of old Norwegian farm culture. The Nasjonalgalleriet (National Gallery) in Oslo (p. 130) owns more than 100 of his works.

Another Norwegian painter, Nikolai Astrup (1880–1928), was also a neo-Romantic, preferring clear, strong colors in his landscapes. A pioneer among female artists was Harriet Backer (1845–1932), who was influenced by impressionism, though most of her work is classified as realist.

Another woman is among the most distinguished of all Norwegian artists today. Born in 1971, Marianne Aulie sells works for millions of Norwegian kroner, although the art historian Stig Andersen calls her paintings "soft pornography." Her repertoire includes everything from abstract paintings to Madonnas and images of clowns. She likes to bathe her paintings in champagne to get a particular texture from the alcohol reacting to acrylic paint.

Sculpture in Norway appeared as dragons on bedposts, carved chairs, and drinking vessels shaped like Viking ships, and on reliquaries in the form of churches.

Norway's first sculptor enjoying an international reputation was Adolf Gustav Vigeland (1869–1943), whose great works remain the statuary groups he created for Vigelandsparken (p. 133) in Oslo. The chief treasure here is his Vigeland Monolith. Naked figures, entwined and struggling, cover the obelisk.

A distinguished Norwegian-Danish sculptor, Stephan (Abel) Sinding (1846–1922), was considered "too modern" by many traditional Norwegian art critics. But Danish beer baron Carl Jacobsen thought otherwise, and that is why the largest collection in the world of Sinding sculptures reside today in the Ny Carlsberg Glyptotek in Copenhagen. However, you can see the Sinding statue of Henrik Ibsen at the National Theater in Oslo.

ARCHITECTURE

As a sparsely populated country on the northern edge of Europe, Norway, did not distinguish itself in architecture the way countries such as Germany and Italy to the south did.

Little survives of early Christian architecture in Norway. Constructed in the 11th century, the first building of importance was **Nidaros Domkirke** (p. 362) in Trondheim. This cathedral was reconstructed (1282–1320) in the late Norman style, at which time it incorporated many Gothic features.

Norwegian architecture flourished in its stave churches (*stavkirker*), which were built before the Reformation, using as inspiration ancient pagan temples. The churches were constructed on a framework of staves, or heavily wooded posts, supporting the walls and roofs. There are 28 well-preserved stave churches remaining today, constituting Norway's most important contribution to world architectural history.

These churches were characterized by their many storied and steeply sloping roofs. Gables, pinnacles, and cupolas were used in abundance. After the construction of these churches, Norwegian architecture fell into a slumber that lasted 3 centuries.

In the early part of the 1800s, architecture in Norway fell under the influence of the Swedish monarch Charles XIV (1763–1844). Norway was locked into a political union with Sweden, which dominated the country. In the development of Christiania (later Oslo) as the capital of Norway, the king imposed a neoclassical style in architecture.

Fun Facts In Their Footsteps

Edvard Munch (1863–1944), the "world's greatest expressionist" and the "handsomest man in Norway," wrote, "Illness, madness, and death were the black angels who stood guard over my cot, and they have followed me throughout my life." A one-man show in 1889, when he was 25, launched his career. His influence on the development of modern expressionism was considered as great as that of van Gogh. He became Scandinavia's greatest painter, and his series of paintings, *From Modern Spiritual Life,* established his genius.

- **Birthplace:** Loten, Norway (December 12, 1863).
- **Favorite Haunts:** Grand Café in Oslo, where he joined a group of "radical bohemians"; provincial villages along the Oslofjord.
- **Resting Place:** The Ground of Honor, Vår Frelsers Gravlund, Oslo, where he was buried in an unadorned tomb—after his sister refused an offer from the Nazi-collaborationist regime for a state funeral.

However, in the countryside, vernacular architecture consisted mainly of wood structures, which can still be seen in many open-air museums throughout the country, including the Norsk Folkesmuseum (p. 132), in Oslo, and Maihaugen (p. 196), in Lillehammer.

Around the turn of the 20th century, *Jugendstil,* a variant of Art Nouveau, came into vogue, especially when the port of Ålesund, which had burned to the ground, was almost entirely rebuilt in that style. In the 1920s, modernism prevailed, which in Norway was called *funkis.* This simplified functional style would prevail until 1940, when Norway was conquered by Nazi Germany.

After the war, modern buildings were often multistoried, with wings, using timber or brick. New housing developments were set in long rows rather than in rectangular blocks to get the maximum of light and sunshine.

Impressions

November always seemed to me the Norway of the year.

—Emily Dickinson, 1864

The architecture of the 21st century can be daringly avant-garde, as evoked by the futuristic Oslo Opera House. With its marble-clad surface and enormous glass facade sporting solar panels, the building evokes a Norwegian iceberg rising from the cold Arctic Sea.

4 THE LAY OF THE LAND

Norway is one of nature's last great frontiers in Europe—mountains, glaciers, and lakes cover 70% of its land. Less than 4% of its territory, mostly in the south-central area, is arable. Within Norway's Jutunheimen range are the highest mountain peaks in Europe north of the Alps. Norway has about 17,000 glaciers. Along the western coast, some 50,000 islands protect the mainland from some of the worst storms in the North Atlantic.

Norway has a varied and changing climate. The coastal zones in the west and east normally experience cool summers and temperate winters. Inland, summers are warm, and winters cold and dry. In the extreme north, 100 days of snowfall each year isn't uncommon.

The fjords are not only a distinguishing feature of Norway's landscape, but also a special attraction to visitors. These were created thousands of years ago when the ocean flowed into glacial valleys. These "fingers" of water cut deep into the landscape. The most intriguing of the fjords, the Sognefjord, is more than 160km (99 miles) long and extremely deep.

Norway's rivers tend to be short and volatile. A smooth flow of water is often "agitated" by waterfalls and patches of white water. Because they're not suited for transportation, rivers are primarily sources of food, principally salmon. The longest river in Scandinavia, the Glomma, runs through southwestern Norway.

Norway's position on the globe has earned it the nickname "Land of the Midnight Sun." In summer, towns in northern Norway, such as Tromsø, experience 24 hours of sunshine, followed by 24 hours of darkness in winter. Even in southern Norway, the summer days are long, and the winter nights may last more than 17 hours.

Thick birch and pine forests cover the mountains; in the lowlands, oak forests abound. Spruce forests cover the southeast and middle regions. The steep mountains in the east are among the tallest in Europe and the site of some of the world's most

Did You Know?

- Norwegians have one of the highest per-capita incomes in the world.
- While medieval alchemists were trying to make gold, they discovered *akevitt* (aquavit, or schnapps), the national "firewater" of Norway.
- Norway has the world's largest foreign trade per capita.
- The average population density is only 13 inhabitants per square kilometer (almost 1/2 sq. mile), compared with 96 for Europe as a whole.
- Norway and Russia share a short land border and have disputed control of a sea area the size of Belgium, Switzerland, and Austria combined.
- Hammerfest is the world's northernmost town.

challenging alpine ski runs. There is excellent hiking in the Vassafaret district around Fløm, where the mountains are rounded, gentle, and dotted with alpine lakes and rivers.

The mountains are also home to ravens, eagles, grouse, and gyrfalcons. They serve as a migratory home to the pure-white snowy owl. Norway's countryside and forests teem with Arctic animals such as reindeer, arctic fox, wolves, bears, lynx, elk, beavers, and otters. Along the coast are nesting grounds for puffins and cormorants; whales, salmon, and cod frolic in the icy seas offshore. Through Norway's conservation efforts and strict regulations regarding the environment, these animals and fish flourish much as they have in the past.

5 NORWAY IN POPULAR CULTURE: BOOKS, FILM & MUSIC

BOOKS

If runic inscriptions, dating from the 1st and 2nd centuries A.D., are to be counted, Norway has the oldest literary tradition of all the Scandinavian countries. The Vikings had a poetic tradition that was almost entirely oral. Legends were told by each generation, sagas of great heroes and mighty adventures, mostly at sea.

Court minstrels, called *scalds,* wrote down compositions to be sung before kings, including Harald I (850–933), the first king of Norway.

The Vikings, by Johannes Brondsted, is one of the best written documents about the age of the Vikings. Viking fans will also be drawn to *The Vinland Sagas: The Norse Discovery of America,* translated by Magnus Magnuson and Hermann Palsson, an incredible saga detailing how Viking age Norwegians sailed in their long ships to the eastern coast of "Vinland" (America) in the 10th century.

The Middle Ages in Norway brought the spread of Christianity with a large body of literature. In the secular realm, stories from the Arthurian cycle and French romances were adopted. Following Norway's union with Denmark at the end of the 14th, a cultural decline began. Danes abolished the Old Norse tongue. When the Reformation came, many ancient Norwegian manuscripts were destroyed. Only the peasants kept national culture alive. The country didn't even have a printing press until 1643.

In the 18th century, a towering figure emerged in Norwegian literature in the form of Ludvig Holberg (1684–1754). Norway's voice in the Age of Reason, Holberg was a satirist, poet, playwright, and prose writer. Living mainly in Denmark, this Norwegian had a tremendous impact on Danish drama. His literary influence in Norway centered on historical writings and essays.

By the 19th century, Norwegian writing began to be appreciated by the world. *The Governor's Daughter,* by Camilla Collett, published in 1854, became the first modern Norwegian novel. Two towering writers emerged: playwright Henrik Ibsen (1828–1906) and Bjornstjerne Björnson (1832–1910).

Ibsen was the first Norwegian to devote himself entirely to theater writing. His verse-plays, *Brand* and *Peer Gynt,* established his greatness, and these were followed by a number of plays, the most famous of which are *A Doll's House, Hedda Gabler,* and *The Master Builder.* Ibsen's plays today are performed all over the world and are available in various editions in book form.

Björnson won the Nobel Prize for literature in 1903. A poet, playwright, journalist, and politician, he was also deeply involved in social and religious problems. There are English translations of some of his most evocative creations, including his celebrated rustic novel *Arne,* first published in 1859, and his *The Fisher Maiden,* published in 1868.

The best female novelist to emerge between the two world wars was Sigrid Undset (1882–1949). She was awarded the Nobel Prize for literature in 1928. She was a Christian writer, and her values were not political. Today she is mainly praised for her three-volume masterpiece *Kristin Lavransdatter,* which tells of love and religion in medieval Norway. Her later works include such widely known books as *Ida Elisabeth,* in 1932, and *The Faithful Wife,* in 1936. With the coming of the Nazis, her books were banned and she fled Norway.

Norwegian travel writing has been linked to voyages of discovery. Both Fridtjof Nansen (1861–1930) and Roald Amundsen (1872–1928) published detailed accounts of their travels. Nansen's books, such as *The First Crossing of Greenland* (1890), are still widely read, as are the works of Amundsen, including *The South Pole* (1912).

The Kon-Tiki Expedition by Thor Heyerdahl details the saga of a modern-day Viking, who set out on a balsa raft with five comrades and sailed 6,920km (4,290 miles) in 1947—all the way from Peru to Polynesia. *Kon-Tiki Man: An Illustrated Biography of Heyerdahl,* by Thor himself, highlights his attempt to document his

Fun Facts **In Their Footsteps**

Henrik Ibsen (1828–1906) attained towering stature as a world dramatist. *Brand* (1866) and *Peer Gynt* (1867) are recognized as two of the finest plays of the 19th century. *A Doll's House* (1879) expressed his belief in the hollowness of the marriage morality of his day. Other masterpieces include *Ghosts* (1881), *Hedda Gabler* (1890), and *The Master Builder* (1892).

Birthplace: Skien, Norway (March 20, 1829).

Favorite Haunts: The Bergen Theater (1851–57); Dresden, Germany (1868–91); Oslo (1891–1906), where he patronized the Grand Café twice a day.

Resting Place: The Ground of Honor, Vår Frelsers Gravlund, in Oslo.

Famous Norwegians

Bjørnstjerne Bjørnson (1832–1910): A major Norwegian writer, he recorded and adapted into literary forms many of the folk tales that later inspired Henrik Ibsen. In 1857, he took over Ibsen's post as director of the Bergen Theater. His historical plays brought him world acclaim, and he became radically involved in Norwegian nationalism, campaigning for a country politically independent of its colonial links with Denmark. One of his poems was adopted as the national anthem of Norway, *"Ja, Vi Elsker Dette Lanet"* ("Yes, I Love This Land"). He won the Nobel Prize in 1903.

Kirsten Flagstad (1895–1962): The greatest Wagnerian singer in the history of opera was born in Hamar, Norway. Her 1933 performance at the Wagner Festival in Bayreuth, Germany, brought her world acclaim. She made her debut at the Metropolitan Opera House in New York City in 1935 as Sieglinde in *Die Walküre.*

Edvard Grieg (1843–1907): Norway's national composer, aka the "Chopin of the North," became famous for adapting musical themes from Norwegian folk tunes, as in *The Peer Gynt Suite,* for example. He was born in Bergen to an English father and a Norwegian mother.

Knut Hamsun (1859–1952): In 1888, a Danish magazine published a portion of his novel, *Hunger.* Hamsun was 19 years old. This novel, along with *Growth of the Soil* and *The Women at the Well,* earned him international fame. In 1920, he won the Nobel Prize for literature.

Thor Heyerdahl (1914–2002): In 1937, this Norwegian ethnologist began laying the groundwork for a series of research expeditions to the Pacific, the most important of which, in 1947, involved the *Kon-Tiki* expedition from Peru to the islands of Polynesia. In 1951, he won an Academy Award for his documentary (see the *Kon-Tiki* Museum in Chapter 6). In 1969 and 1970, he led two *Ra* expeditions. Many of his books have become bestsellers, including *Aku Aku,* a study of the tribal ethnologies of Easter Island, eventually translated into 32 languages.

idea that Polynesia was settled by people migrating west from South America.

Among contemporaries, the best-selling author today is Norwegian fantasy writer Margit Sandemo, whose novel *Spellbound* has been translated into English. Some 40 million copies of her novels are in print. Two other popular writers today are Dag Solstad, who has a great ability to describe modern consciousness, and Herbjørg Wassmo, who enjoys international acclaim for her novels such as *Dina's Book* (1989), which was made into a film in 2002 with French actor Gérard Depardieu.

Finally, *The Norwegians,* by Arthur Spencer, is the best book on the market today for understanding the Norwegian people and their advanced society.

FILM

Lagging far behind its siblings, Sweden and Denmark, Norway only in recent

Henrik Ibsen (1828–1906): One of the greatest modernist-realist playwrights, he was the author of *A Doll's House, Hedda Gabler, The Master Builder,* and *Peer Gynt.*

Trygve Lie (1896–1968): Lie was a leading Labor party lawyer and politician. In 1940, he was named foreign minister of a Norwegian government in exile during the Nazi occupation. In 1946, he was elected secretary-general of the United Nations for 5 years. In 1950, he undertook a "great peace mission," and also supported the United Nations effort to send troops to Korea. In 1951, his term was extended as secretary-general, but he resigned because of ongoing Soviet refusal to recognize him.

Edvard Munch (1863–1944): The greatest Scandinavian painter's most famous works include the gut-wrenching *The Scream* (1893) and *The Bridge* (1901), each conveying a sense of horror that became consistent with the philosophies of the existentialists. His murals are on display at Oslo University.

Fridtjof Nansen (1861–1930): A world explorer, he dreamed of crossing the ice caps of Greenland, a remarkable feat that brought him glory in 1889. He led the Norwegian delegation to the first assembly of the League of Nations in 1920, and in 1922 was awarded the Nobel Peace Prize for his work repatriating prisoners of war.

Liv Ullmann (b. 1938): The famous Norwegian actress made her stage debut in 1957 and became known in the 1960s for her work with the National Theater. World acclaim came through roles in films of Ingmar Bergman, her lover at the time. These included *Cries and Whispers, Scenes from a Marriage,* and *Persona.* She has appeared on Broadway and has written two volumes of memoirs.

Sigrid Undset (1882–1943): *Kristen Lavransdatter* is considered this writer's masterpiece.

Adolf Gustav Vigeland (1869–1943). This sculptor, whose monumental works viewed collectively are one of Oslo's major sights, was a controversial artist—some claim a genius, others a madman. See his obelisk in Frognerpark.

years has begun to impress the world. In olden days, talented Norwegian film directors ended up in Hollywood.

One of the first Norwegian films to attract world attention was the 1951 *Kon-Tiki,* exploring the epic voyage of Thor Heyerdahl. It received the Academy Award that year for a documentary.

It wasn't until 2006 that another Norwegian film won another Oscar, this time for Best Animated Short Film, *The Danish Poet,* narrated by Norwegian screen legend Liv Ullman.

Another great Norwegian film, Nils Gaup's *Pathfinder,* made in 1987, was based on the legend of the Lapps. It was an enormous international success and the second Norwegian film nominated for an Oscar.

Peter & the Wolf, produced in Norway, received an Oscar for Best Animated Short Film in 2008.

More and more Norwegian films are finding world audiences, including world releases of such films as Alexander Rosler's *Mendel*, Pal Sletaune's *Junk Mail*, and Erik Skoldbjaerg's *Insomnia*. Some film critics have hailed this avalanche of new films as a "Norwave in cinema."

Impressions

I know the Norwegians from Illinois, and I know that no immigrants have advanced America more than they.

—Abraham Lincoln

MUSIC

Norwegian music made little impact on the world until the 19th century. Ole Bull (1810–80) attracted major attention and even performed on a concert tour in America. He was one of the finest violinists of his time, composing mainly virtuoso pieces for the violin.

Norway's first composer to achieve world renown, however, was Edvard Grieg (1843–1907). He produced a specifically Norwegian type of music as evoked by his "Peer Gynt Suite" (1888). His piano "Concerto" and three sonatas for violin and piano are his finest works.

After Grieg's death, the major composer was Christian Sinding (1856–1941), who achieved fame for his composition for piano, "Rustle of Spring."

The most distinguished composer of the 20th century was Fartein Valen (1887–1952), who is known for his contribution to atonal music.

In the countryside, Norway, of course, has been known for centuries for its folk music tradition. Folk music is usually performed by soloists, and instrumental is commonly played on the Hardanger fiddle, the national musical instrument of Norway.

Norwegian musicians today have an impact on the international music scene, and Norwegian jazz festivals are attended by audiences worldwide. Pop, rock, hip-hop, metal, R&B, and electronic enjoy wide popularity. Metal traditionally has been one of Norway's biggest musical exports, with such bands as Red Harvest and Enslaved performing.

6 EATING & DRINKING IN NORWAY

MEALS & DINING CUSTOMS Most working Norwegians seldom go out to lunch; instead they grab a quick open-face sandwich, or smørbrød, at their offices. But in major towns and cities, lunch is generally served from 1 to 3pm. The *middag,* the main meal of the day, is generally eaten between 4:30 and 6pm. Many restaurants serve this popular *middag* from 1 to 8pm. In late-closing restaurants, it's possible to dine much later, until around midnight in Oslo. Long after *middag* time, a Norwegian family will have *aftens,* a smørbrød supper that will see them through the night.

THE CUISINE The chief criticism leveled against Norwegian cooking is that it's too bland. The food is always abundant (the Norwegians are known for their second helpings), substantial, and well prepared—but no threat to the French for a Cordon Bleu prize. Today, instead of their own cuisine, Norwegians often turn to the Continent or even Asia to satisfy their taste buds. Foreign restaurants, especially in such cities as Oslo and Bergen, are all the rage.

Norwegians are proud—and rightly so—of many of their tempting specialties, ranging from boiled cod (considered a

Tips — Frommer's Smart Traveler: Restaurants

Value-conscious diners may want to consider the following when eating in Norwegian restaurants:

- Look for the *dagens* menu or daily special, which are reasonably priced and usually prepared fresh each day.
- Order fixed-price menus, especially at lunch. Often, you can dine in some of the most expensive restaurants by patronizing them at lunch and ordering from the set menu.
- Do as the Norwegians do: Order one or two *smørbrød* (open-face sandwiches) for lunch.
- Watch the booze—it can add greatly to the cost of any meal.
- Go ethnic—there are hundreds of affordable foreign dining spots. Norwegian restaurants tend to be expensive.
- Best bet for a quick and inexpensive meal is a *konditori,* or bakery tearoom. Look for self-service cafeterias as well.
- Fill up at the traditional Norwegian *koldtbord* (cold board) at breakfast buffets, so you'll need only a light lunch.

delicacy) to reindeer steak smothered in brown gravy and accompanied by tart little lingonberries, which resemble wild cranberries.

Norway relies on fish, both freshwater and saltwater, for much of its food supply. Prepared in countless ways, fish is usually well cooked and always fresh—a good bet indeed. Try, in particular, the aforementioned boiled cod; it's always—emphasis on *always*—served with boiled potatoes.

In early summer, *kokt laks* (boiled salmon) is a highly rated delicacy. *Kreps* (crayfish) is another big production (as it is in Finland), and *ørret* (mountain trout), preferably broiled and served with fresh lemon, is a guaranteed treat. A recommendation for top-notch fare: *fiske-gratin* (fish soufflé), delicately seasoned.

Norwegians love their fatty smoked eel *(roket al),* although many foreigners have a tendency to whip by this one on the *smörgåsbord* table. The national appetizer is brine-cured herring with raw onions.

You may want to try reindeer steak or *faar-i-kaal,* the national dish, a heavily peppered cabbage-and-mutton stew served with boiled potatoes. A fisher's or a farmer's favorite is *lapskus* (hash, to us), prepared with whatever's left over in the kitchen. The North American palate seems to take kindly to *kjøttkaker,* the Norwegian hamburger—often pork patties—served with sautéed onions, brown gravy, and boiled potatoes.

The boiled potato is ubiquitous. Incidentally, the Norwegian prefers it without butter—just a bit of parsley. Nowadays fresh vegetables and crisp salads are a regular feature of the Norwegian diet as well.

Rumgraut is a sour-cream porridge covered with melted butter, brown sugar, and cinnamon. If they're in season, try the good-tasting, amber-colored *muiter* (cloudberries). An additional treat, well made in Norway, is a pancake accompanied by lingonberries.

Frokost (breakfast) is often a whopping *koldtbord,* the famous cold board, consisting of herring and goat's milk cheese, and such fare as salmon and soft-boiled eggs, plus *wienerbrød* (Danish pastry). At this time, most visitors encounter the ever-popular *flatbrød,* paper-thin crisp rye bread. Many visitors may not want to spend the extra kroner for this big spread, but those going on glacier expeditions need this early-morning fortification.

Incidentally, smorgasbord and smørbrød are very popular in Norway, although they seem to be served here without the elaborate ritual typical of Denmark and Sweden. Customarily, smorgasbord in Norway is only a prelude to the main meal.

DRINK Norway has strict laws regarding the sale of alcohol. Beer and wine may be served in hotels and restaurants 7 days a week, but hard liquor can be sold only between 3 and 11:45pm—and never on Sunday. Visitors can buy the precious stuff from the Vinmonopolet, the state liquor-and-wine monopoly (see below). The restriction on hard liquor may be a bonus for budgeters, as Norwegian prices are sky-high, in line with all the Scandinavian countries. ***Warning:*** Unless visitors ask for a favorite brand of gin or scotch, they may be served a sour-tasting Norwegian home brew.

The Norwegians, like the Danes, are essentially beer drinkers. *Pils,* a light lager, is fairly low in alcohol content, but the *lagerøl* is so low in alcoholic content (less than 2.5%) that it's a substitute for water only. The stronger Norwegian beer is called Export and is available at higher prices. Two other types of beer are Brigg and Zero.

The other national drink is *akevitt* (sometimes written as *aquavit* or *schnapps*). Who would ever think that potatoes and caraway seeds could knock a person under the table? It's that potent, although it's misnamed the "water of life." Norwegians gulp down beer as a chaser. Aquavit (try Linie Akevitt) is sloshed around in oak vats all the way to Australia and back—for added flavor.

The stores of **Vinmonopolet,** the monopoly that sells wines and spirits, are open Monday through Wednesday from 10am to 5pm, on Thursday from 9am to 6pm, and on Friday from 9am to 5pm. The Vinmonopolet is closed on Saturday in all towns except Kirkenes, Bodø, Ålesund, Trondheim, Haugesund, and Arendal. Liquor is not sold to anyone under 20 years of age; for beer and wine, the cutoff is 18.

Planning Your Trip to Norway

In the pages that follow, we've compiled the essentials of what you need to know about the practical details of planning your trip—airlines, a calendar of events, details on currency, and more.

1 VISITOR INFORMATION

In the **United States,** contact the **Scandinavian Tourist Board,** 655 Third Ave., Ste. 1810, New York, NY 10017 (© **212/885-9700;** www.goscandinavia.com), at least 3 months in advance for maps, sightseeing pointers, ferry schedules, and other information.

In the **United Kingdom,** contact the **Norwegian Tourist Board** (a division of the Scandinavian Tourist Board), Charles House, 5 Lower Regent St., London SW1Y 4LR (© **0207/839-6255;** cost 50p per min.). You might also try the tourist board's official website: **www.visitnorway.com**.

In **Canada, Innovation Norway** has replaced the Norwegian Tourist Board. You can reach Innovation Norway at 2 Bloor St. West, Ste. 504, Toronto, Ontario M4W 3E2, Canada (© **416/920-0434;** www.emb-norway.ca).

If you get in touch with a **travel agent,** make sure the agent is a member of the American Society of Travel Agents (ASTA). If a problem arises, you can complain to the consumer affairs department of the Society at 1101 King St., Ste. 200, Alexandria, VA 22314 (© **703/739-2782;** www.astanet.com).

MAPS Many tourist offices supply free maps of their district. You can also contact the Norwegian Automobile Club, Storgata 2, N-0155 Oslo 1 (© **22-34-14-00**), which offers free or inexpensive road maps. Some of Norway's most reliable maps are published by Cappelen.

2 ENTRY REQUIREMENTS

PASSPORTS

Citizens of the United States, Canada, Ireland, Australia, and New Zealand, and British subjects need a valid **passport** to enter Norway. You need to apply for a visa only if you want to stay more than 3 months.

For information on how to get a passport, go to "Passports" in the "Fast Facts" section of appendix A—the websites listed provide downloadable passport applications and the current fees for processing passport applications. For an up-to-date, country-by-country listing of passport requirements around the world, go to the International Travel Web page of the U.S. Department of State at http://travel.state.gov (click on "International Travel for U.S. Citizens").

It's always wise to have plenty of documentation when traveling with children in today's world. For changing details on entry requirements for children traveling abroad, go to the U.S. Department of State website at http://travel.state.gov, and click on "Children & Family."

A British Visitor's Passport is also valid for holidays and some business trips of less than 3 months. The passport can also include your spouse, and it's valid for 1 year. Apply in person at a main post office in the British Isles, and the passport will be issued that day.

Your current domestic **driver's license** is acceptable in Norway. An international driver's license is not required.

CUSTOMS

What You Can Bring into Norway

With certain food exceptions (such as meat, meat products, and cheese), personal effects intended for your own use can be brought into Norway. If you plan to take them with you when you leave, you can bring in cameras, binoculars, radios, portable TVs, and the like, as well as fishing and camping equipment. Visitors of all nationalities can bring in 200 cigarettes, or 250 grams of tobacco and 200 sheets of cigarette paper, or 50 cigars; and 1 liter of spirits or 1 liter of wine. Upon leaving, you can take with you up to NOK25,000 ($5,000/£2,500) in Norwegian currency.

What You Can Take Home from Norway

U.S. Residents

Returning U.S. residents who have been away for at least 48 hours are allowed to bring back, once every 30 days, $800 worth of merchandise duty-free. You'll be charged a flat rate of 4% duty on the next $1,000 worth of purchases. Any dollar amount beyond that is dutiable at whatever rates apply. On mailed gifts, the duty-free limit is $200. Be sure to have your receipts or purchases handy to expedite the declaration process. ***Note:*** If you owe duty, you are required to pay on your arrival in the United States, by cash, personal check, government or traveler's check, or money order, and in some locations a Visa or MasterCard.

To avoid having to pay duty on foreign-made personal items you owned before you left on your trip, bring along a bill of sale, insurance policy, jeweler's appraisal, or receipts of purchase. Or you can register items that can be readily identified by a permanently affixed serial number or marking—think laptop computers, cameras, and CD players—with Customs before you leave. Take the items to the nearest Customs office or register them with Customs at the airport from which you're departing. You'll receive, at no cost, a Certificate of Registration, which allows duty-free entry for the life of the item.

With some exceptions, you cannot bring fresh fruits and vegetables into the United States. For specifics on what you can bring back and the corresponding fees, download the invaluable free pamphlet *Know Before You Go* online at **www.cbp.gov**. Or contact the **U.S. Customs & Border Protection (CBP),** 1300 Pennsylvania Ave., NW, Washington, DC 20229 (✆ **877/287-8867**), and request the pamphlet.

Canadian Residents

For a clear summary of Canadian rules, write for the booklet *Be Aware and Declare,* issued by the **Canada Border Services** (✆ **800/461-9999** in Canada, or 204/983-3500; www.cbsa-asfc.gc.ca). Canada allows its residents a C$750 exemption, and adults are allowed to bring back duty-free one carton of cigarettes, one can of tobacco, 40 imperial ounces of liquor, and 50 cigars. In addition, you're allowed to mail gifts to Canada valued at less than C$60 a day, provided they're unsolicited and don't contain alcohol or tobacco (write on the package "Unsolicited gift, under C$60 value"). Declare all valuables on the Y-38 form before departure from Canada, including serial numbers of valuables you already own, such as expensive foreign cameras. ***Note:*** The C$750 exemption can be used only once a year and only after an absence of 7 days.

U.K. Residents

U.K. residents who are **returning from a European Union country** go through a separate Customs Exit (the "Blue Exit") especially for E.U. travelers. In essence, there is no limit on what you can bring back from an E.U. country, as long as the items are for personal use (this includes gifts) and you have already paid the necessary duty and tax. However, Customs law sets out guidance levels. If you bring in more than these levels, you may be asked to prove that the goods are for your own use. Guidance levels on goods bought in the E.U. for your own use are 3,200 cigarettes, 200 cigars, 400 cigarillos, 3 kilograms of smoking tobacco, 10 liters of spirits, 90 liters of wine, 20 liters of fortified wine (such as port or sherry), and 110 liters of beer.

For information, contact **HM revenue Customs** at ✆ **0845/010-9000** (from outside the U.K., 02920/501-261), or visit www.hmrc.gov.uk.

Australian Residents

The duty-free allowance in Australia is A$900. Residents can bring in 250 cigarettes or 250 grams of loose tobacco, and 2.25 liters of alcohol. If you're taking valuables you already own, such as foreign-made cameras, you should file form B263. A helpful brochure available from Australian consulates or Customs offices is *Know Before You Go*. For more information, call the **Australian Customs Service** at ✆ **1300/363-63,** or go to www.customs.gov.au.

New Zealand Residents

The duty-free allowance for New Zealand is NZ$700. Residents 18 and over can bring in 200 cigarettes, 50 cigars, or 250 grams of tobacco (or a mixture of all three, if their combined weight doesn't exceed 250g); plus 4.5 liters of wine and beer or 1.125 liters of liquor. New Zealand currency does not carry import or export restrictions. Fill out a certificate of export listing the valuables you are taking out of the country; that way, you can bring them back without paying duty. Most questions are answered in a free pamphlet available at New Zealand consulates and Customs offices: *New Zealand Customs Guide for Travellers, Notice No. 4*. For more information, contact **New Zealand Customs Service**, the Customhouse, 17–21 Whitmore St., Box 2218, Wellington (✆ **04/473-6099** or 0800/428-786; www.customs.govt.nz).

3 WHEN TO GO

CLIMATE

In the summer, the average temperature in Norway ranges from 57° to 65°F (13°–18°C). In January, it hovers around 27°F (2°C), ideal weather for winter sports.

The Gulf Stream warms the west coast, where winters tend to be temperate. Rainfall, however, is often heavy here. Above the Arctic Circle, the sun shines night and day from mid-May until late July. For about 2 months every winter, the North Cape is plunged into darkness.

From May to mid-June, the scenery in Norway is at its most spectacular, with fruit trees in blossom, snow in the mountains, and meltwater swelling the waterfalls. There are several public holidays in May, and the Norwegians make full use of them to celebrate springtime after a long winter. In particular, National Day, on May 17, is marked by parties, music, and street parades, with many people dressed in beautiful national costumes. Low-season rates apply during this period.

Late June to early August is the high season in Norway, when the weather is warmest and the schools are on holiday. The most popular tourist places can be busy, but finding peace and quiet, if you wish, is easy. All the man-made tourist attractions are open, and public transport services are more frequent.

Mid-August to October is a time when accommodations and ferries are at mid- or low-season rates. There is so little traffic that you may feel as if you have the whole country to yourself. The temperature drops slowly through September, making for good berry- and mushroom-picking weather. The glorious colors of autumn are at their best in October.

Norway's summer weather is variable and unpredictable, with a number of surprising features. The Atlantic Gulf Stream keeps the western fjord area and the coast up into the Arctic North much warmer than you might expect. The west coast receives the most rain, but the area farther east is drier. The sea temperature can reach 64°F (18°C) or higher on the south coast, where swimming is a popular pastime. Surprisingly, the water is often calm, as most of the inhabited places in Norway are sheltered from the prevailing wind by mountains and forest.

The warmest and most stable weather occurs on the eastern side of the southern mountains, including the south coast between Mandal and Oslo. Even in the north, summer temperatures are pleasantly warm; however, as nearly all of this area is near the west coast, the weather can be wet and changeable. Be sure to take waterproof clothing. If you should be unlucky with the weather, remember a wise Norwegian saying, "There is no such thing as bad weather, only bad clothing."

In winter, much of Norway is transformed into a snow-clad paradise from November to April. Undoubtedly, the best way to enjoy it is on skis, but there are many other things to do as well. Just sitting by the fire in a warm and cozy log cabin is a pleasure for some, as is the friendly, relaxed atmosphere of the hotel bar. Children of all ages (and many grown-ups) never get tired of just playing in the snow. Active types can go tobogganing, skating, ice fishing, ice climbing, dog sledding, and more.

THE MIDNIGHT SUN In the summer, the sun never fully sets in northern Norway; and even in the south, the sun may set around 11pm and rise at 3am. Keep in mind that although the sun shines at midnight, it's not as strong as at midday. Always bring a warm jacket or sweater.

Norway's Average Daytime Temperatures (°F/°C)

		Jan	Feb	Mar	Apr	May	June	July	Aug	Sept	Oct	Nov	Dec
Oslo	Temp. (°F)	25	26	32	41	51	60	64	61	53	42	33	27
	Temp. (°C)	–4	–3	0	5	11	16	18	16	12	6	1	–3
Bergen/	Temp. (°F)	35	35	38	41	40	55	59	58	54	47	42	38
Stavanger	Temp. (°C)	2	2	3	5	4	13	15	14	12	8	6	3
Trondheim	Temp. (°F)	27	27	31	38	47	53	58	57	50	42	35	31
	Temp. (°C)	–3	–3	–1	3	8	12	14	14	10	6	2	–1

Fun Facts Land of the Midnight Sun

In these locations, you can see the whole disk of the sun on the given dates:

Place	From	To
Nordkapp	May 13	July 29
Hammerfest	May 16	July 26
Vardo	May 17	July 25
Tromsø	May 20	July 22
Harstad	May 24	July 18
Svolvær	May 28	July 14
Bodø	June 3	July 8

NORWAY CALENDAR OF EVENTS

Dates are approximate. Check with the local tourist office before making plans to attend a specific event.

January

Northern Lights Festival, Tromsø. Classical and contemporary music performances by musicians from Norway and abroad. Visit www.nordlysfestivalen.no for details. Late January.

February

Kristiansund Opera Festival. Featuring Kristiansund Opera's productions of opera and ballet, plus art exhibitions, concerts, and other events. Visit www.olk.no for details. Early February.

March

Holmenkollen Ski Festival, Oslo. One of Europe's largest ski festivals, with World Cup Nordic skiing and biathlons, international ski-jumping competitions, and Norway's largest cross-country race for amateurs. Held at Holmenkollen Ski Jump on the outskirts of Oslo. To participate, attend, or request more information, contact Skiforeningen, Kongeveien 5, Holmenkollen, N-0787 Oslo 3 (✆ **22-92-32-00;** www.skiforeningen.no). Early March.

Narvik Winter Festival. Sports events, carnivals, concerts, and opera performances highlight this festival dedicated to those who built the railway across northern Norway and Sweden. Visit www.vinterfestuka.no for details, or call ✆ **76-95-03-50.** Second week of March to mid-April.

Birkebeiner Race, Rena to Lillehammer. This historic international ski race, with thousands of participants, crosses the mountains between Rena and Lillehammer, site of the 1994 Olympics. It's a 53km (33-mile) cross-country trek. For details, call ✆ **41-77-29-00** or go to www.birkebeiner.no. Mid-March.

April

Voss Jazz Festival. Three days of jazz and folk music performances by European and American artists. Visit www.vossajazz.no, or call ✆ **56-52-99-11** for details. First week of April.

May

Bergen International Festival (Bergen Festspill). A world-class music event, featuring artists from Norway and around the world. This is one of the largest annual musical events in Scandinavia. Held at various venues in Bergen. For information, contact the Bergen International Festival, Slottsgaten 1,

4055, Dregen N-5835 Bergen (✆ **55-21-06-30;** www.fib.no). Late May to early June.

June

Faerder Sailing Race. Some 1,000 sailboats participate in this race, which ends in Borre, by the Oslofjord. Call ✆ **23-27-56-00,** or go to www.kns.no for details. Mid-June.

North Cape March. This trek from Honningsvåg to the North Cape is one of the world's toughest. The round-trip march is 68km (42 miles) long. Details at www.nordkapp.no. Mid-June.

Emigration Festival, Stavanger. A festive commemoration of Norwegian emigration to North America, with exhibitions, concerts, theater, and folklore. Mid-June.

Midsummer Night, nationwide. Celebrations and bonfires explode all over Norway in honor of the midnight sun. June 23.

Emigration Festival, Kvinesdal. Commemorates the Norwegian emigration to the United States. Late June to early July.

Midnight Sun Marathon, Tromsø. This marathon in northern Norway starts at midnight and draws eager runners from over 30 countries. For details, call ✆ **77-67-33-63** or go to www.msm.no. Mid-June.

July

Kongsberg International Jazz Festival. International artists participate in one of the most important jazz festivals in Scandinavia, with open-air concerts. Call ✆ **32-73-31-66,** or visit www.kongsberg-jazzfestival.no for details. Early July.

Exxon Mobil Bislett Games, Oslo. International athletic competitions are staged in Oslo, with professional participants from all over the world. For details, call ✆ **22-59-17-59** or visit www.bislettgames.com. Early to mid-July.

Molde International Jazz Festival. The "City of Roses" is the site of Norway's oldest jazz festival. It attracts international stars from both sides of the Atlantic every year and is held at venues in Molde for 6 days. For details, contact the Molde Jazz Festival, Box 415, N-6401 Molde (✆ **71-20-31-50;** www.moldejazz.no). Mid-July.

Norway Cup International Youth Soccer Tournament, Oslo. The world's largest youth soccer tournament attracts 1,000 teams from around the world to Oslo. Call ✆ **22-28-90-57,** or visit www.norway-cup.no. Late July to early August.

August

Telemark International Folk Music Festival, Bø. An international festival of folk music and folk dance takes place in the home of many famous fiddlers, dancers, and singers. Call ✆ **33-95-19-19,** or visit www.telemarkfestivalen.no. Early August.

Peer Gynt Festival, Vinstra. Art exhibitions, evenings of music and song, parades in national costumes, and other events honor Ibsen's fictional character. Call ✆ **61-29-47-70,** or visit www.peergynt.no for details. Early August.

Oslo Jazz Festival. This annual festival features music from the earliest years of jazz (1920–25), as well as classical concerts, opera, and ballet. For details, call the Oslo Tourist Bureau, at ✆ **81-53-05-55,** or visit www.oslojazz.no. Second week of August.

Chamber Music Festival, Oslo. Norwegian and foreign musicians perform at Oslo's Akershus Castle and Fortress, which dates from A.D. 1300. Call ✆ **23-10-07-30,** or visit www.oslokammermusikkfestival.no for details. Mid-August.

September

Oslo Marathon. This annual event draws some of Norway's best long-distance runners. Call ✆ **22-69-31-20-21,**

Tracing Your Norwegian Roots

If you're of Norwegian ancestry, you can get information on how to trace your family history from the nearest Norwegian consulate. In Norway, contact the **Norwegian Emigration Center,** Strandkaien 31, N-4005 Stavanger (✆ **51-53-88-60;** www.emigrationcenter.com), for a catalog of information about Norwegian families who emigrated to the United States.

In the United States, the **Family History Library of the Church of Jesus Christ of Latter-day Saints,** 35 N. West Temple, Salt Lake City, UT 84150 (✆ **801/240-2331;** www.familysearch.org), has extensive records of Norwegian families that emigrated to the United States and Canada. The library is open to the public without charge for genealogical research. Mormon churches in other cities have listings of materials available in Salt Lake City; for a small fee, you can request pertinent microfilms, which you can view at a local church.

or visit www.oslomaraton.no. Mid-September.

DECEMBER

Nobel Peace Prize Ceremony, Oslo. A major event on the Oslo calendar, attracting world attention. Attendance is by invitation only. For information, contact the Nobel Institute, Henrik Ibsen Gate 51, N-0255 Oslo 2 (✆ **22-12-93-00;** http://nobelprize.org). Held at Oslo City Hall. December 10.

4 GETTING THERE & GETTING AROUND

GETTING THERE BY PLANE

All transatlantic flights from North America land at Oslo's Fornebu Airport. **SAS** (✆ **800/221-2350** in the U.S.; www.flysas.com) flies nonstop daily from Newark to Oslo. The trip takes about 7½ hours. Most other SAS flights from North America go through Copenhagen. Flying time from Chicago is 11 hours; from Seattle, it's 12 hours, not including the layover in Copenhagen. From New York, **Continental** (✆ **800/525-0280;** www.continental.com) flies 4 days a week in the summer (Thurs–Sun) to Oslo direct. In winter there are New York–to-Oslo flights on Saturday, Sunday, and Thursday.

If you fly to Norway on another airline, you'll be routed through a gateway city in Europe and will sometimes continue on a different airline. **British Airways** (✆ **800/AIRWAYS** in the U.S.; www.britishairways.com), for example, has dozens of daily flights from many North American cities to London, where you can continue to Oslo. **Icelandair** (✆ **800/223-5500** in the U.S.; www.icelandair.com) can be an excellent choice, with connections through Reykjavik. **KLM** (✆ **800/225-2525** in the U.S.; www.klm.com) serves Oslo through Amsterdam.

For passengers from the U.K., **British Airways** (✆ **0844/493-0787** in the U.K.) operates at least four daily nonstops to Oslo from London. **SAS** (✆ **0870/6072-7727** in the U.K.) runs four daily flights

Tips Getting Through the Airport

- Arrive at the airport at least 2 hours before an international flight; if you show up late, tell an airline employee and he or she will probably whisk you to the front of the line. You can check the average wait times at your airport by going to the TSA **Security Checkpoint Wait Times** site (www.tsa.gov/travelers/waittime.shtm).
- Know what you can carry on and what you can't. For the latest updates on items you are prohibited to bring in carry-on luggage, go to **www.tsa.gov/travelers/airtravel.**
- Beat the ticket-counter lines by using airport electronic kiosks or even online check-in from your home computers, from which you can print out boarding passes in advance. Curbside check-in is also a good way to avoid lines.
- Bring a current government-issued photo ID such as a driver's license or passport. Children under 18 do not need government-issued photo IDs for flights within the U.S., but they do for international flights to most countries.
- Help speed up security before you're screened. Remove jackets, shoes, belt buckles, heavy jewelry, and watches, and place them either in your carry-on luggage or the security bins provided. Place keys, coins, cellphones, and pagers in a security bin. If you have metallic body parts, carry a note from your doctor. When possible, pack liquids in checked baggage.
- Use a TSA-approved lock for your checked luggage. Look for Travel Sentry–certified locks at luggage or travel shops and Brookstone stores (or online at www.brookstone.com).

from Heathrow to Oslo. Flying time from London to Oslo on any airline is around 2 hours.

Summer (generally June–Sept) is the peak season and the most expensive. Norway's off season is in winter (about Nov 1–Mar 21). Shoulder season is in both spring and fall. In any season, midweek fares (Mon–Thurs) are lowest.

Flying for Less: Tips for Getting the Best Airfare

Passengers sharing the same airplane cabin rarely pay the same fare. Travelers who need to purchase tickets at the last minute, change their itinerary at a moment's notice, or fly one-way often get stuck paying the premium rate. Here are some ways to keep your airfare costs down:

- Passengers who can book their ticket **far in advance,** who can **stay over Saturday night,** or who **fly midweek** or **at less-trafficked hours** may pay a fraction of the full fare. If your schedule is flexible, say so, and ask if you can secure a cheaper fare by changing your flight plans.
- You can also save on airfares by keeping an eye out in local newspapers for **promotional specials** or **fare wars,** when airlines lower prices on their most popular routes. You rarely see fare wars offered for peak travel times, but if you can travel in the off-months, you may snag a bargain.
- Search the **Internet** for cheap fares. The most popular online travel agencies are **Travelocity.com** (www.travelocity.ca or www.travelocity.co.uk), **Expedia.com** (www.expedia.ca or www.expedia.co.uk), and **Orbitz.com**. In the U.K., **Travelsupermarket** (✆ **0845/345-5708;** www.

travelsupermarket.com) is a flight search engine that offers flight comparisons for budget airlines whose seats often end up in bucket-shop sales. Other websites for booking airline tickets online include **Cheapflights.com, SmarterTravel.com, Priceline.com,** and **Opodo** (www.opodo.co.uk). Meta search sites (which find and then direct you to airline and hotel websites for booking) include **Sidestep.com** and **Kayak.com**—the latter includes fares for budget carriers such as jetBlue and Spirit as well as the major airlines. **Site59.com** is a great source for last-minute flights and getaways. In addition, most **airlines** offer online-only fares that even their phone agents know nothing about. British travelers should check **Flights International** (✆ **0800/0187050;** www.flights-international.com) for deals on flights all over the world.

- **Consolidators,** also known as bucket shops, are great sources for international tickets, although they usually can't beat the Internet-only fares within North America. Start by looking in Sunday newspaper travel sections; U.S. travelers should focus on the *New York Times, Los Angeles Times,* and *Miami Herald.* For less-developed destinations, small travel agents who cater to immigrant communities in large cities often have the best deals. ***Beware:*** Bucket-shop tickets are usually nonrefundable or rigged with stiff cancellation penalties, often as high as 50% to 75% of the ticket price, and some put you on charter airlines, which may leave at inconvenient times and experience delays. Several reliable consolidators are worldwide and available on the Net. **STA Travel** (✆ **800/781-4040;** www.sta.com) is now the world's leader in student travel, thanks to the purchase of Council Travel. It also offers good fares for travelers of all ages. It also has "local" websites in 12 countries. **FlyCheap** (✆ **800/FLY-CHEAP;** www.1800flycheap.com) is owned by package-holiday megalith MyTravel and has especially good access to fares for sunny destinations. **Air Tickets Direct** (✆ **800/778-3447;** www.airticketsdirect.com) is based in Montreal and leverages the weaker Canadian dollar for low fares.
- Join **frequent-flier clubs.** Frequent-flier membership doesn't cost a cent, but it does entitle you to free tickets or upgrades when you amass the airline's required number of frequent-flier points. You don't even have to fly to earn points; **frequent-flier credit cards** can earn you thousands of miles for doing your everyday shopping. But

Tips Security Measures

Because of increased security measures, the Transportation Security Administration has made changes to the prohibited items list. All liquids and gels—including shampoo, toothpaste, perfume, hair gel, suntan lotion, and all other items with similar consistency—**are prohibited** from carry-on baggage and the security checkpoint, unless packed in 3-ounce containers (or smaller) that, in turn, fit into a zip-top, quart-size clear plastic bag. Pack larger items in your checked baggage. Carrying oversized liquids of any sort to the screening checkpoint will cause you delays and will most likely result in the item being confiscated. See www.tsa.gov/311 for more details.

keep in mind that award seats are limited, seats on popular routes are hard to snag, and more and more major airlines are cutting their expiration periods for mileage points—so check your airline's frequent-flier program so you don't lose your miles before you use them. ***Inside tip:*** Award seats are offered almost a year in advance, but seats also open up at the last minute, so if your travel plans are flexible, you may strike gold. To play the frequent-flier game to your best advantage, consult the community bulletin boards on **FlyerTalk** (www.flyertalk.com) or go to Randy Petersen's **Inside Flyer** (www.insideflyer.com). Petersen and friends review all the programs in detail and post regular updates on changes in policies and trends.

GETTING THERE BY CAR

If you're driving from the Continent, you must go through Sweden. From **Copenhagen,** take the E47/55 express highway north to Helsingør and catch the car ferry to Helsingborg, Sweden. From there, the E6 runs to Oslo. From **Stockholm,** drive across Sweden on E18 to Oslo.

GETTING THERE BY TRAIN

Copenhagen is the main rail hub for service between Scandinavia and the rest of Europe. There are three daily trains from Copenhagen to Oslo. All connect with the Danish ferries operating to Norway through either Helsingør or Hirtshals.

Most rail traffic from Sweden into Norway follows the main corridors between Stockholm and Oslo and between Gothenburg and Oslo.

If you plan to travel a great deal on Norwegian railroads, it's worth securing a copy of the *Thomas Cook European Timetable of European Passenger Railroads.* It's available online at www.thomascooktimetables.com.

Thousands of trains run from Britain to the Continent, and at least some of them go directly across or under the Channel, through France or Belgium and Germany into Denmark, where connections can be made to Norway. For example, a train leaves London's Victoria Station daily at 9am and arrives in Copenhagen the next day at 8:25am. Another train leaves London's Victoria Station at 8:45pm and arrives in Copenhagen the next day at 8:20pm. Both go through Dover-Ostende, or with a connection at Brussels. Once you're in Copenhagen, you can make rail connections to Oslo. Because of the time and distances involved, many passengers rent a couchette (sleeping berth). Designed like padded benches stacked bunk-style, they're usually clustered six to a compartment.

Rail Passes for North American Travelers

EURAILPASS The Eurailpass permits unlimited first-class rail travel in any country in western Europe except the British Isles (good in Ireland). Passes are available for purchase online (www.eurail.com) and at various offices/agents around the world. Travel agents and railway agents in such cities as New York, Montreal, and Los Angeles sell Eurailpasses. You can purchase them at the North American offices of CIT Travel Service, the French National Railroads, the German Federal Railroads, and the Swiss Federal Railways. It is strongly recommended that you purchase passes before you leave home as not all passes are available in Europe; also, passes purchased in Europe will cost about 20% more. Numerous options are available for travel in France.

The **Eurail Global Pass** allows you unlimited travel in 20 Eurail-affiliated countries. You can travel on any of the days within the validity period which is available for 15 days, 21 days, 1 month, 2 months, 3 months, and some other possibilities as well. Prices for first-class adult travel are $745 for 15 days; $965 for 21 days; $1,199 for 1 month; $1,695 for 2 months; and $2,089 for 3 months. Children 4 to 11 pay half-fare; those 3 and under travel for free.

A **Eurail Global Pass Saver,** also valid for first-class travel in 20 countries, offers a special deal for two or more people traveling together. This pass costs $629 for 15 days; $819 for 21 days; $1,019 for 1 month; $1,439 for 2 months; and $1,785 for 3 months.

A **Eurail Global Youth Pass** for those 12 to 25 allows second-class travel in 18 countries. This pass costs $485 for 15 days; $625 for 21 days; $779 for 1 month; $1,099 for 2 months; and $1,359 for 3 months.

The **Eurail Select Pass** offers unlimited travel on the national rail networks of any three, four, or five bordering countries out of the 22 Eurail nations linked by train or ship. Two or more passengers can travel together for big discounts, getting 5, 6, 8, 10, or 15 days of rail travel within any 2-month period on the national rail networks of any three, four, or five adjoining Eurail countries linked by train or ship. A sample fare: For 5 days in 2 months you pay $469 for three countries. **Eurail Select Pass Youth** for travelers under 26 allows second-class travel within the same guidelines as Eurail Selectpass, with fees starting at $305. **Eurail Select Pass Saver** offers discounts for two or more people traveling together—first-class travel within the same guidelines as Eurail Selectpass—with fees starting at $399.

WHERE TO BUY RAIL PASSES Travel agents in all towns and railway agents in major North American cities sell all these tickets, but the biggest supplier is **Rail Europe** (✆ **877/272-RAIL;** www.raileurope.com), which can also give you informational brochures.

Many different rail passes are available in the United Kingdom for travel in Britain and continental Europe. Stop in at the **International Rail Centre,** Victoria Station, London SWIV 1JY (✆ **0870/5848-848** in the U.K.). Some of the most popular passes, including Inter-Rail and Euro Youth, are offered only to travelers under 26 years of age; these allow unlimited second-class travel through most European countries.

SCANRAIL PASS If your visit to Europe will be primarily in Scandinavia, the Scanrail pass may be better and cheaper than the Eurailpass. This pass allows its owner a designated number of days of free rail travel within a larger time block. (Presumably, this allows for days devoted to sightseeing scattered among days of rail transfers between cities or sites of interest.) You can choose a total of any 5 days of unlimited rail travel during a 15-day period, 10 days of rail travel within a 1-month period, or 1 month of unlimited rail travel. The pass, which is valid on all lines of the state railways of Denmark, Finland, Norway, and Sweden, offers discounts or free travel on some (but not all) of the region's ferry lines as well. The pass can be purchased only in North America. It's available from any office of **RailEurope** (✆ **800/848-7245**) or **ScanAm World Tours,** 108 N. Main St., Cranbury, NJ 08512 (✆ **800/545-2204;** www.scandinaviantravel.com).

Depending on whether you choose first- or second-class rail transport, 5 days in 10 days costs $249 to $329, 8 days out of 2 months costs $180 to $360, 10 days out of 22 days costs $359 to $489, and 21 consecutive days of unlimited travel costs $469 to $629. Seniors get an 11% discount, and students receive a 30% discount.

Rail Passes for British Travelers

If you plan to do a lot of exploring, you may prefer one of the three rail passes designed for unlimited train travel within a designated region during a predetermined number of days. These passes are sold in Britain and several other European countries.

An **InterRail Pass** is available to passengers of any nationality, with some restrictions—they must be under age 26 and able to prove residency in a European or North African country (Morocco, Algeria, and Tunisia) for at least 6 months before buying the pass. It allows unlimited travel through Europe, except Albania and the republics of the former Soviet Union. Prices are complicated and vary depending on the countries you want to include. For pricing purposes, Europe is divided into eight zones; the cost depends on the number of zones you include. For ages 25 and under, the most expensive option (£399) allows 1 month of unlimited travel in all eight zones and is known to the staff as a "global." The least expensive option (£159) allows 5 days of travel within 10 days.

Passengers age 26 and older can buy an **InterRail 26-Plus Pass.** The cost varies from £359 to £489 for 16 days to £599 to £809 for 1 month. Passengers must meet the same residency requirements that apply to the InterRail Pass (described above).

For information on buying individual rail tickets or any of the just-mentioned passes, contact **National Rail Inquiries,** Victoria Station, London (✆ **08705/848-848**). Tickets and passes also are available at any of the larger railway stations, as well as selected travel agencies throughout Britain and the rest of Europe.

GETTING THERE BY SHIP & FERRY

FROM DENMARK The trip from Frederikshavn at the northern port of Jutland in Denmark to Oslo takes 11 hours. Call **Stena Line** (✆ **96-20-02-00;** www.stenaline.com) for general reservations.

FROM SWEDEN From Strømstad, Sweden, in the summer the daily crossing to Sandefjord, Norway, takes 2½ hours. Bookings can be made through **Color Line,** Tollbugata 5, N-3210 Sandefjord (✆ **47-22-94-42-00;** www.colorline.com).

FROM ENGLAND **SeaEurope Holidays,** 6801 Lake Worth Rd., Ste. 107, Lake Worth, Florida 33467 (✆ **800/533-3755;** www.seaeurope.com), is a U.S.–based company that will arrange a variety of seagoing options for you, all before you land in mainland Europe. For example, if you'd like to sail from Newcastle in England to Bergen in Norway, these trips can be arranged.

GETTING THERE BY CRUISE SHIP

Norway's fjords and mountain vistas are among the most spectacular panoramas in the world. Many ship owners and cruise lines offer excursions along the Norwegian coast.

One of the most prominent lines is **Cunard** (✆ **800/7CUNARD** in the U.S. and Canada; www.cunard.com, or ✆ 0845-071-0300; www.cunard.co.uk in the U.K.).

Ten-day cruises are offered on the new Cunard flagship, *Queen Mary 2* (from $3,422/£1,711 in summer). This vessel re-creates the grandeur of those old queen liners, *Queen Mary* and *Queen Elizabeth,* but on a larger, more modern scale. The 150,000-ton ship carries a total of 2,620 passengers.

Departing from Southampton, England, the ship calls at Oslo and Bergen and cruises the North Sea. En route it also stops at the most frequently visited fjords, including the Eidfjord. Prices for the 6-day cruise (starting at $1,294/£647 in summer) include round-trip airfare to London on British Airways from 79 gateway cities throughout the world.

In its tour of Baltic capitals, **Norwegian Cruise Line** (✆ **866/234-0292;** www.ncl.com) stops at Helsinki, Stockholm, and Copenhagen, but, ironically, doesn't go as far as Norway itself.

GETTING AROUND BY PLANE

The best way to get around Norway is to take advantage of air passes that apply to the whole region. If you're traveling extensively, special European passes are available.

SAS'S "VISIT SCANDINAVIA" FARE The vast distances encourage air travel between Norway's far-flung points. One of the most worthwhile promotions is SAS's **Visit Scandinavia Pass.** Available only to travelers who fly SAS across the Atlantic, it includes up to six coupons, each of which is valid for any SAS flight within or between Denmark, Norway, and Sweden. Each coupon costs $60, $80, or $100, depending on the route. The pass is especially valuable if you plan to travel to the far northern frontiers of Sweden or Norway; in that case, the savings over the price of a regular economy-class ticket can be substantial. For information on buying the pass, call **SAS** (© **800/221-2350;** www.flysas.com).

WITHIN NORWAY Norway has excellent domestic air service. In addition to SAS, an independent airway, **Wideroe Flyveselskap,** provides quick and convenient ways to get around a large country with many hard-to-reach areas. For more information, call © **47-75-11-11-11** or visit www.wideroe.no.

GETTING AROUND BY TRAIN

Norway's network of electric and diesel-electric trains runs as far as Bodø, 100km (62 miles) north of the Arctic Circle. (Beyond that, visitors must take a coastal steamer, plane, or bus to Tromsø and the North Cape.) Upgraded express trains (the fastest in the country) crisscross the mountainous terrain between Oslo, Stavanger, Bergen, and Trondheim. For information and reservations, contact the Norwegian State Railways (NSB; © **81-50-08-88;** www.nsb.no).

The most popular and most scenic run covers the 483km (299 miles) between Oslo and Bergen. Visitors with limited time often choose this route for its fabled mountains, gorges, white-water rivers, and fjords. The trains make frequent stops for passengers to enjoy breathtaking views.

Second-class travel on Norwegian trains is recommended. In fact, second class in Norway is as good as or better than first-class travel anywhere else in Europe, with reclining seats and lots of unexpected comforts. Of course, first-class train travel in Norway is better, though not necessarily *that* much better, than second class. For those who want the added comforts and can afford it, first class is the way to go.

The one-way second-class fare from Oslo to Bergen is NOK739 ($148/£74), plus a mandatory seat reservation of NOK40 ($8/£4). Another popular run, from Oslo to Trondheim, costs NOK813 ($163/£81) one-way in second class. First class from Oslo to Bergen costs NOK814 ($163/£81), and from Oslo to Trondheim NOK888 ($178/£89).

One of the country's obviously scenic trips, from Bergen to Bodø, is not possible by train because of the terrain. Trains to Bodø leave from Oslo. Express trains are called *Expresstog,* and you have to read the fine print of a railway schedule to figure out whether an Expresstog is much faster than a conventional train.

On express and other major trains, you must reserve seats at the train's starting station. Sleepers are priced according to the number of berths in each compartment. Children 4 to 15 years of age and seniors are granted reduced fares.

There are special compartments for persons with disabilities on most medium- and long-distance trains. People in wheelchairs and others with physical disabilities, and their companions, may use the compartments. Some long-distance trains offer special playrooms ("Kiddie-Wagons") for children, complete with toys, games, and books.

EURAIL NORWAY PASS A restricted rail pass applicable only to the state railway lines, the Eurail Norway Pass is available for 3 to 8 days of unlimited rail travel in 1 month. It's suitable for anyone who wants to cover the long distances that separate Norwegian cities. The pass is available in North America through **Rail Europe** (© **800/848-7245;** www.rail europe.com). The cost is $299 for adults in second class for any 3 days in 1 month. For 4 days of travel in 1 month, the second-class cost is $325. For 5 days of travel in 1 month, the second-class cost is $359. For 6 days of travel in 1 month, the second-class cost is $405. For 8 days of travel in 1 month, second class is $455. Children 4 to 15 years of age pay half the adult fare; and those under 4 ride free. Discount passes are available for youth 16 to 25 (Norway Youth Pass) and for travelers over 60 (Norway Senior Pass).

MINIRPIS TICKETS NSB's regional trains offer unlimited travel for NOK199 to NOK299 ($40–$60/£20–£30). The offer is valid for a limited number of seats. You can purchase the ticket by logging on to www.nsb.no. Tickets are often sold out, so make reservations as soon as possible. At this price, tickets are not refundable and a change of reservation is not possible. A supplement of NOK75 ($15/£7.50) will grant you access to the NSB "Komfort Class" section.

GETTING AROUND BY BUS

Where the train or coastal steamer stops, passengers can usually continue on a scenic bus ride. Norway's bus system is excellent, linking remote villages along the fjords. Numerous all-inclusive motorcoach tours, often combined with steamer travel, leave from Bergen and Oslo in the summer. The train ends in Bodø; from there you can get a bus to Fauske (63km/39 miles east). From Fauske, the Polar Express bus spans the entire distance along the Arctic Highway, through Finnmark (Lapland) to Kirkenes, near the Russian border, and back. The segment from Alta to Kirkenes is open only from June to October, but there's year-round service from Fauske to Alta. Passengers are guaranteed hotel accommodations along the way.

Buses have air-conditioning, toilets, adjustable seats, reading lights, and a telephone. Reservations are not accepted on most buses, and payment is made to the driver onboard. Fares depend on the distance traveled. Children under 4 travel free, and children 4 to 16 and seniors pay half-price. For the Oslo-Sweden-Hammerfest "Express 2000," a 30-hour trip, reservations must be made in advance.

For more information about bus travel in Norway, contact **Norway Buss Ekspress AS,** Karl Johans Gate (© **81-54-44-44;** www.nor-way.no) in Oslo, or **Passage Tours of Scandinavia** (© **800/548-5960** in the U.S.; www.passagetours.com).

GETTING AROUND BY CAR & FERRY

Dazzling scenery awaits you at nearly every turn if you drive through Norway. Some roads are less than perfect (dirt or gravel is frequent), but all are passable (you'll even be able to drive to the North Cape). Most mountain roads are open by May 1; the so-called motoring season lasts from mid-May to the end of September. In western Norway, hairpin curves are common, but if you're willing to settle for doing less than 240km (149 miles) a day, you needn't worry. The easiest and most convenient touring territory is in and around Oslo and south to Stavanger.

Bringing a car into Norway is relatively uncomplicated. If you own the car you're driving, you must present your national driver's license, car registration, and proof that the car is insured. (This proof usually takes the form of a document known as a "Green Card," which Customs agents will refer to specifically.) If you've rented a car in another country and want to drive it into Norway, be sure to verify at the time of rental that the registration and insurance documents are in order—they probably will be. Regardless of whether you own or rent the car you're about to drive into Norway, don't assume that your private North American insurance policy will automatically apply. Chances are good that it will, but in the event of an accident, you may have to cope with a burdensome amount of paperwork.

If you're driving through any of Norway's coastal areas, you'll probably have to traverse one or many of the country's famous fjords. Although more and more bridges are being built, Norway's network of privately run ferries is essential for transporting cars across hundreds of fjords and estuaries. Motorists should ask the tourist bureau for the free map *Norway by Car* and a timetable outlining the country's dozens of car-ferry services. The cost for cars and passengers is low.

RENTALS Avis, Budget, and Hertz offer well-serviced, well-maintained fleets of rental cars in Norway. Prices and terms tend to be more favorable for those who reserve vehicles from home before their departure and who present evidence of membership in such organizations as AA (Automobile Association), AAA (American Automobile Association), or AARP. The major competitors' prices tend to be roughly equivalent, except for promotional deals scheduled from time to time.

The prices quoted here include the 23% government tax. The major U.S.-based car rental firms are represented in Norway, including **Budget** (✆ **800/527-0700** in the U.S. and Canada; www.budget.com), **Hertz** (✆ **800/654-3001** in the U.S.; www.hertz.com), and **Avis** (✆ **800/331-1212** in the U.S.; www.avis.com). Despite pressure from the telephone sales representative, it pays to ask questions and shop around before you commit to a prepaid reservation. Each company maintains an office at the Oslo airport, in the center of Oslo, and at airports and city centers elsewhere around the country.

Note: Remember that prices and the relative merits of each company can and will change during the lifetime of this edition, depending on promotions and other factors.

An auto supplier that might not automatically come to mind is **Kemwel** (✆ **800/678-0678;** www.kemwel.com), an auto-rental broker that monitors the availability of rental cars in markets across Europe, including Norway. Originally established in 1908 and now operating in close conjunction with its affiliated company, **Auto Europe** (✆ **800/223-5555;** www.autoeurope.com), it offers convenient and prepaid access to thousands of cars, from a variety of reputable car-rental outfits throughout Europe; sometimes you'll find more favorable rates than those you might have gotten by contacting those companies directly.

Car rentals are reserved and prepaid, in dollars or pounds, prior to your departure for Europe, thereby avoiding the confusion about unfavorable currency conversions and government tax add-ons that you might have discovered after your return home. You're given the option at the time of your booking of whether you want to include collision-damage and other forms of insurance. Most car rentals can be picked up either at the airport or in the downtown offices of cities throughout Norway, and there's usually no penalty for one-way rentals.

DRIVING RULES Driving is on the right, and the law requires that you keep your headlights on at all times. Every passenger, including infants, must wear seat belts. Children 5 years of age and under must ride in the back. A driver must yield to cars approaching from the right. On most major highways, the maximum speed

Tips Winter Motoring in Norway

If you're going to drive in Norway in winter, you must be prepared for the conditions. Most of the main roads are kept open by snowplows year-round, but the road surface will often be hard-packed snow and ice. Journey times will be much longer than in summer, 50km (31 miles) per hour is a typical average, and in bad weather there can be long delays over mountain passes. Most Norwegians use winter tires with metal studs, which come with all rental cars. Temperatures as low as 25°F (–3°C) are common. A good ice scraper and snow brush are essential, as is a diesel engine.

limit is 90kmph (55 mph). On secondary routes, the speed limit ranges from 70kmph (43 mph) to 80kmph (50 mph). Do not drink and drive. Norway has perhaps the strictest laws in Europe about drinking and driving, and there are roadside checks. Speeding is also severely punished, and most highways are monitored by radar and cameras.

GASOLINE (PETROL) There are plenty of gas stations in Norway, and unleaded gasoline *(blyfri bensin)* and diesel fuel are sold from self-service pumps. Those pumps labeled *kort* are open day and night. Most of them accept regular bank credit cards or else oil company credit cards. In the countryside of Norway, gas stations' hours of operation vary widely.

5 MONEY & COSTS

The Norwegian currency is the **krone** (plural: **kroner**), written as NOK. There are 100 **øre** in 1 krone. Bank notes are issued in denominations of 50, 100, 200, 500, and 1,000 kroner. Coins are issued in denominations of 50 øre, 1 krone, and 5, 10, and 20 kroner.

CURRENCY EXCHANGE

Banks offer the best rates for performing currency exchanges. Most hotels will exchange money but usually at an unfavorable rate.

Many hotels in Norway simply do not accept a dollar- or pound-denominated personal check; those that do will certainly charge for making the conversion. In some cases, a hotel may accept countersigned traveler's checks or a credit or charge card.

If you're making a deposit on a hotel reservation, it's cheaper and easier to pay with a check drawn from a Norwegian bank. This can be arranged by a large commercial bank or by a specialist such as **Ruesch International,** 700 11th St. NW, Fourth Floor, Washington, DC 20001 (✆ **800/424-2923** or 202/408-1200; www.ruesch.com), which performs a wide variety of conversion-related tasks, usually for about $15 per transaction.

If you need a check payable in a Norwegian currency, call Ruesch's toll-free number, describe what you need, and write down the transaction number. Mail your dollar-denominated personal check (payable to Ruesch International) to the Washington, D.C., office. When it's received, the company will mail you a check denominated in the requested currency for the specified amount, minus the $3 charge. The company can also help you with wire transfers, as well as converting VAT (value-added tax) refund checks. Information is mailed upon request.

The Norwegian Kroner and Other Currencies

At press time for this edition, faced with some of the greatest fiscal instability since before World War II, U.S. and Norwegian currency experts held widely varying opinions about the 2-year outlook for the interrelated values of the kroner, the dollar, the pound, and the euro. With that in mind, we compiled the following chart as a very rough guide for how the Norwegian kroner might stack up against other international currencies.

For American readers: At the time of this writing, US$1 = approximately 5NOK (or stated differently, 1NOK = approximately 20¢). This was the rate of exchange used to calculate the simplified dollar values provided throughout this edition.

For British readers: At this writing, £1 = approximately 10NOK (or 1NOK = approximately 10p). This was the rate of exchange used to calculate the pound-designated values within the chart below and throughout this edition.

Regarding the Euro: At the time of this writing, 1€ = 10NOK (or stated differently, 1NOK = 10 eurocents).

These monetary relationships can and probably will change during the lifetime of this edition. For more on exact ratios between these and other currencies, check an up-to-date source at the time of your arrival in Norway.

NOK	US$	UK£	Euro€	NOK	US$	UK£	Euro€
1	0.20	0.10	0.10	75.00	15.00	7.50	7.50
2	0.40	0.20	0.20	100.00	20.00	10.00	10.00
3	0.60	0.30	0.30	125.00	25.00	12.50	12.50
4	0.80	0.40	0.40	150.00	30.00	15.00	15.00
5	1.00	0.50	0.50	175.00	35.00	17.50	17.50
6	1.20	0.60	0.60	200.00	40.00	20.00	20.00
7	1.40	0.70	0.70	225.00	45.00	22.50	22.50
8	1.60	0.80	0.80	250.00	50.00	25.00	25.00
9	1.80	0.90	0.90	275.00	55.00	27.50	27.50
10	2.00	1.00	1.00	300.00	60.00	30.00	30.00
15	3.00	1.50	1.50	350.00	70.00	35.00	35.00
20	4.00	2.00	2.00	400.00	80.00	40.00	40.00
25	5.00	2.50	2.50	500.00	100.00	50.00	50.00
50	10.00	5.00	5.00	1,000.00	200.00	100.00	100.00

In England, contact **Ruesch International Ltd.,** Lower Cookham Road, Maidenhead Berkshire SL6 8XY (✆ **0845/880-0400**).

ATMS

PLUS, Cirrus, and other networks connecting automated teller machines (ATMs) operate throughout Norway. The easiest and best way to get cash away from home is from an ATM. The **Cirrus** (✆ **800/424-7787;** www.mastercard.com) and **PLUS** (✆ **800/843-7587;** www.visa.com) networks span the globe; look at the back of your bank card to see which network you're on, and then call or check online for

ATM locations at your destination. Be sure you know your personal identification number (PIN) before you leave home, and be sure to find out your daily withdrawal limit before you depart. Also keep in mind that many banks impose a fee every time a card is used at a different bank's ATM, and that fee can be higher for international transactions (up to $5 or more) than for domestic ones. On top of this, the bank from which you withdraw cash may charge its own fee. To compare banks' ATM fees within the U.S., use www.bankrate.com. For international withdrawal fees, ask your bank.

You can also get cash advances on your credit card at an ATM. Keep in mind that credit card companies try to protect themselves from theft by limiting the funds cardholders can withdraw outside their home country, so call your credit card company before you leave home. And keep in mind that you'll pay interest from the moment of your withdrawal, even if you pay your monthly bills on time.

Important note: Make sure that the PINs on your bank cards and credit cards will work in Norway. You'll need a **four-digit code** (six digits won't work); if you have a six-digit code, you'll have to go into your bank and get a new PIN for your trip. If you're unsure about this, contact Cirrus or PLUS (above). Be sure to check the daily withdrawal limit at the same time.

CREDIT CARDS

Credit cards are a safe way to carry money. They also provide a convenient record of all your expenses, and they generally offer relatively good exchange rates. You can also withdraw cash advances from your credit cards at banks or ATMs, provided you know your PIN. If you've forgotten yours, or didn't even know you had one, call the number on the back of your credit card and ask the bank to send it to you. It usually takes 5 to 7 business days, though some banks will provide the number over the phone if you tell them your mother's maiden name or some other personal information. Keep in mind that when you use your credit card abroad, most banks assess a 2% fee above the 1% fee charged by Visa, MasterCard, or American Express for currency conversion on credit charges. But credit cards still may be the smart way to go when you factor in such things as exorbitant ATM fees and higher traveler's check exchange rates (and service fees).

For tips and telephone numbers to call if your wallet is stolen or lost, see "Lost & Found" in the "Fast Facts" section of appendix A.

Emergency Cash—the Fastest Way

If you need emergency cash over the weekend, when all banks and American Express offices are closed, you can have money wired to you from **Western Union** (**© 800/325-6000;** www.westernunion.com). You must present valid ID to pick up the cash at the Western Union office. However, in most countries you can pick up a money transfer even if you don't have valid identification, as long as you can answer a test question provided by the sender. Be sure to let the sender know in advance that you don't have ID. If you need to use a test question instead of ID, the sender must take cash to his or her local Western Union office rather than transfer the money over the phone or online.

What Things Cost in Oslo	US$	UK£
Taxi from Gardermoen Airport to the city center	120.00	60.00
Bus from Gardermoen Airport to the city center	26.00	13.00
Double room at the Grand Hotel (very expensive)	420.00	210.00
Double room at the Thon Hotel Cecil (moderate)	359.00	179.50
Double room at the Cochs Pensjonat (inexpensive)	144.00	72.00
Lunch for one at Brasserie France (moderate)	78.00	39.00
Lunch for one at Mamma Rosa (inexpensive)	50.00	25.00
Dinner for one, without wine, at restauranteik (expensive)	90.00	45.00
Dinner for one, without wine, at 3 Brødre (moderate)	45.00	23.20
Dinner for one, without wine, at Santino's Spaghetteria (inexpensive)	24.00	12.00
Pint of beer (draft pilsner) in a bar	9.00	4.50
Coca-Cola in a restaurant	4.50	2.25
Cup of coffee in a bar or cafe	4.00	2.00
Admission to the Viking Ship Museum	10.00	5.00
Movie ticket	18.00	9.00
Theater ticket	30.00	15.00

TRAVELER'S CHECKS

You can buy traveler's checks at most banks. They are offered in denominations of $20, $50, $100, $500, and sometimes $1,000. Generally, you'll pay a service charge ranging from 1% to 4%.

The most popular traveler's checks are offered by **American Express** (✆ **800/528-4800** or 800/221-7282 for cardholders). At the latter number, which accepts collect calls, services are offered in several foreign languages, and Amex gold and platinum cardholders may be exempted from the 1% fee. Other popular traveler's check providers include **Visa** (✆ **800/732-1322;** AAA members can obtain Visa checks for a $9.95 fee for checks up to $1,500 at most AAA offices or by calling ✆ **866/339-3378**) and **MasterCard** (✆ **800/223-9920**).

American Express, Thomas Cook, Visa, and **MasterCard** offer **foreign currency traveler's checks,** which are useful if you're traveling to one country, or to the Euro zone; they're accepted at locations where dollar checks may not be.

If you carry traveler's checks, keep a record of their serial numbers separate from your checks in the event that they are stolen or lost. You'll get a refund faster if you know the numbers.

6 HEALTH

STAYING HEALTHY

Norway is viewed as a "safe" destination, although problems, of course, can and do occur anywhere. You don't need to get shots, most food is safe, and the water in cities and towns is potable. It is easy to get a prescription filled in towns and cities, and nearly all places throughout Norway contain hospitals with English-speaking doctors.

General Availability of Health Care

If a medical emergency arises, your hotel staff can usually put you in touch with a reliable doctor. If not, contact the American embassy or a consulate; each one maintains a list of English-speaking doctors. Medical and hospital services aren't free, so be sure that you have appropriate insurance coverage before you travel.

Contact the **International Association for Medical Assistance to Travelers (IAMAT; ✆ 716/754-4883** or, in Canada, 416/652-0137; www.iamat.org) for tips on travel and health concerns in the countries you're visiting, and for lists of local, English-speaking doctors. The United States **Centers for Disease Control and Prevention** (**✆ 800/311-3435** or 404/498-1515; www.cdc.gov) provides up-to-date information on health hazards by region or country and offers tips on food safety. **Travel Health Online** (www.tripprep.com), sponsored by a consortium of travel medicine practitioners, may also offer helpful advice on traveling abroad. You can find listings of reliable medical clinics overseas at the **International Society of Travel Medicine** (www.istm.org).

WHAT TO DO IF YOU GET SICK AWAY FROM HOME

For travel abroad, you may have to pay all medical costs up front and be reimbursed later. Medicare and Medicaid do not provide coverage for medical costs outside the U.S. Before leaving home, find out what medical services your health insurance covers. To protect yourself, consider buying medical travel insurance (see "Medical Insurance," under "Travel Insurance," earlier).

Very few health insurance plans pay for medical evacuation back to the U.S. (which can cost $10,000 and up). A number of companies offer medical evacuation services anywhere in the world. If you're ever hospitalized more than 150 miles from home, **MedjetAssist** (**✆ 800/527-7478;** www.medjetassistance.com) will pick you up and fly you to the hospital of your choice virtually anywhere in the world in a medically equipped and staffed aircraft 24 hours day, 7 days a week. Annual memberships are $225 individual, $350 family; you can also purchase short-term memberships.

U.K. nationals will need a **European Health Insurance Card** (EHIC; **✆ 0845/606-2030;** www.ehic.org.uk) to receive free

Avoiding "Economy-Class Syndrome"

Deep vein thrombosis, or as it's known in the world of flying, "economy-class syndrome," is a blood clot that develops in a deep vein. It's a potentially deadly condition that can be caused by sitting in cramped conditions—such as an airplane cabin—for too long. During a flight (especially a long-haul flight), get up, walk around, and stretch your legs every 60 to 90 minutes to keep your blood flowing. Other preventative measures include frequent flexing of the legs while sitting, drinking lots of water, and avoiding alcohol and sleeping pills. If you have a history of deep vein thrombosis, heart disease, or another condition that puts you at high risk, some experts recommend wearing compression stockings or taking anticoagulants when you fly; always ask your physician about the best course for you. Symptoms of deep vein thrombosis include leg pain or swelling, or even shortness of breath.

Healthy Travels to You

The following government websites offer up-to-date health-related travel advice.

- **Australia:** www.dfat.gov.au/travel
- **Canada:** www.hc-sc.gc.ca/index_e.html
- **U.K.:** www.dh.gov.uk/en/Policyandguidance/Healthadvicefortravellers
- **U.S.:** www.cdc.gov/travel

or reduced-costs health benefits during a visit to a European Economic Area (EEA) country (European Union countries plus Iceland, Liechtenstein, and Norway) or Switzerland. The European Health Insurance Card replaces the E111 form, which is no longer valid. For advice, ask at your local post office or see www.dh.gov.uk/travellers.

We list **hospital** and **emergency numbers** under "Fast Facts: Norway," in appendix A.

If you suffer from a chronic illness, consult your doctor before your departure. Pack **prescription medications** in your carry-on luggage, and carry them in their original containers, with pharmacy labels—otherwise they won't make it through airport security. Carry the generic name of prescription medicines, in case a local pharmacist is unfamiliar with the brand name.

7 SAFETY

STAYING SAFE

Norway has a relatively low crime rate, with rare but increasing instances of violent crime. Most crimes involve the theft of personal property from cars or residences or in public areas. Pickpockets and purse-snatchers often work in pairs or groups, with one distracting the victim while another grabs valuables. Often they operate in or near major tourist attractions like in central Oslo, especially at restaurants, museums, bars, and buses, and on subway trains. Hotel breakfast rooms and lobbies attract professional, well-dressed thieves who blend in with guests and target purses and briefcases left unguarded by unsuspecting visitors and business travelers. Valuables should never be left unguarded in parked vehicles.

The loss or theft abroad of a passport should be reported immediately to the local police and your nearest embassy or consulate. U.S. citizens may refer to the Department of State's pamphlet, *A Safe Trip Abroad,* for ways to promote trouble-free journeys. The pamphlet is available by mail from the Superintendent of Documents, U.S. Government Printing Office, Washington, DC 20402, via the Internet at www.access.gpo.gov, or via the Bureau of Consular Affairs home page at http://travel.state.gov.

8 SPECIALIZED TRAVEL RESOURCES

There are a number of resources and organizations in both North America and Britain to assist travelers with special needs in planning their trips to Norway.

TRAVELERS WITH DISABILITIES

Norway has been in the vanguard of providing services for people with disabilities. In general, trains, airlines, ferries, department stores, and malls are accessible. For information about wheelchair access, ferry and air travel, parking, and other matters, contact the appropriate tourist board (see "Visitor Information," earlier in this chapter). The **Norwegian Association of the Disabled,** Schweigaardsgt #12, 9217 Grønland, 0185 Oslo (✆ **24-10-24-00;** www.nhf.no), also provides useful information.

If you're flying around Norway or Europe in general, the airline can help with such things as reserving seats with enough space, while ground staff can help you on and off planes; but you must arrange for this assistance *in advance* through the airline.

Many travel agencies offer customized tours and itineraries for travelers with disabilities. **Flying Wheels Travel** (✆ **507/451-5005;** www.flyingwheelstravel.com) offers escorted tours and cruises that emphasize sports, and private tours in minivans with lifts. **Access-Able Travel Source** (www.access-able.com) offers extensive access information and advice for traveling around the world with disabilities. **Accessible Journeys** (✆ **800/846-4537** or 610/521-0339; www.disabilitytravel.com) caters specifically to slow walkers and wheelchair travelers and their families and friends.

Organizations that offer assistance to travelers with disabilities include **MossRehab** (✆ **800/CALL-MOSS;** www.mossresourcenet.org), which provides a library of accessible-travel resources online; **SATH (Society for Accessible Travel and Hospitality;** ✆ **212/447-7284;** www.sath.org; annual membership fees: $45 adults, $30 seniors and students), which offers a wealth of travel resources for all types of disabilities and informed recommendations on destinations, access guides, travel agents, tour operators, vehicle rentals, and companion services; and the **American Foundation for the Blind** (**AFB;** ✆ **800/232-5463;** www.afb.org), a referral resource for the blind or visually impaired that includes information on traveling with Seeing Eye dogs.

For more information specifically targeted to travelers with disabilities, the community website **iCan** (www.icanonline.net) has destination guides and several regular columns on accessible travel. Also check out the quarterly magazine ***Emerging Horizons*** (www.emerginghorizons.com) and ***Open World Magazine,*** published by SATH.

FOR BRITISH TRAVELERS The **Royal Association for Disability and Rehabilitation (RADAR),** Unit 12, City Forum, 250 City Rd., London EC1V 8AF (✆ **020/7250-3222;** www.radar.org.uk), publishes three holiday "fact packs." The first provides general information, including tips for planning and booking a holiday, obtaining insurance, and handling finances; the second outlines transportation available when going abroad and equipment for rent; and the third deals with specialized accommodations. Another good resource is **Holiday Care Service,** Seventh Floor, Sunley House, 4 Bedford Park, Croydon, Surrey CR0 2AP (✆ **0845/124-9971;** www.holidaycare.org.uk), a national charity advising on accessible accommodations for seniors and persons with disabilities. Annual membership is £37.

GAY & LESBIAN TRAVELERS

As one of the most sophisticated countries on the planet, it naturally follows that Norway is also one of the most gay-friendly. Most Norwegians are tolerant of the lifestyles of others, including their sexual preference. Obviously, an urban center such as Oslo will accommodate a more openly gay life than in rural areas.

In Norway, gays and lesbians have the same legal status as heterosexuals, with the exception of adoption rights. Legislation passed in 1981 protects gays and lesbians from discrimination. In 1993, a law was passed recognizing the "partnerships" of homosexual couples—in essence, a recognition of same-sex marriages. The age of consent for both men and women in Norway is 16 years of age.

The International Gay and Lesbian Travel Association (IGLTA; ✆ 954/630-1637; www.iglta.org) is the trade association for the gay and lesbian travel industry, and offers an online directory of gay- and lesbian-friendly travel businesses and tour operators.

Many agencies offer tours and travel itineraries specifically for gay and lesbian travelers. **Above and Beyond Tours (✆ 800/397-2681;** www.abovebeyondtours.com) are gay Australia tour specialists. San Francisco–based **Now, Voyager (✆ 800/255-6951;** www.nowvoyager.com) offers worldwide trips and cruises. And **Olivia (✆ 800/631-6277;** www.olivia.com) offers lesbian cruises and resort vacations.

Gay.com Travel (✆ 415/834-6500; www.gay.com/travel or www.outandabout.com) is an excellent online successor to the popular ***Out & About*** print magazine. It provides regularly updated information about gay-owned, gay-oriented, and gay-friendly lodging, dining, sightseeing, nightlife, and shopping establishments in every important destination worldwide.

The Canadian website **GayTraveler** (www.gaytraveler.ca) offers ideas and advice for gay travel all over the world.

The following travel guides are available at many bookstores, or you can order them from any online bookseller: ***Spartacus International Gay Guide*** (Bruno Gmünder Verlag; www.spartacusworld.com/gayguide) and ***Odysseus: The International Gay Travel Planner, 17th Edition*** (Odysseus Enterprises, Ltd.); and the ***Damron*** guides (www.damron.com), with separate, annual books for gay men and lesbians.

For more gay and lesbian travel resources, visit Frommers.com.

SENIOR TRAVEL

Mention the fact that you're a senior when you first make your travel reservations. All major airlines and many Norwegian hotels offer discounts for seniors. In Norway, people over age 67 are entitled to 50% off the price of first- and second-class train tickets. Ask for the discount at the ticket office.

Members of **AARP,** 601 E St. NW, Washington, DC 20049 (**✆ 888/687-2277;** www.aarp.org), get discounts on hotels, airfares, and car rentals. AARP offers members a wide range of benefits, including *AARP The Magazine* and a monthly newsletter. Anyone over 50 can join.

Many reliable agencies and organizations target the 50-plus market. **Elderhostel (✆ 800/454-5768;** www.elderhostel.org) arranges worldwide study programs for those ages 55 and over.

People to People: Reaching Out

Established in 1971, **Friends Overseas** matches American visitors and Norwegians with similar interests and backgrounds. For more information, write to Friends Overseas, 68–04 Dartmouth St., Forest Hills, NY 11375 (www.friendsoverseas.org). To enroll, send a self-addressed, stamped, business-size envelope to Friends Overseas and include your age, occupation or occupational goals, approximate dates of your visit, and names of your traveling companions.

INTRAV (© **800/680-2858;** www.tourvacationstogo.com) is a high-end tour operator that caters to the mature, discerning traveler, not specifically seniors, with trips around the world that include guided safaris, polar expeditions, private jet adventures, small boat cruises down jungle rivers, and trips to the Norwegian fjords.

Recommended publications offering travel resources and discounts for seniors include the quarterly magazine ***Travel 50 & Beyond*** (www.travel50andbeyond.com) and the bestselling paperback ***Unbelievably Good Deals and Great Adventures That You Absolutely Can't Get Unless You're Over 50 2009–2010, 18th Edition*** (McGraw-Hill), by Joan Rattner Heilman.

Frommers.com offers more information and resources on travel for seniors.

FAMILY TRAVEL

The family vacation is a rite of passage for many households, one that in a split second can devolve into a *National Lampoon* farce. But as any veteran family vacationer will assure you, a family trip can be among the most pleasurable and rewarding times of your life.

Most Norwegian hoteliers will let children 12 and under stay in a room with their parents for free; others will not. Sometimes this requires a little negotiation at the reception desk.

Norwegians like kids but don't offer a lot of special amenities for them. For example, a kiddies' menu in a restaurant is a rarity. However, you can order a half portion, and most waiters will oblige. At attractions—even if it isn't specifically posted—inquire if a kids' discount is available. European Union citizens under 18 are admitted free to all state-run museums.

Babysitting services are available through most hotel desks or by applying at the Tourist Information Office in the town where you're staying. Many hotels have children's game rooms and playgrounds.

To locate those accommodations, restaurants, and attractions that are particularly

Frommers.com: The Complete Travel Resource

It should go without saying, but we highly recommend **Frommers.com,** voted Best Travel Site by *PC Magazine.* We think you'll find our expert advice and tips; independent reviews of hotels, restaurants, attractions, and preferred shopping and nightlife venues; vacation giveaways; and an online booking tool indispensable before, during, and after your travels. We publish the complete contents of over 128 travel guides in our **Destinations** section covering nearly 3,600 places worldwide to help you plan your trip. Each weekday, we publish original articles reporting on **Deals and News** via our free **Frommers.com Newsletter** to help you save time and money and travel smarter. We're betting you'll find our new **Events** listings (http://events.frommers.com) an invaluable resource; it's an up-to-the-minute roster of what's happening in cities everywhere—including concerts, festivals, lectures, and more. We've also added weekly **podcasts, interactive maps,** and hundreds of new images across the site. Check out our **Travel Talk** area featuring **Message Boards** where you can join in conversations with thousands of fellow Frommer's travelers and post your trip report once you return.

kid-friendly, refer to the "Kids" icons throughout this guide.

Recommended family travel Internet sites include **Family Travel Forum** (www.familytravelforum.com), a comprehensive site that offers customized trip planning; **Family Travel Network** (www.familytravelnetwork.com), an award-winning site that offers travel features, deals, and tips; **Traveling Internationally with Your Kids** (www.travelwithyourkids.com), a comprehensive site offering sound advice for long-distance and international travel with children; and **Family Travel Files** (www.thefamilytravelfiles.com), which offers an online magazine and a directory of off-the-beaten-path tours and tour operators for families.

9 SUSTAINABLE TOURISM

Sustainable tourism is conscientious travel. It means being careful with the environments you explore, and respecting the communities you visit. Two overlapping components of sustainable travel are **ecotourism** and **ethical tourism.** The **International Ecotourism Society (TIES)** defines ecotourism as responsible travel to natural areas that conserves the environment and improves the well-being of local people. TIES suggests that ecotourists follow these principles:

- Minimize environmental impact.
- Build environmental and cultural awareness and respect.
- Provide positive experiences for both visitors and hosts.
- Provide direct financial benefits for conservation and for local people.
- Raise sensitivity to host countries' political, environmental, and social climates.
- Support international human rights and labor agreements.

You can find some eco-friendly travel tips and statistics, as well as touring companies and associations—listed by destination under "Travel Choice"—at the **TIES** website, www.ecotourism.org. Also check out **Ecotravel.com**, which lets you search for sustainable touring companies in several categories (water-based, land-based, spiritually oriented, and so on).

While much of the focus of eco-tourism is about reducing impacts on the natural environment, ethical tourism concentrates on ways to preserve and enhance local economies and communities, regardless of location. You can embrace ethical tourism by staying at a locally owned hotel or shopping at a store that employs local workers and sells locally produced goods.

Responsible Travel (www.responsibletravel.com) is a great source of sustainable travel ideas; the site is run by a spokesperson for ethical tourism in the travel industry. **Sustainable Travel International** (www.sustainabletravelinternational.org) promotes ethical tourism practices, and manages an extensive directory of sustainable properties and tour operators around the world.

In the U.K., **Tourism Concern** (www.tourismconcern.org.uk) works to reduce social and environmental problems connected to tourism. The **Association of Independent Tour Operators (AITO;** www.aito.co.uk) is a group of specialist operators leading the field in making holidays sustainable.

Volunteer travel has become popular among those who want to venture beyond the standard group-tour experience to learn languages, interact with locals, and make a positive difference while on vacation. Volunteer travel usually doesn't require special skills—just a willingness to work hard—and programs vary in length from a few days to a number of weeks. Some programs provide free housing and food, but many require volunteers to pay for travel expenses, which can add up quickly.

Tips It's Easy Being Green

Here are a few simple ways you can help conserve fuel and energy when you travel:

- Each time you take a flight or drive a car greenhouse gases release into the atmosphere. You can help neutralize this danger to the planet through "carbon offsetting"—paying someone to invest your money in programs that reduce your greenhouse gas emissions by the same amount you've added. Before buying carbon offset credits, just make sure that you're using a reputable company, one with a proven program that invests in renewable energy. Reliable carbon offset companies include **Carbonfund** (www.carbonfund.org), **TerraPass** (www.terrapass.org), and **CoolClimate** (http://coolclimate.berkeley.edu).
- Whenever possible, choose nonstop flights; they generally require less fuel than indirect flights that stop and take off again. Try to fly during the day—some scientists estimate that nighttime flights are twice as harmful to the environment. And pack light—each 15 pounds of luggage on a 5,000-mile flight adds up to 50 pounds of carbon dioxide emitted.
- Where you stay during your travels can have a major environmental impact. To determine the green credentials of a property, ask about trash disposal and recycling, water conservation, and energy use; also question if sustainable materials were used in the construction of the property. The website **www.greenhotels.com** recommends green-rated member hotels around the world that fulfill the company's stringent environmental requirements. Also consult **www.environmentallyfriendlyhotels.com** for more green accommodations ratings.
- At hotels, request that your sheets and towels not be changed daily. (Many hotels already have programs like this in place.) Turn off the lights and air-conditioner (or heater) when you leave your room.
- Use public transport where possible—trains, buses, and even taxis are more energy-efficient forms of transport than driving. Even better is to walk or cycle; you'll produce zero emissions and stay fit and healthy on your travels.
- If renting a car is necessary, ask the rental agent for a hybrid, or rent the most fuel-efficient car available. You'll use less gas and save money at the tank.
- Eat at locally owned and operated restaurants that use produce grown in the area. This contributes to the local economy and cuts down on greenhouse gas emissions by supporting restaurants where the food is not flown or trucked in across long distances.

For general info on volunteer travel, visit **www.volunteerabroad.org** and **www.idealist.org**.

Before you commit to a volunteer program, it's important to make sure any money you're giving is truly going back to the local community, and that the work you'll be doing will be a good fit for you. **Volunteer International** (www.volunteerinternational.org) has a helpful list of questions to ask to determine the intentions and the nature of a volunteer program.

10 PACKAGE TOURS FOR THE INDEPENDENT TRAVELER

For travelers who feel more comfortable if everything is prearranged—hotels, transportation, sightseeing excursions, luggage handling, tips, taxes, and even meals—a package tour is the obvious choice, and it may even help save money.

FROM THE U.S. One of the best tour operators to Norway is **ScanAm World Tours** (✆ **800/545-2204;** www.scanam tours.com). Its best and most highly sought-after itinerary is its **Norway in a Nutshell Fjord Tours.** These tours, which cost $218 to $480 per person from May to September, take 2 days and 1 night. They include a tour of the famous Flåm Mountain Railroad and a 2-hour cruise on the Aurland Fjord and the Naeroy Fjord. Tours are operated from Oslo to Bergen or vice versa. The company also operates many other tours, the most useful being the 9-day, 8-night tour of Oslo and Bergen, plus the fjord country, for those wanting to cover just the highlights of Norway. Prices include only land and begin at $915 per person.

Grand Circle Travel (✆ **800/959-0405;** www.gct.com) offers 17 day tours of the Norwegian fjords and Lapland, with carefully chosen hotels and big Norwegian breakfasts. Highlights of this tour are Bergen, Trondheim, the Lofoten Islands, and Geirangerfjord.

Surprisingly, the major carrier to Norway, **SAS Airlines,** does not offer tours to Norway. Although **American Express** (✆ **800/335-3342**) also doesn't itself offer package deals to Norway, Amex agents can customize a special package just for you. For holiday tours and packages, turn to **Icelandair** (✆ **800/223-5500**) and see what deals are being offered at the time of your visit.

For a vast array of other tours of Norway, many of them appealing to the active vacationer and special-interest traveler, refer to "The Active Vacation Planner," below.

FROM THE U.K. The oldest travel agency in Britain, **Cox & Kings,** Gordon House 10, Greencoat Place, London SW1P 1PH (✆ **020/7873-5000;** www.coxandkings.co.uk), was established in 1758. Today the company specializes in unusual, if pricey, holidays. Its offerings in Norway include cruises through the spectacular fjords and waterways, bus and rail tours through sites of historic and aesthetic interest, and visits to the region's best-known handcraft centers, Viking burial sites, and historic churches. The company's staff is noted for its focus on tours of ecological and environmental interest.

Another reliable tour operator is **Scan-Tours, Inc.** (✆ **020/7554-3530;** www.scantours.co.uk).

11 THE ACTIVE VACATION PLANNER

From dog-sled racing to canoeing, from curling to speed skating to skiing, Norway is the most sports-oriented country in Europe. Nearly half of the four million people of Norway are members of the Norwegian Sports Federation, and three out of four Norwegian children take part in sporting activities. Winter sports are dominated by skiing, of course, along with ice hockey and curling. In the too-short summer, virtually all Norwegians head for the outdoors while the sun shines. They sail, swim, or canoe, and trails fill with hikers or mountain bikers.

SKIING Norway is the birthplace of skiing, predating the sport in Switzerland or Austria. It boasts 30,000km (18,600 miles) of marked ski trails.

From November until the end of May, cross-country and downhill skiing are both available, but don't expect the brilliant sun of the Alps. The days get long just before Easter, when skiing is best. Lights illuminate many of the tracks for winter skiers, proving to be especially helpful in January and February.

From December to April, daylight is limited, but it's still possible to have a full day's skiing if you start early. The bigger resorts have at least one floodlit downhill slope, and many towns and villages have a floodlit cross-country track *(lysløype)*. The days lengthen rapidly in January and February. Mid-February is the most popular period, and accommodations prices are higher then. Early March offers a combination of good skiing conditions and low prices. Easter time is popular with Norwegians, and hotel prices are very high then. Beginning Easter Monday, low-season rates apply again. Skiing in the higher elevations is possible until May, and you can even ski all summer in a few places. For information about summer skiing, get in touch with **Stryn Sommerskisenter** (**© 57-87-79-00;** www.strynefjellet.com). The largest mainland glacier in Europe is at Jostedalsbreen, near Stryn.

Snowboard and skiing facilities in the country are excellent overall. The winter season is longer than in southern Europe. The bigger resorts in Norway have plenty to interest beginners and intermediate skiers for a week or more, and there are many black-diamond runs for the more experienced. Families can find free lift passes and helmets for kids under 7, plus plenty of nursery slopes and day-care centers. Lift passes are relatively inexpensive, rental equipment is often cheaper than in other ski countries, queues are usually short, and the slopes are uncrowded.

Norway is best known for its cross-country skiing, which is superb at ski resorts everywhere. An endless network of marked trails *(skiløyper)* crosses rolling hills, forests, frozen lakes, and mountains. Numerous small ski centers offer inexpensive ski rentals and tuition. All the downhill resorts also have extensive trail networks.

Norwegian ski resorts are known for their informality, which is evident in the schools and the atmosphere. The emphasis is on simple pleasures, not the sophistication often found at alpine resorts. (Incidentally, the word *ski* is an Old Norse word, as is *slalom.*)

Geilo and **Hemsedal** are the best-known downhill resorts for keen downhill skiers. Geilo has the most extensive lift system, but Hemsedal has steeper runs and more spectacular scenery. There is also good cross-country skiing near both resorts. The huge mountain area of **Golsfjellet,** between Hemsedal, Gol, and Valdres, is excellent for experienced cross-country skiers. The main railway between

Fun Facts The Cradle of Skiing

A 4,000-year-old rock carving from Nordland shows that Norwegians were already using skis then. Telemark county is regarded as the "cradle of skiing," because Sondre Nordheim from Morgedal created an interest for the sport there in the 1870s and 1880s. He devised a binding that made it possible to turn and jump without losing the skis, and also designed a ski with inwardly curved edges—the Telemark ski—that became the prototype of all subsequent skis.

Oslo and Bergen serves Geilo directly and Hemsedal via a bus connection from Gol (3–4 hr.).

Geilo is our favorite ski resort in Norway because you can step off a train and onto a ski lift. Voss, its rival, has more folklore and better architecture. A lot of Geilo consists of large structures that evoke army barracks. But, in winter, the white snow is all forgiving, and you will have arrived at an alpine paradise. The best slope at Geilo is the Skiheiser, with 24km (15 miles) of some of the best skiing this side of the Swiss Alps. With 18 lifts and 33 ski runs, Geilo is competitive with any resort in Norway.

Trysil, in eastern Norway, is less famous than Geilo and Hemsedal, but it also offers good downhill skiing and a particularly fine choice of self-catering chalets and apartments with skiable access to the lifts. Trysil is easy to reach by a direct express bus service from Oslo airport (3 hr.). Of course, Trysil is more of a backwater and doesn't possess the après-ski life of more established resorts such as Voss and Geilo.

The **Valdres** area between Hemsedal and Lillehammer is famous for its scenery of rolling forested hills with high mountains in the distance. The Aurdal ski center has the unbeatable combination of superb cross-country terrain and good downhill facilities. A good base for both is one of the excellent chalets at the top of the downhill slopes. Direct bus service connects Valdres to central Oslo (3 hr.).

The owners of ski resorts in Voss, Geilo, and Lillehammer aren't going to fall over dead out of fear that Valdres is going to take over all their business (it hasn't happened so far). But many world-class skiers are increasingly frequenting this resort to avoid the crowds and to enjoy slopes at a more leisurely pace.

Lillehammer has been well known since the Winter Olympics in 1994, and the competitive facilities are world-class. The main downhill slopes are at **Hafjell,** 15km (9¼ miles) north of Lillehammer. The cross-country skiing through the gentle hills, scattered forests, and lakes of the Sjusjøen area is endless and particularly good for beginners. Lillehammer itself is more cosmopolitan than the other ski towns and has a wide range of shops and places to eat and drink.

Impressions

Skiing is the most Norwegian of all our sports, and a glorious sport it is; if any merits being called the sport of sports, this is surely the one.

—Explorer Fridtjof Nansen after crossing Greenland on skis in 1880

We love Geilo's small-scale winter charm, but no other resort in Norway can compete with all the multifarious offerings of Lillehammer. Facilities here are more wide ranging and better organized than in Voss or Geilo. Lillehammer might lack charm, but it more than makes up for that with experienced instructors in its ski schools, good lifts and smooth alpine slopes, and sheer vastness. (It has 402km/249 miles of prepared, illuminated cross-country tracks.)

North of Lillehammer is the Gudbrandsdal valley, surrounded by extensive cross-country areas linked by two long-distance trails: "Troll løype" to the east and "Peer Gynt løype" to the west. Skiers of all abilities enjoy this area, and downhillers find several good ski centers. This region, including **Gålå** and **Fefor,** is especially well served by mountain hotels.

For those traveling with their own car, the **Telemark** area is easily accessible from Haugesund or Kristiansand (3–5 hr.). **Gaustablikk,** near the town of Rjukan, is the best all-around center, with several lifts and downhill runs of all standards, plus many kilometers of cross-country trails to suit all abilities. Although the skiing is good here, it lacks much in après-ski life, restaurants, and hotels.

Frommer's Favorite Offbeat Adventures

- **Dog Sledding:** Traveling over the frozen tundra or through snow-laced forests at the speed of a dog can be one of the great experiences of the Nordic world. You can be a passenger bundled aboard a sled or a driver urging on a team of huskies. An outfitter that specializes in the experience, usually as part of midwinter camping trips under a canopy of stars, is **Muir's Tours,** Nepal House, 97A Swansea Rd., Reading, Berkshire RG1 8HA England (© **0118/950-2281;** www.nkf-mt.org.uk). Five-day all-inclusive tours are conducted in winter for £749 ($1,498) per person. You're given your own team of four to six Huskies for this safari. As you ride along, you'll likely see reindeer along the side of your trail.
- **Observing Musk Oxen:** A remnant of the last ice age, the musk ox had become nearly extinct by the 1930s. Between 1932 and 1953, musk oxen were shipped from Greenland to the Dovrefjell (a national park that's about an hour's train ride south of Trondheim), where about 60 still roam. On a safari you can observe this thriving herd—take along some binoculars—as well as Norway's purest herd of original mountain reindeer. The park, another remnant of the last ice age, is Europe's most bountiful wildflower mountain. Accommodations in or near the park can be arranged through **Borton Overseas** (© **800/843-0602;** www.bortonoverseas.com). Hotel staff members can direct you to where you're most likely to see the herds.
- **Rafting:** Norway's abundant snow and rainfall and its steep topography feed dozens of roaring white-water streams. Experience these torrents firsthand as part of white-water treks downriver. One of Norway's most respected river outfitters is **Norwegian Wildlife and Rafting AS,** Varphaugen Gard, N-2670 Ofta (© **61-230-700**). Based in central Norway, about a 90-minute drive north of Lillehammer, the company has a flotilla of devices suitable for helping you float, meander, or shoot down the white-water streams. Whatever conveyance you can imagine (paddle boards, kayaks, canoes, or inflatable rafts), this company can provide it. Trips last from 1 to 8 days.

Voss is well known and easily reached from Bergen in about 90 minutes by car or train, but the location near the west coast suffers from unreliable weather, particularly early and late in the season. It is well worth considering for a short break, though, or if you want to combine skiing with a winter visit to the fjord area.

Even though it's trying hard, Voss still has a long way to go before it overtakes either Geilo or Lillehammer. Nonetheless, it offers ski lifts, chairlifts, and an aerial cableway that can carry skiers up to 788m (2,585 ft.). We are especially fond of Mjølfjell, reached by going up the Raundalen Valley. This area offers some of the best cross-country skiing in Norway. Voss also emphasizes Norwegian folklore more than either Geilo or Lillehammer.

FISHING With a quarter of Norway's coastline at your disposal, nearly 14,000km (8,680 miles), you obviously have plenty of opportunities for sea fishing.

- **Trekking the Fjords:** Two respected U.S.-based outfitters, **Borton Overseas** (✆ **800/843-0602;** www.bortonoverseas.com) and **Five Stars of Scandinavia** (✆ **800/722-4126;** www.5stars-of-scandinavia.com), offer 7- and 8-day treks through Norway, designed to acquaint you with the country's heritage and its thousands of scenic wonders. Amid the cliffs and waterfalls of the fjords, you can participate in point-to-point guided treks that average around 24km (15 miles) per day. En route you'll visit wooden churches, mountain hamlets, and, in some cases, snowfields and slow-moving glaciers. Depending on your budget and your tastes, overnight accommodations range from first-class hotels to simple mountain huts favored by rock climbers and many trekkers.
- **Bicycling in the Lofoten Islands:** Some of the weirdest and most isolated tundra and lichen-covered rock formations in Norway lie within the Lofoten archipelago, north of the Arctic Circle. Berkeley, California–based **Backroads Travel** (✆ **800/GO-ACTIVE;** www.backroads.com) conducts 6-day hiking-and-biking (they refer to them as "multisport") tours of the isolated archipelago at least twice a year, during July and August, with an emphasis on ecology and natural beauty. Washington state–based **Five Stars of Scandinavia** (✆ **800/722-4126;** www.5stars-of-scandinavia.com) offers comparable tours and tends to be cheaper than Backroads. Both operators house their participants in simple mountain huts and lodges.
- **Going on a Moose Safari:** Norway's largest animal, the moose, can weigh up to 600 kilograms (1,323 lb.). These forest dwellers are shy toward people and best spotted at night. If you'd like to go on a moose safari, contact **Daesbekken Villmarksenter** in Finneskogen (✆ **62-95-48-57;** www.villmarksenter.hm.no), east of Oslo, near the Swedish border. Individual visitors can arrange tours from July to September; otherwise, it's strictly group bookings.

Norway has long been famous for its salmon and trout fishing, with more than 100 salmon rivers flowing into its fjords. The best months for salmon are June, July, and sometimes August. Sea-trout fishing takes place from June to September and is best in August. The brown-trout season varies with altitude.

Fishing in the ocean is free. To fish in lakes, rivers, or streams, anyone over 16 must have a fishing license. The cost of a license to fish begins at NOK200 ($40/£20). National fishing licenses can be purchased at local post offices. For more information, contact the **Bergen Angling Association,** Fosswinckelsgate 37, M-5004 Bergen (✆ **55-32-11-64;** www.bergensportsfiskere.no).

A U.S.-based company that can arrange fishing (as well as hunting) excursions anywhere within Norway and the rest of Scandinavia is **Five Stars of Scandinavia,** 13104 Thomas Rd., KPN, Gig Harbor, WA 98329 (✆ **800/722-4126;** www.5stars-of-scandinavia.com). For a truly unusual fishing experience, consider renting one of their old-fashioned fishermen's cottages in the isolated Lofoten Islands. The rustic-looking, fully renovated cottages each lie adjacent to the sea and evoke 19th-century isolation. Five Stars will rent you a cottage for as short a period as 1 night, but we recommend a minimum stay of 3 nights to appreciate this offbeat adventure.

The best salmon-fishing tours take place in central Norway, especially along the Guala River, one of the country's best-known salmon-fishing rivers. **Ursus Major** (✆ **99-22-49-60;** www.ursus-major.no) offers weeklong fishing tours in Trondheim, which cost from NOK1,500 to NOK24,900 ($300–$4,980/£150–£2,490) per person, including meals and accommodations.

The River Gudbrandsdalslågen, running through a beautiful valley and Hafjell Hunderfossen, is one of the best fishing rivers of Europe, set against a backdrop of the Øyer Mountains, with its many fishing lakes and rivers. The main types of fish caught are burbot, trout, char, and grayling. Many lakes in the mountains have rowboats for free use, and permits are easily obtainable at gas stations, grocery stores, hotels, or inns. For more information, contact the **Øyer Tourist Office** at ✆ **61-27-70-00.**

BIKING For the serious cyclist, there are two great routes in Norway: the North Sea Cycleway and the Old Navvy Road. Each of them is only partially paved. The coastal route is much easier, whereas the Old Navvy Road runs across open mountains, passing through pastures and meadows en route down to the nearest fjord. Pick up detailed maps of routes and how to reach them in tourist offices throughout Norway.

Because the Old Navvy Road follows the Bergen-Oslo train tracks for most of the way, the usual starting point is Haugastøl, known for its herring and jazz.

The North Sea Cycleway stretches for 296km (184 miles) and is mostly rural, with woodland, moors, and crags, passing many a meadow. It runs through such ports as Flekkefjord and Egersund, passing such larger towns as Sandnes and Stavanger.

The Old Navvy Road, called Rallarvegen in Norwegian, was built from 1895 to 1902, starting in the tree-lined east and climbing into the open mountains, with panoramic views of snow-covered slopes; high-altitude, incredibly blue lakes; and the Hardangerjøkulen glacier. The most dramatic point along the route is from Vatnahalsen, where the road descends the 21 hairpin bends of Myrdalskleiva, continuing down the Flamsdal Valley to Flåm. The road has been a cycle track since the 1970s.

Bike rentals abound in Norway. Inquire at your hotel or the local tourist office. The Norwegian Mountain Touring Association (see "Hiking," below) provides inexpensive lodging for those on overnight bike trips. For suggestions on tours, maps, and brochures, contact **Den Rustne Eike,** Vestbaneplassen 2, N-0458 Oslo (✆ **98-63-19-69;** www.denrustneeike.no). They can arrange guided tours in the Oslo area and elsewhere in Norway. Tours last from 3 hours to 14 days.

In July and August, 7-day bike trips run through the Lofoten Islands. They offer moderately rolling terrain, dramatic scenery, traditional *rorbuer* (fishing cottage) lodging, and hearty regional cuisine. Prices begin at NOK17,000 ($3,400/£1,700). Tours are offered by **Backroads** (✆ **800/GO-ACTIVE;** www.backroads.com).

To cycle through the splendors of Norway, you can join Britain's oldest (1878) and largest association of bicycle riders, the **Cyclists' Touring Club,** CTC Parklands, Railton Rd., Guildford, Surrey GU2 9JX (✆ **0844/736-8450;** www.ctc.org.uk). The fees for membership start at £35, which includes information, maps, a subscription to a newsletter packed with practical information and morale boosters, plus recommended cycling routes through virtually every country in Europe. The organization's knowledge of scenic routes is especially comprehensive. Membership can be arranged over the phone with a credit card.

One of the best bets for mountain biking is the Setesdal region, with its many small roads and forest trails. **Setesdal Rafting Centre** (✆ **37-93-11-77;** www.troll-mountain.no), 7km (4¼ miles) north from Evje on the main road (Rte. 9), is an expert in the area, offering both guided trips and bikes for rent with helmets from mid-April to late October.

The Øyer Mountains are also excellent for cycling, and the scenery is splendid. For more information, including suggested cycle tours in the Øyer Mountains, consult the **Øyer Tourist Office** (✆ **61-27-70-00**), and rent bikes from **Hafjellsporten Sports** (✆ **61-27-70-93**).

BIRD-WATCHING Some of Europe's noteworthy bird sanctuaries are on islands off the Norwegian coast or on the mainland. Rocky and isolated, the sanctuaries offer ideal nesting places for millions of seabirds that vastly outnumber the local human population during certain seasons. Foremost among the sanctuaries are the **Lofoten Islands**—particularly two of the outermost islands, Vaerøy and Røst—and the island of Runde. An almost .5km (¼-mile) bridge (one of the longest in Norway) connects **Runde** to the coastline, a 2½-hour drive from Ålesund. Runde's year-round human population is about 150, and the colonies of puffins, cormorants, razor-billed auks, guillemots, gulls, and eider ducks number in the millions. Another noteworthy bird sanctuary is at **Fokstumyra,** a national park near Dombås.

The isolated island of **Lovund** is a 2-hour ferry ride from the town of Sandnesjøen, south of Bødo. Lovund ("the island of puffins") has a human population of fewer than 270 and a bird population in the hundreds of thousands. You can visit Lovund and the other famous Norwegian bird-watching sites on your own, or sign up for one of the organized tours sponsored by **Borton Overseas,** 5412 Lyndale Ave., Minneapolis, MN 55419 (✆ **800/843-0602** or 612/882-4640; www.bortonoverseas.com).

Brochures and pamphlets are available from the tourist board **Destination Lofoten** (✆ **76-06-98-00;** www.lofoten.info).

CANOEING, KAYAKING & RAFTING Canoeing and kayaking, two increasingly popular sports, allow visitors to reach places that are otherwise almost inaccessible. Both activities should provide you with a unique opportunity to observe Norway's animals and birds without frightening them with the sound of an engine.

Some of our best experiences out on a canoe have been with the **Setesdal Rafting Center** (✆ **37-93-11-77;** www.trollaktiv.no), 7km (4¼ miles) north from Evje on the main road, Rte. 9. The region of Setesdal, known for its mountains, rivers, and varied wildlife, contains a stunning stretch of the River Otra—ideal for canoeing extending from the rafting center south to the village of Evje. En route you'll pass several osprey nests and beaver lodges. The center is also the best place in southern Norway for white-water rafting from mid-April to late October. From late June until September, water temperatures can reach 68°F (20°C), which makes the River Otra the warmest in Norway. Both half-day and full-day trips can be arranged. **Crossing Latitudes,** 420 W. Koch St., Bozeman, MT 59715 (✆ **800/572-8747** or 406/585-5356; www.crossinglatitudes.com), is another source for sea-kayaking and backpacking expeditions.

If you'd like to go rafting on the Sjoa River, billed as "the wildest in Norway," you can obtain full information from the **Vågå Tourist office,** Vågavegen 37, N-2680 in Vågå (✆ **61-21-29-90;** www.visitvaga.no), which also provides information about horseback riding, mountain or glacier climbing, mountain biking, and canoeing.

The rivers around Voss resort, in Norway's fjord country, have some of the finest river rafting. **Voss Rafting Center** (✆ **56-51-05-25;** www.vossrafting.no) offers rafting and other watersports such as river-boarding and canyoning. Overnight stays in the wild along with meals can be arranged.

Norwegian Summers: 23 Hours of Daylight

The Norwegian summer has magnificent long, sunny days. Temperatures often reach 86°F (30°C). Daylight on the longest days can last 23 hours, warming the lakes and fjords for all watersports.

GOLFING Norway has more than two dozen 18-hole golf courses, and the **Norwegian Golf Federation** (✆ **22-73-66-20;** http://golf.no) can provide information on all of these. Many golf clubs are open to foreign guests. Greens fees tend to be moderate. Our two favorite clubs are the 18-hole **Oslo Golf Klubb,** at Bogstad, Oslo (✆ **22-51-05-60;** www.oslogk.no), and the 18-hole **Meland Golf Club,** Meland/Frekhaug (✆ **56-17-46-00;** www.melandgolf.no), 36km (22 miles) north of Bergen.

HIKING Norway's mountains and wilderness are among the most spectacular in the world. The **Norwegian Mountain Touring Association,** Storgata 7, N-0101 Oslo (✆ **22-82-28-22;** www.turistforeningen.no), maintains affiliations with all the hiking associations of Norway and provides maps and advice. The association offers guided hikes that last from 5 to 8 days. They cost from NOK605 to NOK1,035 ($121–$207/£61–£104), including meals and lodging. Local associations mark the routes and operate a network of cabins for hikers to share.

Blue Marble Travel, 222A Race St., Philadelphia, PA 19106 (✆ **215/923-3788;** www.bluemarble.org), features reasonably priced biking and hiking trips in Norway. **European Walking Tours,** 1401 Regency Dr. E., Savoy, IL 61874 (✆ **800/231-8448** or 217/398-0058; www.walkingtours.com), sponsors walking tours for the mature traveler in Norway. The operator, Jacqueline Tofté, is a native of the Swiss Alps and has charted routes across meadows, through remote valleys, over mountain passes, and alongside serene lakes. The tours include searches for wildflowers, birds, and mountain animals, with lessons in local architecture, traditions, and history thrown in as well.

HORSEBACK RIDING Throughout Norway you'll find riding schools with horses for rent. Many country hotels in Norway also keep a few horses for the use of guests. Many organizations offer horseback tours of Norway's wilderness, enabling visitors to see some of the more spectacular scenery. Tours can range from a few hours to a full week. Luggage is transported by car. One tour organizer is **Borton Overseas,** 5412 Lyndale Ave., Minneapolis, MN 55419 (✆ **800/843-0602** or 612/882-4640; www.bortonoverseas.com).

Our favorite place to go mountain riding is offered by **Voss Fjellhest** outside the resort of Voss (✆ **56-51-91-66;** www.vossfjellhest.no). In Panoramic fjord and mountain scenery, you'll be taken on day or weekend rides, where everything is arranged for you, including accommodations and meals.

SAILING Norway's long coast can be a challenge to any yachting enthusiast. The most tranquil havens are along the southern coast. To arrange rafting trips or boat trips, along with boat rentals and evening parasailing, contact **SeaAction** (✆ **94-36-85-14** or 33-33-69-93; www.seaaction.com).

WHALE-WATCHING In Norway, you can catch a glimpse of 20m (66-ft.), 40,000-kilogram (88,185-lb.) sperm whales, the largest toothed whales in the world. You can also see killer whales, harbor porpoises, minke whales, and white-beaked dolphins. Whale researchers conduct 6-hour whale-watching tours in the Arctic Ocean.

For information and bookings, contact **Passage Tours of Scandinavia,** 239 Commercial Blvd., Fort Lauderdale, FL 33308 (✆ **800/548-5960** or 954/776-7070; www.passagetours.com). Whale-watching in the Lofoten Islands can be arranged by **Borton Overseas,** 5412 Lyndale Ave., Minneapolis, MN 55419 (✆ **800/843-0602** or 612/882-4640; www.borton overseas.com).

12 STAYING CONNECTED

CELLPHONES

The three letters that define much of the world's wireless capabilities are GSM (Global System for Mobiles), a big, seamless network that makes for easy cross-border cellphone use throughout dozens of countries worldwide. In general reception is good.

For many, **renting** a phone is a good idea. (Even worldphone owners will have to rent new phones if they're traveling to non-GSM regions.) While you can rent a phone from any number of overseas sites, including kiosks at airports and at car-rental agencies, we suggest renting the phone before you leave home. North Americans can rent one before leaving home from **InTouch USA** (✆ **800/872-7626** or 703/222-7161; www.intouch global.com) or **RoadPost** (✆ **888/290-1616** or 905/272-5665; www.roadpost.com). InTouch will also, for free, advise you on whether your existing phone will work overseas.

Buying a phone can be economically attractive, as many nations have cheap prepaid phone systems. Once you arrive at your destination, stop by a local cellphone shop and get the cheapest package; you'll probably pay less than US$100 for a phone and a starter calling card. Local calls may be as low as 10¢ per minute, and in many countries incoming calls are free.

Wilderness adventurers might consider renting a **satellite phone** (aka, "satphone"). It's different from a cellphone in that it connects to satellites and works where there's no cellular signal or ground-based tower. You can rent satellite phones from RoadPost (see above). InTouch USA (see above) offers a wider range of satphones but at higher rates. Per-minute call charges can be even cheaper than roaming charges with a regular cellphone, but the phone itself is more expensive. Satphones are outrageously expensive to buy, so don't even think about it.

INTERNET & E-MAIL

With Your Own Computer

More and more hotels, cafes, and retailers are signing on as Wi-Fi (wireless fidelity) "hot spots." Mac owners have their own networking technology: Apple AirPort. **T-Mobile Hotspot** (www.t-mobile.com/hotspot or www.t-mobile.co.uk) serves up wireless connections at coffee shops nationwide. **Boingo** (www.boingo.com) and **Wayport** (www.wayport.com) have set up networks in airports and high class hotel lobbies. iPass providers (see below) also give you access to a few hundred wireless hotel lobby setups. To locate other hot spots that provide **free wireless networks,** go to **www.jiwire.com**.

For dial-up access, most business-class hotels offer Wi-Fi for laptop modems. In addition, major Internet service providers (ISPs) have **local access numbers** around the world, allowing you to go online by placing a local call. The **iPass** network also has dial-up numbers around the world. You'll have to sign up with an iPass provider, who

Online Traveler's Toolbox

Veteran travelers usually carry some essential items to make their trips easier. Following is a selection of handy online tools to bookmark and use.

- **Airplane Food** (www.airlinemeals.net)
- **Airplane Seating** (www.seatguru.com and www.airlinequality.com)
- **Foreign Languages for Travelers** (www.travlang.com)
- **Maps** (www.mapquest.com)
- **Subway Navigator** (www.subwaynavigator.com)
- **Time and Date** (www.timeanddate.com)
- **Travel Warnings** (http://travel.state.gov, www.fco.gov.uk/travel, www.voyage.gc.ca, or www.dfat.gov.au/consular/advice)
- **Universal Currency Converter** (www.xe.com/ucc)
- **Visa ATM Locator** (www.visa.com), **MasterCard ATM Locator** (www.mastercard.com)
- **Weather** (www.intellicast.com and www.weather.com)

will then tell you how to set up your computer for your destination(s). For a list of iPass providers, go to www.ipass.com and click on "Individuals Buy Now." One solid provider is **i2roam** (✆ **866/811-6209** or 920/233-5863; www.i2roam.com).

Wherever you go, bring a **connection kit** of the right power and phone adapters, a spare phone cord, and a spare Ethernet network cable—or find out whether your hotel supplies them to guests.

Without Your Own Computer

To find cybercafes check **www.cybercaptive.com** and **www.cybercafe.com**. Cybercafes are found in all large cities, especially Oslo and Bergen. But they do not tend to cluster in any particular neighborhoods because of competition.

Aside from formal cybercafes, most **youth hostels** and **public libraries** have Internet access. Avoid **hotel business centers** unless you're willing to pay exorbitant rates.

Most major airports now have **Internet kiosks** scattered throughout their gates. These give you basic Web access for a per-minute fee that's usually higher than cybercafe prices.

13 TIPS ON ACCOMMODATIONS

Hotel passes (see below) can save you big money. In addition, there are several imaginative lodging possibilities other than hotels that are not only workable, but a lot of fun and a change of pace.

BOOKING A HOTEL The Norwegian Tourist Board does not provide a hotel-booking service. Your local travel agency will be able to do this for you, or ask one of the tour operators. Alternatively, you can book accommodations directly by post, fax, or telephone. Practically everyone in Norway speaks English, so you will rarely encounter any difficulty communicating. If you're traveling in the high season (mid-June to mid-Aug), it's advisable to book in advance. Information offices in Norway often have a reservation service. You can also make bookings at the website www.visitnorway.com.

HOTEL PASSES In Norway, you will find several passes, discount schemes, and check systems in operation that are valid at hotels and offer reduced prices. For further information, contact your local travel agency or the following addresses:

Best Western euro Guestcheque, Best Western Hotels Norway (✆ **800/WESTERN** in the U.S. and Canada; www.bestwestern.com); **Norway Fjord Pass,** Fjord Tours Strømgt 4, Bergen, NO-5015 Bergen (✆ **55-815-68-22;** fax 55-31-20-60; www.fjordpass.no); **Scan + Hotel Pass,** Norlandia Hotellene, P.O. Box 6615, St. Olavs Plass, NO-0129 Oslo (✆ **22-98-97-00;** www.norlandia.no); **Scandic Club Card,** Scandic Booking Services (✆ **517-517-20;** www.scandic-hotels.no); **Rica Hotellferie Pass,** Rica Hotels, Slependv 108, NO-1375 Billingstad (✆ **66-85-45-00;** www.rica.no); or **Nordic Hotel Pass,** Choice Hotels ASA, P.O. Box 2454 Solli, NO-0201 Oslo (✆ **22-33-42-00;** www.choicehotels.no).

CHALET HOLIDAYS Norway offers one of the least expensive vacation bargains in all of Europe. Ideal for outdoors-loving families or groups, log-cabin chalets are available throughout the country, on the side of a mountain or by the sea, in a protected valley or woodland, or by a freshwater lake. Some lie in what are known as chalet colonies; others are set on remote and lofty peaks. At night, by paraffin lamplight or the glow of a log fire, you can enjoy aquavit or an early supper, as many Norwegians do. Some cabins are fully equipped with hot and cold running water, showers, and electricity; others are more primitive, evoking pioneer living. Naturally, the price of the rental varies according to the amenities, as well as the size (some come with as many as three bedrooms, most with tiered bunks). The price range is NOK2,900 to NOK10,000 ($580–$2,000/£290–£1,000) weekly, the latter price for completely modern structures. There are chalets in most parts of the country—in the mountains, near lakes, along the coast, and in the fjord country. For a catalog with prices, locations, and other data, write to **Novasol,** Postboks 309, Sentrum, N-0103 Oslo (✆ **81-54-42-70;** www.novasol.com).

FISHERMEN'S CABINS In the Lofoten islands in northern Norway, you can rent a traditional former fisherman's cabin, called a *rorbu.* The fishermen used to come to Lofoten from other parts of the coast for the winter cod-fishing season from January to April and would make these cabins their temporary homes for the duration. Most have been modernized, and a number of them have their own shower and toilet. Nowadays you also find newly built fishermen's cabins, too. Although most *rorbuer* are in the Lofoten islands, you can rent these cabins all along the coast of Norway from north to south. The cabins are by the seashore and, therefore, boast excellent fishing. Prices range from NOK130 to NOK286 ($26–$57/£13–£29) per night. Local regional tourist boards will supply you with further information, or you can call the Lofoten Rorbuferie resort (✆ **76-07-84-44;** www.lofoten-rorbuferie.no).

THE B&B WAY The B&B system in Norway isn't as highly developed as it is in such countries as England. Generally, when you arrive at a town in Norway, you can go to the local tourist office, which will give you a list of private homes that receive guests. Most often they will also book you into one of these accommodations for a small fee. Or you can look for accommodations signs displayed along roads or directly outside houses, reading ROM or HUSROM.

In larger towns, private rooms are priced from NOK650 to NOK900 ($130–$180/£65–£90) for a double, breakfast included. A B&B guidebook for Norway titled *Bed & Breakfast Norway* has full details; copies are available in Norway at general bookshops. For more information, contact **B&B Norway AS,** P.O. Box 92, N-6659, Rindal, Norway (✆ **99-23-77-99;** www.bbnorway.com).

The list of private homes serving as B&Bs can change from week to week. Also, Norwegians will sometimes open their homes only briefly for the few weeks that summer lasts. Therefore, recommending permanent B&Bs that receive guests year-round is not always reliable. Actually, some of the best B&Bs are located in ugly industrial towns. As such, they tend to attract mainly commercial clients and not the adventurous visitor who wants to explore Norway's scenery.

Clarion Collection Hotel Gabelshus (p. 109) is one of our favorite places to stay in Oslo. In other parts of Norway, other favorites include: **Gjestehuset Ersgård** in the summer and winter ski resort of Lillehammer; **Ullensvang Gjesteheim** (p. 303), at Loftus, one of the best B&Bs in the western fjord country; **Ulvik Fjord Pensjonat** (p. 309), another idyllic B&B in the fjord country; **Norrøna,** in the far northern city of Bodø beyond the Arctic Circle; and **Gamle Prestegård** (p. 426) in the remote Lofotens.

FARM HOLIDAYS Farm holidays in Norway are many and varied, but all serve as escapist (and often isolated) destinations for those who want to venture into the remote hinterlands to discover what is called "the real Norway." Farms all over the country offer accommodations, ranging from western farms in the mountains, sometimes with impressive fjord views, to farms in northern Norway facing the open sea. Guests usually stay in their own comfortable cabin or house, complete with kitchen facilities, in or near the farmyard. Some farms provide breakfast. Many offer the chance to participate in activities and aspects of daily life on a farm. The standards, activities, and prices vary a great deal. Contact the local tourist information office, or visit www.visitnorway.com.

We've stayed in enough farmhouses to have some particular favorites. **Hardangerfjord og Fjellferie BA,** Sjusetevegan 145, N-5610 Øystese (✆ **56-55-58-65**) is actually a complex where five owners offer 14 units for rent in restored farmhouses and modern cabins in Øystese and Norheimsund in the Hardangerfjord district (one of Norway's most beautiful fjords). You can also visit www.hff.no for more information.

Outside Bergen, we recommend **No. 17 Grønnestølen Gård,** Grønnestølsveinen 17, N-5073 (✆ **55-28-66-00**). Lying about 4km (2½ miles) from the center, this complex of wood-sided buildings in tranquil surroundings lies in beautiful countryside.

In the Telemark district in the south of Norway, our favorite is a typical old farm with log houses and turfed roofs, the **Uppigard Natadal,** Flatdal, N-3841 Flatdal (✆ **35-06-59-00**).

Another real charmer is **Kårøyan Fjellgård,** Kårøydalen, N-7203 Vinjeøra (✆ **72-45-44-60**), lying in the beautiful, rugged countryside at the end of the Kårøydalen Valley. This place is ideal for families. You'll get rustic accommodations and country food, with plenty of farm animals. Mountains and white-water rapids lie nearby for walking and rafting outings.

A final favorite is **Lilland Gård,** Lilland N-4120 Tau (✆ **51-74-20-00**), a farm dating from the Viking Age. The king, Erik "Blood-Axe," had his estate nearby. In idyllic surroundings, you can enjoy rustic accommodations and an old-fashioned Norwegian breakfast.

CAMPING Norway has more than 12,000 campsites, so you're sure to find somewhere to stay in the area you want to visit. The sites are classified with one to five stars, depending on the standards, facilities, and activities available. There is no standard price, and rates vary. Normally, the fixed charge per site for two to three stars is NOK85 to NOK170 ($17–$34/£8.50–£17), and four to five stars is NOK120 to NOK350 ($24–$70/£12–£35), with additional charges per person.

Many campsites have cabins that can be booked in advance. Most cabins have electricity and heating, but note that you may need to bring bedding. Check when making your booking.

The **Camping Card (Norsk Campingkort)** entitles you to a faster check-in service along with special deals. The Camping Card can be ordered before traveling from the Norwegian Hospitality Association (Reiselivsbedriftenes Landsforening, or RBL), Essendropsgt 6, N-0305 Oslo (✆ **23-08-86-20;** fax 23-08-86-21; www.camping.no). The 1-year stamp can be purchased from participating campsites for NOK100 ($20/£10). RBL also provides a camping guide with extensive information.

Our favorite campsite in Norway is **Lone Camping,** located between Espeland and Haukeland, Hardangerveien 697, Haukeland (✆ **55-39-29-60;** www.bergen-guide.com), because it lies among some of the most dramatic landscapes in the fjord country. If you tire of the country, you can always head for Bergen, which is 20km (12 miles) away and is reached by public bus no. 900. The bus runs to town every half-hour during the day.

While you're in the area, you might also check out **Bratland Camping,** Bratlandsveien 6, Haukeland (✆ **55-10-13-38;** www.bratlandcamping.no), which lies nearby and is also reached by bus no. 900. Here you can rent tent sites or simply furnished cabins, costing from NOK80 to NOK120 ($16–$24/£8–£12). This site is well equipped and lies 4km (2½ miles) south of the town of Lone.

Still in fjord country, a final favorite takes you to the summer resort and winter ski center at **Voss** (p. 310). **Voss Camping,** Prestegårdsalléen 40 (✆ **56-51-15-97;** www.vosscamping.no), has a lakeside location and is convenient to the attractions and sports of the resort (p. 311). Cabins cost NOK500 ($100/£50) and tent sites cost NOK140 to NOK190 ($28–$38/£14–£19). In the same area, **Tvinde Camping** (✆ **56-51-69-19;** www.tvinde.no) is one of the most scenic campsites in central Norway, as it lies beside a waterfall 12km (7½ miles) from the center of Voss (p. 311). Both tent sites and cabins are rented here. Cabins cost NOK375 to NOK495 ($75–$99/£38–£50), and tent sites are NOK130 ($26/£13). This camp is reached by the public bus marked VOSS-GUNVANGEN.

HOME STAYS **Friendship Force,** 34 Peachtree St. NW, Ste. 900, Atlanta, GA 30303 (✆ **404/522-9490;** www.friendshipforce.org), is a nonprofit organization that encourages friendship among people worldwide. Dozens of branch offices throughout North America arrange visits, usually once a year. Because of group bookings, the airfare to the host country is usually less than the cost of individual APEX tickets. Each participant spends 2 weeks in the host country, the first as a guest in the home of a family and the second traveling in the host country.

Servas, 1125 16th St., Ste. 201, Arcata, CA 95521 (✆ **707/825-1714;** www.usservas.org), is an international nonprofit, nongovernmental, interfaith network of travelers and hosts whose goal is to help promote world peace, goodwill, and understanding. Servas hosts offer travelers hospitality for 2 days. Travelers pay an $85 annual fee and a $25 list deposit after filling out an application and being approved by an interviewer (interviewers are located across the U.S.). They then receive Servas directories listing the names and addresses of Servas hosts.

HOME EXCHANGES One of the most exciting breakthroughs in modern tourism is the home exchange. Sometimes the family automobile is even included. Of course, you must be comfortable with the idea of having strangers in your home, and you must be content to spend your vacation in one place. One potential problem, though, is that you may not get a home in the area you request.

Intervac USA, 30 Corte San Fernando, Tiburon, CA 94920 (✆ **800/756-HOME;** www.intervacus.com), is part of the largest worldwide exchange network. It contains over 10,000 homes in over 36 countries. Members contact each other directly. The cost is $85 plus postage, which includes the purchase of three of the company's catalogs, plus the inclusion of your own listing in whichever catalog you select. If you want to publish a photograph of your home, there is an additional charge of $15. Fees begin at $90, going up to $150.

The Invented City (✆ **415/846-7588;** www.invented-city.com) publishes home-exchange listings three times a year. For the $50 membership fee, you can list your home with your own written descriptive summary.

Home Link, 2937 NW 9 St., Fort Lauderdale, FL 33311 (✆ **800/638-3841** or 954/566-2687; www.homelink.org), will send you five directories a year for $130.

Suggested Norway Itineraries

Vacations are getting shorter, and a lean-and-mean schedule is called for if you want to experience the best of any country in a condensed amount of time. If you're a time-pressed traveler, as most of us are, with only 1 or 2 weeks for Norway, you may find the first two itineraries most helpful, as they take in the best of either eastern or western Norway. If you have time for only a 1-week driving tour, make it the western district, as that contains the fjord country, one of the greatest tourist attractions in all the world.

1 THE REGIONS IN BRIEF

WESTERN NORWAY Western Norway is fabled for its fjords, saltwater arms of the sea that stretch inland. Many date from the end of the last ice age. Some fjords cut into mountain ranges as high as 1,006m (3,300 ft.). The longest fjord in western Norway is the Sognefjord, north of Bergen, which penetrates 177km (110 miles) inland. Other major fjords in the district are the Nordfjord, Geirangerfjord, and Hardangerfjord. The capital of the fjord district is **Bergen,** the largest city on the west coast. **Lofthus,** a collection of farms extending along the slopes of Sørfjorden, offers panoramic views of the fjord and the **Folgefonn Glacier.** Hiking is the primary activity in this region. The area north of the **Hardangerfjord** is a haven for hikers. Here you'll find Hardangervidda National Park, on Europe's largest high-mountain plateau, home to Norway's largest herd of wild reindeer. The town of **Voss,** birthplace of the American football great Knute Rockne, is surrounded by glaciers, fjords, rivers, and lakes.

CENTRAL NORWAY Fjords are also common in central Norway; the two largest are the Trondheimsfjord and Narnsfjord. It's not unusual for roads to pass waterfalls that cascade straight down into fjords. Many thick forests and snowcapped peaks fill central Norway. The town of **Geilo,** halfway between Bergen and Oslo, is one of Norway's most popular ski resorts. It boasts more than 129km (80 miles) of cross-country trails. **Trondheim,** central Norway's largest city, is home to Nidaros Domen, the 11th-century cathedral that was once the burial place for kings. **Røros** is a well-preserved 18th-century mining town. The medieval city of **Molde,** Norway's capital during World War II, plays host to one of Europe's largest jazz festivals. **Geiranger,** site of the Seven Sisters waterfall, is one of Norway's most popular resorts.

EASTERN NORWAY On the border with Sweden, eastern Norway is characterized by clear blue lakes, rolling hills, and green valleys. In some ways, it's the most traditional part of the country. Because of its many fertile valleys, it was one of the earliest areas to be settled. Some of the biggest valleys are Valdres, Østerdal, Hallingdall, Numedal, and Gudbrandsdalen. Campers and hikers enjoy the great forests of the Hedmark region, site of Norway's longest river, the Glomma (Gløma), which

EUROPE
0
100 mi
0
100 km
North Cape
Honningsvåg
Vardø
Vadsø
Hammerfest
Norwegian Sea
Kirkenes
Lakselv
Alta
E6
Karasjok
RUSSIA
Tromsø
Kautokeino
Lofoten
Vesterålen
NORTH
Harstad
Abisko
FINLAND
Svolvær
Narvik
Kiruna
Skutvik
ATLANTIC OCEAN
Bodø
Fauske
Svartisen
ARCTIC CIRCLE
Luleå
Mo i Rana
E6
NORWAY
SWEDEN
E6
Umea
Gulf of Bothnia
Trondheim
Kristiansund
Sundsvall
Røros
Molde
Oppdal
Ålesund
Åndalsnes
CENTRAL
Nordfjord
E6
Balestrand
Gävle
Sognefjord
Lillehammer
E16
Hamar
WEST
Voss
Gjøvik
Uppsala
Geilo
Bergen
Hardangerfjord
EAST
Stockholm
Oslo
Karlstad
Tønsberg
Baltic Sea
Haugesund
Skien
Fredrikstad
Sandefjord
Stavanger
Skara
SOUTH
Arendal
North Sea
E6
E18
Gotland
Kristiansand
Gothenburg

runs about 580km (360 miles). The area has many ski resorts, notably **Lillehammer,** site of the 1994 Winter Olympics. Norway's most visited destination is the capital, **Oslo,** which rises from the shores of the Oslofjord. The city of **Fredrikstad,** at the mouth of the Glomma, was once the marketplace for goods entering the country. Its 17th-century Kongsten Fort was designed to defend Norway from Sweden. **Tønsberg,** Norway's oldest town, dates to the 9th century. This area is also the site of the **Peer Gynt Road,** of Ibsen fame, and the mountainous region is home to numerous ski resorts.

SOUTHERN NORWAY Southern Norway is sometimes referred to as "the Riviera" because of its unspoiled and uncrowded—but chilly—beaches. It's also a favorite port of call for the yachting crowd. **Stavanger,** the oil capital of Norway, is the largest southern city and is also quite popular. There's much to explore in this Telemark region, which is filled with lakes and canals popular for summer canoeing and boating. **Skien,** birthplace of the playwright Henrik Ibsen (1828–1906), is primarily an industrial town. In Skien, you can board a lake steamer to travel through a series of canals. The southern part of **Kristiansand** links Norway with continental Europe. Close by is 10km (6¼-mile) **Hamresanden Beach,** one of the longest uninterrupted beaches in Europe. More fjords lie along the western half of the district, notably the Lysefjord, Sandefjord, and Vindefjord.

NORTHERN NORWAY The "Land of the Midnight Sun" is a region of craggy cliffs that descend to the sea and of deep, fertile valleys along the deserted moors. It has islands with few, if any, inhabitants, where life has remained relatively unchanged for generations. The capital of the Nordland region is **Bodø,** which lies just north of the Arctic Circle; it's a base for Arctic fishing trips and visits to the wild Glomfjord. Norway's second-largest glacier, **Svartisen,** is also in this region, as is the city of **Narvik,** a major Arctic port and the gateway to the **Lofoten Islands.** The islands, which have many fishing villages, make up one of the most beautiful areas of Norway. Visitors come here from all over the world for sport fishing and bird-watching.

TROMS Troms is the name of the province, and **Tromsø,** from which polar explorations are launched, is its capital. Troms contains one of Norway's most impressive mountain ranges, the Lyngs Alps, which attract winter skiers and summer hikers. **Alta,** site of the Altafjord, is reputed to have the best salmon-fishing waters in the world.

FINNMARK At the top of Norway is the Finnmark region, home of the Sami. Settlements here include **Kautokeino** (the Sami town) and **Hammerfest,** the world's northernmost town. Most tourists come to Finnmark to see the **North Cape,** Europe's northernmost point and an ideal midnight-sun viewing spot. **Vardø** is the only Norwegian mainland town in the Arctic climate zone. In the 17th century, Vardø was the site of more than 80 witch burnings. The town of **Kirkenes** lies 274km (170 miles) north of the Arctic Circle, close to the Russian border.

2 EASTERN NORWAY IN 1 WEEK

Before beginning any driving tour, you'll want to spend at least 2 or 3 days in **Oslo** (see coverage in chapters 5 and 6). Use the following itinerary to make the most out of a week in eastern Norway, but feel free to skip a place or two if you require some downtime. One week provides just enough time to see some of the significant sights of this region, from dramatic parks to fabled old Viking towns along the Oslofjord.

The highlights of the north include the Olympic resort of **Lillehammer** (one of the most famous towns in Norway) and some of the country's greatest national parks—**Jutunheimen** and **Rondane.** Time is also allotted for a visit to **Røros,** Scandinavia's most colorful mining town, which is preserved on the World Heritage List.

Heading back to Oslo (going south along the Oslofjord), you can take in other attractions, including **Fredrikstad,** Norway's oldest fortified town, and **Tønsberg,** the ancient Viking town and former royal coronation site.

Day ❶: Olympic Resort of Lillehammer ★★

On the morning of **Day 1,** leave Oslo and head north to the winter and summer resort of **Lillehammer,** at the northern end of Lake Mjøsa, where the 1994 Winter Olympics were staged. The trip is a drive of 169km (105 miles). From Oslo, follow the E6, an express highway, to Lillehammer, where you can check in to a hotel for the night. The major attraction here is the **Maihaugen Open-Air Museum** (p. 196), which will take about 2 hours. If you have time remaining on the clock, hook up with an 1850s paddle steamer, the **White Swan of Lake Mjøsa** (see "Sailing on Norway's Oldest Paddle Steamer" for more details; p. 190).

Day ❷: Jutunheimen National Park ★★★

Leave Lillehammer on the morning of **Day 2,** heading northwest toward the resort of **Lom,** a distance of 180km (112 miles), by continuing along the E6 until you reach the junction of Rte. 15. Here you will head west for the final stretch into Lom, where you can check in to a hotel in the small town itself or somewhere nearby for the night.

Lom lies in the center of **Jotunheimen,** with its foreboding glaciers and towering mountain peaks. This is the prize jewel among the national parks of Norway. For details about experiencing the best of the park in a short time, refer to "Jotunheimen National Park: 'Home of the Giants'" (p. 209).

Day ❸: The Ice Age Park of Rondane ★★

Leave Lom on the morning of **Day 3** and drive all the way to the village of **Lesja,** a distance of 159km (99 miles). To reach Lesja, exit Lom via Rte. 15 east, then enter the express highway, E6, heading northwest. At the roundabout, connect to the E136 heading west into Lesja. Check into one of the region's hotels for the night. With its towering peaks, deep valleys, and waterfalls, **Rondane Nasjonalpark** is one of the most visited parks in Norway. See "Exploring the National Parks" (p. 212).

Day ❹: The Ancient Mining Town of Røros ★★

On the morning of **Day 4,** leave Lesja and head for the old mining town of **Røros,** a distance of 193km (120 miles). Take the E136 east, then the E6 northeast, entering onto Rte. 29 as the road continues east. At the junction with Rte. 3, head north, continuing on the highway as it turns into Rte. 30, which will take you into Røros. Fortunately, Røros is signposted along these complicated routes.

Check in to a hotel for the night and set out to explore Scandinavia's most famous old mining town, with its collection of 80 antique houses, some of which date from the 1600s. For a survey of the attractions, including the first smelting works in the area, the **Røros Museum Smelthytta,** see our reviews beginning on p. 216.

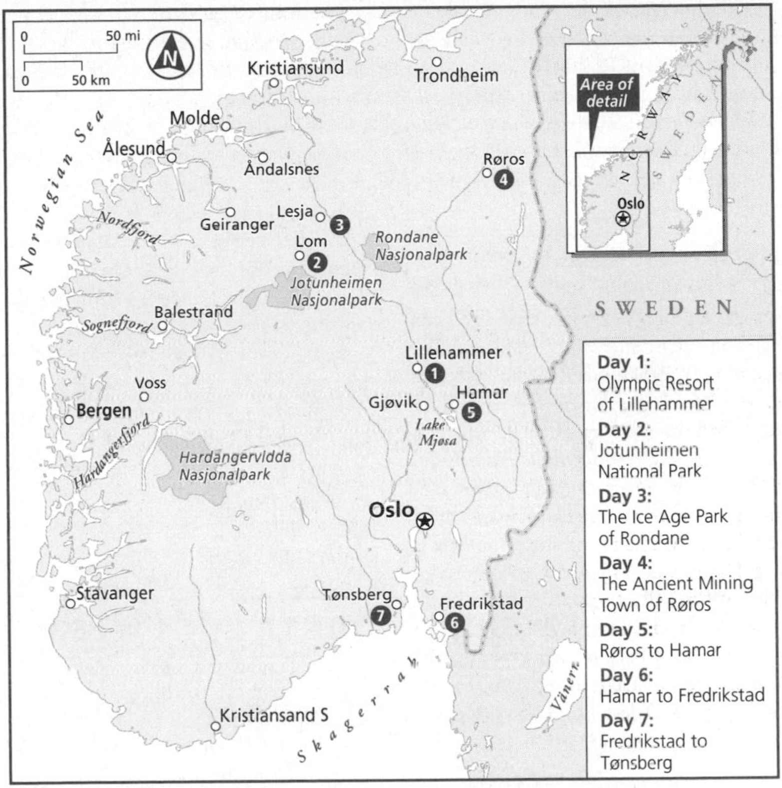

Day 5: Røros ★★ to Hamar

On the morning of **Day 5,** leave Røros and drive 275km (171 miles) to the resort of **Hamar,** the gateway to central Norway's **Lake Mjøsa,** an area of particular beauty. At this point, you'll be only 134km (83 miles) north of Oslo. From Røros, take Rte. 30, heading southwest to the junction with Rte. 3. Rte. 3 will take you south to the junction with Rte. 25, which you follow southeast into Hamar. In Hamar, check in to a hotel for the night. Mostly you come here to enjoy the beauty of the lake. But if you have time for any of the minor sights, visit the **Hedmarksmuseet & Domkirkeodden** (p. 190) and the **Kirsten Flagstad Museum** (p. 191). Of minor interest is the **National Railway Museum** (p. 191).

Day 6: Hamar to Fredrikstad ★

To conclude this 1-week tour, we continue south of Oslo to the two oldest and most intriguing cities along the Oslofjord, **Fredrikstad** and **Tønsberg.** Leave Hamar on the morning of **Day 6,** following the E6 south to Fredrikstad, a driving distance of 216km (134 miles). Check in to a hotel in Fredrikstad for the night. What brings us here is **Gamlebyen,** or the Old Town of Fredrikstad, at the mouth of the Glomma River. As the oldest fortified town in Norway, Old Town is one of the best preserved in eastern Norway. You should allow 3 hours to tour its precincts, including stopovers at the **Fredrikstad Museum** (p. 172) and **Fredrikstad Domskirke** (p. 172). The Old Town is also known as a center for artisans and highly skilled craftspeople. You'll want to devote part of your time to exploring local shops, which sell some of the most original hand-crafted merchandise in Norway.

Day ❼: Fredrikstad ★ to Tønsberg ★

For your final look at eastern Norway, you will have to cross from the east bank of the broad Oslofjord to the west bank. On the morning of **Day 7,** leave Fredrikstad and head for the fjord town of Moss, a distance of 39km (24 miles). From Fredrikstad, follow the E6 north to the junction with Rte. 19, which you will take west into Moss. Once there, head for the port where you can board one of the frequent ferries crossing the fjord to the opposite port of Horten on the west bank.

At Horten, take Rte. 19 south into **Tønsberg,** a distance of only 18km (11 miles), where you can check in to a hotel for your final night. Tønsberg, a former Viking settlement, is Norway's oldest town. In the late morning, you can take in its major sights, including **Slottsfjellet** (p. 180), hailed as the "acropolis of Norway"—although the views from the **Slottsfjelltårnet** are the real show-stealer here. You can spend an hour wandering through the **Nordbyen** (p. 181), or the Old Town, with its historic houses; drop in also to see **Sem Church** (p. 181), the oldest in Vestfold. With its Viking and whaling treasures, **Vestfold Fylkesmuseum** (p. 181) is the most intriguing. After an overnight in Tønsberg, you can drive back to Oslo, which, most likely, is your transportation hub for making your way home.

3 WESTERN FJORD COUNTRY IN 1 WEEK

This driving tour of the fjords of western Norway, one of the world's greatest tourist attractions, is far more scenic than the environs of Oslo in the east previously visited. The Ice Age really outdid itself in carving out this wonderland of nature. Of course, one of the grandest experiences of it may be found in a boat—not a car—traversing the most scenic of the fjords, such as Sognefjord.

If all the fjords were laid out in a straight line, they would measure 21,347km (13,235 miles), roughly the distance between the north and south poles. Throw in Europe's largest glacier, little fjordside farming villages, and jagged snow-capped peaks, and you've got beauty galore.

Day ❶: Ålesund ★★: Top of the Fjord Country

Spread over three islands and opening onto two bright blue fjords, **Ålesund,** lying 1,186km (735 miles) northwest of Oslo, is a good launchpad for a driving tour of the fjord country. Because it is such a long distance from Oslo (and because there are no rail lines to Ålesund), it's best to fly here and rent a car before beginning your tour.

Before heading out from Ålesund, you can explore the rebuilt Art Nouveau town, including its most important attraction, the **Sunnmøre Museum** (p. 337), one of the fjord country's best open-air museums.

Day ❷: Åndalsnes and Romsdalsfjord ★

Leave Ålesund on the morning of **Day 2,** and drive east to the resort of **Åndalsnes,** a distance of 127km (79 miles), following

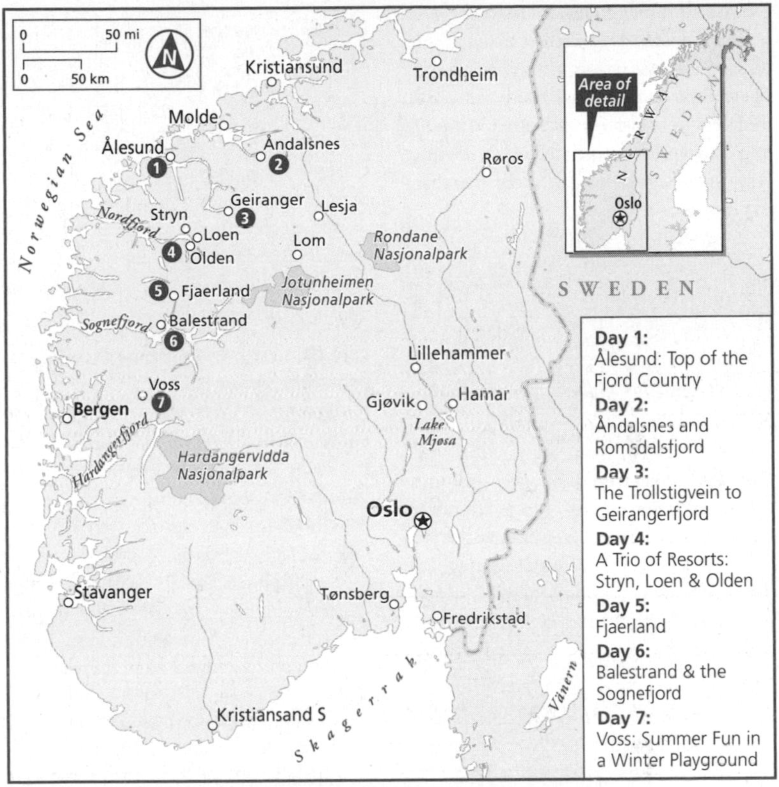

the A69. Once here, check in to a hotel for the night. At Åndalsnes, try to hook up with a summer excursion, especially one involving a hike through the **Romsdalen Alps** (p. 334) that envelop the town. The summit of **Nesaksla Mountain** towers over Åndalsnes at 715m (2,345 ft.). You can ask about the boat trips on **Romsdalsfjord,** one of the most beautiful waterways in western Norway.

Day ❸: The Trollstigvein ★ to Geirangerfjord ★★★

On the morning of **Day 3,** leave Åndalsnes and head south on one of the greatest road trips in Norway, the **Trollstigvein,** a 20-hour drive along Rte. 63 to the fjord resort of **Geiranger** (p. 330), a distance of 85km (53 miles) from Åndalsnes. At one point, the highway climbs a breathtaking 620m (2,034 ft.). When it opened in 1952, the **Ørnevein,** or Eagle's Road, section of Rte. 63 was heralded as a marvel of engineering—and so it is today. Nearly one dozen hairpin turns await you, opening onto panoramic views over **Geirangerfjord.**

Once at the resort town of **Geiranger,** explore the area in the afternoon after checking in to a hotel for the night. Its waterfalls, such as the **Seven Sisters,** are among the world's most dramatic. If it's summer and you arrive late, an evening tour of the Geirangerfjord is available.

Day ❹: A Trio of Resorts: Stryn, Loen & Olden

On the morning of **Day 4,** leave Geiranger and take the ferry across the Geirangerfjord to Hellesylt, a scenic hour's boat ride. At Hellesylt, follow the signs south along Rte. 60 to **Stryn,** a distance of 50km (31 miles). You can check in to a hotel for the night at Stryn or at Loen or Olden; the cluster of resorts are close together.

From your home base in Stryn, you are poised to explore one of the natural wonders of Norway, the ice plateau of **Jostedalsbreen National Park.** See p. 324 for details on how to tour this wonder that lies between Sognefjord and Nordfjord. The glacier is the largest in Europe, and you must have a qualified guide to tour it.

Day ❺: Fjaerland ★★

On the morning of **Day 5,** head 60km (37 miles) to the south to **Fjaerland,** where you can book a hotel room for the evening. For directions, see "Getting There," under Fjaerland (p. 323). Once at Fjaerland, you can spend the afternoon touring **Bøyaøyri Estuary,** a protected nature reserve north of the village. Have some more time? You can also take in the exhibits at the **Norwegian Glacier Museum** (p. 324).

Day ❻: Balestrand ★★ & the Sognefjord ★★★

On the morning of **Day 6,** leave Fjaerland and journey by car ferry to **Balestrand;** the scenic boat ride takes about 45 minutes. Check your luggage in to a hotel for the night before setting out to explore one of the world's deepest and most beautiful fjords, the famous **Sognefjord.** This fjord stretches for 205km (127 miles), and a scenic boat ride on it will comfortably fill your afternoon.

Day ❼: Voss ★: Summer Fun in a Winter Playground

On **Day 7,** it's just a 90km (56-mile) drive south to Voss, where you can choose a hotel for the night. Rte. 13 links Balestrand to Voss, but the section between Vanganes and Balestrand is serviced by car ferry. A wide range of activities awaits you in Voss. Refer to "Seeing the Sights" (p. 310) and "Other Outdoor Pursuits" (p. 311) for the full array of choices. Voss is also a good connecting point for travel back to either Bergen or Oslo, one of which can be your transportation hub for leaving Norway.

4 THE ROUTE TO THE NORTH CAPE ★★ IN 1 WEEK

The drive from **Trondheim** to the **North Cape,** along a narrow and very long strip of land, is one of the most scenic and dramatic in northern Europe. This itinerary should be undertaken only in summer, when the Midnight Sun will light your way.

That said, the weather along this coast has been called "wild and unpredictable," even in summer. Except for the long drive between **Trondheim** and **Mo i Rana,** we've paced the stopovers between towns so that you won't have long treks every day. Many motorists begin this drive in Oslo, but that makes for a 552km (342-mile) jaunt to Trondheim. To eliminate that long trek, many visitors take a train or else fly to Trondheim, where they rent a car before setting out to points north.

Day ❶: Trondheim ★★★: Norway's Most Historic City

Arriving in **Trondheim** for **Day 1,** reserve your hotel room for the night, and then set out to see the city. Begin at Scandinavia's grandest cathedral, **Nidaros Domkirke** (p. 362), dating from the 11th century, and follow that up with a visit to

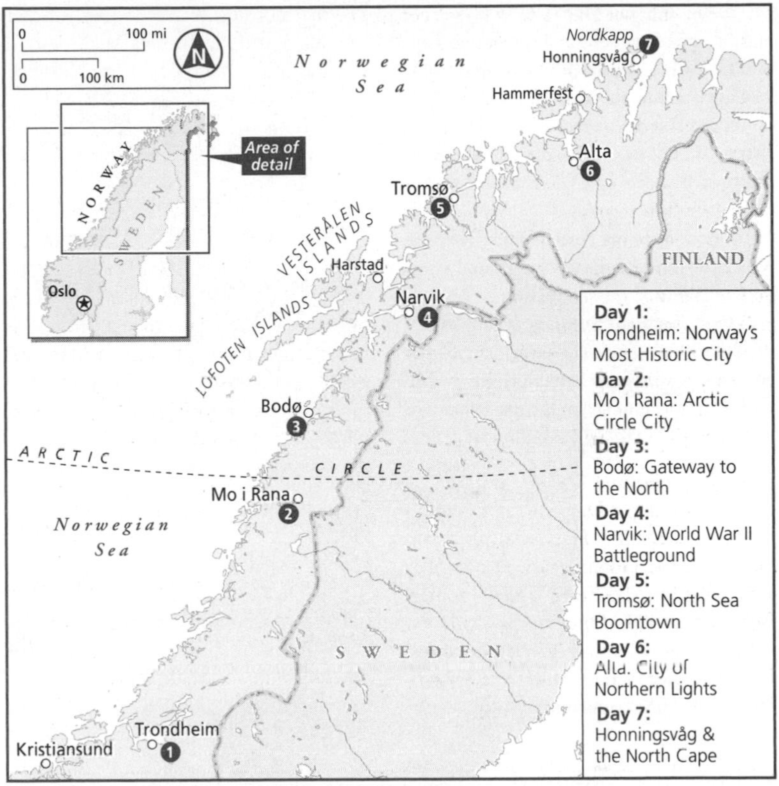

the nearby **Archbishop's Palace** (p. 359). These two sights alone will fill your morning schedule. In the afternoon, you can explore the eclectic collections of the **Nordenfjeldske Kunstindustrimuseum** (p. 363) and wander the grounds of one of Norway's finest folk-culture museums, the **Sverresborg Trøndelag Folk Museum** (p. 364).

Day 2: Mo i Rana: Arctic Circle City

Leave Trondheim on the morning of **Day 2** and head north for 450km (279 miles). Obviously, most of the day will be spent on the highway, taking in the scenery as you motor along the express highway E6. **Mo i Rana,** the third-largest city in the cold north of Norway, is your gateway to the Arctic Circle, which slices the city's boundaries from east to west. The city itself is no beauty, but its setting offers high drama in its towering mountains, stark glaciers, and coastline, as rugged as anything a Maine fisherman has ever seen. Overnight at Mo i Rana before setting out the next morning on your northward journey.

Day 3: Bodø ★: Gateway to the North

Leave Mo i Rana on the morning of **Day 3** and head for the major stopover and refueling stop of **Polarsirkelsenteret,** which lies along the E6, just 80km (51 miles) north of Mo i Rana. In this bleak countryside, stop at the Polarsirkelsenteret, or Arctic Circle Center, in the Saltfjellet mountains. It's a bit corny, but many motorists pick up a certificate showing that they've crossed the Arctic Circle, in case the folks back home need proof of that.

From Polarsirkelsenteret, it is still a drive of 174km (108 miles) north to **Bodø.** After leaving Polarsirkelsenteret, follow the route north to Fauske and cut onto Rte. 80 west, which will take you along the Skjerstadfjord into Bodø, where you can check into a hotel for the night.

The major attraction here is the famous **Maelstrom** (p. 404). This is one of the most powerful maelstroms in the world and is one of the most dramatic natural sights in the north of Europe. If time remains in your day, you can also explore the **Norwegian Aviation Museum** (p. 402), perhaps the best flight-related museum in Norway.

Day ❹: Narvik: World War II Battleground

On the morning of **Day 4,** leave Bodø and travel for 301km (187 miles) northeast to **Narvik,** an ice-free seaport on the Ofotfjord, which was the scene of one of the infamous sea battles of World War II on April 9 and 10 in 1940 when the British attacked the Nazis there. A rebuilt Narvik awaits you today.

To reach Narvik from Bodø, drive east once again along Rte. 80 until you reach Fauske, at which point you head north along E6 to Bognes. Here you transfer to a car ferry taking you to the opposite bank and the beginning of the E10, which will carry you northeast into Narvik, where you can check into a hotel for the night.

You should still have time to take a ride on the **Gondolbanen cable car** (p. 407), transporting you to the top of **Fagernesfjell mountain,** at 640m (2,100 ft.), for a panoramic view. If you still have some energy, you can go on to also visit the **War Museum** (p. 408).

Day ❺: Tromsø ★★: North Sea Boomtown

On the morning of **Day 5,** leave Narvik heading north to **Tromsø,** a distance of 421km (262 miles). Take the E6 from Narvik, cutting northwest at the junction with E8 leading directly into Tromsø.

Book your room, stow your bags, and set out to explore Norway's gateway to the Arctic, the port from which famous explorers have set forth, often to their deaths. Take the cable car to **Fjellheisen** (p. 386) for one of the most panoramic views in all of Norway. Later you can knock off the major attractions of Tromsø, including the **Arctic Cathedral** (p. 386), the northernmost **Mack's Brewery** (p. 387), and the Disney-esque **Polaria** (p. 387). If time remains, visit the **Polarmuseet** (p. 388).

Day ❻: Alta: City of Northern Lights

On the morning of **Day 6,** leave Tromsø and set out for a long drive of 329km (204 miles) to the far northern outpost of **Alta.** From Tromsø, follow E8 southeast to the junction with E6, heading northeast along the rugged coast into Alta, where you can check in to a hotel for the night. Spend a day taking in its sights, which include prehistoric rock carvings at **Hjemmeluft** (p. 428) and a riverboat excursion up the Alta River to **Sautso-Alta Canyon** (p. 428), the Grand Canyon of Scandinavia.

Day ❼: Honningsvåg & the North Cape ★★

On the morning of **Day 7,** leave Alta and drive northeast along the E6 to the junction with E69, which leads north into **Honningsvåg,** the world's northernmost village, a distance of 210km (130 miles) from Alta.

Once your lodging is secured, set out to explore the **North Cape.** In addition to the cape itself, you can visit such satellite attractions as the visitor center at **Nordkapphallen** (p. 437) and the **Nordkappmuseet** (p. 438).

If you made arrangements in Trondheim to return your car in Tromsø, you can fly back to Oslo for your transportation connection to destinations worldwide. Otherwise, prepare for a long drive back from the North Cape.

5 NORWAY FOR FAMILIES IN 1 WEEK

Norway is loaded with attractions that the entire family can enjoy. Surveys have shown that if kids have a vote, Oslo and Bergen are their favorite stopovers. From Viking ships to open-air folkloric parks and from cable-car rides into the mountains to amusement parks, Norway is filled with summer fun. The only problem may be that at midsummer the sun doesn't set, and it may be hard to get kids to go to bed.

Beginning in **Oslo** in the east, this itinerary traverses the south coast of Norway, with overnight stopovers in **Kristiansand S** and **Stavanger** before a descent onto **Bergen,** where we'll spend 3 nights. Using Bergen as a base will allow time to explore Norway's greatest attraction, the fjord district, which appeals to all ages.

Days ❶ & ❷: Oslo ★★★: Gateway to Norway

Flying into Oslo, you can spend 2 busy days having fun even before renting a car and setting out on a motor trip through the southern regions to the fjord district in the west, centering on Bergen. After checking into an Oslo hotel for 2 nights, set out on a Viking adventure. Reached by ferry from the harbor at Oslo, Bygdøy is your best bet. Once on this peninsula, you can spend 3 to 4 hours and also have lunch here. That amount of time will allow you to explore the polar exploration ship ***Fram*** (p. 141), the world-famous balsa log raft ***Kon-Tiki*** (p. 141), the **Norwegian Maritime Museum** (p. 142), the **Norwegian Folk Museum** (p. 132), and the **Viking Ship Museum** (p. 134). The latter seems to have special fascination for kids of all ages. In the afternoon, head for **Tryvannstårnet** (p. 141), the loftiest lookout tower in Scandinavia, with a viewing gallery at 570m (1,870 ft.). You can even see Sweden in the east, and the views of the Oslofjord are panoramic.

In the early evening, take the entire family for a walk along the complex of restaurants and shops that line the harbor at **Aker Brygge.** This is one of the most colorful parts of the city and an ideal place to have a Norwegian seafood dinner. The restaurants serve meat, too, though kids may balk at eating reindeer, a meat as popular in Norway as steak in Texas.

On the morning of **Day 2,** plan a **2-hour summer cruise** (see "Cruises Around the Fjord," p. 153), which will take in the blue beauty of the Oslofjord, with its islands and narrow sounds. You'll be back in Oslo in time for lunch. After a meal, take kids to see the **Children's Art Museum** (p. 146), designed especially for them. Later go for a stroll along the precincts of **Akershus Castle & Fortress** (p. 139). Cap the afternoon by going to **Norgesparken Tusenfryd** (p. 146), the largest amusement park in Norway. It's a smaller version of Copenhagen's fabled Tivoli Gardens.

Day ❸: Kristiansand S ★: The Summer City

Get an early start on the morning of **Day 3** and prepare for a long but scenic drive along the southeastern coast of Norway—all the way to the country's fifth-largest city, **Kristiansand S,** lying 342km (212 miles) southwest of Oslo. Kristiansand is reached by following the E18 all the way.

Norway for Families in 1 Week

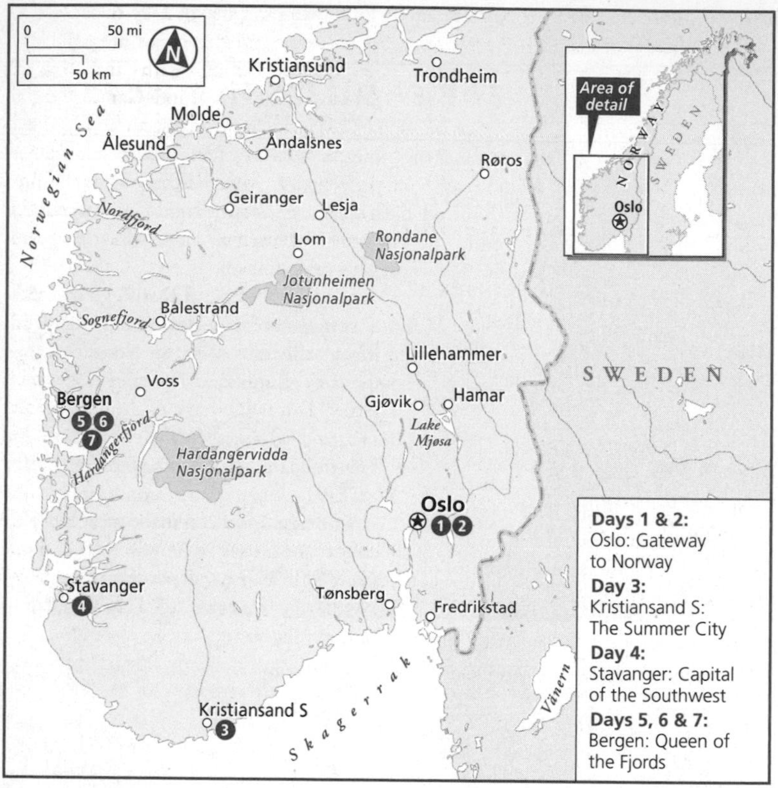

After lunch, set out for some summer fun by booking a ticket on the **Setesdalsbanen** in Grovane (p. 235), an 1894 locomotive running on a narrow-gauge track for 4.8km (3 miles). Follow that up with a stroll through the **Agder Museum of Natural History and Botanical Garden** (p. 233) before rounding off the late afternoon and early evening with a visit to the **Kristiansand Zoo and Amusement Park** (p. 234), the biggest family attraction in the south. It's been called Norway's version of Disneyland. Overnight in Kristiansand before heading west the following day.

Day 4: Stavanger ★★: Capital of the Southwest

On the morning of **Day 4,** leave Kristiansand and drive northwest along E18 into **Stavanger,** a distance of 247km (153 miles). Anchor into a hotel for the night and set out to explore. The most important pilgrimage is to **Preikestolen** (p. 256), or "Pulpit Rock," towering 609m (1,998 ft.) over beautiful Lysefjord. It's more scenic to take the boat trip instead of a bus or car to the destination. Back in Stavanger, you can spend 2 hours exploring **Gamle Stavanger** (p. 250), or Old Town, one of the northern Europe's best preserved, with a visit to its **Domkirke** (p. 249) or cathedral. You can visit the **Norwegian Children's Museum** (p. 250), the greatest playpen in Norway for kids 5 to 12 years old.

Days ❺, ❻ & ❼: Bergen ★★★: Queen of the Fjords

On the morning of **Day 5,** leave Stavanger and head for **Bergen,** a journey by car and ferry that locals can do in 4½ hours, although most foreign visitors spend at least 6½ hours because of stopovers. The trip is complicated but the most scenic in the southwest of the country. For detailed instructions, see "Getting There" in chapter 11, on Bergen.

Once you finally arrive in Bergen, check into a hotel for 3 nights. If you arrive in the late afternoon, you'll still have time to take the **Fløibanen funicular** to the top of Fløien, one of Bergen's famous seven hills. Follow up with an early evening stroll along the historic **Bryggen waterfront,** where you may want to have a family dinner.

On the morning of **Day 6,** set out to explore some of the major attractions of Bergen, beginning with the **Bergen Aquarium** (p. 277) and **Gamle Bergen** (p. 282), the latter a collection of wooden houses from the 18th and 19th centuries set in a park. In the afternoon, visit **Troldhaugen** (p. 286), Edvard Grieg's beautiful Victorian summer villa, which makes a pleasant excursion.

On the morning of **Day 7,** go out with a bang: Take a 1-day tour, lasting 12 hours, through some of Norway's most dramatic fjords and towering mountain peaks. This will be one of the most scenic journeys of your lifetime. For details on how to do this, see "Norway in a Nutshell" (p. 297).

In Bergen, you can make train or plane connections back to Oslo, which most likely will be your departure point from Norway.

5

Settling into Oslo

Over the years, we've watched Oslo, the capital of Norway, grow from a sprawling country town into the sophisticated metropolis it is today. Fueled by oil money from the "black gold" of the North Sea, Oslo today is permeated with a Nordic *joie de vivre* in contrast to its staid, dull reputation of yesteryear.

Along with population growth, urban sprawl has come to Oslo. But Oslo still manages, in spite of its growing numbers, to have more green belts than any other European capital. There are still virgin forests in Oslo and hundreds of hiking trails that lead you to fjords or mountains.

No slouch in the cultural department, either, Oslo has some of the greatest museums in all of northern Europe. The only problem is that Oslo is one of the most expensive cities in Europe. Proceed with caution if you're on a strict budget.

Oslo was founded in the mid-11th century by a Viking king and became the capital around 1300 under Haakon V. In the course of its history, the city burned down several times; fire destroyed it in 1624. The master builder Christian IV, king of Denmark and Norway, ordered the town rebuilt near the Akershus Castle. He named the new town Christiania (after himself), its official name until 1924, when the city reverted to its former name.

In 1814, Norway separated from Denmark and united with Sweden, a union that lasted until 1905. During that period, the Royal Palace, the House of Parliament, the old university, the National Theater, and the National Gallery were built.

After World War II, Oslo grew to 454 sq. km (177 sq. miles); it now has 530,000 inhabitants. That makes it one of the largest of world capitals in acreage—not in population.

Oslo is also one of Europe's most heavily forested cities, and its citizens relish this standing. Oslovians love nature in both summer and winter. When the winter snows fall, they bundle up and take to their nearby ski slopes. During their brief summer, they're quick to shed their clothes and head to the pine-covered hills in the north for long hikes and picnics, or else for sails on the blue waters of Oslofjord to the south. After a long winter slumber, the fjord suddenly becomes clogged with hundreds of sailboats, motorboats, and windsurfers, and dozens of sunbathers stripped down on the rocks, taking in the few precious days of summer sun Oslovians are granted.

1 ORIENTATION

ARRIVING

BY PLANE Planes from all over the world fly into **Oslo International Airport** in Gardemoen (✆ **91-50-64-00**), about 50km (31 miles) east of downtown Oslo, a 45-minute drive from the center. All domestic and international flights coming into Oslo arrive through this much-upgraded airport, including aircraft belonging to SAS, British Airways, and Icelandair.

Tips High-Speed Link from Stockholm

The first high-speed train between Stockholm and Oslo has reduced travel time to 4 hours and 50 minutes between these Scandinavian capitals. Depending on the day, there are two to three trains daily in each direction. This high-speed train now competes directly with air travel.

There's frequent bus service, departing at intervals of between 15 and 30 minutes throughout the day, into downtown Oslo. Bus service is maintained by **SAS** (✆ **81-50-01-76;** www.flybussen.no), whose buses deliver passengers to the Central Railway station and to most of the SAS hotels within Oslo. The cost is NOK130 ($26/£13) per person. There's also a high-speed railway service between Gardemoen and Oslo's main railway station, requiring a transit time of only 20 minutes, priced at NOK160 ($32/£16) per person each way. If you want to take a taxi, be prepared for a lethally high charge of around NOK600 to NOK700 ($120–$140/£60–£70) for up to four passengers plus luggage. If you need a "maxi-taxi," a minivan that's suitable for between 5 and 15 passengers plus luggage, you'll be assessed NOK900 ($180/£90).

BY TRAIN Trains from the Continent, Sweden, and Denmark arrive at **Oslo Sentralstasjon,** Jernbanetorget 1 (✆ **81-50-08-88** for train information), located at the beginning of Karl Johans Gate, in the center of the city. The station is open daily from 4:30am to 1am. From the Central Station, trains leave for Bergen, Stavanger, Trondheim, Bodø, and all other rail links in Norway. You can also take trams to all major parts of Oslo. Lockers and a luggage office are available at the station, where you can exchange money, if needed.

BY CAR If you're driving from mainland Europe, the fastest way to reach Oslo is to take the car ferry from Frederikshavn, Denmark. From Frederikshavn, car ferries run to several towns near Oslo and to Gothenburg, Sweden. You can also take a car ferry from Copenhagen to several points in western Sweden, or from Helsingør, Denmark, to Helsingborg, Sweden. Hwy. E6 runs the length of Sweden's western coast from Malmö through Helsingborg and Gothenburg, right up to Oslo. If you're driving from Stockholm to Oslo, take E3 west to Örebro, where it connects with E18 to Oslo. Once you near the outskirts of Oslo from any direction, follow the signs into the Sentrum.

BY FERRY Ferries from Europe arrive at the Oslo port, a 15-minute walk (or a short taxi ride) from the center. From Denmark, Scandinavia's link with the Continent, ferries depart for Oslo from Copenhagen, Hirtshals, and Frederikshavn.

From Strømstad, Sweden, in the summer the daily crossing to Sandefjord, Norway, takes 2½ hours; from Sandefjord, it's an easy drive or train ride north to Oslo.

VISITOR INFORMATION

Assistance and information for visitors are available at the **Tourist Information Office,** Fridtjof Nansens Plass 5, N-0160 Oslo (www.visitoslo.com). Free maps, brochures, sightseeing tickets, and guide services are available. The office is open June to August daily 9am to 7pm, April to May and September Monday to Saturday 9am to 5pm, and October to March Monday to Friday 9am to 4pm. The information office at the **Oslo Sentralstasjon (Central Station),** Jernbanetorget 1, is open daily from May to

September 8am to 8pm and October to April daily 8am to 6pm. The centralized phone number to call all the tourist offices in Oslo is ✆ **81-53-05-55.**

CITY LAYOUT

See the "Oslo Attractions" map on p. 128 for a breakdown of these neighborhoods.

MAIN ARTERIES & STREETS Oslo is at the mouth of the Oslofjord, which is 97km (60 miles) in length. Opening onto the harbor is **Rådhusplassen (City Hall Square),** dominated by the modern City Hall, a major attraction. Guided bus tours leave from this point, and the launches that cruise the fjords depart from the pier facing the municipal building. You can catch Bygdøy-bound ferries from the quay at Rådhusplassen. On a promontory to the east is **Akershus Castle.**

Karl Johans Gate, Oslo's main street (especially for shopping and strolling), is north of City Hall Square. This boulevard begins at Oslo Sentralstasjon (Central Station) and stretches all the way to the 19th-century Royal Palace at the western end.

A short walk from the palace is the famed **Studenter Lunden (Students' Grove),** where seemingly everybody gathers on summer days to socialize. The University of Oslo is nearby. Dominating this center is the National Theater, guarded by statues of Ibsen and Bjørnson, the two greatest names in Norwegian theater. South of the theater, near the harbor, is **Stortingsgaten,** another shop-filled street.

The main city square is **Stortorvet,** although it's no longer the center of city life, which has shifted to Karl Johans Gate.

At a subway stop near the National Theater, you can catch an electric train to **Tryvannstårnet,** the loftiest lookout in Scandinavia, and to the **Holmenkollen Ski Jump.**

FINDING AN ADDRESS Street numbers begin on the southern end of streets running north-south and on the eastern end of streets running east-west. Odd numbers are on one side of the street, and even numbers on the other. Where large buildings hold several establishments, different addresses are designated with A, B, and C.

STREET MAPS Maps of Oslo are distributed free at the tourist office (see "Visitor Information," above). For extensive exploring, especially of some back streets, you may need a more detailed map. Opt for a pocket-size map with a street index that can be opened and folded like a wallet. Such maps are sold at most newsstands in the central city. If you can't find a map, go to the city's most central bookstore, **Tanum Karl Johan,** Karl Johans Gate 43 (✆ **22-41-11-00**).

NEIGHBORHOODS IN BRIEF

Oslo is made for walking—in fact, you can walk from the Central Station all the way to the Royal Palace (Slottet) in a straight line. Except for excursions to the museum-loaded Bygdøy peninsula and the Holmenkollen Ski Jump, most attractions can be covered on foot.

Oslo is not neatly divided into separate neighborhoods or districts. It consists mainly of **central Oslo,** with the Central Station to the east of the city center and the Royal Palace to the west. Karl Johans Gate, the principal street, connects these two points. Central Oslo is the heart of the city—the most crowded and traffic-congested, but also the most convenient place to stay. Those on the most rushed of schedules—the average visitor spends only 2 days in Oslo—will book accommodations in the center. It's not a real neighborhood, but it's the core of the city, as Piccadilly Circus is to London. Most Oslo hotels and restaurants are here, as are almost 50 museums and galleries—enough to fill many a rainy day. The best of the lot include Akershus Castle, the Historical Museum, and the National Gallery.

The streets Drammensveien and Frognerveien lead northwest to Frogner Park (Frognerparken), whose main entrance is on Kirkeveien. This historical area is the site of the Vigeland Sculpture Park, which displays some of Gustav Vigeland's masterpieces.

The **Old Town** (or Gamlebyen) lies south of the Parliament Building (the Stortinget) and Karl Johans Gate. This section contains some of the city's old-fashioned restaurants, along with the Norwegian Resistance Museum and the Old Town Hall. A stay here is the same as staying in central Oslo (see above). The only difference is that the streets of the Old Town have more old-fashioned Norwegian flavor than the more modern parts of central Oslo.

Aker Brygge is Oslo's newest neighborhood, an excellent place for dining and diversions, but not for hotels as it is sadly lacking in those. For sights along the waterfront, it's the best place for long walks to take in the port life. It emerged near the mouth of the Oslofjord in the old wharf area formerly used for shipbuilding yards. Fueled by oil wealth, steel-and-glass buildings now rise from what had been a relatively dilapidated section. Some of the best shops, theaters, restaurants, and cultural attractions are here, along with apartments for such well-heeled owners as Diana Ross.

The main attractions in **Eastern Oslo** are the Botanisk Hage (Botanic Garden), the Zoological Museum, and the Munch Museum in Tøyen—little more is worth seeing here. Unless you're interested in seeing those sights mentioned, you might skip eastern Oslo. However, thousands of visitors head here just to see the Munch Museum (p. 130).

The **West End** is a chic residential area graced with some of the city's finest hotels and restaurants. It's a more tranquil setting than the center and only 15 minutes away by public transportation. Many visitors who stay here don't mind the short commute and prefer this area to the more traffic-clogged center. However, for walking and sightseeing, central Oslo and its port are more alluring. There is little to see in the West End unless you like walking up and down pleasant residential streets.

Farther west—6km (3³/₄ miles) by car, but better reached by car ferry—is the **Bygdøy** peninsula. Here you'll find such attractions as the Norwegian Folk Museum, the Viking ships, the polar ship *Fram,* and the *Kon-Tiki* Museum. Break up your sightseeing venture with a meal here, but plan to stay elsewhere.

The suburb of **Frogner** begins .8km (¹/₂ mile) west of Oslo's center and stretches for a mile or so. Unless you specifically have business here, you can probably skip this section of the city.

Lying behind the S-station, the main rail station for Oslo, is the **Grønland district,** where many Oslovians go for ethnic dining. There is little of sightseeing interest in this ghettolike area. Many refugees from Pakistan and India, among other countries, fill the area; however, the town's best Indian and Pakistani restaurants lie within more upscale neighborhoods. Come here for affordable dining, not for long, leisurely walks. On a hurried visit, you could afford to skip Grønland entirely without suffering any cultural loss.

At last, once-staid Oslo has grown big and diverse enough to have its own trendy, counterculture district. Lying in east Oslo is trendy **Grünerløkka,** which most of its inhabitants refer to affectionately as "Løkka." This once-rundown sector of Oslo traditionally was known as the worker's district. Today many professional Oslovians are moving in to restore apartments, and the district is the site of several fashionable cafes and restaurants. If you're young with a roving eye at night, you might want to check out some of the establishments in this area.

Many Oslo neighborhoods lie along the **Oslofjord,** which stretches more than 97km (60 miles) north from the Skagerrak to Oslo. Basins dotted with islands fill the fjord. (There are 40 islands in the immediate Oslo archipelago.) Chances are, you won't be staying or dining along the fjord, but might consider a boat trip along the water, as it's a grand attraction on a summer day.

Nearly all visitors want to see **Holmenkollen,** a wooded range of hills northwest of the city rising to about 226m (741 ft.). You can reach it in 35 minutes by electric train from the city center. Skiers might want to stay here in winter, lodging at the Holmenkollen Park Hotel Rica (p. 109). Otherwise, visit for the view and perhaps make it a luncheon stopover, then head back to the historic core.

Marka, Oslo's forest, is a sprawling recreation area with hiking, bicycle riding, skiing, fishing, wild-berry picking, jogging trails, and more. It contains 343 lakes, 500km (310 miles) of ski trails, 623km (386 miles) of trails and roads, 11 sports chalets, and 24 ski jumps and alpine slopes. If you like to go for long walks on summer days, Marka's the spot for you. It's also one of the best places in Greater Oslo for a picnic.

2 GETTING AROUND

BY PUBLIC TRANSPORTATION

Oslo has an efficient citywide network of buses, trams (streetcars), and subways. Buses and electric trains take passengers to the suburbs; from mid-April to October, ferries to Bygdøy depart from the harbor in front of the Oslo Rådhuset (City Hall).

DISCOUNT PASSES The **Oslo Pass** can help you become acquainted with the city at a fraction of the usual price. It allows free travel on public transportation, free admission to museums and other top sights, discounts on sightseeing buses and boats, a rebate on your car rental, and special treats in restaurants. You can purchase the card at hotels, fine stores, and tourist information offices; from travel agents; and in the branches of Sparebanken Oslo Akershus. Adults pay NOK220 ($44/£22) for a 1-day card, NOK320 ($64/£32) for 2 days, and NOK410 ($82/£41) for 3 days. Children's cards cost NOK95 ($19/£9.50), NOK115 ($23/£12), and NOK150 ($30/£15).

BY BUS, TRAM & SUBWAY Jernbanetorget is Oslo's major **bus and tram** terminal stop. Most buses and trams passing through the heart of town stop at Wessels Plass, next to the Parliament, or at Stortorvet, the main marketplace. Many also stop at the National Theater or University Square on Karl Johans Gate, as well as stopping through Oslo's suburbs.

The **subway (T-banen)** has four branch lines to the east. The Western Suburban route (including Holmenkollen) has four lines to the residential sections and recreation grounds west and north of the city. Subways and trains leave from near the National Theater on Karl Johans Gate.

For public transit schedule and fare information, call **Trafikanten** (✆ **81-50-01-76;** www.trafikanten.no). Automated machines cancel tickets. Drivers sell single-trip tickets for NOK30 ($6/£3); children travel for half-fare. An eight-coupon Flexi card costs NOK160 ($32/£16) and is half-price for children. Maxi cards can be used for unlimited transfers for 1 hour from the time the ticket is stamped.

BY TAXI

If you need a taxi, call ✆ **23-23-23-23,** available 24 hours a day. Reserve at least an hour in advance.

Hiring a taxi is very expensive in Oslo. Tariffs start at NOK30 ($6/£3) for hailed taxis in the streets or at NOK50 ($10/£5) if you summon one in advance. In addition to regular fares, there are lethal surcharges between 5 and 10pm costing NOK110 ($22/£11), or between 10pm and 4am costing NOK210 ($42/£21). All taxis have meters, and Norwegian cab drivers are generally honest. When a cab is available, its roof light goes on. Taxis can be hailed on the street, provided they're more than 91m (298 ft.) from a taxi rank. The most difficult time to hail a taxi is Monday to Friday 8:30 to 10am and 3 to 5pm, and Saturday 8:30 to 10am.

BY CAR

Driving is not a practical way to get around Oslo because parking is limited. The efficient public transportation system makes a private car unnecessary. You can reach even the most isolated areas by public transportation.

Among the multistory parking lots in the city center, the best is **Vestre Vika Bilpark,** Dronning Mauds Gate (✆ **22-83-35-35**). The cost of parking a car in a public garage is NOK50 ($10/£5) per hour or NOK178 ($36/£18) for 24 hours. Illegally parked cars are towed away. For car problems, call the **NAF Alarm Center** (✆ **22-34-14-00**), available 24 hours a day.

BY FERRY

Beginning in mid-April, ferries depart for Bygdøy from Pier 3 in front of the Oslo Rådhuset. For schedules, call **Båtservice** (✆ **23-35-68-90**). The ferry or bus to Bygdøy is a good choice because parking there is limited. Other ferries leave for various parts of the Oslofjord. Inquire at the **Tourist Information Office,** Fridtjof Nansens Plass 5, N-0160 Oslo (✆ **24-14-77-00**).

Fast Facts Oslo

American Express American Express Reisebyrå, Maribores Gate 13 (✆ **22-98-35-00**), is open Monday to Friday 9am to 6pm, Saturday 10am to 4pm.

Area Code The country code for Norway is **47.** If you're calling from outside the country, the city code for Oslo is **2.** Inside Norway, no area or city codes are needed. Telephone numbers have eight digits.

Babysitters Hotels can often enlist the help of a housekeeper for "child-minding." Give at least a day's notice, or two if you can. You can also contact the tourist office (see "Visitor Information," above), which keeps a list of available sitters on file.

Bookstores Oslo has many bookstores. The most central and one of the best stocked is **Tanum Karl Johan,** Karl Johans Gate 43 (✆ **22-41-11-00**).

Currency Exchange **Banks** will exchange most foreign currencies or cash traveler's checks. Bring your passport for identification. If banks are closed, try automated machines at the Oslo Sentralstasjon to exchange currency. For foreign currency exchange go to **Forex,** at Oslo Sentralstasjon, Jernbanetorget 1 (✆ **22-17-64-00**).

Dentists If you're having a dental emergency, you can contact either of these organizations at extended hours, usually 24 hours a day, for the address of a dentist who can take a new client on short notice: **Volvat Medisinske Senter (Volvat Medical Center),** Borgenveien 2A (✆ **22-95-75-00**); and **Oslo Legevakt (Oslo Emergency Hospital),** Storgten 40 (✆ **22-11-80-80;** ask for emergency services).

Doctors Some larger hotels have arrangements with doctors in case a guest becomes ill, or try the 24-hour **Oslo Akuttetaten (Emergencies),** Storgata 40 (✆ **22-93-22-93**). A privately funded alternative is **Oslo Akutten,** Nedre Vollgate 8 (✆ **22-00-81-60**). For more routine medical assistance, you can contact the biggest hospital in Oslo, **Ullaval,** Kirkeveien 166 (✆ **22-11-80-80**). To consult a private doctor (nearly all of whom speak English), check the telephone directory or ask at your hotel for a recommendation.

Drugstores A 24-hour pharmacy is **Jernbanetorvets Apotek,** Jernbanetorget 4A (✆ **22-41-24-82**).

Embassies & Consulates See "Fast Facts: Norway," in Appendix A.

Emergencies Dial the Oslo **police** at ✆ **112;** to report a **fire,** call ✆ **110;** call an **ambulance** at ✆ **113.**

Eyeglass Repair **Synsam Karl Johan,** Karl Johans Gate 20 (✆ **22-00-83-10**), is a big eyeglass supplier. Most contact lenses are in stock, too. Unusual prescriptions take about 2 days. Hours are Monday and Wednesday to Friday 9am to 5pm, Tuesday 9am to 6pm, and Saturday 10am to 3pm.

Internet Access You can tap in free at the Rådhuset, the City Hall on Rådhusplassen (✆ **23-46-16-00**).

Laundry & Dry Cleaning Washing and drying can usually be completed in an hour. You must have your coins ready to put in the machines. Dry cleaning is extremely expensive in Oslo, and many establishments take more than a week to return clothing. Try **American Lincoln Norge,** Østmarkv 25 (✆ **22-27-24-50**), which promises 24-hour service.

Lost Property It's uncertain—even in law-abiding Norway—whether someone will actually return a valuable object that you've lost, but the two most obvious places to begin your search are the Lost Property office at Gardermoen Airport (✆ **64-81-34-77**), which is open daily 7am to 6pm, and the Lost Property office at the Central Railway Station (✆ **81-56-83-40**), open Monday to Friday midnight to 5pm.

Luggage Storage & Lockers Facilities for luggage storage are available at the **Oslo Sentralstasjon,** Jernbanetorget 1 (✆ **81-50-08-88**). It's open daily 4:30am to 1am. Lockers cost NOK40 to NOK70 ($8–$14/£4–£7) per day, depending on size.

Newspapers & Magazines English-language newspapers and magazines are sold—at least, in the summer months—at newsstands (kiosks) throughout Oslo. International editions, including the *International Herald Tribune* and *USA Today,* are always available, as are the European editions of *Time* and *Newsweek.*

Photographic Needs Try **Preus Photo,** Stovner Senter 3 (✆ **22-42-98-04**), for supplies, including black-and-white and color film. Film can be developed in 1 hour. It's open Monday to Friday 9am to 5pm, and Saturday 10am to 3pm.

Police Dial ✆ **112.**

Post Office The **Oslo General Post Office** is at Dronningensgatan 15 (✆ **23-14-90-00** for information). Enter at the corner of Prinsensgate. It's open Monday to Friday 8am to 5pm and Saturday 9am to 2pm; it's closed Sunday and public holidays. You can arrange for mail to be sent to the main post office c/o General Delivery. The address is Poste Restante, P.O. Box 1181-Sentrum, Dronningensgatan 15, N 0101 Oslo, Norway. You must show your passport to collect it.

Safety Of the four Scandinavian capitals, Oslo is widely considered the safest. However, it is still a major city, so don't be lulled into a false sense of security. Be careful, and don't carry your wallet visibly exposed or sling your purse over your shoulder.

Taxes Oslo has no special city taxes. You'll pay the same value-added tax throughout the country (see "Fast Facts: Norway," in Appendix A).

Taxis See "Getting Around," above.

Toilets Clean public toilets can be found throughout the city center, in parks, and at all bus, rail, and air terminals. For a detailed list, contact the Tourist Information Office.

Weather See the temperature chart in section 3, "When to Go," in chapter 3.

3 WHERE TO STAY

By the standards of many U.S. and Canadian cities, hotels in Oslo are very expensive. If you're from London, you'll feel right at home. Oslovian hotels lose most of their business travelers, their main revenue source, during the peak tourist months in midsummer. July is always a month for discounts. Some hotels' discounts begin June 21. Regular pricing usually resumes in mid-August.

Hotels also slash prices on weekends—usually Friday and Saturday, and sometimes Sunday. Again, hotels often change their policies, so it's best to check when you make your reservations. Don't always expect a discount—a quickly arranged conference could lead hotels to increase their prices.

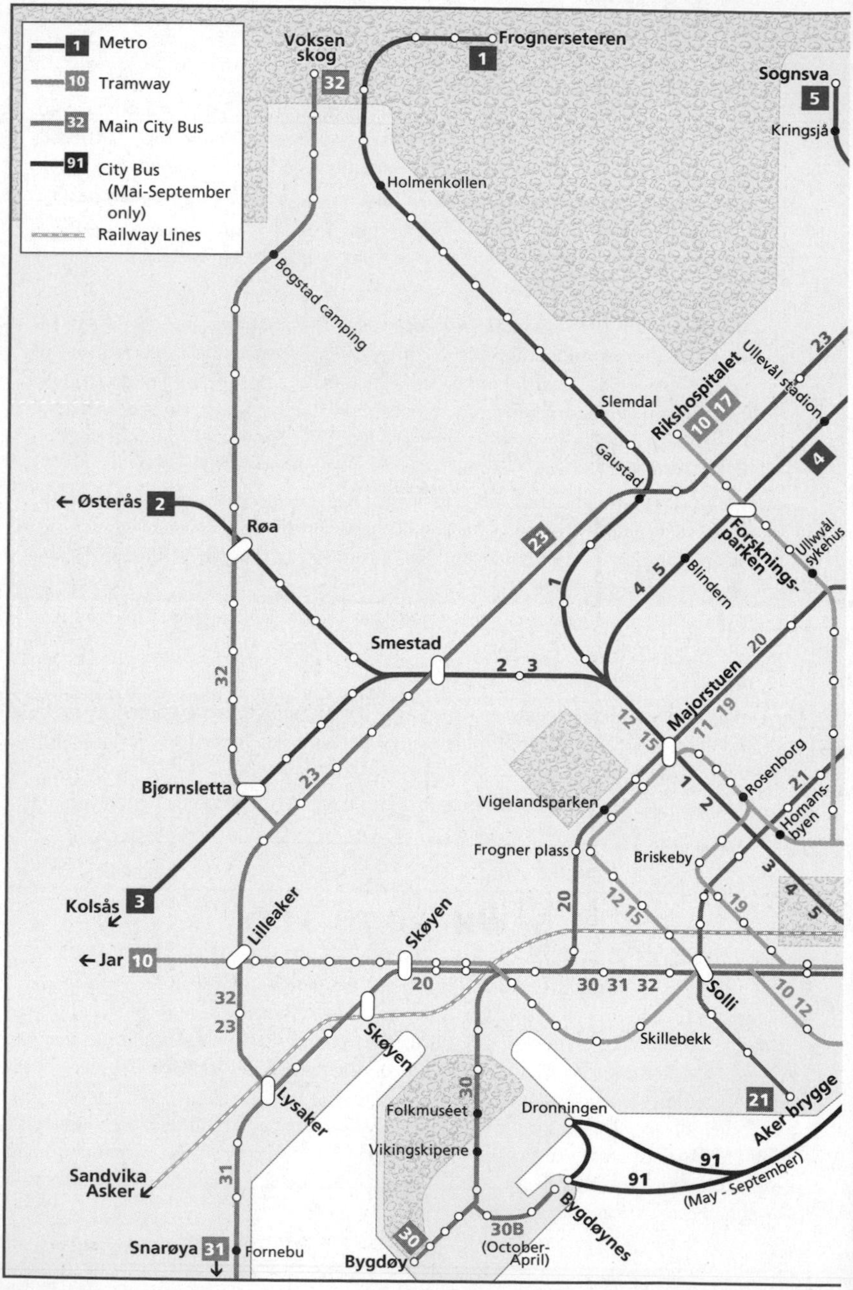
Metro
Tramway
Main City Bus
City Bus (Mai-September only)
Railway Lines
Voksen skog
Frognerseteren
Sognsva
Kringsjå
Holmenkollen
Bogstad camping
Slemdal
Gaustad
Rikshospitalet
Ullevål stadion
Østerås
Røa
Smestad
Forsknings-parken
Blindern
Ullevål sykehus
Majorstuen
Rosenborg
Homans-byen
Vigelandsparken
Bjørnsletta
Frogner plass
Briskeby
Kolsås
Lilleaker
Skøyen
Jar
Solli
Skillebekk
Lysaker
Folkmuséet
Dronningen
Aker brygge
Vikingskipene
Sandvika
Asker
(May - September)
Bygdøynes
30B
(October-April)
Snarøya
Fornebu
Bygdøy

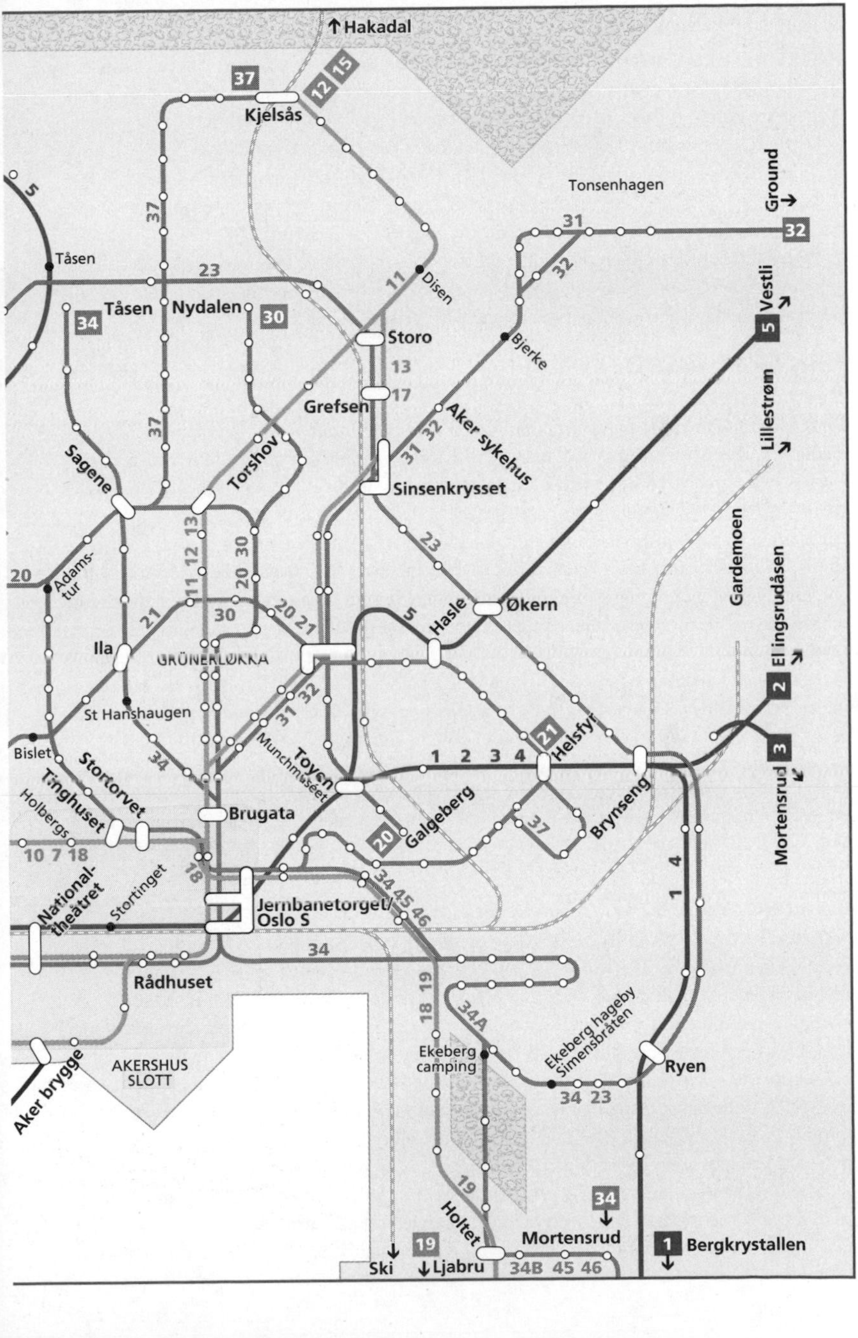
Hakadal
Kjelsås
Tonsenhagen
Ground
Vestli
Lillestrøm
Gardemoen
Ellingsrudåsen
Mortensrud
Tåsen
Nydalen
Disen
Storo
Grefsen
Bjerke
Aker sykehus
Sinsenkrysset
Torshov
Sagene
Adamstuen
Ila
GRÜNERLØKKA
St Hanshaugen
Bislet
Stortorvet
Tinghuset
Holbergs
Hasle
Økern
Helsfyr
Brynseng
Tøyen
Munchmuseet
Galgeberg
Brugata
Nationaltheatret
Stortinget
Jernbanetorget/
Oslo S
Rådhuset
Aker brygge
AKERSHUS
SLOTT
Ekeberg camping
Ekeberg hageby
Simensbråten
Ryen
Holtet
Mortensrud
Ski
Ljabru
Bergkrystallen

The most economy-minded visitors can cut costs by staying at one of the old-fashioned hotels that offer a number of rooms without private bathrooms. Sometimes a room has a shower but no toilet. Even the rooms without bathrooms usually have a sink with hot and cold running water.

HOTEL RESERVATIONS The worst months for finding a place to stay in Oslo are May, June, September, and October, when many business conferences are held. July and August are better, though that's the peak of the summer tourist invasion.

If you happen to arrive in Oslo without a reservation, head for the Oslo Tourist Information Office, Fridtjof Nansens Plass 5 (✆ **24-14-77-00**), which can find you a room in your price category. The minimum stay is 2 days. Don't try to phone—the service is strictly for walk-ins who need a room on the night of their arrival.

Note: Rates quoted below include the service charge and tax. Breakfast—usually a generous Norwegian buffet—is almost always included. Unless otherwise indicated, all our recommended accommodations come with private bathrooms.

CENTRAL OSLO

Very Expensive

First Hotel Grims Grenka ★ Kids Even though it often plays a Norwegian "second fiddle" to the Millennium (see below), this is nonetheless a most desirable address. Because each room comes with a small kitchenette, and family suites have a fairytale theme, the hotel is popular with parents visiting with children in tow. This elegant boutique hotel, whose lobby has a seven-story glassed-in atrium with Oriental carpets, columns, and a fireplace, has a personalized feel. A member of a Sweden-based hotel chain, the hotel has a polite staff and a lot of idiosyncratic style. This is one of the few hotels anywhere where we prefer the regular rooms to the oddly laid-out, curiously spartan suites, where lots of room might be devoted, say, to an interior hallway. Each of the suites is thematically decorated, based on the life of a famous Scandinavian, such as opera and ballet personalities Kirsten Flagstad, Ingrid Bjoner, and Indra Lorentzen. Rooms and suites are accessed via a labyrinthine path of stairs and angled hallways.

Kongensgate 5, N-0153 Oslo. ✆ **23-10-72-00.** Fax 23-10-72-10. www.grimsgrenka.no. 66 units. NOK1,850–NOK2,795 ($370–$559/£185–£280) double, from NOK2,995 ($599/£300) suite. Rates include breakfast. AE, DC, MC, V. Parking NOK170 ($34/£17) per night. T-banen: Stortinget. **Amenities:** Night club; fitness room; wellness center; outdoor Jacuzzi on roof terrace; sauna; massage; laundry service/dry cleaning; nonsmoking rooms. *In room:* A/C, TV, Wi-Fi, minibar, iron.

Grand Hotel ★★★ Kids Famous guests still arrive at Norway's premier hotel, and you are likely to see CEOs, Nobel Prize winners, and movie stars. Tradition and style reign supreme here, as they did when the Grand opened its doors in 1874 in a Louis XVI revival–style building imbued with touches of Art Nouveau. Constant modernization has not managed to erase the original character of the hotel, which stands on the wide boulevard leading to the Royal Palace. In fact, the stone-walled hotel with its mansard gables and copper tower is now one of the most distinctive landmarks of Oslo. Guest rooms are in the 19th-century core or in one of the tasteful modern additions. Newer rooms contain plush facilities and electronic extras, and the older ones have been completely modernized. An eight-story extension contains larger, brighter doubles.

The Hotel Bristol and Hotel Continental are less pretentious than the Grand, lacking such stiff formality and ritualized service. In spite of its formality, many well-heeled families check into the Grand. Children enjoy the indoor heated pool, and the reception staff keeps a list of activities going on in Oslo that will amuse kids. The hotel has several restaurants that serve international and Scandinavian food. The Palmen, the Restaurant Julius Fritzner (p. 111), and the Grand Café (p. 114), the most famous cafe in Oslo, all offer live entertainment.

Karl Johans Gate 31, N-0159 Oslo. ✆ **800/223-5652** in the U.S., or 23-21-20-00. Fax 23-21-21-00. www.grand.no. 289 units. Summer NOK1,545 ($309/£155) double, from NOK3,350 ($670/£335) suite; fall–spring NOK2,100 ($420/£210) double, from NOK3,225 ($645/£323) suite. Rates include buffet breakfast. AE, DC, MC, V. Parking NOK220 ($44/£22). T-banen: Stortinget. **Amenities:** 3 restaurants; 2 bars; nightclub; indoor heated pool; fitness center; health club; sauna; solarium; shopping arcade; room service; babysitting; massage; laundry service/dry cleaning; nonsmoking rooms; rooms for those w/limited mobility; Wi-Fi. *In room:* A/C, TV, minibar, hair dryer, safe, trouser press.

Hotel Continental ★★★ It's not the Grand—what is?—but this deluxe hotel is beautifully appointed and, quite frankly, more fun, attracting the entertainment industry crowd. Although it's been around since 1900, and is still one of Norway's grand old hotels, it has a more modern aura than the stuffier Grand and is the only Norwegian member of the Leading Hotels of the World. It's the only major hotel in Oslo that's still mostly owned by an individual family, making it cozy, a bit inbred, and thoroughly welcoming in its approach to virtually everything. Expect lots of personalized touches, such as a masterful collection of framed original lithographs and woodcuts by Edvard Munch in a salon near the reception area. Bedrooms are plush and intensely well decorated, often with wallpaper and an unerring upper-crust touch, sometimes evoking comfortable bedrooms in private homes. The suites, which absolutely rival those at the Grand, include the Abel Suite named after the famous Norwegian mathematician Niels Henrik Abel. The hotel is entirely nonsmoking.

Stortingsgaten 24-26, N-0117 Oslo. ✆ **22-82-40-00.** Fax 22-42-96-89. www.hotel-continental.no. 154 units. Sun–Thurs NOK2,450–NOK3,000 ($490–$600/£245–£300) double, from NOK3,900 ($780/£390) suite; Fri–Sat NOK1,400–NOK2,160 ($280–$432/£140–£216) double, from NOK2,750 ($550/£275) suite. Rates include breakfast buffet. AE, DC, MC, V. Parking NOK250 ($50/£25). T-banen: Nationaltheatret. **Amenities:** 2 restaurants; 2 bars; 2 cafes; gym; room service; babysitting; laundry service/dry cleaning. *In room:* A/C, TV, Wi-Fi, minibar, hair dryer, safe, trouser press.

Thon Hotel Cecil ★ (Value) This contemporary hotel enjoys a central location, with many restaurants, sights, and shops within a short walk of the main entrance of the hotel. Dating from 1989, it was constructed on the site of a previous hotel destroyed by fire. As if inspired by a much grander Hyatt, most of its rooms are built to open onto a central atrium. Only four rooms on each of the eight floors overlook the street (the sometimes rowdy—at least, at night—Rosenkrantzgate). The well-maintained rooms are cozy and contain neatly kept bathrooms.

Stortingsgate 8 (entrance on Rosenkrantzgate), N-0130 Oslo. ✆ **23-31-48-00.** Fax 23-31-48-50. www.thonhotels.no. 111 units. NOK1,795–NOK2,295 ($359–$459/£180–£230) double; NOK3,595 ($719/£360) suite. AE, DC, MC, V. Parking NOK180 ($36/£18). T-banen: Stortinget. **Amenities:** Laundry service/dry cleaning; nonsmoking rooms; rooms for those w/limited mobility. *In room:* A/C, TV, Wi-Fi, minibar, coffeemaker, hair dryer.

Thon Hotel Stefan (Value) As "Thons" go, this is the low man on the totem pole, but it's a recommendable choice if its siblings are fully booked. We've seen bigger and better hotels in Oslo, but very few that offer comparable comfort at such affordable rates. In an excellent location in the center of the city, this unpretentious hotel never claims to be more than it is. Built in 1952, it has been modernized and much improved over the years. The color-coordinated guest rooms are traditional in style and well furnished and

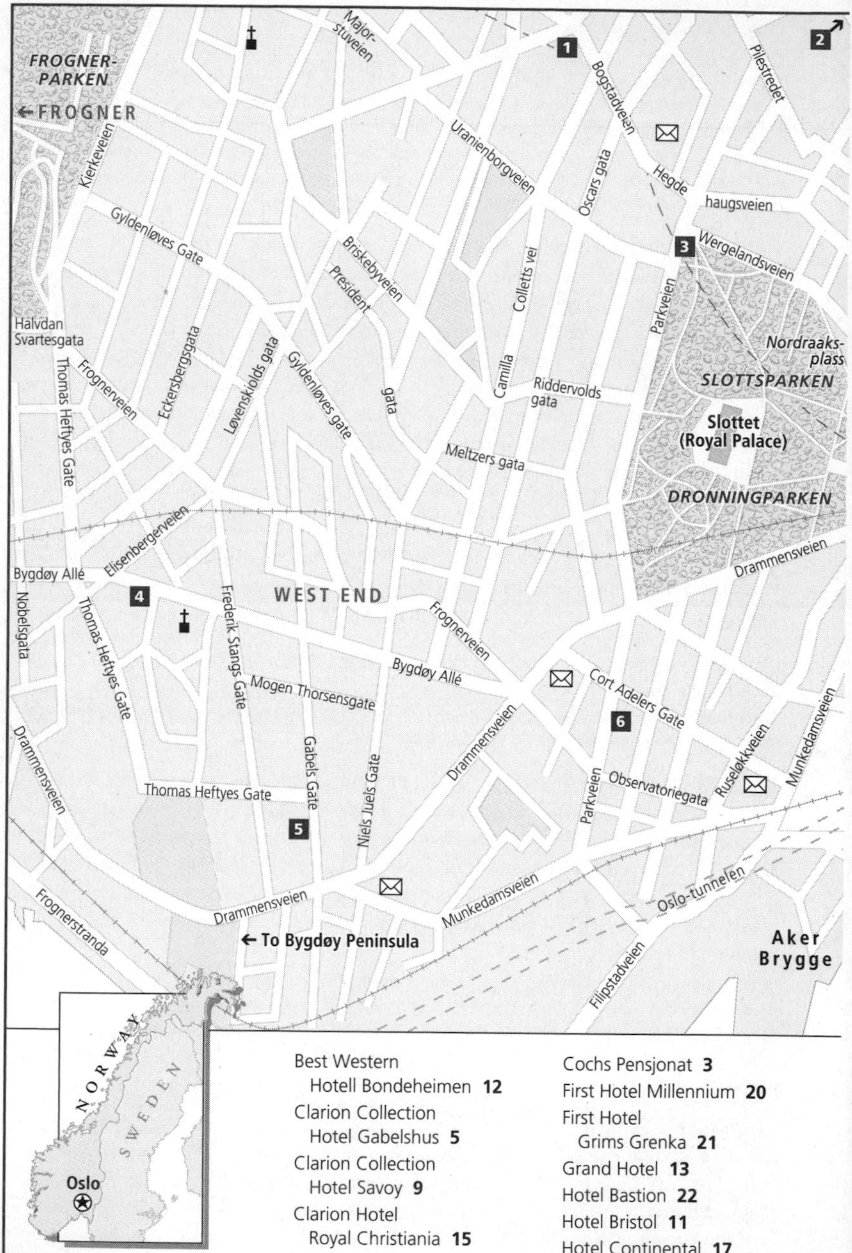

Best Western Hotell Bondeheimen **12**
Clarion Collection Hotel Gabelshus **5**
Clarion Collection Hotel Savoy **9**
Clarion Hotel Royal Christiania **15**
Cochs Pensjonat **3**
First Hotel Millennium **20**
First Hotel Grims Grenka **21**
Grand Hotel **13**
Hotel Bastion **22**
Hotel Bristol **11**
Hotel Continental **17**

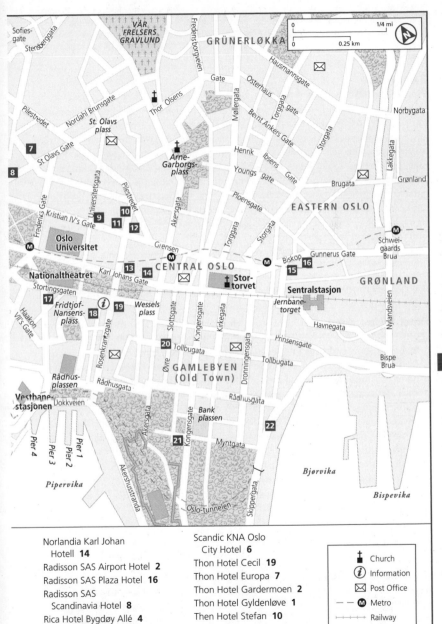

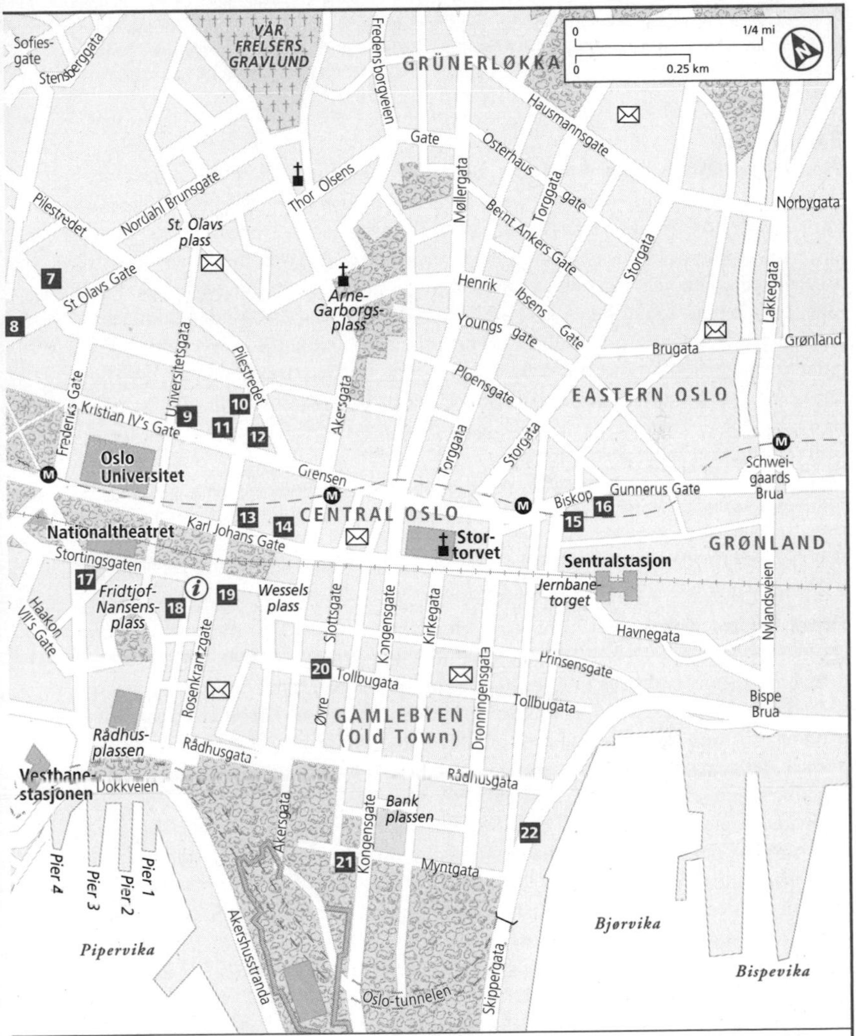

Norlandia Karl Johan Hotell **14**
Radisson SAS Airport Hotel **2**
Radisson SAS Plaza Hotel **16**
Radisson SAS Scandinavia Hotel **8**
Rica Hotel Bygdøy Allé **4**
Rica Victoria Hotel **18**
Scandic KNA Oslo City Hotel **6**
Thon Hotel Cecil **19**
Thon Hotel Europa **7**
Thon Hotel Gardermoen **2**
Thon Hotel Gyldenløve **1**
Then Hotel Stefan **10**

maintained. From May until September 1, weekend rates are granted only to those who make reservations less than 48 hours before arrival.

Rosenkrantzgate 1, N-0159 Oslo 1. ✆ **23-31-55-00.** Fax 23-31-55-55. www.thonhotels.com. 150 units. NOK1,795–NOK2,600 ($359–$520/£180–£260). Rates include buffet breakfast. AE, DC, MC, V. Parking NOK190 ($38/£19). Tram: 10, 11, 17, or 18. **Amenities:** Coffee shop/bar; laundry service/dry cleaning; nonsmoking rooms; rooms for those w/limited mobility. *In room:* A/C, TV, Wi-Fi, minibar, beverage maker, hair dryer, safe.

Expensive

First Hotel Millennium ★★ Kids Because there are two "First" hotels in Oslo, a choice has to be made. If you're given one of the better rooms, we prefer the Millennium to the First Hotel Grims Grenka (see above), as the Millennium is one of Oslo's "personality" hotels, known for its cozy atmosphere and character. In 1998, the owners took over a 1930s office building, successfully transforming it into this comfortable refuge. Rising nine floors behind a pale pink facade, the hotel is noted for a stylish kind of minimalism. Rooms range from standard to superior. The former is comfortable in every way, but the latter is among the most spacious in town, with many Art Deco touches. On the top floor are a dozen accommodations with their own large balconies opening onto cityscape views. Family rooms are also very spacious, with a separate bedroom and living area. All bedrooms feature hardwood flooring.

Tollbugate 25, N-0157 Oslo. ✆ **21-02-28-00.** Fax 21-02-28-30. www.firsthotels.com/millennium. 112 units. NOK1,145–NOK2,095 ($229–$419/£115–£210) double. AE, DC, MC, V. No on-site parking. T-banen: Stortinget. **Amenities:** Restaurant; bar; room service; babysitting; laundry service/dry cleaning; nonsmoking rooms; rooms for those w/limited mobility. *In room:* TV, Wi-Fi, minibar, beverage maker, hair dryer.

Hotel Bristol ★★★ Kids Imbued with character, this 1920s-era hotel competes aggressively and gracefully with two other historic properties, the Grand and the Continental. Of the three, the Bristol consistently emerges as the hippest and the most accessible. Set in the commercial core of Oslo, 1 block north of Karl Johans Gate, the Bristol is warm, rich with tradition, and comfortable. It also isn't as formal as either the Grand or the Continental, attracting the media, arts, and showbiz communities, with a sense of playfulness and fun that's unmatched by either of its rivals.

Bedrooms are comfortable and dignified, but not as plush or as intensely "decorated" as the rooms in either of its grander competitors. Lavish public areas still evoke the Moorish-inspired Art Deco heyday in which they were built. There's enormous life and energy in this hotel—thanks to active restaurants, such as the Bristol Grill (p. 115), piano bars, and a sense of elegant yet unpretentious conviviality.

Kristian IV's Gate 7, N-0164 Oslo 1. ✆ **22-82-60-00.** Fax 22-82-60-01. www.bristol.no. 252 units. Mon–Fri NOK2,275 ($455/£228) double; Sat–Sun NOK1,350–NOK2,275 ($270–$455/£135–£228) double; year-round daily NOK4,000–NOK7,580 ($800–$1,516/£400–£758) suite. Rates include breakfast buffet. AE, DC, MC, V. Parking NOK280 ($56/£28). Tram: 10, 11, 17, or 18. **Amenities:** 2 restaurants; 2 bars; nightclub/dance bar; small-scale exercise room and fitness center; spa; room service; laundry service/dry cleaning; nonsmoking rooms; pianist in the lobby. *In room:* A/C, TV, minibar, hair dryer, trouser press.

Norlandia Karl Johan Hotell ★★ For the sake of this hotel's reputation, it is regrettable that it was built across the street from the finer Grand, to which it is often unfavorably compared. However, put that aside and you'll find a winning address, charm, and grace. As you wander about its stylish public rooms, taking in the stained glass and circular staircase, you'll think you've stumbled into Belle Epoque Paris. The five-story hotel itself is in a renovated building that dates from the late 18th century. The owners have done much to imbue the hotel with character, filling the rooms with Norwegian folk art and installing antiques in every room, both public and private. The medium-size bedrooms have a classic decor with excellent fabrics, double glazing on the windows to cut down on the noise outside, and tiny but marble-clad bathrooms. We prefer the rooms that open onto the front and contain French windows.

Karl Johans Gate 33, N-0162 Oslo. ✆ **23-16-17-00.** Fax 22-42-05-19. www.norlandia.no. 111 units. Mon–Fri NOK1,750 ($350/£175) double; Sat–Sun NOK1,450 ($290/£145) double; year-round daily from NOK2,400 ($480/£240) suite. Rates include breakfast. AE, DC, MC, V. Parking NOK160 ($32/£16) in nearby public garage. T-banen: Nationaltheatret or Stortinget. **Amenities:** Laundry service/dry cleaning; nonsmoking rooms; rooms for those w/limited mobility. *In room:* TV, Wi-Fi, minibar, hair dryer, iron, trouser press.

Radisson SAS Plaza Hotel ★ If for no other reason, we'd check in here for the panoramic views of the city and the Oslofjord. With an exterior sheathed in blue-tinted glass, and a needle-nosed summit that soars high above everything else in Oslo, this is the tallest building in Norway, and the largest hotel in northern Europe. The hotel struggles to permeate its vast, impersonal interior with a sense of intimacy and individuality. Guests do a lot of high-velocity elevator riding, and stay in hermetically sealed heated or air-conditioned rooms high above the city's commercial core, almost immediately next to the city's bus and railway stations. The high-altitude views are sublime, and the comfortable, well-decorated rooms have flair and original works of art. The bar on the 34th floor (Mon–Sat 4pm–1am) has a panoramic view.

Sonja Henies Plass 3, N-0134 Oslo. ✆ **22-05-80-00.** Fax 22-05-80-10. www.radissonsas.com. 673 units. NOK1,095–NOK2,095 ($219–$419/£110–£210) double; from NOK3,500 ($700/£350) suite. Rates include breakfast. AE, DC, MC, V. Parking NOK250 ($50/£25). T-banen: Jernbanetorget. **Amenities:** 2 restaurants; bar; indoor pool; sauna; room service. *In room:* A/C, TV, Wi-Fi (in some), minibar, safe.

Radisson SAS Scandinavia Hotel ★ As the sun sets over Oslo, we like to gather with friends at Summit 21, a bar on the 21st floor, for one of the grandest vistas of Oslo. This black, angular hotel doesn't quite escape the impersonal curse of its 1975 construction, but it tries nobly and succeeds rather well on its interior. Thanks to aggressive, seasonal price adjustments and an appealing setting, this "grandfather" of Oslo's modern hotels boasts an average occupancy rate of 73%, as opposed to the Norwegian national average of only 54%. With 22 floors, this is Oslo's third-biggest hotel (after the Radisson SAS Plaza Hotel and the Clarion Hotel Royal Christiana), the second-tallest building, and the first hotel that most Oslovians think of when they hear the name "SAS Hotel." Bedrooms are relatively large, very comfortable, and come in about a dozen different styles, including Scandinavian, Japanese, ersatz "rococo," Art Deco, and a nautical style inspired by the maritime traditions of Norway.

Holbergsgate 30, N-0166 Oslo. ✆ **23-29-30-00.** Fax 23-29-30-01. www.radissonsas.com. 488 units. NOK1,295–NOK2,095 ($259–$419/£130–£210) double; from NOK3,500 ($700/£350) suite. Rates include breakfast. AE, DC, MC, V. Parking NOK180 ($36/£18). T-banen: Nationaltheatret. **Amenities:** 3 restaurants; bar; indoor heated pool; fitness room; sauna; kids' playroom; underground shopping arcade; room service; laundry service/dry cleaning; nonsmoking rooms; rooms for those w/limited mobility. *In room:* A/C, TV, Wi-Fi, minibar, coffeemaker, safe.

Rica Victoria Hotel ★ If your heart is set on one of the Radissons (see above), this hotel may come as a bit of a letdown. But its interior offers cozy comfort in spite of its foreboding facade. This hotel, built in 1991, enjoys an enviable position midway between the Aker Brygge restaurant and office complex and the Norwegian Parliament.

Some of the best rooms are on the ninth (uppermost) floor, where the sloping walls of the Mansard-style roof add a general coziness. Regardless of their location within the hotel, rooms have wood flooring and tile-covered bathrooms. Rooms are conservative, dignified, and comfortable, with an appealingly nonstandardized format that includes a number of windows, rounded corners, reproduction antiques, and circa-1900s brass lamps.

Rosenkrantzgate 13, N-0121 Oslo. ✆ **24-14-70-00.** Fax 24-14-70-01. www.rica.no. 199 units. NOK1,392–NOK1,760 ($278–$352/£139–£176) double; from NOK1,910 ($382/£191) suite. Rates include breakfast. AE, DC, MC, V. Parking NOK195 ($39/£20) per night. Tram: 10, 12, 15, or 19. **Amenities:** Restaurant; bar; babysitting; laundry service/dry cleaning. *In room:* TV, Wi-Fi, minibar.

Thon Hotel Europa Of the Thon hotels in Oslo, we think the Cecil is a better choice, but this well-run hotel has a lot going for it as well. Few other hotels enjoy a position as quiet yet as convenient to Karl Johans Gate as this redbrick member of the chain. The building faces a large patch of greenery and the front entrances of two of Oslo's museums, the Tekniska Musuet (Technical Museum) and the Nasjionell Galleriet (National Gallery). The hotel was originally built as a complex of private apartments before being transformed in the 1970s into this efficient and well-managed hotel. Bedrooms are small but comfortable, with burl-grained walnut veneers and writing desks.

St. Olavs Gate 31, N-0166 Oslo. ✆ **23-25-63-00.** Fax 23-25-63-63. www.thonhotels.com. 167 units. NOK1,595–NOK1,795 ($319–$359/£160–£180) double; year-round daily from NOK1,995 ($399/£200) suite. AE, DC, MC, V. No on-site parking. T-banen: Stortinget. **Amenities:** Coffee shop; bar; nonsmoking rooms. *In room:* A/C, TV, Wi-Fi, minibar, hair dryer, safe.

Thon Hotel Gyldenløve ★ "The Golden Lion" (its English name) was once a dowdy *hospits* (an inexpensive hotel, but better than a youth hostel). Lying only a 10-minute walk from the Royal Palace, it stands on a tree-lined street in the West End, a highly desirable neighborhood. In its latest reincarnation as part of the ever-growing Thon chain, it has become one of the city's most desirable addresses. Midsize bedrooms are in a modernistic Nordic design, combining a light, airy feeling with Scandinavian pastels.

Bogstadveien 20, N-0355 Oslo. ✆ **23-33-23-00.** Fax 23-33-23-03. www.thonhotels.com. 164 units. NOK1,150–NOK2,345 ($230–$469/£115–£235) double. Rates include breakfast. AE, DC, MC, V. Parking NOK150 ($30/£15). Tram: 11, 13, or 19. **Amenities:** Breakfast room; room service; laundry service; nonsmoking rooms. *In room:* TV, Wi-Fi, minibar.

Moderate

Best Western Hotell Bondeheimen (Value) If you're a devoted member of the Salvation Army, or if you teach Sunday school back home, this is one of the safest and most reliable choices in town. Guests here are more interested in value (not to mention values) than in frills. In the city center, a short block from the Students' Grove at Karl Johans Gate, the Bondeheimen was built in 1913. A cooperative of farmers and students established this hotel, now a Best Western, to provide affordable, teetotalist-friendly accommodations when they visited Oslo from the countryside. Although small, the compact rooms are comfortably furnished, often with Norwegian pine pieces. Bedrooms are larger than standard, with tasteful furniture. All rooms are nonsmoking.

Rosenkrantzgate 8 (entrance on Kristian IV's Gate), N-0159 Oslo 1. ✆ **800/633-6548** in the U.S., or 23-21-41-00. Fax 23-21-41-01. www.bestwestern.com. 127 units. Mon–Thurs NOK1,390 ($278/£139) double; Fri–Sun NOK1,090 ($218/£109) double. Rates include buffet breakfast. AE, DC, MC, V. Parking NOK140 ($28/£14). Tram: 7 or 11. **Amenities:** Restaurant; boutique; laundry service/dry cleaning; rooms for those w/limited mobility. *In room:* TV, minibar, coffeemaker, hair dryer, iron.

Kids Family-Friendly Hotels

First Hotel Grims Grenka (p. 100) The chain-run hotel offers rooms with small kitchenettes for preparing quick meals for the family as well as suites with a fairytale theme for your little prince or princess.

First Hotel Millennium (p. 104) This other "First" in town, the Millenium offers some of the best family rooms in Oslo, with spacious living areas and even a separate bedroom should you want some privacy from your brood.

Grand Hotel (p. 100) The Grand's indoor heated pool provides an outlet for your child's energy. The "solve-everything" concierge can recommend babysitting services as well as diversions for young people.

Hotel Bristol (p. 104) One of the most elegant and comfortable hotels in Oslo welcomes children and lets those under 15 stay free in their parent's room. The chef will even put a "junior steak" on the grill.

Clarion Collection Hotel Savoy ★ This hotel has a tough act to follow now that it's joined that small, select group, Clarion Collection, which operates the superior Hotel Bastion (p. 108). First, try for the Bastion; if no rooms are available there, the Savoy is a viable alternative, though it draws mixed reviews. One former guest found his room "the smallest I have ever stayed in." Another couple loved their room, finding the Savoy "great value, great location," the latter a reference to it standing opposite the National Gallery. Our conclusion is that you'll like the Savoy—or not—depending on your room assignment, so be specific when booking. Some of the bedrooms are spacious and handsomely, even stylishly furnished. The building itself is classic, a traditional-looking structure that was built in the early 20th century, but has been frequently renovated since. On-site is restauranteik (p. 111), serving well-prepared Norwegian and international dishes in a smoke-free atmosphere. The soft upholstered chairs of the hotel's Savoy Bar also attract many nonguests for evening cocktails. The hotel is entirely nonsmoking.

Universitesgata 11, N-0164 Oslo. ✆ **23-35-42-00.** Fax 23-35-42-01. www.choicehotels.no. 80 units. 1,150NOK ($230/£115) double; from NOK1,495 ($299/£150) suite. Rates include buffet breakfast. AE, DC, MC, V. Parking NOK150 ($30/£15). Tram: 11, 13, 18, or 19. **Amenities:** Restaurant; bar; room service; laundry service; rooms for those w/limited mobility. *In room:* TV, Wi-Fi, fridge, hair dryer, iron, safe.

Clarion Hotel Royal Christiania ★ Opposite the main train station, this is one of the leading business and leisure hotels in Oslo, though not where we like to check in. In fairness, it is fine in every way—very convenient—and it certainly has its devotees. But because it's such a mammoth affair, it doesn't have the personalized service of the Grand or the Continental. This is the second-largest hotel in Norway, a soaring 14-story tower built to house athletes and administrators during the 1952 Winter Olympics. Extensively upgraded in the 1990s, with the addition of two nine-story wings, the luxury hotel is now comparable to the nearby Radisson SAS Plaza Hotel (p. 105), but without so much drama. The medium-size guest rooms are as quiet, conservatively decorated, and blandly tasteful as you'd expect from an international chain.

Biskop Gunnerus' Gate 3, N-0106 Oslo. ✆ **23-10-80-00.** Fax 23-10-80-80. www.choicehotels.no. 503 units. Sun–Thurs NOK930–NOK1,440 ($186–$288/£93–£144) double, from NOK2,500 ($500/£250) suite;

Fri–Sat year-round and daily June 15–Aug 1 NOK1,195 ($239/£120) double, NOK1,780 ($356/£178) suite. Rates include buffet breakfast. AE, DC, MC, V. Parking NOK225 ($45/£23). Bus: 30, 31, or 41. **Amenities:** 4 restaurants; bar; indoor heated pool; fitness center; sauna; business center; room service; massage; laundry service/dry cleaning; nonsmoking rooms; rooms for those w/limited mobility. *In room:* TV, Wi-Fi, minibar, coffeemaker, hair dryer.

Hotel Bastion ★★ Finds In 2006, this boutique hotel became a member of the Clarion Collection, a chain of small individual hotels with a personal touch. Under its reincarnation, it is the closest rival to the Bristol (above), which still retains the cutting edge. The owner, Morten Mørch, hand-selected all the hotel's furniture, fabrics, and art. Of course, he got a little assist from Anemone W. Våge, one of the best-known Norwegian designers; she even decorated the apartments of the royal family nearby. In the Old Town of Oslo, within walking distance of Karl Johans Gate, this is a warm, inviting, residential-style property, a true bastion of comfort. The midsize-to-spacious bedrooms are tastefully stylish, yet are also intimate and unpretentious. If you want to go more upmarket, you can ask for one of the junior suites or deluxe suites, among the best in the capital. The hotel is entirely nonsmoking.

Skippergaten 7, N-0152 Oslo. ✆ **22-47-77-00.** Fax 22-33-11-80. www.hotelbastion.no. 99 units. Mon–Thurs NOK1,495 ($299/£150) double, NOK3,995 ($799/£400) suite; Fri–Sun NOK995 ($199/£100) double, NOK2,995 ($599/£300) suite. Rates include buffet breakfast. AE, DC, MC, V. Parking NOK195 ($39/£20). T-banen: Jernbanetorget. **Amenities:** Breakfast lounge; lobby bar; fitness center; Jacuzzi; sauna; room service; laundry service. *In room:* A/C, TV, Wi-Fi, minibar, beverage maker, iron, trouser press.

Scandic KNA Oslo City Hotel This hotel looks deceptively new, thanks to a futuristic-looking mirrored facade that was added in the 1970s to an older core that was originally built in the 1940s by the Norwegian Auto Club. Inside, you'll find a cozy lobby-level bar and restaurant serving Norwegian food, a deeply entrenched kind of informality, and a reception staff that's a bit inexperienced. Bedrooms are simple, well maintained, and a bit spartan-looking. If you're a self-motivated kind of traveler with a clear idea of what you want to see and where you want to go in Oslo, without much need for attention or advice from the staff, this might be an appropriate choice.

Parkveien 68, N-0254 Oslo. ✆ **23-15-57-00.** Fax 23-15-57-11. www.scandic-hotels.com/KNA. 189 units. Sun–Thurs NOK1,790–NOK1,990 ($358–$398/£179–£199) double; Fri–Sat NOK1,250–NOK1,450 ($250–$290/£125–£145) double. Rates include buffet breakfast. AE, DC, MC, V. No on-site parking. Tram: 12 or 15. **Amenities:** Restaurant; bar; health club; sauna; room service; rooms for those w/limited mobility; nonsmoking rooms. *In room:* TV, Wi-Fi, minibar, trouser press.

Inexpensive

Cochs Pensjonat Value One of Norway's best-selling novelists, Lars Saabye Christensen, whose works are translated into English, once claimed in an interview: "I often went past Cochs Pensjonat in my childhood and I always slackened my pace. But I never went in. You couldn't see in. I imagined all sorts of things happening behind the entrance door." He was so impressed that he wrote a novel, *The Half Brother,* in which one of his main characters stayed in Room 502 at Cochs for 4,982 days. There's nothing secretive going on inside. Rather, Cochs is the most famous and most enduring boardinghouse in Oslo, having been launched in 1927 by the Coch sisters. The building has an ornate facade curving around a bend in a boulevard that banks the northern edge of the Royal Palace. This is a comfortable but simple lodging whose newer rooms are high-ceilinged, spartan but pleasant, and outfitted with birch-wood furniture. We infinitely prefer looking out onto Slottsparken from the "Royal Rooms," which were created in 1996 when a large apartment was incorporated into the guesthouse. Expect very few, if any, amenities and services at this hotel—rooms are without telephones. Breakfast is served at KafeCaffé in Parkveien 21.

Parkveien 25, N-0350 Oslo. ✆ **23-33-24-00.** Fax 23-33-24-10. www.cochspensjonat.no. 88 units. Rooms w/private bathroom and kitchenette NOK720 ($144/£72) double, NOK900 ($180/£90) triple, NOK1,100 ($220/£110) quad; rooms w/shared bathroom and no kitchenette NOK620 ($124/£62) double, NOK780 ($156/£78) triple, NOK980 ($196/£98) quad. MC, V. No on-site parking. Tram: 11 or 12. *In room:* TV, kitchenette (in some), no phone.

WEST END

Moderate

Clarion Collection Hotel Gabelshus ★ Finds This member of the Clarion Collection chain may not be as first-class as its previously recommended brethren (see the Savoy, p. 107, or the Bastion, p. 108), but in some ways we prefer it because of its location. It lies a brisk 15-minute walk from the city center in a tranquil location on a tree-lined street. Since its opening as a guesthouse back in 1912, it has greatly expanded through its takeover of an adjoining building. Discreetly conservative, it looks like an English manor house, laced with climbing ivy. The public rooms are filled with antiques, art, burnished copper, and working fireplaces. Guest rooms are decorated with tasteful colors and textiles, and some have terraces. You'll have a choice of Scandinavian modern furniture or traditional styling. The accommodations are well maintained and equipped with double-glazed windows.

Gabels Gate 16, N-0272 Oslo 2. ✆ **23-27-65-00.** Fax 23-27-65-60. www.choicehotels.no. 114 units. Mon–Thurs NOK1,500 ($300/£150) double; Fri–Sun NOK990 ($198/£99) double; NOK2,000 ($400/£200) suite. Rates include buffet breakfast. AE, DC, MC, V. Free parking. Tram: 10. **Amenities:** Breakfast room; lounge; exercise room; sauna; steam room; laundry service/dry cleaning; rooms for those w/limited mobility; nonsmoking rooms. *In room:* TV, Wi-Fi, minibar, hair dryer.

Rica Hotel Bygdøy Allé ★ Finds This accommodation is better equipped than the Gabelshus (see above), but you'll pay more for the privilege of lodging here. The intimate hotel, the smallest in the Rica chain, has the air of an artsy boutique hotel. Its designers shoehorned it into the framework of a late-19th-century Flemish-revival brick structure in Oslo's well-heeled West End. Each of the bedrooms is different in its layout, corresponding to the already-existing towers and gables of the older structure. Room nos. 206, 214, 406, and 414 are among the most sought-after because of their Victorian-era curved walls and bay windows. Other than that, the decor is conservative and predictably upscale—and a bit bland, usually in tones of pale blue.

Bygdøy Allé 53, N-0265 Oslo. ✆ **23-08-58-00.** Fax 23-08-58-08. www.rica.no. 57 units. Sun–Thurs NOK1,760–NOK2,010 ($352–$402/£176–£201) double; Fri–Sat NOK1,070–NOK1,320 ($214–$264/£107–£132) double. Rates include buffet breakfast. AE, DC, MC, V. No on-site parking. Tram: 10. Bus: 30, 31, 32, or 33. **Amenities:** Restaurant; bar; room service; laundry service/dry cleaning; nonsmoking rooms. *In room:* TV, minibar, hair dryer, trouser press.

HOLMENKOLLEN

Expensive

Holmenkollen Park Hotel Rica ★ If you stay here, you'll be both in the city of Oslo and in the country. Just how far out in the country are you? Let's put it this way: At sundown, you are likely to see elks in the distance. On a panoramic hillside crowning Oslo, this hotel sits on forested land that's devoted to recreation, cross-country skiing, and hiking. Its location is a short walk from the Holmenkollen ski jump, at the terminus of tram line no. 1. The hotel was built in 1894, rebuilt after a fire in 1904, reconstructed again in 1948 after a 4-year occupation by the Nazis during World War II, and then massively enlarged with four new wings in 1982, when it was taken over by the Rica hotel chain. Today the oldest part of the hotel (a richly detailed log and timbered building designed in the Viking revival "dragon" style) is used for check-ins and for convention facilities; the remainder contains modern, comfortable rooms and all the facilities you'd expect in a resort hotel. Ranging from comfortable and spacious standards to classically decorated deluxe units, bedrooms are cozy, with lots of exposed wood, and hints of chalet styling.

Kongeveien 26, N-0390 Oslo. ✆ **22-92-20-00.** Fax 22-14-61-92. www.rica.no. 221 units. Mon–Thurs NOK1,695–NOK1,995 ($339–$399/£170–£200) double; Fri–Sun NOK1,435–NOK1,735 ($287–$347/£144–£174) double; from NOK3,200 ($640/£320) suite. Rates include breakfast. AE, DC, MC, V. Parking NOK150 ($30/£15). Tram: 1. **Amenities:** 2 restaurants; cafe; bar; indoor heated pool; health club; sauna; Jacuzzi; babysitting; laundry service/dry cleaning; marked jogging and cross-country ski trails in the vicinity; nonsmoking rooms; rooms for those w/limited mobility. *In room:* A/C, TV, Wi-Fi, minibar, hair dryer, safe, trouser press.

AT THE AIRPORT

Very Expensive

Radisson SAS Airport Hotel ★ To go between the arrivals terminal and the hotel, designed as an integral part of the Gardemoen airport, wheel your luggage along a series of sloping cement ramps and across a busy access road. The architecture is futuristic and well conceived, and rapid checkout (via your TV screen) eliminates a lot of the fuss. Bedrooms have carved headboards in a style that's vaguely Thai or Indonesian, writing tables, plus sleek white-tiled bathrooms. Like any airport hotel, this one is somewhat impersonal.

Hotellvegen, Box 163, N-2061 Gardemoen. ✆ **63-93-30-00.** Fax 63-93-30-30. www.radissonsas.com. 503 units. NOK1,995–NOK2,295 ($399–$459/£200–£230) double; NOK2,895 ($579/£290) junior suite; from NOK4,100 ($820/£410) suite. Rates include buffet breakfast. AE, DC, MC, V. Free parking. **Amenities:** 2 restaurants; bar; health club; sauna; room service; massage; laundry service/dry cleaning; meeting rooms; nonsmoking rooms; rooms for those w/limited mobility. *In room:* A/C, TV, Wi-Fi, minibar, hair dryer, trouser press, safe.

Inexpensive

Thon Hotel Gardermoen Value The Thon chain strikes again with the first budget hotel (opened in 2006) at Gardermoen airport. In spite of its smart, stylish decor, it is an affordable choice, with a shuttle running between the hotel and the airport, a distance of 5 minutes away by bus. Admittedly, it's so large it's a bit of a bed factory. But its rooms are comfortably furnished, albeit a bit small. Rated three stars by the government, its bedrooms are spread out over 13 two-story buildings. The standard singles feature just one bed, but most rooms are doubles with two single beds.

Balder Allé 22, N-2065 Gadermoen. ✆ **64-00-45-00.** Fax 64-00-45-01. www.thonhotels.com. 260 units. NOK895 ($179/£90) double. AE, DC, MC, V. Free parking. **Amenities:** Restaurant; bar; business services; room service; laundry service; nonsmoking rooms; rooms for those w/limited mobility. *In room:* TV, Wi-Fi.

4 WHERE TO DINE

You can now dine internationally without leaving the city of Oslo. The influx of foreigners in recent years has led to the growth of Mexican-, Turkish-, Moroccan-, Chinese-, Greek-, and American-style restaurants. Among European cuisines, French and Italian are the most popular. The biggest concentration of restaurants is at Aker Brygge. This former shipbuilding yard on the harborfront is now the smartest dining and shopping complex in Norway.

Not all restaurants in Oslo are newcomers. Some have long been associated with artists and writers—the Grand Café, for example, was the stamping ground of Henrik Ibsen and Edvard Munch.

At most restaurants, a 15% service charge and 20% value-added tax are included in the bill. It's customary to leave some additional small change if the service has been satisfactory. Wine and beer can be lethal to your final bill, so be careful.

CENTRAL OSLO

Very Expensive

Oro ★★★ CONTINENTAL/MEDITERRANEAN Is this the best restaurant in Oslo, as some critics maintain? We won't go that far (see our review of Bagatelle, p. 120), but Oro is among the top five choices. Gallons of ink have been used in the Norwegian press to describe this hyperstylish restaurant, winner of a Michelin star. Norwegian-born chef Mads Larsson directs the kitchen of a three-faceted establishment that includes a European gourmet restaurant, a separate section called Smak av Oro, and a boutique-style deli (Mon–Fri 11:30am–3pm) for enthusiasts who want to haul some of its raw ingredients back home. The restaurant is a curvaceous, slick-looking testimonial to stainless steel and warm-toned hardwoods. We recommend the fixed-price menus, although be warned that each of them will be prepared only for every member of the table at the same time. One option includes a three-course vegetarian menu at NOK350 ($70/£35). Representative dishes, each one delectable, include lobster ravioli, glazed scallops with Serrano ham, a platter that combines three different versions of foie gras (grilled, *en terrine,* and *en brioche*), and spit-roasted pigeon stuffed with foie gras.

Tordenskiolds 6A (entrance on Kjeld Stubs Gate). ✆ **23-01-02-40.** Reservations required. Fixed-price menus: NOK350 ($70/£35) for 3 courses; NOK470 ($94/£47) for 5 courses; NOK590 ($118/£59) for 7 courses. AE, DC, MC, V. Mon–Sat 6–10pm. T-banen: Stortinget.

restauranteik ★ INTERNATIONAL Located within the Clarion Collection Hotel Savoy (p. 107), one floor above street level, immediately adjacent to Oslo's National Gallery, this is a hip, trendy, expensive, and highly visible restaurant that has attracted such big names as the president of Norway since its opening in 2003. A color scheme of very pale pink and gray offsets a starkly minimalist decor that includes floors and an entire wall that's paneled in walnut. The five on-staff chefs are given free rein to express their creativity in the form of food that's inspired by Thai, Chinese, Japanese, American, Continental, or all-Norwegian culinary motifs. Some dishes that win over palates include pumpkin soup with Serrano ham and tempura-fried onions; delicious spring rolls stuffed with sweet chili, pine nuts, and new cabbage; and entrecote of pork with red-wine bouillon sauce, oyster mushrooms, potato purée, and Norwegian-style glazed apples.

Universitesgata 11. ✆ **22-36-07-10.** Reservations recommended. Set-price menus: NOK370 ($74/£37) for 3 courses; NOK480 ($96/£48) for 4 courses. AE, DC, MC, V. Tues–Sat 6–11pm (last seating). T-banen: Tullenløkka. Closed 1 week at Easter, 1 week at Christmas, and 4 weeks in midsummer.

Restaurant Julius Fritzner ★★ NORWEGIAN/CONTINENTAL Its namesake, Julius Fritzner, opened the Grand Hotel in 1874, so it's only fitting that the present-day owners have named this deluxe restaurant in his honor. Dining at the Grand has long been a marker of tradition. When Roald Amundsen returned to Oslo after his successful expedition to the South Pole in 1912, a banquet here honored him. One of the best and most impressive restaurants in Oslo, it opened in 1995 to rave reviews, and the accolades

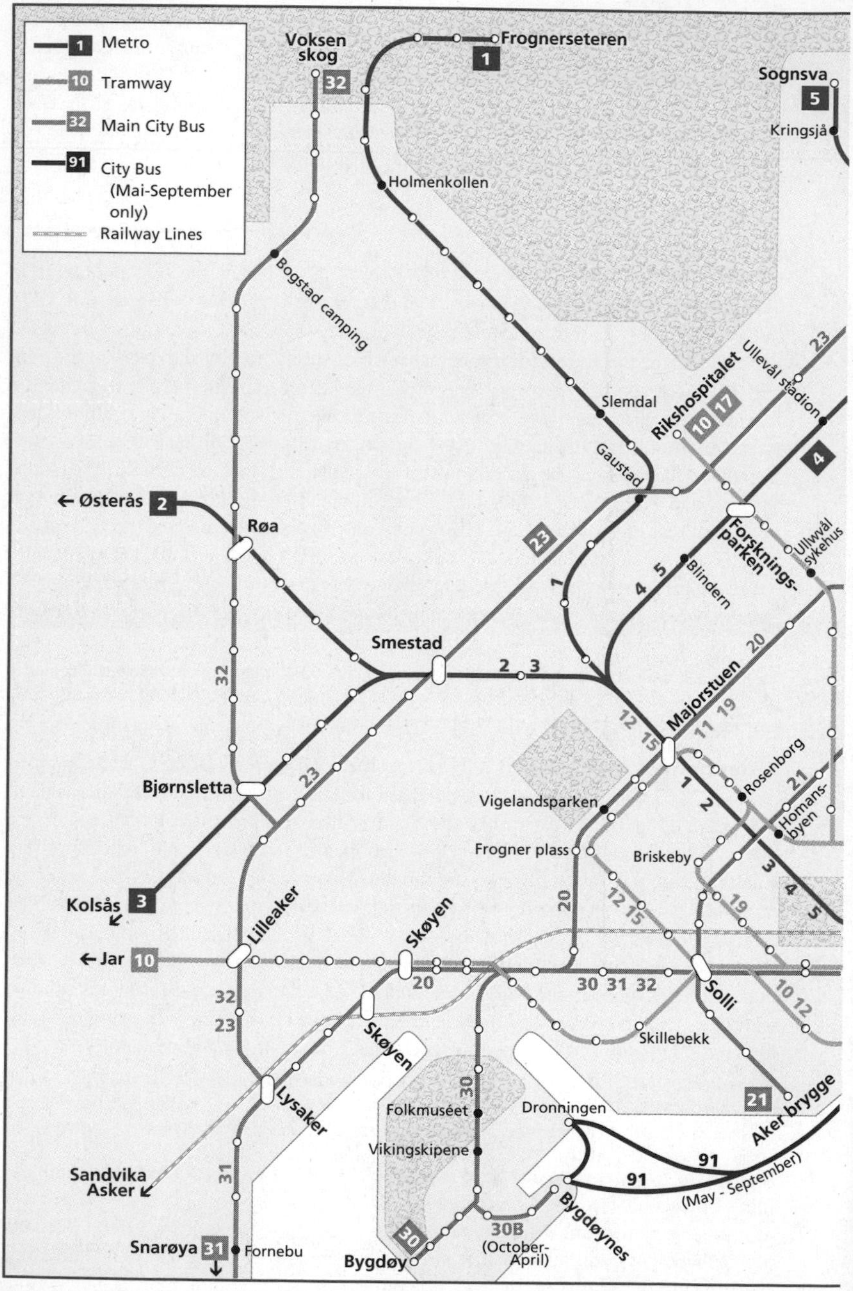
1 Metro
10 Tramway
32 Main City Bus
91 City Bus
(Mai-September
only)
Railway Lines
Voksen
skog
Frognerseteren
Sognsva
Kringsjå
Holmenkollen
Bogstad camping
Slemdal
Gaustad
Rikshospitalet
Ullevål stadion
Østerås
Røa
Forsknings-
parken
Ullwvål
sykehus
Blindern
Smestad
Majorstuen
Rosenborg
Homans-
byen
Bjørnsletta
Vigelandsparken
Frogner plass
Briskeby
Kolsås
Lilleaker
Skøyen
Jar
Solli
Skillebekk
Lysaker
Folkmuséet
Dronningen
Aker brygge
Vikingskipene
Sandvika
Asker
Bygdøynes
(May - September)
30B
(October-
April)
Snarøya
Fornebu
Bygdøy

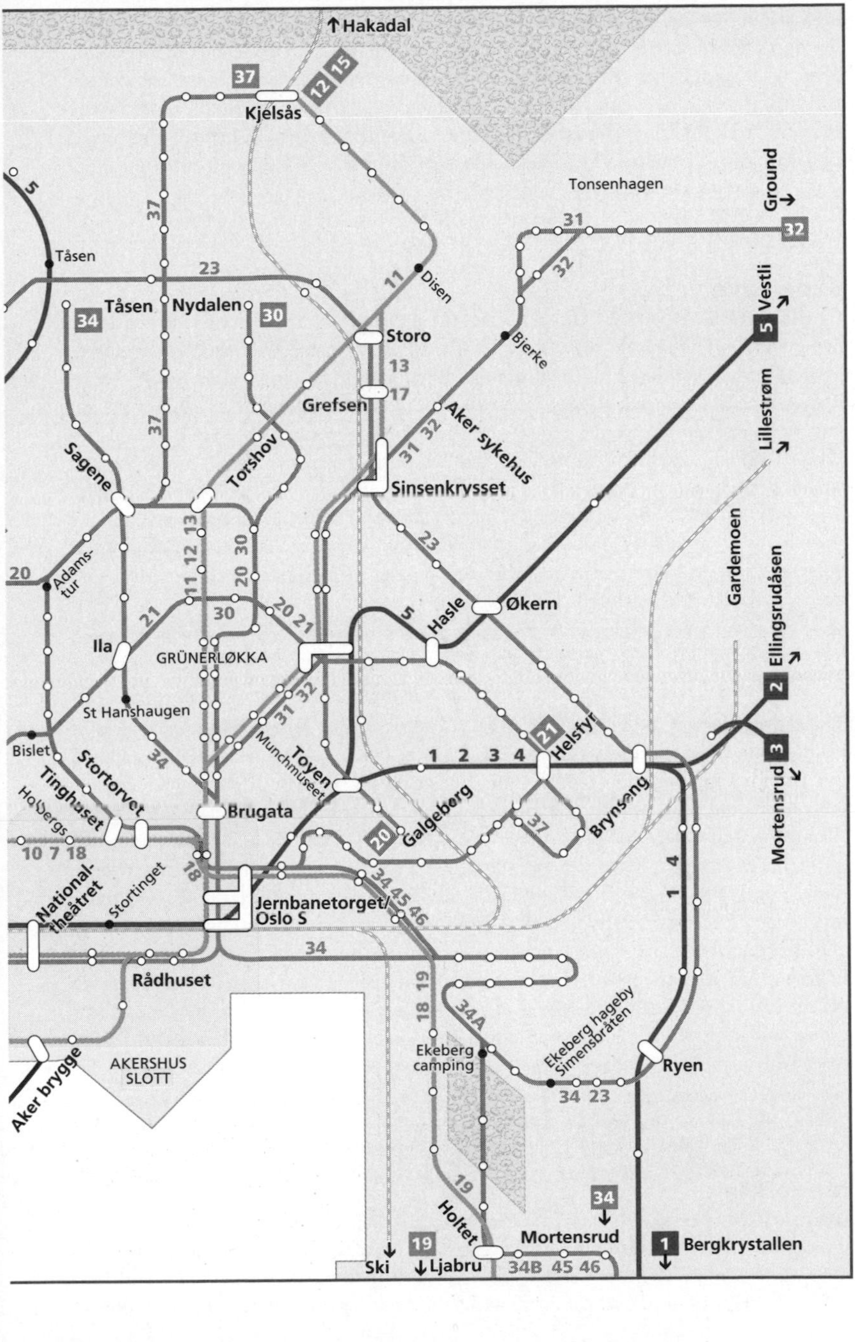

Hakadal
37
12 15
Kjelsås
Tonsenhagen
Ground
31
32
Tåsen
23
Disen
11
Vestli
5
Tåsen
Nydalen
34
30
Storo
Bjerke
13
Grefsen
17
Aker sykehus
31 32
Lillestrøm
Sagene
Torshov
Sinsenkrysset
37
23
Gardemoen
20
Adams-tur
13 12 11
30 20
21
30
20 21
Hasle
Økern
Ellingsrudåsen
2
Ila
GRÜNERLØKKA
St Hanshaugen
31 32
Munchmuseet
Bislet
Stortorvet
34
Tøyen
1 2 3 4
21
Helsfyr
Mortensrud
3
Tinghuset
Holbergs
Brugata
Galgeberg
20
37
Brynseng
10 7 18
Nationaltheåtret
18
Stortinget
Jernbanetorget/ Oslo S
34 45 46
1 4
34
Rådhuset
18 19
34A
Ekeberg hageby Simensbråten
Ekeberg camping
Ryen
AKERSHUS SLOTT
Aker brygge
34 23
19
Holtet
34
Mortensrud
19
Ski
Ljabru
34B 45 46
1
Bergkrystallen

just keep coming. One floor above street level in Norway's most prestigious hotel, the venue is conservative, with a battalion of impeccably trained waiters who maintain their humor and personal touch despite the sophisticated setting. The dishes, all made with the finest Scandinavian ingredients, change with the season and the chef's inspiration. Some of the best dishes are pan-fried turbot, lobster and caviar sauce (how decadent can you get?), crispy fried cod with sautéed vegetables, and a tender roast saddle of lamb with aromatic fresh rosemary. Desserts, which are occasionally theatrical, include a terrine of chocolate with a compote of peaches and sorbet flavored with basil and cinnamon.

In the Grand Hotel, Karl Johans Gate 31. ✆ **23-21-20-00.** Reservations recommended. Main courses NOK295–NOK395 ($59–$79/£30–£40). AE, DC, MC, V. Mon–Sat 5–10:30pm. Closed June 21–Aug 11. T-banen: Stortinget.

Expensive

Grand Café ★★ NORWEGIAN Over the decades, this 1874 cafe has served as the living and dining room for the elite of Kristiania (an old name for Oslo). The country's greatest artists have dined here with foreign diplomats, kings, and explorers. Of course, it's not as chic as it once was (how could it be?), but we're still loyal to it and view a night here as part of our Norwegian experience. A large mural on one wall depicts Ibsen and Edvard Munch, along with other, less famous, former patrons. The atmosphere and tradition here are sometimes more compelling than the cuisine, but if you like solid, honest flavors, this is the place to eat. The menu relies on Norwegian country traditions (how many places still serve elk stew?). Representative dishes include chicken with green asparagus, sun-dried tomatoes, and a basil cream pasta, or herb-marinated monkfish with beans, rice pilaf, and a demi-glace of figs.

In the Grand Hotel, Karl Johans Gate 31. ✆ **23-21-20-00.** Reservations recommended. Main courses NOK165–NOK320 ($33–$64/£17–£32). AE, DC, MC, V. Mon–Fri 11am–11pm; Sat-Sun noon–11pm. T-banen: Stortinget.

Theatercafeen ★ INTERNATIONAL The *New York Times,* with a great deal of justification, listed this cafe as among the 10 most famous on the planet. If you like to eat and drink in opulence, head here for your grand fix. The last of the grand Viennese cafes in the north of Europe, this long-standing favorite was founded a century ago to rival the Grand Café. Each has its devotees, although we like this one better because of its Viennese *schmaltz.* Serenaded by piano and a duet of violins, the style might have pleased the Habsburg emperor Franz-Josef had he ever ventured this far north. It attracts present-day *boulevardiers* and businesspeople. With soft lighting, antique bronzes, cut-glass lighting fixtures, and Art Nouveau mirrors, it's the type of place that encourages lingering. Menu items are well prepared and traditional, and are adjusted accordingly to get the best flavors out of each season. That might mean white wine–steamed mussels or grilled monkfish served with bacon and summer cabbage. Also tantalizing is the fried trout with a truffle hollandaise or marinated salmon with dill-stewed potatoes.

In the Hotel Continental, Stortingsgaten 24. ✆ **22-82-40-50.** Reservations recommended. Main courses NOK242–NOK320 ($48–$64/£24–£32); open-faced sandwiches NOK98–NOK112 ($20–$22/£10–£11) at lunch. AE, DC, MC, V. Mon–Sat 11am–11pm; Sun 3–10pm. T-banen: Stortinget.

Moderate

Brasserie France ★ FRENCH One of our favorite restaurants in town is this most typical of all French bistros with its Art Nouveau decor, French posters, and waiters in long white aprons. The decor is that of a typical French brasserie, the kind you'd find alongside the road in Alsace, complete with tables spilling out onto the sidewalk during the summer months. The brasserie is known for serving the freshest oysters in town. Treat yourself to such dishes as confit of duck leg with cherry tomatoes and green asparagus, or grilled rib-eye with French green beans and a Béarnaise sauce. The best of local ingredients and a strong technique in the kitchen combine to turn out such dishes as pan-fried whole lemon sole with mushrooms and capers, or basil-roasted salmon with a tomato couscous and mussel-laden sauce.

Øvre Slottsgate 16. ✆ **23-10-01-60.** Reservations required. Main courses NOK195–NOK250 ($39–$50/£20–£25). AE, DC, MC, V. Mon–Fri 4:30–11pm; Sat noon–11pm. Bus: 27, 29, 30, 41, or 61.

Bristol Grill ★★ CONTINENTAL This is the premier dining room of the Hotel Bristol (p. 104), one of Oslo's most prestigious hotels. You'll find old-world courtliness, formal service without a lot of flash or frenzy, and elegant decor that evokes a baronial hunting lodge from around 1924, the year the restaurant was founded. A few years later, it evolved into the dining venue you'll see today, with a gentleman's-club allure that eventually welcomed big-name entertainers. You'll pass through a cozy, woodsy-looking piano bar to reach the restaurant. With a culinary focus that has radically improved over the years, the menu continues to be one of the finest in the Norwegian capital as it beautifully adjusts to take advantage of the best ingredients in all four seasons, including winter. There's a spectacular version of bouillabaisse, prepared with Nordic (not Mediterranean) fish and seasoned with saffron, which can be ordered as either a starter or a main course. One of the chef's most successful specialties is medallions of venison sautéed with vanilla and bacon, served on a bed of mushrooms with a terrine of potatoes.

In the Hotel Bristol, Kristian IV's Gate 7. ✆ **22-82-60-00.** Reservations recommended, especially at night. Main courses NOK220–NOK295 ($44–$59/£22–£30). AE, DC, MC, V. Daily 4–11pm. Tram: 10, 11, 17, or 18.

La Sangria ★ Finds SPANISH Established in 1992 in a location across the street from the Radisson SAS Scandinavia Hotel (p. 105), within a dining room sheathed with roughly textured stucco and hand-painted Iberian porcelain, this is the best Spanish restaurant in Oslo. It was launched by two hard-working brothers (Fernando and Juan-Carlos) from Madrid, whose appreciation for both bullfighting and soccer, especially the Real Madrid team, is obvious, to judge by the posters, memorabilia, and photos displayed. Here you can enjoy all our old tapas favorites—snails in garlic butter, fried chorizo sausage, sautéed chicken in garlic. Entrees include paella; prawns with garlic; Serrano ham with Manchego cheese and chorizo sausage; gazpacho; *bacalhau* (cod) alla Vizcaina; and, our favorite, boneless chicken stuffed with ham and cheese in a white-wine sauce.

Holbergsgate 19. ✆ **22-11-63-15.** Reservations recommended. Main courses NOK195–NOK225 ($39–$45/£20–£23). AE, DC, MC, V. Mon–Sat 3–11pm; Sun 3–10pm. Closed Dec 23–Jan 2. Tram: 11 or 19.

Inexpensive

Brasserie 45 ★ Kids CONTINENTAL After taking in an Ibsen play at the National Theater, we always like to head to this nearby restaurant for dinner. Airy and stylish, this second-story bistro overlooks the biggest fountain along downtown Oslo's showplace promenade. This is a family business, and the hard-working owners use their own hands, a dogged courage, and a certain discerning taste to treat you to the best of Mother France's kitchen. In recent years they have wandered the globe for inspiration, finding it in such places as Thailand. Of course, onion soup and chocolate mousse appear on the menu but the uniformed staff also bears steaming platters of ambitious, imaginative cuisine—king prawns in a spicy Thai sauce, anyone? The Norwegian kitchen isn't

Tips Dining Secrets of Oslo

One of Oslovians' favorite pastimes is visiting **Aker Brygge.** Formerly a dilapidated shipbuilding yard, the futuristic complex now combines more shopping, entertainment, and dining diversions in one area than anywhere else in Norway. Many visitors, some with children, come here to check out the restaurants and cafes, watch the people, and listen to music in the bars. Part of the fun is strolling through the complex and picking a restaurant. Norwegian food is served along with a representative selection of foreign food offerings, including American. In the summer visitors and locals fill the outdoor tables overlooking the harbor. There are also many nightlife options (see "Oslo After Dark," in chapter 6). To reach Aker Brygge, take bus no. 27 or walk down from the center west of the Rådhus.

A local favorite here is the **Albertine Café & Bar,** Stranden 3, Aker Brygge (✆ **22-83-00-60**), an informal place on the wharf's edge, offering a panoramic view over the harbor and Akershus fortress. This place consistently serves some of the freshest and tastiest oysters in Oslo. You can drop in for just a hamburger or a full Norwegian seafood dinner. It's also an easy place for meeting singles.

In front of the Rådhuset, you can join Oslovians for a special picnic treat. From 7 to 8am, **shrimp fishermen** pull their boats into the harbor after having caught and cooked a fresh batch of shrimp during their night at sea. You can order shrimp in a bag (it comes in two sizes). Seafood fanciers take their shrimp to the dock's edge, remove the shells, and feast. The fishermen usually stick around until they've sold the last batch, saving just enough for their families.

neglected, either. How about some smoked moose? The chefs turn out such tasty dishes as baked filet of cod with stir-fried vegetables or oven-baked leg of lamb with mushroom sauce. Marinated chicken breast comes with a creamy tomato-glazed sauce and roast potatoes. For dessert in summer, what really beats freshly picked blackberries with ice cream? Families like to come here because of the kids menu.

Stortingsgaten 20. ✆ **22-41-34-00.** Reservations recommended. Main courses NOK169–NOK235 ($34–$47/£17–£24); fixed-price menu NOK270–NOK330 ($54–$66/£27–£33). AE, DC, MC, V. Mon–Thurs 3–11:30pm; Fri–Sat 2pm–midnight; Sun 2–10pm. T-banen: Centrum.

Kristiania Bar & Café CONTINENTAL Set within the oldest part of Oslo's railway (the Østbanehallen, or East Wing), this late-19th-century cafe has one of the grandest decors of any cafe in Oslo, though it's hardly a rival of Theatercafeen. You'll dine and drink beneath a soaring ceiling dotted with cavorting cherubs and elaborate plaster reliefs, at a dark-stained Victorian-era bar that's an antique in its own right. Even this cafe's toilets are historically important and, consequently, ferociously protected against architectural changes. ***Note:*** A staff member will tell you the numeric combinations to punch onto a keypad to enter the bathrooms. Surprisingly for such a lavish setting, the food is relatively simple and much less expensive than at such equally historic cafes as the Grand Café. Menu items focus on burgers, salads, club sandwiches, pastas, milkshakes, and specials of the day. We urge you, if the weather is fine, to opt for a table on this cafe's very large outdoor terrace. It's sunnier and brighter than that of more expensive cafes on nearby narrower, darker streets, and it enjoys a close-up view over one of Oslo's most stunning and monumental fountains.

Østbanehallen, Jernbanetorget 1. ✆ **22-17-50-30.** Reservations not necessary. Main courses NOK95–NOK170 ($19–$34/£9.50–£17). AE, DC, MC, V. Mon–Thurs 11am–midnight; Fri 11am–3am; Sat 11am–1am; Sun 2–11pm. Food service is until 9pm Mon–Sat and 7pm on Sun. T-banen: Jernbanetorget.

Santino's Spaghetteria (Kids) PIZZA/PASTA The food here is good, but we'd visit just to hear the Italian staff speak Norwegian. This overlooked, inexpensive Italian restaurant lies smack in the center of one of the most expensive neighborhoods in Europe. The decor is postmodern and whimsical—a hallucinogenic, rainbow-hued interpretation of a carnival setting in Venice, with warm-colored tones of polished stone, a big circular bar, and a tutti-frutti color scheme run amok. Its menu prices attract clients who don't want to spend a fortune on dinner. Launch yourself with an antipasti, perhaps the mussels steamed in white wine laced with garlic, or melon and Parma ham, always a winner. A fresh minestrone is made daily. The mainly homemade pastas are among Oslo's best, with a wide range of tagliatelle, spaghetti, lasagna, penne, and tortellini, along with fusilli and ravioli. The pizzas emerge piping hot from the oven topped with virtually anything. A special treat is the alla Romana pizza with tomato sauce, mozzarella, smoked baby pork, and arugula.

Tordensskiolds 8. ✆ **22-41-16-22.** Reservations recommended. Main course pizza and pasta NOK119–NOK159 ($24–$32/£12–£16). No credit cards. Mon–Fri 11am–11pm; Sat 1–11pm; Sun 3–10:30pm. T-banen: Stortinget.

OLD TOWN (GAMLEBYEN/KVADRATUREN)

Very Expensive

Statholdergaarden ★★ NOUVELLE NORWEGIAN We know of no grander and more tranquil setting in Oslo for a deluxe restaurant than this restored 17th-century house offering a first-floor dining room that still has the original decor. Beautifully laid tables are placed under period stucco ceilings, whose motifs reappear on the china. The building dates from 1640. At this century-old restaurant (ca. 1901), menu items change frequently, according to what's in season. Some of the best examples of the cuisine here include grilled scallop and Arctic char with artichokes and fennel, or herb-infused lamb in a celery cream sauce. Delicacies include poached turbot with a lime-ginger bouillon, or French pigeon with a corn compote. A zingy filet of lamb, studded with herbs and garlic, is served with orange-glazed fennel. Don't confuse this upscale and prestigious site with the less-expensive bistro Statholderens Krostue (see below), which occupies the building's vaulted cellar.

Rådhusgate 11. ✆ **22-41-88-00.** Reservations recommended. Main courses NOK375–NOK395 ($75–$79/£38–£40); 4-course fixed-price menu NOK895 ($179/£90); 5-course fixed-price menu NOK980 ($196/£98); 6-course fixed-price menu NOK1,050 ($210/£105). AE, DC, MC, V. Mon–Sat 6pm–midnight. Tram: 11, 15, or 18.

Expensive

Det Gamle Rådhus (Old Town Hall) ★ NORWEGIAN One of the oldest restaurants in Oslo, Det Gamle Rådhus is in Oslo's former Town Hall (1641). This is strictly for nostalgia buffs, as the restaurant is not at all cutting edge. It's there for those wanting to see Oslo the way it used to be, who won't mind that the innovative fires died a long time ago. You'll dine within a network of baronial- or manorial-inspired rooms with dark wooden panels and Flemish, 16th-century-style wooden chairs. In the spacious dining room, a full array of open-faced sandwiches is served on weekdays only. A la carte dinner selections can be made from a varied menu that includes fresh fish, game, and Norwegian specialties. If you want to sample a dish that Ibsen might have enjoyed, check out the house specialty, lutefisk—but hold your nose. Old-time Scandinavians eat this traditional dish right before Christmas. To enjoy it, you've got to possess a seriously acquired taste. This Scandinavian dish is made from dried fish that has been soaked in lye and then poached in broth. More to your liking might be smoked salmon (cured right on the premises), a parfait of chicken livers, freshwater pikeperch from nearby streams sautéed in a lime sauce, filet of reindeer with lingonberry sauce, or Norwegian lamb coated with herbs and baked with a glaze.

Nedre Slottsgate 1. © **22-42-01-07.** Reservations recommended. Main courses NOK185–NOK315 ($37–$63/£19–£32); open-faced sandwiches NOK135–NOK270 ($27–$54/£14–£27); fixed-price menus NOK475–NOK575 ($95–$115/£48–£58). AE, DC, MC, V. Mon–Fri 11am–3:30pm; Mon–Sat 5–10:30pm. Kroen Bar Mon–Sat 4pm–midnight. Closed last 3 weeks in July. Bus: 27, 29, 30, 41, or 61.

Statholderens Krostue ★ SWEDISH/DANISH Here you can have a happy return to the culinary past known to Henrik Ibsen. This relatively uncomplicated cellar-level bistro is associated with Statholdergaarden, one of Oslo's most prestigious restaurants (see above). Unlike its more sophisticated sibling, it's open for lunch as well as dinner and features relatively uncomplicated food that's mostly based on traditional Swedish and Danish recipes. The cuisine provides many original and, most of the time, happy combinations of ingredients. Beneath the vaulted Renaissance-era ceiling, you can order *frikadeller* (meatballs), minced veal patties in creamy dill sauce, steak with fried onions, fried eel with potato-and-herb dumplings, and grilled salmon with saffron-flavored noodles. Lunch specialties include platters piled high with Danish or Norwegian ham, herring, boiled eggs, and vegetables, and a selection of *smørbrød* (Danish open-faced sandwiches).

Rådhusgate 11. © **22-41-88-00.** Reservations recommended. Main courses NOK240–NOK300 ($48–$60/£24–£30). AE, DC, MC, V. Tues–Sat 11:30am–10pm. Tram: 11, 15, or 18.

Moderate

Engebret Café NORWEGIAN Regrettably, it's no longer possible to sit, eat, and drink the night away with Henrik Ibsen, Edvard Grieg, and Bjørnstjerne Bjørnson, former patrons of this cafe. A favorite since 1857, this restaurant sits directly north of Akershus Castle in two buildings that have been joined together to form this establishment. The facade of the buildings has been preserved as an architectural landmark. It has an old-fashioned atmosphere and good food, served in a former bohemian literati haunt. During lunch, a tempting selection of open-faced sandwiches is available. The evening menu is more elaborate; you might begin with a terrine of game with blackberry port-wine sauce, or Engebret's always reliable fish soup. Main dishes include a truly savory dish, and red wild boar with whortleberry sauce. Or you can try Norwegian reindeer, salmon Christiania, or Engebret's big fish pot. For dessert, try the cloudberry parfait.

Bankplassen 1. © **22-33-66-94.** Reservations recommended. Main courses NOK235–NOK345 ($47–$69/£24–£35). AE, DC, MC, V. Mon–Sat 11am–11pm. Bus: 27, 29, or 30.

Mamma Rosa (Kids) ITALIAN This is but a lowly trattoria—and no better than it should be—but we like to go here for a change of taste and texture. Established by two Tuscan brothers, this trattoria enjoys the sort of popularity that's a good indication of

Kids Family-Friendly Restaurants

Brasserie 45 (p. 115) This traditional-with-a-twist bistro has a good menu for little ones, especially the picky eaters among them.

Mamma Rosa (p. 118) The best place to fill up on pasta dishes or one of ten kinds of pizzas, each a meal in itself.

Najaden (p. 123) As if being in the Norwegian Maritime Museum weren't enough for kids, those under 12 can also enjoy an elaborate summer lunch buffet here for half-price.

Santino's Spaghetteria (p. 117) Delectable pasta and pizza, served in a quirky setting that kids should love.

Norwegians' changing tastes. The second-floor dining room is decorated in a good approximation of reproduction rococo. You can order 10 kinds of pizza, fried scampi and squid, rigatoni, pasta Mamma Rosa (three kinds of pasta with three sauces), grilled steaks, and gelato. Families, both foreign and Oslovian, frequent this restaurant in large numbers nightly. Children can always find something on the menu to fill up on, especially the pizzas and pastas.

Øvre Slottsgate 12. ✆ **22-42-01-30.** Main courses NOK198–NOK260 ($40–$52/£20–£26); pizzas NOK98–NOK125 ($20–$25/£9.80–£13). AE, DC, MC, V. Mon–Sat noon–11:30pm; Sun 3–10:30pm. T-banen: Stortinget.

Stortorvets Gjæstgiveri ★ NORWEGIAN Many legends surround this nostalgic dining room of yesterday. This is the oldest restaurant in Oslo. The present restaurant is composed of a trio of wood-framed buildings, the most antique of which dates from the 1700s. The inn's upstairs bedchambers with their wood-burning stoves are virtually unchanged since their original construction, although they're now used as private dining rooms. This restaurant changes radically throughout the course of an Oslovian day: Expect a cafe near the entrance; an old-fashioned, charming, and usually packed restaurant in back; and outside dining in good weather. Menu items are traditional, well prepared, and flavorful, and include steamed mussels in white wine and garlic, poached salmon in a butter sauce, or oven-baked halibut with a mussel velouté sauce. A specialty is roast reindeer in a red-wine sauce spiked with wild berries.

Grensen 1. ✆ **23-35-63-60.** Reservations recommended. Small platters and snacks NOK73–NOK130 ($15–$26/£7.50–£13); main courses NOK199–NOK325 ($40–$65/£20–£33). AE, DC, MC, V. Cafe and restaurant Mon–Sat 11am–10:30pm. Tram: 12 or 17.

3 Brødre ★ MEXICAN We used to come here for old-fashioned Norwegian fare. Not anymore. The cuisine is now south of the border—the U.S. border, that is. "Three Brothers" is named after the glove manufacturers who once occupied this building. In their heyday in the 19th century, the brothers were said to have kept more fingers from freezing off than any other manufacturer in Norway. The food may have lost a bit of its punch in traveling so far from Mexico, but this is a favorite among locals. The fare is zesty and well prepared, and you'll get hearty portions at reasonable prices. Get those fajitas you've been hungering for, including one version made with prawns, or dig into double-cheese enchiladas and burritos. The entire street level houses the bustling bar, while a piano bar rests upstairs. Lighter meals, such as snacks and sandwiches, are available on the outside dining terrace in the summer.

Øvre Slottsgate 13. ✆ **23-10-06-70.** Main courses NOK170–NOK285 ($34–$57/£17–£29). AE, DC, MC, V. Mon–Sat 4pm–1am. Street-level bar Mon–Sat 11pm–2:30am. Piano bar Wed–Sat 5pm–2am. Bus: 27, 29, or 30.

AKER BRYGGE

Expensive

Lofoten Fiskerestaurant ★★ SEAFOOD This is the Aker Brygge district's most appealing—and best—seafood restaurant. Opening onto the waterfront, the interior sports nautical accessories that evoke life on an upscale yacht. In good weather, tables are set up on an outdoor terrace lined with flowering plants. Menu items change according to the available catch, with few choices for meat-eaters. The fish is plentiful, served in generous portions, and very fresh. Look for culinary inspirations from Italy and France, and an ample use of such Mediterranean flavors as pesto. Old-guard diners don't find their tried-and-true dishes on the menu but are introduced to Norwegian fish enriched with various sauces and accompaniments, including baked halibut with garlic cream. Other temptations include seabass baked with spices, filet of beef with rosemary jus and pimientos, or baked salmon with horseradish butter.

Stranden 75, Aker Brygge. ✆ **22-83-08-08.** Reservations recommended. Main courses NOK140–NOK265 ($28–$53/£14–£27) lunch; NOK185–NOK298 ($37–$60/£19–£30) dinner. AE, DC, MC, V. Mon–Sat 11am–11pm; Sun noon–10pm. Bus: 27.

Solsiden ★ Finds NORWEGIAN/SEAFOOD The degree to which this wildly popular restaurant is known throughout Oslo seems way out of proportion to its size and season—it's open for 4 months. Part of its fame involves its location within an ugly, cement-sided warehouse opening onto a pier that's directly across the harbor from the bigger, glossier restaurants of the Aker Brygge complex, directly below the imposing bulk of Akershus castle. It's especially appealing on sunny midsummer evenings when sunlight streams onto the pier, while many of the restaurants of Aker Brygge lie in the shadows. The venue features an open kitchen, wide views of Oslo's harbor, the setting sun, and a hard-working staff. Menu items include only fish and shellfish, with no meat of any kind on the menu. The highly theatrical house specialty is a platter of shellfish, prepared for a minimum of two diners at a time, artfully draped with seaweed. Perennial favorites are pan-fried redfish or Norwegian king crab au gratin. Instead of settling for one of the fancier dishes—such as grilled tuna with lemongrass and sesame onions—it's best to simply ask for *Dagens Fisk* (the catch of the day).

Søndre Akershus Kai 34. ✆ **23-33-36-30.** Reservations required. Main courses NOK265–NOK295 ($53–$59/£27–£30); 3-course fixed-price menu NOK445 ($89/£45). May–Aug Mon–Sat 5–10pm; Sun 5–9pm. Closed Sept–Apr. Tram: 10 or 15.

WEST END

Very Expensive

Bagatelle ★★★ FRENCH/CONTINENTAL Though seasons come and go, this longtime favorite is still the best restaurant in Oslo. For years we have been won over by the light, modern cuisine, using market-fresh ingredients, that comes from the imaginative mind of that culinary whiz, Eyvind Hellstrom. Wonderfully aromatic seafood is the star of the menu, including the catch of the day, which the chefs often smoke to perfection. Supreme of fresh cod is made even more divine with truffle butter, and the spit-roasted squab pigeon is voluptuous. Among the more intriguing appetizers are duck foie gras with gingerbread spices or the Norwegian king crab salad with a spicy vinaigrette. The chef's finely honed classic technique is showcased in a delectable herb-roasted Norwegian rack of lamb.

Bygdøy Allé 3. ✆ **22-44-63-97.** Reservations required. Main courses NOK360–NOK420 ($72–$84/£36–£42); 7-course fixed-price menu NOK1,480 ($296/£148). AE, DC, MC, V. Mon–Sat 6–10:30pm. Bus: 30, 31, 45, 72, or 73.

Expensive

Bølgen & Moi Briskeby ★ CONTINENTAL It hardly knocks Bagatelle (see above) out of the running; but when this kitchen is firing on all cylinders, it can turn out cooking to match the best you'll find in Oslo. This is a showcase branch of a chain that's now scattered throughout the urban centers of Norway. Backed by the creative zest of two Norway-born chefs and entrepreneurs (Mr. Bølgen and Mr. Moi), the chain is known for being creative and stylish, and as a haven for the discreetly rich and the sometimes famous denizens of Norway. It's set in the Oslovian suburb of Briskeby, within a redesigned industrial building whose premises are lined with original paintings and photographs by avant-garde artists, most of them Norwegian. The fussiest, most prestigious, and most experimental venue here is the gourmet restaurant, one floor above street level, where only about seven tables accommodate diners for elaborate, drawn-out meals. Frankly, we prefer the street-level brasserie; it's a wee bit less self-consciously grand, and the food is good enough to satisfy all but the most jaded palates. Well-flavored examples include a pork marinated in tamarind with lemongrass glacé; halibut with pickled lemon, or fresh lobster gratinée with a shellfish reduction.

Løvenskioldsgate 26, Briskeby. ✆ **24-11-53-53.** Reservations recommended, required for the gourmet restaurant upstairs. Brasserie main courses NOK225–NOK450 ($45–$90/£23–£45); fixed-price menus NOK465–NOK595 ($93–$119/£47–£60). Gourmet restaurant fixed-price menus NOK465–NOK595 ($93–$119/£47–£60). AE, DC, MC, V. Tues–Fri 7:30am–12:30am; Sat 9am–12:30am. Brasserie closed 3 weeks in July. Gourmet restaurant closed July to mid-Aug. Tram: 19.

Feinschmecker ★★ SCANDINAVIAN One of our local friends, a savvy food critic, has proclaimed this the best restaurant in Oslo. We're not prepared to agree, but will concede that it ranks near the top. One of the most prestigious restaurants in Oslo, Feinschmecker will entertain you with the same style and verve it's produced for such guests as King Harald and his queen, Sonya. The dining room's antique furniture and small-paned windows evoke old-time style despite the building's modernity. Menu items change frequently. Dishes are immaculately presented with a high degree of finish. We found that the quality of materials shines throughout, particularly in such dishes as grilled scallops with crispy potatoes. Even better is the sautéed ocean crayfish tails with apple cider, wild rice, and sun-dried tomatoes. A particularly sought-after main course, and rightly so, is rack of Norwegian lamb.

Balchensgate 5. ✆ **22-12-93-80.** Reservations recommended. Main courses NOK325–NOK395 ($65–$79/£33–£40); fixed-price 4-course menu NOK745 ($149/£75); fixed-price 7-course menu NOK925 ($185/£93). AE, DC, MC, V. Mon–Sat 4:30–11pm. Closed 3 weeks in July. Tram: 12 or 19 to Ilesberg.

Madserud Gård ★ NORWEGIAN This fashionable restaurant is in the vanguard of Norwegian cuisine, lying on the western fringe of Oslo. The cuisine is inventive and prepared with market-fresh ingredients. The chefs are well trained and have some surprising delicacies planned for you, as evoked by such dishes as sautéed scallops with fresh Norwegian caviar on a champagne sabayon. Their set menus are among the most elaborate, fresh, and appealing in town. Start with such delights as the tuna fish carpaccio. Meats, such as reindeer, are superb in flavor and well prepared. Desserts are equally luscious, and there is a fine but expensive wine menu.

34 Madserud Allé. ✆ **22-54-54-22.** Reservations required. All main courses NOK325 ($65/£33); fixed-price 4-course menu NOK695 ($139/£70), fixed-price 7-course menu NOK795 ($159/£80). AE, DC, MC, V. Mon–Sat 6–9pm. Tram: 13.

Moderate

Hos Thea ★ Finds SCANDINAVIAN/SPANISH This century-old building, once a private home, lies in a West End neighborhood 3km (1¾ miles) south of Oslo's center. Is it worth the trip? A lot of foreign foodies who had read about this place in European gourmet magazines think so. The stylish, well-managed restaurant also attracts a loyal crowd of people active in the media and the arts. The waitstaff and chefs share duties, so the person who prepares your meal is likely to carry it to your table as well. Depending on the staff's mood and the season, the superbly prepared menu items might include medallions of veal served with beurre blanc and carrots. That dish is bested by the breast of tender duck in a delectable red-wine sauce. Ingredients arrive fresh from all over, including filets of whitefish flavored in a sauce laced with saffron plucked from the plains of Spain. The venison, which came from the north of Norway, is handled delicately and served with a sauce of mixed Nordic summer berries.

Gabelsgate 11 (entrance on Drammensveien). ✆ **22-44-68-74.** Reservations recommended. Main courses NOK245–NOK265 ($49–$53/£25–£27); fixed-price 4-course menu NOK395 ($79/£40); fixed-price 6-course menu NOK595 ($119/£60). AE, DC, MC, V. Daily 4:30–11pm. Tram: 10 or 13.

Village Tandoori ★ INDIAN You can spend a lot of time admiring the weavings, paintings, chastened brass, and woodcarvings that adorn the walls of this restaurant, a network of dark rooms that evoke an antique house in the Punjab or Rajasthan regions of India. Food is flavorful, exotic, and extremely good, with a wide array of dishes to choose from. Many of the recipes were passed down from someone's mother or—in the case of the lamb tikki marinated in yogurt and spices—somebody's grandmother. Those with a carnivorous streak will opt for the Lahore-style lamb marinated in a tantalizing chili sauce or the spicy Punjabi chicken that is as good as anything this side of Calcutta. Delectable prawns come flavored with either paprika or garlic, and the house specialty, for those who want a taste of everything, is the "village grill" with a three-way marriage of prawns, chicken, and lamb.

Bygdøy Allee 65. ✆ **22-56-10-25.** Reservations recommended only Fri–Sat nights. Main courses NOK165–NOK235 ($33–$47/£17–£24). AE, DC, MC, V. June–Aug daily 5–11pm; Sept–May daily 3–10pm. Tram: 10, 12, or 15.

BYGDØY

Expensive

Lanternen ★ CONTINENTAL Norwegian yachties, who for some unknown reason claim to have the most developed palates in Norway, at least according to their magazines, like this place. So do we. Set close to the arrivals point for the Bygdøy ferry from the quays near Town Hall, within a low-slung white-painted clapboard-covered house from the 19th century, this restaurant is charming, welcoming, and sophisticated. From the windows of its woodsy, modern interior, you'll see about 1,000 privately owned sailboats and motorcraft bobbing in the nearby marina, giving the entire venue a distinctly nautical appeal. Appetizers and main courses are wisely limited but well chosen and intriguing to the taste buds. To begin your meal, try the homemade fish soup or the chili-flavored steamed mussels flavored with fresh garlic and white wine. Fresh, seasonal, and high-quality ingredients characterize the main courses, which range from poached sole with lobster sauce and shrimp to an herb-marinated filet of lamb. We recommend the baked chicken breast, enlivened with the additions of cured ham and mozzarella, and bound with a Madeira-laced sauce.

Huk Aveny 2. ✆ **22-43-78-38.** Reservations recommended. Main courses NOK165–NOK265 ($33–$53/£17–£27). AE, DC, MC, V. Mon–Sat 11:30am–10:30pm; Sun 1–8pm. Closed 1st 2 weeks of Jan. Bus: 30 or the Bygdøy ferry from the quays near Town Hall.

Najaden (Kids) NORWEGIAN In general, we are not turned on by museum restaurants, viewing them as a mere convenience. But Najaden is better than most dining rooms in this category. In the Norwegian Maritime Museum, this restaurant (the name translates as "mermaid") overlooks a room of sculptures removed from 19th-century clipper ships. The popular lunch buffet offers an elaborate array of freshly prepared fish and meat dishes. You won't get a lot of culinary excitement, but the food is fresh and served in generous portions—and the location is unbeatable when you're sightseeing on Bygdøy. This is very much a family-style atmosphere. Kids enjoy the nautical atmosphere and the casual, often noisy dining room. Also, the buffet is large and generous enough for a child, even for the most picky of eaters.

Bygdøynesveien 37. ✆ **22-43-81-80.** Reservations recommended. Main courses NOK210–NOK270 ($42–$54/£21–£27); lunch buffet NOK190 ($38/£19), half-price for children 11 and under. AE, DC, MC, V. May 16–Oct 14 daily noon–6pm; Oct 15–May 15 Mon–Sat 11am–3:30pm. Bus: 30. Ferry: Bygdøy.

FROGNER

Very Expensive

Restaurant Le Canard ★ FRENCH/CONTINENTAL This deluxe restaurant lies in the suburb of Frogner, just about a kilometer (½ mile) west of the center. But if you haul yourself here, you'll encounter a smart, stylish restaurant in one of Oslo's more fashionable neighborhoods. The classically oriented cooking demonstrates first-class workmanship without being showy. The mansion that contains this prestigious restaurant is almost as intriguing as the cuisine. Religious symbols are scattered throughout the building, which was designed in the 1880s by a noted Jewish architect named Lowzow. Look for the Star of David in some of the stained-glass windows, and representations of the Lion of Judah here and there. The always impeccable menu might include lobster with carrot jelly and a watermelon and rosemary vinaigrette or grilled wild turbot from Skaggerrak in a tomato and olive sauce. One enduringly popular dish is a perfectly roasted duck—that is, with most of the fat cooked off—set off to perfection with a blend of mango and olive *jus.*

President Harbitzgate 4. ✆ **22-54-34-00.** Reservations recommended. Main courses NOK240–NOK395 ($48–$79/£24–£40); 4-course fixed-price menu NOK750 ($150/£75); 5-course fixed-price menu NOK850 ($170/£85); 7-course fixed-price menu NOK975 ($195/£98). AE, DC, MC, V. Nov–June Mon–Sat 6–11pm; July–Oct Tues–Sat 6–10:30pm. T-banen: Nationaltheatret.

Expensive

Palace Grill ★★ (Finds) INTERNATIONAL Don't be misled by the word *grill:* This is not a fast-food hamburger joint, but a chic rendezvous. Hip, sophisticated, and unwaveringly upscale, this is a posh but artfully battered neighborhood restaurant, near the Royal Palace, whose clients just happen to have included the crown prince of Norway. Begin with a drink in the high-ceilinged, cowboy rock-'n'-roll bar, which attracts both young-at-heart divorcees and status-conscious young singles. The restaurant, which lies across from the bar within a building that functioned long ago as an elementary school, contains only eight tables and a tiny kitchen, which bustles with a barely controlled creative frenzy. Everything is made fresh for the day of your arrival, from scallops with burnt butter sauce and fresh ginger, to rare-cooked tuna with glazed beets, to breast of duck with red-wine-and-duck-stock sauce.

Solligaten 2, off Drammensveien. ✆ **23-13-11-40.** Reservations not accepted. In Palace Grill, all main courses NOK120 ($24/£12) each. In Palace Reserva, 4-course set-price menu NOK490 ($98/£49). AE, DC, MC, V. Restaurant Mon–Sat 5–10:30pm. Bar daily 3pm–1am. Tram: 11, 12, or 13.

HOLMENKOLLEN

Expensive

De Fem Stuer (Five Small Rooms) ★★ NORWEGIAN/CONTINENTAL Its turn-of-the-20th-century "national romantic" architecture has firmly established this restaurant as something of a historic monument for the diners who trek, ski, or ride uphill on tram no. 1 from Oslo to reach it. On the lobby level of one of our recommended hotels (Holmenkollen Park Hotel Rica, p. 109), the restaurant is in a section that retains its original Viking revival (or "dragon-style") construction. You'll find faded country-Norwegian colors, carved timbers and logs, and a general sense of 19th-century rusticity. As its name implies, the restaurant contains five separate dining areas, four of them small and cozy to the point of being cramped and intimate, the other being high-ceilinged and stately looking. For starters, the chefs make an excellent marinated whale meat in a saffron-and-chili sauce (though some readers may find it politically incorrect to devour this endangered species). You might prefer to try less guilt-inducing dishes such as the guinea hen with foie gras or the pesto-griddled ocean crayfish with tiny peas. Expect such delightful main dishes as a ginger- and chicken-stuffed quail with morels and shiitake mushrooms in a port-wine sauce, or filet of reindeer with parsnips.

In the Holmenkollen Park Hotel Rica Oslo, Kongeveien 26. ✆ **22-92-20-00.** Reservations recommended. Main courses NOK285–NOK350 ($57–$70/£29–£35). AE, DC, MC, V. Mon–Sat noon–2:30pm and 6–11pm. Tram: 1 (to its terminus).

Frognerseteren ★ NORWEGIAN Frognerseteren strikes us as the most Norwegian of all the Norwegian restaurants of Oslo. Set within a short hike (or cross-country-ski trek) from the end of Oslo's tram no. 1, the Frognerseteren rests in a century-old mountain lodge in the Viking revival style. (Richly embellished with dragon and Viking-ship symbolism, the building helped define the Viking revival style that became the architectural symbol of independent Norway.) There's a self-service section and a more formal sit-down area within several small, cozy dining rooms. The chef specializes in succulent game dishes, including pheasant pâté with Cumberland sauce, medallions of reindeer, and filet of elk sautéed in honey and nuts. You can also order poached, marinated, or smoked Norwegian salmon.

Holmenkollveien 200. ✆ **22-92-40-40.** Reservations recommended. Cafe platters NOK60–NOK178 ($12–$36/£6–£18); restaurant main courses NOK235–NOK325 ($47–$65/£24–£33); fixed-price menus NOK535–NOK995 ($107–$199/£54–£100). DC, MC, V. Mon–Sat noon–10pm; Sun noon–9pm. Tram: 1.

Moderate

Holmenkollen Restaurant NORWEGIAN/CONTINENTAL Partially built from logs and local stone, and perched near the summit of a hill outside Oslo, close to the city's world-renowned ski jump, this restaurant evokes a mountain chalet. This restaurant, built in the 1930s, is a frequent target for bus tours whose participants are hauled up to admire the high-altitude view over Oslo and to get a good meal. Main courses in the self-service restaurant include rib-sticking fare that's substantial and unpretentious, including platters of roast meats or fish, but also salads and pastas. Meals in the upstairs dining room might begin with a Caesar salad with herb-roasted chicken and a Parmesan crust or a chilled gazpacho served with pan-fried shrimp. Take delight in the pan-fried trout with spring-fresh asparagus and a chive sauce, or the roasted filet of veal with baby summer vegetables in a wine sauce. Steamed halibut is another delectable treat, with leeks, fresh dill, and a butter sauce.

Holmenkollveien 119. ✆ **22-13-92-00.** Reservations recommended. Main courses in restaurant NOK195–NOK295 ($39–$59/£20–£30); platters in the self-service restaurant NOK90–NOK280 ($18–$56/£9–£28). AE, DC, MC, V. Cafeteria daily 11:30am–4pm; restaurant Mon–Sat 10:30am–10pm, Sun 10:30am–10pm. Tram: 1.

GRÜNERLØKKA

Moderate

Markveien Mat og Vinhus ★ Finds NORWEGIAN/FRENCH/ITALIAN In the heart of the increasingly trendy Grünerløkka area, this restaurant evokes the Oslovian version of the Left Bank bohemian life. The walls are covered with the art of a local painter, Jo Stang, and the waiters welcome diners—in their terms—as "we would in our own home." This is an excellent choice for dining on well prepared cuisine. The ambitious menu includes such delights as roast suckling pig with a mushroom risotto and baked tomato. Everything's flavored with a sauce made of fresh herbs, including a tasty monkfish with boiled new potatoes and a saffron risotto. For something more truly Norwegian, try the reindeer in a green peppercorn sauce, with bacon and Brussels sprouts.

Torvbakkgate 12. ✆ **22-37-22-97.** Reservations recommended. Main courses NOK238–NOK275 ($48–$55/£24–£28); fixed-price menus NOK465–NOK735 ($93–$147/£47–£74). AE, DC, MC, V. Mon–Sat 5–11pm. Closed July 15–Aug 7. Tram: 12.

Südøst NORWEGIAN/INTERNATIONAL In a former bank building in the trendy Grünerløkka district, this place is casual chic, drawing young Oslovian sophisticates to its precincts, especially at night. In summer, Südøst boasts a terrace, filled mainly with people who come here both to eat and drink and take in the view. The people-watching is among the best in town. Food is prepared with a certain zest, including grilled swordfish with a risotto, or grilled tuna fish. The best recommendation, at least for us, is always the fresh catch of the day. The vegetables are often market fresh. You can also order one of the set menus which are rewarding and most filling.

5 Trondheimsveien. ✆ **23-35-30-70.** Main courses NOK189–NOK279 ($38–$56/£19–£28); fixed-price menus NOK395–NOK450 ($79–$90/£40–£45). AE, MC, V. Mon–Thurs 11am–10pm; Fri–Sat 11am–11pm; Sun noon–5pm. Tram: 17.

Sult ★ Finds NORWEGIAN The bar here is called Tørst, meaning "thirst," and the restaurant's name, Sult, means "hunger" in Norwegian. In trendy Grünerløkka, the restaurant attracts lots of young people, as well as artists, writers, and what one member of the staff called "dreamers." No reservations are taken, but you can hang out at the bar next door until one of the small tables becomes available. With its stone floors, pale gray walls, and somewhat rickety wooden chairs, it might remind you more of a cafe than a restaurant, but a glance at its culinary ambitions will quickly dispel any thoughts that this is just a place for drinks. The menu changes every day, depending on what looked good at that day's market. But dishes are well prepared, and everything is made fresh. We've enjoyed beautifully grilled, fresh-tasting scampi, and a tender entrecote with a savory Gorgonzola sauce. Endangered species or not, the menu sometimes features whale steak with red beets.

Thorvald Meyers Gate 26. ✆ **22-87-04-67.** Reservations not accepted. Main courses NOK189–NOK225 ($38–$45/£19–£23); 3-course menu NOK345 ($69/£35). AE, DC, MC, V. Mon–Thurs 4–10pm; Fri 4–11pm; Sat 1–11pm; Sun 1–10pm. Tram: 11, 12, or 13.

OSLOFJORD

Moderate

Ekeberg ★ NORWEGIAN/INTERNATIONAL The view from here of the Oslofjord was said to have inspired Edvard Munch in the creation of his masterpiece, *The Scream.* When the building, designed by Oslovian Lars Backer, was completed in 1929, it was said to be one of the foremost Functionalist buildings in Europe. By the end of the 1990s, the restaurant was closed and left to decay until its new owners took it over and completely renovated it. Today it is a modern building with the classic features retained from 1929.

This complex contains several places to eat, including a bar/lounge, but Ekeberg is clearly the best place for dining. Most foreigners visit just for lunch, enjoying the fish soup, mussels steamed in wine, or the open sandwiches (one made with smoked trout). At night you can dine more festively, enjoying the marinated venison with juniper berry sorbet, or the date-glazed tuna with an apple vinaigrette for a starter, followed by such main courses as dill-baked salmon, or duck confit with a tarragon sauce.

Kongsveien 15. ✆ **23-24-23-00.** Reservations recommended. Lunch main courses NOK118–NOK145 ($24–$29/£12–£15); 3-course fixed-price lunch NOK295 ($59/£30). Dinner main courses NOK145–NOK275 ($29–$55/£15–£28); fixed-price dinner menus NOK320–NOK570 ($64–$114/£32–£57). AE, DC, MC, V. Mon–Sat 11am–midnight; Sun noon–10pm. Tram: 18 or 19.

6

Exploring Oslo

Oslo is most often viewed as a summer destination. Because Oslovians are starved for sunlight, everyone takes to the outdoors in summer, and many of them virtually stay up around the clock this time of year. If you come in winter, you get short days, with darkness descending around 3pm. Oslovians counter the climate by becoming the candlelit center of the world, and the flickering lights make bar-hopping a warm, cozy experience.

To compensate for those long, dark nights, the parties of Oslo become even more frenetic in the winter months. From rock clubs to Mozart concerts, the nightlife in Oslo is more amped up than ever before. The city's cultural activities and special art exhibitions also reach their zenith.

Seasons aside, some travelers would be happy to come to Oslo anytime just for the views of the harborfront city and the Oslofjord. Panoramas are a major attraction, especially the one from Tryvannstårnet, a 117m (384-ft.) observation tower atop 570m (1,870-ft.) Tryvann Hill in the outlying area. Many other attractions are worthy of your time and exploration, too. The beautiful surroundings make these sights even more appealing.

Try to allocate at least 2 or 3 days to exploring Norway's capital. After a stay here, most visitors head west to Bergen and the fjord district or continue east by train or plane to Stockholm, the capital of Sweden.

1 THE BIG SIX

If you've budgeted only a day or two for Oslo—a shame, really—make the most of your time and see only the "platinum" attractions, saving the "gold" and "silver" rated sights for your return visit. We've narrowed the major attractions down to "The Big Six."

Henie-Onstad Kunstsenter (Henie-Onstad Art Center) ★★★ Norway's largest collection of modern art is worth the trip to the museum's beautiful setting beside Oslofjord, 11km (6¾ miles) west of Oslo. It was inaugurated in 1968 to house a gift of some 300 works of art from Sonja Henie, former figure skating champion and movie star, and her husband, shipping tycoon Niels Onstad.

Henie's bequest, beefed up by later additions, virtually spans modern art in the 20th century, from Cubism with Braque to Surrealism with Ernst. In fact, the collection is so vast that it frequently has to be rotated. We're always particularly drawn to the CoBrA Group, with works by its founder, Asger Jorn, and by Karel Appel. You can head downstairs to Henie's trophy room to see her three Olympic gold medals—she was the star at the 1936 skating competition—and ten world championship prizes. Henie garnered 600 trophies and medals, all of which are on display.

Besides the permanent collection, plays, concerts, films, and special exhibits take place. An open-air theater-in-the-round is used in the summer for folklore programs, jazz concerts, and song recitals. A top-notch, partly self-service restaurant, the Piruetten, is also on the premises. Plan to spend about 2 hours here.

Oslo Attractions

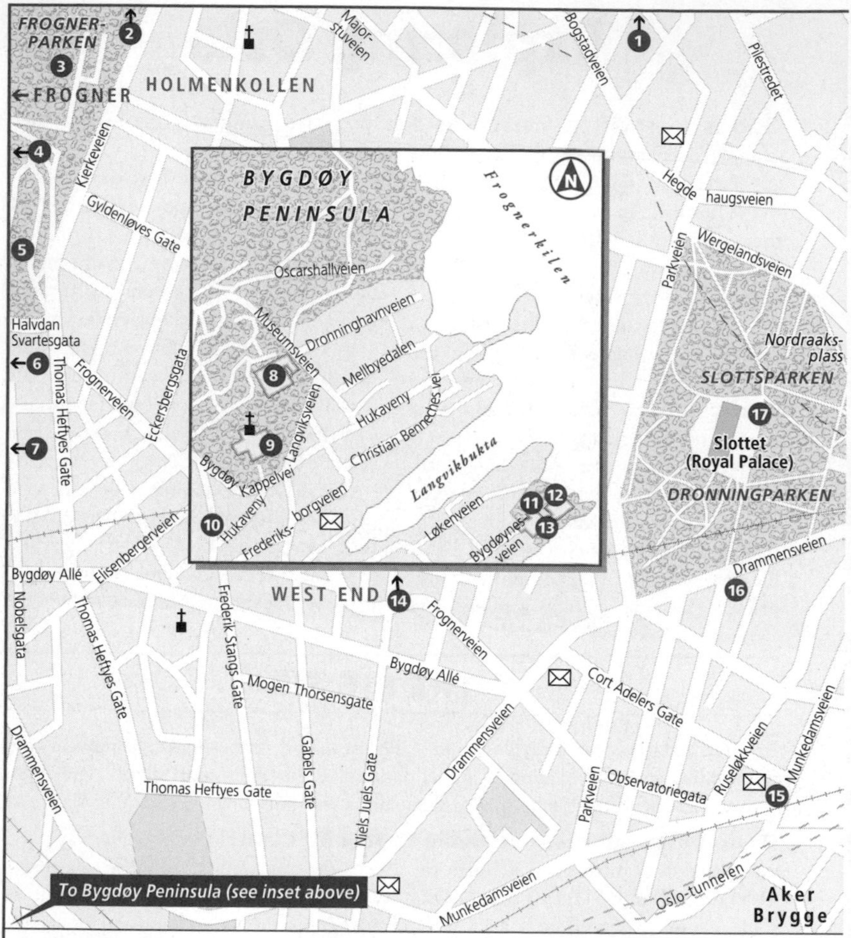

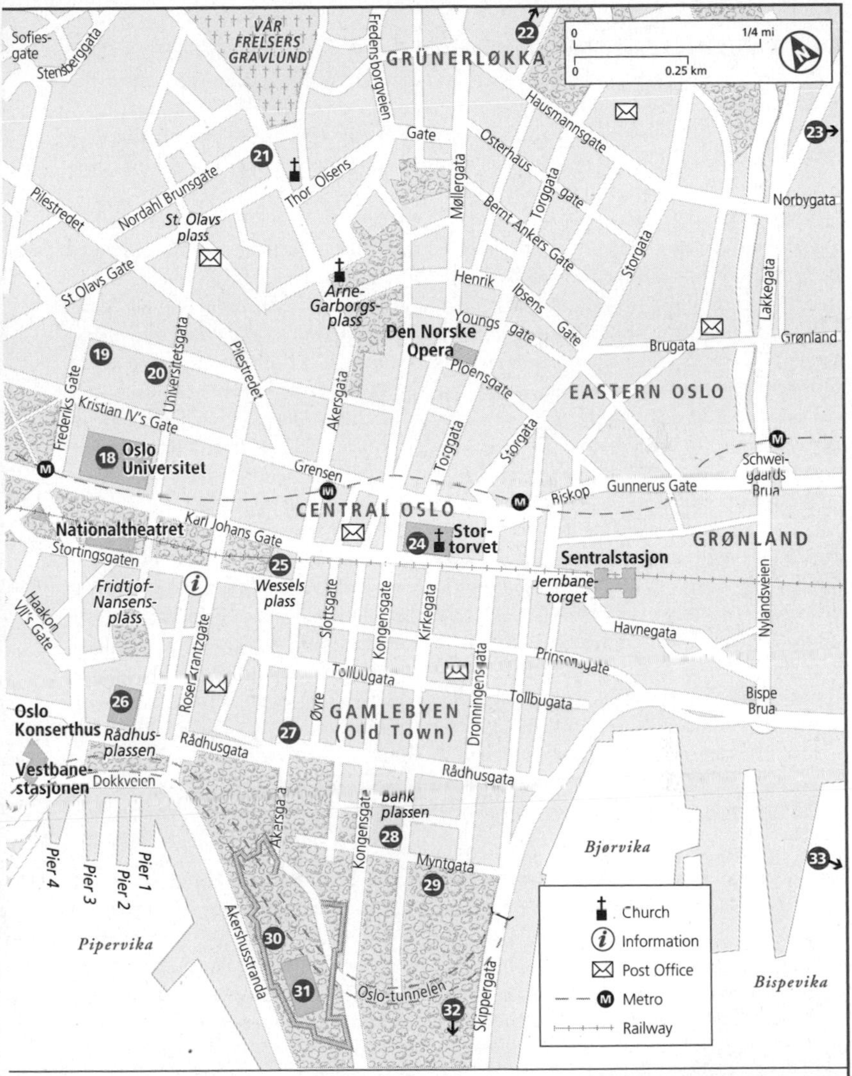

Rådhuset (City Hall) **26**
Skimuseet (Ski Museum) **1**
Skoytemuseet (Ice Skating Museum) **4**
Stenersen Museum **15**
Stortinget (Parliament) **25**
Slottsparken **17**
Teatermuseet i Oslo **27**
Tryvannstårnet (Lookout Tower) **1**
Vigeland Museum **6**
Vigelandsparken **3**
Vikingskiphuset (Viking Ship Museum, University Museum of Cultural Heritage) **9**
Villa Grande **10**

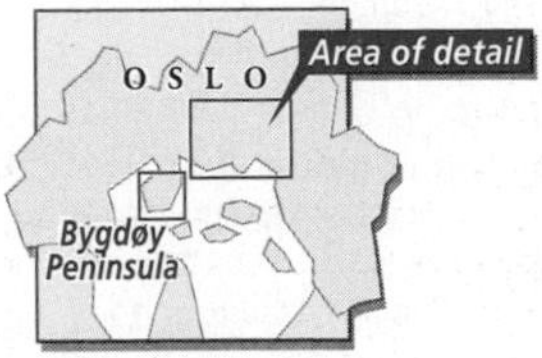

 Høkvikodden, Sonja Henlesvie 31. ✆ **67-80-48-80.** www.hok.no. Admission NOK80 ($16/£8) adults, NOK30 ($6/£3) visitors ages 7–16, free for children 6 and under. Free for all Wed. Tues–Thurs 11am–7pm; Fri–Sun 11am–6pm. Bus: 151, 161, 252, or 261.

Munch Museet (Edvard Munch Museum) ★★★ Edvard Munch (1863–1944) was Scandinavia's greatest painter and, in an act of incredible generosity, donated this collection to his beloved Oslo. The treasure trove is so vast—1,100 paintings, 4,500 drawings, and 18,000 prints—that it can be shown only in rotation. The curators keep a representative sampling of his works on display at all times, so you can trace his development from Impressionism to symbolism.

Love, death, darkness, and anxiety were his overarching themes. The latter was best expressed in his most famous painting, *The Scream,* which is actually a series composed of four versions. This museum's version of the Munch masterpiece is valued at $75 million. Not surprisingly, its August 2004 theft caused a huge international uproar, especially within art communities. Fans of Munch's *The Scream* and his *Madonna* (also nicked by the robbers) can once again gaze upon these paintings, which were recovered in the summer of 2006. Police were cagey at a news conference about how the paintings were recovered. *The Scream* and *Madonna* were part of the artist's "Frieze of Life" series, focusing on the artist's usual themes: sickness, death, anxiety, and love, many of which the museum's curator probably experienced during the paintings' disappearance.

We are especially moved by Munch's early works, such as *At the Coffee Table* (1883), where you can see the preliminary vision that would grow into a future masterpiece. By the 1890s, Munch's paintings had matured into virtual masterpieces. We stand in awe at the *Red Virginia Creeper,* in which the house is being devoured by a plant. *Dagnyi Juel* is his portrait of Ducha Przybyszewska, the Berlin socialite with whom he'd fallen in love (unfortunately, Strindberg was also infatuated with this femme fatale, who would, incidentally, go on to marry a third lover altogether). Most fascinating is a series of self-portraits, which explore his mental state at peak moments of his life, such as *The Night Wanderer* (1923) and *Self-Portrait by the Window* (1940).

Plan to devote at least an hour and a half to Munch.

Tøyengata 53. ✆ **23-49-35-00.** www.munch.museum.no. Admission NOK75 ($15/£7.50) adults, NOK40 ($8/£4) children. Free for all Oct–Mar. June–Aug daily 10am–6pm; Sept–May Tues–Fri 10am–4pm, Sat–Sun 11am–5pm. T-banen: Tøyen. Bus: 60.

Nasjonalgalleriet (National Gallery) ★★★ This museum houses Norway's greatest and largest collection of art. Most visitors flock here to see Edvard Munch's *The Scream,* one of four versions, this one painted in 1893. This painting was stolen in 1994 and, like the version taken from the Munch Museum in 2004 (see above), was subsequently recovered. *The Scream,* which is reproduced in countless posters around the world, still inspires artists today and continues to work its way into popular culture. For example, in a 2006 episode of *The Simpsons,* Bart and his friends steal a copy of *The Scream* in a parody of the real thefts.

Munch has paintings here beyond *The Scream,* a total of 58 of his works, some of them among his most celebrated, including *The Dance of Life, Moonlight,* and *Ashes.* Most of Munch's works on show were painted in the closing years of the 19th century. There are also several self-portraits of Munch—see why he was called "the handsomest man in Norway."

The leading Norwegian Romantic landscape painter Johan Christian Dahl (1788–1857) is in fine form here, but we find his paintings a little too sentimental. Our favorite

So, Who Was This Sonja Henie, Anyway?

Norwegians young and old know the story of one of their most legendary public figures, Sonja Henie (1912–69). In America, however, only the older generation might be able to identify this former figure skater and movie actress who won gold medals for figure skating at the 1928, 1932, and 1936 Winter Olympics.

Henie was born in Oslo, the daughter of a furrier. Having learned skating and dancing as a child, she became the youngest Olympic skating champion when she won her first gold medal at age 15. She became a professional in 1936 on her tour of the United States, performing in ice shows as late as the 1950s. The bright-eyed, bubbly blonde managed to parlay her championships into an effervescent but short motion-picture career.

Twentieth Century Fox ordered writers to tailor film properties for her, to keep the comedy and romance light, and to get her on those skates as much as possible. Often she was teamed with top-rate stars, such as Ray Milland and Robert Cummings in *Everything Happens at Night* in 1939, or Don Ameche, Ethel Merman, and Cesar Romero in the 1938 film *Happy Landing*. The year 1939 also saw her teamed opposite Rudy Valee and Tyrone Power in *Second Fiddle*. Only Shirley Temple and Clark Gable outranked her at the box office that year.

In 1940, when Hitler invaded Norway, she published her autobiography, *Wings on My Feet,* which included a picture of her receiving congratulations from Hitler, surrounded by Nazi officials at the 1936 Olympics. The associations with the Nazis tarnished her reputation during the war, but the outcry against her died down after the war.

In 1960, Henie retired with her third husband, Niels Onstad, a wealthy Norwegian businessman and art patron. In 1968, they founded the Henie-Onstad Kunstsenter (p. 127), near Oslo, as a showcase for Henie's extensive collection of modern art. The next year, at the relatively early age of 57, Norway's most famous daughter died. She was aboard an aircraft carrying her from Paris to Oslo for medical treatment. At the time of her death, she was one of the ten wealthiest women on earth.

is Christian Krohg, who painted it like it was, drawing inspiration from sailors to prostitutes. Scandinavian painting in general is also showcased, with one salon containing works from the Golden Age of Danish painting.

Although not extensive compared to some national collections, European painting in general is on parade, with old masters represented from Van Dyck to Rubens, from El Greco (a remarkable *St. Peter Repentant*) to Cézanne and Matisse. Van Gogh weighs in with a self-portrait, Picasso with his *Guitar.* Look for the works of Gustav Vigeland, although you'll get better acquainted with him at Vigelandsparken (see below).

All the art displayed was created before 1945, the year Norwegians freed themselves from the Nazi yoke. Allow 2 hours for a visit.

Universitetsgaten 13. ✆ **21-98-20-00.** www.nationalmuseum.no. Free admission. Tues–Wed and Fri 10am–6pm; Thurs 10am–7pm; Sat and Sun 11am–5pm. Tram: 10 or 12.

The Man Behind *The Scream*

Scandinavia's greatest artist, Edvard Munch (1863–1944), was a pioneer in the expressionist movement. *The Scream,* painted in 1893, is his best-known painting. There are four known versions of this painting, one of which was stolen from the Munch Museum in August of 2004. The painting, along with another Munch masterpiece, *Madonna,* were recovered by Norwegian police in August of 2006 and returned to the museum. He grew up in Oslo (then called Christiania) and was often ill. Early memories of illness, death, and grief in his family had a tremendous impact on his later works. His father's death may have contributed to the loneliness and melancholy of one of his most famous works, *Night* (1890).

By the early 1890s, Munch had achieved fame (though slight in comparison with his renown today). He was at the center of a *succés de scandale* in Munich in 1892 when his art was interpreted as "anarchistic provocation."

Munch went to Berlin to escape, entering a world of literati, artists, and intellectuals. He met August Strindberg and they discussed the philosophy of Nietzsche, symbolism, psychology, and occultism. The discussions clearly influenced his work. His growing outlook was revealed to the world in an 1893 show in Berlin, where several paintings had death as their theme. His *Death in a Sickroom* particularly created quite a stir.

In 1896, Munch moved to Paris, where he made exquisite color lithographs and his first woodcuts. By the turn of the 20th century, he was painting in a larger format and incorporating some of the Art Nouveau aesthetics of the time. *Red Virginia Creeper* and *Melancholy* reflect the new influences. Prominent people also asked Munch to paint their portraits, and he obliged. His 1904 group portrait of Dr. Linde's sons is a masterpiece of modern portraiture.

A nervous disorder soon sent him to a sanitarium, and he had a turbulent love affair with a wealthy bohemian nicknamed "Tulla." The affair ended in 1902 when a revolver permanently injured a finger on Munch's left hand. He became obsessed with the shooting incident and poured out his contempt for Tulla in such works as *Death of Murat* (1907). Munch also became increasingly alcoholic, and, in 1906, he painted *Self-Portrait with a Bottle of Wine.*

From 1909 until his death, Munch lived in Norway. In his later years, he retreated into isolation, surrounded only by his paintings, which he called "my children." The older Munch placed more emphasis on the monumental and the picturesque, as in landscapes or people in harmony with nature.

In 1940, he decided to leave his huge collection of paintings to the city of Oslo upon his death. Today the Edvard Munch Museum provides the best introduction to this strange and enigmatic artist.

Norsk Folkesmuseum (Norwegian Folk Museum) ★★★ Kids Take a tour of Norway in just 1 day. From all over the country, museum curators moved 155 buildings from their original site and, with great difficulty, transported and reassembled them on

14 hectares (35 acres) on the Bygdøy peninsula. Among the old buildings is the **Gol Stave Church** ★★★, moved here a century ago. Dating from 1200—still with no windows—it came from the town of Gol, 224km (139 miles) northwest of Oslo. One of the oldest such museums in the world, the Folk Museum contains many buildings from the medieval era, including the Raulandstua, one of the oldest wooden dwellings still standing in Norway. Wander the streets of **Gamblebyen** or **Old Town** ★, a reproduction of an early 20th-century Norwegian town. The rural buildings are grouped together by region of origin, and the urban houses are laid out in the form of an old town.

Eventually, the curators decided to make this open-air folk museum a living, breathing entity. They feature a variety of activities, including horse-and-buggy rides, folk music, dancing by men and women in native dress, traditional arts and crafts, and even "Norwegian evenings," a summer food tasting of regional specialties and folk dancing. Artisans demonstrate age-old crafts such as pottery, weaving, silversmithing, and the making of candles, which you can purchase in their workshops. At the Christmas fair, some 120 old-fashioned stands also sell handmade products.

Inside, the museum's 225,000 exhibits capture every imaginable facet of Norwegian life, past and present. Furniture, household utensils, clothing, woven fabrics, and tapestries are on display, along with fine examples of Norwegian rose-painting and woodcarving. Farming implements and logging gear pay tribute to the development of agriculture and forestry. Also look for the outstanding exhibit on Norway's Sami population. You can easily spend 3 hours here.

After the millennium, the museum incorporated the **Bygdo Royal Farm,** with its cultivated fields and grazing lands offering hikes along the trails.

In all, the museum is a living textbook of Norwegian culture that is not to be missed.

Museumsveien 10. ✆ **22-12-37-00.** www.norskfolke.museum.no. Admission NOK95 ($19/£9.50) adults, NOK25 ($5/£2.50) children 16 and under. Jan 2–May 14 and Sept 15–Dec 30 Mon–Fri 11am–3pm, Sat–Sun 11am–4pm; May 15–Sept 14 daily 10am–6pm. Ferry: From Pier 3 facing the Rådhuset (summer only). Bus: 30 from the Nationaltheatret.

Vigelandsparken ★★★ It took us a few years to warm to the sculptures of Gustav Vigeland, the most prominent among Norwegian sculptors of the 20th century. But we finally came around and frequently return to explore this park with 227 of Vigeland's monumental sculptures, mostly devoted to the theme of mankind's destiny. The artist worked for a total of 4 decades on this 30-hectare (74-acre) park but, sadly, died 1 year before his lifetime achievement could be completed.

The chief treasure here is the **Vigeland Monolith** ★★★, a 16m (52-ft.) sculpture composed of 121 colossal figures, all amazingly carved into one piece of stone. The monolith is easy to spot, as it rises on top of the highest hill in the park. Summer lovers

Impressions

I am anchored to my work so that I cannot move. If I walk down the street one day a thousand hands from work hold on to me. I am tied to the studio and the road is never long.

—Gustav Vigeland, 1912

Fun Facts **The Gokstad and the New World**

In 1893, Norwegians built a replica of the *Gokstad* and sailed it to New York harbor, proving how worthy Viking shipbuilding was. From New York, it was transported overland to the World's Fair that year in Chicago.

often visit it at night, as it's floodlit and somehow seems even more dramatic at that time. A set of circular steps envelops the statue. On the steps leading up to the monolith are 36 groups of other figures carved in stone by the great artist. The column itself, with its writhing figures, is said to symbolize the struggle of life, which is one of the main themes running through Vigeland's work.

The "best of the rest" of the sculptures lie along a paved axis stretching for 1km (1/2 mile). These sculptures depict Vigeland's interpretation of life beginning at birth and ending in death. The most famous of these statues, which you'll quickly recognize because it is one of the most reproduced pieces of art in Oslo, is ***The Angry Boy (Sinnataggen)*** ★★. Based on a sketch Vigeland made in London in 1901, it shows a kid stomping his feet and scrunching his face in anger. We don't know why he's so furious, but we love it.

Frogner Park, Nobelsgate 32. ✆ **23-49-37-00.** Free admission to park; museum NOK50 ($10/£5) adults, NOK25 ($5/£2.50) children. Museum free to all Oct–Mar. Park daily 24 hr. Museum June–Aug Tues–Sun 10am–5pm; Sept–May Tues–Sun noon–4pm. Tram: 12.

Vikingskipshuset (Viking Ship Museum, University Museum of Cultural Heritage) ★★★ **Kids** A fascinating chapter in Viking history came alive when three Viking funereal ships were discovered in the Oslofjord between 1867 and 1904. All the vessels, each dating from the 9th century, had been buried in a blue clay that preserved them. The ***Oseberg*** ★★, which required 30 oarsmen to move it through the waters, impresses us the most, with its dragon and serpent carvings. Apparently, the ship was the resting place of a noblewoman; though plundered for much of its booty, many of the queen's burial furnishings are on display.

The finest remaining example of a Viking longship, the ***Gokstad*** ★, when unearthed, had also been sacked by ancient grave-robbers. Among the few artifacts uncovered were bedposts with animal head ornamentation, fragments of a sledge, and even a gaming board (think early Las Vegas). The largest ship of the lot, the *Gokstad* could accommodate 32 oarsmen and travel at a speed of 12 knots. Built around the same time as the *Gokstad,* the *Tune* is less impressive, though it was the tomb of a powerful chieftain. The badly damaged ship was intentionally not restored so that visitors can see the details of shipbuilding in the Viking era.

For kids, the ships here conjure up the legend and lore of the Viking era that flourished in the Middle Ages. We've seen kids stand in awe looking up at the excavated ships long after their parents have taken in the exhibitions. Give or take some time for gawking, you'll spend about an hour here. ***Tip:*** If you go between 11:30am and 1pm, you'll tend to avoid the summer mobs who descend on this building, whose rounded white walls give it the feeling of a burial tomb.

Huk Aveny 35, Bygdøy. ✆ **22-13-52-80.** www.khm.uio.no. Admission NOK50 ($10/£5) adults, NOK30 ($6/£3) children. Oct–Apr daily 10am–4pm; May–Sept daily 9am–6pm. Ferry: From Pier 3 facing the Rådhuset (summer only). Bus: 30 from the Nationaltheatret.

2 OTHER TOP ATTRACTIONS

MUSEUMS

Astrup Fearnley Museum of Modern Art ★ Finds This is one of those special nuggets art lovers stumble across in their travels, wondering why such a place isn't better known. Actually, this privately funded museum has been around since 1993, when Norway's leading architects and designers constructed the stunningly designed building to showcase both Norwegian and international post–World War II art. Works by '60s icon Yoko Ono can be seen here. The equally controversial British artist, a blood-and-guts type of guy, Damien Hirst, is also on view with his installation of *Mother and Child Divided.* The changing exhibitions are often drawn from the museum's permanent collection, much of which is kept in storage. On our last visit, we feasted on another British blood-and-gore type, Francis Bacon, along with the gentler Lucian Freud and Gerhard Richter. Introduce yourself to some locally known Norwegian artists of great stature, especially Knut Rose, Bjørn Carlsen, and Arne Ekeland, our favorites. If you prefer your sculptures oversize, wander through the garden, with such works as Niki de St. Phalle's sparrow. Allow at least 40 minutes.

Dronningensgatan 4. ✆ **22-93-60-60.** http://afmuseet.no. Free admission. Tues–Wed and Fri 11am–5pm; Thurs 11am–7pm; Sat–Sun noon–5pm. T-banen: Stortinget. Tram: 1, 2, 10, or 12. Bus: 27, 29, 38, 51, or 56.

Aula (Great Hall) Admirers of the work of Edvard Munch, like us, will want to see the Great Hall of the university, where Scandinavia's greatest artist painted murals. We've gone here repeatedly over the years just to look at Munch's depiction of *The Sun,* the mural showing rays gently falling over a secluded Norwegian fjord. Until it moved to larger headquarters at the City Hall, this used to be the site of the Nobel Prize award ceremony. Plan on spending 20 minutes here.

University of Oslo, Karl Johans Gate 47. ✆ **22-85-95-55.** Free admission. June 20–Aug 20 daily 10am–4pm. T-banen: Stortinget.

Emanuel Vigeland Museum ★ Finds We'll let you in on something if you promise not to tell. This museum has been accurately dubbed Oslo's best-kept secret, and sometimes we admire the work of Emanuel Vigeland (1875–1948), the younger brother of Gustav, better than his more celebrated sibling's. The main attraction here—besides the fact that Emanuel was the architect of his own museum—is a barrel-vaulted room covered with frescoes that depict human life from conception to death. Some of the scenes are explicitly erotic, and his works have been simultaneously acclaimed and denounced as "decadent." The most curious of the motifs we discovered is on the short wall by the entrance. Still embraced in copulation, a dead couple yields a mighty pillar of smoke and infants. Perhaps Emanuel wanted to link creation, death, and birth as

Impressions

People shall be made to understand the greatness of my art; when facing it, they shall learn to remove their hats, as if in a cathedral.

—Edvard Munch

inseparable. To further a theme, Emanuel decided to turn the museum into his mausoleum. His ashes were laid to rest in an urn above the entrance. It's a shame the museum has such short hours.

Grimelundsveien 8. ✆ **22-14-57-88.** www.emanuelvigeland.museum.no. Admission NOK30 ($6/£3). Sun noon–4pm. T-banen: No. 1 Frognerseteren to Slemdal station (then a 7-min. walk).

Forsvarsmuseet (Armed Forces Museum) In the heart of Oslo at the ancient Akershus Fortress (p. 139), this museum traces the history of Norway from the Viking era up to the occupation of Norway by the Nazis in World War II. Enough artifacts are on view to satisfy any warmonger, and the history of the Nordic wars is depicted. The best part of the museum is the World War II exhibition, which includes guns, tanks, bombs, and fighter planes. Especially moving is a depiction of how the resistance contributed to the final victory for the Allies. It seems a bit ironic that this museum occupies Akershus, which was used by the Germans as their headquarters during the occupation (1940–45). Give yourself at least 40 minutes to explore this museum in a fortress, then head to the on-site cafeteria for some fortification of your own.

Akershus Fortress, Bygning 62. ✆ **23-09-35-82.** www.fmu.mil.no. Free admission. June–Aug Mon–Fri 10am–6pm, Sat–Sun 11am–4:30pm; Sept–May Mon–Fri 10am–3pm, Sat–Sun 11am–4pm. Tram: 1, 2, or 10.

Historisk Museum (University Museum of Cultural Heritage) From the cold Arctic wastelands to the hot, sunny islands of Asia, this museum—owned by the University of Oslo—is a vast treasure trove, containing everything from a carved *stavkirke* (wooden church) to a 1,000-year history of the coins of Norway. Viking artifacts and a display of gold and silver ★ from the 2nd through the 13th centuries are in the Treasure House. In the medieval hall, look for the reddish Ringerike Alstad Stone, which was carved in relief, and the Dynna Stone ★, an 11th-century runic stone honoring the handsomest maiden in Hadeland. There's also a rich collection of ecclesiastical art in a series of portals from stave churches. Grant this museum at least 45 minutes.

Frederiksgate 2 (near Karl Johans Gate). ✆ **22-85-99-64.** Free admission. May 15–Sept 14 Tues–Sun 10am–4pm; Sept 15–May 14 Tues–Sun 11am–4pm. Tram: 11, 17, or 18.

Kunstindustrimuseet (Museum of Decorative Arts and Design) ★ Founded in 1876, this is one of the oldest museums in Norway and among the oldest applied-arts museums in Europe. Since 1876 it has owned the bold, imaginative Baldishol tapestries ★ from the early part of the 12th century. Few Draculas could resist furnishing their home with the antique dragon-style furniture. Royal wardrobe is also on display, including the wedding gown Queen Sonja wore in 1968 (Lady Di had no competition here). The collection of 18th-century Norwegian silver ★, glass, and faience (a type of glazed pottery) is stunning, and there is also an impressive selection of contemporary furniture and crafts. Allow yourself an hour here.

Café Solliløkken and the museum shop on the ground floor are in rooms from the 1830s that originally were in a small country house. The cafe offers light meals, mostly sandwiches and salads, but also some hot Norwegian specialties every day (most often fish). All its pastries are homemade. We opted for the prune Danish, only to be told, "In Norway we don't call it Danish!"

St. Olavs Gate 1. ✆ **22-03-65-40.** www.nationalmuseum.no. Free admission. Tues–Wed and Fri 11am–4pm; Thurs and Sat–Sun 11am–7pm. T-banen: Stortinget. Bus: 37.

Frommer's Favorite Oslo Experiences

Enjoying Fresh Shrimp off the Boats In the morning, head for the harbor in front of the Rådhuset and buy a bag of freshly caught and cooked shrimp from a fisherman. Although this may not be everyone's idea of a good breakfast—sales begin around 7 or 8am and may end in late morning—shrimp lovers will find Valhalla here.

Experiencing Life on the Fjords In the summer, head for the harbor, where boats wait to take you sightseeing, fishing, or to the beach.

Hanging Out in the Students' Grove Summer is short in Oslo, and it's savored. Late-night drinkers sit in open-air beer gardens along Karl Johans Gate, enjoying the endless nights. Our favorite spot for a beer and to watch the passing parade is Studenten, on the corner of Karl Johans Gate and Universitesgata.

Listening to Street Musicians Hundreds of musicians flock to Oslo in the summer. You can enjoy their music along Karl Johans Gate and at the marketplace Stortorvet.

Taking the Ferry to Bygdøy The Bygdøy peninsula offers a treasure trove of attractions, including Viking ships, Thor Heyerdahl's *Kon-Tiki,* seafood buffets, a sailboat harbor, and bathing beaches. At the folk museum are old farmsteads, houses, and often folk-dancing.

Museet for Samtidskunst (National Museum of Contemporary Art) Opened in 1990, this collection of works acquired by the state after World War II presents an array of international and Norwegian contemporary art. Previously grouped together in the National Gallery, the works have more room to breathe here, in what was once the central bank of Norway. We once saw a painting here of a three-headed woman with 14 breasts, but don't worry—exhibits change frequently. Allot 30 minutes to explore the collection.

Bankplassen 4. ✆ **22-86-22-10.** www.nationalmuseum.no. Free admission. Tues–Wed and Fri 11am–5pm; Thurs 10am–7pm; Sat–Sun noon–5pm. Tram: 10 or 12. Bus: 60.

Nobel Peace Center One of Oslo's newest attractions, the ultramodern center presents the history of the founding father of the prize, Alfred Nobel, "the dynamite king," and the biographies and careers of Nobel Peace Prize laureates such as Nelson Mandela. In addition to changing exhibits, a permanent exhibition illustrates the careers of the laureates through film, including recordings of actual Peace Prize ceremonies. If you're lucky, you might catch a glimpse of one of the winners of the Peace Prize who sometimes come to the renovated train station to give lectures.

Radhusplassen. ✆ **48-30-10-00.** Admission NOK80 ($16/£8) 16 and over; NOK55 ($11/£5.50) seniors/students, free 15 and under. June–Sept 15 daily 10am–7pm; off season Tues–Fri 10am–6pm, Sat–Sun 11am–6pm. Tram: 10 or 12.

Norges Hjemmefrontmuseum (Norwegian Resistance Museum) ★ From underground printing presses to radio transmitters, from the German attack in 1940 to the liberation in 1945, the museum documents Norway's World War II resistance activities. Photographs documenting the Nazi attack on Norway have been printed on black iron sheets, and a cluster of German rifles is arranged to form the dreaded swastika that Norwegians grew to hate. The war-time traitor and so-called "minister president," Quisling, is deservedly vilified in the exhibits. We are especially moved by the daring underground newspapers, which appeared as early as the summer of 1940 and continued to publish throughout the dark years of the war. The artifacts here can usually be absorbed in about an hour. Outside is a monument dedicated to Norwegian patriots, many of whom were executed by the Nazis at this spot.

Akershus Fortress. ✆ **23-09-31-38.** www.mil.no. Admission NOK30 ($6/£3) adults, NOK15 ($3/£1.50) children. Sept–May Mon–Fri 10am–4pm, Sat–Sun 11am–4pm; June–Aug Mon–Sat 10am–5pm. Tram: 10, 12, 15, or 19.

Norsk Teknisk Museum (Norwegian Technological Museum) You don't really have to be an engineer to enjoy this museum, which showcases Norway's prime developments in industry, technology, transport, medicine, and science. The first aircrafts, royal automobiles, a Model-T, the first car and tram in Norway, a paddle steamer, even a robot center where you can program your very own robot—all of these exhibits and more are on display here on the outskirts of the city, with views along the banks of the Akerselva River. One intriguing exhibit documents the flight of the *Leiv Eiriksson,* a small plane that was the first ever to travel between America and Norway, flying from New York to Bergen in 1935 in 57 hours.

Kjelsåsvn 143. ✆ **22-79-60-00.** www.tekniskmuseum.no. Admission NOK80 ($16/£8) adults, NOK40 ($8/£4) students and children, family ticket NOK200 ($40/£20). June 20–Aug 20 daily 10am–6pm; Aug 21–June 19 Tues–Sat 10am–4pm, Sun 10am–5pm. Bus: 54.

Skimuseet (Ski Museum) ★ Kids Founded in 1923, this is the oldest ski museum in the world—as such, even the royal family of Norway has added their skis to the collection. At Holmenkollen, an elevator takes visitors up the jump tower for a **panoramic view** ★★★ of Oslo and the fjord, one of the greatest vistas you are likely to experience in Norway. At the base of the ski jump, the Skimuseet displays a wide range of exhibits, including a 4,000-year-old pictograph from Rødøy in Nordland that documents skiing's thousand-year history. The museum also has skis and historical items from various parts of Norway—from the first "modern" skis, dating from about 1870, to a ski dating from around A.D. 600. Artifacts from the Antarctic expeditions of Amundsen are on display, as well as the Scott expeditions into the snowy wastelands. You can even see relics of Fridtjof Nansen's slog across the Greenland icecap. A historical version of Survivorman, he built a boat from his sled and canvas tent to row the final 100km (62 miles) to "the end of the world." Allow 45 minutes.

Kongeveien 5, Holmenkollen. ✆ **22-92-32-64.** www.skiforeningen.no. Admission (museum and ski jump) NOK70 ($14/£7) adults, NOK35 ($7/£3.50) children. May and Sept daily 10am–5pm; June–Aug daily 9am–10pm; Oct–Apr daily 10am–4pm. T-banen: Holmenkollen SST Line 15 from near the Nationaltheatret to Voksenkollen (30-min. ride), then an uphill 15-min. walk.

Skoytemuseet (Ice-Skating Museum) Kids In the land of skaters and skiers, it seems appropriate to have a museum devoted to ice skating. This museum tells the story of many fascinating competitions on ice. You'll learn about the heroes of the speed-skating world, including Axel Paulsen (1855–1938) and Oscar Mathisen (1888–1954), along with their participation in world championships. Kids and adults alike should delight in seeing the first skates ever made in Norway—made with real bone—to the most advanced high-tech skates of today. Opened in 1914, this museum displays artifacts illustrating "major moments" in speed and figure skating. Allot about 30 minutes here.

At the Frogner Stadium, Middelthunsgate 26. ✆ **22-43-49-20.** Admission NOK25 ($5/£2.50) adults, NOK15 ($3/£1.50) children. Tues and Thurs 10am–2pm; Sun 11am–3pm. Tram: 12.

Stenersen Museum ★ Finds Part of the City of Oslo Art Collections, the most avant-garde temporary exhibitions in Oslo are presented here on a regular basis alongside three of the greatest private collections in Norway. Rolf E. Stenersen, a financier, author, and collector (1899–1978), donated some 300 paintings, even watercolors and prints by Edvard Munch, though you can see better Munchs at the National Gallery and the Munch Museum. What you get here are the best examples of Norwegian modernism as it flourished "between the wars," such as 300 paintings and 100 drawings from Amaldus Nielsen, "the painter of the south," whose best works were set in Southern Norway. Finally, the widow of Ludvig O. Ravensburg donated some 160 works by her artist husband (1871–1958). Known for his burlesque humor, he was a relative of Munch. Allow 45 minutes to see this museum.

Munkedamsveien 15. ✆ **23-49 36-00.** www.stenersen.museum.no. Admission NOK45 ($9/£4.50) adults, NOK25 ($5/£2.50) students and children. Free to all Oct–Mar. Tues and Thurs 11am–7pm; Wed, Fri, and Sat–Sun 11am–5pm. Tram: 10 or 12. T-banen: Nationaltheatret.

Teatermuseet i Oslo (Oslo Theater Museum) In the hometown of Bjørnson and Ibsen, theater buffs flock to this museum mainly to view its theatrical memorabilia. A century and a half of Oslovian theatrical history unfolds here, going through the golden years of the Christiania Theater, where many of Ibsen's plays were performed for the first time. The mementos include pictures and costumes, and exhibitions relive the era of the circus, vaudeville, and the marionette theater. The museum has recordings of some of the great highlights in Norwegian theatrical history, with some of the country's most celebrated artists. There's also a rich collection of ballet costumes and portraits of the actors. Plan on an hour's visit.

Christiania Torv 1. ✆ **22-42-65-09.** www.oslomuseum.no. Free admission. Sun and Thurs noon–4pm; Wed 11am–3pm. Tram: 10 or 12.

Vigeland Museum ★ This museum is for connoisseurs who didn't get enough of the monumental artist Gustav Vigeland in Vigelandsparken (p. 133). Opposite the southern entrance to Frognerparken, this was the 1920s former home of the great sculptor and also served as his studio. When he died in 1943, his ashes were placed in the tower of the museum. On the ground floor, nine rooms show a wide medley of his sculptures and drawings, while two rooms upstairs display plastic sketches, drawings, and woodcuts. His apartment upstairs is comprised of two sitting rooms, a library, and a bedroom—not exactly monastic, but not luxurious at all. Of a certain historical interest, Vigeland also sculpted two busts of two of the most famous of all Norwegians, Edvard Grieg and Henrik Ibsen.

Nobels gate. ✆ **23-49-37-00.** www.vigeland.museum.no. Admission NOK45 ($9/£4.50) adults, NOK25 ($5/£2.50) seniors, students, and children 7–16, free for children 6 and under. Free to all Oct–Mar. June–Aug Tues–Sun 11am–5pm; off season Tues–Sun noon–4pm. T-banen: Majorstuen.

HISTORIC BUILDINGS

Akershus Slott og Festning (Akershus Castle & Fortress) ★★ Kids It has withstood fierce battles, drawn-out sieges, and a few fires, and changed shape architecturally since King Hakon V ordered it built in 1299, when Oslo was named capital of

Norway. A fortress, or *Festning,* with thick earth-and-stone walls surrounds the castle, with protruding bastions designed to resist artillery bombardment. Those moats and reinforced ramparts, evoking a Mel Gibson epic, were added in the mid-1700s. For several centuries it was not only a fortress, but also the abode of the rulers of Norway. Now the government uses it for state occasions. From the well-manicured lawns there are **panoramic views ★** of Oslo and the Oslofjorden. In summer, concerts, dances, and even theatrical productions are staged here. Forty-minute English-language guided tours are offered Monday to Saturday at 11am and 1 and 3pm, and on Sunday at 1 and 3pm.

Festnings-Plassen. ✆ **23-09-39-17.** Admission NOK65 ($13/£6.50) adults, NOK15 ($3/£1.50) children. Sept–May Mon–Fri 10am–4pm, Sat–Sun 11am–4pm; June–Aug Mon–Sat 10am–5pm. Tram: 10 or 12.

Oslo Domkirke (Oslo Cathedral) ★ Oslo's restored 1697 cathedral at Stortorvet (the marketplace) contains works by 20th-century Norwegian artists, including bronze doors by Dagfin Werenskiold and a 1950 tempera ceiling by Hugo Louis Mohr. The choir features stained-glass windows crafted by Emanuel Vigeland (not to be confused with the sculptor, Gustav), and in the transepts are those by Borgar Hauglid. The **pulpit and altarpiece ★**, carved in the late 17th century with lovely motifs of acanthus leaves, also remain to delight. The five-story-tall organ dates from the 18th century and would challenge even a budding Norwegian Liberace. Most visits here take half an hour. A bilingual service (in Norwegian and English) is conducted on Wednesday at noon, and an organ recital is presented on summer Saturdays at 1pm. ***Tip:*** For a great panoramic view of Oslo, go to the nightwatchman's room in the steeple, which was added in 1850.

Stortorvet 1. ✆ **23-31-46-00.** www.oslodomkirke.no. Free admission. Daily 10am–4pm. T-banen: Stortinget. Bus: 17.

Rådhuset (City Hall) Inaugurated in 1950, the City Hall, whose architecture combines romanticism, classicism, and functionalism, has been called everything from "aggressively ugly" to the pride of Norway. Aesthetics aside, the whole world looks toward this simple red-brick building with its iconic double towers every December when the Nobel Peace Prize is awarded. Luminaries such as Yasser Arafat (1994); Martin Luther King, Jr. (1964); Nelson Mandela (1993); and Jimmy Carter (2002) have claimed their prizes under this roof. It houses, among other things, a stunning 25×13m (82×43-ft.) wall painted by Henrik Sørensen, and the mural *Life* by Edvard Munch. Tapestries, frescoes, sculpture, and woodcarvings by Dagfin Werenskiold are also on display. Guided tours in English are available. Be sure to check out the astronomical clock and Dyre Vaa's swan fountain in the courtyard. Allow about 20 minutes.

Rådhusplassen. ✆ **23-46-16-00.** Admission NOK40 ($8/£4) adults, free for children 11 and under. May–Sept daily 9am–5pm; Oct–Apr daily 8:30am–4pm. Guided tours Mon–Fri at 10am, noon, and 2pm. Tram: 10 or 12.

Stortinget (Parliament) This yellow-brick building, our favorite parliament building in Europe, sounds a grace note amidst the urban landscape. The original neo-Romanesque exterior, constructed from 1861 to 1866, has been preserved, and the finest artists decorated the interior, with works depicting scenes from the country's history or daily life. You're shown through on a guided tour and can see where some of the world's most progressive and socially conscious politicians meet. The tours, which last 20 minutes, are open to the public. (There's no need to book ahead.)

Karl Johans Gate 22. ✆ **23-31-35-96.** www.stortinget.no. Free admission. Guided tours in English July 1–Aug 15 Mon–Fri 10 and 11:30am, and 1pm; Sept 15–June 15 Sat 10 and 11:30am, and 1pm. Closed Aug 16–Sept 14 and June 16–30. T-banen: Stortinget. Tram: 13, 15, or 19.

ON BYGDØY

Located south of the city, the peninsula is reached by commuter ferry (summer only) leaving from Pier 3, facing the Rådhuset (Town Hall). Departures during the day are every 40 minutes before 11am and every 20 minutes after 11am, and a one-way fare costs 40NOK ($8/£4). The no. 30 bus from the Nationaltheatret also runs to Bygdøy. The museums lie only a short walk from the bus stops on Bygdøy.

For reviews of Bygdøy's **Vikingskipshuset** (p. 134) and **Norsk Folkesmuseum** (p. 132), see "The Big Six," earlier in this chapter.

Frammuseet ★ Go here to see the world's most famous polar ship, *Fram,* dating from 1892. The brave little ship that Fridtjof Nanse sailed across the Arctic from 1893 to 1896 is perfectly preserved in its original condition. The trip made the handsome, fur-coated Viking one of the most renowned of all polar explorers. The noble *Fram* set out on a second expedition, this one headed by Otto Sverdrup, who sailed around southern Greenland to Canada's Ellesmere Island between 1898 and 1902. For its third and most famous journey, from 1910 to 1912, the *Fram* ventured to the Antarctic under the command of Roald Amundsen, who subsequently became the first explorer to reach the South Pole. Plan on spending half an hour here.

Bygdøynesveien. ✆ **23-28-29-50.** www.fram.museum.no. Admission NOK50 ($10/£5) adults, NOK20 ($4/£2) children, NOK100 ($20/£10) family ticket. May–June 15 daily 10am–5:45pm; June 16–Aug daily 9am–6:45pm; Sept daily 9am–5:45pm; Oct–Apr daily 10am–3:45pm. Ferry: From Pier 3 facing the Rådhuset (summer only). Bus: 30 from the Nationaltheatret.

Kon-Tiki Museum ★ Kids *Kon-Tiki* is a world-famous balsa-log raft. In 1947, the young Norwegian scientist Thor Heyerdahl and five comrades sailed it from Callao, Peru, to Raroia, Polynesia (6,880km/4,266 miles). It was not Heyderdahl's aim to discover new lands. He wanted to prove that the people of Polynesia originally came from South America. He showed how ancient civilizations could have done so by using a raft such as *Kon-Tiki.* Besides the raft, there are other exhibits from Heyerdahl's subsequent visits to Easter Island. They include casts of stone giants and small originals, a facsimile of the whale shark, and an Easter Island family cave, with a collection of sacred lava figurines hoarded in secret underground passages by the island's inhabitants. The museum also houses the original papyrus *Ra II,* in which Heyerdahl crossed the Atlantic in 1970. Although kids like to be taken here, adults will find it fascinating as well. For those who

The Loftiest Lookout Tower in Scandinavia

Tryvannstårnet (✆ **22-14-67-11**), at Voksenkollen, dazzles you with its panoramic sweep of Oslofjord and Sweden to its east. The gallery is approximately 570m (1,870 ft.) above sea level. A 20-minute walk down the hill returns you to Frognerseteren, and another 20-minute walk down the hill takes you to the Holmenkollen Ski Jump, where the 1952 Olympic competitions took place. It's also the site of Norway's Holmenkollen Ski Festival.

Admission is NOK40 ($8/£4) for adults or NOK25 ($5/£2.50) for children. Open May to September daily 10am to 5pm, off season daily 10am to 4pm. Take the T-banen to Frognerseteren (SST Line 1) from near the Nationaltheatret to Voksenkollen (a 30-min. ride). From here, it's a 15-minute walk uphill.

Suggested Itineraries for Oslo

If You Have 1 Day

Arm yourself with a bag of freshly cooked shrimp—purchased right off the shrimp boats at the harbor in front of the Rådhus (Town Hall)—and take a ferry over to the Bygdøy Peninsula. Visit some of Oslo's major attractions—they're within walking distance of each other. Explore the Viking ships, the polar ship *Fram,* the *Kon-Tiki* Museum, the Norwegian Maritime Museum, and the Norwegian Folk Museum. In the late afternoon, go to Frognerpark to admire the Vigeland sculptures.

If You Have 2 Days

On your first day, follow the itinerary above. On your second day, take the Frommer's walking tour (p. 146) and have lunch in a Norwegian restaurant. In the afternoon, explore the Edvard Munch Museum. In summer, during clement weather, visit Studenter Lunden, the students' grove near the National Theater, for some beer and fresh air.

If You Have 3 Days

For your first 2 days, follow the itinerary "If You Have 2 Days" (above). On the morning of Day 3, take another Frommer's walking tour (p. 149), eating lunch along the way. In the afternoon, explore Akershus Castle and the adjoining Norwegian Resistance Museum. By late afternoon, visit the lofty lookout tower at Tryvannstårnet and see the Skimuseet at Holmenkollen, taking in the sweeping view of the Oslo environs. Have dinner at Holmenkollen.

If You Have 5 Days

For the first 3 days, follow the itinerary "If You Have 3 Days," above. On Day 4, head south from Oslo for a 1-day excursion to the Oslofjord country, with stopovers at the Old Town at Fredrikstad; Tønsberg, Norway's oldest town; and Sandefjørd, an old whaling town. Head back to Oslo for the night. On Day 5, see the rest of Oslo's major sights, such as the National Gallery, the Historical Museum, and the Henie-Onstad Art Center, 7 miles from Oslo—a major museum of modern art.

get really interested, they can read Heyerdahl's account of his adventures in his book, *Kon-Tiki,* published in countless editions around the world (available in the museum shop, of course). Most visits to this museum take about 45 minutes.

Bygdøynesveien 36. ✆ **23-08-67-67.** www.kon-tiki.no. Admission NOK50 ($10/£5) adults, NOK30 ($6/£3) children. Apr–May and Sept daily 10am–5pm; June–Aug daily 9:30am–5:30pm; Oct–Mar daily 10:30am–4pm. Ferry: From Pier 3 facing the Rådhuset (summer only). Bus: 30 from the Nationaltheatret.

Norsk Sjøfartsmuseum (Norwegian Maritime Museum) ★ Kids Norway is justly proud of its seafaring past, a glorious tradition that lives on at this museum that chronicles the maritime history and culture of the rugged country, complete with a ship's deck with helm and chart house. One gruesome section focuses on shipwrecks. Many boats speak of adventure, including the Gibraltar Boat, a fragile craft in which Norwegian sailors fled Morocco to the safety of British Gibraltar in World War II. There's also a three-deck section of the passenger steamer *Sandnaes,* and a carved-out tree trunk is said to be the oldest surviving Norwegian boat. The Boat Hall features a fine collection of original small craft. The fully restored polar vessel *Gjoa,* used by Roald Amundsen in his search for the Northwest Passage, is also on display. The three-masted schooner *Svanen* (Swan) is moored at the museum. Built in Svendborg, Denmark, in 1916, *Svanen* sailed under the Norwegian and Swedish flags. The ship now belongs to the museum and is used as a training vessel for young people. Visits require about 45 minutes.

Bygdøynesveien 37. © **24-11-41-50.** www.norsk-sjofartsmuseum.no. Admission to museum and boat hall NOK40 ($8/£4) adults, NOK25 ($5/£2.50) children. May–Sept daily 10am–6pm; Oct–Apr Mon–Wed and Fri–Sun 10:30am–4pm; Thurs 11am–6pm. Ferry: From Pier 3 facing the Rådhuset (summer only). Bus: 30 from the Nationaltheatret.

Villa Grande ★ This was once the most notorious address in Norway, the home of Vidkun Quisling, the Norwegian collaborator and Nazi leader who presided over his conquered country during World War II. In Norway, Quisling and the word *traitor* are virtually the same. With historical irony, the government opened Villa Grande, once known as "Gimie," to the public in 2006, turning it into a Holocaust exhibition. Exhibitions focus on the Nazi-led genocide of millions of Jews and the persecution of other minorities. The exhibition begins ominously as you enter and see a picture of the German ship SS *Donau,* shown on November 26, 1942, at a snowy wharf in Oslo. The villa lies on the peninsula of Bygdøy.

Huk aveny 56, Bygdøy. © **22-84-21-00.** www.hlsenteret.no. Admission NOK50 ($10/£5) adults, NOK25 ($5/£2.50) children 11 and under, NOK100 ($20/£10) family ticket. Tues–Fri 10am–4:30pm; Sat–Sun 11am–4:30pm.

3 PARKS & GARDENS

Marka ★★, the thick forest that surrounds Oslo, is just one of the giant pleasure parks in the area. You can also take a tram marked HOLMENKOLLEN from the city center to Oslomarka, a forested area where locals go for summer hikes and for winter skiing. The ride to the stop at Oslomarka takes only 20 minutes, and there are trains every 30 minutes or so, depending on the season. The area is dotted with about two dozen *hytter* (mountain huts) where you can seek refuge from the weather, if needed. **Norske Turistforening,** Storgata 3 (© **22-82-28-22**), sells maps with the hiking paths and roads of the Oslomarka clearly delineated. It's open Monday to Friday 10am to 4pm, Saturday 10am to 2pm. Our favorite trail—and you should have this pinpointed on a map—is a signposted walk to **Sognsvannet ★**, which is a beautiful loch (lake) flanked by forested hills and encircled by an easy hiking trail stretching for 4km (2$^{1}/_{2}$ miles). In winter, the loch is iced over; but, in summer, those with polar-bear blood can take a dip. Even in summer, swimming here is like taking a bath in ice water. In lieu of swimming, then, you might find the banks of this lake better suited for a picnic.

Botanisk Hage og Museum (Botanical Gardens) ★ We go here just to see the more than 1,000 alpine plants gathered from around the world. Complete with waterfalls, the rock garden is an oasis in the heart of Oslo. It's home to many exotic plants, including cacti, orchids, palms, and a "living fossil" from Japan: the Maidenhair Tree, which was planted in 1870. The tree produces lots of seeds, but they remain unfertilized

A Royal Pair: The Un–Fairy Tale Romance

Prince Haakon of Norway may be a direct descendant of Queen Victoria, but he shares little in common with this staunch monarch. Instead of going to Balliol College in Oxford, as did his father, King Garald V, Haakon was a fun-loving young man on campus at the University of California at Berkeley.

When it came to taking a bride, as he did in Oslo on August 25, 2001, he shocked conservative Norway, challenging one of the world's most tolerant and enlightened societies. Crown Prince Haakon married Mette-Marit Tjessem Hoiby (whom he called "the love of my life"), an unconventional royal pairing. The prince had never been married before, but the princess and future queen of Norway was a divorcée and mother. The couple lived together before marriage in the palace with her 3-year-old son by a previous marriage to a convicted cocaine supplier.

Before marrying the prince, Mette-Marit had a "well-known past in Oslo's dance-and-drugs house-party scene," as the Oslo press so delicately phrased it. It was rumored that pressure was brought on the young prince by conservative elements to give up a claim to the throne, eerily evocative of Edward VII's decision to marry the twice-divorced Wallis Warfield Simpson in the 1930s. It is said that Haakon considered renouncing the throne but decided to maintain his status as the heir apparent. "I think this is where I'm supposed to be," he finally said to the press, ending months of speculation.

King Harald was supportive of his son's decision. The future king himself spent a decade trying to persuade his own father, Olav V, to sanction his marriage to his commoner childhood sweetheart. (The present Queen Sonja was born a shopkeeper's daughter.) Olav himself had also intervened when his daughter, Princess Märtha Louise, was cited as a correspondent in a divorce proceeding in London.

The wedding has come and gone, and there is no more talk of revolution at this "scandal." As Ine Marie Eriksen, a law student from Tromsø, explained, "Why should Prince Haakon and Mette-Marit live by rules of the 18th century? That would take away the very thing that the Norwegian people like about our monarchy."

Since their marriage, the royal couple have had two children—Princess Ingrid, born January 21, 2004, and Prince Sverre Magnus, born December 3, 2005. In 1990, the Norwegian constitution was altered, meaning that the eldest child, regardless of gender, takes precedence in the line of succession. The law is not retroactive, however. That means that Crown Prince Haakon is in line for the Norwegian throne, not his sister, Princess Märtha Louise (born 1971). Haakon was born on July 20, 1973.

because the nearest male Maidenhair Tree grows in Copenhagen. There's a museum in the park with a botanical art exhibit. Plan on spending 45 minutes here.

Sars Gate 1. ✆ **22-85-16-30.** www.nhm.uio.no/botanisk. Free admission. Apr–Sept Mon–Fri 7am–8pm, Sat–Sun 10am–8pm; Oct–Mar Mon–Fri 7am–5pm, Sat–Sun 10am–5pm. Bus: 31.

Slottsparken The park surrounding the Royal Palace (Slottet) is open to the public year-round. The changing of the guard, albeit a weak imitation of the changing of the guard at London's Buckingham Palace, takes place daily at 1:30pm. When the king is in residence, the Royal Guard band plays Monday to Friday during the ceremony. The palace was constructed from 1825 to 1848. Some first-time visitors are surprised at how relatively unguarded it is, without walls or rails. You can walk through the grounds but can't go inside unless you have an invitation from the king. The statue at the front of the castle (at the end of Karl Johans Gate) is of Karl XIV Johan himself, who ruled Norway and Sweden. He ordered the construction of this palace but died before it was finished. Allot about 20 minutes.

Drammensveien 1. Free admission. Daily dawn–dusk. T-banen: Nationaltheatret.

4 LITERARY LANDMARKS

See also "Walking Tour 2: In the Footsteps of Ibsen & Munch," below.

Ibsen Museum Now theatergoers from around the world can pay tribute to Ibsen by visiting his former apartment. In 1994, Oslo opened this museum to honor its most famous writer, Ibsen, who lived here from 1895 until his death in 1906. Within walking distance of the Nationaltheatret, the apartment was where Ibsen wrote two of his most famous plays, *John Gabriel Borkman* and *When We Dead Awaken.* The museum curators have tried to re-create the apartment (a longtime exhibit at the Norwegian Folk Museum) as authentically as possible. The study, for example, has Ibsen's original furniture, and the entire apartment is decorated as though Ibsen still lived in it. The attraction has been called "a living museum," and regularly scheduled talks on playwriting and the theater, recitations, and theatrical performances take place here. Allow 25 minutes.

Henrik Ibsens Gate 26. ✆ **22-12-35-50.** www.ibsen.net. Admission NOK85 ($17/£8.50) adults, NOK25 ($5/£2.50) children. Tues–Sun noon–4pm. Guided tours in English at noon, 1, and 2pm. Tram: 13, 15, or 19.

Oslo Bymuseet (City Museum) Housed in the 1790 Frogner Manor at Frogner Park, site of the Vigeland sculptures (see the earlier listing for Vigelandsparken, p. 133), this museum surveys the history of Oslo over the past 1,000 years—the red coats that the city's first policemen wore, the first fire wagon, relics of the great fire of 1624, the exhibits of the Black Death in 1348–50. It also contains mementos of Henrik Ibsen, from the chair and marble-topped table where he sat at the Grand Café to the glasses from which he drank. Frogner Park, with its streams, shade trees, and lawns, is an ideal spot for a picnic. If not that, then go for that delicious ice cream or pastries served at the on-site Café Mathia. It takes about an hour to view the highlights of the museum.

Frognerveien 67. ✆ **23-28-41-70.** www.oslobymuseum.no. Free admission. Tues–Sun 11am–4pm. Tram: 12.

5 ESPECIALLY FOR KIDS

Oslo offers numerous attractions suitable for children and grown-ups alike. Two that can equal the thrill of a fjord trip are seeing the excavated Viking burial ships at the **Vikingskipshuset** (p. 134) and the Boat Hall at the **Norwegian Maritime Museum** (p. 142), both on the Bygdøy peninsula.

Other sights of special interest to children include the polar exploration ship *Fram* at the **Frammuseet** (p. 141); the balsa-log raft *Kon-Tiki* at the **Kon-Tiki Museum** (p. 141); the **Ski Museum** (p. 138), **Lookout Tower** (p. 141), and ski jump at Holmenkollen; the **Norwegian Folk Museum** (p. 132), depicting life in Norway since the Middle Ages; and the ancient **Akershus Castle & Fortress** (p. 139) on the Oslofjord.

Barnekunst Museum (International Children's Art Museum) Kids Here you can see the world through the eyes of a child. The collection in this unique museum consists of children's drawings, paintings, ceramics, sculpture, tapestries, and handicrafts from more than 30 countries, some of which would have pleased Picasso. There's also a children's workshop devoted to painting, drawing, music, and dance.

Lille Frøens vei 4. ✆ **22-46-85-73.** www.barnekunst.no. Admission NOK50 ($10/£5) adults, NOK30 ($6/£3) children. Mid-Jan to late June and Sept–Dec Tues–Thurs 9:30am–2pm, Sun 11am–4pm; June 24–Aug 15 Tues–Thurs and Sun 11am–4pm. Closed Mon, Fri, and Sat year-round and Aug 15–31. T-banen: Frøen.

Norgesparken Tusenfryd Kids This is the largest amusement park in Norway, conceived as a smaller version of Copenhagen's Tivoli. It includes a number of simple restaurants, a roller coaster with a loop and corkscrew, an amphitheater with all-day entertainment by performers such as musicians and clowns, and many games of skill or chance. In the summer, there is also a water park. The park is 19km (12 miles) south of the Central Station.

Vinterbro by E6/E18/Mossevelen. ✆ **64-97-64-97.** www.tusenfryd.no. All-day ticket NOK210–NOK310 ($42–$62/£21–£31) adults, NOK170–NOK245 ($34–$49/£17–£25) children. Late Apr–Sept daily 10:30am–8pm. Closed Oct–late Apr. Bus: Shuttle service from Oslo's Central Station daily 9:30am–4pm; final return shortly after park closes. Fare NOK40 ($8/£4) adults, NOK25 ($5/£2.50) children.

6 OSLO ON FOOT: WALKING TOURS

WALKING TOUR 1 HISTORIC OSLO

START:	**Aker Brygge.**
FINISH:	**Royal Palace.**
TIME:	**2½ hours.**
BEST TIMES:	**Any day when it's not raining.**
WORST TIMES:	**Rush hours (weekdays 7–9am and 5–7pm).**

Start at the harbor to the west of the Rådhuset at:

1 Aker Brygge

This steel-and-glass complex is a rebuilt district of shops and restaurants that was developed from Oslo's old shipbuilding grounds. It has a fine view of Akershus Castle.

Head east along Rådhusplassen, looking to your left at the:

2 Rådhuset

The Oslo City Hall, built in 1950, is decorated with artwork by Norwegian artists.

Climb the steps at the east end of the square and a small hill to see the:

3 Statue of Franklin D. Roosevelt

Eleanor Roosevelt flew to Oslo to dedicate this statue.

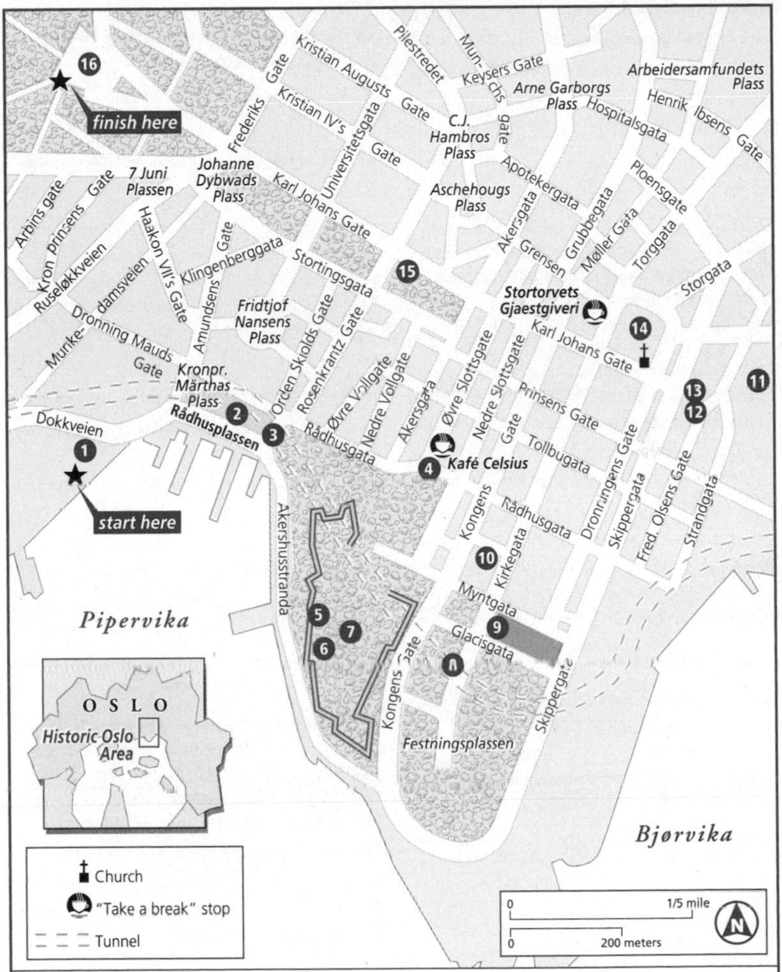

1 Aker Brygge
2 Rådhuset
3 Statue of Franklin D. Roosevelt
4 Christiania Torv
5 Norwegian Resistance Museum
6 Akershus Castle & Fortress
7 Execution Site
8 National Monument to the German Occupation
9 Grev Wedels Plass
10 Bankplassen
11 Oslo Sentralstasjon
12 Karl Johans Gate
13 Basarhallene
14 Oslo Domkirke
15 Norwegian Parliament (Stortinget)
16 Royal Palace (Slottet)

This area is the heart of the 17th-century Renaissance city. Take Rådhusgata east to the traffic hub of:

4 Christiania Torv

The yellow house on your left, the Young Artists Association, was once the home of the dreaded executioner. His fee depended on the type of execution performed.

TAKE A BREAK

To the right of the Young Artists Association is **Kafé Celsius,** Rådhusgatan 19 (✆ **22-42-45-39**), Oslo's oldest residential house. Today it's a charming arts-oriented cafe that serves tasty food. Sandwich prices start at NOK90 ($14/£7.40). You can also order pasta salads and such dishes as ratatouille or tortellini. On cold days, there's a fire in the fireplace. It's open Monday to Saturday 11am to midnight, Sunday 11:30am to 7:30pm.

Continue along Rådhusgata, turning right onto Nedre Slottsgate. Walk to the end of the street. At Myntgata, turn right and pass through a gate. You are now on the greater grounds of Akershus Castle. The first building on the right is the:

5 Norwegian Resistance Museum

The museum has displays on events related to the Nazi occupation of Norway from 1940 to 1945.

Also at the site is:

6 Akershus Castle & Fortress

The structure dates from 1300 but was rebuilt in the 17th century. Take a guided tour and walk the ramparts.

In front of the Norwegian Resistance Museum, pause on the grounds to look at the:

7 Execution Site

Here the Nazis shot prisoners, often Norwegian freedom fighters. There's a memorial to the resistance movement, and you'll have a good view of the harbor in the distance.

Cross the drawbridge to the east, right before Kongensgate, and continue through the castle grounds to the:

8 National Monument to the German Occupation

This commemorates Norway's suffering at the hands of the Nazis.

After seeing the monument, turn left (north) into:

9 Grev Wedels Plass

This is the site of Den Gamle Logen (Freemason's Lodge). In 1850, Ibsen wrote poems here. At no. 9 and Dronningensgatan 4 is the Astrup Fearnley Museum of Modern Art, with changing exhibits of Norwegian and foreign art from the postwar period.

Head north along Kirkegata until you reach:

10 Bankplassen

This former site of the old Bank of Norway is now the Museum of Contemporary Art (Bankplassen 4), with the state collection of international and Norwegian modern art acquired since World War II. This square was once Oslo's social center. Ibsen staged his first play here in 1851 (at a theater that burned down in 1877).

From Bankplassen, turn right onto Revierstredet and left onto Dronningensgatan. At one time the waterfront came up to this point. Go right at the Central Post Office onto Tollbugata. At the intersection with Fred Olsens Gate, turn left and walk to the:

11 Oslo Sentralstasjon

Trains arrive at Oslo's rail hub from the Continent here and depart for all points linked by train in Norway.

Turn left onto the main pedestrian-only street:

12 Karl Johans Gate

The street stretches from the Central Station in the east to the Royal Palace in the west end.

On your right you'll pass the:

13 Basarhallene

Boutiques and shops, hawking everything from food to clothing to crafts, fill this huge complex.

Turn right at Kirkegata, heading for the:

⓮ Oslo Domkirke

This 17th-century cathedral resides at Stortorvet, Oslo's old marketplace. Like the City Hall, the cathedral is decorated with outstanding works by Norwegian artists.

> **TAKE A BREAK**
> Old Oslo atmosphere lives on at the **Stortorvets Gjaestgiveri,** Grensen 1 (✆ **23-35-63-60**), on a busy commercial street. This drinking and dining emporium, dating from the 1600s, is often filled with spirited beer drinkers. A beer costs NOK50 ($10/£5). It's open Monday to Saturday from 11am to 11pm, Sunday (Sept–Apr only) 3 to 9pm.

From Stortorvet, walk west on Grensen until you reach Lille Grensen. Cut left onto this street, returning to Karl Johans Gate. On your left at Karl Johans Gate 22 will be the:

⓯ Norwegian Parliament (Stortinget)

Constructed from 1861 to 1866, it's richly decorated with works by contemporary Norwegian artists.

Continue west along Karl Johans Gate, passing many of the monuments covered on "Walking Tour 2: In the Footsteps of Ibsen & Munch" (see below). Eventually you'll reach Drammensveien 1, the:

⓰ Royal Palace (Slottet)

This is the residence of the king of Norway and his family. The public is permitted access only to the park.

WALKING TOUR 2 IN THE FOOTSTEPS OF IBSEN & MUNCH

START:	**Nationaltheatret.**
FINISH:	**National Gallery.**
TIME:	**2 hours.**
BEST TIMES:	**Any day when it's not raining.**
WORST TIMES:	**Rush hours (weekdays 7–9am and 5–7pm).**

The tour begins at Stortingsgaten 15, just off Karl Johans Gate near the Students' Grove in Oslo's center, site of the:

❶ Nationaltheatret

Study your map in front of the Henrik Ibsen statue at the theater, where many of his plays were first performed and are still presented. The Norwegian Nationaltheatret (✆ **81-50-08-11**), inaugurated in 1899, is one of the most beautiful in Europe.

Facing the statue of Ibsen, continue up Stortingsgaten toward the Royal Palace (Slottet). Cut left at the next intersection and walk along Ruselokkveien. On the right, the **Vika Shopping Terraces,** an unattractive row of modern storefronts tacked onto an elegant 1880 Victorian terrace, used to be among Oslo's grandest apartments. During World War II it was the Nazi headquarters.

Continue along this complex to the end, turning right onto Dronnings Mauds Gate, which quickly becomes Lokkeveien. At the first building on the right, you come to:

❷ Ibsen's private apartment

Look for the blue plaque marking the building. The playwright lived here from 1891 to 1895. When his wife complained that she didn't like the address, even though it was one of Oslo's most elegant, they moved. Ibsen wrote two plays while living here.

Turn right onto Arbinsgate and walk to the end of the street until you reach Drammensveien. At Arbinsgate 1 is the:

❸ Ibsen Museum

In the first building on the left, at the corner of Arbinsgate and Drammensveien, you'll see an Omega store, but look for the blue plaque on the building. Ibsen lived here from 1895 until his death in 1906.

He often sat in the window, with a light casting a glow over his white hair. People lined up in the street below to look at him. The great Italian actress Eleanora Duse came here to bid him a final *adieu,* but he was too ill to see her. She stood outside in the snow and blew him kisses.

The king of Norway used to give Ibsen a key to enter the private gardens surrounding the Royal Palace. Everybody has that privilege today.

Turn right on Drammensveien and continue back to the Nationaltheatret. Take Karl Johans Gate, on the left side of the theater, and walk east. On your left at Karl Johans Gate 47, you'll pass the:

❹ University of Oslo

Aula, the Great Hall of the university, is decorated with murals by Edvard Munch. The hall is open to the public only from June 20 to August 20, daily from 10am to 3pm. For information, call ✆ **22-85-95-55.**

Twice a day Ibsen followed this route to the Grand Café. Admirers often threw rose petals in his path, but he pretended not to see. He was called "the Sphinx" because he wouldn't talk to anybody.

> **TAKE A BREAK**
> The **Grand Café,** Karl Johans Gate 31 (✆ **23-21-20-00**), was the center of social life for the literati and the artistic elite, including Munch. Today a favorite with many visitors, but also with hundreds of Oslovians who appreciate tradition, it is the most famous cafe in all of Scandinavia (see p. 114 for a complete review). On the far wall of the cafe, you can see Per Krogh's famous mural, painted in 1928. Ibsen, with a top hat and gray beard, is at the far left, and Munch—called the handsomest man in Norway—is seated at the second window from the right, at the far right of the window. The poet and playwright Bjørnstjerne Bjørnson can be spotted on the street outside (second window from the left, wearing a top hat), because he wouldn't deign to come into the cafe. You can order food and drink, a big meal, or a snack here.

Returning to the street, note the Norwegian Parliament building (Stortinget) on your right. Proceed left and turn left onto Lille Grensen. Cross the major boulevard, Grensen, and walk straight to:

❺ Akersgata

This street was used for Ibsen's funeral procession. Services were conducted at the Holy Trinity Church on June 1, 1906.

Veer left to see the:

❻ Birthplace of Ibsen's son

On your left, at the corner of Teatergata and Akersgata, is the site of the famous Strømberg Theater, which burned down in 1835. It was also a residence, and Ibsen's son was born here in 1859.

Also on Akersgata is:

❼ Trefoldighetskirken (Holy Trinity Church)

This church was the site of Ibsen's funeral.

A little farther along Akersgata is St. Olav's Church. Turn on the right side of this imposing house of worship onto Akersveien and go to:

❽ Damplassen

This small square—one of the most charming in Oslo—doesn't appear on most maps. Norway's greatest poet, Henrik Wergeland, lived in the pink house on the square from 1839 to 1841.

Take a right at the square and head down:

❾ Damstredet

The antique wooden houses along this typical old Oslo street are mainly occupied by artists.

Damstredet winds downhill to Fredensborgveien. Here, a left turn and a short walk will take you to Maridalsveien, a busy but dull thoroughfare. As you walk north along this street, on the west side look for a large unmarked gateway with wide stone steps inside. Climb to the top, follow a little pathway, and go past gardens and flower beds. Pass a set of brick apartment buildings on the left, and proceed to:

❿ Telthusbakken

Along this little street, you'll see a whole row of early Oslo wooden houses. Look right in the far distance at the green building where Munch used to live.

Walking Tour 2: In the Footsteps of Ibsen & Munch

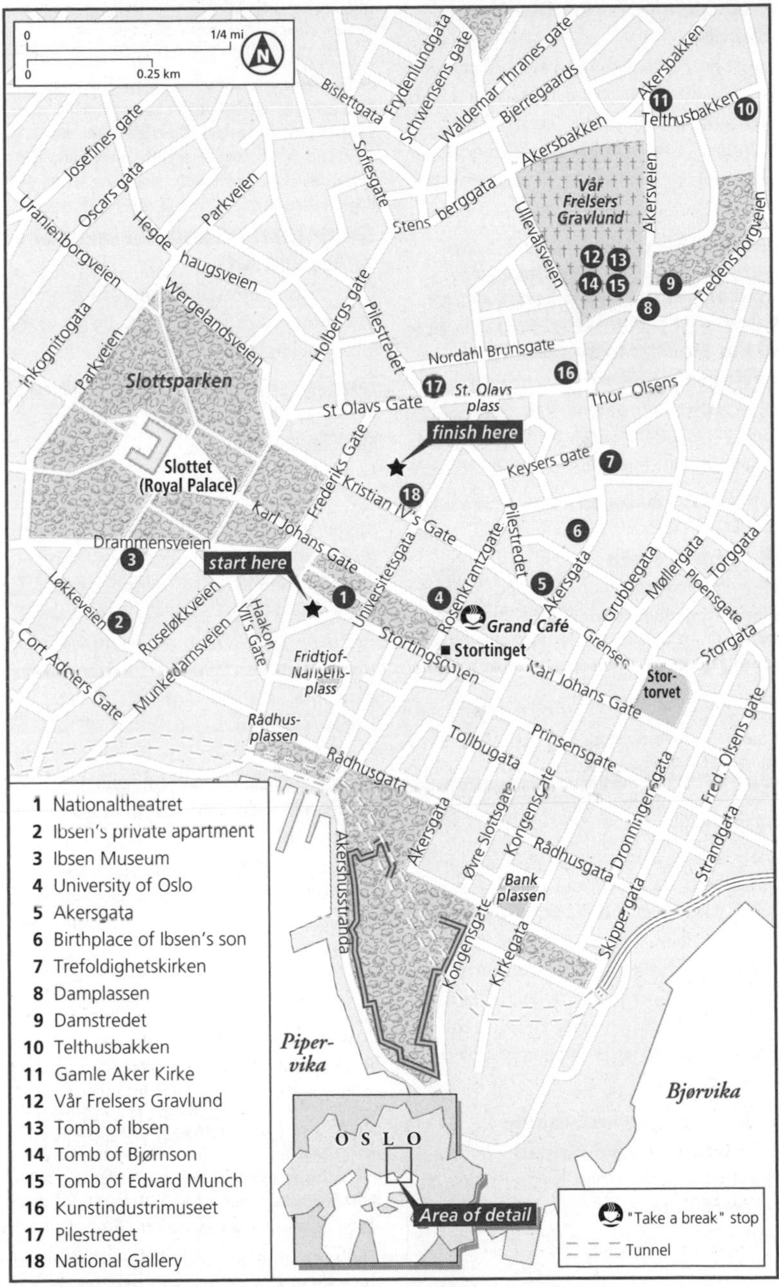

Telthusbakken leads to Akersveien. On your left you can see the:

⓫ Gamle Aker Kirke (Old Aker Church)

Enter at Akersbakken, where Akersveien and Akersbakken intersect. Built in 1100, this is the oldest stone parish church in Scandinavia that's still in use. It stands on a green hill surrounded by an old graveyard and a stone wall.

A short block from the church along Akersbakken (veer left outside the front of the church and go around a corner), you'll come to the north entrance of the city's expansive burial ground:

⓬ Vår Frelsers Gravlund (Our Savior's Cemetery)

In a section designated the "Ground of Honor" are the graves of famous Norwegians, including Munch, Ibsen, and Bjørnson.

Signs don't point the way, but It's easy to see a tall obelisk. This is the:

⓭ Tomb of Ibsen

His wife, Susanna, whom he called "the cat," is buried to the playwright's left. She died in 1914. The hammer on the obelisk symbolizes his work *The Miner,* indicating how he "dug deep" into the soul of Norway.

To the right of Ibsen's tomb is the:

⓮ Tomb of Bjørnson

The literary figure Bjørnstjerne Bjørnson (1832–1910) once raised money to send Ibsen to Italy. Before the birth of their children, Ibsen and Bjørnson agreed that one would have a son and the other a daughter, and that they would marry each other. Miraculously, Ibsen had a son, Bjørnson a daughter, and they did just that. Bjørnson wrote the national anthem, and his tomb is draped in a stone representation of a Norwegian flag.

To the far right of Bjørnson's tomb is the:

⓯ Tomb of Edvard Munch

Scandinavia's greatest painter has an unadorned tomb. If you're visiting on a snowy day, it will be buried because the marker lies close to the ground. Munch died during the darkest days of the Nazi occupation. His sister turned down a request from the German command to give Munch a state funeral, feeling that it would be inappropriate.

On the west side of the cemetery, you'll come to Ullevålsveien. Turn left on this busy street and head south toward the center of Oslo. You'll soon see St. Olav's Church, this time on your left. Stay on the right (west) side of the street. At St. Olavs Gate 1, where Ullevålsveien intersects with St. Olavs Gate, is the:

⓰ Kunstindustrimuseet (Museum of Applied Art)

Even if you don't have time to visit the museum, you may want to go inside to the Café Solliløkken (p. 136).

After visiting the museum, continue along St. Olavs Gate to:

⓱ Pilestredet

Look to the immediate right at no. 30. A wall plaque on the decaying building commemorates the fact that Munch lived here from 1868 to 1875. In this building he painted, among other masterpieces, *The Sick Child.* He moved here when he was 5, and many of his "memory paintings" were of the interior. When demolition teams started to raze the building in the early 1990s, a counterculture group of activists known as "The Blitz Group" illegally took over the premises to prevent its destruction. On its brick-wall side, his masterpiece *The Scream* was re-created in spray paint. The protesters are still in control of the city-owned building, and they are viewed as squatters on very valuable land. It's suspected that if a more conservative government comes into power, officials will toss out the case, throw out the activists, and demolish the building. For the moment, however, they remain in control.

At Pilestredet, turn left. One block later, turn right onto Universitesgata, heading south toward Karl Johans Gate. You'll pass a number of architecturally interesting buildings and will eventually arrive at Universitesgata 13, the:

⓲ National Gallery

The state museum has a large collection of Norwegian as well as foreign art. Two rooms are devoted to masterpieces by Munch.

7 ORGANIZED TOURS

CRUISES AROUND THE FJORD **Båtservice Sightseeing,** Rådhusbrygge 3, Rådhusplassen (✆ **23-35-68-90**), offers a 50-minute boat tour. You'll see the harbor and the city, including the ancient fortress of Akershus and the islands in the inner part of the Oslofjord. Cruises depart from Pier 3 in front of the Oslo Rådhuset (City Hall). They run from mid-May to late August daily on the hour from 10am to 7pm during the high season, less frequently at the beginning and end of the season. Tickets are NOK120 ($24/£12) for adults, NOK60 ($12/£6) for children.

If you have more time, take a 2-hour summer cruise through the maze of islands and narrow sounds in the Oslofjord. From May to September, they leave daily at 10:30am and 1, 3:30, and 5:45pm; the cost is NOK210 ($42/£21) for adults, NOK105 ($21/£11) for children. Refreshments are available onboard.

See the "Summer Evenings on the Oslofjord" box below for information on the outfitter's 3-hour evening fjord cruise, which includes a seafood buffet.

CITY TOURS **H. M. Kristiansens Automobilbyrå,** Hegdehaugsveien 4 (✆ **23-15-73-00**), has been showing visitors around Oslo for more than a century. Both of their bus tours are offered daily year-round. The 3-hour "Oslo Highlights" tour is offered at 10:15am. It costs NOK300 ($60/£30) for adults, NOK150 ($30/£15) for children. The 2-hour "Oslo Panorama" tour costs NOK215 ($43/£22) for adults, NOK105 ($21/£11) for children. It departs at 10:15am. The starting point is in front of the Nationaltheatret. Arrive 15 minutes before departure; tours are conducted in English by trained guides.

8 ACTIVE SPORTS

From spring to fall, the Oslofjord is a center of swimming, sailing, windsurfing, and angling. Daily excursions are arranged by motor launch at the harbor. Suburban forest areas await hikers, bicyclists, and anglers in the summer. In the winter, the area is ideal for cross-country skiing (on marked trails that are illuminated at night), downhill or slalom skiing, tobogganing, skating, and more. Safaris by Land Rover are arranged year-round.

BATHS The most central municipal bath is **Vestkantbadet,** Sommerrogate 1 (✆ **22-56-05-66**), which offers a Finnish sauna and Roman baths. This municipal bath is near the American embassy, just a kilometer (1/2 mile) north from Oslo's center. It's primarily a winter destination and is closed in July. Admission is NOK100 ($20/£10). The baths are open May to mid-August Monday to Friday 1 to 6:30pm, and are reserved Thursday for women only. From mid-August to April, the baths are open Monday and Wednesday 1:30 to 6:30pm, Tuesday and Thursday to Friday 1:30 to 7:30pm, and Saturday 10am to 2:30pm. Prices for massages start at NOK370 ($74/£37) for 30 minutes. If you book a massage (✆ **22-44-07-26**), you can use the baths free.

Frognerbadet, Middelthunsgate 28 (✆ **23-27-54-50**), in Frogner Park, is an open-air pool near the Vigeland sculptures. The entrance fee is NOK80 ($16/£8) for adults and NOK50 ($10/£5) for children. It's open mid-May to mid-August Monday to Friday 7am to 8pm, Saturday and Sunday 10am to 6pm. Take tram no. 2 from the Nationaltheatret.

BEACHES You most likely didn't come to Oslo to go to the beach. Even if you did, you'll find that you often have to swim from a rocky shore. Sun-loving Oslovians, desperate to absorb whatever sun they get on a summer day, often take to whatever remotely

Moments Summer Evenings on the Oslofjord

Summer evenings aboard a boat on the Oslofjord can be restful and exhilarating, but if you happen not to have a private yacht of your own, there are several outfitters who can solve your problem. The best of these is **Båtservice Sightseeing AS** ★, Rådhusbrygge 3 (City Hall Pier no. 3; ✆ **23-35-68-90;** www.boatsightseeing.com), which operates from a low-slung concrete building directly atop one of the piers adjacent to Oslo's City Hall. Between late June and the end of August, weather permitting, they operate nightly cruises that showcase, better than any other means of transportation, the intricate cays, skerries, sandbars, and rocks of the Oslofjord.

You'll travel aboard one of three historic sloops, each of which retains its pinewood masts and complicated 19th-century rigging. During the course of these excursions, you'll be moving by diesel-powered engines, not by wind power. The oldest and most oft-used of the three ships is the *Johanna,* a wood-sided sloop originally built in 1892. Passengers sit at plank-built tables on an open deck, retreating to a glassed-in cabin, or even below decks, if the weather turns foul.

Included in the price are heaping buckets of Norwegian shrimp, served buffet-style from a central table on deck, which you'll peel yourself, and which taste marvelous with the bread, butter, and mayonnaise provided by the cruise director. Beverages come from a cash bar (beer only), and entertainment derives from the vistas and panoramas that unfold on all sides. They include views of the hundreds of private summer homes, often inhabitable only 4 months a year, built alongside the Oslofjord. Departures are nightly at 7pm (late June–Aug only), with a return scheduled for 10pm. The price is NOK355 ($71/£36) per person. Significantly, most of the participants aboard these cruises are likely to be Norwegians, some of them from Oslo, who appreciate the chance for a firsthand view of the midsummer sea and its banks.

resembles a beach. Their few short weeks of summer last until around mid-August, when snow flurries start appearing in the Oslo sky.

Our favorite beach, and the most easily accessible from the center of Oslo, is **Huk,** on Bygdøy peninsula. To reach Huk, take bus no. 30 A—marked BYGDØY—to its final stop. Should you arrive by boat on Bygdøy, follow the signs along Juk Aveny to the beach. Our recommendation is to go over for the day; view the Viking Ship museum, the Folk Museum, and other attractions in the morning; then head for the beach—preferably with the makings of a picnic—for the early afternoon. In case there are any prudes in your party, be duly warned: Half of the beach is reserved for nudists. The nude beach is on the northwestern side. That same warning should go for all beaches in Norway; along with other Scandinavians, Oslovians like to strip down for the beach.

Once you get here, don't expect a traditional Hawaiian beach. The beach is mostly grass lawns and some smooth rocks that you can lie on to sun yourself like a lizard. If the beach at Huk is overcrowded, as it's likely to be on a summer day, take a 10-minute walk through the forest a bit north of where the bus stops. This leads to the more secluded beach at **Paradisbukta.**

These beaches are our favorites mainly because of their proximity to the center, not because they are great sandy strips. But our secret reason to go there is to people-watch. After a day at the beach, you'll soon agree with a common assessment: The people of Norway are among the handsomest and healthiest-looking in the world.

Our second-favorite beach is at **Hovedøya,** on the southwestern shore of the rocky island of Hovedøya. To get here, board boats 92 or 93 leaving from the pier at Oslo called Vippetangen. From late May to mid-August, these boats depart daily from around 6am to midnight.

This is the closest island to the mainland, and it's wildly popular in summer, as ideal for a picnic as it is for walks. The island is riddled with walking paths, most of which lead to the ruins of a 12th-century Cistercian monastery. Our main reason for liking this beach is its fun-loving atmosphere. It's a wonderful break from too much museum-hopping, and it'll give you a good chance to meet with the English-speaking Oslovians (whose initially icy reserve can melt quickly).

You can also reach a number of beaches on the east side of the fjord by taking bus no. 75 B from Jernbanetorget in East Oslo. Buses leave about every hour on weekends. It's a 12-minute ride to **Ulvøya,** the closest beach to the fjord and one of the best and safest for children. Nudists prefer a section here called **Standskogen.**

FISHING Good fishing is to be found in the Oslofjord and in the lakes that envelop Oslo. An especially popular "fishing hole" is the vast area of Marka (see "Skiing," below). You can rent canoes from **Tomm Murstad** at Tryvannsvn 2 at Holmenkollen (✆ **22-13-95-00**) to use for fishing. For information on the nearest place to buy a fishing license, or for more information, contact **Oslomarkas Fiskeadministrasjon** at Sørkeldalen 914, Holmenkollen (✆ **40-00-67-68**).

GYMS Male and female weight lifters call **Harald's Gym,** Hausmannsgate 6 (✆ **22-20-34-96**), the most professional gym in Oslo. Many champion bodybuilders have trained here, and its facilities are the most comprehensive in Norway. Nonmembers pay NOK110 ($22/£11) for a day pass. It's open Monday to Friday from 10am to 9pm, and on Saturday and Sunday from noon to 5pm.

JOGGING Marka, the forest that surrounds Oslo, has hundreds of trails. The easiest and most accessible are at Frogner Park. A great adventure is to take the Sognasvann train to the end of the line, where you can jog along the fast-flowing Sognasvann stream for an hour or so. **Norske Turistforening,** Storgata 3 (✆ **22-82-28-00**), sells maps outlining hiking trails around the capital, and the staff can give you advice about routes.

SKATING Oslo is home to numerous skating rinks. One of the best is the **Narvisen Skating Rink,** Skikersuppa, Karl Johan (✆ **22-33-30-33**), open daily 11am to 9pm, charging adults NOK55 ($11/£5.50) for skate rentals, children NOK30 ($6/£3). The rink is closed from April to November.

SKIING A 15-minute tram or bus ride from central Oslo to Holmenkollen will take you to Oslo's winter wonderland, **Marka,** a 2,579km (1,599-mile) ski-track network. Many ski schools and instructors are available in the winter. You can even take a sleigh ride. Other activities include dogsled rides, snowshoe trekking, and Marka forest safaris. There are 14 slalom slopes to choose from, along with ski jumps in all shapes and sizes, including the famous one at Holmenkollen. For information and updates on ski conditions, you can call Skiforeningen, Kongeveien 5 (© **22-92-32-00**). The tourist office can give you details about the venues for many of these activities.

TENNIS The municipal courts at **Frogner Park** are usually fully booked for the season by the locals, but ask at the kiosk about cancellations. **Njårdhallen,** Sørkedalsceien 106 (© **23-22-22-50**), offers indoor tennis Monday to Thursday from 7am to 10pm, Friday to Sunday 7am to 8pm. Book your court well in advance. During nice weather, you might prefer outdoor tennis at **Njårds Tennis,** Jenns Messveien 1 (© **23-22-22-50**), a cluster of courts that are generally open whenever weather and daylight permit.

9 SHOPPING

THE SHOPPING SCENE

Those who are "born to shop" like Oslo, as it's one of the most shopper-friendly cities in Scandinavia, with traffic-free streets set aside for prospective buyers. The heart of this district is the **Stortorvet,** where more than two dozen shops sell everything from handicrafts to enameled silver jewelry. At the marketplace on Strøget, you can stop for a glass of beer at an open-air restaurant in fair weather. Many stores are clustered along **Karl Johans Gate** and the streets branching off it.

BEST BUYS Look for bargains on sportswear, silver and enamelware, traditional handicrafts, pewter, glass by Hadeland Glassverk (founded in 1762), teak furniture, and stainless steel.

SHIPPING GOODS & RECOVERING VAT Norway imposes a 19.4% value-added tax (VAT), but there are ways to avoid paying it. See "Taxes" in "Fast Facts: Norway," in Appendix A. Special tax-free exports are possible; many stores will mail goods home to you, which makes paying and recovering tax unnecessary.

SHOPPING HOURS Most stores are open Monday to Friday from 9am to 5pm, Saturday 9am to 3pm. Department stores and shopping malls keep different hours—in general, Monday to Friday 9am to 8pm and Saturday 9am to 6pm. Many shops stay open late on Thursday and on the first Saturday of the month, which is called *super lørdag* ("super Saturday"). During the holiday season, stores are also open on Sunday.

SHOPPING MALLS

Mall shopping is a firmly entrenched tradition in Oslo, thanks to the uncertain weather. When it rains or snows, discerning shoppers have several malls from which to choose.

Our favorite place for wandering and shopping in Oslo is **Aker Brygge ★★** (© **22-83-26-80**), a former shipbuilding yard that was recycled into a postmodern complex of steel-and-glass buildings. In all, there are nearly 65 shops here, most of them upmarket fashion boutiques. There are also 40 restaurants, along with pubs, movie houses, and theaters. When it's raining, duck into the indoor shopping mall. Even if you don't buy anything, Aker Brygge makes for a great people-watching experience. The location is right on the harborfront across from the Tourist Information Center at Vestbanen.

Paléet ★★, Karl Johans Gate 37–43, is set on Oslo's most central and most opulent shopping street. The weatherproof complex consists of 45 different shops and boutiques, all of them relatively upscale and flooded with light from skylights. You can purchase candles, incense, sweaters, art, housewares, cosmetics—you name it. Thirteen different restaurants, including burger and beer joints and one serving Indian food, refuel weary shoppers. You can also stop to admire a bronze statue of skating great (and former movie star) Sonja Henie.

Oslo City ★, Stenersgate 1, opposite the Central Station, is the biggest shopping center in Norway—loaded with shops and restaurants. Also near the Central Station, **Galleri Oslo,** at Vaterland, has been called Europe's longest indoor shopping street. Businesses are open daily until midnight, including Sunday. A walkway connects Galleri Oslo to the Central Station.

SHOPPING A TO Z

Antiques

Blomqvist Kunsthandel ★★ Built as an auction house by its original owners in 1870, this place is full of history and style. Its two large rooms have glass ceilings creating tons of natural light. Inside you'll find either one of their six annual auctions or one of their many Norwegian art exhibitions. In 1918, a gallery show released the full collection of an artist by the name of Edvard Munch. His prints and canvasses can still be seen here during temporary exhibitions. While this venue acts as an auction house, items up for bid include antiquities ranging from fine jewelry and paintings to furniture and sculpture. Tordenskiolds 5. ✆ **22-70-87-70.** T-banen: Nationaltheatret.

Arts & Crafts

Baerum Verk ★ Finds For a unique adventure, head outside of town to a restored ironworks site dating from 1610. Here you'll find more than 65 different shops selling handicrafts and other items, including jewelry and woolens, plus exhibitions and six restaurants. If time remains, visit the ironworks museum on-site and see a smelting production dating from the 17th century. Verksgata 15, Baerum Verk. ✆ **67-13-00-18.** Bus: 143 or 153.

Kunstnernes Hus ★★ This is the best place to see and to purchase the latest in cutting-edge Norwegian art. Meaning "Artists' House" in English, this is an artist-run exhibition hall for contemporary art that first opened in 1930 and since that time has been one of the country's major showcases for the presentation of avant-garde national art. On the ground floor are two well-lit galleries and a reception area, and on the floor above are two more sky-lit galleries. Admission is NOK50 ($10/£5) for adults and NOK25 ($5/£2.50) for students and ages 7 to 17. Children 6 and under go in free. Hours are Tuesday and Wednesday 11am to 4pm, Thursday and Friday 11am to 6pm, and Saturday and Sunday noon to 6pm. Wergelandsveien 17. ✆ **22-85-34-10.** T-banen: Sentrum.

Norway Designs ★★★ This is the only store in Norway that came into being as the result of a crafts exhibit. Shortly before it was established in 1957, an exposition of Norwegian crafts went to Chicago and New York, and it attracted a lot of attention. The upscale merchandise here—crystal, pewter, jewelry, and knitwear—emerged from the innovative designs of that exposition. Stortingsgaten 28. ✆ **23-11-45-10.** Tram: 2, 8, or 9.

Books

Bjorn Ringstrøms Antikvariat ★ One of the largest bookstores in Oslo houses a wide selection of Norwegian and Norwegian-American authors. They are also deeply rooted in books pertaining to Norwegian history and politics. A wide range of collectibles can also be found, ranging from antique books and color plates to records and maps. This century-old structure lies directly across the street from the Museum of Applied Art. Sad to report, those days when you could walk in and buy an original edition of Ibsen's plays for $10 have gone with the wind. Ullevalsvn 1. ✆ **22-20-78-05.** T-banen: Stortinget.

Damms Antiqvariat ★★ This is the oldest antiquarian bookstore in all of Norway, in business since 1843. This warm and friendly place is full of history and intrigue, offering a wonderful selection of fiction and travel books. Although they focus mainly on Norwegian titles, you may come across a first edition of a Hemingway or Steinbeck novel. Among some of the more rare treasures, you'll find a page from the *Catholicon,* the first book ever printed with a nonreligious subject matter. Akersg 2. ✆ **22-41-04-02.** T-banen: Stortinget.

Tanum Karl Johan ★ This fine bookstore in the center of town is the largest and most comprehensive in Oslo. It offers a vast selection, including many English titles. Karl Johans Gate 37–41. ✆ **22-41-11-00.** T-banen: Stortinget.

China & Ceramics

Gastronaut This small and intimate space sells an array of its own exclusive china, glass, and cutlery. The china collections from Spain are simple but elegant, and a bit pricey, but worth it if you're serious about your table settings. Spanish olive oils, spices, and specialty foods can also be found here. Bygdøy Alle 56. ✆ **22-44-60-90.** Bus: 30, 31, or 32.

Deli

Fenaknoken ★ This place is the most famous deli in Oslo. Quality, not quantity, is their self-described motto, and they do live up to their words. You'll find everything you need to create the perfect outdoor meal. Cured and smoked meats from all over Europe hang on its walls, along with homemade jams and jellies on their shelves, a wide array of sharp and mild cheeses, and, as they claim, the best smoked salmon ★★★ in the world, although we don't agree with Sean Lennon, who claimed that it is "better than world peace." A specialty of the house is *Fenalnlaar,* cured and seasoned sheep's meat. The only beverage is beer, which is supplied by a local brewery. For your actual picnic, we suggest you take your food to one of the beaches, either **Huk** on the Bygdøy peninsula (p. 154) or **Hovedøya** (p. 155). Tordenskiolds 7. ✆ **22-42-34-57.** T-banen: Nationaltheatret.

Department Stores

GlasMagasinet ★ Claiming that smaller boutiques tend to charge more, locals usually head for this big department store, which specializes in unusual home and kitchen accessories. Since 1739, this has been a leading outlet for knitwear, pewter, traditional rose-painting, and crystal. Today there are more than two dozen fashion shops alone, and **Hadeland Glassverk ★★★** is the largest outlet in Norway for glass goods. You can also find a moderately priced coffee shop and a fairly decent restaurant. Stortorvet 9. ✆ **22-42-53-05.** T-banen: Stortinget. Tram: 11 or 17.

Steen & Strøm ★★ The largest department store in Norway, Steen & Strøm specializes in Nordic items, especially for the outdoors. Look for hand-knit sweaters and caps, hand-painted wooden dishes reflecting traditional Norwegian art, and pewter dinner plates made from old molds. There's a souvenir shop on the ground floor. Kongensgate 23. ✆ **22-00-40-00.** T-banen: Stortinget.

Fashion

For Everyone

H&M This large worldwide chain of stores is very well known for selling fashionable goods at reasonable prices. They carry everything from children's apparel to trendy clothing for men and women. Also on the menu are accessories, including a large selection of handbags and belts. Stenersgate 1 (Oslo City Shopping Center). ✆ **23-15-99-00.** T-banen: Jernbanetorget.

For Men

Peak Performance ★★ This store is definitely the number one choice for the outdoorsman who seeks the most stylish performance clothing. The styles and colors seem limitless: jackets, shirts, accessories, or whatever. Their variety of Gore-Tex and fleece items is also a draw. Jake Gyllenhaal was recently spotted in here, perhaps shopping for a wardrobe for *Brokeback Mountain II.* Bogstadsvn 13. ✆ **22-96-00-91.** T-banen: Majorstuen.

For Women

MA Heavy on Norwegian designers, this fashion boutique also offers some of the best in Italian, Australian, and Belgian designs. Shoes and other accessories are plentiful, too. Prices range from obscene to reasonable. Hegdehaugsvn 27. ✆ **22-60-72-90.** Tram: 15.

Oleana ★ This shop carries the award-winning designs of Solveig Hisdahl. Clothing items are made mainly of wool and silk and include elegant knitwear, skirts, cardigans, and shawls. Other items feature jewelry and silk scarves from some of the top Norwegian designers. Stortingsgaten 8. ✆ **22-33-31-63.** T-banen: Nationaltheatret.

Ove Harder Finseth ★★ This unique clothing store stars the painstaking and laborious productions of designer Ove Finseth. Each one-of-a-kind dress or gown is full of color (no black or gray), intricately detailed, and wonderfully ornate. The client list is quite impressive. Even the princess of Norway had her wedding gown designed here. Custom-made jewelry, bags, and hats are also sold. Pilius Plass 3. ✆ **22-37-76-20.** T-banen: Girneanetorgen.

Soul From Milan to Paris, this store keeps on top of the ever-changing fashion industry. The selection will meet all of your high-fashion needs, from bags by Prada to shoes by D&G. Even Beatle Paul McCartney's daughter Stella is here, with her hot-selling clothing label Chloe. Bygdøy Allé 28. ✆ **22-55-00-13.** Bus: 30, 31, or 32.

Folk Costumes

Heimen Husflid ★★ This leading purveyor of modern and traditional Norwegian handicrafts and apparel carries antique and reproduction folk costumes. More than three dozen different *bunads* (styles) include different regions of Norway, both north and south. Cozy, hand-knit sweaters in traditional Norwegian patterns are a special item. Pewter and brass goods are first-rate. It's about a block from Karl Johans Gate. Rosenkrantzgate 8. ✆ **23-21-42-00.** T-banen: Stortinget. Tram: 7, 8, or 11.

Furniture

Rom for Ide ★★ This is one of those stores that never seems to follow trends but always ends up looking trendy. This furniture outlet, hidden away from the city's shopping streets, specializes in modern yet classic designs. The contemporary and sleek look is the product of Norway's best and brightest new designers. Aside from the furniture, the Norwegian arts and crafts here are also a great buy. Jacob Aallsgate 54. ✆ **22-59-81-17.** T-banen: Majorstuen.

Tanum ★ Finds The furniture sold here is contemporary and stylish. The outlet, which has been in business for 60 years, pushes the envelope when presenting the latest in modern furnishings. Tons of glass-and-steel accents on clean and good-looking pieces are imported from Italy, Germany, Sweden, Denmark, Holland—basically everywhere but Norway. Karl Johans Gate 37. ✆ **22-41-11-00.** T-banen: Stortinget.

Jewelry, Enamelware, Pewter & Silver

David-Andersen ★★★ This outstanding jeweler, established more than a century ago, sells enameled demitasse spoons ★ and sterling silver bracelets with enamel. They're available in many stunning colors, such as turquoise and dark blue. Multicolored butterfly pins are also popular in gold-plated sterling silver with enamel. David-Andersen's collection of Saga silver ★★ was inspired by Norwegian folklore and Viking designs, combined with the pristine beauty of today's design. The store also offers an exquisite collection of pewter items. Karl Johans Gate 20. ✆ **24-14-88-00.** T-banen: Stortinget.

Esaias Solberg ★ Finds Opened in 1849 and long beloved by Oslovians, this is the largest and oldest venue for antique and secondhand gold and silver in Oslo. Brands of watches sold here include Rolex and Patek Phillipe, as well as countless others. They also sell diamond-studded gold and silver necklaces, brooches, and earrings. Outside of jewelry, they also offer some wonderful antique coffee sets, trays, and goblets. The owner of this place has a simple motto: "Antique jewelry is no more expensive than modern jewelry, and any secondhand jewelry sells at half of what it originally cost." Kirkeresten. ✆ **22-86-24-80.** T-banen: Jernbanetorget.

Heyerdahl ★ Want to outfit yourself like a Viking chieftain or bejewel yourself like an ancient queen? Between the City Hall and Karl Johans Gate, this store offers an intriguing selection of silver and gold Viking jewelry. There are articles in pewter and other materials, including Viking vessels, drinking horns, and cheese slicers. The store also has an array of woodcarvings depicting trolls, as well as one of Oslo's largest collections of gold and silver jewelry. Roald Amundsens Gate 6. ✆ **22-41-59-18.** T-banen: Nationaltheatret.

Music

Los Lobos Straight out of 1950s Hawaii, this independent music store caters to all genres and styles of music outside of the mainstream. Aside from music ranging from blues to techno, you'll find cigarette cases, Hawaiian and bowling shirts, tons of denim, belt buckles, snakeskin boots, and much more. Don't expect to find the Top 40 here; this place is for the more alternative music listener. Thorvald Meyers Gate 30. ✆ **22-38-24-40.** Tram: 11 or 12 (to Olaf Ryes).

Norsk Musikforlag This centrally located store's selection of CDs, records, and tapes is the best in Oslo. Kirkergata 30. ✆ **23-60-20-10.** T-banen: Stortinget.

Perfume

Gimle Parfymeri This large and welcoming perfumery is filled with the best in perfume and skin-care items. All employees are trained makeup artists who provide skilled applications and skin-care consultations. They also carry an array of clothing and accessories that are sold exclusively at this store. Bygdøy Allé 39. ✆ **22-44-61-42.** T-banen: Majorstuen.

Souvenirs & Gifts

William Schmidt ★★ Established in 1853, William Schmidt is a leading purveyor of unique souvenirs. It carries pewter items (from Viking ships to beer goblets), Norwegian dolls in national costumes, woodcarvings—the troll collection is the best in Oslo—and sealskin items, such as moccasins and handbags. The shop specializes in hand-knit cardigans, pullovers, gloves, and caps, and a selection of sweaters made from mothproof, 100% Norwegian wool. Fretgof Namser Plass 9. ✆ **22-42-02-88.** Tram: 10 or 12.

Sweaters

Oslo Sweater Shop Some 5,000 handcrafted sweaters are in stock here, close to the Royal Palace. Try them on before you buy. In theory, at least, you can tell the origin of a Norwegian sweater by its pattern and design, but with the increase in machine-made sweaters and the increased sophistication of Norwegian knitwear, the distinctions are increasingly blurred. Here, as in virtually every other sweater shop in Oslo, only about 10% of the sweaters are handmade—the remainder are high-quality and first-rate but most likely were crafted on an electric knitting machine. Sweaters start at around NOK900 ($180/£90), rising to a maximum of NOK3,000 ($600/£300). Other items include necklaces, pewterware, souvenirs, and Norway-inspired trinkets. Next to the Clarion Hotel Royal Christiania, Biskop Gunnerus Gate 3. ✆ **22-42-42-25.** Bus: 30, 31, or 41.

10 OSLO AFTER DARK

Oslo has a bustling nightlife that thrives past midnight. The city boasts more than 100 night cafes, clubs, and restaurants, 35 of which stay open until 4am.

Oslo is also a favorite destination of international performing artists in classical, pop, rock, and jazz music. Autumn and winter are the seasons for cabaret, theater, and concerts. There are four cabarets and nine theater stages throughout the city.

For movie lovers, Oslo has a lot to offer. The city has one of the most extensive selections in Europe, with 30 screens and 5 large film complexes. Films are shown in their original languages, with subtitles.

THE ENTERTAINMENT SCENE

The best way to find out what's happening is to pick up a copy of ***What's On in Oslo,*** detailing concerts and theaters and other useful information. Oslo doesn't have agents who specialize in discount tickets, but it does have an exceptional number of free events. *What's On in Oslo* lists free happenings as well as the latest exhibits at art galleries, which make for good early evening destinations.

The world-famous **Oslo Philharmonic** performs regularly under the leadership of Mariss Janson at the Oslo Konserthus. There are no Oslo performances between June 20 and the middle of August.

If you visit Oslo in the winter season, you might be able to see its thriving opera and ballet company, **Den Norske Opera.** Plays given at the **Nationaltheatret** (where plays by Ibsen are regularly featured) are in Norwegian, so those who know the language should enjoy hearing the original versions of his plays.

THE PERFORMING ARTS

Classical Music

Oslo Konserthus ★★★ Two blocks from the Nationaltheatret, this is the home of the widely acclaimed Oslo Philharmonic. Performances are given autumn to spring, on Thursday and Friday. Guest companies from around the world often appear on other nights. The hall is closed from June 20 until mid-August, except for occasional performances by folkloric groups. The box office is open Monday through Friday 10am to 5pm and Saturday 11am to 2pm. Munkedamsveien 14. ✆ **23-11-31-11.** Tickets NOK200–NOK800 ($40–$160/£20–£80). T-banen: Stortinget.

Opera & Dance

Den Norske Opera & Ballet ★★★ One of the greatest cultural advancements in Norway occurred in the spring of 2008 when this long-awaited opera house opened. It's the new home of the finest opera and ballet troupes in Norway. Built on the Oslo Fjord, the stunning building of avant-garde architecture cost $840 million. The horseshoe-shaped main auditorium seats 1,369 listeners. Stage and theater technology are state of the art. Den Norske plans 300 performances a year. The "Song of Norway" never was better. The box office is open Monday to Friday from 10am to 8pm, Saturday from 11am to 6pm. Kirsten Flagstads Plass 1, in Bjørvika. © **21-42-21-00.** www.operaen.no. Tickets NOK180–NOK450 ($36–$90/£18–£45) except for galas.

Theater

Nationaltheatret (National Theater) ★★★ This theater at the upper end of the Students' Grove opens in August, so it may be of interest to off-season drama lovers who want to hear original versions of Ibsen and Bjørnson. Avant-garde productions go up at the **Amfiscenen,** in the same building. There are no performances in July and August. Guest companies often perform plays in English. The box office is open Monday through Friday from 9:30am to 6pm and Saturday 11am to 6pm. Johanne Dybwads Plass 1. © **81-50-08-11.** Tickets NOK150–NOK400 ($30–$80/£15–£40) adults, NOK85–NOK170 ($17–$34/£8.50–£17) students and seniors. T-banen: Nationaltheatret. Tram: 12, 13, or 19.

SUMMER CULTURAL ENTERTAINMENT

Det Norske Folkloreshowet (Norwegian Evening) performs from July to August at the Norwegian Folk Museum, Museumsveien 10 (© **22-12-37-00** for reservations). The performances are on Tuesday, Wednesday, Friday, and Saturday at 5:30pm. Tickets cost NOK250 ($50/£25) for adults, NOK50 ($10/£5) for children (T-banen: Stortinget).

The ensemble at the **Norwegian Folk Museum,** on Bygdøy, often presents folk-dance performances at the open-air theater in the summer. See *What's On in Oslo* for details. Most shows are given on Sunday afternoon. Admission to the museum includes admission to the dance performance. Take the ferry from Pier 3 near the Rådhuset.

SPECIAL & FREE EVENTS

Oslo has many free events, including summer jazz concerts at the Nationaltheatret. In front of the theater, along the Students' Grove, you'll see street entertainers, including singers, clowns, musicians, and jugglers.

Concerts are presented in the chapel of **Akershus Castle & Fortress,** Akershus Command, on Sunday at 2pm. During the summer, promenade music, parades, drill marches, exhibits, and theatrical performances are also presented on the castle grounds.

In August, the **Chamber Music Festival** at Akershus Castle & Fortress presents concerts by Norwegian and foreign musicians.

The **Oslo Jazz Festival,** also in August, includes not only old-time jazz, but also classical concerts, opera, and ballet performances.

FILMS

American and British films are shown in English with Norwegian subtitles. Tickets are sold for specific performances only. Many theaters have showings nightly at 5, 7, and 9pm, but really big films are usually shown only once an evening, generally at 7:30pm.

Because of the city's long winter nights, film-going is big business in Oslo. Two of the city's biggest theaters are the **Saga Kino,** Stortingsgata 28 (T-banen: Nationaltheatret;

© **82-05-00-01**), and Klingenberg kino, Olav V's Gate 4 (T-banen: Nationaltheatret; © **82-05-00-01**). Most tickets cost between NOK90 and NOK130 ($18–$26/£9–£13) for adults and are half-price for children. During matinees (usually on Mon and Thurs) the cost is reduced to NOK70 ($14/£7) for adults and half-price for children.

THE CLUB & MUSIC SCENE

Dance Clubs & Discos

There are standard age requirements to enter clubs and bars in Oslo and throughout Norway. For those taverns or other places holding a liquor license only for beer and wine, a visitor must be 18 years old or older. For establishments serving hard liquor, the minimum age is 20. In some reviews, varying age requirements are cited where appropriate.

Smuget ★ This is the most talked-about nightlife emporium in Oslo, with long lines of the best and brightest, especially on weekends. It's behind the Grand Hotel in a 19th-century building that was once a district post office. There's an active dance floor with disco music and a stage where live bands (sometimes two a night on weekends) perform. The clientele—mostly ages 20 to 30—includes artists, writers, rock stars, and a cross-section of the capital's night owls. The complex is open Monday through Saturday nights. A restaurant serves Thai, Chinese, Norwegian, Italian, and American food from 11am to 3am; live music plays from 10pm to 3am; and there's disco music from 10pm till very late. Half-liters of beer cost NOK45 ($9/£4.50); main courses run NOK135 to NOK249 ($27–$50/£14–£25). Rosenkrantzgate 22. © **22-42-52-62.** Cover NOK80–NOK120 ($16–$24/£8–£12). T-banen: Stortinget.

Jazz & Rock

Blå ★ This is the leading jazz club in Oslo. Dark and industrial, with lots of wrought iron and mellow lighting, this place books some of the best jazz acts in the world. The crowd is a mix of young and old, dressed in casual but sophisticated attire. The weeknights focus strictly on jazz, with the weekend providing more of a disco atmosphere, recruiting DJs from all over the world to spin the best in techno and house. It's open nightly 11am to midnight. Brenneriveien 9C. © **40-00-42-77.** Cover NOK80–NOK120 ($16–$24/£8–£12). Tram: 11, 12, or 13.

Café Mono If you're looking for a relatively underfinanced punk-rock nightclub with beer-stained walls and a decor that could withstand, undisturbed, an invasion from a foreign army, this is it. It's a haven for the alternative, boozy, and occasionally alienated youth culture of Oslo. There's recorded music virtually all the time, a changing roster of live bands (many of them from the U.S.) appearing every Sunday to Thursday beginning around 10:30pm, and recorded house and garage-style dance music every Friday and Saturday. Whenever there's live music, the cover varies from NOK50–NOK90 ($10–$18/£5–£9); otherwise, it's free. It's open Monday to Saturday 3pm to 3:30am. Pløensgate 4. © **22-41-41-66.** T-banen: Stortinget.

Herr Nilsen ★ This is one of the most congenial spots in Oslo and a personal favorite, in that it hosts some of the top jazz artists in Europe—and America, too. Overlooking the courthouse square, it's the perfect place to while away a snowy evening. The Dixieland music played here evokes New Orleans. Open Monday to Saturday 2pm to 3am, Sunday 3pm to 3am. C. J. Hambros Place 5. © **22-33-54-05.** Cover NOK100–NOK150 ($20–$30/£10–£15). T-banen: Stortinget.

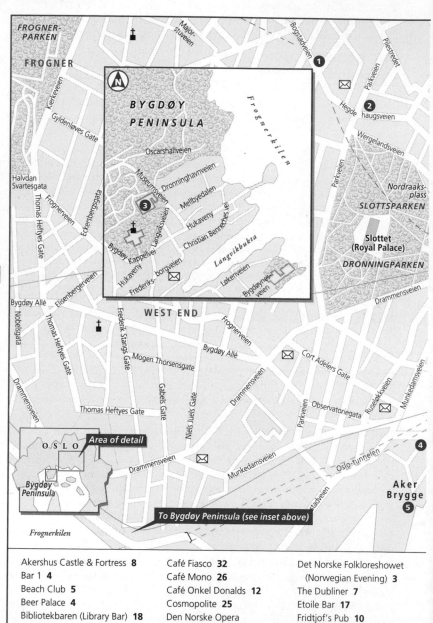

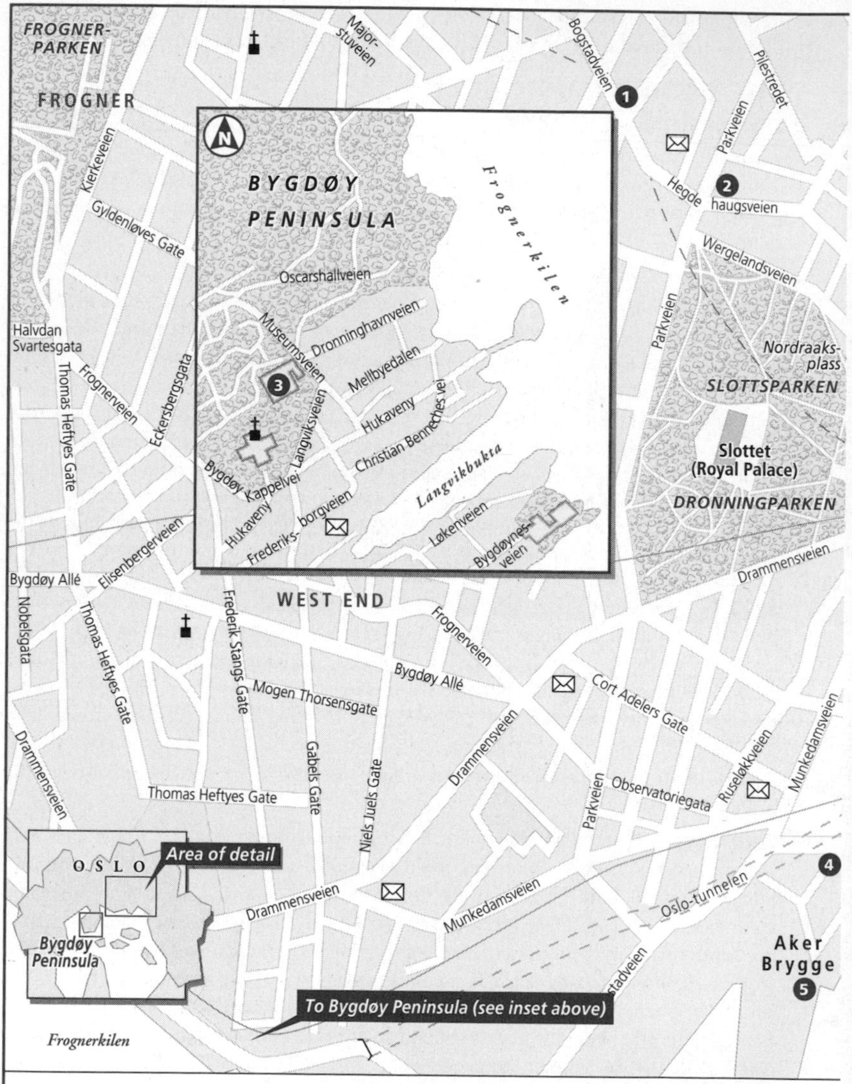

Akershus Castle & Fortress **8**
Bar 1 **4**
Beach Club **5**
Beer Palace **4**
Bibliotekbaren (Library Bar) **18**
Blå **28**
Café-Bar Memphis **29**
Café Fiasco **32**
Café Mono **26**
Café Onkel Donalds **12**
Cosmopolite **25**
Den Norske Opera (Norwegian National Opera) **27**
Det Norske Folkloreshowet (Norwegian Evening) **3**
The Dubliner **7**
Etoile Bar **17**
Fridtjof's Pub **10**
Herr Nilsen **21**
Klingenberg Kino **11**

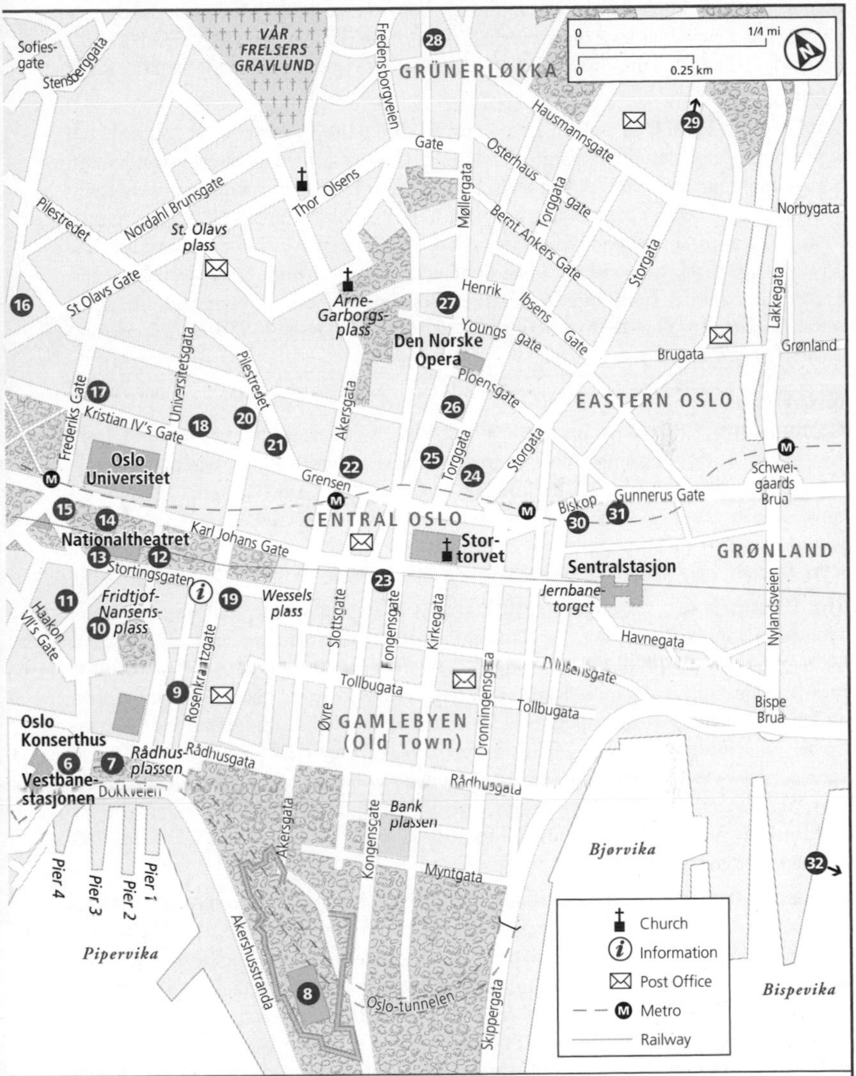

Limelight **30**
London Pub **20**
Lorry **2**
Muddy Waters **22**
Nationaltheatret (National Theater) **14**
Norwegian Folk Museum **3**
Oro Bar **9**
Oslo Konserthus **6**
Oslo Mikrobryggeriet **1**
Restauranthuset Scotsman **23**
Rockefeller/John Dee **24**
Saga Kino **13**
Sir Winston Pub & Piano Bar **15**
Skybar **31**
Smuget **19**
Summit 21 **16**

Muddy Waters ★ If you long for blues music, make your way to this club, with its two fully equipped stages. At least one live band plays almost every night, often with big names, both local and international. This is not necessarily a club for moppets, as a slightly older crowd (at least those over 30) flocks here. Beer costs NOK55 ($11/£5.50). Open daily 2pm to 3am. Grensen 13. ✆ **22-40-33-70.** Cover Fri–Sat usually NOK90 ($18/£9). T-banen: Sentrum.

Rockefeller/John Dee With a capacity of 1,200 patrons, this concert hall and club is one of the largest establishments of its kind in Oslo. It's one floor above street level in a 1910 building, formerly a public bath. Live concerts feature everything from reggae to rock to jazz. When no concert is scheduled, films are shown on a wide screen. Simple foods, such as pasta and sandwiches, are available in the cafe. Most of the crowd is in the 18-to-40 age bracket. It's usually open Sunday to Thursday from 8pm to 2:30am, and Friday and Saturday from 9pm to 3:30am. Showtime is about an hour after the doors open. Torggata 16. ✆ **22-20-32-32.** Tickets NOK100–NOK600 ($20–$120/£10–£60), depending on act. T-banen: Stortinget.

Nightclubs

Cosmopolite This lively international club plays music from all over the world, from Lapland to Africa. A young crowd in their 20s and early 30s flocks here to hear folk music, tango from Argentina, jazz, funk, or whatever. Latin American salsa is often featured, and there's a big dance floor. The club is run by Miloud Guiderk, a North African who truly appreciates the music of the world. Open nightly 8pm to 3am. Møllergata 26. ✆ **22-11-33-08.** Cover NOK50 ($10/£5). T-banen: Jernbanetorget.

The Dubliner ★ This cozy and rustic bar is one of the oldest Irish pubs in Oslo. Housed in a building dating from 1666, the Dubliner holds true to its traditional Irish ancestry once you're inside. The crowd here does vary in age from 20 to 50 but consists mostly of Oslo's Irish and English communities. It offers a typical pub-grub type of menu and plenty of Irish beers on tap. On Friday and Saturday nights, traditional and contemporary Irish music can always be heard. On Tuesday, they hold "jam sessions," where local musicians can bring their instruments and play at being rock stars for the night. It's open Sunday and Monday noon to 1am, Tuesday to Thursday noon to 2am, and Friday and Saturday noon to 3am. Rådhusgata 28. ✆ **22-33-70-05.** Cover Fri–Sat NOK65 ($13/£6.50). T-banen: Stortinget.

Restauranthuset Scotsman The huge, chaotic Scotsman offers several floors of entertainment. For a la carte dining, with an emphasis on beef, head to the cellar restaurant. For nightly live music and a colorful clientele, check out the English-style pub on the first floor. If dancing is your thing, you'll want to stop in the second-floor disco. For gamblers, the third floor features pool tables and off-track horse betting. The fourth floor is strictly for private parties. The fifth and sixth floors have a fully equipped fitness center to help you burn off your trip to the cellar. Open daily 10am to 3am. Karl Johans Gate 17. ✆ **22-47-44-77.** T-banen: Nationaltheatret.

THE BAR SCENE

Pubs & Bars

Bar 1 For a connoisseur of brandy, this small cognac-and-cigar bar is the ultimate. You'll find close to 300 different varieties of cognac, plus a selection of the finest whiskeys. Accompany your libation with one of their wide selection of Cuban and

Dominican cigars. As you could imagine, you'll find a subdued yet sophisticated post-40 crowd here. It's open daily 4pm to 3:30am. Holmensgate 3. ✆ **22-83-00-02.** Tram: 22.

Beach Club This place embodies a classic American diner with Norwegian flair. Its large booths and tables are welcoming—and the burgers are great. There is a bar but not much of a social scene, with mostly businessmen having drinks. Mellow, loungy music plays every night. It's open Tuesday to Friday 11am to 11pm, Saturday and Sunday noon to 11pm. Aker Brygge. ✆ **22-83-83-82.** T-banen: Nationaltheatret.

Beer Palace As you might guess, beer is the main draw at this English-style pub attracting people 20 to 30. The atmosphere is intimate and cozy, with exposed brick walls and couches in the upstairs lounge. A dartboard and pool table provide excitement and entertainment on the first floor. Softly played rock 'n' roll completes the mood. It's open Monday to Thursday 1pm to 1:30am, Friday 1pm to 3am, and Saturday noon to 3am. Holmensgate 3. ✆ **22-83-71-55.** Tram: 10 or 12.

Bibliotekbaren (Library Bar) In a lobby that evokes the Edwardian era, this is a perfect spot for people-watching—that is, middle-aged-people-watching. Sheltered behind racks of leather-bound books, which you can remove and read, you'll feel like you're in a well-furnished private club. There's live piano music at lunchtime, when you can order from a selection of open-faced sandwiches for NOK60 to NOK100 ($12–$20/£6–£10). It's open daily from 10am to midnight; alcohol service starts at 1:30pm. A beer will cost you NOK50 ($10/£5); mixed drinks begin at NOK90 ($18/£9). In the Bristol Hotel, Kristian IV's Gate 7. ✆ **22-82-60-22.** T-banen: Stortinget.

Etoile Bar This elegant bar with a Far Eastern motif is attached to Norway's most famous hotel, the Grand. You might see members of Parliament from across the street. The "Star Bar" has views of historic Oslo. Business people from out of town mingle at night with a young, spirited Oslo crowd. To reach the bar, you take a special elevator to the right of the hotel entrance. Beers cost NOK59 ($12/£5.90); stronger drinks run from NOK95 ($19/£9.50). Open Monday to Thursday 3pm to 1am, Friday and Saturday 3pm to 2am, Sunday 6pm to 2am. In the Grand Hotel, Karl Johans Gate 31. ✆ **23-21-20-00.** T-banen: Stortinget.

Fridtjof's Pub This Norwegian pub offers a cozy retreat for a late-night drink. It consists of a ground floor with deep red walls, comfortable sofas, and some tables and chairs. The second floor has much of the same, providing an unobstructed view of the crowd below whose ages range from 20 to 50. Both floors have interesting photos of polar expeditions, mainly because it's named after Fridtjof Nansen, the first Norwegian to successfully explore the North Pole. In summer, the party usually moves outside, where you can enjoy views of the harbor and city hall directly across the street. It's open daily noon to 1am. Fridtjof Nansen's Plass 7. ✆ **93-25-22-30.** T-banen: Nationaltheatret.

Limelight Steeped in the atmosphere of the theater, this fashionable bar next door to the Oslo Nye Theater is a favorite rendezvous for drinks before or after a show. It draws mainly a middle-aged crowd and is open Tuesday to Saturday 6pm to 1am. Closed June 21 to August 11. Beer and mixed drinks cost from NOK80 ($16/£8) and up. In the Grand Hotel, Karl Johans Gate 31. ✆ **23-21-20-00.** T-banen: Stortinget.

Oro Bar This glamorous tapas bar, associated with the restaurant Oro, evokes the stylish and hip locales of warmer climates. An intensely fashionable crowd in their 30s and 40s—and in intensely expensive clothing—drops in for meals and people-watching. You can eat or just have a drink. A heaping platter of assorted tapas is NOK160 to NOK220

($32–$44/£16–£22). It's open Monday to Saturday 6pm to 2am. Tordenskiolds 6A (entrance on Kjeld Stubs Gate). ✆ **23-01-02-40.** T-banen: Stortinget.

Oslo Mikrobryggeriet This small, English-style pub attracts a mixed, 30-something crowd. Aside from some cognac and whiskey, offerings include six in-house beers, the most popular being "Oslo Pils." With its cozy and warm atmosphere and good music, this brewery is sure to please. It's open daily 3pm to 1am. Bogstadvn 6. ✆ **22-56-97-76.** T-banen: Majotsstuem.

Sir Winston Pub & Piano Bar In the style of a traditional English pub, this place has a cozy, friendly atmosphere with comfortable couches and laid-back lounge music. You'll find anyone here from slick businessmen sipping martinis to neighborhood college kids putting back a few pints while watching the game. Books and pictures of Sir Winston Churchill crowd the wall. An open fireplace provides warmth on cold Norwegian nights. Open Monday to Wednesday 11am to 1am, Thursday 11am to 2am, Friday and Saturday 11am to 3am, and Sunday noon to 1am. Karl Johans Gate 10. ✆ **22-41-14-41.** T-banen: Jernbanetorget.

Skybar ★ On the top floor of the Radisson SAS Plaza Hotel, this bar is known as the most vertigo-inducing and panoramic in Oslo. And at 100m (328 ft.) above the ground, it's also one of the tallest bars in Europe. In the ultramodern interior, surrounded by a glass ceiling and walls, you'll find Oslo's young, professional elite in their 20s, 30s, and 40s. The view and people-watching are worth the trip. It's open Monday to Thursday 4pm to 1am, Friday and Saturday 4pm to 1:30am. Sonja Henie Plass 3. ✆ **22-05-80-00.** T-banen: Central Station.

Summit 21 ★ On the 21st floor of the Radisson SAS Scandinavia Hotel, this bar boasts one of the best crowds and views in town. However, it's mainly known for serving Oslo's best strawberry daiquiris and for its view of the city from the men's-room window. Frequented by businesspeople, and almost everyone else between the ages of 30 to 60, the lively bar is also popular with out-of-towners. It's open Monday to Thursday 4pm to 1am, Friday and Saturday 4pm to 2am. Holbergsgate 30. ✆ **23-29-30-00.** T-banen: Nationaltheatret.

Cafes

Café-Bar Memphis This is a hip, industrial-looking bar with a fondness for such U.S.-derived kitsch as Elvis memorabilia and late, late drunken nights that feature Jack Daniels and beer. There's a limited roster of menu items (seafood pastas, scrambled eggs with ham or bacon and toast), but most of the clients come to sip cocktails, priced at NOK75 to NOK95 ($15–$19/£7.50–£9.50), with friends and acquaintances. It's open Monday to Thursday 11am to 1am, and Friday and Saturday 11am to 3am. Thorvald Meyers Gate 63. ✆ **22-04-12-75.** Tram: 11, 12, 13, or 30.

Café Fiasco Although the owners established this cafe to cater to commuters, the business goes way beyond just serving a fast glass of beer to travelers waiting for their trains. It's oddly located on a sloping, pedestrian ramp that interconnects the bus and railway stations, with views of the surrounding skyscrapers. Inside you'll find a welcome jolt of humanity and a sense of multiculturalism. Reggae, soca, and hip-hop music blare over a sometimes scruffily dressed crowd that's far from bourgeois. Coffee, depending on what's in it, costs from NOK16 to NOK76 ($3.20–$15/£1.60–£7.60); cocktails begin at NOK76 ($15/£7.60). Late at night, long after the commuter trade has ended, the place and surrounding pedestrian passageways become an aggressive singles scene. It's open Monday to Thursday 9am to 1am, Friday 9am to 3am, Saturday 11am to 3am, and Sunday noon to 1am. Schweigaardsgate 4. ✆ **22-17-66-50.** T-banen: Jernbanetorget.

Café Onkel Donalds Of the many bars and pubs that flourish after dark in Oslo, this is the most artfully designed (in this case, by well-known Norwegian architect Petter Abrahamsen in 2001). Its soaring interior spaces evoke the entranceway to a postmodern opera house, and a network of short staircases will take you from the surging energy of the glossy-looking main bar to a series of more intimate mezzanines. The house special cocktail is an Onkel Donald, a head-spinner combining vodka, peach liqueur, cranberry juice, and sour mash. Lots of romances have credited this bar as their catalyst. It's open Monday to Wednesday 11am to midnight, Thursday to Saturday 11am to 3am, and Sunday noon to 2am. Universitesgata 26. ✆ **23-35-63-10.** T-banen: Nationaltheatret.

Lorry This busy, suds-drenched cafe was established 120 years ago as a working-class bar. Since then, the surrounding neighborhood (virtually across the street from the park that flanks the Royal Palace) has zoomed upward in prestige and price. Now the cafe's low-slung, wood-sided building is tucked among villas. There's an outdoor terrace for warm weather dining, but the heart and soul of the place is its Victorian, black-stained interior. Offerings include 130 kinds of beer, 12 of which are on tap. The menu consists of a short list of platters of the day, priced at NOK112 to NOK219 ($22–$44/£11–£22) each, but from around 10:30pm to closing, all everybody seems to do here is drink. It's open Monday to Saturday 11am to 3:30am, and Sunday noon to 1:30am. Parkveien 12. ✆ **22-69-69-04.** Tram: 11.

Gay & Lesbian Bars

This city of slightly more than 500,000 residents has few gay bars. Pick up a copy of *Blick* for NOK35 ($7/£3.50), available at most newsstands within the central city. Otherwise, call Gay/Lesbian Visitor Information, Kongensgate 12, 0153 Oslo (✆ **23-10-39-39**), Monday to Friday 9am to 4pm.

London Pub This is the most consistent and reliable gay pub in Oslo, with a relatively mature crowd of unpretentious gay men and—to a much lesser extent—women. Set within the cellar of a building a few steps from the prestigious Bristol Hotel, it contains a battered looking, beer hall–style trio of underground rooms with two bar areas and a pool table. At its best—during busy periods, usually late in the week—this place can be fun, convivial, and genuinely welcoming to newcomers from faraway places. At its worst, it can be glum and depressing. Whether you like it or not, this is a mainstay of gay life in Oslo. It's open daily from 3pm to 4am. Another bar, **Chairs,** is upstairs and is a bit more animated and festive than its downstairs cousin. It's open daily 3pm to 3:30am. C. J. Hambros Plass 5 (entrance on Rosenkrantzgate). ✆ **22-70-87-00.** T-banen: Stortinget.

Side Trips from Oslo

The fjord towns within easy striking distance of Oslo are filled with history and rich in the lore of the area's Viking past. You can explore the east or west side of the Oslofjord. With time for only one, we suggest the historic east side, centering around Fredrikstad and Halden.

Stretching for 100km (62 miles), Oslofjord is Oslo's link to the open sea. Touring the fjord's western and eastern banks is richly rewarding. The eastern shore also has many beaches with fine sands frequented by Oslovians in summer, especially in July. Even then, however, the waters may be too cold for you if you come from hotter climes than Norway. The western side of the fjord was the site of several Viking settlements, and some of their remains or ruins can be seen today.

1 FREDRIKSTAD: NORWAY'S OLDEST FORTIFIED TOWN ★

96km (60 miles) S of Oslo; 34km (21 miles) S of Moss

If your busy schedule allows you to visit only one mellow old town along the Oslofjord, make it this one. Lying at the mouth of Glomma River, Fredrikstad is Norway's oldest fortified town. Visitors come here mainly to see the Old Town **(Gamlebyen),** one of the best preserved in eastern Norway.

King Fredrik II founded the town as a trading post between the mainland of Europe and western Scandinavia. Its characteristic landmarks are the 1880 cathedral and its delicate, silver-arched Glomma Bridge, which stretches 824m (2,703 ft.) from end to end and rises 40m (131 ft.) over the water.

ESSENTIALS

GETTING THERE Trains from Oslo's Central Station depart for Fredrikstad about every 2 hours. The trip takes about 1 hour from central Oslo. Call ✆ **81-50-08-88** or visit www.nsb.no for rail information.

Frequent bus service operates daily from Oslo to Fredrikstad, the trip taking 1½ hours. Take Hwy. E6 south from Oslo and head toward Moss. Continue past Moss until you reach the junction at Rte. 110, and follow the signs south to Fredrikstad. Visit www.nor-way.no for information.

VISITOR INFORMATION The **Fredrikstad Turistkontor** is Tøihusgata 41 (✆ **69-30-46-00;** www.fredrikstad-hvaler.no). It's open June 10 to August 24 Monday to Friday 9am to 5pm, Saturday to Sunday 11am to 4pm. The rest of the year, it's open Monday to Friday from 9am to 4:30pm. You can also rent bikes here.

SPECIAL EVENTS During the second week of every July, the **Glomma Festival,** named for the town's river, takes place in Fredrikstad. Many Oslovians drive south to attend this 1-week program of events, highlighted by musical performances. Ritual "duels" are staged, along with sailing-ship exhibitions and regattas.

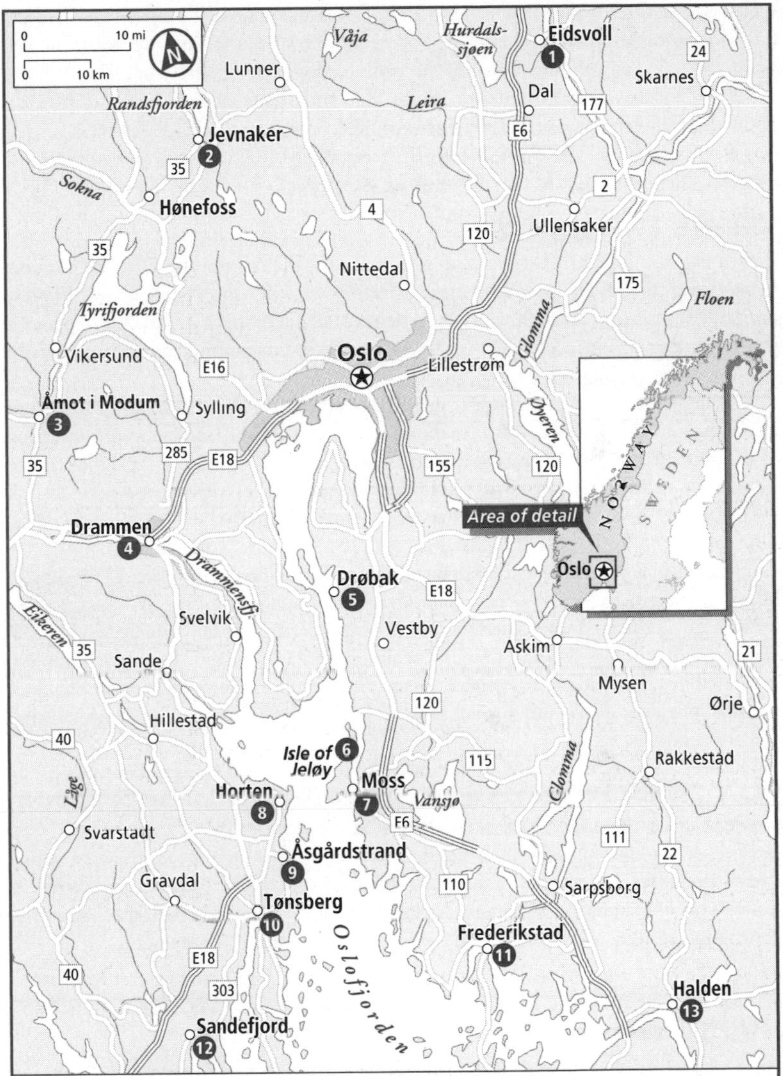

Åmot i Modum **3**
Åsgårdstrand **9**
Drammen **4**
Drøbak **5**
Eidsvoll **1**
Frederikstad **11**
Halden **13**
Horten **8**
Isle of Jeløy **6**
Jevnaker **2**
Moss **7**
Sandefjord **12**
Tønsberg **10**

GETTING AROUND Across the river on the west is the modern industrial part of town; although a bridge links the areas, the best way to reach the Old Town is by ferry, which costs NOK20 ($4/£2). The departure point is about 4 blocks from the Fredrikstad railroad station at Strandpromenaden. Follow the crowd out the main door of the station, turn left, and continue down to the bank of the river. The ferry operates Monday to Friday 5:30am to 11pm, Saturday 7am to 1am, and Sunday 9:30am to 11pm. You can also travel between the two areas by bus (nos. 360 or 362).

To call a **taxi,** dial © **69-36-26-00.** If the weather is fair, we recommend renting a **bicycle.** They're available at the tourist office (see above).

SEEING THE SIGHTS

Fredrikstad was founded in 1567 as a marketplace at the mouth of the River Glomma. **Gamlebyen** (the **Old Town**) ★ became a fortress in 1663 and continued in that role until 1903, boasting some 200 guns in its heyday. It still serves as a military camp and is the best-preserved fortress town in Scandinavia, but the moats and embankments make for an evocative walk.

The main guardroom and the old prison contain part of the **Fredrikstad Museum,** Tøihusgata 41 (© **69-95-85-00**). At the southwestern end of Gamblebyen is a section of the museum in a former guardhouse from 1731. Inside is a model of the old town and a collection of artifacts, both civilian and military, collected by city fathers over a span of 300 years. It's open Tuesday to Sunday from 11am to 4pm; closed October to April. Admission is NOK40 ($8/£4) for adults, NOK20 ($4/£2) for children.

The cathedral of Fredrikstad, **Fredrikstad Domskirke,** Ferjestedsveien (© **69-30-02-80**), was constructed in 1860 in a flamboyant Gothic Revival style. Its most notable features are its stained-glass windows by Emanuel Vigeland, the younger and lesser-known brother of Norway's most famous sculptor, Gustav Vigeland. The church was also decorated by other leading Norwegian artists. The Domkirke lies on the western bank of the Glomma and opens onto a small park. It is open Tuesday to Friday 11am to 3pm, and admission is free.

Outside the gates of the Old Town stands what remains of **Kongsten Festning,** the fortress of Fredrikstad, which was constructed on Gallows Hill and used by the townspeople as an execution site for criminals. When the Swedes took over the site in 1677, they fortified the stronghold with 20 cannons, underground chambers, passages, and a strong arsenal. Today you can scramble among the embankments, walls, stockades, and turrets. It is always open, charging no admission. To reach it, walk 15 minutes beyond the Gamlebyen drawbridge, turning off Tornesveien at the Fredrikstad Motell & Camping.

Finds Insegran: Famous in Norse Sagas

If you like to read Norse sagas, visit the ruins of the 13th-century fortress **Insegran** on an island directly west of Gamlebyen. This once-mighty fortress stood as a fortification against the advancing Swedish armies of the mid-1600s. Various installations are exhibited here in the summer. Insegran is only 400m (1,312 ft.) west of the Old Town, but there is no ferry link. You have to drive south on Rte. 108 until you see the signposted turnoff.

SHOPPING

Since Fredrikstad's heyday as a trading port and merchant base, the Old Town has attracted craftspeople and artisans, many of whom create their wares in historic houses and barns. Many of these glassblowers, ceramic artists, and silversmiths sell their products at local shops.

Glashytta This rustic shop acts as a retail store and glassblowing studio whose merchandise is sold all over the country. The artisans specialize in everything glass, such as stemware and carafes, plates, bowls, and paperweights. You can also specify what you need and watch your custom creation come to life through the skilled hands of local craftspeople. The glass comes in a wide array of colors. Shop hours are Monday to Saturday 8am to 5pm. Torsnesvn 1. ✆ **69-32-28-12.** Bus: 541.

WHERE TO STAY

Hotel City ★ This is no mere hotel, but rather the entertainment center of town. Situated in the town center near the rail station, this stylish and modern hotel offers well-appointed accommodations. All rooms are furnished with good taste and comfort in mind. Each unit is well maintained and equipped with tidy bathrooms. The fifth floor is known as the "safari floor." Not only is this the one floor where smoking is permitted, but also each room is done in a jungle theme with wicker-accented furnishings, tiger-print carpeting, and wall art depicting jungle landscapes and wildlife. The hotel also has two good restaurants, one serving an a la carte international menu, the other with lighter pizza-and-burger fare.

Nygard 44-46, N-1600 Fredrikstad. ✆ **69-38-56-00.** Fax 69-38-56-01. www.hotelcity.no. 110 units. Sept–May NOK1,450 ($290/£145) double; June–Aug NOK1,100 ($220/£110) double. AE, DC, MC, V. Parking NOK140 ($28/£14). Bus: 31. **Amenities:** 3 restaurants; 4 bars; nightclub; sauna; laundry service/dry cleaning; nonsmoking rooms; rooms for those w/limited mobility. *In room:* TV, Wi-Fi (in most), minibar (in some), hair dryer (in some).

Victoria Hotel ★ Established in 1883 near the cathedral park, this Art Nouveau structure is the town's oldest hotel. We prefer its antique style and homey comfort over the Hotel City (see above). Like its competitor, the Victoria lies in the heart of town and affords wonderful views of the grounds of the Fredrikstad cathedral. Many renovations have resulted in the welcoming and cozy hotel you'll find today. Each comfortable guest room is well furnished in a classic English style, and all of them contain neatly kept bathrooms.

Turngaten 3, N-1600 Fredrikstad. ✆ **69-38-58-00.** Fax 69-38-58-01. 65 units. Sept–May NOK1,500 ($300/£150) double; June–Aug NOK1,100 ($220/£110) double. Rates include buffet breakfast. AE, DC, MC, V. Parking NOK120 ($24/£12). Bus: 31. **Amenities:** Restaurant; bar; laundry service/dry cleaning; nonsmoking rooms. *In room:* TV, Wi-Fi, hair dryer.

WHERE TO DINE

Balaklava Guestgiveri ★ NORWEGIAN/INTERNATIONAL For tradition and atmosphere, this restaurant has no competition in the Old Town (although Engelsviken Brygge, below, outside of town is even more atmospheric). It was built in 1803 as the home of the village priest in a style known in North America as "carpenter Gothic." Over 200 years later, simple but flavorful meals are served near a massive fireplace in the cellar or, weather permitting, in the outdoor courtyard. The well-prepared fare includes baked salmon with dill sauce, filet of sole with lemon-butter sauce, and fish-and-clam casserole with herbs. An assortment of fresh game dishes is served when the autumn winds blow.

Faergeportgaten 78. ✆ **69-32-30-40.** Reservations recommended. 3-course set-price menu NOK495 ($99/£50); 4-course set-price menu NOK585 ($117/£59). AE, DC, MC, V. Summer daily 11am–10pm; winter daily 6–11pm.

Engelsviken Brygge ★ Finds SEAFOOD This hideaway restaurant is set at the edge of the crescent-shaped bay that's dominated by the fishing hamlet of Engelsviken, population about 400 hardy souls. Despite its remote locale, it's sought out for its atmosphere by diners from as far away as Oslo. It originated a century ago as a simple fisherman's cottage, but in the mid-1990s, its owners added big windows overlooking the sea, enlarged its premises to include a modern kitchen, slapped on some coats of bright red paint, and started serving fish dishes that have since become legendary. One good example is the creamy fish soup loaded with chunks of fish and shellfish; you can order this excellent dish as a starter or main course. Other offerings include grilled Atlantic halibut with a Béarnaise sauce; a risotto-inspired shrimp and oyster rice; a "symphony" platter loaded high with filet of salmon, catfish, and sea devil; and grilled, poached, or fried versions of most of the fresh local fish. For anyone not particularly interested in seafood, there's also a juicy version of fried beefsteak studded with chunks of garlic and served with a creamy peppercorn sauce.

Engelsvikveien 6, in the hamlet of Engelsviken, 15km (9¼ miles) northwest of Fredrikstad. ✆ **69-35-18-40.** www.engelsvikenbrygge.no. Reservations recommended. Main courses NOK185–NOK395 ($37–$79/£19–£40). AE, DC, MC, V. Daily noon–midnight. From Fredrikstad, follow the signs to Oslo for 4.8km (3 miles), and then turn left onto the road signposted ENGELSVIKEN.

Majorstuen Kids INTERNATIONAL Sizzling pizzas and fresh fish platters draw both locals and visitors to this 18th-century house at the edge of Old Town. Its warm-weather outdoor terrace is one of the most popular places in town. Inside is both a pub and a large dining room that attracts a lot of families with small children for its unpretentious but plentiful food. Among the most popular dishes are pizzas, filet of beef served with vegetables and salad, Wiener schnitzel, and marinated whale steak in black peppercorn sauce (eco-unfriendly as it may be). Majorstuen is the only restaurant in the region that offers whale steak year-round.

Vollportgatan 73. ✆ **69-32-15-55.** Reservations recommended. Main courses NOK160–NOK280 ($32–$56/£16–£28); pizzas (for 1–4 people) NOK155–NOK195 ($31–$39/£16–£20). AE, DC, MC, V. Sun–Thurs noon–9pm; Fri–Sat noon–10pm.

SIDE TRIPS FROM FREDRIKSTAD

Fredrikstad is most often visited on a day trip from Oslo. However, if you'd like to stay at one of the few hotels in Fredrikstad (see above), you can enjoy a day or two exploring some intriguing nearby sights.

The most concentrated collection of archaeological monuments in Norway lies along Rte. 110 between Fredrikstad and Sarpsborg to the east. Norwegians have dubbed the highway **Oldtidsveien,** or **"Old Times Way" ★**. Along this historic sunken road between the two towns, many ancient stoneworks and rock paintings have been found. Look for the signposts as you drive along.

The most idyllic way to tour the Oldtidsveien is by bike if the weather is fair. (If it's not, you really shouldn't even make this trip.) Bike rentals are possible at the Fredrikstad tourist office (see above).

If you take Rte. 110, you will approach all the clearly marked attractions below. Along the trail you'll come first to **Solberg,** a hamlet with a trio of panels featuring nearly 100 carved figures, thought to be 3,000 years old. In the village of **Gunnarstorp,** you can see

Fun Facts Bridge by Leonardo da Vinci

In Tuscany, Leonardo da Vinci drew the plans for a bridge in 1502. It was never built in his day. However, in 2001, da Vinci's stunningly modern pedestrian bridge opened in Norway, of all places.

The 99m (325-ft.) laminated timber bridge links Norway with its eastern neighbor, Sweden, at the town of **Aas,** a 26km (16-mile) drive south of Oslo. Many Oslovians, who have no real intention of going to Sweden, drive down to walk across this remarkable piece of Renaissance engineering.

Of course, da Vinci had a 216m (708-ft.) stone span in mind to cross the Golden Horn inlet at the mouth of the Bosporus between Peta and Istanbul. Sultan Bejazet II, at that time a patron of da Vinci, feared that it was impractical to build such a bridge. The plan died until the original da Vinci drawings were uncovered among some documents in the late 1950s.

Although only a scaled down version of what da Vinci designed, it's a stunning bit of engineering, standing 8m (26 ft.) high at its pinnacle.

several standing stones, including a few dating from the Iron Age as well as a Bronze Age burial ground. Other ancient attractions are found at the village of **Begby,** which has some depictions of ancient people, including boats and wild animals. Rock paintings at **Hornes** depict nearly two dozen ancient boats with oarsmen.

The hamlet of **Hunn** contains the largest archaeological site in Norway, with 4,000-year-old remains of Stone-Age civilization, Viking grave mounds and stone circles, and even signs of ancient cultivation methods. At a nearby hill, you can look at the ruins of the Ravneberget fortification, with walls dating from the 4th century A.D.

Along this road you can also visit some more modern attractions. Midway between Fredrikstad and Sarpsborg, you can visit the **Roald Amundsen Centre** at Framveien 9 (✆ **69-34-83-26**), the 1872 birthplace of Amundsen, who, in 1911, was the first explorer to reach the South Pole. A monument is dedicated to him, and the house is filled with memorabilia of his exploits. You'll approach Hvidsten 7km (4½ miles) east of Fredrikstad along Rte. 110. The center is open from April to September, Monday to Thursday from 10am to 8pm. Admission is NOK50 ($10/£5) for adults, NOK30 ($6/£3) for children.

If you end your exploration in Sarpsborg, at a point 14km (8½ miles) east of Fredrikstad, you can visit the **Borgarsyssel Museum,** Gamlebygata 8 (✆ **69-11-56-50**), which is open from June to August, Tuesday to Saturday 10am to 4pm and Sunday noon to 4pm. This museum of the province of Østfold is an open-air exhibit filled with 30 period structures moved here from various parts of southern Norway. Many cultural artifacts are exhibited, and you can also walk through an herbal garden. Kids should also enjoy the petting zoo. On-site are the ruins of King Øystein's St. Nikolaus Church, built in 1115 but torched by the advancing Swedish army in 1567. There is no admission charge; however, a guided tour costs NOK50 ($10/£5), and you must call ahead.

En route back to Fredrikstad, you can stop off at the **Storedal Cultural Centre,** at Storedal (✆ **69-16-92-67**), 8km (5 miles) east of Fredrikstad. This was the birthplace of King Magnus in 1117. He became king of Norway at the age of 13. But 5 years later he was blinded and since then called King Magnus the Blind. The center is dedicated to blind people as well as those suffering from other disabilities. On-site is a beautiful botanical garden; it costs NOK30 ($6/£3) to enter. Two artists, Arne Nordheim and Arnold Haukeland, designed *Ode to the Light,* a "sound sculpture" that translates the fluctuations of natural light into music. The center is signposted from Rte. 110. It's open June to August daily 10am to 5pm, charging no admission.

2 HALDEN: THE BURNING CITY ★

30km (19 miles) S of Fredrikstad; 144km (89 miles) S of Oslo; 2km (1¼ miles) W of Swedish border

Halden lies at the Iddefjord in the far southeasterly corner of Østfold, bisected by the Tista River and hemmed in by forested hills. The town of 27,000 people makes an idyllic stopover for those touring the eastern bank of the Oslofjord. If you have time for only one stopover, make it Fredrikstad, as it has more attractions. But if time is available, head for Halden, especially on a summer day when yachties from Oslo fill its pretty little picture-postcard harbor.

Historically, Halden was a frontier outpost that was heavily fortified to fend off attacks by the Swedes. It was—and still is—known for Fredriksten fortress, where Norwegian patriots successfully held off Sweden's frequent attacks from the east. These regional fighters made a bold decision in 1659. To drive out the attacking Swedes, they set fire to their own town. The Swedes retreated, although the fortress withstood the siege and the town fire. Attacked by the Swedes again in 1716, the townspeople of Halden once again torched their city to halt the Swedish advance into Norway. These incidents, along with numerous fires set by Mother Nature, gave the town its nickname: "The Burning City."

Today a prosperous little border town, Halden has the dubious distinction of being the site of the country's oldest nuclear power station. In 1959, nuclear energy was introduced here to fuel regional wood-based industries. It is now used for research purposes only.

ESSENTIALS

GETTING THERE **By Rail** Halden is a stopover on the main rail links between Oslo and Gothenburg, Sweden, on that country's western coast. Depending on the time of day, trains depart Oslo once every hour or once every 2 hours. The trip takes 1¾ hours, a one-way ticket costing NOK219 ($44/£22). Call ✆ **81-50-08-88** or visit www.nsb.no for rail schedules. The train is quicker and much preferred over the bus.

By Bus **Nor-Way Buss Ekspress** (✆ **81-54-44-44;** www.nor-way.no) in Oslo runs buses every 3 hours during the day to the town of Svinedsun. Once in Svinedsun, you must take a local bus for the final approach to Halden.

By Car Motorists from Oslo can follow E6 south to reach Halden. Driving time is about 1½ hours.

By Ferry From the middle of May until the middle of August, you can enjoy a day's adventure by taking a ferry, **MS *Sagasund*** (✆ **90-99-81-00**), departing from Halden and sailing over to Strömstad on the west coast of Sweden. Strömstad used to belong to Norway until 1658. Today it's a colorful seaside resort and an embarkation point for the remote Kloster Islands, Sweden's most westerly isles, where cars are prohibited. The warming waters of the Gulf Stream give these islands their luxuriant vegetation. The ferry runs on Wednesday only at 11am and takes 45 minutes; a round-trip fare costs NOK240 (\$48/£24). Call the tourist office (below) for more details.

VISITOR INFORMATION The tourist office at Torgat 2 (✆ **69-19-09-80**) is open June to August 9am to 4:30pm Monday to Friday. From September to May, it's open Monday to Friday 9am to 3:30pm.

SEEING THE SIGHTS

The most idyllic place when the sun is shining is **Busterudpark** at Busterudgaten in the center of town. This century-old park serves as a reminder of how life used to be in this town and is complete with a bandstand from 1879. In the summer, a military band often holds concerts here. The sculptor, Dyre Vaa, erected a monument in the park in 1939 to honor F. A. Reissiger and Oscar Borg for their efforts to promote music in Halden. The park is hardly memorable or filled with attractions, but we like to come here with the makings of a picnic just like the townspeople did back in the 19th century.

Fredriksten Festning (Fredriksten Fortress) ★ Dominating a forested hill, this crowning citadel of Halden was built in 1661 by King Frederick III to protect the Danish-Norwegian kingdom against sieges from Sweden, which had already unsuccessfully attacked Oslo and Copenhagen. The king called in engineers from the Netherlands to build what he hoped—successfully so—would become an impregnable fortress. It took 10 years for the Dutchmen to create this network of labyrinthine passages and perimeter walls so thick they could withstand cannonballs. The gates were also heavily fortified, as were the bastions. They designed the complex of buildings in the shape of a star at the highest point in the sprawling town along two ridges.

In a former prison in the eastern curtain wall, you'll find the **War History Museum.** Exhibits depict the history of battle in Halden from the 1600s through the Nazi takeover in 1940. Another museum, **Dyen Brenner** ("the town is on fire"), explores the history behind the town's unfortunate nickname.

An **apothecary** has been installed in the former Commandant's Residence, which dates from 1754. Modern exhibits trace the history of pharmacology from early folk remedies that relied on bird claws to 20th-century advances in medicine. **Bakery** and **brewery** exhibits are also housed within the complex. The bakery could turn out bread for some 5,000 men, and the brewery could produce 3,000 liters of beer a day.

There is no more idyllic place for lunch in Halden than at the fort's own **Fredriksten Kro,** a mellow old pub with outdoor seating in fair weather.

To reach the fortress, take the steep footpath beginning at Peder Colbjørnsens Gate going up to the principal gatehouse. The stronghold is still in use by the Norwegian army, so not all of the complex can be visited. You can easily spend 2 hours here, although most visitors absorb it in less than an hour.

Peder Colbjørnsens Gate. ✆ **69-18-31-49.** Admission NOK50 (\$10/£5) adults, NOK25 (\$5/£2.50) children. Guided tours NOK50 (\$10/£5) adults, NOK25 (\$5/£2.50) children. May 18–Aug 22 daily 10am–5pm.

Tips **Keep Your Eye on Your Kid**

One thing prevents the Fredriksten Fortress from being truly kid-friendly: The towering bastions are not fenced in and can be dangerous. If you visit with your children, make sure to watch over them carefully.

Fun Facts The Mysterious Death of King Karl XII

You can see a monument within Fredriksten Fortress marking the spot where Swedish King Karl XII was shot during a 1718 siege. Many Norwegian guides tell you that it wasn't their countrymen who killed the king, but one of his own men. A warmongering monarch, Karl had exhausted his troops and tested their loyalty on the battlefield. Many soldiers were tired of him and his endless battles. It has never been proven where the fatal bullet was fired. Swedes maintain that a soldier within the fortress killed Karl. There is strong speculation, however, that he was assassinated by a Swedish soldier eager to return to home and hearth.

Rød Manor ★ Finds This is one of the most impressive and best-preserved manor houses in southeastern Norway, and its gardens, at least to us, are the most impressive in southern Norway. The exact age of the historic core of this building is unknown, although the east wing was added in 1733. Today much of the place looks as it did in 1750, when the Tank and Ankers families resided here. Still elegant, it has lovely interiors filled with objets d'art, hunting trophies, and one of the largest private collections of weapons in Scandinavia. You can see the house only by guided tour. On your own, you can stroll the beautiful **English-style gardens** ★★ with their towering deciduous trees or walk a pathway bordered by hazelnut trees. The symmetrical, baroque-style walkways evoke the gracious living of a grander era (assuming you were rich). The location is signposted 1.5km (1 mile) west of the town center. Plan to spend about 45 minutes here.

Rød Herregård. ✆ **69-18-54-11.** Admission NOK50 ($10/£5) adults, NOK10 ($2/£1) children. Tours June 25 to mid-Aug Tues–Sun noon and 2pm (additional Sun tour at 3pm); May 20–June 24 and mid-Aug to Sept Tues–Sun noon, 1, and 2pm.

WHERE TO STAY

Grand Hotel The Grand isn't all that grand anymore, but since 1898 it's been putting up rail passengers who arrived at the terminus across the street. It's still well maintained and tries to stay up-to-date, although the Park (see below) is now the hotel of choice. The rooms are simple and clean, with modern furnishings and well-kept bathrooms with shower units. Dinner is not served here, but the standby Dickens restaurant (see below) is nearby. The hotel seems to make up for this lack by serving one of the best breakfast buffets in town.

Jernbanetorget 1, N-1776 Halden. ✆ **69-18-72-00.** Fax 69-18-72-59. www.grandhotell.net. 33 units. Mon–Thurs NOK1,110–NOK1,190 ($222–$238/£111–£119) double; Fri–Sun NOK970 ($194/£97) double. Rates include buffet breakfast. AE, MC, V. **Amenities:** Breakfast room; bar; lounge. *In room:* TV.

Park Hotel ★ This is the more comfortable and up-to-date of Halden's two hotels, with a location in a pleasant garden at the center of town. It was originally built in the 1970s; about half of the rooms lie within a new wing that was added in 2000. The four-story weatherproof building offers increased amenities and more diversions than its only other competitor. There is an exceptionally helpful and well-informed staff. Each of the spacious rooms has wooden floors and pastel color schemes.

Marcus Thranes Gate 30, N-1776 Halden. ✆ **69-21-15-00.** Fax 69-21-15-01. www.park-hotel.no. 64 units. Mon–Thurs NOK1,350 ($270/£135) double; Fri–Sun NOK1,010 ($202/£101) double; NOK1,570 ($314/£157) suite. Rates include buffet breakfast. AE, DC, MC, V. **Amenities:** Restaurant; bar; exercise room; sauna; babysitting; laundry service/dry cleaning; garden. *In room:* TV, Wi-Fi, minibar, hair dryer.

WHERE TO DINE

Dickens INTERNATIONAL You won't find grand cuisine here, but those dependable favorites often consumed by Norwegians with a mug of beer: a Dickens burger with bacon, nachos with jalapeños, or a chicken salad with crispy bacon. More substantial fare includes baked trout with an herbal and wine sauce, or pepper filet steak. Lamb steak is another tasty choice, flavored with garlic, thyme, and rosemary. In winter, diners retreat into the 17th-century cellar to enjoy well-prepared and affordable meals. In summer, an outdoor table is preferred on a barge floating in the harbor. Visitors predominate in the summer months, with regulars returning when the wind blows cold.

Storgata 9. ✆ **69-18-35-33.** Reservations recommended Sat–Sun. Main courses NOK197–NOK265 ($39–$53/£20–£27). AE, DC, MC, V. Mon–Thurs 11am–10pm; Fri–Sat 11am–11pm; Sun 1–9pm. Closed Christmas.

HALDEN AFTER DARK

Siste Reis Pub Next to the Grand Hotel building, this is a small, cozy, and friendly Irish-style pub decorated with pictures of local musicians along with classic advertising posters. Close to the train depot, the pub offers many different brews on tap, from Irish Guinness to Danish Tuborg, and especially the local favorite, Borg, a new taste sensation for many first-time visitors to Norway. Most of the patrons, ranging in age from 18 to 40, come here to talk but also to listen to Irish folk music on the weekdays, or recorded

Munch's Little Summer Cottage

In one lazy afternoon, you can explore the little coastal town of Åsgårdstrand, located just outside the doorway of its larger neighbor, Horten. The town achieved fame in the 17th century when shipping and sailing companies were based here. In time, it was discovered by artists, one of whom was Edvard Munch, Scandinavia's most famous painter, who found inspiration along the coast for some of his best-known works.

Today you can still visit **Lykkehuset (Munch's Little House),** at Edvard Munch Gate 25 (✆ **33-08-53-72**). Once a summer house and studio where Munch spent seven seasons, it's been turned into a museum of Munch memorabilia. It was here that he painted his masterful *Girls on the Bridge, Dance of Life,* and *Melancholy.* When Munch died in 1944, the house remained as it was—basically a primitive fisherman's cabin that the artist had purchased in 1897. Called "the handsomest man in Norway" at the time, the artist is said to have taken advantage of his good looks to romance the local girls during his summer sojourns here.

The house is open Tuesday to Sunday 11am to 6pm from June to August, and Saturday and Sunday 11am to 7pm from September to May. Admission is NOK50 ($10/£5). Little Åsgårdstrand lies 10km (6¼ miles) south of Horten. Horten itself lies 35km (22 miles) south of Oslo's "bedroom community" of Drammen, which is 40km (25 miles) southwest of Oslo. Take E18 south from Oslo via Drammen.

 rock 'n' roll on Friday and Saturday. Snacks are served along with the brew. It's open Monday to Thursday 6pm to 1am, Friday 6pm to 3am, Saturday 11am to 3am, and Sunday 1pm to 1am. Jernbanetorget 1. ✆ **69-17-53-07.**

3 TØNSBERG: THE FIRST SETTLEMENT ★

102km (63 miles) S of Oslo

Tønsberg is Norway's oldest town. And just how old is it? No one is certain. But documentation—including the *Saga of Harald Hårfagre,* by Snorre Sturluson—puts the date around 871, when King Harald Fairhair united parts of the country and the Viking town became a royal coronation site.

The renowned Viking ships *Gokstad* and *Oseberg,* on display in Oslo's Bygdøy peninsula, were discovered at a site near Tønsberg on the western bank of the Oslofjord. King Olav of Vestfold and King Sigrød of Trøndelag, both killed in battle, have their tombs at Haugar.

In the Middle Ages, Tønsberg became a major Hanseatic trading post for eastern Norway, with links to Rostock along the Baltic. In the 1600s, it was known as a major port in eastern Norway, worthy of Bergen in the west. By the mid-1800s, Tønsberg was a port for whalers in the Arctic and Antarctic Seas, rivaling Sandefjord (see below). It was also the headquarters of Svend Foyn, known as the "father of Norwegian sealing and whaling."

However, don't be completely misled by the town. Tønsberg is also quite up-to-date with the 21st century and not mired in antiquity. Modern Tønsberg is a 104-square-kilometer (41-sq.-mile) town with some 32,000 residents. It consists of a historic area filled with old clapboard-sided houses and a commercial center with a marketplace. Foodies around the world seek out the Jarlsberg cheese that is made here.

In 3 hours, you can see it all.

ESSENTIALS

GETTING THERE **By Train** Trains depart for Tønsberg from Oslo's main railway station at intervals of between 60 and 90 minutes from 6am to 11:30pm every day, requiring a travel time of about 90 minutes and a fare of NOK199 ($40/£20) each way. The railway station is in the town center. For information and schedules, call ✆ **81-50-08-88** or visit www.nsb.no.

By Bus There is no NOR bus service from Oslo.

By Car Take Rte. 18 south from Oslo via Drammen.

VISITOR INFORMATION Tønsberg **Tourist Information** is at Nedre Langgate 36B, N-3100 Tønsberg (✆ **33-35-45-20**). It's open in July daily 10am to 5:30pm and August to June Monday to Friday 8:30am to 4pm. A little tourist kiosk on the island of Tjøme provides information in July daily from 11am to 5pm. Also visit www.visittonsberg.com for information.

SEEING THE SIGHTS

Slottsfjellet, a huge hill fortress near the train station, is touted as "the Acropolis of Norway." In its heyday, these 13th-century ruins blossomed as the largest medieval fortifications in Norway, attracting the victorious Swedes across the border who came to

Moments Going to the End of the World

In just a half-hour drive, you can leave Tønsberg and travel to what locals call **Verdens Ende ★**, or "World's End." It lies at the southernmost tip of Tjøme, the southernmost island among the low-lying islands and skerries, or rocky islets, jutting out into the Oslofjord, where it empties into the sea. This is a particularly dramatic spot. Usually the wind is blowing rather strong, stirring up the blue-black waters. Old fishing jetties can be seen in the distance. You'll also view an array of rocky islets and big rocks worn smooth by the turbulent waves. This is romantic Viking country and the setting for many summer homes. No one comes here for the excitement: It's just a scenic hideaway. If you don't have a car, take bus no. 101 from Tønsberg; the ride takes 45 minutes and costs NOK65 ($13/£6.50) one-way. Once here, you'll see a "17th-century" lighthouse. Actually, the original is gone and this is a copy from 1932.

destroy it in 1503. It has only some meager ruins today, and most people visit for the view from the 1888 lookout tower, **Slottsfjelltårnet** (✆ **33-31-18-72**), rising 17m (56 ft.) tall. It's open May 15 to June 25 Monday to Friday from 10am to 3pm, June 26 to August 20 daily from 11am to 6pm, August 21 to September 15 Saturday and Sunday from noon to 5pm, and September 16 to September 29 Saturday and Sunday from noon to 3pm. Admission is NOK40 ($8/£4) for adults, NOK20 ($4/£2) for children.

Nordbyen is the old, scenic part of town, with well-preserved houses. **Haugar Cemetery,** at Møllebakken, in the center of town, contains the Viking graves of King Harald's sons, Olav and Sigrød.

Sem Church, Hageveien 32 (✆ **33-36-93-99**), the oldest church in Vestfold, was built of stone in the Romanesque style around 1100. It's open Thursday and Friday 10am to noon, but inquire at the vestry if it's not open during these hours. Admission is free.

Another attraction is **Fjerdingen,** a street of charming restored houses near the mountain farmstead. Tønsberg was also a Hanseatic town during the Middle Ages, and some houses have been redone in typical Hanseatic style—wooden buildings constructed along the wharfs as warehouses to receive goods from fellow Hanseatic League members.

Haugar Vestfold Kunstmuseum This museum is good for a rainy day. The main reason to visit is to introduce yourself to "Odd Nerdrum," an internationally known figurative painter hailed as "the Rembrandt of Norway." The museum displays two of his best-known works, including *Man Imitating Cloud* and *Woman with Doorknob.* One of his most curious works is called *Hermaphrodite.* One wing of the museum is devoted entirely to Odd Nerdrum, but there are also 160 pieces of works by other artists. Tønsberg's art museum lies in the center of town in a building from 1918. Nearby are two Viking grave sites, said to hold the bodies of Olaf and Sigrød, sons of the king, Harald Hårfagre.

Gråbrødragate 17. ✆ **33-30-76-70.** www.haugar.com. Admission NOK50 ($10/£5). June–Aug Mon–Fri 11am–5pm; Sept–May Tues–Fri 11am–4pm; Sat–Sun noon–5pm year-round.

Vestfold Fylkesmuseum ★ Tønsberg hails its once glorious past with the relics of yesterday on display at this museum. Lying at the foot of Slottsfjellet, it features many Viking and whaling treasures. One of the chief sights is the skeleton of a blue whale, the world's largest mammal. The weight of this particular whale can't be determined, but some whales caught off the coast of Norway have weighed in at 150 tons. There's also a Viking ship, the *Klastad* from Tjolling, built about A.D. 800.

In the rural section of the museum, visit the **Vestfold Farm,** which includes a 1600 house from Hynne, a timbered barn from Bøen, and a storehouse from Fadum (with the characteristic apron, or platform). The Heierstadloft (ca. 1350) is the oldest preserved timbered building in Vestfold, and there's a smithy with a charcoal shed, a grain-drying house, and a mountain farmstead.

You can have lunch here at a real mountain farmstead. A typical meal includes *rumgraut* (porridge made with sour cream)—definitely an acquired taste—and other farm foods. The area is perfect for a picnic on a summer day.

Frammannsveien 30. ✆ **33-31-29-19.** Admission NOK50 ($10/£5) adults, NOK10 ($2/£1) children. Mid-May to mid-Sept Mon–Sat 10am–5pm; Sun and holidays noon–5pm. Closed mid-Sept to mid-May.

WHERE TO STAY

Hotel Maritim (Value) This hotel has long been a local favorite—since 1955, in fact—but the opening of the Quality Hotel Tønsberg has put it in second place. Operated by a Norwegian seamen's association, it is a bastion of modern comfort and convenience—all offered for an affordable price. Located on a square beside the ruins of the Church of St. Olav, the hotel occupies a five-story building that's a 10-minute walk east of the rail station on the main pedestrian street. The rooms, which are frequently renovated, are well furnished and have a color scheme to rival the spring flowers of Norway. Some of the units are quite large, and each comes with a small bathroom with shower. Fregatten, a good restaurant offering a Norwegian, Japanese, and Chinese cuisine, is on the ground floor. The helpful staff can arrange boat trips or bikes for guests.

Storgata 17, N-3126 Tønsberg. ✆ **33-00-27-00.** Fax 33-31-72-52. www.maritimhotell.com. 34 units. NOK990–NOK1,090 ($198–$218/£99–£109) double; NOK1,490 ($298/£149) suite. Rates include continental breakfast. AE, DC, MC, V. Closed Dec 22–Jan 5 and 4 days at Easter. **Amenities:** Restaurant; bar; laundry service/dry cleaning. *In room:* TV, minibar.

Quality Hotel Tønsberg ★ This hotel—the best in the area—is a member of the Quality chain in Norway. Whenever you see the Quality brand, you can expect a stylish hotel in the Nordic minimalist fashion. This one is scenically located along the waterfront at the southern end of town. In spite of its location, it is rather tranquil at night. Launched in 2002, the five-story structure is the latest hotel to grace the cityscape of Tønsberg. Its bedrooms are large, and most of them open onto views of the fjord. All are decorated in pastels, and most have carpeting, except for the two dozen units that are set aside for those suffering from allergies. Typical Norwegian food is served at the on-site restaurant.

Ollebukta 3, N-3126 Tønsberg. ✆ **800/228-5151** or 33-00-41-00. Fax 33-00-41-01. www.choicehotels.no. 233 units. NOK1,150–NOK2,105 ($230–$421/£115–£211) double. Children 4 and under stay free in parent's room. Rates include continental breakfast. AE, DC, MC, V. **Amenities:** Restaurant; bar; outdoor heated pool; fitness center; sauna; business center; babysitting; nonsmoking rooms. *In room:* TV, Wi-Fi, minibar, hair dryer, safe.

WHERE TO DINE

Brygga CONTINENTAL/NORWEGIAN This rustic-looking restaurant with an outdoor terrace that opens onto a harbor view is your best choice in town. The Norwegian-style decor includes light gray tones, light-colored woods, and walls covered with modern paintings by local artists. But be warned, Tønsberg is not a hot address for discerning foodies. During the week, Brygga feels like a pub, especially when soccer matches are shown on a big TV screen. The chefs try to please most palates, offering everything from the town's best pizzas to the notable filet of reindeer and moose. If you like meat, the chefs will prepare you an excellent beefsteak with béarnaise sauce and a salad. We prefer their shellfish dishes, especially their seafood salad studded with shrimp, among other delectable items.

Nedre Langgate 32. ✆ **33-31-12-70.** Reservations recommended. Main courses NOK195–NOK270 ($39–$54/£20–£27). AE, DC, MC, V. Daily 11am–10pm.

Himmel & Hav NORWEGIAN/INTERNATIONAL This minimalist-style cafe decorated in bright colors features house specialties that would probably never make the menu of a Greenpeace luncheon: reindeer, for example, or even whale steak. (Their whale specialty is unappetizingly called "Free Willy.") Less controversial dishes include a surf and turf of filet of beef, sautéed with bacon and served with scampi in a Madagascar pepper sauce. On our last visit, we were impressed with the chef's handling of a freshly caught grilled halibut. During the day, classical or jazz music plays in the adjoining Café del Mar.

Nedre Langgate 32. ✆ **33-00-49-80.** Reservations recommended. Main courses NOK95–NOK200 ($19–$40/£9.50–£20) at lunch, NOK220–NOK300 ($44–$60/£22–£30) at dinner. AE, DC, MC, V. Cafe daily noon–3:30am; kitchen service until 10:30pm.

4 SANDEFJORD ★

125km (78 miles) S of Oslo; 24km (15 miles) S of Tønsberg

Although a modern town today, Sandefjord was one of the most famous stamping grounds of the Vikings in the Middle Ages. Its natural harbor along a 9.8km (6-mile) fjord made it the whaling capital of the world at one time. A monument remains at the harbor to the once prosperous whaling industry, which made Sandefjord the richest city in Norway. Today it has built up the third-largest merchant fleet in Norway.

This old port still has a bit of 19th-century charm and character. Considering its rich history, it should have more. But much of the old was torn down to make way for modern developments.

You can afford to skip most of the town and concentrate on the waterfront, a breezy section of green parks and beautifully maintained gardens. If the day is sunny, what we like to do is rent a bike (inquire at the tourist office), make a picnic basket with some seafood from the "fishtraders" who hang out by the harbor, and set off along the coast for an adventure. You might also poke about in the little stores and shops, ducking into one of the cozy harborfront cafes for a warming coffee, and stroll along, admiring the many sculptures that dot the waterfront.

Sandefjord attracts summer visitors seeking boating fun in its archipelago and on its many beaches. The archipelago is studded with 115 so-called "islands," but most of these are mere rocky outcroppings—not real islands at all. We asked a longtime local boatman which island was his favorite among dozens of possibilities. "The one that gets the most sun on any given day," he said. "After a long cold winter, we in Norway want sun. So we stop our boats off at the hottest rock and take a little sunbath, often in just our underwear, if that."

Locals call the town "Bathing City" (*Badebyen* in Norwegian). Yachties from Oslo also fill up the harbor in summer after having sailed through the skerries, or rocky islets.

On a summer day, we always like to stroll along its waterfront, enjoying the fresh salt air and the beautiful parks and gardens. You'll see a magnificent compound of buildings constructed in 1899 in the dragon motif so popular in Norway. The baths were closed in 1940, at the beginning of the Nazi occupation, and the site today is the civic center.

ESSENTIALS

GETTING THERE The country's second-busiest international airport is **Sandefjord Airport Torp** (✆ **33-42-70-00**). Some budget airlines such as Good Jet and Ryanair use this smaller airport rather than the one in Oslo. In addition to its air link, there is one daily **ferry connection** to Strömstad, Sweden, taking 2½ hours. For schedules and information, call **Color Line,** Tollbugata 5 (✆ **81-00-08-11;** www.colorline.no).

From Oslo there are several **express trains** reaching Sandefjord in 2 hours. For information and schedules, call ✆ **81-50-08-88** or visit www.nsb.no. Frequent **buses** also run between Oslo and Sandefjord daily, and there are also good bus connections between Tønsberg and Sandefjord. Visit www.nor-way.no for information.

VISITOR INFORMATION The **Sandefjord Tourist Information Office** is at Torvet (✆ **33-46-05-90;** www.visitsandefjord.com). In summer, it's open Monday to Friday 9am to 6pm, Saturday 10am to 4:30pm, and Sunday 12:30 to 4:30pm. Off season it's open only Monday to Friday 9am to 4pm.

SEEING THE SIGHTS

Lying off Storgata, **Commander Christensen's Whaling Museum,** Museumsgaten 39 (✆ **33-48-46-50**), has a life-size replica of a mighty **blue whale ★**, its tongue alone weighing 3½ tons. The museum chronicles the controversial whaling industry that nearly drove this mammoth sea beast to extinction. In the heyday of whaling, as we learned, Sandefjord sent out vast "floating factories" to process the whale meat and its by-products. Admission is NOK50 ($10/£5) for adults, NOK25 ($5/£2.50) for ages 7 to 17, and free for those 6 and under. A family ticket costs NOK125 ($25/£13). From June to August hours are daily 10am to 5pm; September daily 10am to 4pm; October to May daily 11am to 3pm.

Sandefjord preserves a slice of its past at **Øvre Myra Cotter's Farm,** Solvangveien 8 at Nyphen. In use since 1770, this is the last cotter's farm in the area. (A cotter was a hired hand who occupied a cottage in return for services on the farm.) Inquire at the tourist office (see above) about joining one of the guided tours in summer to this homestead.

OUTDOOR PURSUITS

After all this maritime history, you, too, can head for the water if the day is fair. The best beach, **Langeby,** lies 7km (4¼ miles) from the center, and buses from Sandefjord go there hourly. You'll find dozens of other beaches along the 146km (91-mile) coastline. Our favorite public beach—arm yourself with a map from the tourist office—is at **Søllokka,** reached along RV 303 by following the directions north to Tønsberg. We also like **Granholmen,** reached along RV 303 following the directions south to Larvik, the latter the hometown of Thor Heyerdahl, of *Kon-Tiki* fame.

The area is a popular site for scuba divers. The best outfitter is **Neptun Dykkersenter,** Hegnasletta 13 (✆ **33-46-14-90**), which will rent all the equipment needed to qualified divers. There is no regular place to rent boats, but you might inquire here about rentals, or else check with the tourist office to see what might be available if you'd like to go boating. Outdoor activities are a casual thing at Sandefjord, a sort of do-it-yourself operation that changes from season to season.

WHERE TO STAY

Clarion Collection Hotel Atlantic ★★ Kids This obvious market leader in town is also the most atmospheric in its reverence for the maritime tradition of the city. Built on the site of an older structure, this hotel respected its 1914 origins in its brand-new design. The tasteful interior takes a whaling theme as its motif. Bedrooms have sleek modern styling, and each comes with a private bathroom with shower (six units also have a tub). Suites have their own fireplaces and Jacuzzis. Children under 12 stay free, but a rollaway bed is an additional fee. The on-site dining room serves a light supper in the evening that is free to guests.

Jernbanealleen 33, N-3200 Sandefjord. ✆ **33-42-80-00.** Fax 33-42-81-00. www.choicehotels.no. 109 units. NOK1,595 ($319/£160) double; NOK2,795 ($559/£280) suite. Rates include continental breakfast and light supper. AE, DC, MC, V. **Amenities:** Dining room; sauna; laundry service/dry cleaning; nonsmoking rooms; rooms for those w/limited mobility. *In room:* TV, Wi-Fi, minibar, hair dryer, trouser press.

Hotel Kong Carl ★ This is a long-time favorite of ours, bringing back memories of our first stay here when fishermen were (practically) still harpooning whales. Near the town center and marketplace, this white clapboard-sided house dates from 1690 and has been an inn since 1721. The frequently refurbished hotel's cathedral ceilinged annex is used extensively as a conference center. Bedrooms are tastefully and comfortably furnished and come in a wide range of sizes. Most of the accommodations are at least partially furnished with antiques. Lunch and dinner is served Monday to Saturday in a regional restaurant; you can also enjoy a beer on the summer terrace.

Torvgaten 9, N-3201 Sandefjord. ✆ **33-46-31-17.** Fax 33-46-31-19. www.kongcarl.no. 29 units. NOK990–NOK1,500 ($198–$300/£99–£150) double; NOK1,900 ($380/£190) suite. Rates include continental breakfast. AE, DC, MC, V. Closed Dec 22–Jan 2 and 1 week at Easter. **Amenities:** Restaurant. *In room:* TV, minibar, hair dryer.

Rica Park Hotel Although a chain, this hotel still manages to offer personalized service. Idyllically positioned overlooking the harbor and a city meadow, the hotel still has the lingering aura of its birthday in 1958. Dark wood pieces stand in contrast to the pastel-colored walls. Each bedroom is furnished with rich fabrics, thick carpeting, and comfortable furnishings. Bathrooms are up-to-date and well equipped, with three-fourths of them having a tub as well as a shower. Many locals patronize the hotel's gourmet restaurant, Park Garden, for special occasions. Even if you're not a guest, consider dropping in here for entertainment. During the summer, live shows are staged with local bands, international artists, and Norwegian cabaret acts.

Strand Promenaden 9, N-3201 Sandefjord. ✆ **33-44-74-00.** Fax 33-44-75-00. www.rica.no. 233 units. NOK1,645–NOK2,045 ($329–$409/£165–£205) double; NOK2,700 ($540/£270) suite. AE, DC, MC, V. **Amenities:** 2 restaurants; bar; piano bar; saltwater indoor pool; fitness center; sauna; babysitting; laundry service/dry cleaning; nonsmoking rooms; rooms for those w/limited mobility. *In room:* A/C (in some), TV, minibar, hair dryer.

WHERE TO DINE

Solvold's ★★★ FRENCH/ASIAN FUSION This is the best restaurant along Oslofjord. The chef, Odd Ivar Solvold, has won three national culinary championships, and he certainly deserves his acclaim. For this new building, the chef chose Sven Lund as his architect, the same man who also designs for the king of Norway.

The dining is quite formal, and the wine cellar is on the same floor as the dining area. Foodies celebrate Solvold for his seafood, and he secures the finest catches. His lemon-baked turbot with a carrot and coriander cream is a prize-winning dish indeed, as is his pan-fried seawater crayfish with a crustacean emulsion. Savor his filet of tuna, or opt for a meat course, none better than the rack of venison in a tangerine sauce. For dessert, we were enthralled by his pickled peach with vanilla and apricot-mascarpone ice cream. Attached to Solvold's is Smak, a less formal restaurant, featuring international dishes such as carpaccio, paella, and sushi.

Thor Dalsgate 9. ✆ **33-46-27-41.** Reservations required. Main courses NOK225–NOK285 ($45–$57/£23–£29). AE, DC, MC, V. Tues–Sat 6–11pm.

5 EIDSVOLL: CRADLE OF INDEPENDENCE

80km (50 miles) N of Oslo

To appreciate this site, you might need to have true Norwegian blood flowing through your veins, as many Americans do. Reached from Oslo via the E6, motorists arrive at **Eidsvoll,** Carsten Ankers vagen (✆ **63-92-22-10**), where, on May 17, 1814, the country's constitution was written after 6 intense weeks. It was the most liberal constitution the world had ever known and today is the oldest existing constitutional charter in Europe.

Even if you're not interested in the political implications of Norway, a visit to the manor house **Eidsvoll-bygningen** is worthwhile for its insiderish view of the lifestyles of the upper crust of the early 1800s.

The two-floor house with 30 rooms was constructed of timber. Portraits of the members of the 1814 Norwegian parliament are on display here, but far more intriguing is the collection of objects used to furnish the house, including a well-stocked library, elegant dining rooms, lavish bedrooms, English antiques, and murals depicting figures from Greek mythology.

The cast-iron stoves are works of art. The Ankers family, who lived in the house, also owned the local ironworks, and they insisted on only the best for themselves.

You can also visit the Room of the Constitutional Committee, where the original wooden benches are still in place, along with a series of paintings of Norwegian landscapes.

The house is open May to August daily from 10am to 5pm; September to April Tuesday to Friday 10am to 4pm, Saturday and Sunday 10am to 5pm. Admission is NOK70 ($14/£7).

If you're not driving, you can reach the manor house by taking train no. 450 from the central station in Oslo to Eidsvoll. Trains run every 1 to 2 hours for the 50-minute journey. From here you can take a local bus to the nearby town of Eidsvoll Verk. The manor house lies 4km (2½ miles) east of the E6 on the edge of this Eidsvoll Verk.

6 JEVNAKER: NORWAY'S OLDEST GLASSWORKS

70km (42 miles) NW of Oslo

With the glories of the banks of the Oslofjord behind you, head northwest from Oslo along the scenic banks of yet another fjord, **Tyrifjord,** enjoying some of the best land and seascapes in eastern Norway before arrival at **Hadeland Glassverk** ★, Rte. 241, Jevnaker (✆ **61-31-66-00**).

In operation since 1762, this is one of the oldest glassworks in Scandinavia. To launch the company, most of the workers were brought in from Germany. Until 1814, the company was owned by the king of Denmark and Norway.

This place is a real family attraction, and many activities are specifically designed for children. Kids and adults alike will be fascinated watching some of Norway's most skilled glass blowers practice their art at the Glass Hut. Kids can blow their own glass or dye their own candles here. ***Note:*** The pre-Christmas scene is particularly active here, so plan on crowds that time of year.

Other highlights include a visit to "Honey House" to enjoy a freshly baked confection, or a trip to the Factory Shop to browse for bargains. Children can also play in a house designed for them, watch a tinsmith at work in the Pewter Workshop, or take rides on the gentle horses in the park out back during the summer.

On the main square of the glassworks is the **Hadeland Glassworks Art Gallery,** opened in 1997, with an exhibition of the works of 50 internationally known artists.

Admission is free, and the glassworks can be visited Monday to Friday 10am to 5pm, Saturday 10am to 4pm, and Sunday 11am to 5pm. To reach Jevnaker, motorists can follow E16 toward Hønefoss, then Rte. 241 into Jevnaker.

8

Lillehammer & the Peer Gynt Road

One of the premier wildernesses of Europe, this is a region to visit if you love the great outdoors. From its Olympic ski conditions on snow-capped mountains to the glaciers in its national parks, expect high-adrenaline thrills in both winter and summer. Visitors arrive at the likes of Jotunheimen National Park specifically seeking a close encounter with nature.

When touring the area, you might even meet up with the rare musk ox. But keep your distance and admire him from afar. If threatened, the shaggy creature can charge at the rate of 60kmph (37 mph).

This chapter will guide you through some of Norway's highest mountain peaks, which are a hiker's paradise in summer and a ski mecca in winter. In addition to its many resorts and enchanting wooden villages, this section of Norway is filled with hidden gems such as the town of Røros, a former copper-mining site that is now preserved as a UNESCO World Heritage Site.

Lying to the east of the western fjord district, eastern central Norway is the virtual playground of Scandinavia, embracing the greatest national parks, the fabled ski resort at Lillehammer, and some of the nation's most panoramic scenery. At times it may seem remote and distant, but much of it is within an easy 1- or 2-hour drive to the immediate south of Oslo.

1 HAMAR: GATEWAY TO LAKE MJØSA

134km (83 miles) N of Oslo; 58km (36 miles) SE of Lillehammer

Hamar is no beauty itself, but it's at the center of a beautiful region of central Norway. If it's a choice between Lillehammer and Hamar, make it Lillehammer. But if you have that extra day to spare, journey to Hamar, if for no other reason than to enjoy Lake Mjøsa.

Located on the large and scenic Lake Mjøsa, Hamar is the capital of Hedmark County and one of Lillehammer's rivals for the winter-sports enthusiast. It makes a good stopover en route from Oslo to Lillehammer, but it also has many attractions in its own right if you'd like to base yourself here and drive up to the more crowded Lillehammer.

In the Middle Ages, Hamar was the seat of a bishopric, and some ecclesiastical ruins remain from those glory days. Hamar was also the home of Kirsten Flagstad, one of the world's most famous operatic sopranos back in the days when *soprano* suggested something other than a hit TV show.

Hamar's Viking ship–shaped ice-skating hall was the site of skating events during the 1994 Winter Olympics.

Hamar is a good center not because of its great architecture (it doesn't have any), but because of its natural setting. Its most charming assets are its marinas and waterside cafes, which, at least in summer, capture some of the charm of Norway. If you want to see old Norway, explore the ruins at the Hedmarksmuseet (see below).

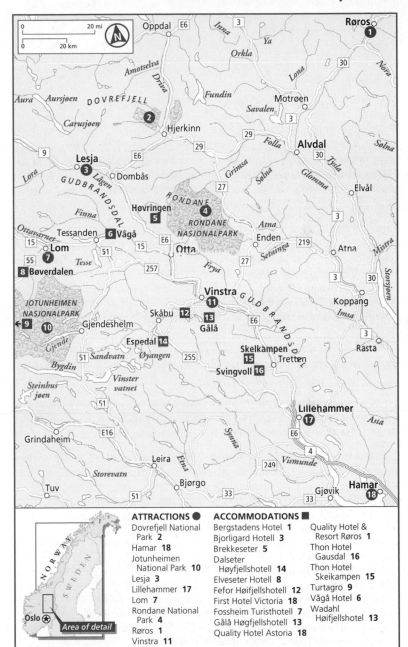

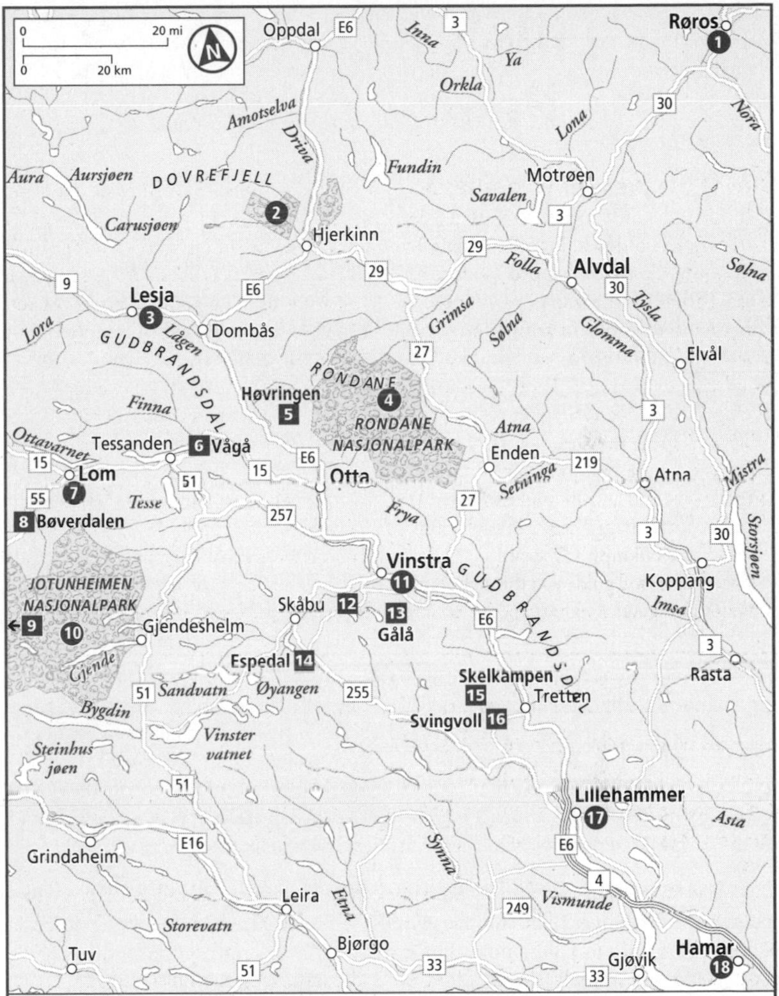

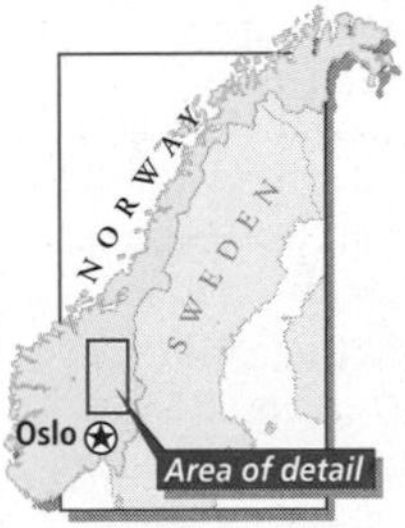

ATTRACTIONS ●

- Dovrefjell National Park **2**
- Hamar **18**
- Jotunheimen National Park **10**
- Lesja **3**
- Lillehammer **17**
- Lom **7**
- Rondane National Park **4**
- Røros **1**
- Vinstra **11**

ACCOMMODATIONS ■

- Bergstadens Hotel **1**
- Bjorligard Hotell **3**
- Brekkeseter **5**
- Dalseter Høyfjellshotell **14**
- Elveseter Hotell **8**
- Fefor Høifjellshotell **12**
- First Hotel Victoria **18**
- Fossheim Turisthotell **7**
- Gålå Høgfjellshotell **13**
- Quality Hotel Astoria **18**
- Quality Hotel & Resort Røros **1**
- Thon Hotel Gausdal **16**
- Thon Hotel Skeikampen **15**
- Turtagro **9**
- Vågå Hotel **6**
- Wadahl Høifjellshotel **13**

More alluring than the rather dull modern buildings of Hamar itself is the surrounding fertile farmland, riddled with forests and pastures. In such a bucolic setting, it is easy to understand why many Oslovians build summer homes here and use Lake Mjøsa as their playground during the few short weeks of sun they have. Many towns, such as Hamar, are used as mere refueling stops for visits to the nearby national parks and lakes.

ESSENTIALS

GETTING THERE Frequent trains run between Oslo and Hamar, costing NOK215 ($43/£22) one-way and taking 1¼ hours. Visit www.nsb.no for schedules. Nor-Way Buss Ekspress runs daily from Oslo. Visit www.nor-way.no for schedules. Motorists should take the E north from Oslo until they see the signposted turnoff for Hamar.

VISITOR INFORMATION The local tourist office is at Vikingskipet (✆ **62-51-75-03**), open Monday to Saturday 8am to 4pm. From mid-May to mid-August, hours are Monday to Saturday 8am to 6pm. Or visit www.norway.com/hamar for information.

SEEING THE SIGHTS

Hamar Olympiahall This modern sports arena hosted events during the 1994 Winter Olympics. While that seems like a long time ago, folks around here will be talking about it for years to come. The arena is built in the shape of a Viking ship, lying within walking distance of the town center. Today it is the site of numerous sports events, performances, and exhibitions, and can hold some 10,000 spectators. It's been called a "sports cathedral without equal." Visits are possible when events aren't being staged.

Åkersvikaveien. ✆ **62-51-75-00.** Admission NOK35 ($7/£3.50); ice-skating (late July to mid-Aug) NOK50 ($10/£5). June 30 to mid-Aug daily 8am–8pm.

Hedmark Kunstnersenter (Hedmark Artists' Center) This restored center for the arts offers changing exhibitions featuring regional artists, mainly painters and sculptors. Check with the tourist office to see what's currently showing. The center is beautifully situated by Lake Mjøsa, west of town, which makes for an idyllic walk along the lake.

Parkgate 21. ✆ **62-54-22-60.** www.kunstbanken.no. Admission NOK30 ($6/£3) adults, NOK20 ($4/£2) students and seniors, free for children 15 and under. Tues–Fri 11am–5pm; Sat–Sun noon–5pm.

Hedmarksmuseet & Domkirkeodden West (1.5km/1 mile) of the town center, the ruins of the nearly 1,000-year-old Hamar Cathedral jut out into Lake Mjøsa. The

Moments **Sailing on Norway's Oldest Paddle Steamer**

The best way to travel to Hamar is aboard the world's oldest paddle steamer, *Skibladner*★★ (✆ **61-14-40-80**), which calls not only at Hamar, but also at Eidsvoll and Lillehammer, among other points. The ship was built in 1854 and is still in good shape, stretching 50m (164 ft.) long and measuring 5m (16 ft.) wide. It has a cruising speed of 12 knots and sails from the middle of June to the middle of August. Onboard is a luxurious 70-seat restaurant that's fully licensed and serves regional specialties. The most popular route is between Hamar and Lillehammer, taking 4 hours and costing NOK230 ($46/£23) per person one-way.

sight can be reached by a scenic walk, or you can take bus no. 6 leaving from the Hamar Library, costing NOK60 ($12/£6) one-way. These ruins are evocative and call attention to Hamar's once-important role in Norway's ecclesiastical world. The church was constructed of locally quarried limestone, with Romanesque architecture, although later additions were Gothic.

The ruins are protected by a steel-and-glass cover provided in 1998. This protective umbrella is the largest glass construction in Europe, fanning out for 2,600m (8,528 ft.). Adjoining is an archaeological museum displaying artifacts found in the area, and also an open-air folk museum featuring 18th- and 19th-century houses. In an organic garden you can see nearly 400 different types of herbs. The best time to visit these ruins is in summer when concerts or plays are also presented.

Strandveien 100. ✆ **62-54-27-00.** www.hedmarksmuseet.no. Admission NOK75 ($15/£7.50) adults, NOK35 ($7/£3.50) children, NOK185 ($37/£19) family ticket. May 24–June 15 Tues–Sun 10am–4pm; June 16–Aug 17 daily 10am–5pm; Aug 18–Sept 14 Tues–Sun 10am–4pm.

Kirsten Flagstad Museum If you've never heard the music of Norway's greatest opera diva Kirsten Flagstad (1895–1962), it's worth it to come here and listen to her operatic recording in a special room. This museum of Flagstad memorabilia lies 46m (151 ft.) from the marketplace and a 10-minute walk from the rail station. On the ground floor you can purchase records, books about the star, and souvenirs. A special costume room is of particular interest because the Metropolitan Opera contributed some of the gowns that Kirsten wore in her most famous performances. Memorabilia and photographs, including the star's private albums, letters, contracts, and magazine and newspaper publicity, round out the exhibit. The collection of recordings here is the largest Flagstad trove in the world, covering her entire career from her first recordings in 1914 to her last memorable recordings in San Francisco.

Kirkegata 11. ✆ **62-53-32-77.** www.kirsten-flagstad.no. Admission NOK50 ($10/£5) adults, NOK30 ($6/£3) children, family pass NOK110 ($22/£11). June 1–Sept 1 Tues–Sun 11am–4pm; Sept 2–May 31 Tues–Fri noon–3:30pm.

NSB Jernbanemuseet (National Railway Museum) About the last profession we'd want to follow is that of a Norwegian railroad engineer, blasting through mountains and rugged terrain to lay tracks or carve out tunnels; but for the railroad buff, this museum is pure bliss. Established in 1896 on the shores of Lake Mjøsa, it collects and displays bits of Norwegian rail history dating from its beginnings in the 1850s. Vehicles include models from 1861 to 1950, among them three royal coaches and several steam locomotives weighing up to 150 tons. There is a museum park with several station buildings, railway tracks, and other exhibits, as well as a "dining car" serving snacks and refreshments. A small train travels along the grounds of the amusement park.

Strandveien 163. ✆ **62-51-31-60.** www.norsk-jernbanemuseum.no. Admission NOK75 ($15/£7.50) adults, NOK40 ($8/£4) children. July to mid-Aug daily 10am–5pm; June and mid-Aug to Sept 18 daily 10am–3:30pm. Closed Sept 19–May. Take bus 1 from the railway station or walk 30 min. from the town center going north along the shore of Lake Mjøsa.

WHERE TO STAY

First Hotel Victoria Set between the edge of the lake and the town's main pedestrian shopping street, this hotel originated in the 1850s as a small inn and grew over the years into the seven-story, modern-looking, gray-sided chain hotel you'll see today. The well-known Norwegian "Skagen painter," Christian Krohg, always stayed at Victoria when he

The Voice of the Century

Kirsten Flagstad (1895–1962), to whom there's a museum of memorabilia dedicated in Hamar, remains one of the all-time legends of opera. Interpreting the operas of Henry Purcell or Richard Wagner, among other composers, Flagstad had no equal in her day. At the age of 40, she was planning to retire but was invited to perform at New York's Metropolitan Opera on February 2, 1935. The rest is history. Her performance was broadcast across Canada and the United States, and it created a sensation, with music critics labeling her "the Voice of the Century." Her Brunhild in San Francisco ensured her lasting fame in America. Along with Lauritz Melchior, Flagstad is credited with keeping the Metropolitan Opera alive in New York during its difficult days of the Depression on the eve of World War II.

Her popularity waned when she returned to Nazi-occupied Norway to be with her husband, Henry Johansen. It was a naive decision that would harm her incredible popularity in the United States for the rest of her life. During the war she never sang for the Germans. But her husband, Johansen, in ill health, was arrested by the Norwegians at the end of the war and labeled a war profiteer, even though he'd aided the Allied resistance. He died a year later.

On Flagstad's return to postwar America, a political campaign, labeled in the press as one of "extreme vituperation," was waged against her. Demonstrations marred each one of her performances in New York and San Francisco. Nevertheless, her devoted fans still clung to her. At age 54, when most divas are in retirement, Flagstad continued to perform with the San Francisco Opera, scoring some of her greatest successes with *Tristan und Isolde* and *Die Walküre.* During the tragic years of the war, her voice had "darkened" and lost some of its brilliant upper register. But all of her concerts were still sold out by die-hard fans.

Fortunately, her recorded voice remains to win new generations of fans among opera lovers. Many music critics now hail her as "the diva of the 20th century." Flagstad's recorded voice has become "immortal," glowing with richness, power, and an expressiveness that is not only beautiful, but also intensely dramatic.

visited the region. From his regular table he gazed out over Lake "Mjøsa" and found inspiration for his art. Parts of the hotel are rather grand, especially some of the paneled, big-windowed public rooms whose deep sofas evoke a well-upholstered room in a private home or social club. Three of the rooms sport a frilly decor that the staff defines as "feminine-looking." The remainder are soothing, contemporary, monochromatic, and favored by (usually male) business travelers from other parts of Scandinavia.

The hotel restaurant, large, contemporary, attractively formal, and outfitted with large windows, is open daily for lunch and dinner.

Strandgata 21, N-2317 Hamar. ✆ **62-02-55-00.** Fax 62-53-32-23. www.firsthotels.com. 115 units. Mon–Thurs NOK1,253 ($251/£125) double, NOK1,700 ($340/£170) suite; Fri–Sun and mid-June to mid-Aug daily NOK853 ($171/£85) double; NOK1,500 ($300/£150) suite. Rates include buffet breakfast. AE, DC, MC, V. Free parking. **Amenities:** Restaurant; bar; room service; laundry service/dry cleaning; nonsmoking rooms; rooms for those w/limited mobility. *In room:* TV, Wi-Fi, minibar.

Quality Hotel Astoria ★ Stay at the Victoria (above) if you want tradition, but at the Astoria if you prefer your hotels sleek and modern. Originally built in the early 1970s in the commercial center of town, this hotel was radically renovated in the late 1990s into a well-managed, middle-bracket enclave of efficiency and warmth. Because of its renovations, it promotes itself as "the newest hotel in town." Each room has a writing table; comfortable, contemporary-looking furniture; and a monochromatic color scheme, depending on the floor it's on, of pale yellow, green, or soft red. The in-house restaurant, Big Buffalo, is separately recommended in "Where to Dine," below.

Torggata 23, N-2317 Hamar. ✆ **62-70-70-00.** Fax 62-70-70-01. www.choicehotels.no. 78 units. NOK1,180–NOK1,780 ($236–$356/£118–£178) double. Rates include buffet breakfast. AE, DC, MC, V. Nearby parking NOK50 ($10/£5). **Amenities:** 2 restaurants; cocktail bar; the "Dirty Nelly" pub; nightclub; laundry service/dry cleaning; nonsmoking rooms; rooms for those w/limited mobility. *In room:* TV, Wi-Fi, minibar, trouser press.

WHERE TO DINE

Big Buffalo STEAKHOUSE This restaurant is not mere "hotel dining," but a step above that. Part of its allure derives from the cozy decor with dark woods and photos of Mexico, and part of it derives from savory preparations of such local ingredients as elk, beefsteak, venison, chicken, and veal. The menu changes with the seasons, but the best specialties include Mexican pepper steak with three kinds of pepper, served with fried tomatoes and corn, or three lamb chops in a rosemary sauce. You can also order grilled chicken breast on a bed of onions, peppers, and mushrooms.

In the Quality Hotel Astoria, Torggata 23. ✆ **62-70-70-00.** Reservations recommended Fri–Sat. Main courses NOK110–NOK350 ($22–$70/£11–£35). AE, DC, MC, V. Daily 4–11pm.

Bykjeller'n NORWEGIAN/INTERNATIONAL This is the largest and most imaginative dining, drinking, and disco venue in Hamar. It was built in 1849 as an inn, and the high-ceilinged interior was transformed into its present incarnation in the 1970s. Many visitors never get beyond the street-level pub, whose thick beams and rustic artifacts make up the setting for foaming mugs of beer, and pub items that include salads, pizzas, sandwiches, and meal-size platters of fish, steak, pasta, and game. In summer, a beer garden sprawls out into what used to be a stable yard in back. Relatively elaborate dining is available in the stone-vaulted cellar, which was originally conceived as a coal cellar and which today is artfully illuminated with a mixture of candles and electric lights. Menu items vary with the seasons but are likely to include lutefisk (especially at Christmas); sausages and meatballs; pork spareribs in barbecue sauce; smoked, dried, and thin-sliced mutton; tenderloin steaks; and venison with port wine sauce.

There's a disco on the top floor of the restaurant, floored with massive oaken planks and ringed with a wraparound mezzanine that's favored by voyeurs who gaze down at the dancers and the flirts who try to engage them in conversation. The disco is open Friday and Saturday nights from 10pm to 3am. There's a cover charge of NOK90 ($18/£9) that's imposed only on Saturday (not on Fri). Entrance to the disco is free for anyone who dines in the cellar.

Torggata 82. ✆ **62-54-31-00.** Reservations recommended Fri–Sat. Main courses NOK85–NOK200 ($17–$40/£8.50–£20) at lunch, NOK225–NOK325 ($45–$65/£23–£33) at dinner. AE, DC, MC, V. Street-level pub daily 11am–10:30pm. Dinner in cellar-level restaurant daily 6–10:30pm. Disco Fri–Sat 10pm–3am.

For the largest drinking and dining venue in town, refer to Bykjeller'n under "Where to Dine," above.

The well-attended **Irishman Pub,** Strandgata 31 (✆ **62-52-33-92**), draws a lively crowd, usually in the 30- to 50-year-old bracket, to its 1930s-era precincts. The decor? Classic Irish pub, down to the pictures of famous Irishmen lining the walls. Recorded music plays in the background except on Friday, when live music is heard. On one night, the singers owed massive inspiration to The Beatles and Bob Dylan. Of course, Guinness and Irish whiskeys rule the night. Open Sunday and Monday noon to 8pm, Tuesday to Thursday noon to 12:30am, and Friday and Saturday noon to 2:30am.

2 LILLEHAMMER OF OLYMPIC GLORY ★★

169km (105 miles) N of Oslo; 363km (225 miles) S of Trondheim

Surrounded by mountains, Lillehammer is one of Europe's favorite resorts and our own choice for many a vacation. The town, at the head (northern end) of Lake Mjøsa, became internationally famous when it hosted the 1994 Winter Olympics. Today the sports sites and infrastructure benefit greatly from the two-billion-kroner investment that the government put into Lillehammer to make it worthy of the games. Skiers in winter can take advantage of many of these improvements.

Even with all its upgrades, Lillehammer's appeal still lags far behind the popularity of such chic alpine resorts as St. Moritz in Switzerland or St. Anton in Austria. Those great alpine retreats have far more dramatic skiing, an array of first-class and deluxe hotels, fabulous restaurants, and a glittering après-ski life. Compared to them, Lillehammer is just a country town. Yet for many skiers, it has great appeal because of its natural ski conditions. Sadly, "Winter City," as Lillehammer is called, doesn't get much of that famous alpine sunshine.

However, even if you're not considering it for a ski holiday, Lillehammer is an attractive venue for summer vacationers, as it has a number of attractions (see below) and a broad appeal for families.

With a population of 23,000, Lillehammer is surrounded by forests, farms, and small settlements. Its main pedestrian street, **Storgata** ★, is known for its well-preserved wooden buildings.

At the southern end of the Gudbrandsdal valley, Lillehammer was founded as a trading post back in 1827. Over the years, Lillehammer has attracted many artists, such as Jakob Weidemann, who were drawn to its beautiful landscapes and special Nordic light. The most famous artist who lived here was Sigrid Undset, who won the Nobel Prize for literature.

If you're driving into Lillehammer, you may be completely confused by the maze of convoluted traffic patterns, one-way streets, and tunnels. It's better to park as soon as you can and explore Lillehammer on foot. It's easy to navigate, and, frankly, there isn't that much to see in the very center once you've walked the Storgata. Lillehammer's greatest attractions, such as its ski slopes and the Maihaugen Folk Museum, lie on the outskirts.

At the peak of summer, the streets, which contain both attractive wooden structures and a lot of ugly modern buildings, are full of people shopping, eating, or drinking. In winter, skiers take over. Frankly, considering the fame of Lillehammer, many visitors expect a far more beautiful town than they discover here.

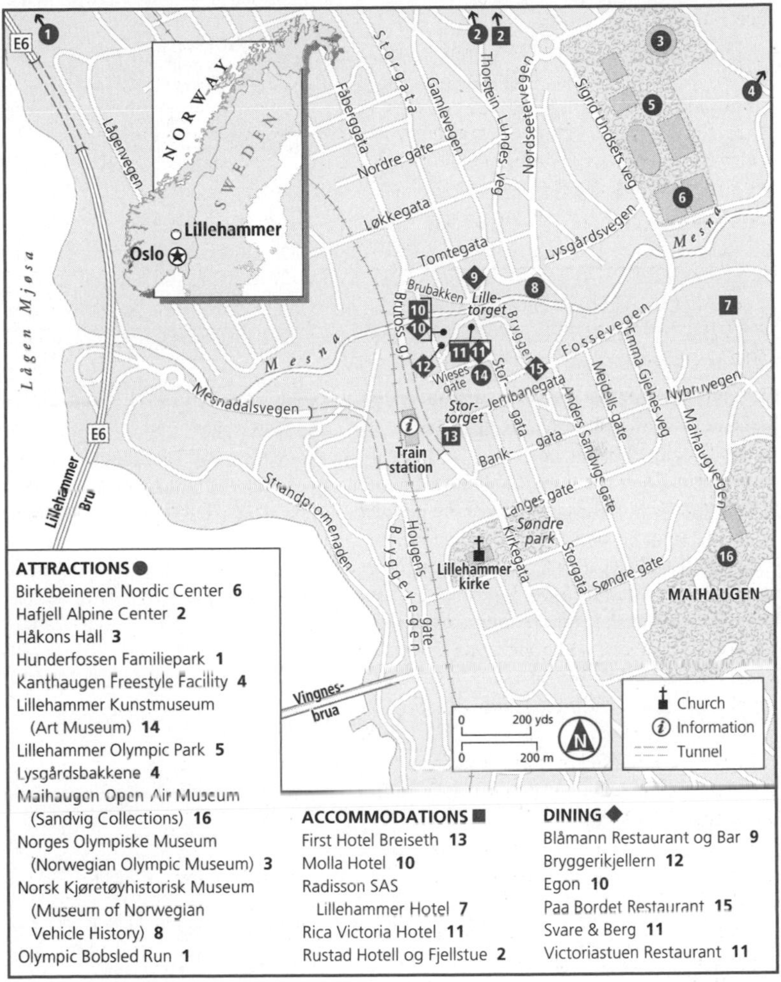

What you'll see in Lillehammer is shop after shop, some 250 in all, crowding the Storgata or streets branching off from it. Some of these stores, such as those selling crafts, will be of interest to visitors. Others are merely there to serve the population living in the province—hardware stores and the like.

ESSENTIALS

GETTING THERE **By Train** From Oslo, express trains take about 2 hours and 20 minutes, and local trains take about 3 hours. Depending on the time of year, there are five to eight trains per day. Call ✆ **81-50-08-88** or visit www.nsb.no for information.

By Bus Bus trips between Oslo and Lillehammer take about 2½ hours and depart two or three times a day. Visit www.nor-way.no for information.

By Car Head north from Oslo along E6.

VISITOR INFORMATION The Lillehammer Tourist Office is adjacent to the railway station at Torget 2 (✆ **61-28-98-00;** www.lillehammerturist.no). From mid-June to mid-August, it is open Monday to Saturday 9am to 7pm, Sunday 11am to 6pm. Off-season hours are Monday to Friday 9am to 4pm and Saturday 10am to 2pm.

SEEING THE SIGHTS

During the peak summer season, usually June 20 to August 20, the tourist bureau schedules several excursions. These include trips to the **Maihaugen Open-Air Museum (Sandvig Collections)** and voyages on **Lake Mjøsa** aboard the *White Swan of Lake Mjøsa,* an 1850s paddle steamer. See "Sailing on Norway's Oldest Paddle Steamer," earlier in this chapter, for more details. Ask the tourist office (see "Visitor Information," above) for a list of activities.

Hunderfossen Familiepark (Hunderfossen Family Park) Kids At this kiddie fun park, you'll find a presentation of the most popular Norwegian fairy tales, more than 50 activities for children and adults, and lots of space to roam around. There are a merry-go-round and Ferris wheel, as well as carnival booths, a cafeteria, and a swimming pool. A 12m-tall (39-ft.) troll at the gate welcomes visitors. The park is 12km (7½ miles) north of Lillehammer on E6.

Fåberg. ✆ **61-27-72-22.** www.hunderfossen.no. Admission NOK300 ($60/£30) adults, NOK195 ($39/£20) seniors, NOK245 ($49/£25) children 3–13, free for children 2 and under. May–Sept daily 10am–6pm. Closed Oct–Apr. Bus: Hunderfossen from Lillehammer.

Lillehammer Kunstmuseum (Art Museum) This museum of art is better than most provincial museums in Norway because so many great artists, including Edvard Munch, were inspired by the area. In 1963, it opened as a contemporary museum but later expanded into an annex designed by Snøhetta. To bridge the gap between the two buildings, Bard Breivik, the sculptor, created a sculpture garden using the elements of water and stone. In the center of town, the museum displays one of Norway's largest collections of national art, with pieces dating from the 1830s to the present. Some of Norway's major artists are represented, including Axel Revold, Erik Werenskjold, and Christian Krogh. But most international visitors seek out works by Edvard Munch. The collection includes four of his paintings, including *Portrait of Ida Roede.* This gallery also possesses one of the biggest collections of paintings from the so-called Norwegian Romantic period. Opened in the winter of 1992, it was one of the major cultural venues during the 1994 Olympics.

Stortorget 2. ✆ **61-05-44-60.** www.lillehammerartmuseum.com. Admission NOK60 ($12/£6) adults, NOK50 ($10/£5) students and seniors, free for children 15 and under. June 24 to mid-Aug daily 11am–5pm; mid-Aug to June 23 Tues–Sun 11am–4pm.

Maihaugen Open-Air Museum (Sandvig Collections) ★★ Many Norwegian towns have open-air museums featuring old buildings that have been moved and put on display. This is one of the best of them. This museum consists of 180 buildings, from manor houses to the cottage of the poorest yeoman worker, and there are more than 40,000 exhibits. The houses reassembled here and furnished in 17th- to 18th-century style came from all over the Gudbrandsdal (Gudbrands Valley). Of particular interest is the Garmo Stave Church, built in 1200.

You can also visit 37 old workshops, displaying activities ranging from gunsmithing to wood engraving, and a large exhibit covering Norwegian history from 10,000 B.C. to the present. The museum lies about 10 minutes on foot from the town center or a 20-minute walk from the train station. Head up Jernbanegata, turn right onto Anders Sandvigs Gate, and then go left up Maihaugvegen following the signposts. The city's concert hall is also at the museum, and two on-site cafeterias serve Norwegian food.

Maihaugveien 1. ✆ **61-28-89-00.** www.maihaugen.no. Admission NOK80–NOK100 ($16–$20/£8–£10) adults, NOK40–NOK50 ($8–$10/£4–£5) children 6–16, free for children 5 and under. May 18–Sept daily 10am–5pm; Oct–May 17 (indoor museum only) Tues–Sun 11am–4pm. Bus: 007.

Norsk Kyøretøyhistorisk Museum Norway's only vehicle museum illustrates the development of transportation from the first sledges and wagons to modern-day cars. The most intriguing to us, and perhaps sad, exhibitions are the cars left over from Norway's attempt to build up an automobile-manufacturing industry. Most famous of these is the strange "Troll Car," a kissing cousin of Sweden's Saab. The last ones were made in the 1950s and are viewed as collectors' vehicles today. The museum is east of the town center; from the bus stop, head out on Elvegata.

Lilletorget 1. ✆ **61-25-61-65.** Admission NOK40 ($8/£4) adults, NOK20 ($4/£2) children 7–14, free for children 6 and under. June 15–Aug 20 daily 10am–6pm; Aug 21–June 14 Mon–Fri 11am–3pm, Sat–Sun 11am–4pm.

OLYMPIC SITES

The **Lillehammer Olympic Park** ★★ was the site of the 1994 games and is today one of the major centers for sports in Norway. In **Håkons Hall,** there are facilities for fitness training, squash, badminton, football, handball, volleyball, and other pursuits. Visitors can attend various sporting events here, especially hockey matches, but also indoor golfing events. Check with the tourist office to see what might be in the offing at the time of your visit.

Also in the hall is **Norges Olympiske Museum (Norwegian Olympic Museum),** Olympiaparken (✆ **61-25-21-00**), the only such museum in Scandinavia, with exhibitions not only about Lillehammer's role as host of the games in 1994, but also on the entire history of the Olympics up to the present day. In all, there are some 6,000 individual exhibits, as well as documentaries of the games. Admission is NOK75 ($15/£7.50) for adults and NOK35 ($7/£3.50) for children. It's open June to August daily from 10am to 6pm. Off-season hours are Tuesday to Sunday 11am to 4pm.

Lysgårdsbakkene, the ski jump tower (✆ **61-05-42-00**), is open daily from mid-June to mid-August 9am to 8pm, charging NOK15 ($3/£1.50) for admission. You can take a chairlift to the top of the big ski jump for a **panoramic view** ★★ of Olympic Park and the surrounding area. The chairlift costs NOK45 ($9/£4.50) for adults and NOK40 ($8/£4) for children. Although you can also take the chairlift back down, it makes a lovely stroll to walk down instead.

In the upper part of the park, the **Lillehammer Skiklub** (✆ **61-27-58-00**) has areas for cross-country skiing, plus a ski lodge and a cafeteria. The **Kanthaugen Freestyle Facility** (✆ **61-05-42-00**) is one of the most compact facilities of its type in the world, with hills for aerials, moguls, and "ballet." Skiing instruction is offered on the ballet hill.

The **Olympic Bobsled Run** (contact Lillehammer's Olympic Park, ✆ **61-05-42-00**) is not in the park, but at Hunderfossen, 15km (9¼ miles) north of the town. This is northern Europe's only artificially refrigerated bobsled and luge track. The track is 1,365m (4,477 ft.) long, and the height difference from start to finish is 114m (374 ft.). The track has 16 curves. From October to March, visitors can try bobsledding or "bobrafting." The bobraft is a rubber bob that to us looks like a big bathtub. Even in the warmer months, from April to September, you can still try the wheelbob (a bobsled on wheels), which takes four passengers per trip at a speed of 100kmph (62 mph). Rates for the bobraft facility (winter only), bobsled run (winter only), and wheeled bobsled (summer only) are the same: NOK190 ($38/£19) per person.

OUTDOOR ACTIVITIES

BIKING & HIKING The best mountain-biking and hiking possibilities are from the **Nordseter Hyttegrend (Nordseter Activity Center),** lying 15km (9¼ miles) northeast of the town center of Lillehammer. Follow the signs to Nordseter at the approach roads to Lillehammer.

Once at this lakefront sporting complex (✆ **61-26-40-37**), you'll find many options for biking, hiking, boating, hill climbing, and canoeing. From here you can hike to Mount Neverfjell at 1,089m (3,572 ft.). In summer, a 21-gear mountain bike rents for NOK180 ($36/£18) per day; a rowboat or canoe for excursions on the waters of lake Nevelvaten rents for NOK200 ($40/£20).

Free maps (and advice) are available for anyone who wants to ramble along any of the well-marked hiking trails radiating outward and into the surrounding hills. Likewise, the best biking routes in the area can be plotted for you.

SKIING Lillehammer has a 94m (308-ft.) slope for professionals and a smaller jump for the less experienced. The lifts take skiers 457m (1,499 ft.) above sea level up the slalom slope, and more than 402km (249 miles) of marked skiing trails are packed by machines. The Lillehammer Ski School offers daily classes, and several cross-country tours are held weekly. Ask at the tourist office (see "Visitor Information," above) for details.

Hafjell Alpine Center (✆ **61-27-47-06**) was the main venue for Olympic alpine competitions in 1994. It has seven lifts and 20km (12 miles) of alpine slopes. The location is 15km (9¼ miles) north of town. A "ski bus," costing NOK50 ($10/£5) one-way and taking 20 minutes, runs here from the center of Lillehammer about six times per day. Lillehammer is also the starting point for 402km (249 miles) of prepared cross-country tracks, 5.8km (3.5 miles) of which are illuminated.

Lillehammer gears up in December for its winter sports season. In addition to the ski center, there's an admission-free **skating rink** where you have to bring your own skates. It's open in the winter Monday to Friday from 11am to 9pm, Sunday 11am to 5pm. In the winter, you'll also discover festivals, folklore nights, and ski races.

In winter, **Nordseter** is the focal point of two separate slopes—for both the beginner and the intermediate-level downhill skier. It also has a vast network of cross-country ski trails. A lift pass, valid for a full day, costs NOK340 ($68/£34) per person, and ski equipment (either downhill or cross country) rents for NOK305 ($61/£31) per day.

SHOPPING

In the center of Lillehammer, a respected name in Norwegian handcrafts, is **Husfliden ★★**, Storgata 47 (✆ **61-26-70-70**), presenting a vast array of Norwegian products, ideal as gifts or souvenirs. The location is near Sigrid Undsets Plass. One of Norway's oldest established jewelers, in business since 1868, is **Gullsmed Frisenberg ★★**, Storgata 74 (✆ **61-25-03-36**), now run by the fourth generation of the founding family. Merchandise includes some of the best jewelry selections from Scandinavia's leading designers.

Sport og Fritid, Kirkegata 55 (✆ **61-25-76-87**), opposite the Lillehammer Art Museum, offers a huge selection of winter and summer attire. Whatever you need in the realm of sports gear, you are likely to find here. **Belsvik Match,** Storgata 72 (✆ **61-26-63-00**), is Lillehammer's oldest and biggest clothing outlet. Merchandise comes in a wide range of price categories. Most visitors prefer to come here for the traditional Norwegian knitwear.

WHERE TO STAY

First Hotel Breiseth ★ At the time of its opening in 1898, this was the most fashionable hotel in Lillehammer, and it became known as a summer gathering place for artists. Though more modern hotels are now numero uno, the Breiseth is still a winning choice. Within an easy walk of Olympia park, and also close to the bus and train terminals, its location is more convenient than panoramic. Remodeling has been very successful. However, traditional touches remain, as evidenced by the turn-of-the-20th-century public rooms, with artwork on the walls and marble pillars holding up ceilings. In winter, we always gravitate to the blazing fireplace in the parlor. Guest rooms are small to midsize but are completely fresh and tastefully furnished with many wooden pieces, along with tiled bathrooms. One wing caters specifically to those with allergies, with natural-fiber linens and a strict no-smoking-or-pets policy.

1–5 Jernbanegaten 1, N-2609 Lillehammer. ✆ **61-24-77-77.** Fax 61-26-95-05. www.firsthotels.no/breiseth. 89 units. Sun–Thurs NOK1,398 ($280/£140) double, NOK1,598 ($320/£160) suite; Fri–Sat NOK1,298 ($260/£130) double, NOK1,498 ($300/£150) suite. Rates include buffet breakfast. AF, DC, MC, V. **Amenities:** Restaurant; bar; sauna; room service, laundry service/dry cleaning; nonsmoking rooms; rooms for those w/limited mobility. *In room:* TV, Wi-Fi, minibar, beverage maker, hair dryer, trouser press.

Molla Hotel ★★ Though not the equal of the Radisson SAS (see below), this is one of the most modern and desirable hotels in this vast area, rising 11 floors from its location in the town center. It was constructed in 1992 to host visitors to the 1994 Winter Olympics. The hotel is the second-tallest building in town and the site of one of Lillehammer's most sought-after restaurants, Egon, which is recommended separately (p. 201). Bedrooms come in pleasing pastels and are tastefully and comfortably furnished. Rooms are not as luxurious as you might wish for, but contain such grace notes as pine furnishings, quilted bedspreads, and regional art. The location is the most romantic in town, a converted mill dating from 1863 set by a rushing stream and waterfall. Another winning feature is the panoramic rooftop bar.

Elvegaten 12, N-2609 Lillehammer. ✆ **61-26-92-94.** Fax 61-26-92-95. www.mollahotel.no. 58 units. Mon–Thurs NOK1,050 ($210/£105) double; Fri–Sun NOK1,345 ($269/£135) double. Rates include buffet breakfast. AE, DC, MC, V. **Amenities:** Restaurant; bar; sauna; room service; laundry service/dry cleaning; nonsmoking rooms; rooms for those w/limited mobility. *In room:* TV, minibar, hair dryer.

Radisson SAS Lillehammer Hotel ★★★ Kids Set at the halfway point between the open-air museum at Maihaugen and the Olympic Park, this is the best hotel in Lillehammer, opening onto a 3.5-hectare (8½-acre) park. Lying 600m (1,968 ft.) from the main street, it is the most traditional hotel in Lillehammer, having known a previous life as the Lillehammer Hotel. In its latest reincarnation, it is better than ever, a smoothly running and efficient operation with the best facilities in town. A small midrise, it greets you with a fountain at the entrance, a nice touch that sets the tone for the interior. Paintings, paneling, artifacts, and carpeting add to the style of the hotel. Bedrooms are well organized and exhibit the epitome of comfort and taste, with bright fabrics and homelike touches throughout. The drinking and dining facilities are top rate.

Turisthotelveien 6, N-2609 Lillehammer. ✆ **61-28-60-00.** Fax 61-25-73-33. www.radisson.com. 303 units. Sun–Thurs NOK1,300–NOK1,575 ($260–$315/£130–£158) double; Fri–Sat NOK1,600–NOK1,875 ($320–$375/£160–£188) double. AE, DC, MC, V. **Amenities:** 2 restaurants; 4 bars; 2 heated pools (1 heated indoor); fitness room; sauna; children's programs; room service; laundry service/dry cleaning; nonsmoking rooms; rooms for those w/limited mobility. *In room:* TV, Wi-Fi, minibar, hair dryer.

Rica Victoria Hotel ★ Established in 1872, this is an old, traditional choice for vacationers, but it's kept up with the times. The biggest changes occurred in 1963 and 1976 when new wings were added, but there have been regular rejuvenations since. The complex consists of an older concrete building along with a more modern six-floor structure. The interior is more gracious than the exterior, with heavy beams, brown-leather sofas, and brass chandeliers, in addition to paintings. Guests gather near the fireplace in the lounge when it's cold outside. Some of the facilities are used by nonguests as well as locals, including a pub-style steakhouse and a disco. We prefer the bedrooms in the original house to the more sterile newer units. Still, all the rooms are comfortable, featuring small bathrooms. The Victoriastuen Restaurant, reviewed separately below, offers guests excellent on-site dining.

Storgata 84B, N-2615 Lillehammer. ✆ **61-25-00-49.** Fax 61-25-24-74. www.rica.no. 109 units. NOK1,445–NOK1,695 ($289–$339/£145–£170) double. Rates include buffet breakfast. AE, DC, MC, V. **Amenities:** Restaurant; bar; disco; room service; laundry service/dry cleaning; nonsmoking rooms; rooms for those w/limited mobility. *In room:* TV, minibar, hair dryer.

Rustad Hotell og Fjellstue ★ Finds This has more of a Klondike feeling than the sleek first-class hotels previously recommended, and we actually prefer it for that reason. You can settle into the wilderness at this favorite spot 18km (11 miles) north of Lillehammer. The log-and-timber chalet is on the edge of a lake, with a dock for swimming and boats. The property is surrounded by private grounds with views of the water or the mountains. Hiking trails are available in many directions, and there are some 300km (186 miles) of well-prepared cross-country tracks in winter. The staff can arrange swimming, canoe and boat trips, fishing, and a winter ski school. Skis can be rented on-site. The bedrooms are small to midsize, each comfortably furnished.

Sjusjøen, N-2612 Lillehammer. ✆ **62-36-34-08.** Fax 62-36-35-74. www.rustadhotel.com. 46 units. June–Aug NOK1,050 ($210/£105) double; Sept–May NOK1,300 ($260/£130) double. Rates include buffet breakfast. AE, DC, MC, V. **Amenities:** Restaurant; bar; sauna. *In room:* TV, minibar (in some).

WHERE TO DINE

Blåmann Restaurant og Bar MEXICAN/NORWEGIAN Quesadillas with beef and reindeer may seem like an odd juxtaposition of culinary traditions, but this long-standing favorite more or less succeeds in its offerings (although we've had far better quesadillas than those served here). Housed in an old-fashioned building, it offers views of the river on one side of the restaurant. In summer, there is outdoor seating in a "hang" over the Mesna River. A delicious hunter's soup is made with mushrooms, reindeer, and spices, and served with sour cream. Our favorite dish is the mountain trout served in a sour-cream sauce with cucumber salad and potatoes. Some of the more exotic main dishes include breast of ostrich, and you can also order succulent Norwegian lamb. In summer, no dessert tops the "Berry Trip," a mixed-berry medley with homemade ice cream.

Lilletorvet 1. ✆ **61-26-22-03.** Reservations recommended. Main courses NOK235–NOK325 ($47–$65/£24–£33). AE, DC, MC, V. Mon–Sat 11am–11pm; Sun 1–10pm.

Bryggerikjellern NORWEGIAN This 1814 brewery, a 7-minute walk east of the train station, was transformed in 1969 into a pub/restaurant, offering beer, steaks, and tasty main dishes. It's done a roaring business ever since and is especially popular in winter with skiers. In fact, when the weather's bad and no one can ski or climb in the hills, this is one of the most popular watering holes in town. The joint especially attracts those to whom suds are more vital than the food. The Norwegian fare is rather typical, and salads are the only appetizers. They'll feed you well in generous portions, and most dishes are priced at the lower end of the scale.

Disco Brenneriet (The Distillery) is linked to the restaurant. It's open Friday and Saturday from 11pm to 3am. On Friday there's a NOK70 ($14/£7) cover charge, going up to NOK80 ($16/£8) on Saturday.

Elvagata 19. ✆ **61-27-06-60.** Reservations not accepted. Main courses NOK180–NOK410 ($36–$82/£18–£41). AE, DC, MC, V. Mon–Sat 6–11pm; Sun 3–10pm.

Egon ★ Kids NORWEGIAN/INTERNATIONAL Housed in a grinding mill from 1863 and connected to the Molla Hotel (which lies immediately next door) by a covered passageway, this restaurant offers three floors of seating, lots of cozy nooks and crannies, big-windowed views from every floor of a river, and a lingering memory of then–First Lady Hillary Clinton, who came here for food and drink during the 1994 Olympics. There's outdoor seating in summer, and a worthy collection of rustic country antiques and mill implements hanging from the ceiling beams and rafters. Patrons order their food from the counter near the entrance (which happens to be on the restaurant's uppermost—that is, third—floor). Subsequent to that, a waitstaff will carry your order, when it's ready, to wherever you happen to be sitting on any of three cozy floors. Members of the waitstaff are strategically scattered throughout all levels of the dining room to fetch additional food orders throughout the course of your meal.

Menu options involve access to a set-price salad and pizza buffet; a children's menu comprised of simple burgers, franks, and pastas; and an a la carte menu for adults. Specialties include a "black and white" platter that's composed of filets of veal and filet mignon, served with béarnaise sauce; rack of Norwegian lamb; and some rather banal, diet-conscious fish dishes such as baked salmon with broccoli and a lemon-flavored white wine sauce.

In the Molla Hotel, Elvegata 12. ✆ **61-25-23-40.** Reservations recommended. Main courses NOK125–NOK259 ($25–$52/£13–£26). AE, DC, MC, V. Mon–Sat 11am–11pm; Sun noon–11pm.

Paa Bordet Restaurant ★ NORWEGIAN/INTERNATIONAL This restaurant is housed in a timbered, rustic building dating from 1880. It's long been known locally for its excellent cuisine prepared with quality ingredients. On our visit, we were delighted with the marinated wild salmon and enjoyed a zesty beet root salad as well. Full-flavored dishes include crispy breast of duck with fresh cabbage, baked apple, and an orange sauce, or roasted filet of elk served with creamed Brussels sprouts. All the dishes our party sampled were made with consummate skill, including the pan-fried skate with lobster sauce and fresh green beans. For dessert, try the delightful white chocolate confection with raspberry sorbet.

Bryggerigata 70. ✆ **61-25-30-00.** Reservations recommended. Main courses NOK185–NOK310 ($37–$62/£19–£31); 3-course fixed-price menu NOK450 ($90/£45); 4-course fixed-price menu NOK550 ($110/£55). AE, DC, MC, V. Mon–Sat 6–10:30pm. Closed July.

Svare & Berg NORWEGIAN/MEXICAN A popular bar with a fireplace for evening drinkers, this is also a reliable restaurant in a traditional setting. It's cozy and casual, and the food is good. The two most popular—justifiably so—main courses are the filet of reindeer and the roast salmon served with a butter sauce. For a change of pace, order the Mexican fajitas with beef or chicken. The crepes with berries "from the woods," served with ice cream, is a summer delight.

Sharing the same kitchen is **Nikkers,** a bar/restaurant with a lighter menu that truly attracts all kinds—a moose walked in one night looking for dinner. It offers live music on Friday and Saturday nights and is open Monday to Saturday 11am to 2am and Sunday 1pm to midnight.

Elvegata 18. ✆ **61-24-74-30.** Reservations recommended. Main courses NOK89–NOK299 ($18–$60/£8.90–£30). AE, DC, MC, V. Mon–Wed 11am–11pm; Thurs 11am–midnight; Fri–Sat 11am–2am.

Victoriastuen Restaurant ★ NORWEGIAN/INTERNATIONAL Located in the recommended Rica Victoria Hotel (p. 200), this lively lobby-level restaurant offers some of Lillehammer's finest dining year after year, with its windows opening onto the town center. The restaurant is nostalgically outfitted in what Norwegians refer to as "farmer's colors"—that is, strong blues and reds with an antiquelike patina. The location is only a 3-minute walk north of the rail station, so it's a convenient address. The kitchen provides quality cuisine, using regional produce whenever possible. Our mountain trout, fried and served in a sour-cream sauce, was a delight, as was the fresh catfish in a butter sauce with a cucumber salad. *Frikadeller* (meatballs) are a filling and tasty pleasure, or you may prefer a succulent chateaubriand if you have a more demanding palate and a full wallet.

Charging less, Victorianhjørnet (Victorian Corner), one floor above, is a pub, pizzeria, and steakhouse. It provides good food in far less formal surroundings.

In the Rica Victoria Hotel, Storgata 84B. ✆ **61-25-00-49.** Reservations recommended. Main courses NOK220–NOK350 ($44–$70/£22–£35). AE, DC, MC, V. Daily 11am–2pm and 3–11pm.

LILLEHAMMER AFTER DARK

Felix Pub & Scene A pub since 1984, this major venue for the alternative rock scene is housed in a historic building from 1832. Visited by musicians, students, and others, it often stages live concerts on the ground floor of its two floors. Patrons range in age from 18 to 30, and they listen to recorded music—rock, punk rock, whatever—when there are no live bands. Another potent lure for young people is that the pub offers the cheapest pints in Lillehammer, at NOK45 ($9/£4.50) per half liter. It's open daily 10:30am to 2am. Storgata 31. ✆ **61-25-01-02.** Cover NOK50–NOK100 ($10–$20/£5–£10) for live music concerts.

Marcello Nightclub This is the major nightclub for the district, holding at capacity anywhere from 250 to 300 patrons on its dance floor. The dancers, ranging in age from 30 to 45, move to recorded music, which runs the gamut from pop to country. Only beer and wine are sold, and the doorman assured us, "It's easy to get in unless you're too drunk." Open Thursday to Sunday 10pm to 3am. Storgata 86. ✆ **61-25-90-90.** Cover NOK80 ($16/£8) Fri, NOK85 ($17/£8.50) Sat.

Toppen Bar This bar offers panoramic views, with vistas of Lillehammer, the Olympic areas, and Lake Mjøsa. It's called "Lillehammer's highest watering hole," located on top of the Molla Hotel. Like the highest bars we know in the Rocky Mountains, the suds can go to your head fast at this elevation. It's open Monday to Saturday 8pm to 2am. Elvegata 12. ✆ **61-26-92-94.**

3 VINSTRA: THE PEER GYNT ROAD

220km (136 miles) NW of Oslo; 61km (38 miles) NW of Lillehammer

As much as we enjoy Lillehammer, our hearts are won over, too, by the wildness of the Peer Gynt country, where you'll encounter nature in some of its rawer aspect. Although this is primarily known as a ski area, summer—when you can travel along mountain roads, past old farmsteads and fish-filled lakes, enjoying the alpine flowers and the wild birds—is equally delightful.

The Peer Gynt Road ★★★, between Lillehammer and the little town of Vinstra, takes you right into the heart of Peer Gynt country. Henrik Ibsen came this way when he was researching his masterpiece *Peer Gynt,* published in 1867 and later set to music by Edvard Grieg. Ibsen based his tale in part on the exploits of one Per (spelled with only one *e*) Gynt Haga, a real-life Norwegian folk hero noted for such exploits as riding on the backs of reindeer at breakneck speed.

As you drive through the Gudbrandsdal (Gudbrands Valley), you can travel the same route that bewitched the original hero, and outside Vinstra you can visit a monument to Per Gynt Haga, the Peer Gynt prototype, in the cemetery adjoining the Sødorp Church, 1.5km (1 mile) south of town. The road passes two large resorts, **Skeikampen/Gausdal** and **Golå/Wadahl,** before rejoining E6 at Vinstra.

The Peer Gynt country is an unspoiled mountain region with altitudes varying from 769m to 1,499m (2,522–4,917 ft.). This is one of Norway's oldest and best-known sports districts. The skiing center at Fefor was opened in 1904, and it was here that the adventurous Capt. Robert Falcon Scott tested the equipment for his expedition to the South Pole.

ESSENTIALS

GETTING THERE **By Train** Following more or less the same route as the buses but taking a bit less time, trains travel from Oslo's Central Station to Gardermoen to Lillehammer to Vinstra, taking about 3¼ hours and charging around NOK458 ($92/£46) each way. That price includes the fee for reserving a seat, which, in light of the many weekenders who go to Peer Gynt country from Oslo, is a good idea. For railway information throughout Norway, call ✆ **81-50-08-88** or visit www.nsb.no.

By Bus Buses depart from Oslo's central bus station, which is immediately adjacent to the town's railway station. They make a stop at the bus station at Gardermoen Airport, then continue on to Lillehammer and then on to Vinstra. There are between three and four of these per day, each maintained by Norway Buss Ekspress. One-way fares for the 3½-hour bus trip are NOK290 ($58/£29) per person. Call ✆ **81-54-44-44** for reservations and information, or visit www.nor-way.no. Otherwise, call the Vinstra tourist office for schedules or click on the region's website (www.peergynt.no) for a limited schedule.

By Car From Lillehammer, continue northwest along E6 into Vinstra.

By Taxi Note that once passengers arrive in Vinstra, at either the bus or the railway station (they're adjacent to each other), they'll usually have to migrate by taxi to their hotel. Most hotels are in isolated spots up in the mountains. A taxi fare from Vinstra to Golå, for example, costs from NOK335 ($67/£34) and carries up to four passengers if they don't have too much luggage, and two to three persons if they do have a lot of luggage. Usually a hotel will send a van down to meet its passengers as part of the cost of their hotel package.

VISITOR INFORMATION The best source of information about touring in the area is found at the **Vinstra Turist og Messekontor,** N-2640 Vinstra (✆ **61-29-47-70**), open Monday to Friday 8:30am to 5pm from June to August, and Monday to Friday 8:30am to 4pm from September to May.

OUTDOOR ACTIVITIES

The **Peer Gynt Ski Area ★★★** is ideal for those who'd like to combine cross-country skiing with alpine skiing. All the facilities in the ski region are within easy reach of all the hotels in the area. A ski bus links the resorts of Espedalen, Fefor, and Gålå. In all, there are 28km (17 miles) of slopes, 8 lifts, 1 chairlift, and 24 slopes. In the entire area there are 460km (285 miles) of well-prepared trails and 170km (105 miles) of stick-marked trails in beautiful surroundings. Skiers rate the Peer Gynt Trail as Norway's best cross-country skiing area, and floodlit trails in Espedalen and in Gålå make it possible to ski even after dinner.

To ski the area, you can purchase a 1-day Troll Pass, costing NOK320 ($64/£32) for adults and NOK265 ($53/£27) for children. The pass entitles you to all the lifts in the area. Check with the local resorts for further information. You can pick up maps and other data at the tourist center at Vinstra (see above).

In summer, **Norske Bygdeopplevelser** (✆ **61-28-99-70**) offers cycling trips and mountain hikes through the Peer Gynt land.

SEEING THE SIGHTS

Much revered by the Norwegians, Bjørnstjerne Bjørnson, the author of the national anthem of Norway, lived at an old farmstead, **Aulestad,** in Gausdal, 18km (11 miles) northwest of Lillehammer, from 1875 until his death in 1910. Bjørnson purchased the farm with his wife, Karoline. He won the Nobel Prize for literature in 1903. In 1934, the house was opened as a national museum, and today it is filled with Bjørnson memorabilia. It's signposted near the hamlet of Follebu. Aulestad (✆ **61-22-30-83**) is open in late May and September daily 11am to 2:30pm, and June to August daily 10am to 5pm. Admission is NOK75 ($15/£7.50) adults, NOK35 ($7/£3.50) for children under 16.

WHERE TO STAY & DINE

Most people travel the Peer Gynt Road as an excursion from Lillehammer. But if you'd like to stay around for a few days, here are several recommended accommodations. These recommendations are scattered throughout the area at various hamlets and resorts.

Dalseter Høyfjellshotell (Kids) There are far grander hotels in the area than this inviting oasis in the wilderness, but the staff at this homelike hotel does more to hook you up with the best outdoor activities in the area. Ski trails start right outside the entrance to the hotel, and in summer the hotel sells fishing permits for those who want to try their luck with trout, char, and perch. Mountain biking expeditions can be arranged by staff, who also give advice on marked trails where you can hike among the

Bjørnstjerne Bjørnson: Yes, We Love This Land

Ranking along with author Henrik Ibsen, 1903 Nobel Prize winner for literature Bjørnstjerne Bjørnson (1832–1910) has left part of his world behind at this old farmstead at Aulestad (see above), which the public can now visit in Gausdal. The author is a towering figure in the history of Norway, having achieved fame as a poet, dramatist, novelist, journalist, editor, public speaker, and theater director.

His immortality was ensured when his poem "Ja, vi elsker dette landet" ("Yes, We Love This Land") was selected as the Norwegian national anthem.

The son of a pastor, Bjørnson grew up in a farming community, later the setting for several of his novels. From 1857 to 1859, he became Ibsen's successor as artistic director of the Bergen Theatre, where he married the actress Karoline Reimers in 1858.

Later, from 1866 to 1871, he was director of the Christiania Theatre in Oslo. While in self-imposed exile between 1860 and 1863, he wrote some of his most enduring works. Some of his best-remembered works today are *The Heritage of the Kurts,* written in 1884, and *In God's Way,* written in 1889.

Later in life, he became an ardent socialist, working for peace and international understanding. Although he enjoyed worldwide fame in his life and his plays helped to bring "social realism" to Europe, his international reputation today pales when compared to his sometimes friend and always rival, Ibsen.

flora and fauna. Or you can just sit and breathe the fresh mountain air. This family-run hotel, built in 1963 but considerably modernized since, is set on a hillside overlooking panoramic forests and mountains. The bedrooms are outfitted in a cozy, comfortable Norwegian regional style, with lots of heat during the Arctic winters. In winter, evening dance music contributes to a festive ski-lodge atmosphere, and meals of well-prepared country fare are served in a warm, inviting room. The hotel is entirely nonsmoking.

Gudbrandsdalen, N-2658 Espedal. ✆ **61-29-99-10.** Fax 61-29-99-41. www.dalseter.no. 88 units. NOK705–NOK990 ($141–$198/£71–£99) double. Rates include buffet breakfast. Children 4 and under stay free in parent's room; 3-night minimum stay. DC, MC, V. Closed May–June and Oct–Dec 21. **Amenities:** Restaurant; bar; heated indoor pool; 2 tennis courts; exercise room; 2 saunas; large kids' playroom; rooms for those w/limited mobility. *In room:* TV.

Fefor Høifjellshotell ★ (Kids) The core of this hotel dates from 1891, when it was a modest-size plank-sided mountain inn, sheltering summer hikers and winter skiers from a location beside the Fefor Innsjø (Fefor Lake), 13km (8 miles) east of Vinstra. Today, greatly expanded by a series of modern wings that contain the accommodations, it's an upper-middle-bracket refuge with the most charming old central hotel cores in the region. Designed in the Norwegian nationalist style, it features red Nordic dragons on the roof of its oldest wing, blazing fireplaces, and heavy iron chandeliers. Bedrooms are cozy, wood-trimmed, and contemporary, with views over the lake and the mountains. Access to the ski lifts requires a 12-minute hike across flat ground from the hotel. On the grounds of this hotel are 20 wood-sided, bare-boned cabins, each with cooking facilities, available for 6 to 12 people each year-round. If you enjoy rustic, outdoorsy surroundings, these just might be the perfect accommodations for you. Cabins, designed for those who like to rough it a bit, accommodate up to seven guests and are rented only by the week, costing NOK9,050 ($1,810/£905).

N-2640 Vinstra. ✆ **61-29-33-00** or 61-29-17-60. www.fefor.no. 120 units. Mon–Thurs NOK2,190 ($438/£219) double; Fri–Sun NOK2,590 ($518/£259) double. Rates include half-board. AE, DC, MC, V. **Amenities:** Restaurant; bar; indoor heated pool; 2 saunas; children's programs; boating facilities; skating rink; squash hall; nonsmoking rooms. *In room:* TV.

Gålå Høgfjellshotell ★★★ (Kids) This resort is the preferred choice in the area, a luxurious hotel combined with a historic core, making for some old-fashioned nostalgia wedded to elegance and modern comfort. There's more of a sense of the 19th-century Norwegian nationalist style scattered around this hotel than there is in other hotels nearby. Its architectural style derives from its origins around 1870 as a high-altitude sanatorium for tuberculosis patients and its transformation in the 1890s, into a hotel. Another part of its allure is its location—within a short walk of the ski lifts, and easily accessible from the slopes on skis. Accommodations are nostalgically furnished in a rustic, old-fashioned style, and much about this place evokes a skier's and hiker's boutique hotel. Its Mor Aases Restaurant is the best in the area, with freshly caught organic trout from Lake Gålå, seasonal game, and fresh berries and herbs.

Despite its relatively intimate size, the hotel functions as a manager and rental agent for about 130 self-catering cabins, suitable for between 6 and 10 occupants, scattered throughout the nearby district. Each has a kitchen, and amenities range from bare-boned to relatively plush. They're favored by families and extended groups of friends traveling together. Depending on the season and their size, they cost NOK3,475 to NOK18,735 ($695–$3,747/£348–£1,874) per week without meals or services.

N-2646 Gålå. ✆ **61-29-81-09.** Fax 61-29-76-01. www.gala-resort.com. 42 units. NOK550–NOK1,060 ($110–$212/£55–£106) double in summer; rates include buffet breakfast. NOK2,200–NOK2,450 ($440–$490/£220–£245) double in winter; rates include half-board. AE, DC, MC, V. **Amenities:** Restaurant; bar; outdoor heated pool; tennis court; sauna; children's programs; laundry service/dry cleaning; cross-country skiing; easy-access downhill ski slopes. *In room:* TV, hair dryer.

Thon Hotel Gausdal ★★ There are now two Thons in the area, though Gausdal is the market leader. Lying 8km (5 miles) northwest from the town of Svingvoll, it is still one of the most traditional lodges in the area. Its original core is from 1876 but was burned to the ground by the Nazis. The oldest wing that survived is from 1921. Other wings were added in 1956, 1984, and the mid-1990s, creating a cohesive, well-operated unit. The hotel lies in the center of the small but popular mountain resort of Gausdal, 16km (10 miles) west of Tretten, the nearest railroad station. If you notify them, the owners will send a car to pick you up. Bedrooms are comfortably and tastefully furnished, offering views of the mountains. Each comes with a shower and bathtub. Kilometers of hiking or ski trails surround the hotel, and provisions can be made for downhill or cross-country skiing in winter and horseback riding or hill climbing in summer. There is immediate access to ski lifts, a sports center with a ski school, and ski-rental facilities. Even if you're passing through just for the day, you might want to stop in to sample the hotel's smorgasbord. The hotel is entirely nonsmoking.

Skeikampen, N-2652 Svingvoll. ✆ **61-05-51-50.** Fax 61-05-51-51. www.thonhotels.no. 129 units. NOK1,370 ($274/£137) double. Rates include buffet breakfast. AE, DC, MC, V. **Amenities:** Restaurant; bar; indoor heated pool; 18-hole golf course; 3 tennis courts; sauna; 1 room for those w/limited mobility. *In room:* TV, Wi-Fi, minibar (in some), hair dryer.

Thon Hotel Skeikampen ★ Kids This is the more affordable of the two Thons in the area, and it has its devotees. One of the few hotels remaining open all year, this establishment remains one of the finest places to lodge in the ski region. It offers attractive public rooms filled with antique and modern furniture, and acres of woodland grounds. The snug and cozy bedrooms, decorated in "Nordic light" pastels, are distributed in such a way that most of them open onto scenic views. Sports lovers will find a ski lift adjacent to a smaller rope tow for beginners and a ski school with child-care facilities. The hotel is right at the timberline, and forested and rocky paths both are well marked for climbers. On the premises is a Spanish-inspired bodega, with the best wine stock in the region. Wine-tasting parties and semiformal dinners are held here at least three times a week. The hotel lies 38km (24 miles) from the rail station at Tretten, and arrangements can be made to have a car pick you up.

N-2652 Svingvoll. ✆ **61-28-50-00.** Fax 61-28-50-01. www.thonhotels.no. 115 units. NOK1,530 ($306/£153) double. Children 4 and under stay free in parent's room. Rates include buffet breakfast. AE, DC, MC, V. **Amenities:** Restaurant; bar; fitness room; spa; sauna; laundry service/dry cleaning; nonsmoking rooms; rooms for those w/limited mobility. *In room:* TV, minibar (in some), Wi-Fi, hair dryer.

Wadahl Høifjellshotel ★★ This is one of the more luxurious of the several hotels positioned on the ski slopes around Lillehammer, with an isolated hillside location that allows residents to ski from the hotel's front door to the ski lifts, and then ski back to the hotel from the upper reaches of the surrounding slopes. The hotel is only a few minutes away from the Gålå Høgfjellshoteel, with identical access to hiking and cross-country trails. If faced with a choice between the two, we'd choose the Gålå for its superior cuisine.

Cozy and rustic, with a sports-conscious clientele that often drives from as far away as Oslo for weekend getaways, the Wadahl was originally established in 1900 as a survival station for the high mountains around it. It was transformed into a resort hotel in 1930 and has been enlarged several times, most recently in 1999 but with minor refurbishments post-millennium. Rooms are comfortably furnished and modern-looking, each with an immaculately kept bathroom. Midwinter and midsummer are equally desirable high seasons here, and unlike most other urban hotels in Norway, weekend visits are more, rather than less, expensive than weekdays.

N-2646 Gålå. ✆ **61-29-75-00.** Fax 61-29-75-01. www.wadahl.no. 100 units. Mon–Thurs NOK700–NOK825 ($140–$165/£70–£83) per person; Fri–Sun NOK1,750–NOK2,600 ($350–$520/£175–£260) for 2 persons. AE, DC, MC, V. Closed Nov–Dec and May Mon–Thurs. **Amenities:** Restaurant; bar; large outdoor heated pool; indoor heated pool; outdoor lighted tennis courts; sauna; horseback-riding facilities; activity center for access to hiking, hill climbing, and cross-country skiing; nonsmoking rooms; rooms for those w/limited mobility. *In room:* TV, minibar.

4 LOM ★ & JOTUNHEIMEN NATIONAL PARK ★★★

62km (38 miles) NW of Otta; 180km (112 miles) NW of Lillehammer

With its towering peaks and foreboding glaciers, **Jotunheimen National Park,** one of the greatest parks in Norway, lies in Lom municipality. Lom can also be your gateway to the fjord country, as two of the grandest fjords in Norway, **Geiranger** and **Sognefjord** (see chapter 12), are a short drive to the west.

Continuing northwest from our last stopover at Vinstra, we turn off the E6 onto Rte. 15 heading west into **Lom,** which lies in the center of the Jotunheimen National Park. In one of the most colorful settings of any rustic little village in Norway, Lom straddles the Prestfossen Waterfall and the Bøvra River. A village of great and traditional charm, despite heavy tourist traffic, Lom has retained much of its log-cabin architecture and boasts a stave church from 1170.

Some 905km (562 miles) of its municipal border are covered by glaciers and mountains, the most important and dramatic of which are **Glittertind,** at 2,452m (8,043 ft.), and **Galdhøpiggen,** at 2,469m (8,098 ft.).

ESSENTIALS

GETTING THERE **Nor-Way Buss Ekspress** (✆ **81-54-44-44;** www.nor-way.no) buses pass through Lom from Oslo at the rate of three per day, costing NOK485 ($97/£49) one-way and taking 6½ hours. From Lillehammer or Vinstra, continue northwest along E6 until the junction with Rte. 15, at which point you head west into Lom.

VISITOR INFORMATION For information about the area, including hiking, head for the **Jotunheimen Reiseliv** (✆ **61-21-29-90;** www.visitlom.com), in the Norsk Fjellmuseum (see below). You can also purchase hiking maps here, which are necessary if you plan to tour Jotunheimen Nasjonalpark.

SEEING THE SIGHTS

In the center of Lom, **Stavkyrke** (✆ **97-07-53-97**) dates from 1170 but was enlarged in 1635 when it was restyled in a cruciform shape. In 1667, two naves were added. The church is admired for its early-18th-century paintings and Jakob Saeterdalen's pulpit and chancel from 1793. Charging NOK45 ($9/£4.50) for adults, but free for children 14 and under, it is open June 15 to August 15 daily 9am to 8pm, August 16 to September 15 daily 10am to 4pm.

An even more impressive sight is the **Fossheim Steinsenter** ★ (✆ **61-21-14-60;** www.fossheimsteinsenter.no), with Europe's biggest and most varied exhibition of rare and stunningly beautiful rocks, along with gems, minerals, and fossils, plus jewelry on sale. Part of the museum is devoted to exotic geological specimens gathered from all over the world. The owners take pride in the national stone of Norway, thulite, which was first discovered in Lom in 1820 and is now quarried. (Manganese gives thulite its reddish color.) Admission is free, and the center is open mid-June to mid-August daily 9am to 8pm. In the off season, hours are Monday to Friday 10am to 3pm.

Norsk Fjellmuseum in Lom (✆ **61-21-16-00;** www.fjell.museum.no) is the visitor center for Jotunheimen National Park (see below). The center has a dual role as a museum filled with intriguing exhibits about mountaineering and an information center for hikers in the park. Exhibits relate both the culture of the mountain people and the

Impressions

It [Besseggen Ridge] cuts along with an edge like a scythe for miles and miles . . . and scars and glaciers sheer down the precipice to the glassy lakes, 1,600 feet below on either side.

—Henrik Ibsen

park's natural history. A 10-minute mountain slide show is also presented. Admission is NOK50 ($10/£5) for adults and NOK30 ($6/£3) for children under 14. It is open mid-June to mid-August Monday to Friday 9am to 7pm, Saturday and Sunday 10am to 7pm. Off-season hours are Monday to Friday 10am to 3pm, Saturday and Sunday by appointment only.

JOTUNHEIMEN NATIONAL PARK: "HOME OF THE GIANTS"

Norway's greatest national park is dominated by the **towering peaks ★★** of **Galdhopiggen** and **Glittertind.** It is a land of glaciers, mountains, lakes, and waterfalls. It has more than 60 glaciers and is crisscrossed by valleys that split it up into ridges and high plateaus.

A heavily frequented area since 1813, it has become one of the best-developed wilderness tour areas in the north of Europe, with its "linkage" of hotels, tourist huts, and private cabins lying along well-marked trails. It attracts both the neophyte and the more advanced mountain hiker, along with the glacier and rock climbers who descend upon the park in summer.

The beauty of the park, especially its wildflowers in spring, has inspired some of Norway's most famous composers and writers, including Edvard Grieg and Henrik Ibsen. Although its wild reindeer have departed, flocks of tame reindeer are kept on farmsteads by farmers in Vågå or Lom. Fishermen come to the park to catch red char or mountain trout.

First-timers like to take the high and panoramic **Sognefjellet ★★**, a road linking Lom with Lustrafjorden. Built in 1939 by unemployed youth, this is the best access to the northern tier of the park. The road peaks at 1,434m (4,704 ft.), making it the highest mountain road in the north of Europe. In fact, the elevation is so high that the snow doesn't melt until early July. It can even snow here during the hottest period of the summer.

In all, the park encompasses 3,900 sq. km (1,521 sq. miles), with an amazing number of towering peaks, some 200 of which rise to 1,900m (6,232 ft.). Norway's highest waterfall, **Vettisfossen ★★**, is also found in the park, with its 275m (902-ft.) drop. The waterfall lies a short walk from the Vetti Lodge on the western frontier of the park.

The most popular hike in Norway is along the **Besseggen Ridge ★★** towering over Lake Gjende. The trail links the mountain lodges of Memurubu and Gjendesheim. One of the most famous lakes in Norway, Gjende appears in the writings of Henrik Ibsen. The author had his Peer Gynt tumble from the ridge into the lake on the back of a speeding reindeer. The lake is 18km (11 miles) long and 146m (479 ft.) deep. Its emerald-green waters are fed by glaciers. In summer, you can rent boats along the lakefront.

Obtain complete and detailed maps from the tourist office before setting out into the park, and know that the weather can change at a moment's notice. You can also arrange with the tourist office to hire a guide, which is highly recommended.

WHERE TO STAY

Elveseter Hotell ★★ (Finds) In one of the untouched wilderness areas of Jotunheimen National Park, this is one of the most exceptional hotels in Central Norway. In its role as a hotel, it accepted its first overnight guest in 1870, while it simultaneously functioned as a farmstead whose workers and overseers were completely snowbound for at least 6 months of the year. What you'll see today is a compound of 19 Tolkienesque buildings, many antique, all of them plank-sided, and some of them with sod roofs. They nestle beside a river on a valley floor that's flanked on both sides by some of the most jagged and snow-covered mountains in Norway. Two of the buildings boast foundations from 1579 and 1640, respectively. Others are newer structures fancifully trimmed in the Norwegian nationalist style, with Viking-inspired motifs.

The compound's centerpiece is the *Sagasøyla* (Saga column), rising 30m (98 ft.) and capped with bronze statues of Viking lords. It presents a figurative history of Norway from 872 to 1814. Depending on your point of view, the decor of this place is either richly historic—a period piece that revels in the Norwegian national aesthetic—or a slightly dated piece of Scandinavian kitsch. A wide range of outdoor activities is available here, including midsummer cross-country skiing on the high altitudes nearby or on glaciers, every kind of trekking and climbing, and river rafting. Folkloric shows, presented within an on-site theater, occur frequently.

Elveseter, 2687 Bøverdalen. ✆ **61-21-99-00.** Fax 61-21-99-01. www.elveseter.no. 88 units. NOK980 ($196/£98) double; from NOK2,000 ($400/£200) suite. Rates include buffet breakfast. Evening buffet in dining room NOK240 ($48/£24) per person. AE, DC, MC, V. Closed mid-Sept to late May. Bøverdalen lies 24km (15 miles) from Lom. From the hamlet of Bøverdalen, drive 3.3km (2 miles) southwest and follow the signs to Elveseter. **Amenities:** Buffet-style restaurant; bar; indoor heated pool; theater for movies and folkloric expositions; sports facilities that include options for hiking, trekking, and rafting. *In room:* No phone.

Fossheim Turisthotell ★★ Finds The bearded Svein Garmo, often seen uncorking a wine bottle, is the third-generation owner at Fossheim. He extends his hand to guests, welcoming them to "enjoy the good life." That's just how things are done in a hotel founded back in 1897. The site was once run as both a farm with seven bedrooms and a hotel, but it has seen dramatic improvements and expansion over the years. A new addition called "Amerika" was designed to attract post–World War II American visitors who demanded rooms with private bathrooms. The main building is still accented with stout ceiling beams and Norwegian antiques. You can select a room here or else choose a log house built according to ancient traditions. All the rooms, regardless of your choice, are tasteful, comfortable, and cozily decorated. One of the reasons to stay here is to enjoy the cuisine; see "Where to Dine," below.

N-2688 Lom. ✆ **61-21-95-00.** Fax 61-21-95-01. www.fossheimhotel.no. 46 units. NOK1,040–NOK1,350 ($208–$270/£104–£135) double. Rates include buffet breakfast. AE, DC, MC, V. **Amenities:** Restaurant; 2 bars. *In room:* TV, no phone.

Turtagro Value Beginning in the 1800s, this area was on the vanguard of mountain sports in Norway. In 1876, William Cecil Slingsby from Britain came here to climb Store Skagastølstind, which put the area on the tourist maps. For nature lovers who want a Norwegian alpine setting against a backdrop of snow-covered peaks and glaciers, one of the most isolated hotels in Norway occupies a forested, mountainside site 9.5km (6 miles) northeast of the hamlet of Fortun and 59km (37 miles) northeast of the village of Sogndal. It originated in 1887, when it functioned as an emergency station for mountaineers and trekkers in the surrounding hills and mountains. What you'll see today is a trio of red-painted, wood-sided buildings, one of which is exclusively devoted to the housing of the hardworking staff. The more comfortable lodgings are within the artfully minimalist conventional bedrooms, each of which has wood paneling and a no-frills decor. The budget accommodations are at the Swiss Chalet, built in 1889, containing a total of 66 beds with shared bathrooms. The dining room serves hearty food, flavorful and plentiful.

N-6877 Fortun. ✆ **57-68-08-00.** Fax 57-68-08-01. www.turtagro.no. 19 units, plus 66 dormitory-style beds in a nearby outbuilding. NOK885–NOK1,085 ($177–$217/£89–£109) per person double; NOK570 ($114/£57) per person for bed in dormitory-style outbuilding. Rates include buffet breakfast. AE, DC, MC, V. Closed Oct–Mar. **Amenities:** Restaurant; bar; babysitting; laundry service. *In room:* No phone.

Vågå Hotel (Value) We've always been sentimentally attached to this place where we came years ago to climb our first Norwegian mountain. Country comfortable, big-windowed, and well respected, this is the only hotel, and one of the most oft-recommended restaurants, in the hamlet of Vågå, where about half of the county's population of 4,000 people lives. Substantial-looking and solid, it was originally built in the 1950s, then enlarged and radically reconfigured twice, in the 1960s and again in the 1970s. Its interior is cozy and richly paneled, in ways that make it seem older than it actually is, with local pine. A fireplace, completely sheathed in heat-conductive ceramic tile, throws off a welcome midwinter heat. The comfortably furnished but rather minimalist bedrooms are small to midsize. There's a large indoor swimming pool, the kind you can swim laps in. Because the local downhill ski lifts are about 32km (20 miles) away, this hotel attracts fewer downhill skiers than cross-country skiers.

N-2680 Vågå. ✆ **61-23-95-50.** Fax 61-23-95-51. www.vagahotel.no. 56 units. NOK1,200 ($240/£120) double. Rates include buffet breakfast. AE, DC, MC, V. From Lom, drive 32km (20 miles) east, following Rte. 15 and the signs to Otta. **Amenities:** Restaurant; 2 bars; indoor heated pool. *In room:* TV (in some).

WHERE TO DINE

Fossheim Restaurant ★★★ NORWEGIAN An enticing aroma originating in the kitchen spreads across the hills, luring visitors here. Set within the cozy, old-fashioned dining room of the Fossheim Turisthotell (see above), amid a scattering of 19th-century Danish and Norwegian antiques, this is the most famous and well-recommended restaurant in the region. It owes much of its renown to head chef Kristoffer Hoyland, whose imaginative use of local fish and game has been publicized, thanks to local and national newspapers, throughout Norway. Despite frequent modernizations, at least some of the building's original late-19th-century character remains, including lavish use of pinewood paneling and big-windowed views of the mountains and the local stave church. Main courses vary with the seasons, yet all are redolent of the bracing mountain climate of central Norway. The best examples include baked wild salmon served with fresh vegetables and a creamy sauce; whole fried mountain trout served with herbs and a sour cream sauce; and award-winning versions of reindeer filet and breast of wild ptarmigan served pinky-rare, each with a creamy game sauce that's enriched with wild mushrooms.

N-2686 Lom. ✆ **61-21-95-00.** Reservations recommended. Fixed-price menus NOK340–NOK1,500 ($68–$300/£34–£150). AE, DC, MC, V. Daily 1–3pm and 7–10:30pm (until 10pm in winter).

5 RONDANE ★★ & DOVREFJELL ★ NATIONAL PARKS

Lesja: 159km (99 miles) N of Lom

The last Ice Age carved out one of Norway's most dramatic landscapes in the Rondane and Dovrefjell national parks. With their barren mountains, narrow canyons, and deep cirques, they bring out the adventurer in us.

Jotunheimen should eat up most of your time, but Rondane is vastly impressive with its towering peaks, waterfalls, and deep valleys. We've found the best alpine hiking at Rondane, a glaciated landscape with 125 bird species and nearly 3 dozen mammals, including the reindeer.

Rondane gets the most visitors, and hikers prefer it, but bird watchers flock to Dovrefjell because of a recent expansion. It took into its boundaries the **Fokstumyra**

marshes ★★, home to nearly 75 species of birds who nest in the area. Some 50 other species have been spotted, such as the loon bird, the lapwing, the great snipe, and the ruff. Allow about 2 days for Rondane and at least one for Dovrefjell to scratch the surface of these wildernesses.

ESSENTIALS

GETTING THERE Two buses a day (9:45am and 3:15pm) run from the little town of Otta, lying on the E6 northwest of Lillehammer, and the settlement of Mysusaeter, ending at the Spranghaugen Car Park. This is the start of the most frequented routes through Rondane. The trip takes 45 minutes and costs NOK60 ($12/£6) one-way. There is no public transportation to Dovrefjell. Motorists can reach such gateway towns as Lesja or Dombås by taking the E6 northwest of Lillehammer. For bus information, call ✆ **81-54-44-44** or visit www.nor-way.no.

VISITOR INFORMATION For details on exploring both Rondane and Dovrefjell, you can go to the **Nasjonalparksenter,** Sentralplassen, in the town of Dombås (✆ **61-24-14-44**). Open mid-June to mid-August Monday to Saturday 9am to 8pm, Sunday 9am to 4pm; mid-August to mid-June Monday to Friday 9am to 4pm.

EXPLORING THE NATIONAL PARKS

If you have time for only one of these parks, make it Jotunheimen (see above), but if you stay on, you're in for some more scenic glory. The little town of Lesja can be your gateway to **Rondane Nasjonalpark,** which lies to its southwest. Henrik Ibsen called Rondane "palace piled upon palace." Created in 1962, the 572-sq.-km (223-sq.-mile) park was the first to open in Norway.

The park is divided into a trio of different mountain areas, all more than 2,011m (6,596 ft.) in elevation. To the east of the Rondane massif rise the peaks of **Rondeslotteet,** at 2,178m (7,144 ft.). To the west are such mountains as **Veslesmeden,** at 2,016m (6,612 ft.); **Storsmeden,** at 2,017m (6,617 ft.); and **Sagtinden,** at 2,018m (6,619 ft.). All these mountains are linked by narrow "saddles." The third group is split by the deep valley of Lunggluрdalen and crowned by **Midtronden Mountain,** at 2,114m (6,934 ft.).

One of Norway's great areas for hikers, Rondane has poor soil, and the ground is often covered with lichens instead of more luxuriant flora. The park is peppered with little lakes and rivers, the landscape broken in part by dwarf birch trees.

The area has been inhabited for thousands of years, as ancient Viking burial mounds and centuries-old reindeer traps reveal. More than 2 dozen types of animals, including reindeer and some 125 species of birds, now populate the park.

Most visitors to the park begin their hikes at the Spranghaugen Car Park, near Mysusaeter, which is reached by bus. From this point, the most popular hike in the park is the 6km (3¾-mile) jaunt to **Rondvassbu,** followed by a 5-hour return climb to the summit of **Storronden,** at 2,138m (7,013 ft.).

The **Sjoa,** Europe's best river for rafting, cuts through the park, centered at Heidal with its rushing white waters. The rafting season starts in mid-May and lasts until the end of September. **Sjoa Rafting** in Heidal offers trips through the gorge and other activities in the park. Rafting trips along a 11km (6¾-mile) stretch of the Sjoa run 3½ hours and cost NOK650–NOK700 ($130–$140/£65–£70). Call ✆ **61-23-61-70** for more information.

The other national park, **Dovrefjell Nasjonalpark,** was enlarged in 2002 to take in more of the surrounding area. The park now includes territory in three counties, making it the largest continuous protected area in Norway. Although still called Dovrefjell, its full name in Norwegian is actually Dovrefjell-Sunndalsfjella National Park.

The core of the park was set aside for protection in 1974. The aim was to safeguard the highlands around Snøhetta, which soars to a height of 2,286m (7,498 ft.). Hikers can ascend to Snøhetta in about 6 hours.

The park is home to wolverines, arctic foxes, and reindeer. It is also the habitat of the rare musk ox. This animal, which can survive at amazingly cold temperatures, also lives in parts of Greenland and Alaska. It can weigh up to 446 kilograms (983 lb.). Obviously, its coat is incredibly thick.

In 1931, 10 musk oxen were introduced to Dovrefjell, having been shipped over from Greenland. Because these animals once inhabited Dovrefjell, they were bred successfully. The herd is now estimated to number about 80. It is highly unlikely you'll come across the elusive wolverine or the arctic fox, however.

In another section of the park, the Knutshøene rises 1,690m (5,543 ft.), lying to the east of the main route, E6. This section of the park is Europe's most diverse intact alpine ecosystem. Before setting out to explore the park, arm yourself with a good map from the visitor center (see above).

One of the most intimate ways to explore the national park—and our favorite way of doing it—involves participating in one of the 5-hour guided tours offered by the **Moskus Safari Dovrefjell (Dovrefjell Park Musk Ox Safari Company)**, N-2660 Dombås (✆ **99-70-37-66**). Between mid-June and mid-August every summer, they make daily departures at 9am, usually from the Spranghaugen Car Park, near Mysusaeter, or—with prior reservations—from one of the area's hotels. After a 40km (25-mile) bus or van ride, participants get out for short hiking treks across the tundra (sturdy shoes and protective rain gear are recommended) for close-up observation of the musk oxen and their natural habitats. The cost is NOK300 ($60/£30) per person, lunch is not included in the experience, and participants are usually redeposited either in the Spranghaugen Car Park or back at their hotels sometime between 1 and 2pm. For information on other sporting or sightseeing options within the park, contact the Dombås tourist information office at ✆ **61-24-14-44.**

OTHER ATTRACTIONS

In the center of the historic town of Lesja, you can visit **Lesja Bygdatun** (✆ **61-24-31-53**), consisting of a dozen houses moved to this site and revealing how life was lived in the 18th and 19th centuries. You can explore farm dwellings, cookhouses, barns, storehouses, and a forge hammering out wrought-iron products. Archaeological finds unearthed in the region are also displayed here. An association of farm women bakes and cooks daily at the coffeehouse and restaurant, which serves waffles and other traditional baked goods. On Saturday, they serve the famous *rumgraut* (porridge made with sour cream). There is also a craft shop selling embroideries, painted china and glass, wooden bowls, and other items made in Lesja. From June 20 to August 18, it is open daily from 10am to 5pm, charging NOK40 ($8/£4) to enter. Children 15 and under enter free.

WHERE TO STAY & DINE

In addition to the choices below, the **Rondane Spa** (✆ **61-20-90-90**) at the gateway to the Rondane National Park is the only spa-hotel in this region of central Norway.

Bjorligard Hotell ★ This is the area's most appealing hotel. We liken it to a large, contemporary chalet, thanks to exposed planking, weathered siding, and a design that

Sigrid Undset Country

Winner of the Nobel Prize for Literature in 1928, Sigrid Undset (1882–1949) still enjoys an international audience. She lived and wrote about this area in central Norway and was known for her novels about Scandinavia in the Middle Ages. Her *Kristin Lavransdatter* became an international bestseller. Her books have been translated into all the major languages of the world. Undset wrote 36 books and was a great storyteller who was particularly adept at exploring human psychology.

Born in Denmark the same year as James Joyce and Virginia Woolf, Undset came to Norway at age 2, where in time she devoured Norse sagas, finding inspiration for her later work.

In 1919, she moved to Lillehammer, after a life in Oslo, the subject of many of her novels. An outspoken critic of Nazi Germany, she fled in April 1940, when the Germans invaded her country. She went to neutral Sweden, not wanting to be taken hostage by the Germans. In the 1940s, she came to the United States to plead her occupied country's cause. Upon her return to Norway in 1945, she lived for another 4 years but never wrote another word.

You can recapture some of the atmosphere of Undset's prize-winning trilogy, *Kristin Lavransdatter,* by visiting the **Jørundgard Middelalder Senter** at Sel (✆ **61-23-37-00**). This medieval farm was re-created in 1995 for the Liv Ullmann film *Kristin Lavransdatter.* The film helped put Undset back on the Norwegian cultural map, especially among young people.

The farm lies in Nord-Sel, 15km (9¼ miles) north of Otta, which is reached along E6. The center consists of 16 buildings and a consecrated stave church. You can join in a guided tour and taste foods of the Middle Ages. The center (✆ **61-23-37-00**) is open for guided tours, costing NOK90 ($18/£9), daily from 10am to 5pm from June to mid-August.

might have been inspired by a mountainside lodge in Switzerland. Redecorated and renovated, it lies within a 7-minute walk from the village ski lifts, attracting a sports-oriented and, in many cases, rather youthful clientele. Public areas contain paneling, a blazing fireplace, rustic artifacts, and cozy comfortable seating nooks. Bedrooms range from midsize to spacious, including 16 units with four-poster or king-size double beds; all come with views over the surrounding landscapes.

N-2669 Bjorli. ✆ **61-24-44-00.** Fax 61-24-44-01. www.bjorligard.no. 56 units. NOK1,100 ($220/£110) double. AE, DC, MC, V. Closed May and Nov. Bjorli lies northwest of Lesja along E6. **Amenities:** Restaurant; bar; indoor heated pool; sauna; fitness room; Jacuzzi; all nonsmoking rooms. *In room:* TV, coffeemaker, kitchenette.

Brekkeseter ★ Kids The origins of this hotel date from 1772, when its central core functioned as a farm for the midsummer production of hay, and the spring and autumn gathering of moss (used as cattle feed) from the surrounding mountains. Today, set directly atop the tree line (where the forest ends and the rocky uplands begin), the site comprises 25 separate buildings, each an old-fashioned plank-sided testimonial to the building techniques of yesteryear. The largest of these, built in stages between 1772 and 1995, functions as a small-scale, conventional hotel. None of the rooms in this part of the hotel has a TV or phone, but the simple but cozy decor reflects the barren but beautiful landscape outside.

If you opt to rent one of the conventional bedrooms, it will come as part of a highly unusual "three-quarter pension" plan, wherein breakfast, a full dinner, and a boxed lunch (which you'll pack yourself from a wide choice of raw ingredients) is included in the rates. If you opt to rent one of the cabins, it will contain a full kitchen and space for between 2 and 10 occupants, ideal for large or small families. Its price will not include any meals.

N-2673 Høvrigen. ✆ **61-23-37-11.** Fax 61-23-43-13. www.brekkeseter.no. 12 units, 17 cabins. NOK1,560–NOK3,600 ($312–$720/£156–£360) double; NOK800–NOK4,400 ($160–$880/£80–£440) cabin (2–10 occupants). Rates for double include 3/4 board; cabin rates do not include meals. AE, MC, V. Hotel closed Easter to mid-June and mid-Oct to Jan, but cabins are available. **Amenities:** Restaurant; babysitting; laundry service; trekking guides. *In room:* No phone.

6 RØROS: NORWAY'S GREAT MINING TOWN ★★

159km (99 miles) SE of Trondheim; 399km (247 miles) N of Oslo

Exploring a mining town might sound like a put-off, but this relic of another day is the finest of its kind in Scandinavia. As you strolled through the National Gallery in Oslo, you may have been struck by the arresting paintings crafted by the Norwegian artist Harald Sohlberg. His paintings made Røros famous internationally, and a statue of him stands at Harald Sohlberg Plass.

Tucked away in the mountains of eastern Norway, the old mining town of Røros is now part of UNESCO's World Cultural and Natural Heritage List. It is the most famous and evocative of Norway's mining towns.

More than 3 centuries old, it is known for its collection of 80 well-preserved buildings from the 17th and 18th centuries. Many of Norway's old wooden towns have long burned to the ground, but the Old Town of Røros is still so authentic that film companies regularly use the town as an authentic backdrop. One such film was *An-Magrit,* starring Liv Ullmann, adapted from the work of Røros's best-known author, Johan Falkberget, who lived in the town until his death in 1967. Some of Astrid Lindgren's *Pippi Longstocking* classics were filmed in Røros as well, and it was used as a setting for Siberia in Solzhenitsyn's *A Day in the Life of Ivan Denisovich.*

Røros lies at the northern tier of the Osterdal, a valley to the east of Gudbrandsdalen. It is famous because of its rich copper mines, which were launched in 1644 and ran until going bankrupt in 1977.

ESSENTIALS

GETTING THERE **By Plane** Røros Airport (✆ **72-41-39-00**) is a 4-minute drive from the center of town. **Widerøe Airlines,** a partner of SAS, flies to and from Oslo daily.

By Train Røros has rail links with Oslo and Trondheim. Three trains per day arrive Monday through Saturday from Trondheim, taking 2½ hours, and three trains come in from Oslo, taking 5 hours. For train information and schedules, call ✆ **81-50-08-88** or visit www.nsb.no.

By Bus Three buses per day connect Trondheim and Røros Monday through Saturday, taking 3¼ hours. Visit www.nor-way.no for information.

By Car From Trondheim, take E6/Rte. 30 south for 2½ hours.

VISITOR INFORMATION For information, go to the **Røros Reiseliv Turistkontorget,** Peder Hiortsgata 2 (✆ **72-41-11-65**), a block from the train station. From June 25 to August 19, hours are Monday to Saturday 9am to 6pm, Sunday 10am to 4pm. The rest of the year, hours are Monday to Friday 9am to 3pm and Saturday 10:30am to 12:30pm. Also visit www.rorosinfo.com for information.

SEEING THE SIGHTS

The best way to see Røros is to take a guided walk through the Old Town starting at the local tourist office (see above). In summer, tours leave several times daily, costing NOK60 ($12/£6); free for children. In the off season, only Saturday tours are conducted.

In town you can also visit **Røros Kirke,** Kjerkgata (no phone), which dates from 1650. It was established to cater to the workers in the smelting works. More than a century later, it was substantially rebuilt in the baroque style, seating 1,600 worshippers, an amazingly large congregation for a town of this size. It is an eight-sided stone structure with a pulpit sitting over the altarpiece. Admission is free, and it is open June 21 to August 15 Monday to Saturday from 10am to 5pm and Sunday 2 to 4pm.

Røros offers several other attractions, including **Røros Museum-Smelthytta,** Malmplassen (✆ **72-40-61-70**), site of the first smelting works in the area, dating from 1646. A model exhibition here illustrates old mining and smelting technology, including ore hoists, waterwheels, horse-drawn winches, and furnaces. One section displays regional costumes from the 1800s. The building is a reconstruction of the original structure, which burned in a fire in 1953. Admission is NOK60 ($12/£6) for adults or NOK30 ($6/£3) for children under 15. It's open mid-June to August daily 10am to 7pm; in other months, it's open Tuesday to Friday 11am to 3pm and Saturday and Sunday 11am to 2pm.

For us, a highlight of a visit to Røros is a side trip to **Olavsgruva,** or Olav's Mine, Kojedalen (✆ **72-40-61-70**), lying 9.5km (6 miles) east of Røros. A guided tour will take you through 3 centuries of mining. The system here consists of two mines, Nyberget and Crown Prince Olav's mine. Nyberget is by far the oldest, as Prince Olav mine was begun only in 1936. The tour on foot takes you 50m (164 ft.) below the surface of the earth and 500m (1,640 ft.) into the cavern, where miners of yore toiled in miserable conditions. The temperature is about 41°F (5°C) all year. Sound-and-light effects help re-create the mood of the old mines. Mine tours cost NOK80 ($16/£8) for adults and free for children under 15. Tours are conducted five times daily from June 1 to mid-August, and two times daily from mid-August to September. In the off season, tours are conducted only on Saturday. If you're driving, follow the signs along Rte. 31 to the mines northeast from the center of Røros. Otherwise, a round-trip by taxi will cost NOK400 ($80/£40).

Johan Falkberget Museum (✆ **72-41-46-31**) honors the area's favorite son. The author (1879–1967) was reared at Trondalen Farm in the Rugel Valley outside Røros. Translated into 20 languages, he became a famous author around the world, his most celebrated book being *An-Magrit,* which was made into a 1969 film starring Liv Ullmann. It tells of a peasant girl who transported copper ore in the Røros mines. Falkberget's early poverty and toil in the mines colored all his works. The trilogies *Christianus Sextus* (1927–35) and *Bread of Night* (1940–59) concern mining life in the 17th and

18th centuries. They emphasize the virtues of hard work and Christian love. The Falkberget museum lies beside Lake Rugelsjø. Admission is NOK60 ($12/£6) for adults and NOK30 ($6/£3) for children. Tours are July 1 to August 5 daily at noon, 1, and 2pm. From August 6 to 12, tours are daily at noon. Local trains from Røros will take you to Rugeldalen Station, lying 20km (12 miles) north of Røros. You can take a signposted track leading up to the museum. Except for the Røros Museum, all tours for local attractions must be arranged through the tourist office.

SHOPPING

Silversmiths, woodcarvers, painters, potters, and glass blowers abound in Greater Røros. Pottery, sculpture, and wall decorations, all of high quality, are sold at **Per Sverre Dahl Keramikk,** Mørkstug. 5 (✆ **72-41-19-89**).

WHERE TO STAY

Bergstadens Hotel This hotel is the center of social life in Røros. In the center of town near the train station, this landmark hotel was built before World War II but was brought up-to-date during extensive renovations. A cozy, well-run choice, it is furnished in a modern Nordic style with light pastels. Half of the bedrooms open onto views of the mountains, and some have balconies. The staff is helpful in arranging outdoor activities such as horseback riding. The hotel houses the largest concentration of eating and drinking establishments in town. Three on-site bars include Barny Dancing, with recorded music; Nilsenhjørnet Bar; and the combined Hiort Pub & Moskusen Nuppe. The hotel's main restaurant, Bodegaen Mat & Vin, serves a classic and bountiful Norwegian cuisine.

Oslovein 2, N-7374 Røros. ✆ **72-40-60-80.** Fax 72-40-60-81. www.bergstaden.no. 90 units. June–Aug NOK1,300 ($260/£130) double; Sept–May NOK1,500 ($300/£150) double. Children 3 and under stay free in parent's room. Rates include continental breakfast. AE, DC, MC, V. **Amenities:** 2 restaurants; 3 bars; indoor heated pool; sauna; room service; nonsmoking rooms. *In room:* TV, minibar, hair dryer.

Quality Hotel & Resort Røros ★ Luxury may not be the right word for this well-established hotel, but its accommodations are the finest in the area. Frankly, Bergstadens is more fun, but, as chain hotels go, this Quality Hotel is a cut above most of its brethren. This hotel enjoys good views from its high-altitude position over the town, north of the rail station. It was built in the mid-1950s but has been enlarged and improved many times. The bedrooms are decorated in light pastels, opening onto a view of the Old Town. Furnishings are comfortable and tasteful, each unit coming with a small bathroom. The hotel is used by locals as a sort of dining and dancing center after 9pm.

An-Magrittsvei, N-7361 Røros. ✆ **72-40-80-00.** Fax 72-40-80-01. www.choicehotels.no. 167 units. May–Aug NOK1,150 ($230/£115) double, NOK1,450 ($290/£145) suite; Sept–Apr NOK1,395 ($279/£140) double, NOK1,895 ($379/£190) suite. Children 3 and under stay free in parent's room. Rates include buffet breakfast. AE, DC, MC, V. Closed Dec 19–28. **Amenities:** 2 restaurants; 2 bars; indoor heated pool; sauna; babysitting; nonsmoking rooms; rooms for those w/limited mobility. *In room:* TV, Wi-Fi, minibar, hair dryer (in some), trouser press.

WHERE TO DINE

Vertshuset Røros NORWEGIAN If you're seeking the most authentic Norwegian experience for dining or lodging, this is your most atmospheric choice. **Vertshuset Røros** offers well-prepared food and comfortable lodgings within one of the oldest and most nostalgically decorated dining and overnight venues in town. Whereas the restaurant directly fronts the street, the hotel is contained within a completely separate, also red-clapboard, building in back, in a central location not far from the village church. Frankly, the place is most famous as a restaurant, with attentive service, lots of early-20th-century decorative objects, and a menu that focuses on fish and game caught, trapped, or shot within the region. Stellar examples include filets of reindeer or elk in juniper berry sauce; grilled trout and salmon caught in local waters, sometimes served meunière style; and succulent preparations of lamb. Beefsteaks are always a good bet, and the selection of wines comes from throughout Europe. The bedrooms, 17 in all, within the separate annex in back, rent for NOK1,100 to NOK1,180 ($220–$236/£110–£118), double occupancy, with breakfast included. In-room amenities include TV with cable connection and a telephone.

Kjerkgata 34, N-7374 Røros. ✆ **72-41-93-50.** Reservations recommended. Main courses NOK230–NOK350 ($46–$70/£23–£35). AE, DC, MC, V. Daily noon–10pm.

EASY EXCURSIONS

Norway's second-largest lake is part of **Femundsmarka Nasjonalpark** ★ (✆ 62-45-88-96), lying to the immediate southwest of Norway bordering Sweden. It became a national park in 1971 and has long been a retreat for falconry. In the park, we've seen wild reindeer grazing at the upper elevations. In summer, nearly three dozen musk oxen call the park home before migrating during the winter months.

From June 13 to August 24, a limited number of buses go between Røros and Synnervika, a hamlet that is the gateway to the park. Once at the park, you can take the ferry, MS *Foemund II* (✆ **72-41-37-14;** www.femund.no), a diesel-engine boat that sails from the northern shore of Lake Femunden. The boat sails daily from June 13 to August 22, allowing you to take in the shores of this beautiful lake. Fares start at NOK125 ($25/£13), with children under 15 sailing for half-price. The cost of a ticket depends on how far you ride.

9

Southern Norway

The Norwegians themselves go to the south in summer for their vacations, as this part of the country gets more sunshine than any other. Norwegians refer to this vacation spot as Sørlandet, a land of valleys, mountains, rivers, and lakes. Gulf Stream temperatures make taking a dip possible in summer.

Though there is much for the foreign visitor to see and do here, the sheer drama of other regions, including the western fjord district and the region north of the Arctic Circle, far outweighs the more modest attractions of southern Norway.

But if you've got an extra week, you're in for a good time, especially in Rogaland, the southwestern part of the country, which has been called "Norway in a Nutshell," with its wide variety of attractions. Bathed in a mild climate (at least, for Norway), it is a land of fjords, mountains, green valleys, beaches, old towns, and villages—and is also a great place to go fishing.

The coastal lands of southern Norway, shaped geographically like a half-moon, are studded with beaches, bays, and sailing opportunities. Within this area, the Telemark region is known for its lakes and canals, which are used for summer boating and canoeing. A port city, Larvik is the hometown of one of Norway's most famous sons, Thor Heyerdahl, the explorer who conducted the *Kon-Tiki* expedition, among other famous voyages. From Skien, visitors can explore this water network. Arendal is a charming old town with a harbor near some of the best beaches. Kristiansand S is a link between Norway and the rest of Europe. The Christianshholm Fortress has stood here since 1674, and the town is near Haresanden, a 10km-long (over 6¼-mile) beach.

The district lives today in the technological future, thanks to its oil industry, but it also harks back to the country's oldest inhabitants. Here, the Viking king Harald Fairhair gathered most of Norway into one kingdom in A.D. 872. The locals say that it was from here that the Vikings sailed to discover America.

Rogaland also consists of the hilly Dalane in the south, the flat Jaeren (farmland), the beautiful Ryfylke, and Karmøy and Haugesund in the north.

1 LARVIK: HOME OF A GREAT EXPLORER

15km (9¼ miles) S of Sandefjord; 130km (81 miles) SW of Oslo

As you head south, consider stopping over for 2 hours or so to check out the charm of this old port. This is a main port for ferries sailing for Frederikshavn, Denmark, and it's also famously associated with its favorite homegrown boy, Thor Heyerdahl (1914–2002), whose *Kon-Tiki* you may have already seen on the Bygdøy peninsula in Oslo. Heyerdahl organized and led the expedition by the balsa raft *Kon-Tiki* from Peru to Polynesia in 1947 to demonstrate the possibility of aboriginal South American voyages to the Oceanic Islands.

In addition to Heyerdahl, Larvik's largest export is a stone called Larvikitt that's 270 million years old. The stone quarry here is the town's largest industry.

Larvik is a major transportation hub and communications center for southeastern Norway. It also makes a good center for exploring such small but colorful ports as Stavern to its immediate south.

GETTING THERE Chances are, you might arrive from Hirtshals in Denmark, as the **Color Line**(© **81-00-08-11;** www.colorline.com) offers service between the two cities. The line runs one or two daily ferries, taking 3 hours, 45 minutes. Trains, often 20 a day, pull in from Oslo and arrive at the terminus on Storgata, also the site of the bus station. The trip takes 2 hours and costs NOK262 ($52/£26) one-way. If you set out heading south from Oslo along E18, you should pull into Larvik some 2 hours later. Visit www.nsb.no for information.

VISITOR INFORMATION For information, go to the **Larvik Tourist Office,** Storgata 48 (© **33-13-91-00;** www.visitlarvik.no), opposite the ferry terminal. It's open Monday to Friday from 8:30am to 4pm.

GETTING AROUND Do as many of the locals do in summer and rent a bike from the tourist office (see "Visitor Information," above). The Vestfold district is riddled with well-mapped-out trails for biking, stretching from one end of the province to the other end. Before setting out, purchase the map *Sykkelkart Vestfold,* available for NOK95 ($19/£9.50) from the tourist office.

SEEING THE SIGHTS

The major attraction is the **Larvik Museum ★** (© **98-23-12-90**), which is a three-in-one cultural attraction. The classic baroque-timbered **Herregården Manor House,** Herregården 6, was built between 1674 and 1677 as the home of Ulrik Frederik Gyldenløve, the Norwegian governor general. As the illegitimate son of King Fredrik IV of Denmark, he became the duke of Larvik and was shipped off to Norway to escape the intrigue of the Danish court. The house is filled with 17th- and 18th-century antiques.

Larvik Sjøfartsmuseum (Maritime Museum), Kirkestredet 5, is housed in Larvik's oldest brick building from 1730. On the idyllic little island of Tollerodden east of the harbor, this museum displays models of ships, paintings of sailing vessels, and other nautical artifacts to bring the port's maritime history alive. One section of the museum is devoted to the daring exploits of Larvik-born Thor Heyerdahl.

Finally, the **Fritzøe Museum** on Langestrand Island displays tools, equipment, drawings, and models illustrating the iron-production era in Larvik from 1670 to 1870.

All three museums charge a combined ticket of NOK40 ($8/£4) for adults or NOK10 ($2/£1) for children under 16.

If time remains, consider a visit to **Larvik Kirke,** Kirkestredet (© **33-17-30-00**), which is the port's Trinity Church. Commissioned in 1677, it was finished in 1763 when a tower was added. Inside its chief treasure is *Suffer the Little Children to Come Unto Me,* an altarpiece painting by Lucas Cranagh that was commissioned by Duke Gyldenløve. A monument outside was the creation of Arne Vigeland, who was commissioned to erect a memorial to Norwegians who died in World War II. Admission is free, and the church is open June 25 to August 10 daily from 11am to 1pm and 6 to 8pm.

WHERE TO STAY & DINE

Hotell Greven ★ One hotel here can serve all your needs for lodging, drinking, and dining. Still going strong after 2 centuries, Hotell Greven is not only the most traditional choice, but also the best in the area, as it has kept abreast of the times. In spite of countless

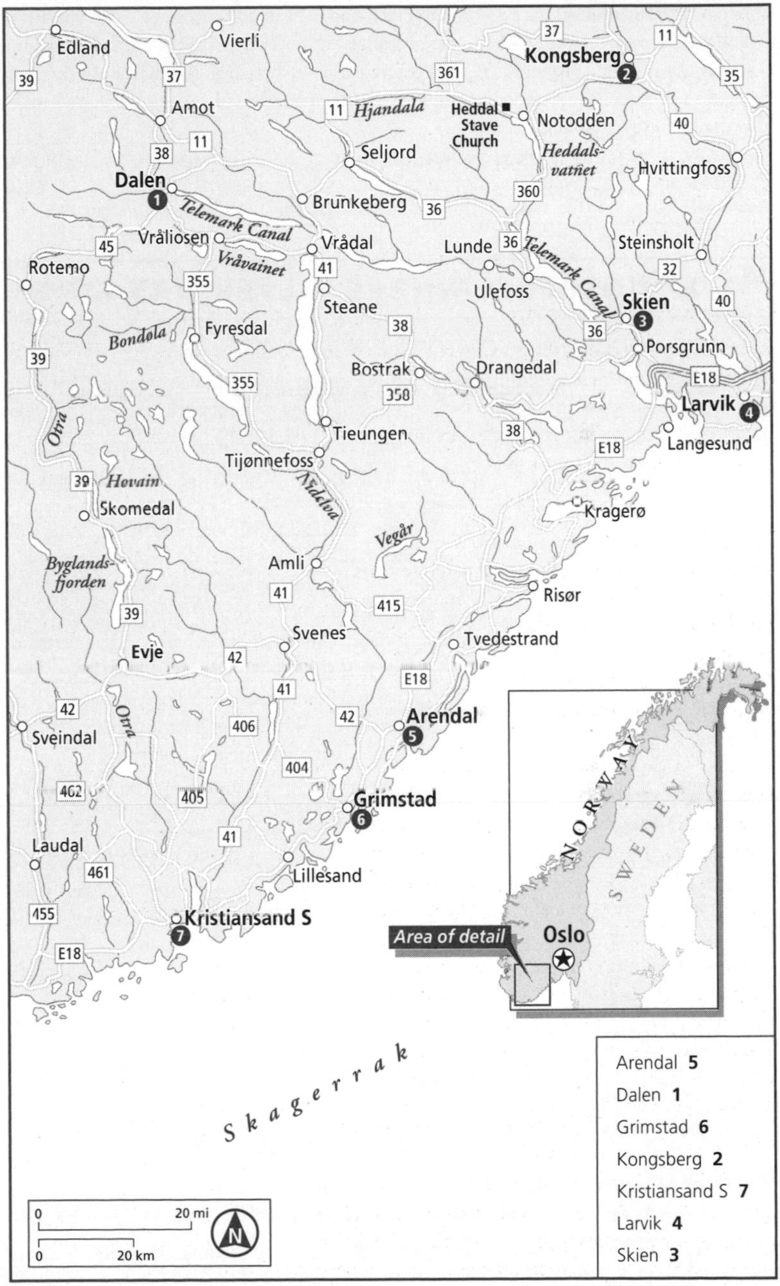
Edland
Vierli
Amot
Dalen
Telemark Canal
Vråliosen
Vråvainet
Rotemo
Bondøla
Fyresdal
Hjandala
Seljord
Brunkeberg
Vrådal
Steane
Heddal Stave Church
Notodden
Heddalsvatnet
Kongsberg
Hvittingfoss
Lunde
Ulefoss
Steinsholt
Skien
Porsgrunn
Bostrak
Drangedal
Larvik
Langesund
Tieungen
Tijønnefoss
Nidelva
Otra
Høvain
Skomedal
Byglandsfjorden
Vegår
Kragerø
Amli
Risør
Svenes
Tvedestrand
Evje
Arendal
Sveindal
Grimstad
Laudal
Lillesand
Kristiansand S
Skagerrak
NORWAY
SWEDEN
Oslo
Area of detail
0 20 mi
0 20 km
N
Arendal 5
Dalen 1
Grimstad 6
Kongsberg 2
Kristiansand S 7
Larvik 4
Skien 3

 renovations, its public lounges and bedrooms still retain an old-fashioned aura—and that's how the locals prefer it. There is style and grace here, and the prices are very reasonable for this part of the country. Each good-size bedroom is tastefully furnished. The chefs have abandoned those old-time Mother Norway recipes; in both of their restaurants, they feature a savory continental cuisine, Dolce Vita serving Italian specialties and Kreta offering food from the Greek islands where many Norwegians now vacation. The piano bar on-site makes this the liveliest venue in Larvik.

Storgata 26, N-3256 Larvik. ✆ **33-18-25-26.** Fax 33-18-04-94. www.hotell-greven.no. 24 units. NOK900 ($180/£90) double; NOK1,100 ($220/£110) suite. Rates include continental breakfast. AE, DC, MC, V. **Amenities:** Bistro; piano bar; dance bar; room service; laundry service/dry cleaning. *In room:* TV.

2 KONGSBERG: WHERE SILVER WAS KING

84km (52 miles) SW of Oslo; 40km (25 miles) W of Drammen

For more than 2 centuries, Kongsberg was the silver-mining town of Norway. Back in 1623, two children here spotted a big ox butting a cliff with his horns, uncovering a silver vein. Their father hoped to profit from the windfall, but the king heard the news and promptly dispatched his soldiers to force the man to reveal the location of the mother lode.

Suddenly, Kongsberg was overrun. Between the 1623 discovery and 1957, some 1.35 million kilograms (1,488 tons) of pure "wire" silver filled the king's purse. Even today, though the mines are closed, Kongsberg is still home to the Royal Norwegian Mint, which has been operating in the town since 1686.

Today some 4,000 workers are employed in high-tech companies located here, and instead of silver you'll find industries such as aerospace and car-part production.

The falls of the Lågen River divide the town into two parts. The oldest district, lying west of the river, is the site of the major attractions. The newer part in the east encompasses the visitor information center, the traffic hubs, and the best shops.

ESSENTIALS

GETTING THERE From the Central Station in Oslo, **trains** leave every 2 hours during the day, taking 1½ hours to reach Kongsberg at a cost of NOK159 ($32/£16) for a one-way ticket. For more information, call ✆ **81-50-08-88** or visit www.nsb.no. There is also bus service from Oslo aboard **Nettbuss Telemark** (✆ **35-02-60-00;** www.nettbuss.no/telemark), taking 1½ hours and costing NOK145 ($29/£15) per one-way ticket. Motorists can take the E18 southwest of Oslo to Drammen. From Drammen, continue southwest along Rte. 11.

VISITOR INFORMATION The **Kongsberg Tourist Office,** Schwabesgate 2 (✆ **32-29-90-50;** www.visitkongsberg.no), is open as follows: May 1 to June 20 and mid-August to mid-September Monday to Friday 9am to 4pm, Saturday 10am to 2pm; June 21 to mid-August Monday to Friday 9am to 7pm and Saturday and Sunday 10am to 2pm. During the rest of the year, it's open Monday to Friday 9am to 4pm.

GETTING AROUND You can walk around the Old Town or rent a bike from the tourist office (see "Visitor Information," above) at a cost of NOK170 ($34/£17) per day.

SPECIAL EVENTS Now beginning its fourth decade, the **Kongsberg International Jazz Festival** in July is attended by some of the most important jazz artists in Europe.

The King's Mine and the baroque church are among the choice concert venues for this major musical event. In 2009, the festival will take place from July 2 to 5. Call ✆ **32-73-31-66** for complete details.

SEEING THE SIGHTS

Kongsberg Kirke★★, Kirketorget (✆ **32-73-19-02**), an elaborate baroque and rococo church, evokes something you might find in Bavaria, hardly in a more minimalist Norway. But this church is one of the sightseeing wonders of the south, and we recommend a stopover here even if you don't have time to check out the rest of town. The largest baroque church in Norway lies in the old city on the western bank of the Lågen River. Seating a 2,400-member congregation, this 1761 church bears witness to the silver-mining prosperity of Kongsberg. The beautiful interior is made all the more stunning because of three huge, glittering glass chandeliers created at the Nøstetangen Glassworks.

As a curiosity, note that the rococo altar joins the large pulpit, altarpiece, and organ pipes on a single wall. Constructed in the shape of a cross, the church has a tower surmounting one of its transepts. You can still see the royal box, reserved for visits from the king, and the smaller boxes, meant for the top mining officials. Naturally, the church owns many valuable pieces of silver. In olden days, it took six strong men to ring the church's mammoth bell, which was cast in Denmark. Admission to the church costs NOK30 ($6/£3) for adults and NOK10 ($2/£1) for persons under 16. There's usually an informed English-speaking guide on the premises dispensing information, in oral or printed form, about the church. From mid-May to late August, it's open Monday to Friday 10am to 4pm, Saturday 10am to 1pm, and Sunday 2 to 4pm. The rest of the year, it's open Tuesday to Thursday 10am to noon. If your arrival in Kongsberg doesn't correspond to any of these opening hours, the tourist office might be able to open the church for you if you phone them in advance.

You'll find four museums housed in a single converted building that once belonged to the Silver Mining Company at the **Norsk Bergverksmuseum ★**, Hyttegata 3 (✆ **32-72-32-00**).

The **Norwegian Mining Museum** traces 3 centuries of silver mining. You might think only specialists would be interested in visiting here, but hundreds of visitors like to wander about, learning about mining. One 18th-century working model illustrates the entire process of mining and smelting the precious silver ore. The machinery used in the smelting process can still be seen in the basement. Some of the specimens on exhibit are made of pure silver.

Also on-site is **Den Kongelige Mynts Museum,** devoted to the Royal Mint, which was relocated here in 1685. The museum contains a rare collection of coins minted in town. A third museum, the **Kongsberg Arms Factory Museum,** traces the city's industrial history from 1814 onward.

Finally, a fourth museum, **Kongsberg Skimuseum,** honors many local skiers such as Birger Ruud and Petter Hugsted, who went on to Olympic glory and world championships. A historic collection of skis and equipment is on view. The most recent exhibition details the daring exploits of Børge Ousland and Erling Kagge on their ski expeditions to the North and South Poles, where they attracted world attention.

Admission to all four museums costs NOK70 ($14/£7) for adults and NOK20 ($4/£2) for children under 16. From mid-May until the end of August, hours are 10am to 5pm daily; off-season hours are noon to 4pm daily.

You might also want to explore **Lågdalsmuseet (Lågdal Folk Museum),** Tillischbakken 8–10 (✆ **32-73-34-68**), a 12-minute stroll southeast from the rail depot. Nearly three dozen antique farmhouses and miners' cottages were moved to this site. This is the most history-rich exhibit of how life used to be lived in the scenic Numedal Valley, which was mainly home to the families of miners and farmers. The 19th-century workshops you'd expect (most open-air museums in Norway have these), but the optics museum and the World War II Resistance Museum come as a surprise to us. Admission is NOK40 ($8/£4) for adults and NOK10 ($2/£1) for children. From June 23 to August 15, the museum is open daily from 11am to 5pm. From mid-May to June 22 and August 16 to August 31, it is open Saturday and Sunday 11am to 5pm. In the off season, hours are Monday to Friday 11am to 3:30pm.

Other than the church, the town's raison d'être is still **Kongsberg Sølvgruver ★★** (✆ **32-72-32-00**), the old silver mines that put Kongsberg on the map in the first place. To reach these mines, you can take an Expressen Bus from Kongsberg to the hamlet of Saggrenda, a distance of 8km (5 miles) taking 10 minutes and costing NOK55 ($11/£5.50). Departures are hourly from Kongsberg. Once at Saggrenda, it is a 10- to 15-minute walk to the entrance to the mines, where you can take a guided tour lasting 90 minutes. You can also drive from Kongsberg to Saggrenda, a distance of 8km (5 miles) to the southwest following Rte. 11.

The tour of the mines begins with a ride on a little train going 2.3km (1½ miles) inside the mountain containing the King's Mine, a journey back in time. The train stops at a depth of 342m (1,122 ft.) below ground. This is the entrance to the King's Mine, which reaches a total depth of 1,070m (3,510 ft.) below the earth. You can still see the *Fahrkunst,* invented by German miners. Dating from 1880, it was the first "elevator" to carry miners up and down. You'll also see the old mining equipment on display.

Regardless of the time of year, wear warm clothing before descending into the mines. You visit the mines by conducted tour, but the hours are a bit irregular: May 18 to June 30 daily 11am and 1 and 3pm; July 1 to August 14 daily 11am, noon, and 1, 2, 3, and 4pm; August 15 to 31 daily 11am and 1 and 3pm; September Saturday and Sunday noon and 2pm; October Sunday only noon and 2pm. The rest of the year, the mines are completely closed. Tours, including the ride aboard the underground train, cost NOK140 ($28/£14) for adults and NOK80 ($16/£8) for persons under 16.

WHERE TO STAY

Best Western Gyldenløve Hotell This long-standing favorite, hardly an exciting choice, stands in the town center, still evoking the 1950s era in which it was built. However, it's been remodeled over the years and is a fine and serviceable choice if your expectations aren't too high. Bedrooms are medium in size and furnished like standard motel rooms—not stylish but comfortable, each equipped with a midsize bathroom with a tub or shower. The hotel also has a small pharmacy on-site, a whirlpool, and a sauna where guests can meet fellow guests while turning lobster red. The on-site full-service restaurant serves a respectable international cuisine.

Hermann Fossgate 1, N-3600 Kongsberg. ✆ **800/237-8483** or 32-86-58-00. Fax 32-86-58-01. www.bestwestern.com. 62 units. NOK965–NOK1,650 ($193–$330/£97–£165) double. Rates include buffet breakfast. AE, DC, MC, V. **Amenities:** Restaurant; exercise room; sauna; laundry service/dry cleaning; nonsmoking rooms; rooms for those w/limited mobility. *In room:* TV, Wi-Fi, minibar, beverage maker, hair dryer, iron.

Quality Hotel Grand ★ This chain hotel is the best in the area, with more style, comfort, and facilities than Gyldenløve, but it also carries a higher price tag. All of its bedrooms have been renovated; some of them open onto views of a waterfall, the others open onto views of the mountains. Each room is tastefully and comfortably furnished, although accommodations tend to be a bit small. Thirty percent of the units contain bathrooms with tub/showers; the rest have only showers. The hotel also offers the best drinking, dining, and entertainment facilities in town. Its piano bar is a nightly attraction, and on Friday and Saturday nights from 9pm to 3am, there is disco action. You also have a choice of light dining in a lounge or more formal Norwegian and international cuisine in the hotel's main restaurant.

Christian August Gate 2, N-3611 Kongsberg. ✆ **32-77-28-00.** Fax 32-73-41-29. www.quality-grand.no. 176 units. NOK1,415–NOK1,975 ($283–$395/£142–£198) double; NOK2,800 ($560/£280) suite. Children 11 and under stay free in parent's room. Rates include continental breakfast. AE, DC, MC, V. **Amenities:** 2 restaurants; 2 bars; indoor heated pool; sauna; laundry service/dry cleaning; nonsmoking rooms; rooms for those w/limited mobility. *In room:* TV, minibar, hair dryer.

WHERE TO DINE

Big Horn Steak House ★ STEAK/NORWEGIAN/INTERNATIONAL A chain-run restaurant, Big Horn unexpectedly serves the best steaks in the area, in a setting inspired by an American steakhouse. Naturally, the chefs secure the best-quality beef available in Norway, and some of the portions of beef we've seen consumed here are amazing. For non-beef options, choices are not surprisingly more lackluster, though you'll find the marinated pork ribs with barbecue sauce tasty, as you will the grilled scampi served with chili sweet corn. Like in a U.S. eatery, starters include buffalo wings served with bleu cheese. You might also opt for the French vineyard snails flavored with garlic and gorgonzola, the latter a bit overpowering. For desserts, the house favorite is ice cream Grand Canyon or a chocolate mousse with blackberries.

Thomesvn. 4. ✆ **32-72-30-60.** Reservations recommended. Main courses NOK208–NOK557 ($42–$111/£21–£56). AE, DC, MC, V. Daily 4–11pm.

EASY EXCURSIONS: HEDDAL STAVE CHURCH ★★★

Even if you have to skip the mines, head for the greatest man-made attraction in southern Norway. The **Heddal Stave Church** lies 33km (20 miles) west of Kongsberg, reached by taking Rte. 134 toward Notodden. This medieval architectural masterpiece is still in use today. Rising 25m (82 ft.) high and 19m (62 ft.) long, Heddal is the largest of the 28 stave churches remaining in Norway.

The oldest part of the church, the chancel, was built of wood in 1147. About a century later, the church was enlarged to its present format. Runic inscriptions reveal that the church was consecrated in 1242 and dedicated to the Virgin Mary. Inside are a beautiful wooden carved chair from 1200, a baptismal font from 1850, and two of the original pillars from the church. The altarpiece is the work of an unknown artist in 1667, and the wall painting, also by an unknown artist, is from 1668. Dragons and serpents, along with grotesque human heads, decorate the portals.

The church (✆ **35-02-00-93**) charges admission of NOK50 ($10/£5) for adults, NOK20 ($4/£2) for children. From June 21 to August 20, it is open 9am to 7pm daily. From May 20 to June 20 and August 21 to September 10, hours are 10am to 5pm daily.

3 SKIEN: MEMORIES OF HENRIK IBSEN

138km (86 miles) S of Oslo; 30km (19 miles) W of the Larvik-Frederikshavn (Denmark) ferry connection

Long proud of its association with playwright Henrik Ibsen (1828–1906), who was a native of Skien, this bustling industrial town and government center for Telemark is visited not only for its literary associations, but also because it is the principal gateway to Telemark.

Skien is an old town, dating from 1100, although it wasn't until 1358 that it received its royal charter. Fire and floods ravaged Skien over the centuries, destroying the entire town at times. The last disastrous fire occurred in 1886, and a new town had to be created out of the debris. Skien covers an area of 786 sq. km (307 sq. miles), with nearly 50,000 inhabitants.

The main reason most visitors go to Skien today, other than its Ibsen associations, is that it is the gateway to the **Telemark Canal** (p. 228) and the starting point for many trips.

ESSENTIALS

GETTING THERE Trains run every hour or two from Oslo to Skien, taking 2³/₄ hours and costing NOK285 ($57/£29) one-way. Call ✆ **81-50-08-88** for schedules, or visit www.nsb.no. Motorists take the E18 south from Oslo to Larvik until the signposted turnoff (Rte. 36) heading northwest into Skien. You can also fly to the small Sandefjord Airport (✆ **33-42-70-00**), lying near Skien. Even though it's small, it is the country's second-busiest international airport. From the airport, buses run into the center of Skien.

VISITOR INFORMATION For information, go to the **Skien Tourist Office,** Nedre Hjellegate 18 (✆ **35-90-55-20;** www.grenland.no), which is open during July and August Monday to Friday 8:30am to 7pm, Saturday 10am to 4pm, and Sunday 11am to 4pm. The rest of the year, it's open Monday to Friday 10am to 4pm.

SEEING THE SIGHTS

Ibsen left Skien in 1843 when he was 15 years old, returning only briefly as part of an unsuccessful attempt to borrow some money to enter prep school in Oslo. He lived at several addresses in Skien, including a small house in an old neighborhood, Snipetorp 27, near the town center. The house on Snipetorp is one of several in the neighborhood that have been proclaimed protected monuments. Ibsen's former home is now a cultural center and an art gallery.

Bø Sommarland (Kids) This is the country's largest water park, drawing families from all over Norway during the summer. More than 100 different activities await you here, including a kids' water park (ideal for small children) and Bøverstranda ("the Beach"), along with water slides and Sommarlandelva, a 250m-long (820-ft.) artificial river. Near the entrance is the scenic lake, Steinjønn, where you can borrow a canoe for a ride. The Flow Rider is for those who love skateboarding, snowboarding, and surfing. Of course, the waves here are artificial, but they are said to be the best of their kind in the world. You can also experience Europe's first roller-coaster flume.

The latest draw is the Space Ball, a centrifugal slide that creates the illusion of being in a whirlpool. The attraction begins as visitors enter a dark tunnel before being thrown into the Space Ball, which spirals down toward the center and drops visitors into a deep pool. There's also a big amusement area, Las Bøgas, with a Ferris wheel, an amusement arcade, merry-go-rounds, and lots of games. Family-friendly entertainment, from clown shows to band performances, is also presented daily. The park lies 50km (31 miles) from Skien and 25km (16 miles) from Notodden.

Bø. ✆ **35-06-16-00.** www.sommarland.no. Admission NOK285 ($57/£29) adults, NOK190 ($38/£19) children 15 and under. June–Aug daily 8am–dusk.

Brekkeparken ★ This 1780 manor house, the headquarters of the Telemark Museum, attracts everybody from fans of Ibsen's *A Doll's House* to botanists and devotees of Norwegian folk art. Luring theater buffs from around the world, it allows you to visit Ibsen's reconstructed study and the bedrooms from his Oslo apartment, as well as his "blue salon." In addition, there's a **remarkable collection of folk art from the 1700s and 1800s ★**, including many authentic pieces such as national costumes, textiles, handcrafts, and woodcarvings. As you wander the park in late spring, especially in May, you can take in the largest **tulip park ★★** in Scandinavia. In addition to the main building, there are some 20 old structures that have been moved here from different districts in Telemark.

Øvregate 41. ✆ **35-54-45-00.** Admission NOK60 ($12/£6) adults, NOK25 ($5/£2.50) children 15 and under. Mid-May to Aug daily 10am–6pm.

Venstøp ★ Ibsen's childhood home, Venstøp Farm, lies 5km (3 miles) northwest of Skien. The house is furnished with objects actually used by the Ibsen family when they lived here from 1835 to 1843. The building itself dates from the early 19th century, and the dark attic was the inspiration for the playwright's *The Wild Duck.* Two paintings are by Ibsen—he had originally wanted to become an artist, but his wife ("the cat") insisted that he become a playwright. In her words, she "gave" the world a great dramatic talent but spared it a mediocre artist.

Venstøp. ✆ **35-52-57-49.** Admission NOK50 ($10/£5) adults, NOK20 ($4/£2) children 15 and under. Mid-May to Aug daily noon–6pm.

WHERE TO STAY

Clarion Collection Hotel Bryggeparken Because it's constructed in a traditional style, this hotel near the harbor and river looks much older than it is. In actuality, the five-story brick structure was both built and opened in 2001. If you want older and more traditional accommodations, check into the Thon Hotel Høyers (see below). Offering the freshest rooms in town, it is furnished in a contemporary style. Some of the rooms have balconies opening onto water views. All of them are comfortable and tasteful, with small bathrooms, 28 of which contain tubs and showers, with the rest containing showers only. From 6 to 9pm nightly, guests can enjoy a light evening meal, which is included in the rate.

Langbryggen 7, N-3724 Skien. ✆ **35-91-21-00.** Fax 35-91-21-01. www.choicehotels.no. 103 units. Mon–Thurs NOK1,795 ($359/£180) double; Fri–Sun NOK1,395 ($279/£140) double; NOK2,195 ($439/£220) suite. Rates include continental breakfast. AE, DC, MC, V. Closed Dec 20–Jan 2. **Amenities:** Restaurant; bar; indoor heated pool; sauna; laundry service/dry cleaning; nonsmoking rooms; rooms for those w/ limited mobility. *In room:* TV, Wi-Fi, minibar, hair dryer, iron.

Thon Hotel Hoyers ★ In a structure dating from 1853, this much renovated and improved hotel is the leading choice in town, and our personal favorite. It stands in the center of gardens stretching to the water and lies a 3-minute taxi ride from the rail station. Its bedrooms are comfortably and attractively furnished. The bedrooms range from midsize to spacious and are freshened up every year with firm mattresses, new carpeting, and draperies as needed. The hotel's restaurant, Madame Blom (see below), boasts some of the finest dining and drinking in Skien. The hotel is entirely nonsmoking.

Kongensgate 6, N-3701 Skien. ✆ **35-90-58-00.** Fax 35-90-58-05. www.thonhotels.com. 73 units. NOK1,510 ($302/£151) double; NOK2,400–NOK2,800 ($480–$560/£240–£280) junior suite. Rates include continental breakfast. AE, DC, MC, V. Closed Dec 22–Jan 2. **Amenities:** Restaurant; bar; 1 room for those w/limited mobility. *In room:* TV, Wi-Fi (in some), minibar, coffeemaker (in some), hair dryer.

WHERE TO DINE

Madame Blom ★ Value NORWEGIAN This restaurant at the oldest hotel in Telemark is your best option for moderately priced food. In the Thon Hotel Hoyers (see above), it lies almost 1km (about 1/2 mile) south of the railroad station. During the day many locals drop in for a feast of smørbrød—open-faced sandwiches. The kitchen also turns out more substantial and rib-sticking fare. We were enticed by the appetizer of smoked trout, served with a creamy apple-and-celery salad. The main courses are well prepared and concentrate on ingredients from Norway's field and stream. Try the filet of reindeer steak with mushrooms and steamed vegetables, or the filet of river trout stuffed with shrimp and crayfish. For something more exotic, sample the halibut shipped over from Greenland and served with a mustard and dill sauce. The dessert specialty is vanilla ice cream with raisins, marinated ginger, and a dash of rum.

Kongensgate 6. ✆ **35-90-58-00.** Reservations recommended. Main courses NOK182–NOK290 ($36–$58/£18–£29). AE, DC, MC, V. Mon–Fri noon–2pm; Mon–Sat 4–10pm.

EASY EXCURSIONS: THE TELEMARK CANAL ★★

Skien is the gateway to the Telemark Canal, which was completed in 1892. Five hundred men labored for 5 years on this canal, blasting their way through mountains. Today it contains a total of 28 lock chambers, and the route runs from Skien in the east to the ancient Norwegian town of Dalen in the west. The canal affords a sailing route of 105km (65 miles) with an elevation difference of 72m (236 ft.).

At the turn of the 20th century, the canal became known as the "fast route" between eastern and western Norway. Nostalgic canal boats, the MS *Victoria,* the MS *Henrik Ibsen,* and the MS *Telemarken,* will take you from Skien to Dalen, a 10-hour trip on this historic waterway, costing around NOK880 ($176/£88) round-trip. Although not the equivalent of the Panama Canal, we highly recommend this trip. It's a comfortable, easy way to penetrate some of the lakes and rivers of inland Norway. As you sail along, you'll pass farmland so neat it appears landscaped, and a countryside dotted with scenic summer homes (often owned by residents of Oslo) and churches. Along the way you'll also encounter panoramic vistas in many directions, with views of deep, dark forests, which some Norwegians claim are still inhabited by trolls. Swift-flowing streams add to the landscape drama, as do forested hillsides and deep valleys, some of which draw skiers in winter. The engineer in you may also be fascinated by viewing the original stone walls of the canal, as well as the closing mechanisms.

For information and bookings, contact **Telemarkreiser,** Handelstorget (✆ **35-90-00-30** or 35-90-00-20) in Skien.

Where to Stay & Dine in Dalen

Dalen Hotel ★★ At the terminus of the Telemark Canal, with dragon heads and Viking-inspired gingerbread dripping from its eaves, this historic hotel has some similarities with Norway's medieval stave churches. This hotel is often cited as a fine example of the Norwegian nationalist style. Built in 1894, it was a lodging for prominent guests interested in seeing the natural beauty of a region that had just opened thanks to the completion of the Telemark Canal. Today, thanks to 2 decades of ongoing renovations, its ocher-and-brown, mostly wood premises still evoke the fantasy and whimsy of the late Victorian age. It is graced with symmetrical towers, soaring turrets, wide verandas, and high ceilings. Rooms come in various shapes and sizes, all decidedly old-fashioned but well maintained.

Furnished in a traditional Norwegian style, with lots of wood, the on-site Dalen Restaurant is the best place to eat in the area. It serves a market-fresh cuisine of Norwegian and international specialties. On warm summer days we prefer meals under the branches of a willow in the garden outside, with a terrace that opens toward a swan-filled lake. The cooking is not fancy, but it's affordable and tasty. Set meals, which are changed daily, cost from NOK190 to NOK400 ($38–$80/£19–£40).

N-3880 Dalen I Telemark. ✆ **35-07-70-00.** Fax 35-07-70-11. www.dalenhotel.no. 38 units. NOK1,550–NOK2,000 ($310–$400/£155–£200) double; NOK1,845–NOK2,645 ($369–$529/£185–£265) suite. Rates include buffet breakfast. AE, DC, MC, V. Closed Nov–Mar. **Amenities:** Restaurant; bar; easy access to fishing, hill climbing, and trekking. *In room:* Hair dryer.

4 ARENDAL & MERDØY ISLAND

239km (148 miles) SW of Oslo; 69km (43 miles) E of Kristiansand S

"I have found heaven on earth," Harald Hagerup, a local painter, assured us on our first visit to Arendal. After spending some time here, we concur that it is a worthwhile little stopover.

Arendal, the government center of the Aust-Agder district, was once known as "the Venice of Scandinavia." At the time it was riddled with canals, but following a disastrous fire, these canals were filled in and turned into wide streets. That move took away a lot of the charm, but much remains to enchant.

For the best look at old Arendal, visit **Tyholmen** ★★, in the center, with its handsomely preserved 18th-century wooden houses. Many artists and craftspeople have moved here from Oslo, taking over the wood-framed structures and restoring them. In summer, the harbor, **Pollen,** is filled with boats and people, as this is one of the most popular centers for domestic tourism in Norway. Many Norwegians come here to take boat trips among the neighboring rocks, and they also traverse the delta of the Nid River.

In addition to Ibsen, the region's second-most-famous son was Knut Hamsun, called the "Balzac of Norway." He won the Nobel Prize in 1918. His novels give a vivid portrait of 19th-century Norwegian values, and his works are still very popular in Germany, almost more so than they are in Norway.

ESSENTIALS

GETTING THERE **By Train** Four trains a day arrive from Oslo, requiring a change of trains at Nelaug. Trip time, including the transfer, is 4½ hours. For schedules and information, call ✆ **81-50-08-88** or visit www.nsb.no.

By Bus Nor-way Buss Ekspress (✆ **81-54-44-44;** www.nor-way.no) buses travel between Oslo and Arendal, taking 4 hours and costing NOK370 ($74/£37) for one-way passage.

By Car From Skien (see above), our last stopover, E18 continues south into Arendal.

VISITOR INFORMATION For helpful advice about Arendal and the surrounding area, go to the **Arendal Turistkontor,** Peder Thomassons 1 (© **37-00-55-44;** www.arendal.com), open mid-June to mid-August Monday to Saturday 9am to 6pm and Sunday noon to 6pm. Otherwise, hours are Monday to Friday 9am to 4pm.

SEEING THE SIGHTS

Arendal Rådhus In the center of town, the Rådhus, or Town Hall, is better known as the second-largest timber building in Norway and the country's single tallest timber structure. It was originally built in 1815 by a rich shipowner but became the town hall in 1844. Regrettably, the city fathers of the late 1800s made some unfortunate decisions, such as flattening the dramatic domed ceiling. The elegant original staircase remains, and the hall also contains about 300 antique portraits, many from the 19th century—and some of them quite amusing. If you're Norwegian, look for some of your ancestors.

Rådhusgata 19. © **37-01-30-00.** Free admission. Mon–Fri 9am–3pm.

Aust-Agder Museum ★ Finds This is an unusual museum, a result of the fact that the town's sailors were asked to bring home curios from their global sailing that might interest those left behind. These seafarers succeeded so admirably, this museum was opened in 1932. In addition to finds from around the world, the museum showcases the folk art of the region and is filled with memorabilia of the history of the town, mainly artifacts from its seafaring heyday. One exhibit is dedicated to the ill-fated slave ship the *Fredensborg,* which sank off Tromøy in 1768. The museum lies about 1.5km (1 mile) north of the center; to reach it, follow the signs in the direction of Oslo.

Parkveien 16. © **37-07-35-00.** Admission NOK35 ($7/£3.50) adults, NOK15 ($3/£1.50) children. June 20–Aug 20 Mon–Fri 9am–5pm; Sun noon–5pm; Aug 21–June 19 Mon–Fri 9am–3pm, Sun noon–3pm.

WHERE TO STAY

Clarion Collection Hotel Tyholmen ★ Two highly regarded chain hotels compete for your patronage here. We give our nod to the Clarion Collection. Enjoying panoramic views of one of Norway's loveliest harbors, this hotel is the best in the area for an overnight stopover. Architecturally, it was inspired by the 1800s, the heyday of the sailing vessels that put Arendal on the map. The decor of each bedroom reflects the history of a different ship constructed in Norway, and each unit is named for a particular vessel. All of the accommodations are decorated in soothing pastels, with modern furnishings and midsize bathrooms. The hotel's restaurant, Tre Seil (see below), is popular in the area during the summer. The dining facilities here are so excellent that you may want to patronize the hotel for food and drink even if you're not a guest. The location is a 2-minute walk south of the bus station. This hotel is entirely nonsmoking.

Teaterplassen 2, N-4800 Arendal. © **37-07-68-00.** Fax 37-07-68-01. www.choicehotels.no. 60 units. NOK1,050–NOK1,890 ($210–$378/£105–£189) double. Rates include buffet breakfast. AE, DC, MC, V. **Amenities:** Restaurant; bar; sauna; laundry service/dry cleaning; rooms for those w/limited mobility. *In room:* A/C, TV, Wi-Fi, minibar, hair dryer, safe, trouser press.

Thon Hotel Arendal Under new Thon management, this hotel has been improved, though it continues to evoke the decade of its creation, the 1960s (no great compliment). Only three of its five floors contain bedrooms; the remaining two floors are entirely devoted to conference and convention facilities, making it a frequent host for corporate conventions from throughout Norway. The medium-size bedrooms come in monochromatic tones of pale blue, pale green, and earth tones. Each of the tiled bathrooms has its own shower, and a few (only 10) have bathtubs as well. The hotel's restaurant, Serdinand, is separately recommended below.

Fiergangen 1, N-4800 Arendal. ✆ **37-05-21-50.** Fax 37-05-21-51. www.thonhotels.com. 84 units. NOK1,150–NOK1,745 ($230–$349/£115–£175) double. AE, DC, MC, V. **Amenities:** Restaurant; bar; nightclub; lobby bar w/pianist; business center; laundry service/dry cleaning; nonsmoking rooms; 1 room for those w/limited mobility. *In room:* TV, Wi-Fi (in most), minibar, hair dryer.

WHERE TO DINE

Serdinand NORWEGIAN/INTERNATIONAL This is Arendal's most popular steakhouse. Set on the street level of the Thon Hotel Arendal (see above), it boasts a mustard- and brown-colored decor, exposed paneling, a pleasant staff, and a warm and cozy setting. Many of the robust dishes served here are native to Norway, including lamb grown in local meadows and salmon caught in nearby waters. Reindeer is shipped down from the far north. Fish dishes, except for the salmon, are more limited but likely to include succulent trout and tasty catfish, prepared either with butter, with white wine sauce, or blackened.

In the Thon Hotel Arendal, Fiergangen 1. ✆ **37-05-21-50.** Reservations recommended. Main courses NOK120–NOK165 ($24–$33/£12–£17) at lunch, NOK220–NOK300 ($44–$60/£22–£30) at dinner. AE, DC, MC, V. Mon–Fri 10am–10:30pm; Sat 10am–11pm; Sun 3–10pm.

Tre Seil ★ NORWEGIAN "Three Sails," located in the Clarion Collection Hotel Tyholmen (see above), is the most prestigious restaurant in town. With its nautical decor, it offers big windows looking out over the moored yachts and boats bobbing in the harbor. You'll enjoy excellent cuisine and formal service. The upper-crust clientele frequently orders the steak—the best in the area. For a recommended main course, we suggest the herb-marinated filet of lamb with squash, onions, and peppers in a creamy game sauce. You might also try the salmon with a sour-cream sauce and Norwegian crabs. We're especially fond of the chef's large prawns gratinée with garlic, herbs, and butter. For a real "taste of Norway," opt for the grilled filet of reindeer saddle or the perfectly grilled filet of salmon caught in Norwegian fjords.

In the Clarion Tyholmen Hotel, Teaterplassen 2. ✆ **37-07-68-00.** Reservations recommended. Main courses NOK180–NOK310 ($36–$62/£18–£31). AE, DC, MC, V. Daily 11am–11pm.

EASY EXCURSIONS

In the bay of Arendal, **Merdøy Island** ★ is like a time capsule. Virtually intact architecturally from its days as a prosperous 19th-century town, the island's clapboard-sided houses retain their allure today.

There are no restaurants, only a small cafe, and there's a lovely bathing beach nearby where you can picnic.

The **Merdøgaård Museum** (✆ **37-07-35-00**) on the island is run by the Aust-Agder Museum (see above). The museum is the perfectly preserved early-19th-century house of a long-departed sea captain, with the furnishings still intact. A guardian lives on the premises and will show you around. It's open June 23 to August 12 daily from noon to 4pm. Admission is NOK20 ($4/£2) adults, NOK10 ($2/£1) children.

To reach the island, take a ferry departing for Pollen at Arendal's harborfront. Departures are every 30 minutes from 9am to 6pm mid-June to mid-August, and the boat makes stops at two or three other islands before reaching Merdøy. The ferry costs NOK45 ($9/£4.50) each way, and the trip takes 20 minutes. For schedules and more information, contact the tourist office.

Lying 20km (12 miles) west of the center of Arendal is Grimstad, site of the **Grimstad Bymuseum-Ibsenhuset,** Henrik Ibsen Gate 14 (✆ **37-04-04-90**), in the center of town. Henrik Ibsen worked in this town at a pharmacy while pursuing the pharmacist's daughter. Ibsen also wrote his first play, *Catalina,* here. The Grimstad museum includes the old pharmacy and Ibsen's house. Admission is NOK50 ($10/£5) for adults, NOK20 ($4/£2) for children. Open May 23 to September 14 Monday to Saturday 11am to 5pm, Sunday noon to 5pm.

5 KRISTIANSAND S: THE SUMMER CITY ★

526km (326 miles) SE of Bergen; 342km (212 miles) SW of Oslo

The fifth-largest city in Norway, with some 75,000 inhabitants, is called *Sommerbyen,* or "the Summer City." We agree with this appellation, having been here on a winter visit when many of the attractions were closed for the season.

Visitors heading to Bergen and the fjord country often arrive in Norway at Kristiansand S (not to be confused with Kristiansund N in the north). The biggest city and an important port of Sørtlandet (the south coast), Kristiansand S offers the most attractions, the largest number of hotels and restaurants, and the most activities of any town along the southern coast.

Founded by King Christian in 1641, Kristiansand S is a busy port and industrial center, yet it has many charming old streets and antique houses clustered cozily together.

Kristiansand S is the largest town in the south and Norway's largest ferry port. **Kvadraturen,** "the quadrant," is known for its right-angled street plan that was influenced by the Renaissance period's strict adherence to form. **Markens** is the town's pedestrian precinct and meeting place.

ESSENTIALS

GETTING THERE **By Plane** Kristiansand Airport lies at Kjevik, 16km (10 miles) east of the city center. SAS Scandinavian Airlines Norge (✆ **05400;** calls from within Norway only) flies from Oslo to Kristiansand. An airport bus runs between Kjevik and the heart of Kristiansand.

By Train Anywhere from three to six trains link Oslo and Kristiansand daily, taking 4½ hours, with a one-way ticket costing NOK601 ($120/£60). Call ✆ **81-50-08-88** for more information or visit www.nsb.no.

By Bus Nor-Way Buss Ekspress buses (✆ **81-54-44-44;** www.nor-way.no) travel down from Oslo in 5½ hours, with a one-way ticket costing NOK320 ($64/£32). Buses run two to four times daily.

By Ferry International ferries link Kristiansand to Hirtshals in the northern reaches of Denmark's Jutland peninsula. Ferries run three to four times daily, depending on the time of year, with the sea voyage taking 4 hours. **Color Line** (✆ **22-94-44-00;** www.colorline.com) operates these ferries. This is the shortest ferry link between Norway and Denmark. Depending on the time of year, fares can range from NOK350 to NOK650 ($70–$130/£35–£65). The highest fares are charged on weekends from mid-June to mid-August.

By Car From our last stopover at Arendal, the E18 continues southwest in Kristiansand.

VISITOR INFORMATION For help, go to **Destinasjon Sørlandet,** Rådhusgata 6 (✆ **38-12-13-14;** www.sorlandet.com), which also distributes bus, train, and ferry schedules. Open June 18 to August 12 Monday to Friday 8:30am to 6pm, Saturday 10am to 6pm, and Sunday noon to 6pm. Otherwise, hours are Monday to Friday 8:30am to 3:30pm.

GETTING AROUND Municipal buses go through the center taking you from point to point at a ticket cost of NOK15 ($3/£1.50) per ride. Contact the tourist office (see above) for information.

SIGHTS & OUTDOOR ACTIVITIES

Although Kristiansand S has plenty of museums, churches, and other activities, many visitors come here for outdoorsy activities in summer. Our favorite sport is biking. In the area are 70km (43 miles) of bike trails. You can pick up maps of the area at the tourist office (see above). Many head toward the hills with their bikes, but we always prefer to take the coastal route. Bikes can be rented at **Kristiansand Sykkelsenter,** Grim Torv 3 (✆ **38-02-68-35**).

If you're a fisherman, you can obtain a permit at the tourist office, which will allow you to fish at **Vestre Grievann.** This is a lake north of the city that is known for its excellent catches in perch, trout, and eel.

For watersports, head for **Kulholmen Marina** at Roligheden Camping (✆ **38-09-67-22**), which rents everything from water skis to small boats and water scooters.

Another pleasurable experience is to go horseback riding at **Islandshestsenteret** at Søgna (✆ **38-16-98-82**). Stables here hold the rare Icelandic horse, which is smaller than most breeds of horses.

Agder Naturmuseum og Botaniske Hage (Agder Museum of Natural History and Botanical Garden) The present exhibitions, which opened in 1990, show part of the natural history of southern Norway. Colorful minerals are on display, and the museum includes a beautiful botanical garden. The complex contains the largest collection of cacti in Norway. As part of the package, you can visit the neighboring **Gimle Estate** ★, a 19th-century manor house filled with elegant, antique-heavy interiors, with a historic **rose garden** ★★ planted in 1850. From the center of town, motorists can take the E18 east, crossing a bridge. After the bridge, turn right and follow the signs. Bus no. 22 also runs there.

Gimleveien 23. ✆ **38-09-23-88.** www.naturmuseum.no. Admission to museum NOK40 ($8/£4) adults, NOK15 ($3/£1.50) children; admission to house and garden NOK55 ($11/£5.50) adults, NOK20 ($4/£2) children. June 20–Aug 20 daily 11am–5pm; Aug 21–June 19 Tues–Fri 10am–3pm, Sun noon–4pm. Closed Dec 16–Jan 7.

Christiansholm Festning (Christiansholm Fortress) The present "defenders" of this fortress are a lot friendlier than they were in the early 1940s, during the darkest days of the Nazi occupation of Norway. At that time, the Germans took over this fortress and trained their guns to the sea, expecting an Allied invasion that never came. A landmark along the Strandepromenaden, this fortress dates from 1674. The installation was ordered by King Christian IV of Denmark. The job of the defenders was to protect the Skagerrak Straits from invasion, not only from pirates but also from the roving Swedes. That threat of invasion never came, except once during the Napoleonic Wars of 1807. The walls are 5m (16 ft.) thick, and the fortress was created by both the labor of the local citizenry as well as heavy taxes.

Festningsgata. ✆ **38-07-51-50.** Free admission. May 15–Sept 15 daily 9am–9pm.

Kristiansand Domkirke Constructed in a neo-Gothic style in 1884, this Domkirke is the third-largest church in Norway, seating 1,800 worshippers. You may want to check it out, especially when there is organ practice at 11am on summer weekdays. You can climb the tower for NOK20 ($4/£2) for a **panoramic view ★** of the area. Summer concerts are also presented here, especially at the weeklong International Church Music Festival in mid-May, with organ, chamber, and gospel music on tap.

Kirkegata. ✆ **38-10-77-50.** Free admission. June–Aug daily 11am–2pm.

Kristiansand Dyrepark (Kristiansand Zoo and Amusement Park) ★ Kids Today the major family attraction in the south of Norway, Kristiansand Dyrepark has been billed by some as Norway's Disneyland. It's no Disneyland, but it does provide summer amusements for the area. The highlight is Nordisk Vilmark, a simulated wilderness area where you can walk on boardwalks over the habitats of wolverines, lynx, wolves, and moose. The zoo itself contains many exotic specimens, including some Arctic species, and diverse animals roam in large enclosures. The park covers an area of 60 hectares (148 acres). Children should delight in the *Kardemomme by* (Cardamom town), a recreated "town" suggesting a hamlet in Africa. The town is based on a well-known children's story by Thorbjørn Egner, and famous characters from Egner's story stroll about, greeting visitors. A pirate ship, a circus, a play land, giraffes, a farm, and other amusements, including a bobsled track and water slide, also await you here.

Signposted along E18. ✆ **38-04-97-00.** www.dyreparken.com. Admission, including all activities, NOK120–NOK310 ($24–$62/£12–£31) adults, NOK100–NOK240 ($20–$48/£10–£24) children. Mid-May to Aug daily 10am–7pm; Sept to mid-May daily 10am–3pm. Take the Dyreparkbussen from the center. The park is signposted off E18 at a point 9km (5½ miles) east of the center of town.

Kristiansand Kanonmuseum (Cannon Museum) Lying 8km (5 miles) south of town, the Cannon Museum recalls the dark days of World War II when the occupying Nazi forces were installed here, as well as Christiansholm Festning (see above). The museum preserves the German's heavy "Vara Battery" cannons, which gave them control over the strategic Skagerrak Straits. The 337-ton cannons could fire at a range of 55km (34 miles). You can also visit the bunkers where 600 German soldiers and 1,400 laborers lived. You can even see their scribbling, in German, on the wall.

Møvik. ✆ **38-08-50-90.** www.kanonmuseet.no. Admission NOK80 ($16/£8) adults, NOK40 ($8/£4) children. June 17–Aug 15 daily 11am–6pm; Aug 16–Sept Mon–Wed 11am–3pm, Thurs–Sun 11am–5pm; Oct–June 16 Sun 11am–5pm.

Moments Walking the Streets of the Old Town

The best-preserved district of the city is **Posebyen ★**, along the river in the northeastern part of town. It survived a disastrous fire in 1892 that swept over Kristiansand. The streets are filled with the original one- and two-story houses that accommodated workers in the 19th century. You'll see small-paned windows, iron fences, benches, and flower boxes. The kitchens and bedrooms were built in the rear, with separate doorways leading to little gardens. The most interesting parts of the area lie between Festningsgaten and Elvegata and between Rådhusgaten and Tordenskiolds. The best time to visit is on a Saturday mid-June to August when a market is held with street stalls and all kinds of produce for sale.

Moments **Heading for the Fish Market**

On a lovely summer evening, stroll down to the Fish Market at Grovane where you can purchase fresh shrimp from one of the vendors and enjoy them on the pier as you people-watch and breathe the fresh air of Norway's all-too-fleeting summer. Small bridges lead to wooden maritime-inspired structures painted in red and yellow, housing a series of restaurants and shops by the canal. There's no better way to spend an evening in Kristiansand than to spend it here.

Oddernes Kirke ★ Finds It may not be bigger than the Domkirke (see above), but it's a lot prettier. One of the oldest parish churches of Norway lies 1.5km (1 mile) east of the town center, reached by bus no. 22. The church, whose nave and choir were built around 1040, was dedicated to Saint Olav, the patron saint of Norway. After viewing the church's interior, be sure to wander the grounds, particularly the ancient cemetery with its impressive rune stones.

Oddernesvn. ✆ **38-05-87-50.** Free admission. May–Aug Sun–Fri 11am–2pm.

Vest Agder Fylkes-Museum ★ If you are growing a bit jaded with open-air museums in Norway, note that this is one of the largest and best, lying 4km (2½ miles) east of town on E18. From all over the Setesdalen region, nearly 50 antique farm and town dwellings were moved to this site. Some are furnished with provincial pieces, illustrating life as it was lived in the 18th and 19th centuries. Traditional costumes of the region are also displayed, along with other artifacts from the past. Folk dancing is staged Wednesday at 6pm from mid-June to mid-August. The major building houses thematic exhibitions, devoted to 18th- and 19th-century Norwegian life, once a year.

Vigeveien 22B. ✆ **38-10-26-80.** Admission NOK50 ($10/£5) adults, NOK25 ($5/£2.50) children, NOK120 ($24/£12) family ticket. June 20–Aug 20 Mon–Sat 10am–6pm, Sun noon–6pm; off season Sun noon–5pm.

NEARBY ATTRACTIONS

The **Setesdalsbanen** in Grovane (✆ **38-15-64-82**) runs a steam train along 4.8km (3 miles) of narrow-gauge track. The locomotive, built in 1894, starts its run at Grovane, 20km (12 miles) from Kristiansand. It travels for 78km (48 miles) between Kristiansand and Byglandsfjord, providing a vital link between Setesdalen (the Setesdal Valley) and the southern coast. At one time it transported nickel from the mines along with other exports such as timber. In July, departures from Grovane are at 6pm Tuesday to Friday. From June 17 to June 30 and from August 1 to 27, the train also operates on Sunday at 11:30am, and 1:15 and 3:10pm. A round-trip fare is NOK100 ($20/£10) for adults and NOK50 ($10/£5) for children.

The countryside around Kristiansand is rich with rolling meadows, birch-clad hills, deep valleys, and mountain moors. You'll see panoramic scenery along the E18 going east or west. Our favorite spot for a hike is in the **Baneheia Skog,** or Baneheia Forest. The trail begins only a 15-minute walk north of the city center. Trails are cut through the forest, which is studded with evergreens and graced with small lakes. You can make this walk easy or lazy, or a challenge if you head up some of the steeper hills. It's best to pick up the makings of a picnic before heading here.

Another favorite place for hikers is **Ravnedalen,** or Raven Valley, which is signposted just northwest of Kristiansand. This is a lush park that bursts into wildflower bloom in spring. You can wander its narrow, winding trails for hours. The climax comes when you climb 200 steps to a 93m (305-ft.) lookout point. You're rewarded with one of the most **panoramic vistas ★★** along the southern coast.

You can also drive along the E18 to **Mandal,** 42km (26 miles) southwest of Kristiansand, Norway's southernmost town. Here you can walk the streets of its historic center, with its old wooden houses, and stroll its long sandy beach, Sjøsanden.

At the southernmost point in Norway is **Lindesnes Fyr** (**✆ 38-25-77-35**), Norway's first lighthouse, dating from 1656. Inside is an exhibition of lighthouse artifacts. Admission is NOK50 ($10/£5) for adults and free for children under 12. It's open July and August daily 9am to 9pm, June and September daily 10am to 7pm, and May daily 10am to 6pm.

In summer, boat trips are offered to visit the archipelago of offshore skerries (isolated rock islands). Visits are possible to Lillesand to the east and to the island of Brogøy, which lies right off the coast of Kristiansand and offers many scenic strolls and places for sunbathing. You can sail aboard the M/S *Maarten* from Kristiansand daily in the summer at 10am and 2pm. The trip costs NOK230 ($46/£23) for adults or NOK115 ($23/£12) for children. Departures are from the fish quay. This is the best bet for passengers who'd like to absorb some of the scenery of the rugged southern coast of Norway.

SHOPPING

The largest shopping center in southern Norway lies 12km (7½ miles) east of Kristiansand. **Steen and Strøm Sørlandssenteret** (**✆ 38-04-91-00**) offers 100 stores plus 10 restaurants and cafes, even such centers as a solarium. Closer to the center of town is **SlottsQuartalet,** Tordenskiolds 9 (**✆ 38-02-79-99**), at the top end of the Markens pedestrian street. You'll find various shops and cafes here.

WHERE TO STAY

Clarion Hotel Ernst ★★ Kings, diplomats, Americans (Nelson Rockefeller, Hubert Humphrey), even Nazi officers during World War II have chosen this hotel as their favorite. The only hotel in town with a doorman, the Ernst first opened its doors in 1859. Even though it's received frequent renovations since then, its owners have taken care to preserve its classic look. Beautifully run and managed, it is preferred by those who shun the more sleekly modern look as exemplified by the Radisson SAS Caledonian Hotel. All the bedrooms come in different sizes with individual color schemes, but each one contains a midsize, well-maintained bathroom. The location is ideal, lying 180m (590 ft.) from the central bus terminal, rail station, and ferry dock. It is the only hotel in the area that has a restaurant and bars that rival the drinking and dining facilities at the SAS Caledonian. The hotel is a nonsmoking establishment.

Rådhusgaten 2, N-4611 Kristiansand S. **✆ 38-12-86-00.** Fax 38-02-03-07. www.ernst.no. 135 units. Sun–Thurs NOK1,290–NOK1,590 ($258–$318/£129–£159) double; Fri–Sat NOK1,090 ($218/£109) double. Rates include buffet breakfast. AE, DC, MC, V. Parking NOK125 ($25/£13). **Amenities:** Restaurant; 2 bars; nightclub; room service; babysitting; massage; laundry service/dry cleaning; rooms for those w/limited mobility. *In room:* A/C, TV, Wi-Fi, minibar, beverage maker, hair dryer, trouser press.

Quality Hotel Kristiansand ★ Kids There is no better address for families with small children in all of southern Norway, although the managers of the Rica Dyreparken, reviewed below, would make the same claim for themselves. This establishment bills itself as a "children's hotel." Of course, adults can stay here, too. The hotel is one of Sørlandet's biggest, lying 11km ($6^3/_4$ miles) east of the town center. The building is modern, and the bedrooms are freshly and comfortably furnished with cheerful pastels and wooden furnishings. Everything is geared to families with children, including a large playroom, organized kiddie activities, and even a special buffet for youngsters in the dining room. Visitors can also take advantage of toys located on the grounds, which are provided by the hotel. The hotel is entirely nonsmoking.

Sorlandsparken, N-4696 Kristiansand S. ✆ **38-17-77-77.** Fax 38-17-77-80. www.quality-kristiansand.no. 210 units. NOK1,012–NOK1,560 ($202–$312/£101–£156) double; NOK2,300–NOK2,600 ($460–$520/£230–£260) suite. AE, DC, MC, V. Free parking. **Amenities:** Restaurant; bar; outdoor heated pool; sauna; children's center and programs; business center; babysitting; laundry service/dry cleaning; rooms for those w/limited mobility. *In room:* TV, Wi-Fi, minibar, hair dryer.

Radisson SAS Caledonian Hotel ★★ Located in the city center, the largest hotel in the area is the best hotel in southern Norway, although our hearts still belong to the Clarion Hotel Ernst. Built in 1968 near the fish market, it remains smart and stylish because of frequent renewals. A stay here is very convenient, as the hotel is within walking distance of the train and bus stations, as well as the ferry terminal, theaters, cinemas, and the best shopping. The good-size bedrooms are furnished stylishly with contemporary pieces and midsize bathrooms. The hotel's restaurant is far superior to a typical hotel dining room, and the drinking facilities, including a pub, disco, and piano bar, are the best in the city.

Vestre Strandgate 7, N-4601 Kristiansand S. ✆ **38-11-21-00.** Fax 38-11-21-01. www.radisson.com. 205 units. Sun–Thurs NOK1,595–NOK1,945 ($319–$389/£160–£195) double; Fri–Sat NOK1,195–NOK1,695 ($239–$339/£120–£170) double; NOK2,700 ($540/£270) suite. AE, DC, MC, V. Parking NOK120 ($24/£12). **Amenities:** Restaurant; 2 bars; room service; babysitting; laundry service/dry cleaning; nonsmoking rooms; rooms for those w/limited mobility. *In room:* A/C, TV, Wi-Fi, minibar, hair dryer.

Rica Dyreparken Hotel ★ Kids This novelty hotel is sure to delight as many as it will alienate. Lying right in one of the most popular holiday parks in Norway, this hotel, which opened in April 2000, was architecturally inspired by Noah's Ark. Staying here should delight animal lovers of all ages. All the public lounges and bedrooms have motifs relating to the animal kingdom—you might opt to stay in a monkey room or a horse room. Or, choose to relax on an African safari bed or recline in a tiger-striped chair in one of the Jungle Jim bedrooms. The hotel even has its own bridge along the water, as well as a large bar terrace where you can sit out on a summer night enjoying the fresh air. The Norwegian in-house restaurant is named—you guessed it—Noah's Ark.

Dyreparken, N-4609 Kristiansand S. ✆ **38-14-64-00.** Fax 38-14-64-01. www.rica.no. 160 units. Summer NOK1,295–NOK1,620 ($259–$324/£130–£162) double. Rates include buffet breakfast. AE, DC, MC, V. Free parking. **Amenities:** Restaurant; bar; children's center; babysitting; laundry service/dry cleaning; nonsmoking rooms; rooms for those w/limited mobility. *In room:* TV, minibar, hair dryer.

WHERE TO DINE

Bakgården ★ FRENCH/INTERNATIONAL The interior of this well-established restaurant is accented with oil-burning lamps, creating a mellow atmosphere. The cuisine is an unending festival celebrating southern Europe, and the chefs frequently add flair, borrowing recipes from around the world, although dishes are tailored to local palates. The chefs continue to come up with intriguing flavor combinations, including tournedos of angelfish wrapped in parma ham and served with langoustine, a basil sauce, and beetroot foam. Another worthy choice is pan-fried cod with cauliflower and a potato puree with mustard. Fried scamp is marinated in chili peppers and ginger and served with a black pasta with a spicy lime and bell pepper sauce. Don't overlook the starters, especially the smoked cod soup. The pricey wine list may elicit a gasp from you—in Norway, wine is priced like liquid gold.

Tollbødgate 5. ✆ **38-02-79-55.** Reservations required. Main courses NOK279–NOK295 ($56–$59/£28–£30); 5-course fixed-price menu NOK675 ($135/£68), NOK1,060 ($212/£106) with wine. AE, DC, MC, V. Mon–Sat 6–11pm.

Bølgen & Moi ★★ CONTINENTAL When champagne soup arrives as a starter, you know you're in a special place. This is a member of a chain of fine-dining restaurants that now stretches across Norway. It occupies a big-windowed replica of a 19th-century warehouse, set within the "tourist zone" of Kristiansand, on the docks, almost immediately adjacent to the waterfront. Inside, within a color scheme of white, dark wooden paneling, and touches of apple green, a uniformed and cheerfully hardworking waitstaff manages to be simultaneously informal, unpretentious, and chic. Menu items derive from the culinary canon of two of Norway's preeminent chefs and restaurant entrepreneurs, Trond Moi and Toralf Bølgen, and change at the beginning of every month, according to the season. Worthy examples include breast of duck with red-currant sauce; creamy lobster stew served with lobster-stuffed ravioli; fried salmon steaks with Asian spices; and roasted venison served with a forest mushroom sauce.

Sjølystveien 1A. ✆ **38-17-83-00.** Reservations recommended. Main courses NOK220–NOK329 ($44–$66/£22–£33). AE, DC, MC, V. May–early Sept daily 5–10pm (last order); early Sept–Apr Tues–Sun 5–10pm.

Sjøhuset (Sea House) ★ NORWEGIAN Set directly on the harborfront in the center of town, this restaurant is housed in a century-old former salt warehouse whose oxblood-red walls are very distinctive. Inside you'll see the massive structural beams of the restaurant's original construction and a blazing stone-sided fireplace. In summer, we prefer the waterfront terrace. Specialties include filet of halibut with a balsamic glace topped with crayfish gratinée or pan-fried redfish in a red wine glace. Another delight is a plate of lamb chops marinated in garlic and herbs and served with a mustard aïoli or else poached chicken breast whose flavor is enhanced by lemon foam.

Østre Strangate 12. ✆ **38-02-62-60.** Reservations required in summer. Main courses NOK259–NOK389 ($52–$78/£26–£39). AE, DC, MC, V. Daily 11:30am–11pm.

KRISTIANSAND S AFTER DARK

There is cultural life here—the acclaimed **Kristiansand Symfoniorkester (Kristiansand Symphony Orchestra)** performs year-round at Kongensgate 6 (✆ **38-07-70-00**). Musical concerts are also presented year-round at **Musikkens Hus,** Kongensgate 54 (✆ **38-14-87-30**). If you're interested, check with the tourism office (p. 233) to see if any performances are scheduled at the time of your visit. **Telfords Pub,** in the Radisson SAS Claedonian Hotel, Vestre Strandgate 7 (✆ **38-11-21-00**), is a watering hole with an authentic Scottish interior and atmosphere, attracting a heavy-drinking crowd (20s–40s). If you'd like to dance all night, try the amusingly named **Dr. Fjeld,** in the Clarion Hotel Ernst, Rådhusgata 2 (✆ **38-12-86-00**). Many young people come here, mixing with guests of all ages from the hotel itself. The best piano bar is **Lobbybaren,** Vestre Strandgate 7 (✆ **38-11-21-00**), also in the Radisson SAS Caledonian Hotel, attracting an older crowd.

10

Stavanger

Who would have thought that the once sleepy, provincial city of Stavanger, fourth largest in Norway, would ever be named European Capital of Culture for 2008? The old Stavanger is gone forever. Today it's a bright, cosmopolitan city and one of our favorites in Norway.

What brought about this miraculous change? "Black gold" (oil, that is) from the North Sea. Packing riches and economic clout, Stavanger has become the oil capital of Norway.

The good news is that it still retains a bit of its old charm as a famous seaport set in some of the most beautiful fjord and mountain country in Norway. Since the 9th century, fresh fish and vegetables have been sold at the old marketplace. Many of its low wooden houses, some of which have been around for 9 centuries, still remain.

Stavanger has also burst out with some of the most intriguing museums in the Southwest, although it's hardly a rival of Bergen in that regard. Nothing is finer in Stavanger than its historic harbor, where you can see ships both new and old.

Long before the North Sea oil boom, it was the herring fishermen who put Stavanger harbor on the map. In the 19th century, this harbor bustled, its wharves teaming with net makers and menders, coopers, and smiths. The port today not only constructs the rigs for those offshore oilfields, but refines the oil as well.

You can wander the narrow streets of Stavanger for hours, visiting its shops, bars, restaurants, cafes, and art galleries. Budget at least 1 busy day for this bustling old seaport on the Ryfyllkefjord.

1 ORIENTATION

ARRIVING

BY PLANE Flights land at **Stavanger International Airport** at Sola, 14km ($8^1/_2$ miles) south of the city center. **SAS Scandinavian Airlines Norge** (✆ **91-50-54-00**) flies between Oslo, Bergen, Kristiansand S, and Stavanger. **Widerøe** (✆ **81-00-12-00**) flies from Bergen to Stavanger. These airlines also serve Stavanger from London, Newcastle-upon-Tyne, and Aberdeen, Scotland. A taxi from the airport to the city center goes for NOK200 to NOK250 ($40–$50/£20–£25).

BY TRAIN Direct trains from Oslo require seat reservations and take 8 hours, traveling via Kristiansand S. A one-way fare costs NOK846 ($169/£85). About three trains per day arrive from Oslo in Stavanger, and there is one overnight service. For rail information, call ✆ **81-50-08-88** or visit www.nsb.no.

BY BUS There is no direct bus link between Oslo and Stavanger. However, **Nor-Way Buss Ekspress** (✆ **81-54-44-44;** www.nor-way.no) runs a bus service between Oslo and Kristiansand S, taking 5 hours and costing NOK310 ($62/£31) one-way. From Kristiansand S, you can continue on another bus to Stavanger, taking 4 hours and costing NOK355 ($71/£36).

BY BOAT From Bergen, **Flaggruten** (© **51-86-87-88**) runs an express catamaran to Stavanger, taking 4½ hours and costing NOK680 ($136/£68) for a one-way trip.

BY CAR Because of the jagged coastline of western Norway, access by car from Bergen to Stavanger requires a 149km (92-mile) detour, incorporating high-speed motorways and three different ferry crossings. It usually takes 6½ to 7 hours to drive to Stavanger from Bergen. Access in the east from Kristiansand S is much easier. You continue west from Kristiansand S until you reach the end of E18.

ESSENTIALS

VISITOR INFORMATION You can get all sorts of visitor information at **Stavanger tourist Office,** Domkirkeplassen 3 (© **51-85-92-00;** www.destinasjon-stavanger.no). From June to August it is open daily 7am to 8pm; September to May Monday to Friday 9am to 4pm, Saturday 9am to 2pm.

CITY LAYOUT Most of Stavanger's attractions lie within an easy walk of the historic harbor. **Vågen Gamle Stavanger,** the old town, is on the western side of Vågen. Ferries to the United Kingdom leave from this point. This historic harbor is now a colorful marina with two sailing ships at anchor and a fish market held daily until 4pm.

Ferries to Haugesund and Bergen depart from the eastern part of town, across a body of water known as **Byfjorden.**

In the center of Stavanger, to the immediate north of the train station, is a large pond called **Breiavann.** Both the bus and train stations lie on the southern side of this pond, about a 10-minute walk from the main harbor.

GETTING AROUND Most of the historic central core of Stavanger is walkable, which is about the only way to get around unless you take a taxi. The historic town is filled with narrow streets and pedestrian walkways. If you don't have a rented car, you'll find that local buses fan out to the suburbs, including such neighboring communities as Sola, the site of the airport. Fares start at NOK30 ($6/£3). For more information, call © **51-51-65-30.**

If the weather is fair and you'd like to use a bike to get around, you can rent one at **Nordsjøvegen,** Vågsgata 22 (© **51-66-20-95**), costing NOK85 ($17/£8.50) per day. If you'd like to do more extensive biking, go to the visitor information center (see above) and request a *Sykkelkart* or cycling map of the area.

For a **taxi,** call **Norgestaxi Stavanger** at © **08000** or Stavanger Taxicentral at © **51-90-90-90.**

SPECIAL EVENTS Stavanger is called festival city, or *festivallryen,* and celebrations take place all year. For complete listings at the time of your visit, ask at the visitor information center (see above). Spring's best festival is **MaiJazz,** beginning the second week of May, when internationally known musicians come to Stavanger to perform top-quality jazz. Around mid-June the **Great Norwegian Humor Festival** takes place, with well-known artists performing. There are revues, street entertainers, and shows for children. The **International Chamber Music Festival** occurs in mid-August, an event that attracts some of the world's most acclaimed classical artists to Stavanger. Some 20 concerts are staged within the course of a week. The **Stavanger Wine Festival,** beginning in mid-March and lasting 10 days, celebrates all things grape.

Fast Facts Stavanger

Banks One of the most central banks for exchanging money is **SpareBank,** Domkirkeplassen (✆ **51-67-67-00**). You can also exchange money from June to August at the visitor information center (see above).

Car Repair Call ✆ **51-53-88-88,** a 24-hour hot line.

Consulates There is no U.S. representative. Brits can go to the **United Kingdom Consulate** at Prinsens Gate 12 (✆ **51-52-97-13**).

Dental Service There is a dentist open every day to handle emergencies. The name of the dentist is published in the Saturday newspapers. Otherwise, call for an appointment at the office of Ognedal Hans Kristian, Kongsgate 44 (✆ **51-52-03-17**).

Doctor In an emergency, call ✆ **51-51-02-02.** Otherwise, ask your hotel staff to recommend a doctor, all of whom speak English.

Emergencies Call ✆ **110** for fire, ✆ **112** for the police, and ✆ **113** for an ambulance.

Laundry If your hotel doesn't have facilities, go to **Renseriet,** Kongsgate 40 (✆ **51-89-56-53**).

Left Luggage Go to **Byterminalen** (no phone), the city terminus, Monday to Friday 7am to 8pm, Saturday 8am to 10pm.

Pharmacy Your best bet is **Vitusapotek Løven,** Olav V's Gate 11 (✆ **51-91-08-81**), open daily 9am to 11pm or 8pm on public holidays.

Post Office The main post office is at Haakon VII's Gate 9, open Monday to Wednesday and Friday 8am to 5pm, Thursday 8am to 6pm, and Saturday 9am to 1pm.

2 WHERE TO STAY

Because Stavanger is an oil boomtown and full of businesspeople for most of the year, you'll find expensive hotels and a dearth of good, moderately priced choices. That's the bad news. The good news is that in the summer months and on weekends, the first-class and better-rated hotels slash their prices, and nearly all of them fall into the "moderate" category during peak tourism season.

EXPENSIVE

Clarion Hotel Stavanger ★★ This is Stavanger's second-tallest building and better than the Radisson SAS sisters, below. It's a smoothly contemporary blockbuster that's on every corporate list as a well-managed hotel. (About 70% of its clients work in the oil or oil services industries.) Set 2½ blocks uphill from the harbor, it lies within a 7-minute walk to every attraction in the Old Town. It's a tall, elegant, contemporary hotel with 14 stories and a decor that's accented with lots of polished stone, burnished copper, and Nordic birch. Ironically, it's positioned midway between two of its most powerful competitors, the also-recommended Radisson SAS Atlantic and the Radisson SAS Royal hotels. Pahr Iversen, a locally famous artist, crafted the paintings in the lobby and the tile work in most of the bathrooms.

Ny Olavskleiv 8, N-4004 Stavanger. ✆ **51-50-25-00.** Fax 51-50-25-01. www.choicehotels.no. 249 units. Mid-Aug to mid-June Mon–Thurs NOK1,595–NOK2,095 ($319–$419/£160–£210) double; Fri–Sun year-round and daily mid-June to mid-Aug NOK995 ($199/£100) double, NOK3,600 ($720/£360) year-round suite. Rates include buffet breakfast. AE, MC, V. Parking NOK70 ($14/£7) per night. **Amenities:** 2 restaurants; bar; health club w/saunas and a view over the town; laundry service/dry cleaning; nonsmoking rooms; rooms for those w/limited mobility. *In room:* A/C, TV, Wi-Fi, minibar, beverage maker, hair dryer, iron, trouser press.

Radisson SAS Atlantic Hotel ★ The largest and most traditional deluxe hotel in Stavanger is this behemoth, though of the two, we gravitate more to its sibling, the Royal (see below). Until its height was surpassed around the turn of the millennium by a taller contender in the suburbs, its 13 stories made it the tallest building in town. Everything about it evokes the artfully spare minimalism of the heyday of Scandinavian modern design, thanks to lots of carefully finished hardwood and stone, plus glass and stainless steel. Bedrooms here are well conceived and very comfortable. If you're able to afford one of the suites, you'll find them large and supremely comfortable refuges, replete with leather upholsteries, macho-looking hardwoods, and, in many cases, big-windowed views over the town. Restaurant Mortepumpen serves seasonal specialties alongside panoramic views of Lake Brelavannet. The King Oscar Bar & Salon and the Alexander Pub are glamorous places to meet for a drink.

Olav V's Gate 3, P.O. Box 307, N-4002 Stavanger. ✆ **51-76-10-00.** Fax 51-76-10-01. www.radisson.com. 354 units. Mon–Thurs NOK1,995–NOK2,495 ($399–$499/£200–£250) double; Fri–Sun and daily mid-June to mid-Aug NOK995 ($199/£100) double; year-round NOK2,500–NOK4,990 ($500–$998/£250–£499) suite. AE, DC, MC, V. Parking NOK120 ($24/£12) per night. **Amenities:** Restaurant; cafe; pub; reduced rates at a nearby health and exercise club; sauna; room service; laundry service/dry cleaning. *In room:* TV, Wi-Fi, minibar, beverage maker, hair dryer, iron, safe (in some).

Radisson SAS Royal Hotel ★★★ Built in 1987 and radically renovated, this is the smallest and the most plush of Stavanger's Radisson SAS hotels. Its rooms rise around an atrium-style lobby that's outfitted with pale oak paneling and pale blue carpets and upholsteries. Bedrooms are outfitted in four different decorative styles: a warm but minimalist version of Scandinavian modern, a generic Oriental (Pan-Asian) style, a high-tech design, and a style that the hotel refers to as "ecological," featuring lots of hand-crafted ceramics and weavings made from nonsynthetic materials. The eight suites here, with separate sitting areas and business-class amenities, are the best in the city if the dividends from your North Sea oil investment just came in.

Løkkeveien 26, P.O. Box 307, N-4002 Stavanger. ✆ **51-76-60-00.** Fax 51-76-60-01. www.radisson.com. 204 units. Mid-Aug to mid-June Mon–Thurs NOK1,595–NOK2,595 ($319–$519/£160–£260) double; Fri–Sun year-round and daily mid-June to mid-Aug NOK995–NOK1,695 ($199–$339/£100–£170) double; year-round NOK2,500–NOK3,600 ($500–$720/£250–£360) suite. Rates include buffet breakfast. Parking NOK120 ($24/£12). AE, DC, MC, V. **Amenities:** 2 restaurants; bar; indoor heated pool; fitness room; sauna; Jacuzzi; business center; room service; laundry service/dry cleaning. *In room:* TV, Wi-Fi, minibar, beverage maker, safe, trouser press.

Skagen Brygge Hotell ★★★ (Finds) No hotel in Stavanger has the charm and character of this favorite, which is as modern as tomorrow in comfort but lives in the past architecturally (even if its white wooden "wharfhouses" are merely replicas). This is the most architecturally distinctive and the most visible hotel in town, thanks to its prime harborfront location in the center of Stavanger's historic core. About 10 of its rooms occupy a 19th-century brick building that's partially concealed on the hotel's back side.

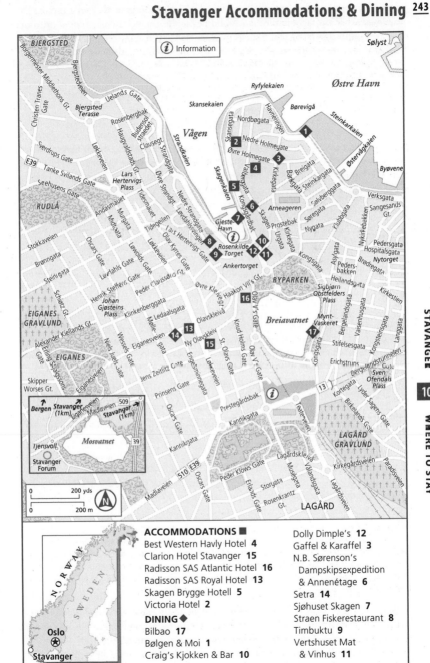

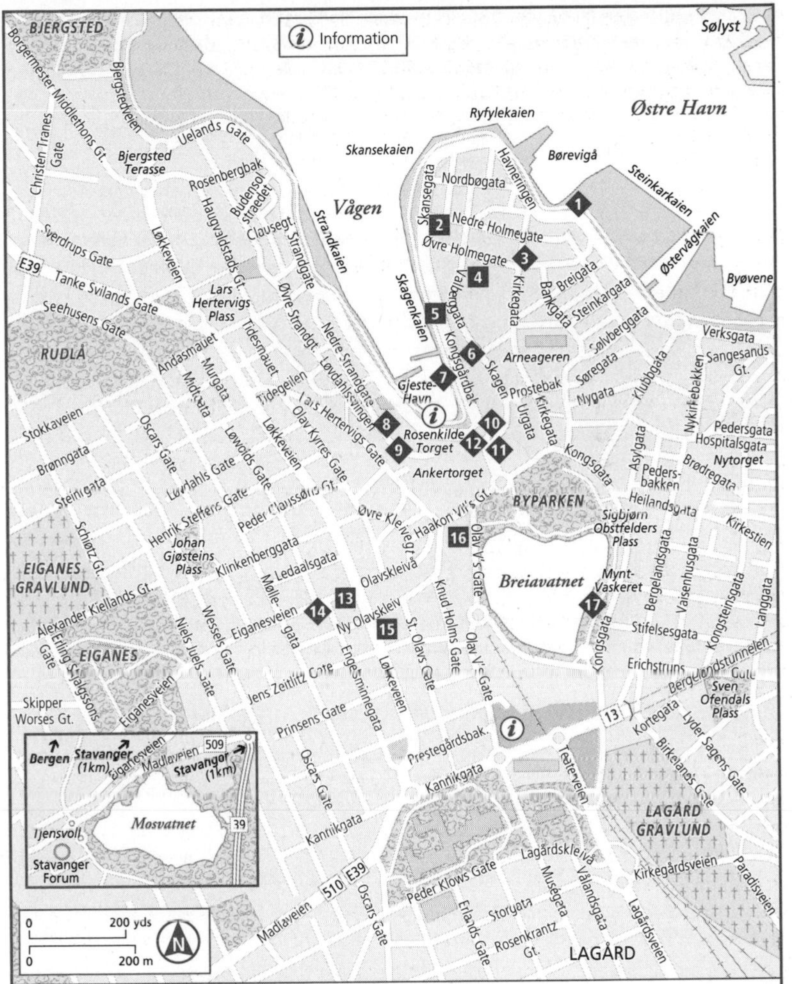

ACCOMMODATIONS ■

Best Western Havly Hotel **4**
Clarion Hotel Stavanger **15**
Radisson SAS Atlantic Hotel **16**
Radisson SAS Royal Hotel **13**
Skagen Brygge Hotell **5**
Victoria Hotel **2**

DINING ◆

Bilbao **17**
Bølgen & Moi **1**
Craig's Kjokken & Bar **10**
Dolly Dimple's **12**
Gaffel & Karaffel **3**
N.B. Sørenson's Dampskipsexpedition & Annenétage **6**
Setra **14**
Sjøhuset Skagen **7**
Straen Fiskerestaurant **8**
Timbuktu **9**
Vertshuset Mat & Vinhus **11**

But the genuinely dramatic part of this hotel fronts the harbor. As a replacement for warehouses that, throughout the decades, burned to the ground, architects duplicated the look of an interconnected series of steep-gabled, tall and narrow town houses, modernized with oversize windows and a sense of postmodern flair. Older rooms are cozy, and warm, with exposed masonry and flowered Laura Ashley fabrics. Sunnier, more dramatic, and more panoramic are the big-windowed accommodations in the newer section, some of which might evoke greenhouses if it weren't for their leather-upholstered furniture, hardwood floors, Oriental carpets, and sense of high-tech flair.

Skagenkaien 30, N-4004 Stavanger. ✆ **51-85-00-00.** Fax 51-85-00-01. www.skagenbryggehotell.no. 110 units. Sun–Thurs NOK1,830 ($366/£183) double; Fri–Sun year-round and daily July NOK1,115 ($223/£112) double; year-round NOK1,980–NOK3,500 ($396–$700/£198–£350) suite. Rates include buffet breakfast. AE, DC, MC, V. No on-site parking. **Amenities:** Exercise area w/sauna and Turkish bath; laundry service/dry cleaning. *In room:* A/C, TV, minibar, safe.

MODERATE

Best Western Havly Hotel (Value) This comfortable hotel is hardly the best, but it's the most affordable in a town where virtually every hotel room is pricey. The only member of the Best Western hotel chain in town is positioned on a street that runs parallel to the wharves of the Vågen (harbor), 1 block uphill. Small-scale, boxy, and modern, it was built in the 1960s in a low-rise design that doesn't interfere (too much) with the otherwise antique buildings of old Stavanger that rise around it on every side. There's no bar, no restaurant, and very few amenities, but in light of the well-maintained accommodations, and because of the many bars and restaurants that lie within a few blocks, no one seems to care. It attracts business travelers from other parts of Scandinavia, and there's an aura of brisk, matter-of-fact efficiency permeating a decor that includes smallish, weather-tight windows (without any particularly panoramic view) that you might have expected in a Best Western in, say, a cold-climate region of the Pacific Northwest.

Valberggate 1, N-4006 Stavanger. ✆ **51-93-90-00.** Fax 51-93-90-01. www.havly-hotell.no. 42 units. Mid-Aug to May Mon–Thurs NOK1,660 ($332/£166) double, Fri–Sun NOK1,030 ($206/£103) double; June to mid-Aug 1,030NOK ($136/£72) double. Rates include buffet breakfast. AE, DC, MC, V. No on-site parking. **Amenities:** Laundry service/dry cleaning; nonsmoking rooms. *In room:* TV, Wi-Fi, beverage maker, hair dryer, iron.

Victoria Hotel ★ This hotel was the oldest in Stavanger, and once it was *the* place to stay. But its competitors, recommended above, have long since outpaced it. Nonetheless, it remains a durable favorite. It is not a hotel where a rock star would be catered to, but if you're a hardworking sales rep for an oil-service company or a leisure traveler without huge expectations, it will work just fine. It was inaugurated in 1900 in the redbrick-with-stone-trim building that's now carefully preserved as a town landmark. It's set prominently at the edge of the harbor, but in a less-touristed waterfront area used for the mooring of fishing boats and supply ships servicing the North Sea oil platforms. Over the years, the hotel's role in Stavanger has changed: Once its clientele was primarily concerned with the herring and canning industries; now about 85% of its clients are middle-bracket employees within the oil service industries. Expect a thoroughly decent, muted hotel with a helpful staff, and a lobby that's outfitted in a paneled style that you might have expected from a 19th-century hotel in England. Rooms are well maintained and not overly large, each with conservative traditional furniture. Each has a floor plan that, thanks to the hotel's U-shaped layout and antique shell, is different from each of its neighbors.

Skansekaien 1, N-4001 Stavanger. ✆ **51-86-70-00.** Fax 51-86-70-10. www.victoria-hotel.no. 107 units. Mon–Thurs NOK1,350–NOK1,550 ($270–$310/£135–£155) double, NOK2,200 ($440/£220) suite; Fri–Sun NOK895–NOK1,095 ($179–$219/£90–£110) double, NOK1,995 ($399/£200) suite. Rates include buffet breakfast. AE, DC, MC, V. Parking NOK50 ($10/£5). **Amenities:** Restaurant; bar; laundry service/dry cleaning; nonsmoking rooms. *In room:* TV, Wi-Fi, minibar.

3 WHERE TO DINE

EXPENSIVE

Bilbao ★★ SPANISH/INTERNATIONAL One of our favorite restaurants in Stavanger occupies a white clapboard-sided house, originally built in 1860, set directly beside the Breavent (the small pond that's a focal point for Stavanger's town center). The earthier and less formal of the two dining venues is the basement-level bodega, outfitted with ceramic tiles and thick plaster-sheathed walls. More formal and stylish is the gourmet restaurant upstairs, where a collection of avant-garde art and a sweeping view over the pond add to the dining allure. Food in the bodega includes *bacalao* (Iberian-style cod), paella prepared for one or more diners at a time, fish soup, paper-thin slices of Serrano ham, and a highly appealing array of tapas. Upstairs, a roster of more elaborate dishes features cream of shellfish soup with crabmeat-stuffed ravioli; filet of halibut in orange sauce; or scallops with red beets.

Kongsgate 41. ✆ **51-53-33-00.** Reservations recommended for the formal restaurant. In gourmet restaurant, main courses NOK250–NOK280 ($50–$56/£25–£28), fixed-price menus NOK465–NOK525 ($93–$105/£47–£53); in Spanish bodega, servings of tapas NOK70–NOK200 ($14–$40/£7–£20), main courses NOK150–NOK330 ($30–$66/£15–£33). AE, DC, MC, V. Mon–Sat 6–11pm (from 5pm for the bodega).

Bølgen & Moi ★★ CONTINENTAL It might be a member of a chain, but it's hardly McDonald's—in fact, it serves the finest cuisine in Stavanger's increasingly competitive culinary market. This restaurant—a member of a high-quality and elite dining chain that now stretches across Norway—lies on the ground floor of the avant-garde premises of Stavanger's oil museum. Its interior is as spare, angular, metallic, and minimalist as the museum itself. Part of its drama derives from its position, straddling a pier and a rocky headland jutting into Stavanger's harbor. Illuminated mostly by candles, the setting is a foil for cuisine that's more elaborate and cutting-edge than what you'll find at many nearby competitors. You know you're going to dine well when you're served such starters as potato soup with sautéed foie gras and white truffle oil, or asparagus with poached quail eggs and a chive-studded hollandaise. To see the heights that the chef can reach, order the skate with fresh herbs from the garden and extra-virgin olive oil, or the honey-glazed duck breast.

In the Norsk Oljemuseum (Norwegian Petroleum Museum), the harborfront, Kjeringholmen. ✆ **51-93-93-51.** Reservations recommended. Small platters NOK149–NOK159 ($30–$32/£15–£16); main courses NOK285–NOK305 ($57–$61/£29–£31); fixed-price menus NOK495–NOK695 ($99–$139/£50–£70). AE, DC, MC, V. Daily 11am–5pm; Tues–Sat 5pm–midnight. Bar until midnight.

Craig's Kjokken & Bar ★ (Finds) INTERNATIONAL Oklahoma-born Craig Whitson is a local hit, and he illustrates his down-home style of humor with a dozen dried pigs' heads hanging on the wall. Once you get by that jolt, prepare yourself to "pig out" on some good food. The American sofas with tables can be used for dining, and there is an array of other unusual tables and chairs. There are more than 600 bottles of wine in the cellar, with such major regions of Europe as Alsace or the Rhone represented along with many Tuscan vintages. A homemade soup of the day hits the spot on a cold day, or try one of the nightly appetizers fashioned from langoustines or fresh scallops—the menu changes frequently. A popular dish is a rib-and-sausage plate with gnocchi, or baked cod cooked in a zesty tomato bouillon. The spring lamb burger is another tasty treat. For dessert, there's nothing finer than the vanilla-laced crème brûlée.

Breitorget 6. ✆ **51-93-95-90.** Reservations recommended. Main courses NOK220–NOK290 ($44–$58/£22–£29); 5-course fixed-price menu NOK590 ($118/£59). AE, MC, V. Mon–Sat 6–11pm. Closed Dec 22–Jan 3 and 1 week for Easter.

Gaffel & Karaffel ★ NORWEGIAN/INTERNATIONAL The "Fork & Carafe" is one of the hippest restaurants in Stavanger. The wooden tables have no tablecloths, the red halls are hung with knives and forks, and there's a popular bar downstairs. The historic building, from 1871, was originally the private home of a fisherman and his family. High-quality ingredients are skillfully handled by a well-trained staff that might tempt you with its garlic-marinated fresh shrimp as an appetizer. For a main course, a pasta specialty is likely to be featured along with such main-dish staples—each well prepared—as monkfish with bacon served in a pepper sauce, or delightful Norwegian lamb with fresh vegetables in a savory sauce. Also try the popular tapas menu. A dessert specialty is *panna cotta,* a pudding of milk and vanilla with fresh fruit.

Øvre Holmegate 20. ✆ **51-86-41-58.** Reservations recommended. Main courses NOK239–NOK279 ($48–$56/£24–£28); fixed-price menus NOK375–NOK595 ($75–$119/£38–£60). AE, DC, MC, V. Mon–Sat 6–11pm. Closed Dec 22–Jan 8 and 1 week at Easter.

N. B. Sørenson's Dampskipsexpedition & Annenétage ★ Finds NORWEGIAN When the wood-sided warehouse that contains these restaurants was built in 1876, the waters of Stavanger's harbor literally lapped at its foundations, and merchandise could be unloaded directly from ships that could moor beside it. Today a road separates its front entrance from the harbor. The heavy timbers and all-wood interior evoke a rich sense of nostalgia for the 19th-century mercantile days.

The street-level brasserie (Dampskipsexpedition, or "Steamship Expedition") is the more convivial and animated (and cheaper) of the two venues—a warren of varnished pine planks, polished brass, nautical-nostalgic memorabilia, and beer suds. Menu items served in the street-level brasserie include sirloin of beef with gnocchi and a Madeira sauce or else grilled salmon with *beurre blanc* and salmon roe. Upstairs, an interconnected series of late-19th-century Victorian parlors is the setting for Annenétage, a much more rigid and pretentious gourmet restaurant. Food items here are innovative: The best examples include monkfish with cauliflower and scallops flavored with pumpkin and served with avocado. You can also order smoked trout with slices of apple and celeriac; and a dessert specialty of chocolate marquise with espresso sauce.

Skagen 26. ✆ **51-84-38-20.** Reservations recommended. In street-level brasserie, main courses NOK249–NOK292 ($50–$58/£25–£29); in upstairs gourmet restaurant, fixed-price menus NOK675–NOK825 ($135–$165/£68–£83). AE, DC, MC, V. Street-level brasserie daily 11am–midnight; upstairs gourmet restaurant Mon–Sat 6–11pm.

Setra ★ NORWEGIAN/INTERNATIONAL Set in a pink-sided building immediately uphill from the SAS Royal Hotel, this restaurant is elegant, upscale, and richly committed to presenting French food with flair and sensitivity. "Trude" supervises the dining room, and her husband, Steinar, is the hard-working chef. From the kitchens emerge dishes that change with the season but that could conceivably grace some of the grandest tables. Some fine examples include king crab from the North Atlantic or freshly caught fish from the Stavanger region. The owners buy their lamb, beef, chicken, and vegetables (in season) from the best farmers in Rogaland.

Eiganesveien 8. ✆ **51-52-86-26.** Reservations recommended. Main courses NOK340 ($68/£34); fixed-price menus NOK570–NOK850 ($114–$170/£57–£85). AE, DC, MC, V. Mon–Sat 6–11pm.

Straen Fiskerestaurant ★ SEAFOOD This is the best seafood restaurant in Stavanger, its windows opening onto a view of the harbor. It amusingly bills itself as "world famous throughout Norway." The old-fashioned interior is straight from the 1950s, with homelike decor and a grandmotherly touch here and there. Begin, perhaps, with the grilled scallops and mushrooms with a tantalizing Jerusalem artichoke purée. You might proceed to the finest item on the menu: Norwegian grilled lobster with a peppery butter. The other main courses maintain a balance between simplicity and elegance, as exemplified by the crab legs with homemade saffron pasta, fresh garlic, and tomato oil, or the poached halibut with pea lentils and a bacon cassoulet with beets—everything served with orange butter. The food is perfectly cooked and appears in generous portions. There is a nightclub upstairs and a sushi restaurant downstairs that's served by the same kitchen.

Nedre Strandgate 15. ✆ **51-84-37-00.** Reservations recommended. Main courses NOK272–NOK325 ($54–$65/£27–£33); fixed-price 3-course menu NOK475 ($95/£48); 5-course fixed-price menu NOK595 ($119/£60). AE, DC, MC, V. Mon–Sat 6–11pm. Closed Dec 22–Jan 7.

Timbuktu ★ NORWEGIAN/AFRICAN The fixed-price menus here are arguably the best in town. Stylish and popular, this restaurant is set beside a cobble-covered square that opens directly onto Stavanger's Vågen (harborfront). Inside, within a decor of pale birch with ebonized trim, there's a busy bar area (Mon–Sat until between midnight and 1:30am) and somewhat crowded tables. Try the masterly salad of lime- and olive-marinated skate or a platter of very fresh sushi as a main course. Drawing upon the bounty of a rugged land, the chefs will delight you with the catch of the day, such as roasted halibut with pickled fennel in an anise-flavored gravy. You might also savor the roasted lamb with a Madeira-flavored gravy and a side helping of couscous. To wake up your taste buds, opt for the redfish with passion fruit sauce or else filet of pork with a spicy tomato and pear chutney.

Nedre Strandgate 15. ✆ **51-84-37-40.** Reservations recommended. Main courses NOK225–NOK259 ($45–$52/£23–£26). 4-course fixed-price menu NOK659 ($132/£66); 5-course fixed-price menu NOK819 ($164/£82). AE, DC, MC, V. Mon–Thurs 6–1:30am; Fri–Sat 6–10pm.

Vertshuset Mat & Vinhus ★★ CONTINENTAL One of the old town's most appealing restaurants, this "food and wine house" is set on a street running parallel to the old port, within an early-19th-century wooden house. Its interior has been "postmodernized" with a decor that is both high-tech and woodsy-looking. Lunches tend to feature *husmanskost* (grandmother-style) dishes such as Nordic meatballs, filet of reindeer, grilled salmon steaks, and pizzas. Dinners are more elaborate and, at least in terms of cuisine, more stylish, with memorable dishes that include salted filets of cod with mashed potatoes and green peas; salmon with garlic sauce; or perhaps a "symphony" of different kinds of fish, fried, steamed, grilled, or broiled. On-site is the cozy XO Bar.

Skagen 10. ✆ **51-89-51-12.** Reservations recommended. Lunch pizzas and platters NOK125–NOK230 ($25–$46/£13–£23); dinner main courses NOK250–NOK310 ($50–$62/£25–£31). AE, DC, MC, V. Daily 11am–10pm. Bar until midnight or 1am, depending on business.

MODERATE

Dolly Dimple's (Kids) PIZZA This is the Stavanger branch of an enormously popular nationwide chain of pizzerias whose Greek-born owner lives in—guess where—Stavanger. It was established in honor of "the world's most beautiful fat girl," in this case, Celesta Geyer, whom the owner saw as a sideshow attraction at an American circus in the 1970s. Today her pen-and-ink likeness (looking even more zaftig and delectable, thanks to the many pizzas she has consumed since becoming Norway's official representative to the pizza-loving world at large) is displayed in about 60 locations throughout Norway. Pizzas here are delicious, coming in 25 already-defined versions, in various degrees of spiciness, plus any number of custom-designed others that you can build yourself by indicating to a staff member what you want on it. Regulation standards include, among others, "Los Banditos," made from strips of marinated beef, chicken, Mexican-style tomato salsa, jalapeño peppers, and cheese. More Nordic versions are built with, among other food, smoked salmon, crème fraîche, and shrimp.

Kongsgårdsbakken 1. ✆ **04-440** (within Norway only). Medium pizzas (suitable for 1–2 persons) NOK129–NOK193 ($26–$39/£13–£19); large pizzas (suitable for 2–3 persons) NOK163–NOK246 ($33–$49/£16–£25). AE, DC, MC, V. Sun–Thurs noon–11pm; Fri–Sat noon–midnight.

Sjøhuset Skagen INTERNATIONAL Thanks to the folksy-looking and heavily timbered premises that date from the mid-19th century, this place is more atmospheric and cozier than the many other pub/restaurants that compete with it nearby. Inside you'll find a warren of congenially cramped cubicles and mezzanines that hint at its origins as a storage for marine supplies and fish. Frankly, we prefer this place as a drinking-with-snacks venue much more than we do as a restaurant, even though a roster of salads, burgers, and pastas is available, as well as such North Atlantic staples as fish and chips. You can also order filet of trout simmered in sour cream or else spareribs marinated in honey and served with a barbecue sauce and spicy fried potatoes. The place has a lot of charm and historical authenticity.

Skagenkaien 16. ✆ **51-89-51-80.** Lunch main courses NOK110–NOK189 ($22–$38/£11–£19); dinner main courses NOK199–NOK315 ($40–$63/£20–£32). AE, DC, MC, V. Mon–Sat 11:30am–midnight; Sun 1–11pm.

4 OUTDOOR ACTIVITIES

Stavanger has some of the best museums of all the port cities of western Norway. But if you want to skip all of them, you can spend your time in the great outdoors, as locals do during their all-too-short summer. Even if you have to miss some of the town's attractions, try to spend some time along the banks of **Lysefjord** (see "Norway's Most Beautiful Fjord," later). What we like to do is spend a day along Lysefjord and view **Preikestolen.** After arriving back in Stavanger in the late afternoon, you can walk the cobblestone streets of **Gamle Stavanger** (p. 250) and have dinner in one of the city's many good restaurants.

In summer Stavanger is made for walking. The best hiking jaunt is the 4km (2½-mile) walk to **Pulpit Rock**—see Preikestolen (p. 256).

If you want to combine sports with your sightseeing, you can pick up many specialized books and maps at the tourist office (see earlier) that will guide you through a vast area, including the rolling hills of the **Setesdalsheiene** and hundreds of little islands and skerries (rocky islets) of the **Ryfylke archipelago.** The tourist office can even arrange for you to stay at one of three dozen cabins in the area, costing from NOK350 to NOK400 ($70–$80/£35–£40) for a one-room unit with a hot plate and refrigerator.

Fishermen flock to the **Suldalslågen,** the longest salmon river in western Norway, lying north of the center of Stavanger. Salmon season lasts from July to September. The best fishing lodge is at **Lindum,** Lakseslottet Lindum N-4240 Suldalsosen (✆ **52-79-91-61**). Call for information if you're interested in renting a cabin or camping facilities.

The best golf is found at the **Stavanger Golf Klubb,** Longebakke 45, Hafsfjord (✆ **51-93-91-00**), a lush woodland and landscaped park with an 18-hole championship international course.

Finally, call **Fossanmoen,** N-4110 Forsand (✆ **51-70-37-61**), if you'd like to go on horseback-riding jaunts while seated on Iceland ponies. These trips take you through some of the scenic wonders of this vast fjord country. Depending on what you're in for, rides can last from 1 hour to all day. Prices range from NOK500 to NOK1,000 ($100–$200/£50–£100).

5 SEEING THE SIGHTS

Arkeologisk Museum (Museum of Archaeology) (Kids) The Vikings will live on forever here, where 15,000 years of southwestern Norway's culture and natural history is on parade. Models of prehistoric life attract a lot of attention, as do the changing natural history exhibitions. Educational but fun films are shown periodically; call ahead to check the schedule. This museum is also the shelter for the public archive of antiquities for Rogaland. It's very family-friendly, featuring treasure-hunt games and other activities for kids.

Peder Klowsgate 30A. ✆ **51-04-60 00.** Admission NOK50 ($10/£5) adults; NOK20 ($4/£2) seniors, students, and children. June–Aug Tues–Sun 11am–5pm; Sept–May Tues 11am–8pm, Wed–Sat 11am–3pm, Sun 11am–4pm.

Domkirke (Cathedral) ★★★ It's not up there in the celestial ranks with the cathedral of Trondheim, but this is the other great church still left from Norway in the Middle Ages—and it stands proud and relatively intact. Constructed over a decade beginning in 1125, the cathedral was dedicated to Saint Swithun. It is said that Bishop Reinald sailed here from Winchester, England, with relics of the saint, to dedicate the cathedral. He carried with him what was said to be the arm of Swithun.

A fire in 1272 swept over the Romanesque structure, destroying most of it. During the church's reconstruction, a Gothic chancel was added. In the new structure, twin square towers and a mammoth porch at the west end were also added. With the coming of the Reformation, the Domkirke lost its precious relics of the saint along with its bells and several altars. A major restoration from 1938 to 1942 was carried out that, for the most part, returned the church to a Middle Ages look.

We always time our visit here to coincide with the organ recital at 11:15am on Thursday. In such an atmosphere, you'll feel as if you've gone back 8 centuries.

The length of the Dom is 65m (213 ft.), with the chancel measuring 22m (72 ft.). The original nave is striking in its simplicity, but the other parts are more elaborate, including the large round columns and the square capitals. Some of the capitals are carved with such Norse figures as dragons and griffins. See, in particular, the fine memorial tablets and the **famous pulpit** ★, outstanding examples of baroque art in Norway.

The pulpit remains a masterpiece of woodcarving, depicting scenes from the Old Testament and crowned by a baldachin honoring the victories of Christ.

Domkirkeplassen. ✆ **51-84-04-00.** Free admission. June–Aug daily 11am–7pm; Sept–May Tues–Thurs and Sat 11am–4pm.

Gamle Stavanger ★★★ This is northern Europe's largest and most impressive—and best preserved—settlement of old-fashioned wooden houses. In "Old Stavanger" (its English name), more than 170 buildings from the late 18th century and early 19th century are not only preserved, but also fully renovated. The houses were built with money brought back to Stavanger by seafarers who roamed the world. A walk through the narrow streets of Gamle Stavanger is one of the most memorable city experiences in southern Norway. The houses are owned partly by private residents and partly by the city itself.

To reach Old Town, go to the west side of Vågen (the harbor) and climb a steep slope overlooking Strandkaien. Once a district for the working class, the area is now gentrified and rather exclusive, and much attention is focused on these whitewashed wooden houses, often with creepers or geraniums growing in flower boxes. The dollhouse homes are separated by small terraced gardens. In the evening, lampposts from the 1890s light your way through the fog.

Norsk Barnemuseum (Norwegian Children's Museum) ★ Kids This is the greatest playpen in Norway for children ages 5 to 12. In fact, it is one of the best children's museums in all of Europe. Exhibits center around almost anything related to children. You get documentation and exhibitions, of course, but the museum also satisfies a kid's desire to play with toys—it has the largest collection in the country. Storytelling and performances for children are also staged here. Activities include climbing up the "Scary Attic" or visiting a secret treehouse, or kids can even embark on a journey in a toy box or whisper into "a bag of secrets." This is very much a hands-on museum for kids, who are allowed to play with toys as well as paint, sing, write, or whatever. The museum also has more serious exhibits dealing with children's rights around the world.

Sølvberget 2. ✆ **51-91-23-93.** www.norskbarne.museum.no. Admission NOK80 ($16/£8) adults, NOK40 ($8/£4) children. Tues–Sat 11am–3:30pm, Sun noon–4:30pm; mid-June to mid-Aug also Mon 11am–5pm.

Norsk Oljemuseum (Norwegian Petroleum Museum) ★ Finds Opened in 1999, this is one of the most unusual museums in Scandinavia and already a much-photographed landmark in the port. This museum documents how oil was discovered off the coast of Norway in 1969, forever changing the country. The oil industry's celebration of itself, this is a spectacularly dramatic museum, rising as it does directly from the waters of the harbor. It resembles a space-age jumble of tin cans, with hints of an offshore oil platform, and an avant-garde modern combination of stainless steel, granite, and glass. The best parts of the museum are those that convey the huge shock and drama associated with Norway's entrance into the oil industry, which had otherwise been dominated by Arabs and Americans, and Norway's struggle to bone up on the legalities and international agreements.

The museum is not particularly adept at explaining the technicalities of the drilling rituals, and there's something superficial about the science associated with the construction of oil platforms, even though you can wander through a replica of an oil platform that's attached to the main bulk of the museum.

One of the city's finest restaurants, Bølgen & Moi (p. 245), is within the premises of this museum, which "guards" the entrance to Stavanger's harbor in the way that Sydney's Opera House "guards" the entrance to the harbor to that city.

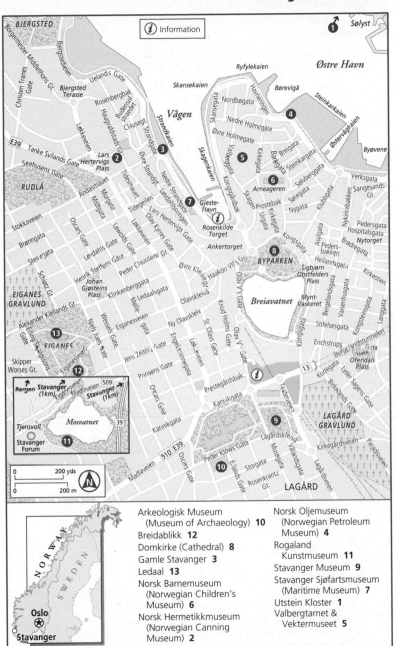

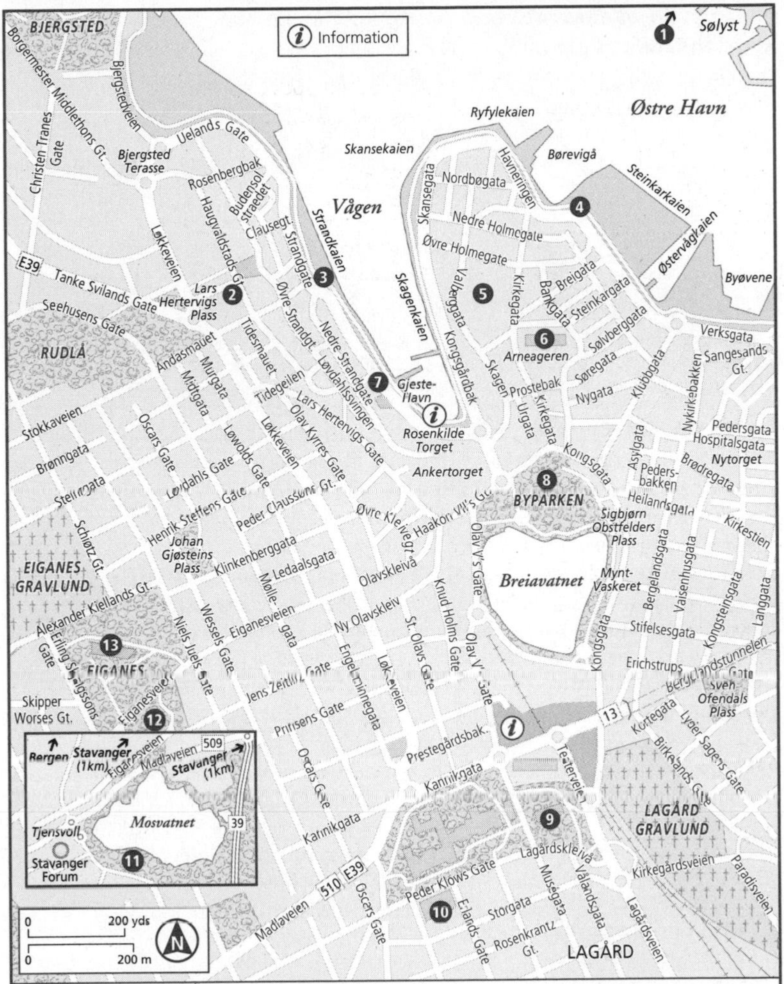

Arkeologisk Museum (Museum of Archaeology) **10**
Breidablikk **12**
Domkirke (Cathedral) **8**
Gamle Stavanger **3**
Ledaal **13**
Norsk Barnemuseum (Norwegian Children's Museum) **6**
Norsk Hermetikkmuseum (Norwegian Canning Museum) **2**
Norsk Oljemuseum (Norwegian Petroleum Museum) **4**
Rogaland Kunstmuseum **11**
Stavanger Museum **9**
Stavanger Sjøfartsmuseum (Maritime Museum) **7**
Utstein Kloster **1**
Valbergtarnet & Vektermuseet **5**

Kjeringholmen. ✆ **51-93-93-00.** www.norskolje.museum.no. Admission NOK80 ($16/£8) adults, NOK40 ($8/£4) children, students, and seniors. June–Aug daily 10am–7pm; Sept–May Mon–Sat 10am–4pm, Sun 10am–6pm.

Rogaland Kunstmuseum ★ This is Stavanger's museum of fine arts, both showing temporary exhibitions as well as maintaining an impressive treasure trove of art. The collection consists of some 2,000 paintings, drawings, and sculptures. Most of these are by Norwegian artists from the beginning of the 19th century to the present. Donated to the museum, the **Halvdan Haftsten Collection ★** includes some 200 paintings and drawings created by eight Norwegian artists between the two world wars. The museum displays the largest and most impressive collection of the **works of Lars Hertervig ★** (1830–1902), one of the greatest romantic painters of Norwegian landscapes, along with an impressive array of the works of Kitty Kielland. The location 3km (1¾ miles) from the city center is at the northern end of the Old Town close to Mos Lake (Mosvannet), off E18.

Henrik Ibsen Weg 55, Mosvannsparken. ✆ **51-53-09-00.** www.rkm.no. Admission NOK50 ($10/£5) adults and students, free for children 15 and under. Tues–Sun 11am–4pm. Bus: 3, 5A, 5B, 7, or 9.

Stavanger Museum ★★ This is a five-part museum that you can visit with just one ticket. If you want to see the entire museum, expect to spend the better part of a day scampering from one point to another across the city. At the main museum, you'll be given a map with the locations of all the museums.

The main museum is called simply the **Stavanger Museum,** Muségata 16 (✆ **51-84-27-00**), open from mid-June to August 15 daily from 11am to 4pm. From June 1 to June 14 and from August 16 to August 31, it is open Monday to Thursday 11am to 3pm and Sunday 11am to 4pm. During other months, the museum is open only on Sunday 11am to 4pm. The ticket for all five museums costs NOK60 ($12/£6) for adults, NOK30 ($6/£3) for students and seniors, NOK10 ($2/£1) for ages 4 to 6 (free for 3 and under).

At the main museum at Muségata, you can see a permanent collection of stuffed birds and animals from all over the world. The centuries-old history of Stavanger, dating from the Viking era, is also presented, along with dramatized sound recordings about Stavanger in the 1800s.

The second museum, **Stavanger Sjøfartsmuseum (Maritime Museum),** Nedre Strandgate 17–19, lies in a converted warehouse dating from 1770. Its permanent exhibition traces the maritime history of Stavanger for the past 2 centuries, from the days of the herring fleets to the booming oil industry of today.

The facade is a trim and shipshape, clapboard-sided, white-painted building directly on the harborfront. Inside there's a battered post-and-beam construction showing how artfully timbers were used by 19th-century craftsmen; a sense of the dust, dirt, and economic mayhem of the Industrial Revolution; and the pervasive scent of tar and turpentine. Expect a claustrophobic, dark-toned interior; hundreds of ship models and 19th-century maritime accessories; and a horrendous sense of how hard life was in 19th- and early-20th-century coastal Norway.

You can visit a general store from the turn of the 20th century, a reconstructed merchant's apartment from the early 1900s, a reconstructed shipowner's home, and a sailmaker's loft, along with a memorial room to the philosopher Henrik Steffens. There is also a children's shop on-site. This museum is closed in December.

Norsk Hermetikkmuseum (Norwegian Canning Museum), Øvre Strandgate 88A, lies in an old canning factory, with exhibitions tracing the fishing industry, Stavanger's

Moments A Bike Ride to the "Three Swords"

On a summer day we like to get the makings of a picnic and set out to see **Sverd I Fjell,** or the Three Swords monument at Hafrsfjord. This is the spot where King Hårald Fairhair united Norway into one kingdom in 872. In 1983 Fritz Røed created this monument, and it was unveiled by King Olav. The monument, standing as a symbol of unification, depicts Viking sword sheaths modeled on actual swords found in various parts of the country. The crowns on the tops of the swords represent the Norwegian districts that took part in the epic battle for unification. From the center of Stavanger, bike along Mosvannet Lake and continue along Rte. 510 toward Sola. Allow about half an hour to reach this monument. The area of Møllebukta itself, in which the monument lies, is a popular outdoor spot of great beauty.

main industry before being replaced by the oil industry, from the 1890s to the 1960s. Some of the machinery is still working, and on the first Sunday of every month, the smoking ovens are stoked up. The public can taste newly smoked brisling straight from the ovens. This is the oddest and quirkiest of Stavanger's museums, and it arouses the most emotion within the Norwegians who visit it. It's also the least polished and the earthiest of the town's museums, and the one that most richly and evocatively portrays the harsh and boring circumstances of factory work during the Industrial Revolution. It's set within a low-slung clapboard building within a neighborhood of increasingly gentrified antique cottages. Inside, about 50 antique machines are displayed, with sepia toned photographs of how they, along with scores of weary workers, fitted sardines, herring, and brislings into the galvanized steel tins that were later shipped to homes throughout Europe. Expect an enduring sense of the soot, grime, grease, and fish guts that once permeated this place with odors that stretched for several blocks in all directions. Overall, this museum is one of the most effective and eloquent tributes in Stavanger to the workaday heroism of 19th- and early-20th-century Norway.

The fourth museum, **Ledaal ★**, Eiganesveien 45, was built by Gabriel Schanche Kielland, a shipowner and merchant, in the years 1799 to 1803. The mansion is a fine example of the neoclassical style as interpreted in western Norway, with interior furnishings that are mainly rococo, Empire, and Biedermeier. This is the official—but rarely used—residence of the Norwegian royal family during their visits to Stavanger and Rogaland counties, of which Stavanger is the capital. It's painted a shade of Pompeian red and set adjacent to one of Stavanger's most evocative cemeteries. It's separated from a road leading into Stavanger, about a 15-minute walk uphill from the harbor, by a wall of very large boulders. The look is country-rustic and baronial, and is completely permeated with a sense of genteel 18th-century aristocracy and all-wood construction; it's closed in December and January.

The fifth museum is **Breidablikk ★**, Eiganesveien 40A. Set across the road from Ledaal (see above), it was built by another merchant and shipowner, Lars Berensten, in 1881 and 1882. Both the exterior and interior of the house are preserved in their original condition. It's a teeny-weeny bit kitschy, thanks to an exaggerated alpine-*gemütlich* style, a coat of almost-too-bright ocher paint (with dark brown trim), and yard upon yard of elaborate gingerbread running along the eaves and verandas. It's Victoriana/Carpenter gone wild and an amusing sightseeing diversion; it's closed December and January.

Utstein Kloster ★ This is Norway's only preserved medieval abbey. In the 9th century, Utstein was one of the royal residences of Harald Hårfagre, the Fairhair, Norway's first monarch. In 1250 it belonged to Magnus Lagabøter (the Lawmender) who as king would draft Norway's first constitution, then the most democratic in the world. Magnus gave Utstein to the canons of an Augustinian order, who constructed their abbey around his fortress at the end of the 1200s. With the coming of the Reformation, Utstein became one of the largest private estates in western Norway. In summer, sporadic concerts featuring leading jazz and classical musicians are staged in its chapel.

Mosterøy. ✆ **51-72-47-05.** Admission NOK50 ($10/£5) adults, NOK20 ($4/£2) children, free for children 6 and under. May to mid-Sept Tues–Sat 10am–4pm; Sun noon–5pm.

Valbergtarnet & Vektermuseet Inhabiting a wooden city, the residents of Stavanger lived in constant fear of fire. So, from 1850 to 1853, they constructed this historic tower, Valbergtarnet, with a panoramic sweep over Stavanger and its harbor. A guard was stationed here 24 hours a day to be on the lookout for a fire. Today the site is visited mainly for its **panoramic view ★★**, one of the most memorable cityscape vistas in southwestern Norway. But a small museum, Vektermuseet, has been installed here as well. The watchman's museum focuses on the guard's duties and the watchman as a symbol of safety.

Valbergjet 2. ✆ **51-89-55-01.** Admission NOK50 ($10/£5) adults, NOK20 ($4/£2) children. Tues–Sat 10am–4pm; Sun noon–5pm. Closed Dec–Mar.

6 SHOPPING

Locals head for the area's major shopping center, **Kvadrat Kjøpesenter** at Lura, lying between Stavanger and Sandnes (✆ **51-96-00-00**). There are nearly 160 shops here selling everything from reindeer hides, sheepskin jackets, and pewter souvenirs, to Norwegian handcrafts such as wooden trolls. Other outlets include restaurants, a state-run wine store, a pharmacy, and even a post office, if you want to mail back some of the cards you can purchase in one of several shops.

Most shops are open Monday to Wednesday and Friday from 9am to 5pm, Thursday 9am to 7pm, and Saturday 9am to 3pm.

Gjestal Spinneri ★ (Finds) Motorists and serious shoppers might want to check out this spinning mill, lying 30km (19 miles) southeast of Stavanger in the little village of Oltedal. Established in 1937, it has since become one of Scandinavia's leading producers in the manufacture of hand-knitting yarn and plaids. The mill uses mostly Norwegian lamb's wool, but also English or New Zealand wool, to create ideal, high-quality wool garments. The outlet sells all types of yarn and ready-made sweaters and other woolen products at 30% to 40% below the prices you'll find in most city stores. On-site is a cafeteria, so you can also make this a luncheon stopover. 4333 Oltedal. ✆ **51-61-22-00.**

Helger Myhre Marine Supplies This shop would never be considered a staple on Stavanger's tourist circuit, and many non–Norwegian shoppers might bypass it immediately in favor of a more luxurious venue. But if you've ever sailed a boat, or if you happen to own a boat, or if you merely happen to be fascinated with the thousands of articles you could stockpile *if* you owned a boat, this place is well worth a visit. Nautical hardware (everything you'd need to winch, ratchet, hoist, or belay a sailing craft) is stocked on the street level. Clothing for men, women, and children is upstairs, and a collection of sometimes kitschy-looking "Ahoy, Mate!" souvenirs, many in brass, is scattered around the store. Skagenkaien 22. ✆ **51-89-07-20.**

Helgi Joensen ★ Sculptural pewter—modern decorative art—reaches its peak in Stavanger at the working studio of this renowned artist who grew up on the coasts of the North Atlantic and found inspiration for his work here. Sculptures are mainly in pewter, and each piece is constructed individually, its texture formed freehand with no casting or molds. One piece of Joensen's sculptural pewter makes for a good heirloom gift. A visit here is also a chance to explore inside the working studio of a Norwegian artist. Ovre Strand Gate 52. ✆ **51-52-98-99.**

7 STAVANGER AFTER DARK

Café Sting ★ Stavanger is not known for its counterculture or bohemian undercurrents, but the little that exists is most visible here. Set atop the highest hill within the town center, a breathless 10-minute trek from the harbor via a flight of winding concrete steps, this cafe lies adjacent to Valbergstårnet, a mock-medieval stone tower that was originally conceived late in the 19th century as a fire-watch station. The low-slung, white-sided clapboard house that contains the cafe was built in 1850. Inside you'll find five different rooms, most on the ground floor, and most lined with strikingly modern paintings. By far the greatest business here derives from the establishment's role as a cafe serving pastries, beer, wine, and coffee, usually to liberal-minded members of Stavanger's arts community. Expect a larger-than-usual percentage of gay men and women here, but only on Friday, Saturday, and Sunday nights, when the place takes on more of a lavender luster. The cellar is home to a disco, usually frequented by straights and (to a much lesser extent) gays in their 20s and 30s, that operates Thursday to Saturday 11pm to 3:30am. The cafe is open Monday to Thursday noon to midnight, Friday and Saturday noon to 3:30am, and Sunday 3pm to midnight. There is no cover. Valberget 3. ✆ **51-89-32-84.**

Checkpoint Charlie Hard Rock Café Mainly a dance place, this club can hold 200 people on a good night. Drawing a crowd in their 20s, it attracts those who like alternative music and hard rock. Music, often rock 'n' roll, is presented live one to two times a week, at which time a small cover, which can range from free to around NOK15 ($3/£1.50), might be imposed. It's open daily 8pm to 2am. Nedre Strandgatan 5. ✆ **51-53-22-45.**

The Irishman This pub, attracting those from their 20s to their 60s, is the expat favorite, drawing a lot of patrons from Ireland, Scotland, and England who are lured by the recorded music they play from those countries—that and the large selection of different whiskeys as well as Scotch single malts. Incidentally, they also sell American bourbon. A house band plays music on Thursday evenings as well as on Saturday afternoon. It's open Monday to Wednesday 5pm to 1am, Thursday and Friday 3pm to 2am, and Saturday and Sunday 1pm to 2am. Holebergatan 9. ✆ **51-89-41-81.**

Newsman Pub ★ This is an earthy British-style pub that its fans have defined as the most literate in Norway. Its decor was inspired by an old-fashioned newspaper office, the kind where lead type was supervised by stooped-over men with green eyeshades. You

Moments Norway's Most Beautiful Fjord ★★★

Poets have been inspired by the 42km (26-mile) **Lysefjord,** or "light fjord," the country's most scenic. The blue waters of the fjord seem to glow even on a gray day as a luminous mist hovers over the fjord. "Time passes at a sedate pace at Lysefjord," or so wrote Olav Pedersen in 1883. "Your thoughts can wander in peace." That statement is still true today. Other writers have claimed that spending time on the majestic fjord allows them to tune in to nature's harmonious symphony. Sunsets here are often a dramatic mauve color tinged with royal purple.

You can take a day trip to the fjord, combining a traditional ferry ride with an express boat. Of course, weather could be a factor in your decision to go or not to go. For information about schedules and tickets, contact the visitor information center (earlier in this chapter) in Stavanger or call **Rogaland Kollektivtrafikk** at ✆ **51-51-65-30.** In summer, 3- to 6-hour boat trips are organized to the fjord, which is accessible only by boat. A typical excursion offered by **Rødne Fjord Cruise** (✆ **51-89-52-70**) costs NOK340 ($68/£34) for adults, NOK240 ($48/£24) for seniors, and NOK175 ($35/£18) for children ages 4 to 15.

can sit around the woodsy-looking bar, within sightlines of the framed front pages of newspapers from around the English-speaking world, including banner headlines announcing the deaths of Winston Churchill and JFK and the resignation of Richard Nixon. It's all very adult, and charming in its re-creation of a 1920s-era kind of aesthetic. Rest your pint of beer on any of several old-fashioned lecterns, and perhaps flip through a copy of any of the English-language papers that are displayed, library style, on rods. There's even *The Newsman,* an in-house paper that focuses on local politics, personalities, and gossip. The only food items served are snack items such as muffins and sandwiches. Open Monday to Saturday noon to 1:30am and Sunday 3pm to 1:30am. Skagen 14. ✆ **51-84-38-80.**

8 SIDE TRIPS FROM STAVANGER

The region surrounding Stavanger, both north and south, is one of the most beautiful in southwestern Norway, with some spectacular natural attractions. Fjord and mountain landscapes come together in a kind of majesty. There are some man-made attractions as well, but Mother Nature wins out over those.

PREIKESTOLEN ★★★ "Pulpit Rock" is a mammoth cube of rock with a vertical drop of 609m (1,998 ft.) over Lysefjord. It can be visited on either a boat or bus trip, or by a car-ferry trip and short drive, taking about 45 minutes from the center of Stavanger. If you want to climb the rock, you can take a boat and bus hiking jaunt. A pathway leads to the top. Jimmy Stewart in the Hitchcock film *Vertigo* would have had a tough time of it here, but if you like panoramic vistas, this rock is for you.

The walk from the car park to Pulpit Rock is 4km (2½ miles) but can take 2 hours each way. The walk has an elevation of 350m (1,148 ft.) and requires both you and your footwear to be in good shape. The last part of the walk passes dizzying drops high above Lysefjord. The weather can change quickly, so remember to bring rainwear.

A bus, costing NOK55 ($11/£5.50) one-way, leaves from the station in Stavanger from late May to early September. The boat is timed to meet ferry departures, which will take you for the final lap of the journey.

You can also sail by the rock on a fjord cruise but it's not as impressive from down below. **Rødine Fjord Cruise** (**© 51-51-65-30**) offers a cruise from Stavanger to Pulpit Rock for NOK340 ($68/£34) for adults, NOK240 ($48/£24) for seniors, and NOK175 ($35/£18) for ages 4 to 15. Call for bookings.

11

Bergen

Bergen—Europe's most underrated city—is enveloped by majestic mountains, the world's most spectacular fjords, and one of Europe's largest glaciers. In summer, when most visitors arrive, the staid image of Bergen as a bourgeois, conservative town fades away and a youthful energy prevails before the deep freeze of winter settles in. Not only that, but the July sun shines all night long—and it's party time, often until morning. The partying doesn't totally end in winter. People just move that party into the beer taverns.

On even the most rushed of itineraries, try to spare at least 2 days for Bergen to experience the natural beauty that is still preserved here.

In western Norway, the landscape takes on an awesome beauty, with iridescent glaciers; deep fjords that slash into rugged, snowcapped mountains; roaring waterfalls; and secluded valleys at the end of twisting roads. From Bergen, the most beautiful fjords to visit are the **Hardangerfjord** (best at blossom time—May and early June), to the south; the **Sognefjord,** Norway's longest fjord, immediately to the north; and the **Nordfjord,** north of that. A popular excursion on the Nordfjord takes visitors from Loen to Olden along rivers and lakes to the **Brixdal Glacier.**

On the Hardangerfjord, you can stop over at a resort such as **Ulvik** or **Lofthus.** From many vantage points, it's possible to see the **Folgefonn Glacier,** Norway's second-largest ice field. It spans more than 260 sq. km (101 sq. miles). Other stopover suggestions include the summer resorts (and winter ski centers) of Voss and **Geilo.** For resorts in the fjord district, see chapter 12, "The West Coast Fjord Country."

Bergen, with its many attractions and excellent transportation, makes the best center in the fjord district. It's an ancient city that looms large in Viking sagas. Until the 14th century, it was the seat of the medieval kingdom of Norway. The Hanseatic merchants established a major trading post here until the 18th century. Seafaring Bergen has given the world two cultural icons—the composer Edvard Grieg and the playwright Henrik Ibsen.

Bergen has survived many disasters, including several fires and the explosion of a Nazi ship during World War II. It's a town with important traditions in shipping, banking, and insurance; its modern industries are expanding rapidly; and its university is one of the academic jewels of Norway.

1 ORIENTATION

ARRIVING

BY PLANE Planes to and from larger cities such as Copenhagen and London land at the **Bergen Airport** in Flesland, 19km (12 miles) south of the city. Dozens of direct or nonstop flights go to just about every medium-size city in Norway on such airlines as **SAS** (**© 91-50-54-00;** www.sas.no).

The World's Longest Tunnel

Thanks to a tunnel, you can now drive from Oslo to Bergen without having to take a ferry across water. Opened in 2001, the **Laerdal Tunnel ★★★**, stretching for 24.5km (15.3 miles), is the longest in the world. It lies on E16, the main road between Bergen and Oslo. The entrance to the tunnel begins at a point 296km (184 miles) northwest of Oslo. Costing $1.1 billion, it is said to be the safest road tunnel on the globe.

Along with high-tech monitoring, fire safety, and air treatment, the tunnel features a trio of large turning caverns (in case you change your mind and want to go back), 16 turning points, and nearly 50 emergency "lay-bys." Some 400 vehicles per hour can go through the tunnel, the ride taking just 20 minutes.

The area up above gets severe weather in winter, but all is calm in the tunnel. The high mountain passes at 1,809m (5,934 ft.) are closed in winter. The panoramic, high-mountain road between Aurland and Laerdal, the so-called "Snow Road," is open only in summer.

Frequent **airport bus** service connects the airport to the Radisson SAS Royal Hotel and the city bus station. Departures are every 20 minutes Monday to Friday and every 30 minutes Saturday and Sunday. The one-way fare is NOK80 ($16/£8).

BY TRAIN Day and night trains arrive from Oslo and stations en route. For information, call ✆ **81-50-08-88.** Travel time from Oslo to Bergen is 8½ hours. Visit www.nsb.no for information.

BY BUS Express buses travel to Bergen from Oslo, Trondheim, Ålesund, and the Nordfjord area. The trip from Oslo takes 11 hours. Visit www.nor-way.no for information.

BY CAR A toll is charged on all vehicles driven into the city center Monday to Friday from 6am to 10pm. A single ticket costs NOK15 ($3/£1.50).

The trip from Oslo to Bergen is a mountain drive filled with dramatic scenery. Because mountains split the country, there's no direct road. The southern route, E76, goes through mountain passes until the junction with Rte. 47, then heads north to Kinsarvik and makes the ferry crossing to E16 leading west to Bergen. The northern route, Hwy. 7, through the resort of Geilo, heads to the junction with Rte. 47, then south to Kinsarvik. Take the ferry and then go west on E16.

Visitors with a lot of time may spend 2 or 3 days driving from Oslo to Bergen. Fjords and snowcapped peaks line the way, and you can photograph waterfalls, fjord villages, and ancient stave churches.

To reduce driving time, motorists can use a tunnel—11km (6¾ miles), the longest in northern Europe—that goes between Flåm (see "Flåm: Stopover on Europe's Most Scenic Train Ride," in chapter 12) and Gudvangen. From Gudvangen, follow E16 southwest to Bergen.

VISITOR INFORMATION

The **Bergen Tourist Office,** Vågsallmenningen 1 (✆ **55-55-20-00;** www.visitbergen.com), provides information, maps, and brochures about Bergen and the rest of the region. It's open June to August daily 8:30am to 10pm, May and September daily 9am to 8pm, October to April Monday to Saturday 9am to 5pm. The Bergen Tourist Office can also help you find a place to stay, exchange foreign currency, and cash traveler's checks when banks are closed. You can also buy tickets for city sightseeing or for tours of the fjords.

CITY LAYOUT

Bergen is squeezed between mountain ranges and bounded by water. The center of the city lies between the harbor, **Bryggen** (check out "Seeing the Sights," later in this chapter); the railway station; and the main square, **Torgalmenningen.**

Like Rome, Bergen is said to have grown up around **seven hills.** For the best overall view, take the funicular to **Fløien.** The northern section of the city is **Sandviken,** which is filled with old warehouses. The area south of central Bergen is being developed at an incredible rate.

In the center of Bergen, walk on cobblestone streets as you explore the quayside with its medieval houses and the open-air Fish Market. The center has colonnaded shops and cafes, and in **Gamle Bergen** you get a taste of the early 19th century.

2 GETTING AROUND

The **Bergen Card** entitles you to free bus transportation and (usually) free museum entrance throughout Bergen, plus discounts on car rentals, parking, and some cultural and leisure activities. It's a good value. Ask for it at the tourist office (see "Visitor Information," above). A 24-hour card costs NOK190 ($38/£19) for adults, NOK75 ($15/£7.50) for children 3 to 15. A 48-hour card is NOK250 ($50/£25) for adults, and NOK100 ($20/£10) for children 3 to 15. Children under 3 travel or enter free.

BY BUS

The **Central Bus Station (Bystasjonen),** Strømgaten 8 (✆ **55-55-90-70**), is the terminal for all buses serving the Bergen and Hardanger areas, as well as the airport bus. The station has luggage storage, shops, and a restaurant. City buses are marked with their destination and route number. For **bus information** in the Bergen area, call ✆ **177.** A network of yellow-sided city buses serves the city center only. For information, call ✆ **55-59-32-00.**

BY TAXI

Taxis are readily available at the airport. To request one, call ✆ **55-99-70-10.** A ride from the Bergen Airport to the city center costs around NOK280 ($56/£28). Sightseeing by taxi costs NOK500 to NOK750 ($100–$150/£50–£75) per hour, depending on the day of week and the time of day.

BY CAR

PARKING Visitors can park on most streets in the city center after 5pm. For convenient indoor parking, try the **Bygarasjen Busstation** (✆ **55-56-88-70**), a large garage near the bus and train stations, about a 5-minute walk from the city center. It's open 24 hours a day and charges NOK20 ($4/£2) per hour. You can park for 24 hours for NOK90 ($18/£9).

RENTAL CARS You might want to rent a car to explore the area for a day or two. **Budget** (© **800/472-3325** in the U.S.; www.budget.com) maintains offices at the airport (© **55-22-75-27**) and downtown at Vestre Strømkaien 5 (© **55-27-39-90**). Its least expensive car is NOK770 ($154/£77) per day, which includes the 23% government tax, collision-damage waiver, and unlimited mileage. Rates per day are lower for rentals of a week or more.

Hertz (© **800/654-3001** in the U.S.; www.hertz.com) has locations at the airport (© **55-22-60-75**) and downtown at Nygårdsgate 89 (© **55-55-08-20**). For a 2-day rental, the smallest car, a Volkswagen Lupo, costs NOK1,795 ($359/£180).

Avis (© **800/331-2112** in the U.S.; www.avis.com) has branches at the airport (© **55-22-76-18**) and downtown at Lars Hillesgate 20 (© **55-55-39-55**). For a 1-day rental, its smallest car, an Opel Corsa, costs NOK1,300 ($260/£130) with unlimited mileage. The price includes the 23% tax and the optional collision-damage waiver. Of course, rates are subject to change. The lowest rates are almost always offered to those who reserve their cars from their home country before they leave.

BY FERRY

You can take a ferry across the harbor Monday to Friday from 7am to 4:15pm; they don't run on Saturday or Sunday. One-way fares are NOK20 ($4/£2) for adults and NOK15 ($3/£1.50) for children. Ferries arrive and depart from either side of the harbor at Dreggekaien and Munkebryggen. For information, call © **55-55-20-00.**

BY COASTAL STEAMER

Bergen is the cruise capital of Norway, home to a flotilla of well-engineered ships that carry passengers, cars, and vast amounts of freight up and down the coast. At least 10 of the boats begin and end their itineraries in Bergen and make about 30 stops en route before landing 5 to 6 days later at Kirkenes, far north of the Arctic Circle, near the Russian border. You can book a berth on any one of these ships for short- or long-haul transits and do a quick bit of sightseeing while the ship docks in various ports.

The most popular tour is a 12-day unescorted northbound cruise—Oslo-Bergen-Kirkenes-Oslo—starting at $2,999 (£1,500) per person, based on double occupancy. It's best to book these cruises through the New York City office of the Bergen Line (© **866/552-0371;** www.hurtigruten.us). The line owns some of the ships and acts as a sales agent for the others. If you're already in Norway, talk to any travel agent. You can make arrangements through Bergen-based **Cruise Spesialisten,** Lillemarkev 1–3 (© **55-23-07-90**) or with its competitor, **Kystopplevelser,** on Strandkaien 4 (© **55-31-59-10**). Both companies distribute brochures and lots of information concerning the stalwart Norwegian cruise ships that make frequent runs up and down the Norwegian coast. They include the *Narvik* (1995); *Nord Norge* (launched in 1997); *Polarys* (1996); *Nordkapp* (1996); *Trollfjord* (2002); *Finmarken* (2002); *Midnatt Sol* (2003); and *Lofoten* (1995), which is sometimes pressed into duty on an as-needed basis.

Other routes head south from Bergen to Stavanger and other ports, and tours go to some of the fjords to the south. For information and reservations, contact the Bergen Line, Cruise Spesialisten (see above), or a local operator. The best operator is **Fjord 1** (© **55-90-70-70**), which runs fast ferries from Bergen to Sognefjord, the world's longest fjord.

Fast Facts Bergen

Area Code The country code for Norway is **47.** Most land-based telephones within Bergen begin with 55. (Cellphones, however, are not bound by that general rule and might begin with virtually anything.) In Norway, all telephone numbers have eight digits, the first two of which are usually defined as the "area code." It's always necessary to dial all eight digits.

Banking Bergen has dozens of banks. The most visible is **Dnb Norske Bank,** Lars Hilles Gate 30 (✆ **55-21-10-00**). Branches of many of its competitors can be found near the Radisson SAS Hotel Norge, on Rådstuplass.

Bookstores One of the best, with a wide range of books in English, is **Norli,** in the Galleriet, Torgalmenningen 8 (✆ **55-21-42-80**). It's open Monday to Friday 9am to 8pm, Saturday 9am to 6pm.

Business Hours Most **banks** are open Monday to Friday from 9am to 3pm, and Thursday until 6pm. Most **businesses** are open Monday to Friday 9am to 4pm. **Shops** are generally open Monday to Wednesday and Friday 9am to 4:30pm, Thursday 9am to 7pm (sometimes also on Fri until 7pm), Saturday 9am to 2pm.

Currency Exchange You can exchange currency at the Bergen Airport. In town you can exchange money at several banks. When the banks are closed, you can exchange money at the tourist office (see "Visitor Information," above).

Dentists Emergency care only is available at **Bergen Legevakt,** Vestre Stromkaien 19 (✆ **55-56-87-00**), from 5 to 10pm.

Doctors For medical assistance, call **Bergen Legevakt,** Vestre Stromkaien 19 (✆ **55-56-87-00**), 24 hours a day. If it's not an emergency, your hotel can make an appointment with an English-speaking doctor.

Drugstores One convenient pharmacy is **Apoteket Nordstjernen,** Strømgate 8 (✆ **55-21-83-84**). It's open Monday to Saturday 8am to 11pm and Sunday 10am to 11pm.

Embassies & Consulates Most foreign nationals, including citizens of the United States, will have to contact their embassies in Oslo (see "Embassies & Consulates," in Appendix A) if they have a problem. Exceptions to this rule include the **United Kingdom,** which maintains a consulate in Bergen, at Øvre Ole Bulls Plass 1 (✆ **55-36-78-10**); and Canada, which has a consulate at Asbjørnsen Gate 20 (✆ **55-29-71-30**).

Emergencies For the **police,** dial ✆ **112;** to report a **fire,** call ✆ **110;** for an **ambulance,** dial ✆ **113.**

Eyeglass Repair A good optician is **Optiker Svabø,** Strandgaten 18 (✆ **55-31-69-51**).

Hairdressers & Barbers One of the best in town is **Prikken Frisørsalong,** Strandkaien 2B (✆ **55-32-31-51**). It's open Monday, Tuesday, Thursday, and Friday 9am to 4pm; Wednesday 10am to 7pm; and Saturday 9am to 2pm.

Hospitals A medical center, **Accident Clinic (Legevakten),** is open around the clock. It's at Vestre Stromkaien 19 (✆ **55-56-87-00**).

Internet Access Your best bet is **Accezzo,** next to the Galleriet shopping mall at Torgallmenningen 8 (✆ **55-31-11-60**).

Laundry Try **Jarlens Vaskoteque,** Lille Øvregate 17 (✆ **55-32-55-04**). It's near the Hotel Victoria in a little alley about 45m (148 ft.) northeast of the 17th-century Korskirken church, off Kong Oscars Gate. It's open Monday, Tuesday, and Friday 10am to 6pm; Wednesday and Thursday 10am to 7pm; and Saturday 10am to 3pm.

Libraries The **Bergen Public Library,** Strømgaten (✆ **55-56-85-00**), is open in July and August on Tuesday, Wednesday, and Friday 10am to 3pm, Monday and Thursday 9am to 7pm, and Saturday 9am to 1pm; the rest of the year, it's open Monday to Friday 10am to 8pm and Saturday 10am to 5pm.

Lost Property Various agencies recover lost objects. For assistance, contact the local police station or **Tourist Information** (✆ **55-55-20-00**).

Luggage Storage & Lockers Rental lockers and luggage storage are available at the **Jernbanestasjonen (railway station),** Strømgaten 1, which is open daily 7am to 11:50pm. The cost ranges from NOK20 to NOK40 ($4–$8/£2–£4) per day, depending on the locker's size.

Police Call ✆ **112.**

Post Office The main post office is on Småstrandgaten (✆ **55-54-15-00**), 1 block from Torget. It's open Monday to Friday 8am to 5pm, and Saturday 9am to 2:30pm. If you want to receive your mail in care of General Delivery, the address is Poste Restante, N-5002 Bergen. You'll need your passport to pick it up.

Taxes Bergen adds no city taxes to the national value-added tax.

Telephone Most locals pay for their calls with debit phone cards, available in various denominations at newspaper kiosks and pharmacies. To call abroad, dial ✆ **00;** to call collect, dial ✆ **115.**

3 WHERE TO STAY

Easily found at Vågsallmenningen 1, the **Bergen Tourist Office** (see "Orientation," earlier in this chapter) books guests into hotels and secures accommodations in private homes. More than 30 families take in guests during the summer. The booking service costs NOK30 to NOK50 ($6–$10/£3–£5), and prospective guests also pay a deposit that's deducted from the final bill. Double rooms in **private homes** usually cost from NOK380 to NOK450 ($76–$90/£38–£45), with no service charge. Breakfast is not served.

The rates quoted for the hotels below include service and tax. Many expensive accommodations lower their rates considerably on weekends and in midsummer. We've mentioned it when these reductions are available, but the situation is fluid, and it's best to check on the spot. All of our recommended accommodations come with private bathrooms unless otherwise indicated.

Bergen Accommodations & Dining

ACCOMMODATIONS ■

Augustin Hotel **7**
Bergen Travel Hotel **22**
Best Western Hotell Hordaheimen **9**
Clarion Collection Hotel Havnekontoret **1**
Clarion Hotel Admiral **8**
Comfort Hotel Holberg **6**
First Hotel Marin **13**
Neptun Hotel **17**
P Hotel Bergen **27**
Park Pension **31**
Quality Edvard Greig Hotel and Suites **32**
Radisson SAS Hotel Norge **20**
Radisson SAS Royal Hotel **2**
Rica Travel Hotel **29**
Scandic Hotel Bergen City **28**
Solstrand Hotel & Bad **32**
Steens Hotel—Bed & Breakfast **13**
Strand Hotel **24**

DINING ◆

Bølgen & Moi **30**
Bryggeloftet and BryggeStuene **3**
Egon **14**
Enhjørningen (the Unicorn) **4**
Escalón Tapas Restaurant **10**
Finnegaardstuene **11**
Holberg-Stuen **16**
Kafe Krystall **12**
Kaffistova **9**
Lucullus **17**
Mago **26**
Naboen **23**
Restaurant Potetkjeller **15**
Ristorante Stragiotti **25**
Smauet Mat & Vinhus **21**
Spisekroken **18**
To Kokker **5**
Wessel-Stuen **19**

ⓘ Information

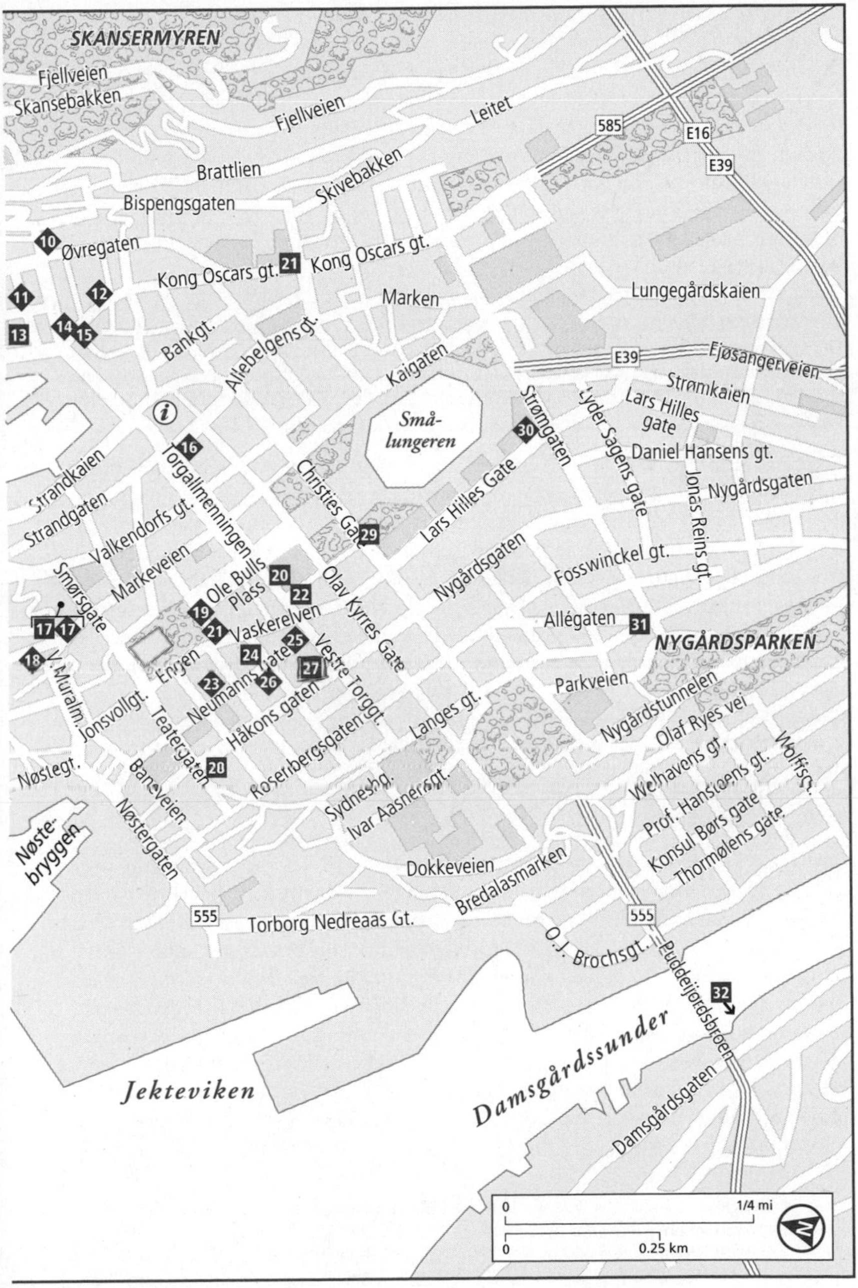
SKANSERMYREN
Fjellveien
Skansebakken
Fjellveien
Leitet
Brattlien
Bispengsgaten
Skivebakken
Øvregaten
Kong Oscars gt.
Kong Oscars gt.
Marken
Lungegårdskaien
Bankgt.
Allebelgens gt.
Kaigaten
E39
Fjøsangerveien
Strømkaien
Lars Hilles gate
Små-lungeren
Strømgaten
Lyder Sagens gate
Daniel Hansens gt.
Strandkaien
Torgallmenningen
Christies Gate
Lars Hilles Gate
Jonas Reins gt.
Nygårdsgaten
Strandgaten
Valkendorfs gt.
Nygårdsgaten
Fosswinckel gt.
Markeveien
Ole Bulls Plass
Olav Kyrres Gate
Smørsgate
Vaskerelven
Allégaten
NYGÅRDSPARKEN
Vestre Torggt.
Engen
Neumanns gate
Parkveien
V. Muralm.
Jonsvollgt.
Håkons gaten
Langes gt.
Nygårdstunnelen
Olaf Ryes vei
Teatergaten
Rosenbergsgaten
Welhavens gt.
Wolffsg.
Nøstegt.
Baneveien
Sydnesbg.
Ivar Aasnergt.
Prof. Hansteens gt.
Konsul Børs gate
Thormølens gate
Nøste-bryggen
Nøstergaten
Dokkeveien
Bredalasmarken
555
Torborg Nedreaas Gt.
555
O.J. Brochsgt.
Puddefjordsbroen
Damsgårdssunder
Jekteviken
Damsgårdsgaten
Damsgårdsgaten
585
E16
E39
0
1/4 mi
0
0.25 km
N
10
11
12
13
14
15
16
17
17
18
19
20
20
21
21
22
23
24
25
26
27
29
30
31
32

EXPENSIVE

Clarion Collection Hotel Havnekontoret ★★★ This has become the most sought-after address in town. Right on the scenic Bryggen harborfront, the hotel was created from the historic house of the Bergen Port Authority. The recycling into a first-class hotel of grace and charm has been remarkable. Architects respected the past style, keeping the neoclassicist features and baronic influences from 1919. Book into one of the tower rooms, as the views over the harbor and the cityscape are spectacular. The six-floor property features rooms with a contemporary, colorful decor, each with a state-of-the-art bathroom. Bedrooms also have all the most up-to-date amenities, including satellite TV with pay movies. The hotel also contains the best fitness equipment in town, and its buffet restaurant serving breakfast and dinner is even patronized by some in-the-know locals.

Slottsgaten 1, N-5835 Norway. ✆ **55-60-11-00.** Fax 55-60-11-01. www.choicehotels.no. 116 units. NOK1,590–NOK2,995 ($318–$599/£159–£300) double; NOK15,000 ($3,000/£1,500) suite. Rates include buffet breakfast. AE, DC, MC, V. Parking NOK110–NOK160 ($22–$32/£11–£16). Bus: 1, 5, or 9. **Amenities:** Restaurant; bar; fitness room; sauna; business center; salon; room service; laundry service/dry cleaning; nonsmoking rooms; rooms for those w/limited mobility. *In room:* TV, Wi-Fi, minibar, beverage maker, hair dryer.

First Hotel Marin ★★ (Kids) Naturally, the hotel is imbued with a maritime theme as befits its location at Bryggen along the waterfront, with several of its bedrooms opening onto views of the harbor and the famous fish market. This is one of the better first-class hotels in town, rising seven floors in a streamlined format on a steep hillside in a brown-brick building. Standard doubles are available, but if you're willing to pay more, you'll get a superior double with more space and upgraded amenities. Each room is tastefully and comfortably furnished in a stylish Nordic modern with immaculately kept tiled bathrooms. Families often book one of the suites (the princess room or the pirate room) that come with a separate bedroom with a large double bed and a living room.

Rosenkrantzgaten 8, N-5003 Bergen. ✆ **53-05-15-00.** Fax 53-05-15-01. www.firsthotels.com. 152 units. NOK1,495–NOK2,295 ($299–$459/£150–£230) double; NOK2,095–NOK3,995 ($419–$799/£210–£400) suite. AE, DC, MC, V. Free parking. Bus: 1, 5, or 9. **Amenities:** 2 restaurants; bar; fitness center; sauna; Turkish bath; Jacuzzi; room service; laundry service/dry cleaning; nonsmoking rooms. *In room:* TV, Wi-Fi, minibar, hair dryer (in some).

Radisson SAS Hotel Norge ★★★ This Radisson SAS is the traditional prestige hotel and an even better address than the Radisson SAS Royal (below). In the city center, near Torgalmenningen, the Norge has been a Bergen tradition since 1885. Built in 1962 and renovated in 2006 and 2007, it continues to be a favorite of local celebrities. Rooms are better than ever after regular refurbishments, with double-glazed windows, bedside controls, and ample bathrooms with showers and, in some cases, bathtubs big enough for a romantic duo. The ninth-floor units open onto private balconies overlooking the flower-ringed borders of a nearby park. The hotel's Ole Bull serves international food, while the FISH offers up some of the town's freshest seafood. There's also an on-site piano bar, the American Bar. The Contra Bar, on the street level, near the reception area, is a leading nightlife venue, and the Metro disco lies in the cellar, both with separate entrances.

Nedre Ole Bulls Plass 4, N-5807 Bergen. ✆ **800/333-3333** in the U.S., or 55-57-30-00. Fax 55-57-30-01. www.radissonsas.com. 347 units. NOK1,995–NOK2,895 ($399–$579/£200–£290) double; from NOK3,495 ($699/£350) suite. Rates include breakfast. Children 17 and under stay free in parent's room. AE, DC, MC, V. Parking NOK150 ($30/£15); reserve with room. Bus: 2, 3, or 4. **Amenities:** 2 restaurants; 2 bars; dance club; heated indoor pool; fitness center; spa; sauna; room service; babysitting; laundry service/dry cleaning; rooms for those w/limited mobility; solarium. *In room:* TV, minibar, hair dryer, trouser press.

Radisson SAS Royal Hotel ★★ Opened in 1982, this hotel was built on the fire-ravaged site of an old warehouse that had stood here since 1702. With the passage of the years, it has kept abreast of changing times and decor, although the Hotel Norge (above) remains the traditional favorite. Lying right at Bryggen in the center of town, the hotel offers a choice of standard rooms, business-class rooms, and suites, the latter decorated with locally made arts and crafts, creating one of the coziest ambiences in Bergen. The guest rooms are beautifully maintained, with lithographs and comfortable, upholstered furniture. The hotel has a nightclub, Engelen, and a pub, Madame Felle, named after a lusty matron who ran a sailors' tavern on these premises during the 19th century. The pub's outdoor terrace does a thriving business in summer.

Bryggen, N-5835 Bergen. ✆ **800/333-3333** in the U.S., or 55-54-30-00. Fax 55-32-48-08. www.radisson.com. 273 units. NOK1,995–NOK2,895 ($399–$579/£200–£290) double; from NOK3,400 ($680/£340) suite. Rates include breakfast. AE, DC, MC, V. Parking NOK120 ($24/£12). Bus: 1, 5, or 9. **Amenities:** 2 restaurants; 2 bars; nightclub; heated indoor pool; fitness center; sauna; room service; babysitting; laundry service/dry cleaning; nonsmoking rooms; rooms for those w/limited mobility. *In room:* TV, Wi-Fi, minibar, hair dryer, trouser press.

Scandic Hotel Bergen City ★ This is a fine stopover any time there isn't a convention in town. Management also runs the Bergen Congress Center. In summer, the hotel fills up with vacationers, attracting mainly commercial travelers in winter. The hotel is convenient for those interested in the Bergen cultural scene, as it lies near the Nationale Theater and Grieghallen. The hotel is stylish and inviting, with midsize bedrooms that are well furnished and kept sparkling clean. The lobby bar is a popular rendezvous area where guests meet fellow guests.

Håkonsgate 2-7, N-5051 Norway. ✆ **55-30-90-80.** Fax 55-30-90-91. www.scandic-hotels.com. 254 units. NOK1,380–NOK2,090 ($276–$418/£138–£209) double, NOK1,990–NOK2,290 ($398–$458/£199–£229) suite. Rates include breakfast. AE, DC, MC, V. No on-site parking. Bus: 2, 3, or 4. **Amenities:** Restaurant; bar; laundry service. *In room:* TV, Wi-Fi, minibar.

MODERATE

Augustin Hotel ★ Finds The clear winner in the moderately priced category for us is the oldest family-run hotel in Bergen. The Augustin has one of the best locations in Bergen—right in the harborfront shopping district—with front rooms that have harbor views. Constructed in 1909 in the Jugendstil or Art Nouveau style, the Augustin rises six floors. In 1995, it more than doubled in size by adding a new wing, with modern rooms (equipped with larger showers and tubs) designed by award-winning Bergen architect Aud Hunskår. More traditional and less desirable rooms remain in the old section. The hotel is decorated with lots of art, much of which comprises pieces from well-known contemporary Norwegian artists. The Altoona tavern, once the haunt of Bergen artists and concertmasters in the 17th century, has been creatively integrated into the hotel. The hotel was built on the Altona's foundation, and its nostalgic memory is evoked in the hotel's wine cellar, which is open to the public. Even if you're not a guest, we'd recommend a visit to the on-site Brasserie No22, with some of the best shellfish and meat grills in town.

Carl Sundts Gate 22–24, N-5004 Bergen. ✆ **55-30-40-00.** Fax 55-30-40-10. www.augustin.no. 109 units. Mon–Thurs NOK1,195–NOK1,750 ($239–$350/£120–£175) double; Fri–Sun NOK990–NOK1,190 ($198–$238/£99–£119) double. AE, DC, MC, V. Parking NOK85 ($17/£8.50). Bus: 2 or 4. **Amenities:** Restaurant; bar; laundry service/dry cleaning; nonsmoking rooms; rooms for allergy sufferers; rooms for those w/limited mobility. *In room:* A/C, TV, minibar, hair dryer, iron, trouser press.

Best Western Hotell Hordaheimen This hotel is a bit staid and not for the party crowd, but it's an enduring favorite. Located near the harbor, it has long been a base for young people from nearby districts. It's operated by the Bondeungdomslaget i Bergen, an association that sponsors cultural and folklore programs, and school and civic groups sometimes reserve nearly all the rooms. The five-story hotel was built at the turn of the 19th century and renovated in stages, with additional rooms completed in 2007. Ongoing refurbishments, as needed, have kept the hotel looking young. Lars Kinsarvik, an internationally known designer, created some of the furniture displayed in the public areas during the late 19th century. The small, simple guest rooms are immaculate, with good beds and tiny bathrooms.

Christian Sundts Gate 18, N-5004 Bergen. ✆ **55-33-50-00.** Fax 55-23-49-50. www.bestwestern.com. 88 units. Mon–Thurs NOK1,650–NOK1,950 ($330–$390/£165–£195) double; Fri–Sun NOK1,050–NOK1,300 ($210–$260/£105–£130) double. Rates include buffet breakfast. AE, DC, MC, V. No on-site parking. Bus: 1, 5, or 9. **Amenities:** Restaurant; lounge; room service; laundry service/dry cleaning; nonsmoking rooms; rooms for those w/limited mobility. *In room:* TV, minibar, hair dryer, safe.

Clarion Hotel Admiral ★ Its location alone is a major selling point, as it lies only minutes from such attractions as the Bergen Fish Market, right on the Bergen harbor, with panoramic views of Bryggen and the old wharf. In 1906, the now-recycled building was one of the largest warehouses in Bergen, with six sprawling floors peppered with massive trusses and beams. It was miraculously transformed into this modern bastion in 1987. Some rooms are small, but others are midsize to spacious, with shiny modern bathrooms. Many rooms lack water views, but the ones that do open onto flower-bedecked balconies—in fact, the best harbor views in town, which is one of the main reasons we like to check in here. This member of the Clarion chain is not as luxurious and well appointed as the Clarion Collection.

Christian Sundts Gate 9, N-5004 Bergen. ✆ **55-23-64-00.** Fax 55-23-64-64. www.choicehotels.no. 211 units. Mon–Thurs NOK1,360 ($272/£136) double, NOK1,600–NOK2,500 ($320–$500/£160–£250) suite; Fri–Sun NOK1,100 ($220/£110) double, NOK1,510–NOK2,550 ($302–$510/£151–£255) suite. Rates include buffet breakfast. AE, DC, MC, V. Parking NOK150 ($30/£15); reserve with room. Bus: 2, 4, or 11. **Amenities:** 2 restaurants; bar; business center; room service; laundry service/dry cleaning; nonsmoking rooms; rooms for those w/limited mobility. *In room:* TV, minibar, hair dryer, safe.

Neptun Hotel ★ Finds The Neptun puts you into the "swim" of things, with a far livelier ambience and decor than the staid Hordaheimen (above). It was built in 1952 long before many of its more streamlined and trend-conscious competitors. Its eight-story premises attract lots of business, especially from Norwegians riding the *Hurtigruten* (coastal steamers), who consider it a worthwhile and solid choice in the upper-middle bracket. Each of the bedrooms has a decorative theme related to its name. For example, rooms named after Ole Bull, Nordahl Grieg, Ludvig Holberg, Salvador Dalí, and Joan Miró have photos or artworks commemorating their namesakes' lives and achievements. Units on the fourth and fifth floors are the most recently renovated. The hotel's premier restaurant, Lucullus, is one of Bergen's best (see "Where to Dine," later); there's also a likable, bustling brasserie named Pascal Mat & Vin.

Valkendorfsgate 8, N-5012 Bergen. ✆ **55-30-68-00.** Fax 55-30-68-50. www.neptunhotell.no. 124 units. NOK1,195–NOK2,010 ($239–$402/£120–£201) double; NOK1,420–NOK4,040 ($284–$808/£142–£404) suite. AE, DC, MC, V. Parking NOK180 ($36/£18). Bus: 20, 21, or 22. **Amenities:** 2 restaurants; bar; room service; laundry service/dry cleaning; nonsmoking rooms. *In room:* A/C, TV, minibar, hair dryer, iron.

Quality Edvard Grieg Hotel and Suites ★ Finds We're surprised that this hotel isn't better known, considering the quality of its accommodations. Savvy business people know of its charm, but its location away from the center might be daunting for the casual sightseer. Opened in 1987, this modern, all-suite hotel—Norway's first—lies 19km (12 miles) south of Bergen and 4.8km (3 miles) from the airport. Luxuriously appointed suites are amply sized, with comfortable beds in the rather small sleeping quarters and a separate lounge. Free airport transfers are arranged for arriving and departing guests Monday to Friday from 7am to 10pm.

Sandsliåsen 50, N-5245 Sandsli. ✆ **55-98-00-00.** Fax 55-98-01-50. www.choicehotels.no. 153 units. NOK1,195–NOK1,495 ($239–$299/£120–£150) suite for 2. Rates include breakfast. AE, DC, MC, V. Free parking. Bus: 30 from the Bergen bus station. **Amenities:** Restaurant; bar; heated indoor pool; fitness center; sauna; bike rentals; laundry service/dry cleaning; nonsmoking rooms; rooms for those w/limited mobility. *In room:* TV, minibar, hair dryer, iron, trouser press.

Rica Travel Hotel (Value) This is hardly a glamorous hotel, but it attracts routine business travelers—not those on expense accounts—and mainly vacationers in summer trying to survive in high-priced Bergen. The location near Torgallmenningen is ideal, as it's close to attractions, shops, bars, and restaurants. Bedrooms are fairly standard, rather comfortable and maintained well, but there aren't a lot of extras or facilities.

Christiesgate 5–7, N-5808. ✆ **55-36-29-00.** Fax 55-36-29-01. www.rica.no. 144 units. NOK1,546 ($309/£155) double. AE, DC, MC, V. Parking NOK140 ($28/£14). Bus: 2, 3, or 4. **Amenities:** Restaurant; bar. *In room:* TV, Wi-Fi, minibar, hair dryer.

INEXPENSIVE

Bergen Travel Hotel (Kids) This is a place to get a good night's sleep for an affordable price—but not a lot more. In the center of Bergen, the five-story building has been a hotel since the 1970s, although it absorbed a building across the street in 2005. Bedrooms come in various sizes, and each has pale colors and contemporary furniture crafted from dark-grained hardwoods. Some of the accommodations used to be small private apartments, so they can generously accommodate four or more people, which makes them a family favorite. Bedrooms have wooden floors and comfortable but simple furnishings, and four of the units come with small kitchens.

Vestre Torgate 20A, N-5015 Bergen. ✆ **55-59-90-90.** Fax 55-59-90-91. www.hotelbergen.com. 63 units. Mon–Thurs NOK1,180–NOK1,350 ($236–$270/£118–£135) double. Fri–Sun NOK880–NOK1,350 ($176–$270/£88–£135) double. Rates include continental breakfast. AE, DC, MC, V. Closed Dec 22–Jan 4. No on-site parking. Bus: 2, 3, or 4. **Amenities:** Pub; laundry service/dry cleaning. *In room:* TV.

Comfort Hotel Holberg ★ Set near the Nykirk, a 15-minute walk from Bergen's Fish Market, this seven-story hotel built around 1995 commemorates the life of the late-18th-century writer and dramatist Holberg, "the Molière of the North," one of the most famous writers in Danish and Norwegian letters. (The writer was born in a since-demolished house on the site of this hotel's parking garage.) The hotel's lobby is a testimonial to the author's life, with an informative biography, memorabilia, and photographs of stage productions based on his works. Bedrooms are a modernized reinterpretation of the Norwegian "farmhouse" style, thanks to wooden floors, rough-textured half-paneling stained in tones of forest green, and big windows, some of them floor-to-ceiling, that swing open directly onto a view of the quiet residential street below.

Strandgaten 190, Pb 1949 Nordnes, N-5817 Bergen. ✆ **55-30-42-00.** Fax 55-23-18-20. www.choicehotels.no. 140 units. NOK1,271–NOK2,345 ($254–$469/£127–£235) double. Rates include buffet breakfast. AE, DC, MC, V. Parking NOK130 ($26/£13). Bus: 1, 5, or 9. **Amenities:** Restaurant; bar; laundry service/dry cleaning; nonsmoking rooms. *In room:* TV, Wi-Fi, minibar, hair dryer, beverage maker.

Park Pension ★ Finds This 1890s hotel lies on the fringe of Bergen in a part of town that is rapidly gentrifying. You can often find rooms here when the hotels in the city center are fully booked. The location isn't that far out—it's a 10-minute walk to the train or bus station. The converted four-story town house is in an attractive university area near Grieghall and Nygård Park. The rooms are traditionally furnished, often with antiques. Accommodations vary in size, but all have good beds and adequate bathrooms. A neighboring building (furnished in the same style) accommodates overflow guests. Breakfast is served in the dining room; later in the day, sandwiches, small hot dishes, and wine and beer are available there.

Harald Hårfagresgaten 35 and Allegaten 20, N-5007 Bergen. ✆ **55-54-44-00.** Fax 55-54-44-44. www.parkhotel.no. 33 units. NOK1,400 ($280/£140) double. Rates include buffet breakfast. AE, DC, MC, V. Parking NOK100 ($20/£10). Bus: 11. **Amenities:** Breakfast room; lounge; nonsmoking rooms. *In room:* TV, hair dryer, iron, safe (in some).

P Hotel Bergen Value This cost-conscious, unpretentious hotel occupies the premises of what functioned for many years as a turn-of-the-20th-century lodging known as the Ambassadeur. In 2006, it was taken over by the P Hotel chain, which performed a few minor upgrades but then left the venue basically unchanged. Everything here is adequate and comfortable, but far from plush. The bathrooms in each room have showers with floor drains rather than tubs. We prefer rooms on the uppermost (fourth) floor beneath the mansard-style roof because of the views over Bergen. Access to these rooms is for the young at heart and involves climbing an additional flight of stairs above and beyond the floor where the elevator ends.

Vestre Torvgate 9, 5015 Bergen. ✆ **800-46-835.** Fax 55-90-05-84. www.p-hotels.com. 48 units. NOK895 ($179/£90) double. Rates include Norwegian breakfast. AE, DC, MC, V. No on-site parking. Bus: 1 or 9. **Amenities:** Breakfast room. *In room:* TV.

Steens Hotel—Bed & Breakfast ★ Value Among the more established B&Bs, the Steens is the best Bergen has to offer. This is a stylish 1890 house that has been successfully converted to receive guests. Owned and operated by the same family since 1950, Steens offers great accommodations at reasonable prices. The bedrooms are moderate in size and comfortable, and the bathrooms, though small, are well maintained. The best rooms are in front and open onto a park; each unit comes with a neatly maintained private bathroom equipped with a shower. The thoughtful, personal touches include hot coffee served throughout the day in the public rooms that evoke a historic aura. The B&B is within a short walk of the bus or rail station.

22 Parkveien, N-5007 Bergen. ✆ **55-30-88-88.** Fax 55-30-88-89. 18 units. www.steenshotel.no. NOK1,200 ($240/£120) double. Extra bed NOK220 ($44/£22). Rates include Norwegian breakfast. AE, MC, V. Free parking. Bus: 1 or 5. **Amenities:** Breakfast room; lounge. *In room:* TV.

Strand Hotel ★ Finds From the rooftop of this first-rate hotel, all of Bergen is laid out before you. This hotel was once a decaying 1920s hulk with a rowdy clientele. After the millennium, the rooms were radically upgraded and the second-floor bar became a stylish watering hole. Bedrooms are cozy, efficiently decorated, and comfortable; some have the added advantage of having views directly over the southern flank of Bergen's famous harbor. Complimentary waffles are available every afternoon from 4 to 6pm.

Strandkaien 2, N-5013 Bergen. ✆ **55-59-33-00.** Fax 55-59-33-33. www.strandhotel.no. 89 units. Mid-June to early Aug daily and year-round Fri–Sun NOK950–NOK1,080 ($190–$216/£95–£108) double; Mon–Thurs NOK1,140–NOK1,440 ($228–$288/£114–£144) double. Rates include buffet breakfast. AE, DC, MC, V. Parking NOK165 ($33/£17). Bus: 1, 5, or 9. **Amenities:** Breakfast room; bar; gym; sauna; laundry service/dry cleaning; solarium. *In room:* TV, minibar, trouser press.

ON THE OUTSKIRTS

Solstrand Hotel & Bad ★★★ Finds This is the most prestigious resort in the region around Bergen. Discerning travelers appreciate its isolated location beside the fjord, as well as its history, which stretches from 1896. The setting evokes a romantic getaway to the countryside. Colors used throughout the hotel are rich and jewel-toned. Bedrooms are cheerfully painted, high-ceilinged affairs, with a sophisticated mixture of antique and modern furniture. The in-house restaurant serves lunch buffets, priced between NOK370 and NOK550 ($74–$110/£37–£55) per person, and a la carte at dinner. Advance reservations are recommended for meals that—especially on Sunday between 1 and 3pm—are a magnet for extended families from the surrounding region. The hotel's many amenities include free use of rowboats and putt-putt motorboats, as well as access to a nearby 9-hole golf course. The hotel is entirely nonsmoking.

N-5200 Os (24km/15 miles south of Bergen). ✆ **56-57-11-00.** Fax 56-57-11-20. www.solstrand.com. 135 units. Late Aug to early June NOK1,849–NOK2,180 ($370–$436/£185–£218) double; mid-June to mid-Aug Mon–Thurs and year-round Fri–Sun NOK1,950 ($390/£195) double. Rates include buffet breakfast. AE, DC, MC, V. Closed Dec 22–Jan 3 and 1 week at Easter. From Bergen, drive south along the E39, following the signs to Stavanger, turning off at the markers to either Os (the region) or Osøyro (the hamlet that functions as the centerpiece of the Os region). Free parking. **Amenities:** Restaurant; bar; indoor heated pool; tennis court; exercise room; spa treatments; saunas; watersports program; laundry service/dry cleaning; fjord-side beach; helicopter landing pad. *In room:* TV, minibar, hair dryer.

4 WHERE TO DINE

VERY EXPENSIVE

Kafe Krystall ★★★ Finds CONTINENTAL This intimate restaurant is a place for a romantic evening. Old-fashioned candlelit table settings, jazz background music, and the quiet ministrations of a single server (Bergen-born owner Vibeke Bjørvik) create the aura of a dignified private home. Menu items change every 3 weeks. Our party sampled a menu that began delectably with a terrine of foie gras and quail, served with a port wine sauce, and was followed by a cream of shellfish soup with lobster-stuffed ravioli. The rest of the menu consists of well-balanced flavors, such as the roasted turbot served with a risotto of chanterelles and red wine sauce; and the filet of lamb with caponata. For dessert, we were won over by the vanilla-and-whisky *panna cotta* with chocolate sauce and a serving of lime-marinated raspberries.

16 Kong Oscarsgate. ✆ **55-32-10-84.** Reservations recommended. Fixed-price menus NOK595–NOK725 ($119–$145/£60–£73). AE, DC, MC, V. May–June and mid-Aug to Sept Mon–Sat 6–10pm; Oct–Apr Mon–Fri 6–10pm. Closed July to mid-Aug. Bus: 20, 21, 22, or 23.

Lucullus ★★★ CONTINENTAL Modern art and a grandmotherly decor incongruously meet in this posh, conservative restaurant in the Neptun Hotel (p. 268), a gourmet citadel named after the most famous gastronome of ancient Rome, Lucullus. Tasteful artwork lines the walls of the mostly blue-and-white room, with touches of dark red. The starters continue the elegant tone, using high-quality ingredients transformed into flavor-filled combinations such as reindeer carpaccio with chutney sauce or Russian king crabmeat with monkfish lasagna. Such classic main dishes as breast of duck with a creamy foie gras sauce would be welcome at a top-rated Parisian bistro. The chef is justifiably proud of his tender and flavorful filet of beef Lucullus, the house specialty, although you might opt for a duo of pheasant with a morel-studded butter sauce or quail with a *foie gras* risotto. For dessert, it doesn't get much better than a warm cloudberry soufflé with house-made white chocolate ice cream. The carefully chosen wine list is the best in Bergen.

In the Neptun Hotel, Valkendorfsgate 8. ✆ **55-30-68-00.** Reservations recommended. Main courses NOK330–NOK360 ($66–$72/£33–£36); fixed-price menus NOK630–NOK850 ($126–$170/£63–£85). AE, DC, MC, V. Mon–Fri 5–10:30pm; Sat 7–10:30pm. Closed July. Bus: 20, 21, or 22.

EXPENSIVE

Enhjørningen (the Unicorn) ★★ SEAFOOD Part of the charm of this restaurant on the Hanseatic wharf derives from the not-level floors, the low doorways, and the inconvenient access via narrow staircases to its second-floor dining room. Set within one of the old wooden buildings of the Bryggen complex, adjacent to the harbor, it boasts a history and a name that were recorded as early as 1304. After several fires and the removal of lots of rotted timbers, the inn has been restored to its 1700s condition. You'll sit in one of several old-fashioned dining rooms set railway-style (end to end) and outfitted like an early-19th-century parlor with framed oil paintings, usually landscapes. It's usually mobbed, especially in midsummer. Choices include savory fresh mussels steamed in white wine with cream, curry, and saffron; cognac-marinated salmon; herb-fried medallions of anglerfish with a mushroom-studded cream sauce; and bacalao (dried cod) served au gratin with a crusty layer of cheese and potatoes. The star offering of the restaurant's small offering of meat dishes is a grilled filet of beef with a pepper-flavored cream sauce. At Christmas, they serve the pungent lutefisk, a whitefish that many Norwegians associate with their childhoods.

Bryggen. ✆ **55-32-79-19.** Reservations recommended. Main courses NOK280–NOK310 ($56–$62/£28–£31); fixed-price menus NOK510–NOK560 ($102–$112/£51–£56). AE, DC, MC, V. Mon–Sat 4–11pm. Closed 2 weeks at Christmas. Bus: 4, 5, 80, or 90.

Finnegaardstuene ★★★ NORWEGIAN/FRENCH This is one of the leading gourmet restaurants on the west coast of Norway. The foundations of this popular restaurant were laid around 1400, when Hanseatic League merchants used it as a warehouse. Today some of the woodwork dates from the 1700s, and four small-scale dining rooms create a cozy atmosphere. The chefs have created magic in sleepy Bergen with their well-thought-out menu and carefully prepared dishes. It changes with the season and the inspiration of the chef. Some of the best dishes might include caramelized halibut served with a tomato and seafood risotto, or tenderloin of venison wrapped in bacon and flavored with sage, the dish served with a morel jus. Another specialty is slow-roasted French pigeon with foie gras.

Rosenkrantzgate 6. ✆ **55-55-03-00.** Reservations recommended. Main courses NOK295–NOK315 ($59–$63/£30–£32); fixed-price menu NOK545–NOK795 ($109–$159/£55–£80). AE, DC, MC, V. Mon–Sat 6–11pm. Closed 1 week at Easter and Dec 22–Jan 8. Bus: 5 or 21.

Restaurant Potetkjeller ★★ Finds INTERNATIONAL Set within a few steps of Bergen's Fish Market, this is one of the oldest, most exclusive, and best restaurants in Bergen. Its oldest feature is an antique flagstone floor (the date of construction is unknown) at the base of a cellar whose vaulted ceiling dates from the mid-1400s. (After most of the city's clapboard-sided houses burned to the ground in 1702, the stone-built cellar was used as a dump for the ashes and debris that remained behind. After extensive renovations in the late 1990s, the cellar is now used for additional seating for the restaurant upstairs.) Menu items from the open kitchen change but are likely to include pan-fried king crab salad; filet of organic pork with potato gnocchi and morel cream; grilled scallops with shellfish sauce and lobster ravioli; filets of roe venison with grilled Jerusalem artichokes and a cream-enriched demi-glace sauce; and a dessert special of baked nectarines with syrup and *semifreddo* (a combination of mascarpone cheese, brandy, espresso, icing sugar, gluten, grated chocolate, and cream). There is a different wine for each course, each selected by the chef. The cellar has 300 different vintages.

Kong Oscarsgate 1A. ✆ **55-32-00-70.** Reservations recommended. Fixed-price menus NOK460–NOK550 ($92–$110/£46–£55) without wine; NOK715–NOK1,105 ($143–$221/£72–£111) with wine. AE, DC, MC, V. Mon–Sat 4–10pm. Bus: 1, 5, or 9.

Spisekroken ★★ (Finds) NORWEGIAN/CONTINENTAL Small-scale, charming, and redolent with the scents and aesthetics of early-20th-century Norway, this highly recommended choice occupies two floors (street level and cellar) of an antique building in Bergen's historic core. We prefer the cellar, where most of the illumination comes from flickering candles; it seems especially cozy on cold winter nights. Menu items show a bit of culinary ambition and flair, and change with the seasons to reflect whatever is fresh and, in many cases, locally available. This is particularly true of the veal, which is purchased from a local farmer and served with preparations such as Parmesan cheese, chanterelle mushrooms, pesto, and *rösti* potatoes. Other recommendable main courses include baby goat baked in white wine and herbs or marinated red deer with a creamy lime sauce and a rhubarb salsa. Another specialty is oven-baked filet of salmon with a crunchy topping and a passion fruit *beurre blanc.* Imaginative appetizers feature marinated scampi served with dried cod and a mango salsa or else king crab with pineapple salsa and a raspberry vinaigrette.

Klostergaten 8. ✆ **55-23-01-15.** Reservations recommended. Main courses NOK139–NOK249 ($28–$50/£14–£25); fixed-price 3-course menu NOK489 ($98/£49). AE, DC, MC, V. Mon–Sat 4–11pm; Sun 1–10pm. Closed 2 weeks at Christmas. Bus: 1, 5, or 9.

To Kokker ★ FRENCH/NORWEGIAN To Kokker ("Two Cooks"—in this case, Norway-born partners Daniel Olsen and Grete Halland) is a favorite with celebrities who have included Matt Dillon, Britain's Prince Andrew, and a bevy of French starlets. Savvy local foodies increasingly gravitate here for the chef's well-considered juxtaposition of flavors and textures. Menu items include such time-tested favorites as foie gras with the traditional accompaniments; lobster soup; whitebait roe with chopped onions, sour cream, and fresh-baked bread; reindeer with lingonberry sauce; and filet of lamb with mustard sauce and *pommes Provençal.* The 1703 building is adjacent to the oldest piers and wharves in Bergen. The classic dining room, one floor above street level, has a warmly tinted decor of deep red and soft orange, old paintings, and a solidly reliable staff.

Enhjørninggården 3. ✆ **55-30-69-55.** Reservations required. Main courses NOK285–NOK330 ($57–$66/£29–£33). AE, DC, MC, V. Mon–Sat 5–10pm. Bus: 1, 5, or 9.

MODERATE

Bølgen & Moi NORWEGIAN This is a franchise restaurant located in the same building as the Bergen Art Museum. If you're visiting the museum, it makes the ideal choice for lunch, but it's also good and affordable enough to return for an evening visit. Many professional workers in the neighborhood patronize the local bar for drinks and conversation. On the lunch menu you can begin with the fish soup, following with a burger or pizza, perhaps one of the well-stuffed sandwiches, our favorite being the shellfish with crayfish, shrimp, and crab. At night the menu grows more elaborate, with such main courses as grilled salmon with salmon caviar or medallions of veal in a morel cream sauce. Braised pork belly might appear with an apple marmalade. Starters include yellowtail tuna tartar with artichoke or else pan-seared scallops with tomato sauce. Desserts are freshly made including, for example, a walnut tart with rhubarb sorbet.

Rasmus Meyers Alle 9. ✆ **55-59-77-00.** Reservations not necessary. Main courses NOK136–NOK198 ($27–$40/£14–£20) lunch; NOK265–NOK319 ($53–$64/£27–£32) dinner; 3-course vegetarian menu NOK399 ($80/£40); fixed-price menus NOK495–NOK645 ($99–$129/£50–£65). AE, DC, MC, V. Tues–Sat 11am–10pm; Sun 11am–5pm. Bus: 1, 5, or 9.

Bryggeloftet and BryggeStuene ★ NORWEGIAN Charming and well managed, this is the best-established restaurant along the harborfront, a two-level affair originally built in 1910 as a warehouse. The street-level dining room (known as the Stuene) has low-beamed ceilings, carved banquettes, 19th-century murals of old Bergen, and dozens of clipper-ship models. The Bryggeloftet, upstairs, showcases high ceilings, wood paneling, and a venue that's a bit more formal and less animated. Come to this traditional place if you're seeking authentic Norwegian flavors. Dinner in either section might include fried *porbeagle* (a form of whitefish) served with shrimp, mussels, and white-wine sauce; roast reindeer with cream sauce; or pepper steak with a salad. Several different preparations of salmon and herring are featured, along with roast pork with Norwegian sour cabbage and various preparations of reindeer, grouse, and elk, depending on the season. Between September and February, the menu offers *lutefisk,* an old-fashioned and strong-flavored Norwegian delicacy that is not for the weak-stomached.

Bryggen 11–13. ✆ **55-30-20-70.** Reservations recommended. Main courses NOK220–NOK360 ($44–$72/£22–£36); lunch smørbrød NOK110–NOK140 ($22–$28/£11–£14). AE, DC, MC, V. Mon–Sat 11am–11:30pm; Sun 1–11:30pm. Bus: 1, 5, or 9.

Egon NORWEGIAN/INTERNATIONAL The 1876 building that contains this member of a well-respected nationwide restaurant chain is one of the most distinctive, with some of the most elaborate carved masonry, along the quays. True to its origins as the city's *Kjøttbasaren* (meat market), the upstairs of the building contains a half-dozen boutique-style butcher shops and fishmongers. During a 20th-century restoration, archaeologists discovered the rotted keel of a 14th-century wooden ship beneath its foundations. Today the building's ground floor contains a restaurant that's either appealing in its coziness and historicity or daunting because of its ever-present mobs. Menu items include grilled poultry and a grilled tenderloin steak, fresh fish, soups, salads, and pastas, all served in generous portions by a staff that often seems more than a bit harassed. Some food items have just a hint of Americanized flair, especially a "party platter" that's piled high with nachos, chicken fingers, and onion rings. There's also a bacon-wrapped tenderloin of beef and Cajun-blackened chicken cutlets.

Vetrlidsalmenning 2. ✆ **55-55-22-22.** Reservations recommended. Main courses NOK195–NOK259 ($39–$52/£20–£26). AE, DC, MC, V. Daily 11am–midnight; bar nightly till 1am. Bus: 5 or 21.

Escalón Tapas Restaurant ★ Finds SPANISH Set immediately adjacent to the lowest stage of the Fløibanen cable car, this is a charming, convivial, and unpretentious bar and tapas joint that has consistently won awards as one of the best restaurants of its type in Bergen. The setting lies a few steps down from street level, allowing diners a pavement-level view out over the neighborhood outside or, if they progress into the back of the place, a cavelike interior that's cozy, warm, and dotted with mostly Iberian paintings. Two or—more often—three tapas platters comprise a full meal, depending on your hunger level. The best examples include grilled mushrooms filled with Manchego cheese, Spanish-style potato omelets, meatballs in salsa, scampi in a garlic wine sauce, tuna marinated in olive oil and capers, and shellfish crepes. A wide assortment of Spanish wines is also available.

A second branch (Lilla Escalón) is at Neumannsgate 5 (© **55-32-90-99**), with the same tapas-based food choices and similar prices. Ironically, despite its name (*lilla* means small), it's almost twice the size of its original counterpart and sits over a cellar that was built in the 18th century for the storage of wine. Lilla Escalón is open daily from noon to 1am.

Vertrlidsalmenningen 21. © **55-32-90-99.** Reservations not accepted. Tapas NOK45–NOK98 ($9–$20/£4.50–£9.80); set-price meal consisting of 3 separate tapas dishes NOK189 ($38/£19). AE, DC, MC, V. Sun–Fri 3pm–1am; Sat noon–1am. Bus: 5 or 21.

Holberg-Stuen NORWEGIAN One floor above street level, this restaurant was established in 1927 midway between the harborfront and Ole Bulls Plass. It was named in honor of the 18th-century writer Ludvig Holberg. He divided his time between Bergen and Copenhagen, and both cities ferociously claim him as part of their cultural heritage. The setting is much like a tavern, with beamed ceilings, an open log fire, lots of exposed wood, and a vivid sense of Old Norway. Some of the most intriguing menu items include grilled stockfish with a bacon and a cabbage stew or else grilled salmon with new potatoes. A local favorite is the pan-fried monkfish with cured ham and a sour cream sauce, or else a shank of lamb in a Provençal sauce. The all-time favorite is sirloin of beef in a red wine or else a pepper sauce. This is a longtime favorite; come here for old-fashioned flavors, not trendy experiments.

Torgalmenningen 6. © **55-55-20-55.** Reservations recommended. Main courses NOK229–NOK279 ($46–$56/£23–£28). AE, DC, MC, V. Mon–Sat 11am–11pm; Sun 2–10pm. Bus: 1, 5, or 9.

Mago ★ NORWEGIAN/MEDITERRANEAN The name of this restaurant means magician in Norwegian. The cuisine isn't magical, but it is exceedingly good, with generally successful flavor combinations. The staff offers a friendly welcome, as they let you order from an ever-changing menu. Fresh fish such as scallops are always on the menu, as is a well-chosen array of meat, poultry, and lamb dishes. Some dishes may be less than brilliant, but they are always based on fresh ingredients competently cooked. The best thing on the menu is the homemade ice cream in many flavors. If you'd like, you can enjoy a beer or a glass of wine on the ground level in front of a large fireplace. The wine selection, much of it by the glass, is one of the best in town.

Neumanns Gate 5. © **55-96-29-80.** Reservations not needed. Main courses NOK180–NOK230 ($36–$46/£18–£23). AE, DC, MC, V. Mon–Sat 4–11pm.

Naboen SCANDINAVIAN/SWEDISH With so many Swedes moving to Norway, it was inevitable that these immigrants would open a restaurant in Bergen. Many classic Scandinavian dishes are served here, along with some specifically Norwegian dishes. But most of the dishes reflect the secrets of the Swedish cuisine from the *Køttbullar* (ping-pong meatballs) to a delectable cured salmon. If you like to eat well, but shun flashiness, this is your place. Offerings change with the season, but locals keep coming back, especially to order from the array of desserts made fresh daily.

Neumannsgate 20. © **55-90-02-90.** Reservations recommended. Main courses NOK168–NOK246 ($34–$49/£17–£25). AE, DC, MC, V. Daily 4–11pm.

Smauet Mat & Vinhus ★ CONTINENTAL/FRENCH/ITALIAN The romantic, cozy atmosphere and high-quality food continue to lure us here. Tempting smells and lots of energy emanate from the open kitchen of this candle-studded restaurant whose decor emulates the style of a 19th-century Norwegian farmhouse. In a place so authentically Norwegian, you wouldn't expect a cuisine this thoroughly Continental. Subtly intermingled flavors emerge in the rack of lamb with creamed artichokes and a shallot confit demi-glace or theme-marinated salmon with a spinach risotto. Other standouts include the monkfish studded with lardoons and served with braised Savoy cabbage; medallions of venison in a port wine sauce; and the cinnamon-scented, pan-fried breast of chicken with pancetta. The location, in a house built in 1870, lies just a few steps from the Ole Bulls Plass.

Vaskerelvsmauet 1–3. ✆ **55-21-07-10.** Reservations recommended, especially on weekends. Main courses NOK189–NOK280 ($38–$56/£19–£28). AE, DC, MC, V. Sun–Thurs 4–10pm; Fri–Sat 5–11pm. Closed 10 days btw. Christmas and New Year's. Bus: 2, 3, or 4.

Wessel-Stuen NORWEGIAN/CONTINENTAL Other and better restaurants have opened to successfully challenge this longtime favorite, but the stube still has its habitués. This restaurant (named for the 18th-c. Danish/Norwegian humorist Peter Wessel) has some of its namesake's framed illustrations and all the trappings of an 18th-century wine cellar. It's decorated in old-tavern style with beamed ceilings, and its adjoining pub is a famous meeting place for locals. The chefs can be experimental at times, and the menu has kept up with the times with more modern ingredients and sauces, but they're also soundly grounded in the classics. Some of the more reliable main dishes include filet of Norwegian haddock gratinated with cheese and served with beet root and a cherry sauce or steamed salmon with the traditional sour cream and cucumber. Stockfish emerges with a celery root purée along with a peach coulis. Two other specialties are filet of pork marinated in chili, and grilled beef ribs with an herb sauce.

Øvre Ole Bulls Plass 8. ✆ **55-55-49-49.** Reservations recommended. Main courses NOK219–NOK289 ($44–$58/£22–£29); fixed-price menus NOK395–NOK415 ($79–$83/£40–£42). AE, DC, MC, V. Mon–Sat 11am–11pm; Sun 2pm–midnight. Bus: 2, 3, or 4.

INEXPENSIVE

Kaffistova (Value) NORWEGIAN This elegant cafeteria looks more like a full-service restaurant, with its linen tablecloths and upscale cutlery. On the ground floor of Hotel Hordaheimen, this no-nonsense place offers aggressively unpretentious and relatively quick meals. Lunchtime features open-faced sandwiches (smørbrød) and simple platters of the day. Dinner offerings are a bit more elaborate, with carved meats, pepper steak, meatballs, and an excellent version of mushroom soup.

In the Hotel Hordaheimen, Christian Sundts Gate 18. ✆ **55-33-50-00.** Reservations not necessary. Lunch main courses NOK70–NOK140 ($14–$28/£7–£14); dinner main courses NOK145–NOK190 ($29–$38/£15–£19). AE, DC, MC, V. Sun–Fri 10am–8pm; Sat 10am–6pm. Bus: 21, 22, or 23.

Ristorante Stragiotti ★ (Finds) ITALIAN This is the best Italian restaurant in Bergen. Michele Stragiotti, an Italian native from Piemonte, owns this eatery, a short walk from the Ole Bulls Plass. Stragiotti's is a trimmed-down minimalist testimonial to post-modern Italian simplicity. The house specialty is Norwegian beef with your choice of four sauces (mushroom, black peppercorn, tomato, or béarnaise). Expect Norwegian rack of lamb (tender and full of flavor), homemade pastas, freshly caught fish, and lots of scaloppine choices, including a savory version with Gorgonzola cheese. A *grigliata di pesce,* wherein Italian cooking techniques are applied to very fresh Norwegian fish, is particularly appealing.

Vestre Torgate 3. ✆ **55-90-31-00.** Reservations recommended. Pizzas NOK110–NOK170 ($22–$34/£11–£17); main courses NOK130–NOK300 ($26–$60/£13–£30); fixed-price menu NOK370–NOK650 ($74–$130/£37–£65). AE, DC, MC, V. Daily noon–midnight. Bus: 2, 3, or 4.

5 SEEING THE SIGHTS

THE TOP ATTRACTIONS

The best way to begin is to take a stroll around **Bryggen ★★★**. This row of Hanseatic timbered houses, rebuilt along the waterfront after a disastrous fire in 1702, is what remains of medieval Bergen. The northern half burned to the ground in 1955. Bryggen has been incorporated into UNESCO's World Heritage List as one of the most significant cultural and historical re-creations of a medieval settlement, skillfully blending with the surroundings of modern Bergen. It's a center for arts and crafts, where painters, weavers, and craftspeople have their workshops, some of which are open to the public.

Akvariet (Bergen Aquarium) ★★ (Kids) A 15-minute walk from the city center, this aquarium contains the most extensive collection of marine fauna in Europe, lying on the outmost reaches of the Nordnes district, with a panoramic view of the entrance to the port of Bergen. The exceptional marine life includes seals, penguins, lobsters, piranhas, and a "bearded" cod. Nothing is uglier than the Norwegian catfish, which wins all those most hideous-looking contests. In the outer hall you can get the feel of the fish—dip your hand into the shallow pool of unpolluted water pumped up from a depth of 120m (394 ft.) in the fjord outside. Nine glass tanks, each containing about 236,250 liters (62,500 gallons) of water, ring the hall. Downstairs, a wide range of marine life in 42 small aquariums demonstrates many colorful forms of sea life and illustrates evolutionary development. Kids should enjoy the seal and penguin feeding time, daily at 11am, and 2 and 6pm in the summer, or in the winter daily at noon and 4pm. Every hour you can watch the 3D film *SOS Planet,* as well as Ivo Caprino's film about the Bergen Aquarium. Not only that, you can attend concerts and folkloric musical performances, a first for us in any aquarium.

Nordnesbakken 4. ✆ **55-55-71-71.** www.akvariet.com. Admission NOK150 ($30/£15) adults, NOK100 ($20/£10) children, NOK400 ($80/£40) family ticket. May–Aug daily 9am–7pm; Sept–Apr daily 10am–6pm. Bus: 11 from the Fish Market.

Bergen Art Museum ★★★ This ever-growing and expanding art museum possesses one of the most impressive collections in Norway. In the tri-level Lysverk Building overlooking Lille Langegard Lake, the museum possesses more than 9,000 works of art.

Bergen Billedgalleri is devoted to both Norwegian and international art extending from the 13th to the 20th centuries. The collection is known for its magnificent **Greek and Russian icons ★** from the 1300s and its **Dutch paintings ★** from the 1700s. Seek out, in particular, *Birch in the Storm,* a famous painting by J. C. Dahl, as well as *Vardøhus Fortress,* by Peder Balke. When the gallery dips into **modern art,** there is a bit of camp, as in their display of poetry and an exhibition by Yoko Ono, as well as Bjørn Carlsen's mixed-media piece *Mother, I Don't Want to Die in Disneyland.* The photography of Tom Sandberg confirms his reputation as one of Scandinavia's greatest photographers.

Impressions

Reaching Bergen we fail to find it particularly attractive. Everything is fishy. You eat fish and drink fish and smell fish and breathe fish.

—Lilian Leland, *Traveling Alone: A Woman's Journey Round the World,* 1890

Bergen Attractions

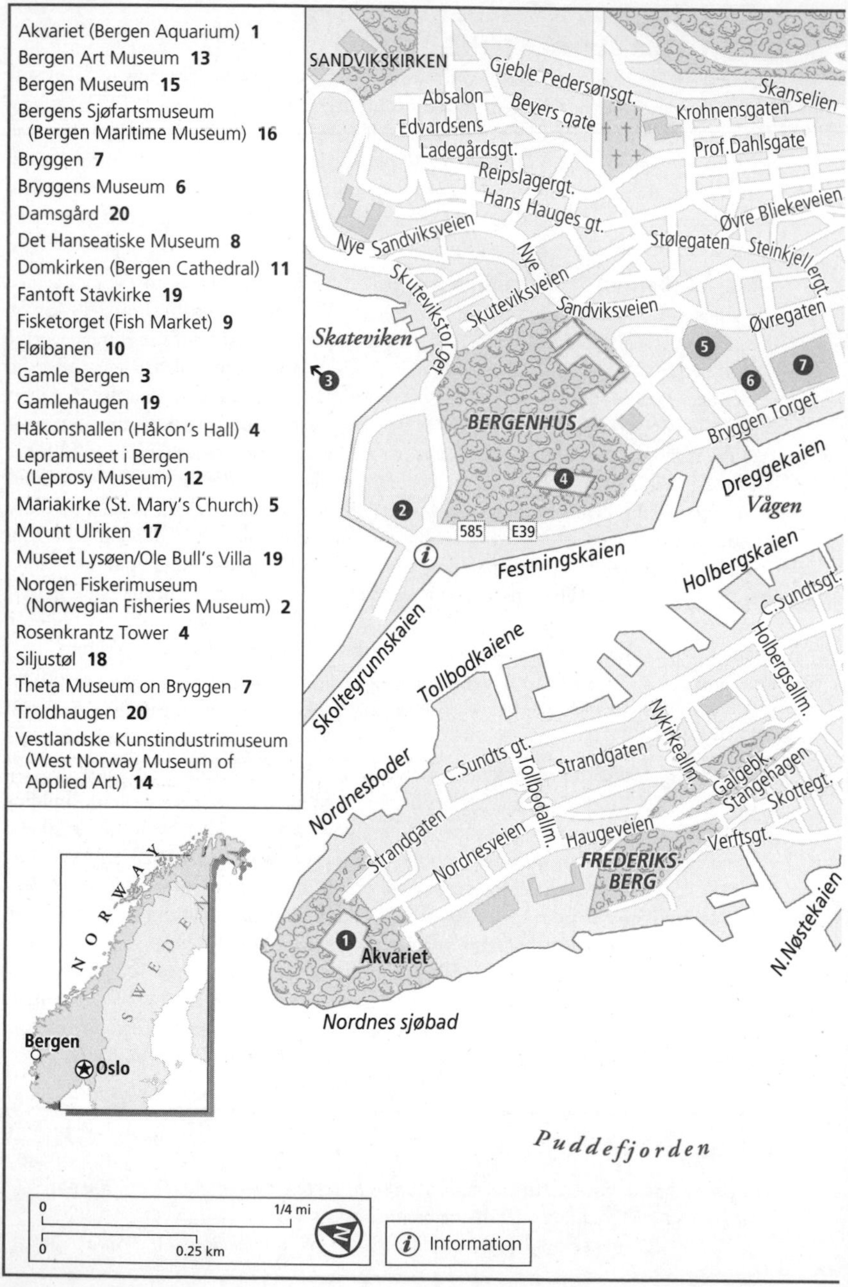
Akvariet (Bergen Aquarium) 1
Bergen Art Museum 13
Bergen Museum 15
Bergens Sjøfartsmuseum (Bergen Maritime Museum) 16
Bryggen 7
Bryggens Museum 6
Damsgård 20
Det Hanseatiske Museum 8
Domkirken (Bergen Cathedral) 11
Fantoft Stavkirke 19
Fisketorget (Fish Market) 9
Fløibanen 10
Gamle Bergen 3
Gamlehaugen 19
Håkonshallen (Håkon's Hall) 4
Lepramuseet i Bergen (Leprosy Museum) 12
Mariakirke (St. Mary's Church) 5
Mount Ulriken 17
Museet Lysøen/Ole Bull's Villa 19
Norgen Fiskerimuseum (Norwegian Fisheries Museum) 2
Rosenkrantz Tower 4
Siljustøl 18
Theta Museum on Bryggen 7
Troldhaugen 20
Vestlandske Kunstindustrimuseum (West Norway Museum of Applied Art) 14
SANDVIKSKIRKEN
Gjeble Pedersønsgt.
Absalon
Beyers gate
Skanselien
Krohnensgaten
Edvardsens
Ladegårdsgt.
Prof.Dahlsgate
Reipslagergt.
Hans Hauges gt.
Øvre Bliekeveien
Nye Sandviksveien
Stølegaten
Steinkjellergt.
Nye Skuteviksveien
Skutevikstorget
Sandviksveien
Øvregaten
Skateviken
BERGENHUS
Bryggen Torget
Dreggekaien
Vågen
585
E39
Festningskaien
Holbergskaien
C.Sundtsgt.
Skoltegrunnskaien
Tollbodkaiene
Holbergsallm.
Nykirkeallm.
Nordnesboder
C.Sundts gt.
Tollbodallm.
Strandgaten
Galgebk.
Stangehagen
Skottegt.
Strandgaten
Nordnesveien
Haugeveien
Verftsgt.
FREDERIKSBERG
N.Nøstekaien
Akvariet
Nordnes sjøbad
NORWAY
SWEDEN
Bergen
Oslo
Puddefjorden
0
1/4 mi
0
0.25 km
Information

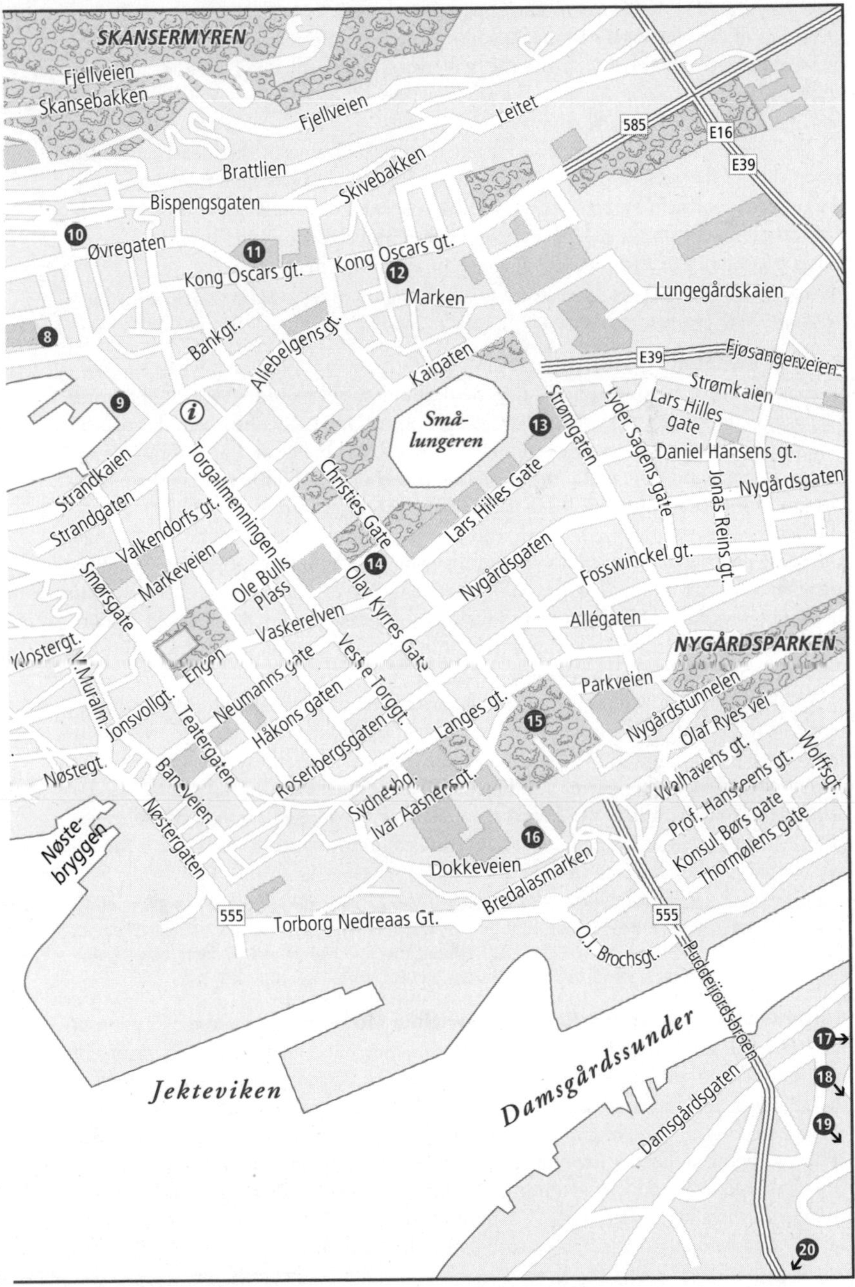
SKANSERMYREN
Fjellveien
Skansebakken
Fjellveien
Leitet
Brattlien
Skivebakken
Bispengsgaten
Øvregaten
Kong Oscars gt.
Kong Oscars gt.
Marken
Lungegårdskaien
Bankgt.
Allebelgens gt.
Kaigaten
Fjøsangerveien
Strømkaien
Lars Hilles gate
Smålungeren
Strømgaten
Lyder Sagens gate
Daniel Hansens gt.
Jonas Reins gt.
Nygårdsgaten
Strandkaien
Strandgaten
Torgallmenningen
Christies Gate
Lars Hilles Gate
Valkendorfs gt.
Markeveien
Ole Bulls Plass
Olav Kyrres Gate
Nygårdsgaten
Fosswinckel gt.
Allégaten
Smørsgate
Vaskerelven
NYGÅRDSPARKEN
V.Muralm.
Engen
Neumanns gate
Vestre Torggt.
Parkveien
Jonsvollgt.
Teatergaten
Håkons gaten
Langes gt.
Nygårdstunnelen
Olaf Ryes vei
Nøstegt.
Rosenbergsgaten
Wolffsgt.
Sydnesh.
Ivar Aasensgt.
Prof. Hansteens gt.
Nøste-bryggen
Nøstergaten
Konsul Børs gate
Thormølens gate
Dokkeveien
Bredalsmarken
585
E16
E39
E39
555
Torborg Nedreaas Gt.
555
O.J. Brochsgt.
Puddefjordsbroen
Jekteviken
Damsgårdssunder
Damsgårdsgaten
8
9
10
11
12
13
14
15
16
17
18
19
20

The impressive Rasmus Meyer Collection features paintings from the 18th century up to 1915. It's worth the visit here to gaze upon **Edvard Munch's masterpieces ★★**, especially the trio *The Woman in Three Stages, Melancholy,* and *Jealousy.* Some of the best paintings of the **Norwegian Romantics** also hang here, including works by J. C. Dahl, Harriet Backer, and Nikolai Astrup, the latter known for depicting dramatic landscapes in western Norway. In addition to the art, note the decorated ceiling and wall painting in the **Blumenthal Room ★** from the 18th century.

The greatest **modern art ★★** in western Norway is found in the Stenersen Collection. Most of the work, by Norwegian and international artists, is from the 20th century and includes northern Europe's most extensive collection of **Paul Klee's works ★★**. The masters of modern art are all here: Picasso, Edvard Munch once again, Joan Miró, Vassily Kandinsky, and Max Ernst, as well as a host of lesser-known artists.

Rasmus Meyers Allé 3–9. ✆ **55-56-80-00.** www.bergenartmuseum.no. Combined ticket to all 3 galleries NOK50 ($10/£5). Tues–Sun noon–4pm. Bus: 1, 5, or 9.

Bergen Museum ★ Everything from Henrik Ibsen mementos and whale skeletons to beautiful Viking age objects and Egyptian mummies awaits you here, as well as some of the best church and folk art in Norway. Part of the University of Bergen, this two-in-one museum consists of both a Cultural History Department and a Natural History Department. Founded in 1825, the museum formed the basis for launching the university in 1946 after the defeated Nazis had ended their occupation.

Naturhistorisk Samlinger is filled with displays and exhibitions from the Ice Age, including prehistoric fossils. However, visitors come here mainly to see the **whale collection ★** (northern Europe's largest collection) and the exhibits of snakes, Norwegian birds, and crocodiles (displayed in various ways—stuffed, fossilized, preserved in jars). The origins of the creatures in the collection range from Greenland to Africa. You can also visit a plant house and a botanical garden.

The Kulturhistork Samlinger features exhibitions and displays on art history, archaeology, and anthropology. For many, this is the best of the museums, as it covers everything from Egyptian mummies to "Ibsen in Bergen," which traces the writer's growth as a playwright during the 6 years he spent from 1851 to 1857 with the Norwegian Theater in Bergen. You'll also find the largest collection of **Norwegian church art ★** in the country, a display of delicate Viking jewelry, and exhibits devoted to such North American cultures as the Aleut and Inuit.

Cultural History Dept., Håkon Sheteligs Plass 10; Natural History Dept., Muséplass 3. ✆ **55-58-31-40** for the Natural History Dept. and the Cultural History Dept. www.bergenmuseum.uib.no. Admission for both museums NOK40 ($8/£4) adults, NOK20 ($4/£2) seniors, free for children and students. May 15–Aug Tues–Sun 11am–4pm; off season Tues–Fri 10am–2pm, Sat–Sun 10am–3pm. Bus: 2, 3, or 4.

Bergens Sjøfartsmuseum (Bergen Maritime Museum) In a scenic location in the middle of the University of Bergen's campus, this museum presents the history of maritime life and seafaring in west Norway. Frankly, the Bergen Museum is so enthralling that this little, lesser museum is too often overlooked. But if you're already on the campus of the university, you might give it a look. Exhibits are arranged to give you a good idea of the shipping industry's importance to port cities and—in a fascinating exhibit—Norway's role in World War II during the Nazi occupation. Displays include artfully arranged and crafted models of the Viking ships that terrorized Europe. Also on display are paintings and marine artifacts rescued from the North Sea.

Haakon Sheteligsplass 15. ✆ **55-54-96-00.** www.bsj.uib.no. Admission NOK30 ($6/£3) adults, free for children 15 and under. June–Aug daily 11am–3pm; Sept–May Sun–Fri 11am–2pm. Bus: 2, 3, or 4.

Bryggens Museum This museum was built on the site of Bergen's first settlement. In digging into the 800-year-old foundation of the original building, the architects uncovered a treasure trove of medieval tools, pottery, runic stones, and even ancient skulls. Everything they dug up from 1955 to 1972 only enhanced the museum's eventual collection. The museum also illustrates the daily and cultural life of Bergen in the Middle Ages. Call ahead to find out about its regularly changing exhibits, as well as its folk-music and dance performances.

Dreggsallmenning 3, Bryggen. ✆ **55-58-80-10.** www.bymuseet.no. Admission NOK50 ($10/£5) adults, free for children 15 and under. May–Aug daily 10am–5pm; Sept–Apr Mon–Fri 11am–3pm, Sat noon–3pm, Sun noon–4pm. Bus: 20, 21, 22, 23, 50, 70, 71, 80, or 90.

Damsgård ★ (Finds) If you have to make choices, visit Edvard Grieg's beloved Troldhaugen. But if you can find the time, Damsgård is an absolute gem. This off-the-beaten-path European palace in miniature from 1770 is the finest example of 18th-century rococo timber architecture in western Norway. The roof is of black glazed tiles from the Netherlands, a sign of grand extravagance back then. In 1983, the municipality of Bergen acquired the house and its furnishings. The interior is painted in a "jolly range of baroque colors." After a visit inside, wander through the lavish **baroque rose gardens ★★**, with their ponds, Grecian sculpture, and flora in common use 2 centuries ago.

Alleen 29, Laksevåg. ✆ **55-58-80-10.** Admission NOK50 ($10/£5) adults, free for children 15 and under. May–Aug daily 11am–5pm (last tour at 4pm). Closed Sept–Apr. Bus: 19, 70, or 71. 3km (1¾ miles) west of Bergen on Rte. 582.

Det Hanseatiske Museum ★ In one of the best-preserved wooden buildings at Bryggen, this museum illustrates Bergen's commercial life on the wharf centuries ago. German merchants, representatives of the Hanseatic League centered in Lübeck, lived in these medieval houses built in long rows up from the harbor. With dried cod, grain, and salt as articles of exchange, fishermen from northern Norway met German merchants during the busy summer season. Life was cold, dark, and grim for the German stockfish tradesmen who lived here in the remote regions of Norway during long, cold winters. Merchants weren't allowed to build fires for fear of setting all the wood-framed buildings along the wharf ablaze. The Black Death eventually swept through the region, destroying their monopoly on the trade. The museum is furnished with authentic articles dating from 1704.

Finnegårdsgaten 1A, Bryggen. ✆ **55-54-46-90.** May–Sept admission NOK50 ($10/£5) adults; Oct–Apr admission NOK30 ($6/£3) adults; free for children 14 and under year-round. June–Aug daily 9am–5pm; Sept–May daily 11am–2pm. Bus: 20, 21, 22, 23, or 24.

Domkirken (Bergen Cathedral) For 9 centuries, this has been a place of worship, but it's amazing that the cathedral is here at all—after all, it's been burned down five times. The first stone church was built in the mid–12th century and dedicated to Olav the Holy, patron saint of Norway. By the 13th century, the Dom was in the hands of the Franciscan brothers, but the fires that swept Bergen in 1248 and again in 1270 caused massive damage.

Under a grant from King Magnus ("the Lawmender"), the friars reconstructed a beautiful church, which stood here in 1301. Regrettably, the massive Bergen fires of 1463 and again in 1488 swept over the church. With the coming of the Lutheran Reformation, the first Lutheran bishop claimed the old Franciscan church and turned it into the cathedral of Norway's oldest diocese. Unfortunately, two more fires destroyed the cathedral in 1623 and 1640. The present building dates from its major restoration in the 1880s, which saw the addition of beautiful stained-glass windows with biblical motifs. All that remains from the 13th century are the Gothic choir stalls and the foundations of the towers. Since the Battle of Bergen in 1665, a cannonball has been embedded in the West Wall.

Kong Oscarsgate and Domkirkegate. ✆ **55-59-32-70.** Free admission. Late May to Aug Mon–Sat 11am–5pm, Sun 10am–1pm; off season Tues–Fri 11am–2pm, Sat 11am–3pm, Sun 10am–2pm. Bus: 1, 5, or 9.

Fantoft Stavkirke ★ Finds This is a rare opportunity to see what a wood-built stave church looked like, even if it's merely a mocked-up version. In the Middle Ages, Norway had a total of 750 stave churches, but only 30 are still standing. Architecturally, these churches were unique, with their "dragon heads," carved doorways, and staves or vertical planks. The original stave church was constructed in Fortun in Sogn in 1150 and moved to Fantoft in 1883 at a point 5km (3 miles) south of Bergen. Regrettably, a self-styled Satanist burned it to the ground on June 6, 1992. As of 2007, Varg Vikernes was serving a 21-year jail sentence for murder and arson. The present church is an exact duplication of the original. Adjacent to the church is a large cross from 1050, which was moved here from Sola in Rogaland.

Fantoftveien 46, Paradis. ✆ **55-28-07-10.** www.fantoftstavkirke.com. Admission NOK30 ($6/£3) adults, NOK20 ($4/£2) students, free for children 6 and under. May 15–Sept 15 daily 11am–2pm and 2:30–6pm. From the bus station in Bergen, take bus 50. Departures are every 20 min. for the 10-min. jaunt to the stave church. Get off at Fantoft. From the bus stop, it's a 10-min. walk up the hill.

Fisketorget (Fish Market) ★ Always one for social programs, Norway enforced a law at Fisketorget between 1630 and 1911: Rich Bergenser living within a 40km (25 miles) range of the market were forbidden to purchase fish there. Only the poor were allowed to buy goods, and for daily house use only. Presumably, rich people could afford to go farther afield to dine on a seafood meal. Now that it is open to everyone in Bergen, head to this bustling market at lunchtime for freshly opened oysters, a real treat from the sea. Another popular option is freshly boiled shrimp to eat as you take in views of the waterfront. Some vendors also offer a baguette for your lunch—none better than smoked salmon with some mayonnaise and fresh cucumber. The market is a photographer's delight, with fishermen in their mackintoshes and Wellington boots, and weather-beaten fishmongers (often women) in dirty long, white aprons having their pictures taken as the catch of the day is hauled in.

Bergen Harbor. Free admission. June–Aug Mon–Fri 7am–5pm, Sat 7am–7pm; Sept–May Mon–Sat 7am–4pm. Bus: 1, 5, or 9.

Fløibanen A short walk from the Fish Market is the station where the funicular heads up to Fløien, the most famous of Bergen's seven hills. We'll miss the old contraption that used to haul us up to the top of the 320m (1,050-ft.) Mount Floyen. But for the first time in its 85-year history, the funicular has upgraded facilities and installed new cable cars. Today two modern carriages featuring glass ceilings and panoramic windows carry visitors to the top to take in the spectacular vista. Once there, you can take one of several paths that provide easy walks through a lovely wooded terrain with views of lakes and mountains in the distance. In summer, you can order lunch at the restaurant here, which is open daily and also serves as a souvenir shop.

Vetrlidsalm 23A. ✆ **55-33-68-00.** www.floibanen.com. Round-trip NOK70 ($14/£7) adults, NOK35 ($7/£3.50) children ages 4–15. May–Aug Mon–Fri 7:30am–midnight; Sat 8am–midnight; Sun 9am–midnight. Sept–Apr, funicular stops every night at 11pm. Bus: 6.

Gamle Bergen ★ This museum offers a rare look at small-town life during the 18th and 19th centuries with various antique dwellings and shops, a bakery, and even the town's local barber and dentist. This collection of more than 40 wooden houses is set in a picture-perfect park. The Old Town is complete with streets, an open square, and narrow alleyways, and some of the interiors are exceptional, including a merchant's living room in the typical style of the 1870s, with padded sofas, heavy curtains, and potted plants. Its old-fashioned, clapboard-sided architecture and renditions of 19th-century domestic life evoke some of the scenes from Ibsen's *A Doll's House*.

Elsesro and Sandviken. ✆ **55-39-43-00.** Admission NOK50 ($10/£5) adults, free for children 4–15 and students. Houses mid-May to Aug only, guided tours daily on the hour 10am–5pm. Park and restaurant daily noon–5pm. Bus: 20, 24, 80, or 90 from the city center (every 10 min.).

Gamlehaugen The king's official Bergen residence was originally occupied in the 19th century by Christian Michelsen, one of the first prime ministers of Norway after it separated from Denmark in 1814. It's open for just a short time each summer, and a visit here will tell you much about how the upper class lived at the beginning of the 19th century. The rambling wood-sided villa lies about 10km (6¼ miles) south of the city, overlooking the Nordåsvannet estuary. The interior is a happy marriage of the once-fashionable National Romanticism combined with an elegant Art Nouveau. Don't make the mistake we did and get caught wandering around the second floor. Security discovered us and promptly sent us scurrying back downstairs. Its gardens are open to the public all year. Don't expect the hoopla you might see at Buckingham Palace—the venue is understated, discreet, and (probably for security reasons) aggressively mysterious.

Fjøsanger. ✆ **55-92-51-20.** Admission NOK50 ($10/£5) adults, NOK25 ($5/£2.50) children 4–15. June–Aug Tues–Sun noon–3pm; Sept–May Sat–Sun noon–3pm. Bus: Fjøsanger-bound bus 60 from the Central Bus Station.

Håkonshallen (Håkon's Hall) Built of local stone, this is the largest secular medieval hall still standing in Norway, though its days of glory are long gone. Once it was the political and social center of the 13th-century kingdom of Norway. Erected between 1247 and 1261, it took its name from its first builder, Håkon Håkonsson. It was used in 1261 as the setting for the wedding and coronation of King Magnus Lagabøte, Håkon's son and co-ruler. By 1520, it had degenerated to a storage depot. Don't expect any great array of artistic treasures here: The hall has had a rough life. It was damaged in a 1944 fire caused by the explosion of an overloaded Nazi munitions ship and was later restored. (The explosion damaged nearly every building in Bergen and sent the ship's anchor flying almost to the top of a nearby mountain.) Guided tours are conducted hourly; call in advance to confirm. The Great Hall is also used for concerts and performances.

Bergenhus, Bradbenken. ✆ **55-31-60-67.** Admission NOK40 ($8/£4) adults, NOK20 ($4/£2) children. Mid-May to Aug daily 10am–4pm; Sept to mid-May daily noon–3pm (Thurs until 6pm). Closed various days in May. Bus: 5.

Lepramuseet i Bergen (Leprosy Museum) Visiting a former lepers' colony might not be your idea of a hot time, but this museum of early medicine has much to fascinate visitors—and not just those who are doctors. Exhibits focus on the country's contribution to leprosy research, especially the work of Dr. Armauer Hansen, who gave his name to Hansen's disease, the modern name for leprosy. In the Middle Ages, St. Jørgens Hospital here was a hospital for lepers, and many of the oldest buildings date from the beginning of the 1700s. The museum also exhibits the Bergen Collection of the History of Medicine.

Kong Oscarsgate 59. ✆ **55-96-11-55.** Admission NOK40 ($8/£4) adults, free for children and students. May 21–Sept 3 daily 11am–3pm. Closed Sept 4–May 20. Bus: 20, 21, 22, 23, or 24.

Mariakirke (St. Mary's Church) ★★ The oldest building in Bergen, perhaps dating from the first half of the 12th century, is also one of the most outstanding examples of Romanesque in Norway. The oldest ornament in the church is the altar, but the **pulpit ★★** is the richest example of baroque decorative art in the country. A gift from Hanseatic merchants, it has carved figures depicting everything from *Chastity* to *Naked Truth*. Organ recitals are presented here every Tuesday from June 24 to August at 7:30pm.

Dreggen. ✆ **55-31-59-60.** Admission NOK20 ($4/£2) adults, free for children 6 and under. May 22–Aug Mon–Fri 9:30–11am and 1–4pm; Sept–May 21 Tues–Fri 11am–12:30pm. Bus: 9, 20, 21, or 22.

Mount Ulriken ★★ Closed down for a long time for extensive repairs, this cable car is slated to reopen in September of 2009. For the grandest view in western Norway, visit Bergen's highest mountaintop, Ulriken, at 642m (2,106 ft.). The attraction lies at Landaas, 5km (3 miles) southeast from the center of Bergen. The Ulriksbanen (✆ **55-20-20-20**), the most famous cable car in western Norway, runs up the mountain. A shuttle bus departs for the Ulriksbanen from the Tourist Information Office in Bergen (p. 259) every hour on the hour, daily from 10am to 5pm from May to September. Off-season departures depend on the weather. From the uppermost station of the cable-car station, you can walk for 4 to 5 hours north along a well-trodden track to the top of the Fløibanen funicular railway, with scenic vistas in all directions. This is our favorite walk in the Bergen area.

Landaas. ✆ **55-20-20-20** for the cable car. Return fare NOK90 ($18/£9) adults, NOK45 ($9/£4.50) children 4–15. Combined cable car and shuttle bus NOK150 ($30/£15) adults, half-price children. Sept–Apr shuttle bus departures every hour on the hour 9am–6pm; May–Aug 9am–9pm. Cable car operates 4–5 times an hour in summer, daily 9am–10pm; off-season cable car operates 3–4 times an hour, daily 10am–5pm.

Norgen Fiskerimuseum (Norwegian Fisheries Museum) This museum is mainly for fishing aficionados, though it does manage to stir up some controversy, as does Norway itself, with its exhibits on whaling and sealing. Norway, along with Japan, has been severely criticized by ecosensitive people concerned with the destruction of endangered species such as the whale. The nature and management of fisheries is presented in detail, as are depictions of the sea and its vast, though diminishing, resources. The processing of fish, such as the vital cod, is revealed along with exportation methods.

Bontelabo 2. ✆ **55-32-12-49.** Admission NOK30 ($6/£3) adults, NOK10 ($2/£1) students and seniors, free for children 15 and under. June–Aug Mon–Fri 10am–6pm, Sat–Sun noon–4pm; Sept–May Sun–Fri 11am–4pm. Bus: 1, 5, or 9.

Rosenkrantz Tower The Middle Ages live on here, and the aura is a bit spooky. We're sure the wretched prisoners held in dungeons here would agree with us. Even if you find the setting foreboding, the stunning **panorama ★★** of Bergen's seaport is worth the trek here. This defense and residential tower was constructed in the 13th century by the governor of Bergenhus (Bergen Castle), Erik Rosenkrantz. Two older structures were incorporated into the tower: King Magnus the Lawmender's keep, from about 1260, and Jørgen Hanssøn's keep, from about 1520. It was rebuilt and enlarged in the 1560s. There are guided tours of the tower and Håkonshallen (see earlier) about every hour.

Bergenhus, Bradbenken. ✆ **55-31-43-80.** Admission NOK40 ($8/£4) adults, NOK20 ($4/£2) children. May 15–Aug 31 daily 10am–4pm; Sept 1–May 14 Sun noon–3pm. Bus: 1, 5, or 9.

Siljustøl ★ Finds Although most visitors rightly flock to Edvard Grieg's former home at Troldhaugen, Bergen has an important Norwegian composer of its own: Harald Saeverud. Born in Bergen in 1897, the young composer studied first in his hometown before going on to Berlin, where he met some of the greatest of the 20th-century German composers. Upon returning to Bergen in 1934, he married wealthy Marie Hvoslef.

Grieg: The Chopin of the North

"I am sure my music has the taste of codfish in it," or so wrote Norway's greatest composer, Edvard Grieg, born in Bergen in 1843, the son of a salt-fish merchant. Like Ole Bull (p. 287), Grieg became the towering figure of Norwegian Romanticism.

Shipped off to the Music Conservatory in Leipzig from 1858 to 1862, Grieg fell under the heavy influence of German Romanticism but returned to Oslo (then called Christiania) with a determination to create national music for his homeland.

Back home he fell heavily under the influence of his country's folk music and "fjord melodies."

When Grieg met the great Norwegian writer Bjørnstjern Bjørnson, the author realized that he'd found the writer to compose music for his poems. Their most ambitious project was a national opera based on the history of the Norwegian king Olav Trygvason.

Meeting Henrik Ibsen for the first time in 1866, not in Norway but in Rome, Grieg agreed to compose the music for Ibsen's dramatic poem *Peer Gynt*. In 1868, he finished *Piano Concerto in A Minor,* his first great masterpiece. In 1888 and 1893, Grieg published *Peer Gynt Suite I* and *II,* which remain popular orchestral pieces to this day. Bjørnson was furious that Grieg had teamed with Ibsen, and the work on their national opera never came to fruition.

During the Nazi occupation, Saeverud wrote a trio of "war-symphonies" and one called "Ballad of Revolt," in honor of the Norwegian resistance to the Nazis. After the war, he composed music for Henrik Ibsen's dramatic poem, *Peer Gynt*. Twelve concert pieces extracted from this work are among the most frequently played orchestral works today.

In 1874, Grieg returned to Bergen, where he created such world-fabled compositions as *Ballad in G Minor,* the *Norwegian Dances for Piano,* the *Mountain Thrall,* and *The Holberg Suite.* He'd married Nina Hagerup, the Norwegian soprano, and together they moved into Troldhaugen, their coastal home that today is one of the major sightseeing attractions of Bergen.

It was at Troldhaugen that Grieg created such works as *Piano Sonata for Violin and Piano in C Minor,* the *Haugtussa Songs,* and the *Norwegian Peasant Dances.* His last work was *Four Psalms,* based on a series of Norwegian religious melodies.

In spite of poor health and the loss of one lung, Grieg maintained a grueling schedule of appearances on the Continent. But he always came back to Troldhaugen for the summer. Eventually, on September 4, 1907, as he prepared to leave for yet another concert, this time in Leeds, England, he collapsed at the Hotel Norge in Bergen and was hospitalized, where he died.

The money for constructing his home, Siljustøl, was a wedding gift to the composer and his new bride. The imposing estate—set on 70 beautiful hectares (173 acres)—is like a piece of west Norway in miniature. Upon completion in 1939, Siljustøl was the largest private home in Norway, with 63 rooms. The house is made of wood and natural stone, and has six toilets, although the composer preferred the more old-fashioned plumbing of Norway—a hole in the floor.

In 1986, Saeverud became the official composer for the Bergen International Music Festival. He lived in Bergen until his death in 1992, at the age of 95. After being given a state funeral, he was buried at Siljustøl, where his grave site is a pilgrimage destination for fans.

Rådal (near Rte. 582 to the airport), 12km (7½ miles) north from the center. ✆ **55-92-29-92.** Admission NOK50 ($10/£5) adults, free for children 15 and under. Late June–late Sept Sat–Sun noon–4pm. Closed late Sept–late June. Bus: 20 from Bergen Bus Station.

Theta Museum on Bryggen ★ Finds Don't miss this museum if you are fascinated by World War II intrigue, sabotage, and mystery. This little cell was the seat of clandestine Bergen resistance during the darkest days of the Nazi takeover of the city in World War II. It is also Norway's tiniest museum. The one room operated until 1942, when it was discovered by the Germans, who destroyed it. The present room is a reconstruction. The freedom fighters called themselves the "Theta Group," and their aim was to establish contact and communication with the Norwegian government in exile in England. The museum is also the hardest to find in Bergen. Look for a carved depiction of a unicorn placed prominently on the facade of an old building directly fronting the quay of Bryggen. Then walk "inland" from the quay, down a narrow alleyway that runs perpendicular to the waterfront until you see a sign directing you to the museum on the third floor. The building stands at the entrance to Enhjørningsgarden.

Enhjørningsgarden. ✆ **55-55-20-80.** Admission NOK20 ($4/£2) adults, NOK5 ($1/50p) children. Mid-May to mid-Sept Tues and Sat–Sun 2–4pm. Bus: 1, 5, or 9.

Troldhaugen (Trolls' Hill) ★★★ This can be the most romantic setting in Norway if you arrive just as Edvard Grieg's music is drifting up from a summer concert in the 200-seat Troldsalen, a concert hall on the grounds. This Victorian house, in beautiful rural surroundings, was the summer villa of composer Edvard Grieg and the site where he composed many of his famous works in a setting on Lake Nordås. The house still contains his furniture, paintings, and other mementos. His Steinway grand piano is frequently used at concerts given in the house during the annual Bergen festival, and at Troldhaugen's summer concerts. Grieg and his wife, Nina, a Norwegian soprano, are buried in a cliff grotto on the estate.

Troldhaugveien 65, Hop. ✆ **55-92-29-92.** Admission NOK60 ($12/£6) adults, free for children 14 and under. Jan 5–Apr 30 and Oct 1–Dec 19 Mon–Fri 10am–2pm, Sat–Sun noon–4pm; May–Sept daily 9am–6pm. Closed Dec 20–Jan 4. Bus 23 or 24 to Hop from the Bergen bus station, platform 20; when you reach Hop exit, turn right, walk about 180m (590 ft.), turn left at Hopsvegen, and follow signs (15-min. walk). Hop is about 5km (3 miles) from Bergen.

Vestlandske Kunstindustrimuseum (West Norway Museum of Applied Art) ★★ Finds Stumble into this museum on a rainy day in Bergen to kill some time—you'll come away singing its praises. The various displays span 5 centuries, the most intriguing of which are devoted to "the Art of China" ★★★. This is one of the largest collections of Chinese applied art outside China itself. A series of huge marble Buddhist temple sculptures was created over a range of centuries. Even an Asian emperor would be impressed by the silk robes embroidered with dragons and the wealth of jade, exquisite porcelain, rare textiles, and delicate paintings. Other treasures inside include Ole Bull's violin ★★. Made in 1562 by the Italian master Saló, the instrument has a head of

Ole Bull: Romantic Musician & Patriot

One of the most colorful characters in the history of western Norway was Ole Bull (1810–70), the founder of Norway's national theater and a virtuoso violinist. Leading one of the most remarkable lives of the 19th century, he was not only a celebrated composer, but also a fervent Utopian socialist and an international ambassador of Norwegian culture on his frequent international concerts. He became friends with Liszt, Schumann, Longfellow, Ibsen, and Hans Christian Andersen, among other celebrated men of the day. Bull, who was noted for both his personal sense of theatrics and his ardent sense of Norwegian nationalism, had a profound influence on Grieg and his music. Bull's best-known musical composition is *Saeterjentens Sondag* for violin and piano.

Born in Bergen, Ole Bull was immediately recognized as a child prodigy. Amazingly, he joined the Bergen Philharmonic Orchestra when he was only 8 years old. One of the great violin virtuosos of all time, a sort of Victorian Mantovani, he won fans in such diverse places as the United States, Cuba, Moscow, and Cairo. He almost single-handedly rekindled an interest in Norwegian folk music both in Norway and abroad. In time, the people of Norway began to regard him as a national symbol.

After his first wife, a French woman, died, Ole Bull married Sara Thorp, of Madison, Wisconsin, and together they built a summer villa at Lysøen in 1872. The strikingly handsome musician let his hyperactive imagination run wild as he created an architectural fantasy he called "Little Alhambra," with its Russian onion dome, pierced-wood Moorish arches, arabesque columns, and elegant trelliswork. It was in Lysøen that he died in 1880. The last of the great Norwegian Romanticists, he was given one of the most-attended funerals in Norway.

Visitors today wander across his "fairy tale" 70-hectare (173-acre) property, with its romantic paths studded with gazebos and white shell sand. In the natural native pine forest, Ole Bull added exotic trees and bushes from all over the world that would grow in Bergen's chilly clime.

You can also visit a statue and fountain dedicated to this virtuoso performer on Ole Bulls Plass in the heart of Bergen.

an angel carved on it by Benvenuto Cellini. There is also an impressive collection of Bergen silverware. The Bergen silversmiths of the 17th and 18th centuries were celebrated for their heavy but elaborate baroque designs. Their collection of tankards, for example, is stunning, and most of them are embossed with flora motifs; others are inlaid with silver coins.

Permanenten, Nordahl Bruns Gate 9. ✆ **55-33-66-33.** Admission NOK50 ($10/£5). May 15–Sept 14 daily 11am–5pm; Sept 15–May 14 Tues–Sun noon–4:30pm.

IN NEARBY LYSØEN

To reach the island of Lysøen, 26km (16 miles) south of Bergen, drive or take a bus (from Platform 20 at the Bergen bus station, marked FANA-OS-MILDE) to Sørestraumen on Rd. 553. Take the Ole Bull ferry across the channel from Sørestraumen, Buena Kai. The round-trip fare is NOK50 ($10/£5) for adults, NOK29 ($5.80/£2.90) for children. When the museum and villa are open, ferry schedules coincide with the site's hours, and boats depart for the mainland at hourly intervals. The last boat leaves a few minutes after the museum closes.

Museet Lysøen/Ole Bull's Villa The villa and concert hall that stand here were built in 1872–73 for the world-famous violin virtuoso and Norwegian national hero Ole Bull. Before going here, read our box "Ole Bull: Romantic Musician & Patriot," a small primer about who this guy was. The building, now a national monument, is preserved as it was when the musician died in 1880. The building itself is an architectural fantasy of the 19th century, with a dome, curved staircase, cutwork trim, and gingerbread gables. Bull built 13km (8 miles) of romantic trails that meander around the island, and, if time remains, you may want to walk them, following in Ole Bull's footsteps.

Lysøen. ✆ **56-30-90-77.** Admission NOK30 ($6/£3) adults, NOK10 ($2/£1) children ages 4–15. Guided tours early May–Aug Mon–Sat noon–4pm; Sun 11am–5pm. Closed Sept–early May. Transportation: See "Organized Tours," below.

ORGANIZED TOURS

For information about and tickets to tours, contact **Tourist Information,** Vågsallmenningen 1 (✆ **55-55-20-00**). The most popular and our most highly recommended tour of Bergen is the 3-hour city bus tour. It departs daily at 10am and covers the major attractions, including Troldhaugen and "Old Bergen." It operates May to September and costs NOK295 ($59/£30) for adults, NOK200 ($40/£20) for children 4 to 15. Between mid-May and the end of August, there's an additional departure every day at 2pm.

WALKING TOUR HISTORIC BERGEN

START:	**The Fish Market.**
FINISH:	**West Norwegian Museum of Decorative Arts.**
TIME:	**1 hour.**
BEST TIME:	**Any day between 8am and 5pm (when it's not raining, of course).**
WORST TIME:	**When cruise ships anchor.**

❶ Fish Market

Around the turn of the 19th century, this broad esplanade at the innermost reaches of Bergen's harbor teemed with fishermen selling their catch, as well as the blood, guts, and carcasses. Today, in a much-sanitized format, it's a venue for crafts, knitwear, carved Siberian and Sami souvenirs, and, to a lesser degree, fish and seafood.

From here, walk west along the Strandkaien, hugging the harborfront on your right side, making a small detour inland at the Strandkaien's end. Within a block, at an angular jog in the avenue known as the Strandgaten, you'll see the solid, partially fortified walls of:

❷ City Wall Gate

This gate was originally built in 1550 as a checkpoint in a once-continuous wall that surrounded Bergen. Today it stands isolated amid the newer buildings and broad avenues that surround it on all sides. There's a cheap-clothing outlet on its ground floor and an obscure, rarely visited museum (the Buekorps Museum) upstairs.

From here, walk west along Strandgaten, noting the many shops that line the street on either side. Within about 5 minutes you'll reach one of Bergen's most visible houses of worship:

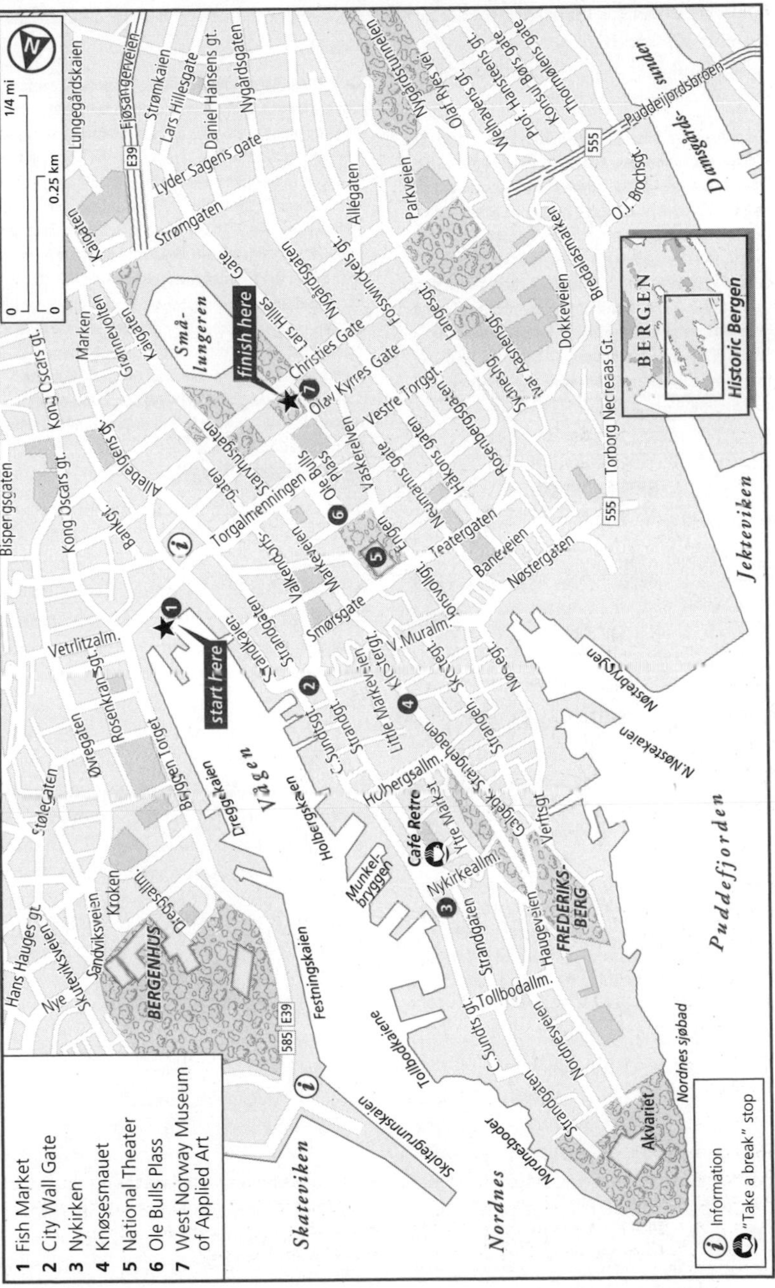
1 Fish Market
2 City Wall Gate
3 Nykirken
4 Knøsesmauet
5 National Theater
6 Ole Bulls Plass
7 West Norway Museum of Applied Art
Information
"Take a break" stop
start here
finish here
Café Retro
0 1/4 mi
0 0.25 km
BERGEN
Historic Bergen
Vågen
Puddefjorden
Skateviken
Nordnes
Jekteviken
Damsgårds-sundet
Smålungeren
BERGENHUS
FREDERIKSBERG
Akvariet

❸ Nykirken

Noteworthy features of this church are the Danish-inspired, mansard roof from around 1761, the copper-capped baroque spire, and its location overlooking the entrance to Bergen's harbor.

From here, walk steeply uphill for a block along the Nykirkeallmenningen, and turn left onto the narrow confines of the cobble-covered Ytre Markeveien, noting the antique wood-sided houses on either side. Walk 4 short blocks to the Kippersmauet, and then turn left, walking down a steep, cobble-covered alleyway where, at nos. 23 and 24, there was a disastrous fire in 2001. (A pair of 14-year-old boys is credited with detecting the fire and pounding on the doors of neighboring houses, an act that saved the entire wood-built neighborhood from burning to the ground.)

> **TAKE A BREAK**
> **Café Retro,** Klosteret 16 (✆ **55-31-16-16**), is loaded with the kitsch and artful debris of the age of Sputnik, with shelves filled with 1950s-era toasters, fans, and ashtrays (all of which are for sale as art objects in their own right). It sells sandwiches made from "ecological" (organic) breads, priced at NOK40 to NOK60 ($8–$12/£4–£6) each, as well as coffee, tea, soda, and pastries. It's open Monday to Friday 10am to 6pm.

Now retrace your steps uphill back to the Ytre Markeveien, and then turn right onto the big square (Holbergsallmenningen), originally conceived as a firebreak. Cross the wide boulevard (Klosteret) and walk east for 1 short block, turning right (sharply downhill) on the impossibly narrow cobble-covered alleyway identified within a few steps as the:

❹ Knøsesmauet

You'll immediately find yourself hemmed in, somewhat claustrophobically, by the antique wooden houses of a district known as the Klosteret. It's composed of compact and, in most cases, impeccably well-maintained wooden houses immediately adjacent to one another. Even today, the risk of fire among the brightly painted historic buildings is a much-feared issue. Especially vulnerable are what local firefighters refer to as "chimney houses"—ones where cement, stucco, or ornamental masonry facades have been added to an otherwise mostly wooden building.

Continue descending the cobble-covered, steeply sloping length of the Knøsesmauet, bypassing brightly painted wooden houses, prefaced, in some cases, with tiny gardens. Cross over the Skottogaten and continue walking downhill. Turn left onto the St. Hansestredet. (Sankt Hanse is the patron saint of the summer solstice, often invoked in midsummer with bouquets of midsummer flowers such as the ones that adorn the sides of the houses along this street.) St. Hansestredet, within 2 short blocks, merges with the busy traffic of the Jonsvollsgaten, a wide commercial boulevard. Walk east for about 3 minutes, cross over the Teatergaten, and continue walking east along Engen, the eastward extension of the Jonsvollsgaten. On your left rises the stately looking, Art Nouveau bulk of the:

❺ National Theater

This arts complex is rich with memories. It was established by violinist Ole Bull, who envisioned it as a showcase for Norwegian-language drama and music. Today performances of Broadway-style musicals alternate with more serious, mostly Norwegian works. Details to look for inside and out include life-size portrait statues of Bjørnson, author of Norway's national anthem, and Ibsen, who served as the theater's director for 5 years. (The stern and magisterial-looking granite sculpture of Ibsen, completed in 1982 and set into the lawns of the theater's eastern side, was considered so ugly that it remained in storage for many years.) On the theater's tree-shaded western side, just outside the entrance to its lobby, is a flattering likeness, in bronze, of Nordahl Grieg, often referred to as the Norwegian version of Winston Churchill because he warned of the Nazi menace before many of his colleagues in the Norwegian Parliament.

If it's open, walk into the theater's lobby, a survivor of a disastrous fire in 1916 and of a Nazi bomb that fell directly into its lobby in 1944. Completely restored in the late 1990s, the lobby has an understated Art Nouveau style and portraits of great Norwegians lining its walls.

Now, with your back to the ornamental eastern side of the theater, walk easterly along the:

6 Ole Bulls Plass

Descend the gradual slope and note the grand commercial buildings that rise on either side. Broad and wide and flanked with flower beds, restaurants, bars, and shops, it was originally laid out, in an era when virtually everything that flanked it was made of wood, as a firebreak. Today it's an architectural showcase of Bergen, named after Norway's first musical superstar.

Descend along the Ole Bulls Plass, past a violin-playing statue of the musical star himself. When the street opens onto the broad esplanade known as Olav Kyrres Gate, note on the right side the turn-of-the-19th-century brick facade of the:

7 West Norway Museum of Applied Art

The statue of a seated male lost in thought set into a niche on the museum's facade commemorates the 19th-century painter J. C. Dahl. It was crafted by one of Norway's first widely celebrated female sculptors, Ambrosia Tønnesen. The abstract sculpture set onto the lawn in front of the museum, composed of a series of rainbow-colored concentric hoops, is in honor of Bergen-born early-20th-century composer Harald Saeverud.

6 OUTDOOR ACTIVITIES

FISHING In the region around Bergen, anyone can fish in the sea without restrictions. If you plan to fish in fresh water (ponds, streams, and most of the best salmon and trout rivers), you'll need a permit. These are sold at any post office. You'll also need the permission of the owner of the land on either side of the stream. The best fjord fishing, where you can angle for such catches as cod, mackerel, haddock, and coalfish, is offered by **Ryfylke Fjord Tour** (✆ **91-35-91-32**). Twice-daily 2-hour fishing trips depart from Bergen Harbor.

Information and fishing permits, which cost NOK105 to NOK170 ($21–$34/£11–£17), are available from **Bergen Sportsfiskere (Bergen Angling Association),** Damsgaardsveien 106 (✆ **55-34-18-08**). It's open Monday to Friday 9am to 3pm. **Ryfylke Fjord Tour** (✆ **91-35-91-32**) offers 2-hour fishing trips departing from Bergen twice daily.

GOLF The best golf course is **Meland Golf Club,** lying 36km (22 miles) north of Bergen at Meland/Frekhaug (✆ **56-17-46-00**). This is an 18-hole, par-73 golf course with a pro shop, lockers, and changing facilities. The setting is on 90 hectares (222 acres) in the midst of forests, lakes, and mountains. Greens fees Monday to Friday are NOK400 ($80/£40), going up to NOK500 ($100/£50) on Saturday and Sunday.

SWIMMING The **Sentralbadet,** Theatersgaten 37 (✆ **55-56-95-70**), has a heated indoor pool. An open-air pool whose season is limited to the fleeting Nordic summer is at **Nordnes Sjøbad,** Nordnes. For hours, check with the Bergen tourist office (p. 259). At either pool, adults pay NOK80 ($16/£8), children NOK42 ($8.40/£4.20).

TENNIS **Paradis Sports Senter,** Hwy. R1, Paradis (✆ **55-91-26-00**), 6.5km (4 miles) south of Bergen, is the best place to get your game on. The club has five indoor courts, four squash courts, four badminton courts, a health club and gym, and a solarium. It's open Tuesday and Thursday 9am to 10pm, Monday and Wednesday 9am to 11pm, Friday 9am to 9pm, Saturday 10am to 6pm, and Sunday 11am to 9pm.

WALKING Only 10 minutes away from town by the funicular, several roads and footpaths lead to **Mount Fløien,** an unspoiled wood and mountain terrace with lakes and rivers. The **Bergen Touring Club,** Tverrgaten 4 (✆ **55-33-58-10**), arranges walking tours farther afield and supplies information on huts and mountain routes all over Norway. It also provides maps and advice on where to hike. The office is open Monday to Friday 10am to 4pm (until 6pm on Thurs).

7 SHOPPING

Shoppers who live outside Scandinavia and spend more than NOK310 ($62/£31) in a tax-free tourist shop can receive a refund up to 18.5% of the purchase price when they leave Norway. See "Fast Facts: Norway," in appendix A, for details.

THE SHOPPING SCENE

Bargain hunters head to the **Fish Market *(Fisketorget)*** ★★. Many local handicrafts from the western fjord district, including rugs and handmade tablecloths, are displayed here. This is also one of the few places in Norway where bargaining is welcomed. The market keeps no set hours, but it is best visited between June and August daily, 7am to 7pm, and September to May, Monday to Saturday, 7am to 4pm. Take bus no. 1, 5, or 9.

HOURS Stores are generally open Monday to Friday from 9am to 6pm (until 8pm Thurs and sometimes Fri), Saturday 9am to 4pm. Shopping centers outside the city are open Monday to Friday 10am to 8pm and Saturday 9am to 6pm. Some food stores stay open until 8pm Monday to Friday and 6pm on Saturday.

SHOPPING A TO Z

Art Galleries

Hordaland Art Center and Café (Kids) An artistic focal point of the historic neighborhood that contains it, this is a publicly funded art gallery that puts on as many as 12 different art exhibitions each year. Originally completed in 1742, it served as a school for the children of the local parish for many years. A children's play area is on-site, and a cafe has pastries, sandwiches, and platters on offer. Schedules are erratic, varying with each exhibition. Klosteret 17, Nordnes. ✆ **55-90-85-90.** A 5-min. walk from Torgallmenningen.

Fashion

Kløverhuset ★★ Next to the Fish Market on the harbor, this four-story shopping center has been Bergen's largest and best fashion store since 1923. Bargains include moderately priced and attractively designed knit sweaters, gloves, and Sami jackets. Strandgaten 13–15. ✆ **55-31-37-90.**

Glassware & Ceramics

Prydkunst-Hjertholm ★★ One of the leading outlets for glassware and ceramics purchases much of its merchandise directly from the artisans' studios. The quality goods include glass, ceramics, pewter, wood, and textiles. Gift articles and souvenirs are also available. Olav Kyrres Gate 7. ✆ **55-31-70-27.**

Tibords Interiør Bergen Storsenter ★★ This outlet has Bergen's best and most extensive collection of glassware, porcelain, and pottery. All the big names are here, including Arabia from Finland or Kosta Boda from Sweden, and even Wedgwood from England. Still, this is a true showcase of Scandinavian design. Much of the merchandise is made by local artisans, and the glass, ceramics, and pottery are of the highest quality. You'll want to pull up a big truck to the store. The price tags will restrain you, however. Torgallmenningen 8. ✆ **55-55-33-41.**

Handicrafts

In and around **Bryggen Brukskunst ★★**, the restored Old Town near the wharf, many craftspeople have taken over old houses and ply ancient Norwegian trades. Crafts boutiques often display Bergen souvenirs, many based on designs 300 to 1,500 years old. For example, we purchased a reproduction of a Romanesque-style cruciform pilgrim's badge. Other attractive items are likely to include sheepskin-lined booties and exquisitely styled hand-woven wool dresses.

Husfliden ★★ Since 1895, Husfliden has been the premier name in Norwegian handicrafts. Top-quality merchandise is sold here, especially hand-woven textiles. The Norwegian sweaters are among the best in town, and there is even a department for national costumes. Many items such as iron bowls and candlesticks are for table settings. Handmade pewter, wooden bowls, hand-woven rugs, and fireplace bellows are other useful items. Well-made, quality wooden toys are also sold here. Vagsallmenningen 3. ✆ **55-54-47-40.**

Jewelry

Juhls' Silver Gallery ★ Finds Next to the SAS Royal Hotel, along the harborfront, Juhls' displays the town's most unusual selection of quality jewelry. The designers take for their inspiration the constantly changing weather of the far north and, in their words, provide "a cultural oasis in a desert of snow." Bryggen. ✆ **55-32-47-40.**

Shopping Mall

Galleriet ★ This is the most important shopping complex in the central Bergen area, with 70 stores offering tax-free shopping. Close to the Fish Market, it displays a wide array of merchandise and features summer sales and special exhibitions. It has several fast-food establishments, too. Torgalmenningen 8. ✆ **55-30-05-00.**

Sportswear

G-Sport Gågaten This store has virtually everything you'd need for every sport available within Norway. Inventory changes radically throughout the seasons, with an emphasis on cycling and hiking in summer and downhill and cross-country skiing in winter. There are special high-energy food supplies (a tablespoon will give you the temporary strength of a gorilla) and high-tech outdoor gear whose high price tag reflects the newest trends in sportswear and rough-weather gear. Strandgaten 59. ✆ **55-23-22-22.**

Finds Shopping Tour

Norway has a centuries-old tradition of crafts, which undoubtedly developed to help people pass the time during the cold, dark winters when farm families were more or less housebound for months. Some of the major crafts were woodcarving, weaving, and embroidery, and these skills live on today at many local artist and crafts centers. Some of the best areas include Hardanger (around the Hardangerfjord, near Bergen), Song (just north of the Sognefjord, also near Bergen), and Telemark (the district around Skien, within a day's drive from Oslo). For a true behind-the scenes look at Norway, **Five Stars of Scandinavia,** 2914 Yelm Hwy. SE, #24, Olympia, WA 98501 (✆ **800/722-4126;** www.5stars-of-scandinavia.com), will set up a self-guided tour for you, factoring in everything they know about local artisans.

8 BERGEN AFTER DARK

THE PERFORMING ARTS

Grieghallen ★★★ The modern Grieg Hall, which opened in 1978, is Bergen's monumental showcase for music, drama, and a host of other cultural events. The stage is large enough for an entire grand opera production, and the main foyer comfortably seats 1,500 guests for lunch or dinner. Snack bars provide drinks and light snacks throughout the performances.

The Bergen Symphony Orchestra, founded in 1765, performs here from August to May, often on Thursday at 7:30pm and Saturday at 12:30pm. Its repertoire consists of classical and contemporary music, as well as visiting opera productions. International conductors and soloists perform periodically. ***Tip:*** Ticket prices on Thursday tend to be at the lower end of the price scale, and prices on Friday and Saturday tend to be at the upper end. Edvard Griegs Plass 1. ✆ **55-21-61-00.** Tickets NOK120–NOK470 ($24–$94/£12–£47). Closed July. Bus: 2, 3, or 4.

Den National Theater ★★ September to June is the season for Norway's oldest theater, founded in the mid-19th century. It stages classical Norwegian and international drama, contemporary plays, and musical drama, as well as visiting opera and ballet productions. Engen 1. ✆ **55-54-97-00.** Tickets NOK250–NOK350 ($50–$70/£25–£35). Bus: 2, 3, or 4.

SUMMER CULTURAL ENTERTAINMENT

Bergen Folklore ★ The Bergen Folklore dancing troupe performs from June to August on Tuesday at 9pm. The program, which lasts about an hour, consists of traditional folk dances and music from rural Norway. Tickets are on sale at the tourist office (see "Orientation," earlier in this chapter) and at the door. Bryggens Museum, Bryggen. ✆ **97-52-86-30.** Tickets NOK100 ($20/£10) adults, free for children. Bus: 1, 5, or 9.

FILMS

Konsertpaleet, Neumannsgate 3 (✆ **55-56-90-83**), shows all films in their original versions. The earliest performance is at 11am, the latest at 11pm. Tickets usually cost NOK85 ($17/£8.50).

THE CLUB & MUSIC SCENE

Café Opera Built in the 1880s, this large stone- and timber-built structure was originally conceived as a warehouse; today it functions as both a restaurant and a cafe. After the kitchen closes, it becomes an animated nightclub that's open Tuesday to Saturday. On Tuesday night, there is an open jam session where musicians can entertain or poets can read. On other nights, DJs mix and blend disparate music, depending on their individual tastes. The cafe is host to international DJs and bands on most Fridays and Saturdays. The 20s and 30s crowd finds this to be one of the more entertaining joints after dark for drinking, talking, and flirting—but very few of them actually get up and dance. Engen 18. ✆ **55-23-03-15.** No cover. Bus: 2, 3, or 4.

Engelen ★ This is one of Bergen's more elegant dance clubs, attracting a somewhat conservative crowd in their 40s, 50s, and 60s. That seems to change a bit on Saturday with the arrival of noisy, fun-seeking 20-somethings who make the place more raucous and animated. Light meals are available, but most people just show up to drink. Cocktail drink prices begin at NOK95 ($19/£9.50), or NOK70 ($14/£7) for a beer. It's open

Wednesday to Saturday 10pm to 3:30am. In the Radisson SAS Royal Hotel, Bryggen.
✆ **55-54-30-00.** Cover NOK75–NOK100 ($15–$20/£7.50–£10), free to hotel guests. Bus: 1, 5, or 9.

Kafe Kippers USF ★ A favorite rendezvous for artists, this club plays some of the best jazz music in Bergen, attracting a wide age group. Every Friday night they have a live jazz artist performing; otherwise, it's the best in "listening jazz." In winter, the club holds 80 patrons in snug comfort inside. In summer, the on-site outdoor restaurant, Kaien, serving a menu that borrows from cuisines throughout Europe and the world, becomes the largest in Bergen, with 500 seats available, opening onto fjord waters. Georgenes Cerft 3. ✆ **55-31-00-60.** Cover NOK80–NOK170 ($16–$34/£8–£17). Bus: 13.

Madam Felle Dark, woodsy-looking, and cozy, this is an animated and crowded pub with limited food service and live music that packs the place with 20- and 30-somethings 4 nights a week. On those nights (always Fri–Sat, plus 2 weeknights whose schedule changes frequently), live music plays between 9 and 11pm, with a cover charge that might be free or that might rise to anywhere between NOK100 and NOK250 ($20–$50/£10)–£25), depending on the season, the mood of the staff, and the fame and reputation of the band that's playing that night. The pub is named after a strong-willed early-20th-century matriarch who became a noted innkeeper at a spot near here, and who's something of a legend in Bergen. Bryggen. ✆ **55-54-30-58.** Bus: 20, 21, 22, 70, 80, or 90.

Rick's Café Sprawling and large enough to hold 1,800 raucous and slightly drunken persons at a time, this is a labyrinth, with rooms devoted to the after-dark pursuit of cabaret and comedy (there are two small stages for live performances), some serious drinking (on cold winter nights, things can get rather sudsy), or a friendly pickup (no doubt encouraged by the bar's potent cocktails). Attracting a crowd of 20- to 40-somethings, it's open daily from 9am, remaining stalwartly open as a cafe throughout the day, then soldiering on as a bar and nightclub beginning around 5pm and continuing till around 2am, depending on business. After 10pm, as many as five separate bar areas dispense alcohol. Veiten 3. ✆ **55-55-31-31.** Cover NOK100 ($20/£10). Bus: 1, 5, or 9.

Rubinen Rubinen is one of Bergen's most popular dance clubs, attracting an over-35 crowd of mostly married couples who come here to whirl their partners across the floor with great determination. It features all kinds of music, including country-western, rock 'n' roll, and occasional bouts of Latin, tango, and formal ballroom dancing. Drinks cost from NOK80 to NOK130 ($16–$26/£8–£13), depending on what's in them. It's open Wednesday to Saturday 10pm to 3:30am, with live music nightly. Rosenkrantzgate 7. ✆ **55-31-74-70.** Cover NOK90 ($18/£9). Bus: 2, 3, or 4.

THE BAR SCENE

Altona Vinbar ★ This is one of the oldest, most deeply entrenched, and best-known bars in Bergen. Some of the stone walls and the wooden ceiling are original, dating from the 1600s. Boasting an association with the site that housed literary lion Ludvig Holberg during his years in Bergen and lying in the basement of the Augustin Hotel, its walls are painted white and the bar is decorated with modern sculptures. Patrons, ranging from 30 to 60 years old, come here to listen to the recorded classical music and to enjoy the elegant drinks, including champagne, cognac, and the best Scotch whisky. It's open Monday to Thursday 6pm to 1:30am and Friday and Saturday 6pm to 2:30am. Strandgaten 81. ✆ **55-30-40-72.** Bus: 2 or 4.

Baklommen This small and cozy bar, with its old Chesterfield chairs, is a quiet and romantic retreat, lying downstairs from the To Kokker restaurant. Despite the fact that increasing numbers of 20-somethings have been spotted here recently, a relatively mature crowd, ages 30 to 60, comes here to escape from a lot of the pub rowdiness of Bergen. In the heart of the Hanseatic Wharf, this bar plays recorded jazz music in the background. It's open Tuesday to Saturday 6pm to 1am. Bryggen. ✆ **55-32-27-47.** Bus: 1, 5, or 9.

Dyvekes Vinkjeller A sense of spookiness permeates this cozy drinking den. In 1849, a famous Norwegian bandit (Gjest Baardsen, the "Robin Hood" of Norway) drank himself to death here. Drinkers have reported sightings of a young serving wench in 17th-century costume who takes drink orders from patrons and then disappears without bringing the desired quaffs. Come here for glasses of wine, priced from NOK65 to NOK220 ($13–$44/£6.50–£22); glasses of beer; colorful patrons (both living and dead)—and in a wide age range—and a genuine sense of Norwegian history. It's open Sunday to Thursday 3pm to 1am, Friday and Saturday noon to 2am. Hollendergaten 7. ✆ **55-32-30-60.** Bus: 20, 21, or 22.

Fotballpuben This is the biggest sports pub in Bergen, a rocking and rolling beer-soaked place with an undeniable affection for football (that is, soccer) and, to a lesser degree, rugby. Feel free to wander through this crowded establishment's labyrinth of inner chambers—joining a 20s-to-50s crowd—whose corners and edges are sometimes upholstered with vinyl padding (installed due to a fear of falls from inebriated sports fans?). Screens blow up the action of sports events in progress (or prerecorded) whenever there's a soccer stadium with an intensely contested match. The staff prides itself on serving the cheapest beer in Bergen, priced from NOK40 to NOK55 ($8–$11/£4–£5.50) per mug, depending on the time of day. It's open Monday to Thursday 9am to 1am, Friday and Saturday 9am to 3am, and Sunday noon to 1am. Vestre Torgate 9. ✆ **55-33-66-61.** Bus: 1 or 9.

Kontoret (The Office) The most frequented pub in the city center, the Kontoret lies immediately adjacent, through a connecting door, to the Dickens restaurant, where platters of rib-sticking English food cost from NOK190 to NOK250 ($38–$50/£19–£25). In the Kontoret, the decor captures the feel of an office from the early 1900s, replete with banged-up manual typewriters and oaken countertops that evoke the green eyeshades and ink-stained printing rituals of an earlier era. The local brew is called Hansa, a half-liter of which costs NOK60 ($12/£6). It's open Sunday to Thursday 4pm to 12:30am, Friday and Saturday 4pm to 2am. 4 Kong Olav V Plass. ✆ **55-36-31-33.**

Stenersens Café You wouldn't expect such a hip nightclub and pub to be within an art museum, but in the case of this large, high-ceilinged cube of a room on the museum's rear side, that's exactly the case. Patrons in their 20s and 30s are drawn to the danceable music

Fun Facts The Brown Scene

What does a Norwegian mean when he refers to a "brown" nightclub? It's a raucous, boozy, semisleazy joint where off-duty prostitutes, bikers, harborfront riff-raff, slumming suburbanites, business travelers on short-term leaves from their spouses, and all manner of fringe society get together for a rollicking and booze-soaked good time. Don't say you haven't been warned.

emerging from a DJ's station on one side; a bar at another end of the room serves beer and sandwiches, and electronic art in kaleidoscopic color is beamed against yet another. It is open Tuesday to Saturday 5pm to 1am, rocking and rolling long after the museum is closed tight like a drum. Windows directly overlook the large, octagonal reflecting pool on the museum's back side. Pastas and salads cost NOK85 to NOK110 ($17–$22/£8.50–£11). In the Bergen Art Museum, Rasmus Meyers Allé 3 and 7. ✆ **55-32-65-70.** Bus: 1, 5, or 9.

9 SIDE TRIPS FROM BERGEN

SOGNEFJORD ★★★

If there's only room for one fjord in your future, make it Norway's longest and deepest fjord, **Sognefjord,** a geologic and panoramic marvel. The terrain soars upward from the watery depths of the North Atlantic, and many waterfalls punctuate its edges with spray. The best way to view the fjord involves a full-day jaunt that's possible only between May 18 and September 15. It combines self-guided travel by boat, bus, and rail. Begin by heading to the Bergen harborfront (the Strandkaien), where you'll board a ferry for the 4½-hour ride to the fjord-side hamlet of Gudvangen. A bus carries participants on to the town of Voss (see "Voss: A Winter Playground," in chapter 12). In Voss, after exploring the town, you can board a train to carry you back to Bergen. Many schedule permutations are possible, but the one that's particularly convenient leaves Bergen at 8:30am and returns at 5:15pm. The combined round-trip fare is NOK1,060 ($212/£106). Details on this and other explorations by public transport are available from the tourist office (see "Orientation," earlier in this chapter).

NORWAY IN A NUTSHELL ★★★

Our most serious recommendation is to have the more prolonged experience instead of a "quickie." That said, no tour we've ever taken in Norway has the drama or excitement of this 12-hour captivating preview of the breadth and diversity of landscapes, encapsulating the majesty of fjords and mountains that look like giant trolls.

Several different transit options operate throughout the day. The one most aggressively recommended by Bergen's tourist office operates year-round. It starts at 8:40am at **Bergen**'s railway station. After a 2-hour train ride, you'll disembark in the mountaintop hamlet of **Myrdal,** where you can take in the natural wonders for about 20 minutes. In Myrdal, you'll board a cog railway for one of the world's most dramatically inclined train rides. The trip down to the village of **Flåm,** a drop of 870m (2,854 ft.), takes an hour and passes roaring streams and seemingly endless waterfalls.

After a 1-hour stopover in Flåm, where you can have lunch or take a brief hike, you'll board a fjord steamer for a ride along the Sognefjord. You'll reach the fjord-side town of Gudvangen after a 2-hour ride. After 30 minutes in Gudvangen, you'll board a bus for the 75-minute ride to Voss. Here you'll spend 30 minutes before boarding a train for the 75-minute ride back to Bergen. Arrival is scheduled for 8:35pm.

Expect only a rushed overview of each town, as there is more scenery than you can digest in a 12-hour day. The round-trip fare, excluding meals, costs NOK895 ($179/£90) for adults, NOK447 ($89/£45) for children 4 to 15, and is free for accompanied children under 4. There are discounts for holders of Eurailpasses or Scanrail passes. For more information, contact Bergen's **Tourist Office** (see "Orientation" earlier in this chapter) or call ✆ **81-56-82-22** (www.norwaynutshell.com).

12

The West Coast Fjord Country

No place in all of Norway holds the enchantment of the fjord country, the single most intriguing region in all of the Scandinavia countries. *National Geographic* did us one better, citing the Norwegian fjords as "the world's best travel destination."

Gouged by glaciers, studded with deep valleys, characterized by rolling fells and rugged mountain plateaus, the fjord country is a land of farmlands, blossoming orchards, small villages, cascading waterfalls, and Scandinavia's most convoluted geography. It's a place to slow down and take your time. Just getting from point to point is a bit of an endeavor—but, oh, those views along the way.

Norwegian fjords are narrow arms of the sea, snaking their way inland. It took 3 million years to form the furrows and fissures that give western Norway its distinctive look. At some points the fjords become so narrow that a boat can hardly pass between the mountainsides.

Fjords have been of enormous significance to Norwegians through the ages. They served as lifelines to those who settled in the harsh mountain landscape. Instead of building roads to each house and village, they used the easily accessible and navigable fjords. Thus, inland and coastal regions were linked together as the fjords enabled commodities to be transported to the old trading stations. Imagine how centuries ago people used to row across their neighborhood fjord to visit church on Sunday mornings.

Bergen is the best departure point for trips to the fjords: To the south lies the famous **Hardangerfjord** and to the north the **Sognefjord,** cutting 178km (110 miles) inland.

Voss, about 1½ hours from Bergen, is a famous ski resort that is also well situated between both the Hardangerfjord and the Sognefjord.

We start in the towns around the Hardangerfjord—**Lofthus, Kinsarvik, Eidfjord,** and **Ulvik**—make a detour to **Voss,** and then move north to the towns around the Sognefjord, including **Balestrand** and **Flåm.**

GETTING THERE Bergen is the traditional gateway to the fjord country. From Bergen, you have a choice of several options for getting about the district; the most expensive is by private car. Most of the towns and villages have road connections, although you'll have to take several car ferries to cross the fjords. Boat excursions, many of which leave from Bergen, are the traditional way to see the fjords. In summer, dozens of possibilities for these excursions await you. Contact the tourist office in Bergen for details (see "Orientation," in chapter 11).

Of the towns recommended in this chapter, Voss, both a winter ski center and a summer mountain resort, has the best rail connections with Oslo and Bergen. All of the fjord towns and villages are also connected by buses that make their way through the mountains and along the fjords, boasting vistas in all directions. Of course, travel by bus from place to place is time-consuming, and often there are only two to five departures a day, depending on business, so you'll have to plan your connections in advance.

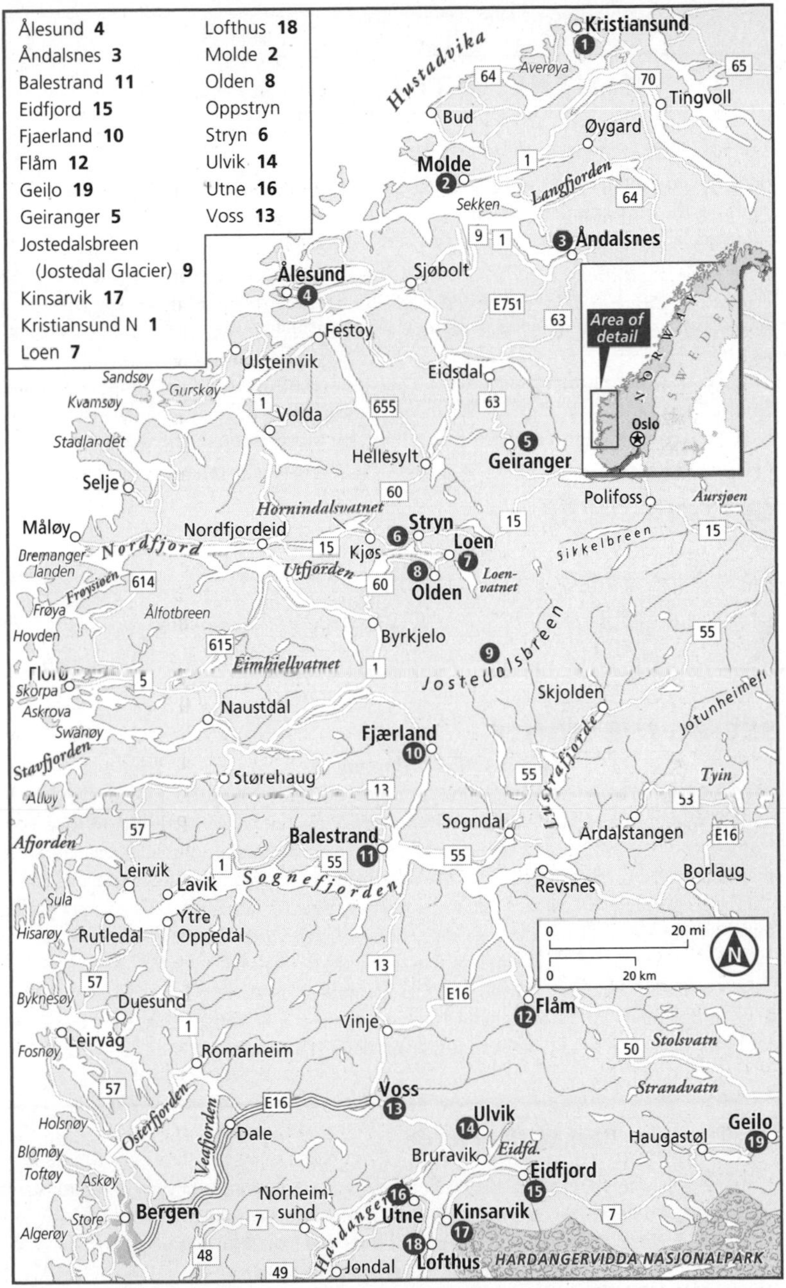
Ålesund 4
Åndalsnes 3
Balestrand 11
Eidfjord 15
Fjaerland 10
Flåm 12
Geilo 19
Geiranger 5
Jostedalsbreen (Jostedal Glacier) 9
Kinsarvik 17
Kristiansund N 1
Loen 7
Lofthus 18
Molde 2
Olden 8
Oppstryn
Stryn 6
Ulvik 14
Utne 16
Voss 13
Kristiansund
Hustadvika
Averøya
Bud
Tingvoll
Øygard
Molde
Langfjorden
Sekken
Åndalsnes
Ålesund
Sjøbolt
Area of detail
NORWAY
SWEDEN
Oslo
Festoy
Ulsteinvik
Eidsdal
Sandsøy
Gurskøy
Kvamsøy
Volda
Stadlandet
Geiranger
Hellesylt
Selje
Polifoss
Aursjøen
Hornindalsvatnet
Stryn
Måløy
Nordfjordeid
Kjøs
Loen
Nordfjord
Dremanger-landen
Utfjorden
Olden
Loen-vatnet
Sikkelbreen
Frøysjoen
Frøya
Ålfotbreen
Hovden
Byrkjelo
Eimhjellvatnet
Jostedalsbreen
Florø
Skorpa
Askrova
Skjolden
Naustdal
Jotunheimen
Swanøy
Stavfjorden
Fjærland
Lustrafjorden
Tyin
Størehaug
Alløy
Sogndal
Årdalstangen
Afjorden
Balestrand
Leirvik
Lavik
Sognefjorden
Revsnes
Borlaug
Sula
Ytre Oppedal
Hisarøy
Rutledal
20 mi
20 km
Byknesøy
Duesund
Flåm
Vinje
Leirvåg
Fosnøy
Romarheim
Stolsvatn
Strandvatn
Voss
Osterfjorden
Veafjorden
Ulvik
Geilo
Holsnøy
Dale
Haugastøl
Blomøy
Bruravik
Eidfd.
Toftøy
Askøy
Eidfjord
Norheim-sund
Utne
Kinsarvik
Store
Bergen
Algerøy
Hardangerfjorden
Lofthus
Jondal
HARDANGERVIDDA NASJONALPARK

Details about bus routes in the fjord district are available at the Central Station in Bergen. Also visit www.nsb.no for train schedules and www.nor-way.no for bus schedules.

1 UTNE: A TRIO OF FJORDS ★

130km (81 miles) E of Bergen; 45km (28 miles) N of Odda

This tiny hamlet is a good place for a first-timer to get acquainted with the unique geography of the fjord country. Utne has a view of the entrances to three fjords: Indre Samla, Granvin, and Eid. Across Utnefjorden, the formidable bulk of Oksen rises from the headland separating the Granvin and the Eid fjords. A great ravine breaches the steep slope of Oksen. Utnefjorden is almost 3.3km (2 miles) wide opposite Utne and nearly 822m (2,696 ft.) deep in places, making it deeper than any other part of the Hardangerfjord.

Utne is at the northern end of the Folgefonn peninsula, with mountains looming nearby. Two valleys converge on the town, Utnedalen to the east and Fossdalen to the west. The river through Fossdalen forms falls as it drops through the woods toward the end of its course, dividing into two branches as it reaches the fjord.

GETTING THERE

In the west, board the **ferry** at Kvanndal; in the east, at Kinsarvik. From Monday to Friday, ferries leave every hour, and on Saturday and Sunday, they leave every 2 hours. **Train** connections are possible from Voss 38km (24 miles) to the east, on the main Bergen-Oslo line. **Bus** connections are made via Odda in the south and from Bergen in the west. By **car,** head east from Bergen along the E16. At Kvanndal, board the ferry for Utne.

SEEING THE SIGHTS

Founded in 1911, the **Hardanger Folk Museum ★**, lying near the ferry quay at Utne (✆ **53-67-00-40;** www.hardanger.museum.no), celebrates the past of Utne and does so with insight and style. It exhibits old timber buildings, furnished according to their eras, from several parts of Inner Hardanger. By the fjord are old boathouses and a general store that once stood on the quay side. In the administrative building are local arts and crafts, national costumes, and data on the fruit-growing industry. The famous Hardanger fiddle, so beloved by Ole Bull and Edvard Grieg, came from this area. The museum owns several of these antique fiddles, and you can also visit a fiddle-maker's workshop here.

The museum charges NOK40 ($8/£4) for adults and is free for children. In May, June, and September, it's open daily 10am to 4pm. In July and August, hours are daily 10am to 5pm. The rest of the year, hours are daily 10am to 3pm.

Tips Your Pass to the Fjords

Some 170 hotels and upmarket B&Bs offer discounted overnight rates to holders of the **Fjord Pass.** The card costs NOK120 ($24/£12) and is valid for two adults and all children 14 and under. The pass is available from **Fjord Tours,** Stromgate 4, N-5015 Bergen (✆ **55-55-76-60;** www.fjord-tours.com).

A Side Trip to Norway's Only Barony

In 1658, Karen Mowat, a rich Norwegian heiress, wed Ludvig Rosenkrantz, a Danish nobleman. Her wedding present was a farmstead at Hattberg, lying in a valley west of Folgefonna. She and her husband built a castle here, which was granted the status of a barony. That castle and all its side attractions can be visited. It is also a cultural center, B&B, and a luncheon or dinner stopover. The descendants of this noble pair donated the estate to the University of Oslo in 1927. The small castle is enveloped by a rose garden and some of the most dramatic scenery in Norway.

The Baroniet holds many concerts in the summer season, and it's also possible to hear plays by Shakespeare in the courtyard. Lunch, based on freshly grown produce from the baronial estate, is served in a greenhouse. You can also have tea in the Tea Room. The specialty is the Baroness's rose tea, served with freshly made pastries. Those who are still around can order dinner at the estate's farm, a three-course meal served beside a 17th-century fireplace. Call ✆ **53-48-29-99** for reservations. You can also be served more elegantly in the manor itself, with a concert in the Red Room preceding a 3- or 5-course dinner in the Blue Room.

Bed-and-breakfast can be arranged at the home farm. Rooms are well furnished, and most have washing facilities, but you have to share the bathrooms in the hallway. Rates are NOK900 ($180/£90) for a double, including breakfast, with an extra bed costing NOK250 ($50/£25).

Baroniet Rosendal, at N-5486 Rosendal (✆ **53-48-29-99;** www.baroniet.no) is open May 3 to June 27 daily 11am to 3pm; June 28 to August 17 daily 10am to 5pm, and August 18 to September 7 daily 11am to 3pm. Admission is NOK100 ($20/£10) for adults, NOK10 ($2/£1) for children 17 and under; concerts range from NOK150 to NOK250 ($30–$50/£15–£25). From Utne, follow Rte. 550 south in the direction of Odda, taking the Folgefonn Tunnel west and going along Rte. 48 into Rosendal where the estate is signposted.

When fjords were the highways of western Norway, Utne was an important junction. The **Utne Hotel** (see below) opened in 1772.

WHERE TO STAY & DINE

Utne Hotel ★★★ Dating from 1722, but renovated in 2006, this is Norway's oldest hotel in continual operation. To settle a war debt, King Christian VII granted Sergeant Børsem permission to operate an inn here, and it's been going strong ever since. Børsem's family ran the hotel until 1995, when new owners took over. Torbjørg Utne (1812–1903)—nicknamed Mother Utne—gave the hotel the romantic character it still possesses today. By the mid-19th century, the hotel offered "the best quarters in the country." That's not quite true anymore, but we'd say that the Utne Hotel and the Hotel Ullensvang (p. 303) are the best places to stay in the fjord country for those seeking a genuine Norwegian west-country ambience. Today a foundation owns the well-preserved hotel, which has a distinctive atmosphere and intimate ambience. Only a few minutes' walk from the ferry quay, the antiques-filled place offers generous hospitality. The well-maintained bedrooms have the gracious comfort of the 19th century. The staff can arrange mountain sightseeing tours as well as boat trips on the fjords.

The Utne Hotel restaurant is one of the major reasons to stay here: It's one of the finest in the fjord country. A complete three-course dinner of Norwegian specialties costs NOK450 ($90/£45), and the dining room is open to nonguests.

N-5779 Utne i Hardanger. ✆ **53-66-64-00.** Fax 53-66-10-89. www.utnehotel.no. 25 units. NOK1,450 ($290/£145) double. Children 11 and under stay free in parent's room. Rates include continental breakfast. AE, DC, MC, V. Closed Dec 24 and Easter. **Amenities:** Restaurant; bar. *In room:* No phone.

2 LOFTHUS ★★: CENTER OF THE HARDANGERFJORD ★★★

379km (235 miles) W of Oslo; 140km (87 miles) E of Bergen

Our favorite spot in the Hardanger district is sleepy Lofthus, once the haunt of Edvard Grieg and other artists. Resting on the fjord, the resort is enveloped by snowcapped mountains, farms, and orchards. Hovering in the background is the Folgefonn Glacier.

Lofthus is actually the collective name for several groups of farms—Helleland, Eidnes, Lofthus, Opedal, Århus, Ullensvang, and Pedal—extending from north to south along the eastern coastal slopes of Sørfjorden, 6 to 8km (3¾–5 miles) south of Kinsarvik Bay.

The discovery of a runic stone at Pedal in the 19th century established that the area has been populated since about A.D. 600. Cistercian monks came to Opedal 7 centuries later and pioneered a fruit-growing industry. Their footpaths are still used, and many visitors have benefited from the 616 steps, the **Monks' Staircase,** that make their way up the steep gradient to the Vidda.

The church and buildings of Ullensvang lie around the mouth of the Opo River. The Gothic stone Ullensvang church was probably built at the end of the 13th century, and the builders may have been Scottish masons. Although the church has irregular hours, it's usually open during the day from May to mid-September. Ullensvang was the name of the ancient farm where the *prestegård* (church farm) stands facing the church. It is now the name of the church, the hamlet, the parish, and the *kommune* (county), and the site of Hotel Ullensvang, the most famous hotel in the region (see "Where to Stay," below).

ESSENTIALS

GETTING THERE Board the ferry at Kvanndal for Kinsarvik, where you can make bus connections south to Lofthus. **Train** connections are possible from Voss, 49km (30 miles) to the east, on the main Bergen-Oslo line, and take 1 hour and 15 minutes. **Bus** service takes 1 hour from Odda in the south, 15 minutes from Kinsarvik in the north. From Bergen you can go by express bus/boat in 2½ hours. **Motorists** can take the E16 east from Bergen to Kvanndal, where you can board a car ferry to Kinsarvik. At Kinsarvik, head south on Rte. 47 to Lofthus.

VISITOR INFORMATION The summer-only **Lofthus Tourist Information Office,** Strandkaiterninalen (✆ **53-66-11-90**), is open daily June to August noon to 5pm.

SEEING THE SIGHTS

An El Dorado for nature lovers and fjord fanciers, Lofthus, along with Ulvik (see "Ulvik: Misty Peaks & Fruity Fjord Farms," later in this chapter), is one of the best centers for taking in the glories of **Hardangerfjord** ★★★. Your hotel can arrange boat trips, or you can go to the tourist office (see above) and see what excursions might be available at the time of your visit.

Flowing in a northeasterly direction, the fjord stretches out for 179km (111 miles). Along the western coast of Norway, the fjord is broad and open, but when its "fingers" dig inland into several branches, it often becomes very narrow. The banks of the fjord are a delight in spring. You'll view not only wildflowers but also lots of blossoming fruit trees along its sloping banks.

The **waterfalls ★★** along both banks are stunning and are reason enough to explore the fjord. When the snows melt in the early spring, the waterfalls that rush down the mountains are at their most powerful.

Motorists can drive along the fjord, taking in its vast panorama. From Skånevik, a small ferry port at the head of Skånevikfjord (a branch of the Hardangerfjord), routes 48, 11, 13, and 7 run for 193km (120 miles) all the way to Northelmsund, the main center of the north side of Hardangerfjord. This road also bypasses Lofthus, as well as Odda, the principal settlement along Hardangerfjord.

You will also be able to take in views of **Folgefonna ★★**, Norway's third-largest glacier. It stretches for 37km (23 miles). At its widest point, it measures 16km (10 miles).

WHERE TO STAY

Hotel Ullensvang ★★★ The composer Edvard Grieg, who knew a thing or two about fjord scenery, chose this hotel for his summer vacation in 1878. He came back over many a summer, finding inspiration for his music such as *Springtime, The Hoberg Suite,* and *Peer Gynt Suite.* His original piano is still kept in a cottage on the grounds. We like to follow his example, returning every other summer to this 1846 hotel, the single-most romantic inn on the edge of the Hardangerfjord (although the Utne Hotel, above, gives it serious competition).

Now a beautifully equipped structure with a garden opening onto the shoreline and with views of the Folgefonna glacier, the hotel has been run by the Utne family for four generations. It offers rooms ranging from standard to deluxe, and are handsomely furnished and come with well-maintained private bathrooms. Scandinavian kings, Emperor Wilhelm II, and European nobility have patronized the hotel. Tours of the surrounding area, including the best beauty spots along Hardangerfjord, can be arranged with local guides, recommended by the hotel. The quality on-site restaurant is reviewed separately below. The hotel is entirely nonsmoking.

N-578 Loftus i Hardanger. ✆ **53-67-00-00.** Fax 53-67-00-01. www.hotel-ullensvang.no. 172 units. NOK1,790–NOK2,510 ($358–$502/£179–£251) double; NOK3,290 ($658/£329) suite. Rates include buffet breakfast and dinner. AE, DC, MC, V. Closed Dec 22–30. **Amenities:** Restaurant; bar; heated indoor pool; tennis court; squash court; gym; spa; sauna; rowboats for fjord cruises; sailboats; game room; salon; room service; laundry service; solarium; rooms for those w/limited mobility. *In room:* TV, minibar, trouser press.

Ullensvang Gjesteheim ★ Value When we first discovered this place years ago, guests from England were sitting in the garden enjoying food and drink. We figured the inn must be a good place—and so it was. Admittedly, it doesn't match the style and charm of the Hotel Ullensvang, but it's a good runner-up. A cozy, homelike guesthouse in the town center, Ullensvang is run with a personal touch. Bedrooms are comfortably furnished, if a bit old-fashioned, and bathrooms in the corridors are shared and most adequate for the job. The dining room serves a Norwegian *koldbord* (cold board) for breakfast and also dishes up home-cooked Norwegian specialties at lunch and dinner, including such dishes as filet of reindeer. Lunch and dinner menus range from NOK100 to NOK170 ($20–$34/£10–£17) for a main course.

 N-5774 Lofthus i Hardanger. ✆ **53-66-12-36.** Fax 53-66-15-19. www.ullensvang-gjesteheim.no. 17 units, all w/shared bathroom. NOK710 ($142/£71) double. Children 4 and under stay free in parent's room. Rates include continental breakfast. AE, DC, MC, V. Closed Dec 23–Jan 1. **Amenities:** Restaurant; bar. *In room:* No phone.

WHERE TO DINE

Restaurant Ullensvang ★ Value NORWEGIAN We find some of the best fjord-country dining at this old inn (see the review for the Hotel Ullensvang). Such famous composers or writers as Edvard Grieg and Bjørnstjerne Bjørnson have sung the praise of these viands. The windows of this three-level restaurant open onto dramatic views of the fjord. Guests flock here for the big buffet spread, where you'll find at least 65 dishes, everything from jellied salmon to homemade cakes. Many of the dishes have a strong regional flavor, as exemplified by the filet of reindeer or the red deer with a rich game sauce laced with herbs. Fish fanciers gravitate to the flounder or catfish with steamed fresh vegetables. In summer, expect those delectable cloudberries that are similar to a yellow raspberry. They can be served as a soufflé or (and we prefer this) just fresh with cream.

Lofthus i Hardanger. ✆ **53-67-00-00.** Reservations required. Buffet NOK450 ($90/£45); main courses NOK295 ($59/£30) a la carte. AE, DC, MC, V. Daily noon–2:30pm and 7–9:30pm. Closed Dec 22–30.

3 KINSARVIK: HOLIDAY ON THE KINSO RIVER

119km (74 miles) E of Bergen; 38km (24 miles) S of Voss; 374km (232 miles) W of Oslo

The main village of **Kinsarvik** stands on a glacier-formed ridge at the mouth of the Kinso River, which flows into four magnificent waterfalls as it drops from the plateau to Husedalen on its way to the sea. Since early times, Kinsarvik has been the marketplace for the region.

Kinsarvik was Hardanger's principal timber port in the 17th and early 18th centuries. When the export of timber was transferred to Bergen in 1750, Kinsarvik developed a shipbuilding industry that continued until 1870, when the village became a center for woodcarving. Today one of its principal manufacturers is a pewter factory.

The plot of grass that slopes to a stony beach near the Kinsarvik ferry terminal is **Skiperstod,** site of a boathouse for naval long ships from about 900 until 1350.

ESSENTIALS

GETTING THERE The **Bergen Railroad** running between Bergen and Oslo will take you to the Voss station, the nearest terminal to Kinsarvik. There are 14 arrivals and departures a day. From Voss, you can journey to Kinsarvik by bus. Trip time from Oslo to Voss is 5½ hours. **Bus** service takes 1¼ hours from Odda, 15 minutes from Lofthus. The bus trip from Bergen consumes 2½ hours, and 50 minutes from Voss, the nearest rail connection. **Motorists** can take E16 east from Bergen to Kvanndal, and then board a car ferry to Kinsarvik. **Boats** leaving from Kvanndal on the northern coast of the Hardangerfjord take about 45 minutes.

VISITOR INFORMATION **Turist-Informasjonen** (✆ **53-66-31-12**), in the village center, is open daily as follows: May 1 to June 20 9am to 5pm, June 21 to August 20 9am to 7pm, and August 21 to September 1 9am to 5pm. At other times, information is available from the **Kinsarvik Library** (✆ **53-67-15-77**), also in the village center.

SEEING THE SIGHTS

Said to be have been constructed by Scottish master builders at the end of the 12th century, **Kinsarvik Church** ★ is one of the oldest stone churches in Norway. The interior was restored in 1961 to its pre-Reformation condition. It has a 17th-century pulpit painted by Peter Reimers, a painted and carved altarpiece, and medieval frescoes. The church is constructed in a vaguely Roman style, and chalk paintings on the walls show the "weighing of souls" in judgment by Archangel Michael. The admission-free church is open daily May to September 15 10am to 4pm.

Borstova, the building on the fjord side of the green facing the church, was constructed partly from the timbers of St. Olav's Guildhall, the meeting place of the local guild until 1680. It's now a council chamber and social center.

The stone **column** ***(minnestein)*** on the green commemorates the local men who fought in the wars that led to the end of Norway's union with Denmark in 1814.

The **Tillegg i Tekst (Hardanger Recreation Park),** in the middle of Kinsarvik, is open daily mid-May to mid-August. It is an ideal place for a picnic on a summer day. You can pick up picnic supplies from the town's only grocery store, **SPAR** (✆ **53-67-11-70**), which is located in the town center, a 2-minute walk from the Best Western Kinsarvik Fjord Hotel (see below).

Lying 6.5km (4 miles) from Kinsarvik on Rte. 13 to Odda, a minor road forks left providing an alternative route to Lofthus. A short distance from the fork is the entrance to the **Skredhaugen Museum** (✆ **90-17-41-15**), a branch of the Hardanger Folk Museum at Utne. A collection of 10 timber houses gathered from the Hardanger area and furnished according to the period can be viewed here. There is also an art gallery of regional works on view. The museum is open June 10 to August 20 Monday to Saturday 11am to 4pm, Sunday noon to 4pm. Admission is NOK45 ($9/£4.50), and free for children.

Kinsarvik is also an excellent base for exploring all the attractions of the Hardangerfjord area, including the Hardangervidda mountain plateau. You can rent rowing boats and canoes here to explore the fjord. The tourist office (see above) will tell you how to reach the **Nykjesøyfossen** waterfall, or the best viewpoint for taking in the panoramic of the better-known **Vøringfossen** waterfall. Many sights in Lofthus, Utne, Eidfjord, and Ulvik can also be easily explored from a base at Kinsarvik.

WHERE TO STAY & DINE

Because of their fjord country charm and isolation, we infinitely prefer to stay at Utne or Lofthus. The downside is that you may not always find accommodations in those places in summer unless you reserve well in advance. A good alternative is to journey to Kinsarvik, where rooms might be more readily available.

Best Western Kinsarvik Fjord Hotel ★ (Kids) This hotel will not excite you but will rarely disappoint you. Even though it's a Best Western chain member, this hotel is still family run, offering personal service and warm fjord hospitality. Built in 1952, it was greatly expanded in 1993. Right by the Hardangerfjord, it's rich in historical interest and is a first-class choice for those seeking the experience of combined fjord and mountain landscapes. It's also one of the best-equipped hotels in the area. Bedrooms are completely modern, some with hardwood floors, others with carpets. Each comes with a remodeled bathroom with a tub/shower combination. Nonguests exploring the area during the day can patronize the hotel's fixed-price lunch for NOK180 ($36/£18) or the dinner buffet of regional fjord specialties for NOK370 ($74/£37). There is live music 7 nights a week in summer.

 N-5782 Kinsarvik. ✆ **800/780-7234** in the U.S. and Canada, or 53-66-74-00. Fax 53-66-33-74. www.bestwestern.com. 70 units. NOK1,450 ($290/£145) double; NOK1,500 ($300/£150) suite. Children 11 and under stay free in parent's room. Rates include continental breakfast. AE, DC, MC, V. Closed Jan. **Amenities:** Restaurant; bar; fitness center; sauna; room service; babysitting; laundry service/dry cleaning; nonsmoking rooms. *In room:* TV, coffeemaker (some units), hair dryer.

4 EIDFJORD: WESTERN GATEWAY TO HARDANGERVIDDA

149km (92 miles) E of Bergen; 336km (208 miles) W of Oslo

North of Kinsarvik, the Eidfjord district, centering around the village of Eidfjord, is one of the oldest settlements in Norway. Stone Age hunters came through here following the migrations of the reindeer to put steaks on their table. Some 1,000 people still inhabit the northern tip of Hardangerfjord, making their living through agriculture and tourism.

Hikers flock here to go into the hinterlands, where they encounter members of Europe's largest herd of wild reindeer. These same hikers also encounter cascading waterfalls, fjord farms, and mountain lodges in and around Hardangerfjorden, which sends "fingers" of deep water into the innermost reaches of the country. Fishermen come here to catch mountain trout that will be cooked for them later that night at their hotel. The town itself enjoys one of the most scenic locations in the district, nestled between a deep fjord and a deep lake, the Eidfjordvatnet.

ESSENTIALS

GETTING THERE Take the **train** from Bergen to Voss, where a connecting bus will take you the rest of the way. The train from Bergen to Voss takes 1 hour and 15 minutes and costs NOK318 ($64/£32). **Buses** for Eidfjord depart three or four times a day from Voss, taking 1¾ hours.

Part of the route across the Eidfjord itself requires a 10-minute ferryboat ride from Ulvik. In summer the ferry departs every 10 minutes, and in winter every 40 minutes. From Odda in the south, **motorists** take Rte. 47 north; from Geilo in the east, go along Rte. 7 west. The drive takes an hour.

VISITOR INFORMATION The **Eidfjord Tourist Office** (✆ **53-67-34-00;** www.eidfjordinfo.com) lies in the town center and is open June to August daily from 9am to 7pm. There are no street names. Also visit the website for information.

SEEING THE SIGHTS

The county contains nearly one-quarter of the **Hardangervidda National Park ★★★**, the largest mountain plateau in Europe, rising 1,000m (3,280 ft.) to 1,200m (3,936 ft.) high and covering an area of 7,500 sq. km (2,925 sq. miles). The park is home to some 20,000 wild reindeer, the herd supplemented in the summer months by horses, goats, and sheep brought here by local farmers to graze. The park is also home to the southernmost habitats of the snowy owl, the arctic fox, the lynx, and other creatures from the frozen tundra of the north, as well as a diverse bird population, ranging from ravens to eagles.

Hiking trails carved centuries ago by footpaths of early settlers cut through the mountainous area, leading to a series of more than a dozen tourist huts (log cabins). The local

Fun Facts Sultry, Tropical Norway

Did you know that some half a billion years ago, Norway was situated south of the equator? You can learn more astonishing facts like this at the Hardangervidda Naturscenter in the Eidfjord district.

tourist office (see above) will provide maps and more information if you want to go hiking.

Before going on a hike, stop in at the **Hardangervidda Naturscenter,** Øvre Eidfjord (© **53-55-59-00;** www.hardangervidda.org), which shows an informative 20-minute movie and offers geological exhibitions of the park. It's open June to August daily 9am to 8pm; from April to May and in September and October, hours are daily 10am to 6pm. Admission is NOK110 ($22/£11) for adults, NOK50 ($10/£5) for children, NOK240 ($48/£24) family ticket. On-site is a restaurant that makes a good luncheon stopover, plus a souvenir shop.

Several canyons, including the renowned **Måbø Valley ★★**, lead down from the Hardangervidda plateau to the fjords. Part of the 1,000-year-old road across Norway, traversing the Måbø Valley, has been restored for hardy hikers. At a point 18km (11 miles) southeast of Eidfjord, you'll see the dramatic **Voringfoss Waterfall ★**, dropping 145m (476 ft.). It's reached along Rte. 7.

Back in the center of Eidfjord, the **Eidfjord Kirke** dates from the 14th century. Built of stone, it can be visited with a guide; ask the tourist office (see "Visitor Information," earlier) to make arrangements. The local tourist office also rents boats and bicycles. Bikes cost NOK100 ($20/£10) per half-day, NOK150 ($30/£15) per day. Kayaks cost NOK150 ($30/£15) per day; canoes are NOK350 ($70/£35) per day.

You can also make an excursion to a small mountain farm at **Kjeåsen Farm ★**, lying 6km (3³/₄ miles) northeast of Eidfjord. This is one of the most panoramic sites in all the fjord country. If you climb to the top of the mountain, allow 3 hours there and back. The climb is extremely difficult and recommended only for those in Olympic-competition physical shape. The farm lies 600m (1,968 ft.) above sea level by the Simafjord.

Numerous lakes and rivers in the county offer good trout fishing. Two rivers, the Eio and the Bjoreio, as well as Eidfjord Lake, boast salmon and trout fishing.

WHERE TO STAY & DINE

Eidfjord Hotel This fairly standard choice for overnighting lacks the upmarket appeal of the Quality Hotel below. But it does have location going for it. Right next door to the Eidfjord bus stop, this hotel was originally built in 1974 to house workers from the Tyssedal Power Station nearby. In 1994, it was converted into this comfortable but uninspired fjord hotel. Bedrooms have wooden floors and solid, comfortable furnishings, with half of the accommodations opening onto views of the fjord. On-site is a well-run dining room serving quite good Norwegian food, with meals starting at NOK185 ($37/£19).

N-5783 Eidfjord. © **53-66-52-64.** Fax 53-66-52-12. www.eidfjordhotel.no. 28 units. NOK1,350 ($270/£135) double. Children 5 and under stay free in parent's room. Rates include continental breakfast. DC, MC, V. Closed Jan. **Amenities:** Restaurant; bar; sauna; room service. *In room:* TV, no phone.

Quality Hotel & Resort ★★ The architects of this hotel angled the building so that most of its rooms could take advantage of the sun. From the windows of the rooms, you can look out onto some of the most panoramic views in the fjord district. This hotel, completed in 2001, lies by the fjord in Nedre Eidfjord, close to the bus station. Since 1880, visitors to Eidfjord have been staying in an old hotel that stood on this spot. But it was completely torn down and rebuilt, although an old-fashioned decor remains, with a plentiful use of antiques. Some 40 of the rooms open onto views of the fjord, and most of them are carpeted and quite large. The 40 rooms that open onto the fjord also contain complete tub/shower combinations; the rest come equipped with a shower. The dinner buffet here is the best tasting and best value, at NOK235 ($47/£24), at the resort. There's often evening entertainment at the piano bar Monday to Saturday.

N-5783 Eidfjord. ✆ **53-67-41-00.** Fax 53-67-41-11. www.choicehotels.no. 81 units. NOK950–NOK1,495 ($190–$299/£95–£150) double; NOK1,500–NOK2,500 ($300–$500/£150–£250) suite. Children 15 and under stay free in parent's room. Rates include continental breakfast. AE, DC, MC, V. Closed Jan. **Amenities:** Restaurant; bar; laundry service; nonsmoking rooms; rooms for those w/limited mobility. *In room:* A/C, TV, Wi-Fi, minibar.

5 ULVIK: MISTY PEAKS & FRUITY FJORD FARMS ★

149km (92 miles) E of Bergen

Ulvik is a rarity—an unspoiled resort. It lies like a fist at the end of an arm of the Hardangerfjord and is surrounded in the summer by misty peaks and fruit farms. It's the beautiful setting, not an array of attractions, that draws visitors. Ulvik's claim to fame? It's where potatoes first grew in Norway. The village's 1858 church is attractively decorated in the style of the region. It's open June to August daily from 9am to 5pm. Classical concerts, often presented by visiting chamber orchestras from other parts of Europe, are offered in summer inside the church. When a concert is to be presented, notices are posted throughout the town. Other than the enchantment of the hamlet itself, the real reason to stay here is for walking and hiking (see below for our favorite trails).

ESSENTIALS

GETTING THERE If you're not driving, you can reach Ulvik by train or bus from Bergen or Oslo. From either city, take a train to Voss, where you can catch a bus for the 40km (25-mile), 45-minute ride to Ulvik. Buses run from Voss daily, five times in the summer, three in the winter. In Ulvik the bus stops in front of the Ulvik church in the town center. There's no formal bus station.

VISITOR INFORMATION Contact the **Ulvik Tourist Office,** in the town center (✆ **56-52-62-80;** www.visitulvik.com). It's open May 15 to September 15 Monday to Saturday from 8:30am to 5pm and Sunday 1 to 5pm; September 16 to May 14 Monday to Friday 9am to 2pm. The office can arrange excursions, from trips on fjord steamers to bus tours of the Osa mountains.

SEEING THE SIGHTS

A number of do-it-yourself excursions begin at Ulvik; see the tourist office for details. They change seasonally and depend on the weather. Our favorite walk is along the northern tip of the Hardangerfjord, a paradise for hikers. It's home to some 1,000 people and the continent's largest herd of wild reindeer. Mountain trout attract anglers to the area. We've been through this area in July when the cherries ripen, followed in just 3 weeks or so by the most delicious-tasting plums, pears, and apples. It's a great opportunity for a summer picnic, and you can stop to buy fresh fruit and other foodstuffs at one of the roadside farm kiosks.

The Ulvik area offers some of the best walks in the fjord country. These are part of what is known as the **Kulturlandskapsplan** ★ and are divided into four different walks, including the stone-covered grave mounds at Nesheim and Tunheim, the cotter's farm at Ljonakleiv, and a restored country mill in Nordallen in Osa. The tourist office sells a manual, *Heritage Trails of Ulvik,* outlining details on all these walks. The same office will provide information about organized walks on Tuesday and Thursday in summer along forest roads and into the mountains.

SHOPPING

In the center of Ulvik is the summer-only **Husfidsnovae** (no phone), a small crafts shop run by locals who spend their long winter nights concocting arts and handicrafts. For most of them, it's only a hobby; for others, the craft work is a full time job. You'll find woven tablecloths and tapestries, Hardanger embroidery, knitwear, crocheted tablecloths, beadworks for Hardanger folk costumes, ceramics, woodwork, and silver jewelry—all handmade in Ulvik. Hours are irregular, but give it a try to see if it's open.

WHERE TO STAY & DINE

Rica Brakanes Hotel ★★★ There's a famous view of the Hardangerfjord and the surrounding forest from this well-recommended hotel. This is one of the most impressive fjord resorts in the area, although it began modestly enough in 1860 when it opened as a five-bedroom inn. Over the years, it grew, but the building came to a terrible end when German warships opened fire on it in April 25, 1940. When money became available in the post-war era, it was reconstructed and reopened in May 1952. With its custom-designed furniture and textiles, and its very stylish interior, it was hailed as Norway's leading fjord hotel. Soon Princess Juliana of the Netherlands checked in, and she later returned when she was elevated to the throne as Queen. Today all that remains of the original building is one small dining room. The new parts of the hotel are airy, sunny, and comfortable. The guest rooms are midsize to spacious and well maintained. In the summer, plane rides over the fjords can be arranged, and windsurfing and boat rentals are available.

N-5730 Ulvik. ✆ **56-52-61-05.** Fax 56-52-64-10. www.brakanes-hotel.no. 143 units. NOK1,660 ($332/£166) double; NOK2,600 ($520/£260) suite. Rates include buffet breakfast. AE, DC, MC, V. **Amenities:** Restaurant; bar; indoor heated pool; 2 tennis courts; fitness center; sauna; nonsmoking rooms; rooms for those w/limited mobility. *In room:* TV, Wi-Fi, minibar.

Ulvik Fjord Pensjonat ★ (Value) This cozy family-run hotel in the town center hardly competes with the Rica Brakanes, but has habitués who would stay nowhere else. The hospitality and home cooking lure guests back each summer, when they wander the extensive grounds and take in the panoramic views of the fjord. Ulvik Fjord Pensjonat, constructed in two stages, in 1946 and 1977, is one of the finest guesthouses along the Hardangerfjord. The rooms are spacious and pleasantly furnished in regional Norwegian style. You'll be welcomed by the Hammer family, who won the Norwegian Hospitality Prize in 1989. More than 20 years later, the family is still in charge and still extending the hospitality that brought them acclaim.

 N-5730 Ulvik. ✆ **56-52-61-70.** Fax 56-52-61-60. www.ulvikfjordpensjonat.no. 19 units, 17 w/private bathroom. NOK860 ($172/£86) double w/private bathroom. Rates include buffet breakfast. MC, V. Closed Oct–Apr. **Amenities:** Restaurant; bar; lounge; free rowing boat; kids' play area. *In room:* Wi-Fi, hair dryer.

6 VOSS: A WINTER PLAYGROUND ★

38km (24 miles) W of Ulvik; 101km (63 miles) E of Bergen

On the main road between east and west Norway, we know of no better pit stop than Voss. It's also the most folkloric. Between two fjords, Voss is a famous year-round resort and the birthplace of the American football hero Knute Rockne. Maybe the trolls don't strike fear in the hearts of farm children anymore, but revelers dressed as trolls still appear in costumed folklore programs to give visitors a little fun.

Voss is a natural base for exploring the two largest fjords in Norway, the **Sognefjord** to the north and the **Hardangerfjord** to the south. In and around Voss are glaciers, mountains, fjords, waterfalls, orchards, rivers, and lakes.

ESSENTIALS

GETTING THERE From Ulvik, take Hwy. 20 to Rte. 13; then follow Rte. 13 northwest to Voss. If you're not driving, there's frequent train service from Bergen (travel time is 1¼ hr.) and Oslo (5½ hr.). There are six daily buses from Bergen (1¾ hr.) and one bus a day from Oslo, which takes 9 hours (call ✆ **56-52-08-00** for the exact time, usually 8am).

VISITOR INFORMATION The **Voss Information Center** is at Hestavangen 10 (✆ **56-52-08-00;** www.visitvoss.no). It's open June to August Monday to Friday 8am to 7pm, Saturday 9am to 7pm, Sunday noon to 7pm; September to May Monday to Friday 8:30am to 3:30pm.

SEEING THE SIGHTS

St. Olav's Cross, Skulegata, near the Voss Cinema, is the oldest relic in Voss, believed to have been raised when the townspeople adopted Christianity in 1023.

A ride on the **Hangursbanen cable car** (✆ **56-53-02-20**) will be a memorable part of your visit. It offers panoramic views of Voss and its environs. The mountaintop restaurant serves refreshments and meals. The hardy take the cable car up and then spend the rest of the afternoon strolling down the mountain, which is our personal favorite of all the walks possible in the area. A round-trip ride costs NOK90 ($18/£9) for adults, NOK55 ($11/£5.50) for children 7 to 15 and is free for children 6 and under. Entrance to the cable car is on a hillside, a 10-minute walk north of the town center. It's open in summer and winter but closes during the often gray and rainy months of May and September to December.

Vangskyrkje Once an ancient pagan temple stood on this site. In 1271, a Gothic-style stone-built church grew up here. This church has suffered, beginning with a 1536 Lutheran Reformation that destroyed much of its original architecture. What remains is a timbered tower, a Renaissance pulpit, a stone altar, and a triptych, along with fine woodcarvings and a painted ceiling. It's a miracle that anything is left after an aerial attack by the invading Nazis destroyed most of Voss—but the church was relatively undamaged. The church lies a 5-minute walk east of the train station.

Vangsgata 3. ✆ **56-51-22-78.** Admission NOK20 ($4/£2) adults, free for children 16 and under. Daily 10am–4pm. Closed Sept–May.

Voss Folkemuseum We've seen bigger and better folks museums than this, but if you have an hour or so in Voss, you might check it out. Almost a kilometer (1/2 mile) north of Voss on a hillside overlooking the town, this museum consists of more than a dozen farmhouses and other buildings dating from the 1500s to around 1870. They were not moved here but were built on this site by two farm families.

Mølster. ✆ **56-51-15-11.** Admission NOK45 ($9/£4.50) adults, free for children. May–Sept daily 10am–5pm; Oct–Apr Mon–Sat 10am–3pm, Sun noon–3pm.

SKIING

Voss continually adds to its facilities and is definitely in the race to overtake Geilo and Lillehammer as Norway's most popular winter playground. Its eight chairlifts, various ski lifts, and aerial cableway carry passengers up 788m (2,585 ft.). In all, there are 40km (25 miles) of alpine slopes, plus two marked cross-country trails.

The town offers what it calls a "ski circus." Beginners take the Hangursbanen cable car; one ski lift (900m/2,952 ft. long) goes from Traastolen to the top of Slettafjell (with a wide choice of downhill runs), the Bavallen lift is for the slalom slopes, and the downhill runs are at Lonehorgi.

Lessons at the **Ski School** (✆ **56-51-00-32**), at the end of the cable-car run, are moderately priced. The tourist office and hotels can arrange bookings. All equipment is available for rent.

Children 8 and older are allowed on the slopes. A special branch of the Ski School handles these youngsters. Babysitting is available for children 6 and under.

OTHER OUTDOOR PURSUITS

This is Valhalla for fishermen, as there are some 500 lakes and rivers in the greater vicinity of Voss. A local fishing license, costing NOK85 ($17/£8.50), is available at the post office or the tourist office. You can catch trout and char with only local tackle. Fishing guides can be booked through the tourist office.

Voss also offers the best paragliding in Norway, with flights conducted daily in summer from 11am to 5pm, costing NOK1,500 ($300/£150) per person for a tandem flight. The starting point is **Nordic Ventures** (✆ **56-51-00-17**), in the center of town.

Parasailing, water-skiing, and banana boating are possible at the Vangsvatnet, in front of the Park Hotel Vossevangen. The season is from May to October. Parasailing costs NOK550 ($110/£55), water-skiing NOK300 ($60/£30), and banana boating NOK800 ($160/£80). For information, call **Nordic Ventures** (✆ **56-51-00-17**).

River sports are big, and there are a number of outfitters, mainly the **Voss Rafting Center** (✆ **56-51-05-25**), offering not only rafting, but canyoning and river-boarding as well, at prices beginning at NOK770 ($154/£77) per person. Their base is near the Park Hotel, a 3-minute walk from the rail station. The season goes from May 1 to October 1. Other outfitters include **Voss Ski & Surf** (✆ **56-51-30-43**), featuring river kayaking for both neophytes and more skilled kayakers, and **Nordic Ventures** (✆ **56-51-00-17**), offering guided sea kayaking through the Sognefjord, past waterfalls and mountain scenery.

The best campsite in the area is **Tvinde Camping, Tvinde,** N-5700 Voss (✆ **56-51-69-19;** fax 56-51-30-15; www.tvinde.no), near the E16 highway. It's one of the most scenic campsites in central Norway, as it lies beside a waterfall, 12km (7 1/2 miles) from the center of Voss. Both tent sites and cabins, the latter in a two-story building with a veranda, are rented here. The cost of the cabins ranges from NOK400 to NOK540

 ($80–$108/£40–£54) a night, with tent sites costing only NOK150 ($30/£15), plus NOK40 ($8/£4) for adults and NOK20 ($4/£2) for children. The sanitary facilities are rated first class by Norwegian camping guides, and facilities include a washing machine and dryer, along with an on-site kiosk selling groceries. This camp is reached by public bus marked VOSS-GUNVANGEN, leaving from the center of Voss.

Almost as good is **Voss Camping,** Prestegårdsalléen 40 N-5702 Voss (✆ **56-51-15-97;** www.vosscamping.no), located lakeside and convenient to the attractions and sports of Voss. Its reception area and the campsite itself are open May to September 8am to 10pm daily. The site is well maintained, and the accommodations are reasonably comfortable. Decent cabins are rented for NOK500 ($100/£50), with tent sites going for NOK140 to NOK190 ($28–$38/£14–£19). On-site are washing machines and dryers. To reach the campsite, turn left after leaving the rail station and walk along the rim of the lake, turning right onto a little gravel road (signposted) at the local Vangskyrkja Church. Follow this road to the campsite itself. Both the Tvinde and Voss camping sites accept only cash.

WHERE TO STAY

Moderate

Fleischers Hotel ★★★ Kids We've spent more nights at this hotel of character than any other in the fjord district because it's been here forever (okay, 1889). With its peaked, chalet-style roofs and dormers, it looks like something you'd encounter along a lake in Switzerland. Still run by the founding fathers, the Fleischers, the hotel was modernized and expanded, but much of its original charm remains, and there is an inviting ambience in the elegant salons. Fleischers can name-drop with the best of them: King Edward of England when he was Prince of Wales in 1885, Emperor Wilhelm II of Germany in 1890 (his private toilet is still displayed in the reception area), and in 1907 the King of Siam. On the lakefront beside the Voss train station, Fleischers Hotel couldn't be more convenient. The gracious frame hotel has a modern wing with 30 units and terraces overlooking the lake. In the older part of the hotel, the rooms are old-fashioned and more spacious. The restaurant serves an a la carte menu; main courses cost NOK180 to NOK405 ($36–$81/£18–£41). In the summer, a buffet of local fish and Norwegian specialties is served for NOK370 ($74/£37). This hotel does more than any other to cater to kids, featuring a children's pool with many activities, including a varied schedule that ranges from activities programs to a playground and even movies to appeal to kids.

Evangervegen 13, N-5700 Voss. ✆ **56-52-05-00.** Fax 56-52-05-01. www.fleischers.no. 90 units. NOK1,550 ($310/£155) double. Rates include buffet breakfast. AE, DC, MC, V. **Amenities:** Restaurant; bar; lounge; indoor heated pool; 2 saunas; children's activities; room service; babysitting; laundry service/dry cleaning; 1 room for those w/limited mobility. *In room:* TV, minibar, hair dryer, trouser press (in some).

Hotel Jarl After Fleischers, the Jarl comes as a bit of a letdown, although it's comfortable and reliable in every way. In the center of Voss, it's been a durable favorite since its opening in 1972. Maintenance is high here, and all the bedrooms, small to midsize, are tastefully furnished, each featuring a well-equipped bathroom with a tub/shower combination. The chefs prepare a menu of regional specialties and international dishes using high-quality produce, and after dinner you can do a bit of dancing at the hotel's pub and disco.

Elvegata, N-5700 Voss. ✆ **56-51-99-00.** Fax 56-51-99-01. www.jarlvoss.no. 78 units. NOK1,550 ($310/£155) double. Rates include buffet breakfast. AE, DC, MC, V. **Amenities:** Restaurant; bar; pub/disco; indoor heated pool; sauna. *In room:* TV, minibar, safe.

Park Hotel Vossevangen ★ If Fleischers is a bit stuffy for you, Park Hotel Vossevangen offers a livelier venue and a younger crowd. The product of a 1990 merger, this hotel consists of two sections (originally the Park Hotel and the Vossevangen Hotel), joined by a covered passageway. With many of its rooms overlooking Lake Vossevangen, the guest rooms are attractively furnished and contain well-kept bathrooms. The hotel is family-owned and houses the best restaurant in town, the Elysée (see "Where to Dine," below). Facilities include the Café Stationen, the Pentagon Dance Bar, the Stallen Pub, and the Pianissimo Bar. It's in the town center, about 90m (295 ft.) from the train station.

Uttrågate, N-5701 Voss. ✆ **56-53-10-00.** Fax 56-53-10-01. www.parkvoss.no. 131 units. NOK1,300–NOK1,650 ($260–$330/£130–£165) double. Rates include buffet breakfast. AE, DC, MC, V. **Amenities:** Restaurant; bar; lounge; babysitting; nonsmoking rooms; rooms for those w/limited mobility. *In room:* TV, minibar.

Inexpensive

Kringsjå Pension (Kids) This three-story guesthouse in the center of Voss is really a glorified B&B, the best in town. Some parts were built in the 1930s, and others are more modern. The public rooms are spacious and airy, and the guest rooms are simply, comfortably furnished, with good beds but small bathrooms with tub/shower combinations. A room with four to five beds is ideal for families. The hall bathrooms are well maintained and are also equipped with tub/shower combinations. A generous breakfast is served daily, and other meals are sometimes available but must be arranged in advance.

Strengjarhaujen 6, N-5700 Voss. ✆ **56-51-16-27.** Fax 56-51-63-30. www.kringsja.no. 18 units. NOK450 ($90/£45) per person double; NOK410 ($82/£41) per person family room. Children 11 and under half-price. Rates include buffet breakfast. AE, DC, MC, V. **Amenities:** Lounge. *In room:* No phone.

ON THE OUTSKIRTS

Stalheim Hotel ★ (Finds) Part of the fun of staying at this old coaching inn on the former postal route between Oslo and Bergen is getting there, traveling on the dramatic but scary Stalheimskleiva Road, taking more than a dozen hairpin turns between Voss and Flåm. The first hotel here opened in 1885, and in time it attracted royalty including Kaiser Wilhelm II who visited 20 summers in a row. In the heart of the fjord district, with views over the Naerøydalen Valley, the present hotel is the fourth in a series on this site. The hotel's own Museum of Norwegian Folk Art is not only one of the largest in the country, but also one of the best. The rooms are beautifully furnished and well maintained, and the cuisine is one of the finest in the area.

N-5715 Stalheim. ✆ **56-52-01-22.** Fax 56-52-00-56. www.stalheim.com. 124 units. NOK1,500–NOK2,300 ($300–$460/£150–£230) double; NOK1,850 ($370/£185) family unit; NOK2,100 ($420/£210) triple; NOK3,000 ($600/£300) suite. AE, DC, MC, V. Lies 32km (22 miles) N of Voss; follow Rte. E16. **Amenities:** Restaurant; bar; shop. *In room:* Hair dryer.

WHERE TO DINE

Moderate

Elysée FRENCH/NORWEGIAN At this, the town's best restaurant, the food is more satisfying than at Fleischers and based on the freshest ingredients available locally. Ever had baked sea scorpion? You can here. But if that frightens you away, try the filet of lamb marinated in honey prepared like cooks did it in the Middle Ages. In season there is always a lusty game dish on the menu, and everything served here is backed up with one of the best wine lists in the area. Nothing satisfies us for a dessert more than the homemade ice cream with fresh berries and a vanilla sauce. The decor of this prestigious restaurant includes *trompe-l'oeil* murals based on a modern interpretation of the Pantheon.

In the Park Hotel Vossevangen, Uttrågate. ✆ **56-51-13-22.** Reservations recommended. Main courses NOK220–NOK300 ($44–$60/£22–£30); lunch smorgasbord NOK320 ($64/£32); fixed-price dinner NOK410 ($82/£41). AE, DC, MC, V. Sun–Thurs 7:30–10am, 1–3pm, and 7–10pm; Fri–Sat 1–11pm.

Fleischers Restaurant ★ NORWEGIAN The dining room of this landmark hotel, a few steps from the Voss train station, hasn't been altered since the hotel opened over a century ago. Long the leading restaurant in the Voss area, the Victorian-style Fleischers remains the traditionalists' favorite. Its lunchtime smorgasbord is a lavish array of all-you-can-eat Norwegian delicacies. Specialties include smoked salmon and filet of beef, lamb, pork, and veal. This is authentic cuisine that would have pleased Ibsen—a real "taste of Norway." What you won't get are dash and culinary sophistication.

Evangervegen 13. ✆ **56-52-05-00.** Reservations recommended. Lunch smorgasbord NOK250 ($50/£25); main courses NOK180–NOK420 ($36–$84/£18–£42); summer buffet NOK370 ($74/£37). AE, DC, MC, V. Mon–Sat 1–10:30pm; Sun 1–9:45pm.

Inexpensive

Vangen Café **Value** NORWEGIAN Fleischers and Elysée are wonderful for that special occasion, but most diners stop off here for roasted reindeer and other traditional Norwegian food such as locally caught fish. Also try the freshly made cakes or afternoon snacks. The *dagen's menu* (menu of the day) is the best food value in town. A 5-minute walk from the train station in the center, this cafeteria-style outlet is one floor above street level over a small souvenir shop and food market. Soft drinks and fruit juices are served, but no alcohol.

Vangen Super-Market, Vangsgata. ✆ **56-51-12-05.** Smorgasbord NOK50–NOK55 ($10–$11/£5–£5.50); *dagen's menu* (daily specials) NOK100–NOK160 ($20–$32/£10–£16). No credit cards. Mon–Fri 10:30am–6pm; Sat 10:30am–4pm; Sun noon–6pm.

7 BALESTRAND: CENTER FOR SOGNEFJORD ★★

90km (56 miles) N of Voss; 219km (136 miles) NE of Bergen; 204km (126 miles) SW of Fjaerland

You'll get fjord fever if you stay here at the junction of Vetlefjord, Esefjord, and the Fjaerlandsfjord. That's a lot of fjords. But there's more. Balestrand lies on the northern rim of the Sognefjord, Norway's longest and deepest fjord. "Just how deep is the fjord?" we asked a local. "A mermaid could swim all the way to China," he said. Call that West Country exaggeration. The fjord actually measures some 1,308m (4,290 ft.) deep.

When Esias Tegnèr wrote of the snow-covered mountains and the panoramic Sognefjord in the saga of Fridtjof the Brave, the book sold widely and sent an array of artists to the area in the mid-19th century.

Soon Hans Gude, Hans Dahl, Johannes Flintoe, and other well-known Scandinavian artists were painting the fjord and mountain landscapes. Their art became so popular that regular visitors started to flock to Balestrand to take in the glories of the area for themselves—and so they have continued to this day.

ESSENTIALS

GETTING THERE From Voss, continue driving north on Rte. 13 to Vangsnes and board a car ferry for the short crossing northwest to Balestrand. You can also take a train from Bergen or Oslo to Voss or Flåm, and then make bus and ferry connections north to Balestrand. Bus and ferry schedules are available at the Voss tourist office (✆ **56-52-08-00**) and the Flåm tourist office (✆ **57-63-21-06**). From Bergen there are daily express boats to Balestrand; the trip takes 3½ hours.

VISITOR INFORMATION The **Tourist Office** (✆ **57-69-16-17** in winter, or 57-69-12-55 in summer) is in the town center. From June to August, it's open daily 8:30am to 10pm; May and September daily 9am to 8pm; October to April Monday to Saturday 9am to 4pm.

SEEING THE SIGHTS

The staff at the tourist office can help you plan a tour of the area and put you in touch with local craftspeople. There you can pick up a list of constantly changing excursions and buy tickets for one of the scheduled 1½-day tours—for example, a taxi plane across the **Jostedal Glacier.** If offered, the taxi plane, which costs NOK900 to NOK1,100 ($180–$220/£90–£110), is the most dramatic ride in the area.

If you'd like to do something less arranged, and if it's a summer day, we suggest a leisurely stroll south along the banks of the fjord. You'll pass many 19th- and early-20th-century homes and gardens along the way. Less than 1km (½ mile) south along the fjord, you'll come to two **Viking Age burial mounds.** One mound is topped by a statue of the legendary King Bele.

If your appetite's whetted by all the apple trees dotting the landscape, you'll also find several idyllic spots for a picnic.

Want still more walks? Take the small ferry that leaves Balestrand and crosses Esefjord to the Dragsvik side. At this point, you can walk along an old country road that is now abandoned but was in use during the early part of the 20th century. This is a scenic stroll through "forgotten" Norway that goes along for 8km (5 miles).

Kaiser Wilhelm II, a frequent visitor to Balestrand, presented the district with two statues of Old Norse heroes, King Bele and Fridtjof the Bold. They stand in the center of town. Another sight is the English church of **St. Olav,** a tiny wooden building that dates from 1897. The church is closed to the public, but its construction can be admired from outside.

You can explore the area by setting out in nearly any direction on scenic country lanes with little traffic or a wide choice of marked trails and upland farm tracks. The tourist office (see earlier) sells a touring map for NOK85 ($17/£8.50). There's good sea fishing, as well as lake and river trout fishing. Fishing tackle, rowboats, and bicycles can all be rented in the area.

Back in Balestrand, near the ferry dock, you can visit the **Sognefjord Aquarium** (✆ **57-69-13-03**), with its exhibition of saltwater fish. Especially mysterious is the marine life from the world's deepest fjord. The cast of denizens of the deep include Esefjord herring "lip fish," eels, and sharks. The exhibition consists of a number of large and small aquaria, both indoors and out on the jetty. The marine environments have been authentically re-created, including the tidal belt at Munken and the sandy seabed around Staken. A man-made model of Sognefjord shows the currents of the fjord and provides an impression of its depth. There is also an audiovisual presentation. The admission of

Fun Facts A Boot for the Kaiser

Kaiser Wilhelm II of Germany was on holiday in the village of Balestrand, visiting a friend, when World War I broke out. Norwegian authorities gave the kaiser an ultimatum to leave their territory by 6pm that very day. Not being a man to have his pleasures cut short, Kaiser Wilhelm took his jolly good time drinking his tea and savoring impressions of the surrounding landscape before heading full steam out on the fjord aboard his yacht, minutes before the deadline expired.

NOK50 ($10/£5) includes an hour of canoeing on the fjord. It's open mid-April to May and mid-August to October daily 10am to 4pm, June to mid-August daily 9:30am to 6pm.

EXCURSIONS ON THE SOGNEFJORD ★★★

The mighty **Sognefjord,** one of the greatest and most impressive—also one of the deepest—fjords in the world, stretches for a total length of 205km (127 miles). It spreads its powerful "fjord fingers" as far as **Jostedalsbreen,** the country's largest glacier, and to Jotunheimen, Norway's tallest mountain range. The widest and most dramatic part of the fjord stretches from the coast to Balestrand. After Balestrand, the fjord grows much narrower.

If you have a choice, opt for a late spring visit when thousands upon thousands of fruit trees can be seen in full bloom along both banks of the Sognefjord. This region is one of the most beautiful on earth when the blossoms burst forth. The entire district is ideal for skiing, sailing, mountain hiking, and other outdoor activities.

The best way to see the fjord is to take a boat from Bergen operated by **Fylkesbaatane** (✆ **55-90-70-70;** www.fjord1.no/fylkesbaatane). Balestrand is a stopover on the Bergen-to-Flåm line, with departures from Bergen leaving once a day, taking 5½ hours and costing NOK600 ($120/£60) per person.

WHERE TO STAY & DINE

Dragsvik Fjordhotell (Kids) Lying right on a peninsula of natural beauty and opening onto the magnificent Sognefjord, the view from this hotel is like a dream. The hotel itself is more down to earth, billing itself as "a home away from home," which it is, to a certain extent. The same family owners—now in the third generation—built this small guesthouse on a vacation farmland in 1953. It eventually grew into the slightly larger complex that greets you today. Almost a kilometer (½ mile) from Balestrand and 270m (886 ft.) from the ferry quay at Dragsvik, this hotel is a bargain. Units are comfortable and well maintained, if small. Tiny bathrooms come equipped with tub/shower combinations; doubles in the new wing have the most up-to-date plumbing. Some of the accommodations are in what management calls "fjord cabins," complete with kitchen, shower, and toilets. Because these might comfortably house anywhere from two to five guests, these are often rented as family units. The large dining room offers a panoramic view of the Fjaerlandsfjord. You can rent bicycles and rowboats from the staff.

Dragsvik, N-6899 Balestrand. ✆ **57-69-44-00.** Fax 57-69-44-01. www.dragsvik.no. 19 units. NOK545–NOK740 ($109–$148/£55–£74) double; NOK640–NOK740 ($128–$148/£64–£74) cabins. Rates include buffet breakfast. AE, MC, V. Closed Nov–Jan. **Amenities:** Restaurant; bar; room service. *In room:* Hair dryer.

Kviknes Hotel ★★ There was an inn on this site back in 1752, and the present owners, the Kvikne family, who took the inn over in 1877, are still in charge today. As each new generation of Kviknes came along, they made changes and alterations, continuing to expand, either reconstructing or adding new buildings. The hotel was built in the Swiss style and continues to respect its origins, even as it became a completely up-to-date facility. Its public rooms are graced with art and antiques. "We are completely modern," the manager assured us, "but with old world charm."

Patrons who have enjoyed the family hospitality over the years include Kaiser Wilhelm II of Germany, movie stars, international artists, royalty, emperors, prime ministers, and even presidents. At its core it's an elaborately detailed building with balconies opening onto the edge of the fjord. All but a few of the guest rooms have fjord views, and they vary widely in size and style. We go for the units in the original structure, with old-fashioned Norwegian style, flowery fabrics, and spacious bathrooms with tub/shower combinations. Some of these accommodations are furnished with antiques. The less personal rooms are in the annex, where a bland Nordic style prevails. Bathrooms tend to be small to medium in size. The hotel has a large dining room with a beautiful fjord view, several lounges, and a dance club. An extensive buffet is served every night; lunches are less elaborate, with brasserie-style meals. Like the cuisine, the chefs are international but use locally grown ingredients whenever possible. Sports such as water-skiing, windsurfing, and fjord fishing can be arranged, as can helicopter flights to the Jostedal Glacier.

Kviknevegen 8, N-6898 Balestrand. ✆ **57-69-42-00.** Fax 57-69-42-01. www.kviknes.no. 200 units. NOK1,590–NOK2,140 ($318–$428/£159–£214) double; NOK2,590 ($518/£259) suite. Rates include buffet breakfast. AE, DC, MC, V. Closed Oct–Apr. **Amenities:** Restaurant; bar; fitness center; Jacuzzi; sauna; room service; babysitting; laundry service/dry cleaning; nonsmoking rooms; rooms for those w/limited mobility. *In room:* TV, hair dryer.

8 FLÅM: STOPOVER ON EUROPE'S MOST SCENIC TRAIN RIDE ★

96km (60 miles) SE of Balestrand; 165km (102 miles) E of Bergen; 131km (81 miles) E of Voss

Flåm (pronounced "Flawm") lies on the Aurlandsfjord, a tip of the more famous Sognefjord. In the village you can visit the old church (1667), with painted walls done in typical Norwegian country style. But, believe us, the thrill is in the getting there, not in any fantastic attractions once you've arrived.

The best and most exciting way to approach Flåm is aboard the **electric train from Myrdal ★★★**, which connects to trains from Bergen and Oslo. The Flåm Railway is the most thrilling train ride in Scandinavia, and possibly the world. The gradient is 55/1,000 (that is, a gradient of 1 in 18) on almost 80% of the line. The twisting tunnels that spiral in and out of the mountain are manifestations of the most daring and skillful engineering in Norwegian railway history. The electric train follows a 19km (12-mile) route overlooking an 883m (2,896-ft.) drop, stopping occasionally for passengers to photograph spectacular waterfalls. The trip takes 50 minutes. In winter, about four or five trains a day make the run to Flåm. In summer, depending on business, service begins at 7:40am and runs throughout the day. Tickets must be purchased in advance. The one-way fare from Myrdal to Flåm is NOK210 ($42/£21).

ESSENTIALS

GETTING THERE By **car** from Balestrand, take Rte. 55 east along the Sognefjord, crossing the fjord by ferry at Dragsvik and by bridge at Sogndal. At Sogndal, drive east to Kaupanger, where you'll cross the Ardalsfjord by ferry, and head south to Revsnes. In Revsnes, pick up Rte. 11 heading southeast. Drive east until you connect with a secondary road heading southwest through Kvigno and Aurland. From Aurland, take Rte. 601 southwest to Flåm. The whole trip takes 2 to 3 hours, depending on weather and road conditions.

Bus travel is less convenient. One **bus** a day Monday to Saturday runs between Aurland and Flåm. The trip takes 30 minutes.

From May to September, two **ferries** per day cross the fjord between Aurland and Flåm. The trip takes 30 minutes.

Flåm can also be reached by high-speed **express boats** from Bergen, Balestrand, and Leikanger. The boats carry passengers only. In Bergen, call **Fylkesbaatane** (✆ **55-90-70-70;** www.fjord1.no/fylkesbaatane); the one-way trip costs NOK625 ($125/£63).

VISITOR INFORMATION The **tourist office** (✆ **57-63-21-06**), near the railroad station, will rent bikes for NOK110 ($22/£11). It's open May to September daily 8:30am to 8:30pm. Also click on www.visitflam.com for information.

SEEING THE SIGHTS

Flåm is an excellent starting point for car or boat excursions to other well-known centers on the **Sognefjord** ★★★, Europe's longest and deepest fjord. Worth exploring are two of the wildest and most beautiful fingers of the Sognefjord: the **Nærøyfjord** and the **Aurlandsfjord.** Ask at the tourist office about a summer-only cruise from Flåm to both fjords. From Flåm by boat, you can disembark in Gudvangen or Aurland and continue by bus. Alternatively, you can return to Flåm by train.

There are also a number of easy walks in the Flåm district. If time is limited, make that walk along the banks of the **Aurlandsfjord,** leaving the "day-trippers" and the crass souvenirs in the center of Flåm far behind. The setting along the shoreline supports apple orchards, little hamlets, a fisherman's cottage here and there, and farmland where you can sometimes stop in and buy freshly picked fruit.

A map with detailed information is available from the tourist office for NOK60 ($12/£6).

SHOPPING

One of the biggest gift shops in Norway, attracting mainly train passengers, is **Saga Souvenirs** (✆ **57-11-00-11**). Here you'll find all those regional products visitors like to haul away from Norway and take back home. There's an excellent selection of knitwear, along with jewelry and the inevitable trolls.

WHERE TO STAY & DINE

Fretheim Hotel ★★★ A gem of a hotel, this is one of the most charming of all the fjord hotels of western Norway, with a pedigree dating from 1866. A modern annex was added in 2002, although the original and cohesive allure of the place remains. We'd stop over here to patronize the bar, if nothing else, as it opens onto a panoramic vista of the fjord waters. The location is just 50m (164 ft.) from the railway station. Long renowned for its hospitality—even King Harald has dropped in—it continues to maintain its high standards.

The staff is most helpful in planning fjord cruises or horseback riding in the area. Rooms are decorated in light colors and range from small to midsize; try, if possible, to get a unit with a balcony opening onto the fjord. All units contain bathrooms with tub/shower combinations. Even if you're a nonguest, consider stopping off to patronize their excellent restaurant, with salmon, of course, being the chef's specialty. Price ranges from NOK120 to NOK290 ($24–$58/£12–£29), but the real deal is the NOK340 ($68/£34) buffet dinner. Live music will entertain you in the bar.

N-5743 Flåm. ✆ **57-63-63-00.** Fax 57-63-64-00. www.fretheim-hotel.no. 118 units. NOK1,090–NOK1,650 ($218–$330/£109–£165) double; NOK2,450–NOK3,850 ($490–$770/£245–£385) suite. Children 5 and under stay free in parent's room. Rates include continental breakfast. AE, DC, MC, V. **Amenities:** Restaurant; bar; room service; laundry service/dry cleaning; nonsmoking rooms; rooms for those w/limited mobility. *In room:* TV, hair dryer, safe.

Heimly Pension (Value) This is the more affordable choice in town, lying next to Aurlandsfjord, only 400m (1,312 ft.) from the Flåm railway. It is a cozy family-run B&B dating from the 1950s and still carrying the aura of that time. Designed in the style of an A-frame chalet, it offers a ground-floor lounge where international travelers gather. The small to midsize guest rooms are tastefully and comfortably furnished, with well-maintained private bathrooms equipped with showers. The best views over the fjord are on the two upper floors. A lively pub and a good restaurant serving home-style meals are in an annex across the road.

N-5742 Flåm. ✆ **57-63-23-00.** Fax 57-63-23-40. www.heimly.no. 25 units. NOK720–NOK990 ($144–$198/£72–£99) double. Rates include buffet breakfast. AE, DC, MC, V. Closed Dec 24–Jan 2. **Amenities:** Restaurant; bar. *In room:* No phone.

9 GEILO: A WINTER WONDERLAND

109km (68 miles) SE of Flåm; 239km (148 miles) E of Bergen; 239km (148 miles) W of Oslo

Most motorists in summer driving between Oslo and Bergen (or vice versa) have to make a choice—Geilo or Voss? After checking out these resorts in both summer and winter over the years, we recommend Voss in the summer, because of all its folkloric activities, instead of Geilo, which can be a bit dull when the July sun shines.

In contrast, we have found Geilo in winter to be the best in the area for skiing. But part of the fun of visiting this town in winter, as it is in any alpine retreat, is to enjoy the lavish après-ski life of drinking and dining. In that regard, Geilo as a resort ranks higher than any other ski area in Norway, even when pitted against the more famous Lillehammer.

Geilo lies some 792m (2,598 ft.) above sea level in the Hol mountain district. Although it's not strictly in the fjord country, it's included here because it's a "gateway" there en route from Oslo to Bergen. The Geilo area boasts 130km (81 miles) of marked cross-country skiing tracks.

ESSENTIALS

GETTING THERE From Flåm, motorists return to Aurland to connect with Rte. 50. It runs southeast through the towns of Steine, Storestølen, Hovet, and Hagafoss. In Hagafoss, connect with Rte. 7 going southwest into Geilo. If you're dependent on public transportation, forget about the meager long-distance bus service and opt for the train connections via Oslo or Bergen. From Oslo, the fare is NOK437 ($87/£44) per person one-way, and the trip takes 3½ hours; from Bergen, it's NOK392 ($78/£39) one-way and takes 3 hours.

VISITOR INFORMATION The **Turistinformasjonen** office is at Vesleslåtteveien 13 in the town center (✆ **32-09-59-00**). It's open June to August daily from 9am to 9pm; September to May Monday to Friday 8:30am to 5pm, Saturday 8:30am to 3pm. The town doesn't use street addresses, but everything is laid out easily enough to find. Also visit www.geilo.no for information.

OUTDOOR ACTIVITIES

Geilo is both a summer and a winter destination, although its claim to fame is as a skiing resort, the main season lasting from January to March. If you plan on doing a lot of skiing, it's best to purchase the **Vinterlandkoret Ski Pass** at the tourist office. This pass, costing NOK340 ($68/£34) per day or NOK1,415 ($283/£142) per week, is good for all five ski centers in the area, as well as the network of slopes in such nearby resorts as Ål, Uvdal, and Hemesdal.

Of the five different ski centers, our most preferred is **Geilo Skiheiser** (✆ **32-09-59-20**), with 24km (15 miles) of slopes, many as good as those in the Swiss Alps, plus 130km (81 miles) of cross-country trails along with 18 lifts and a "ski-board" tunnel.

The favorite area for families is **Vestlia** (✆ **32-09-55-10**), west of Ustedalsfjord. Other ski centers are found at **Havsdalsenternet** (✆ **32-09-17-77**), which Norwegian young people have adopted as their favorite; and **Slaatta**(✆ **32-09-02-02**), with its wide range of alpine and cross-country trails (though not as good as those of Geilo Skiheiser, above).

In all, Geilo, Norway's most popular winter resort, offers 18 lifts and 33 runs. All the ski centers are linked by a free shuttle bus service. Cross-country skiers will find a total of 220km (136 miles) of marked trails through forests, hills, and moors to **Hardangervidda,** Europe's largest mountain plateau. (See "Eidfjord: Western Gateway to Hardangervidda," earlier in this chapter.)

In summer, mountain tracking is the passion. Some of the greatest hikes in central Norway are open to you, and the Geilo tourist office is most helpful in offering expert guidance and furnishing maps. There is a network of marked routes and pathways established since ancient days. Geilo cable cars take you to the top of the resort at 1,060m (3,477 ft.) above sea level. From that vantage point, marked trails split off in many directions.

When you get tired of hiking, you can always take up canoeing, cycling, or horseback riding. To go rafting and canoeing, call **Dagali Rafting** (✆ **32-09-38-20**), which organizes trips in the Dagali and Sjoa areas around Geilo. Depending on the day of the week, trips begin at NOK325 ($65/£33), going up to NOK810 ($162/£81). On your own, you can rent canoes and rowboats at **Fagerli Leirskole,** Skurdalen (✆ **32-09-47-25**).

For horseback riding, call **Hakkesetstølen** (✆ **32-09-09-20**). You can ride the happy trails from June to October.

To go biking in the area, stop by first at the Geilo tourist office for a cycling map. On your rented bike, you can set out to explore summer roads leading into the surrounding mountains. Bikes can be rented in the center of Geilo at **Intersport Geilo** (✆ **32-09-55-80**), costing NOK180 to NOK300 ($36–$60/£18–£30) per day.

Fishermen flock here to try their luck in the region's nearly 100 mountain lakes or stretches of river, which can be fished from June to September. A fishing license costing NOK80 ($16/£8) is available at the tourist office, and fishing boat rentals and tackle are available for rent through **Fagerli Leirskole** (✆ **32-09-47-25**), costing NOK160 ($32/£16) per day.

SEEING THE SIGHTS

The most exciting possibility is to book an organized tour at the tourist office for glacier trekking on **Hardangerjøkulen,** at 1,860m (6,101 ft.). These are available Monday, Wednesday, and Friday from July 1 to September 15. The tour takes 10 hours and costs NOK600 ($120/£60) per person, including a train ride to and from Finse.

A number of other tours are offered as well: rafting from NOK750 to NOK875 ($150–$175/£75–£88), river boarding (a new high-adrenaline sport involving a white-water trip downstream on a high-impact plastic board-cum-flotation device) from NOK730 to NOK810 ($146–$162/£73–£81), and a 2-hour moose safari for NOK450 ($90/£45). This latter jaunt is offered only on Thursday evening (when the moose can be seen) from July 1 to September 15.

Back in the center of town, but only in July, you can visit **Geilojorget,** a 17th-century farm, which is open daily from 11am to 5pm. Some old houses, 2 or 3 centuries old, have been moved to the site and are open for guided tours. You can see how farmers lived at the time and visit such buildings as a storage house or the cattle barn. Cultural activities are also presented at the time, including folk music shows. On-site is a cafe serving old-time dishes; if you've ever wanted to try a sour-cream cookie, this is the place for you.

WHERE TO STAY

Dr. Holms Hotel ★★★ Kids This is our preferred stopover when driving across Norway between Oslo and Bergen. One of the most famous resort hotels in Norway, it is also the area's finest place to stay. Here, near the railroad station, you get elegance, comfort, and traditional styling, as the hotel is filled with art and antiques. Dr. J. C. Holms, a specialist in respiratory diseases who established the resort so that patients could breathe fresh mountain air, opened the hotel in 1909. After being occupied by the Nazis from 1940 to 1945, it was freed by the Norwegian resistance in May 1945. There have been many changes since, including the addition of two wings and a swimming complex. The latest major overhaul took place at the time of the millennium, but since then other smaller improvements have been made to keep the hotel operating in tiptop shape. Original works of art decorate the hotel. Guest rooms, including 11 family rooms, are beautifully furnished in a romantic English style and offer many luxuries.

N-3580 Geilo. ✆ **32-09-57-00.** Fax 32-09-16-20. www.drholms.com. 126 units. NOK1,600 ($320/£160) double; NOK1,850–NOK2,375 ($370–$475/£185–£238) suite. Rates include buffet breakfast. AE, DC, MC, V. **Amenities:** Restaurant; bar; wine cellar; indoor heated pool; children's pool; fitness center; sauna; room service; babysitting; laundry service/dry cleaning; library; nonsmoking rooms; rooms for those w/limited mobility. *In room:* TV, Wi-Fi, minibar.

Highland Hotel ★ Within walking distance of the ski slopes, this hotel is a good, substantial choice, a viable alternative to the very pricey Dr. Holms or the Nye Vestlia. Bedrooms are small to midsize, each comfortably furnished, though nothing lavish. The standard of maintenance is high, and the staff is one of the more efficient in the area. We gravitate to the on-site restaurant, Smiu Biffverksted, a steakhouse with high-quality beef. The hotel is also one of the finest choices if you'd like to stay in at night, as it offers a piano bar and a nightclub.

Lienvegen 11 N-3580 Geilo. ✆ **32-09-61-00.** Fax 32-09-61-01. www.highland.no. 160 units. NOK1,030 ($206/£103) double; NOK1,300 ($260/£130) family room. MC, V. **Amenities:** 3 restaurants; bar; nightclub; indoor heated pool; fitness center; sauna; children's playroom; laundry service. *In room:* TV.

Nye Vestlia Resort ★★★ (Kids) Check into Dr. Holms Hotel for a time-mellowed atmosphere of tradition, but book into this vastly enlarged and modernized hotel for contemporary comfort, including the best spa between Oslo and Bergen. From a hotel originally built in the 1960s, Helene Hennie, one of Norway's most renowned interior architects, designed and worked on the resort. As part of the complex, there are 34 double and family rooms in small cabins surrounding the main hotel building. Eleven slightly worn-down cabins lie in idyllic locations in the birch forest with views over Ustedalsfjord and Geilo itself.

Although the cuisine here doesn't quite match the level of Hallingstuene (see below), it is nonetheless sublime. Chefs use fresh ingredients from the four corners of the world to compose a menu of traditional Scandinavian food and modern international dishes. Those chefs dazzle with everything from a nine-course gourmet international dinner to a classic mountain buffet.

Some of the best cross-country skiing in the area begins at the resort's doorstep. The kid-friendly resort also has the best skiing in Norway for children; there's even a ski lift system suitable for kids and a children's ski club. In summer, guests go hiking, boating, or horseback riding, and most definitely they play golf—one of the reasons many check in here, with programs in this sport for the kiddies as well. The best nighttime entertainment is also provided at Nye Vestlia, including live dance music almost every evening year-round except Sunday.

N-3580 Geilo. ✆ **32-08-72-00.** Fax 32-08-72-01. www.vestlia.no. 120 units. NOK1,025–NOK2,600 ($205–$520/£103–£260) double, including full board. AE, DC, MC, V. **Amenities:** 3 restaurants; dance bar; indoor heated pool; golf course; tennis court; fitness center; exclusive spa; sauna; Jacuzzi; playground; babysitting; laundry service/dry cleaning; solarium; rooms for those w/limited mobility. *In room:* TV, minibar.

Ustedalen Hotel Geilo (Value) This hotel started out in 1890 renting rooms to engineers who were working on the Bergen railroad. Later it became a center for persons seeking convalescence. Converted into a holiday hotel in the 1970s, it is a privately owned establishment that has been upgraded by the addition of a swimming pool. Bedrooms are small but comfortably furnished, each with modern furniture and a private bathroom with shower. On location is a good restaurant serving tasty, traditional mountain food, its windows opening onto a view of the Ustedalsfjord.

Gamleveien 32, N-3580 Geilo. ✆ **32-09-67-00.** Fax 32-09-67-01. www.ustedalen.no. 86 units. NOK520–NOK1,150 ($104–$230/£52–£115) per person. Rates include buffet breakfast. Rates include half-board (minimum 2 nights). MC, V. **Amenities:** Restaurant; dance bar; indoor heated pool; sauna. *In room:* TV.

WHERE TO DINE

Most visitors to Geilo eat in their hotels, but here are a few additional options.

Hallingstuene ★★★ NORWEGIAN/INTERNATIONAL Leading Norwegian food critics agree this is the best eats on the cross-country route between Oslo and Bergen. Set within a red-painted antique house near the railway station, Hallingstuene is the most elegant restaurant in Geilo. You'll dine surrounded by dozens of old-fashioned landscapes in an atmosphere evocative of a mountain cottage in a Norwegian forest. It's the domain of Frode Aga, a celebrity chef. Menu items, many of them composed from locally available ingredients, manage to be simultaneously elegant and rustic. Some fine offerings include grilled mountain trout; carpaccio of reindeer; and an old-fashioned starter, *rake fiske,* which consists of boiled mountain trout that's marinated (or preserved) for 3 months in a mixture of salt brine and sugar. Main courses include a pungent version of grilled filets of either venison or reindeer, served in a wine-flavored game sauce, with forest mushrooms. Dessert might be a delicacy such as boiled and sweetened cloudberries with vanilla ice cream.

Geiloveien 56. ✆ **32-09-12-50.** Reservations recommended. Main courses NOK225–NOK325 ($45–$65/£23–£33). AE, DC, MC, V. Tues–Sun 5–10pm (until 11pm Sat).

Ro Kro Value NORWEGIAN This place doesn't aspire to be more than it is, a mere refueling stop where you can eat through the night—well, at least until 10pm. In a town celebrated for its cuisine, this is no more than a convenience cafeteria. But it's good for what it is, providing succulent pastas and hearty stews, even grills such as reindeer steaks, when you come in out of the cold or stop off after hiking in summer. Many locals come here for the sandwiches or freshly made salads offered throughout the day. Unlike many cafeterias in Norway, this one maintains a full bar and a selection of beers.

In the Ro Hotell, Geiloveien. ✆ **32-09-08-99.** Reservations not accepted. Main courses NOK110–NOK230 ($22–$46/£11–£23). AE, DC, MC, V. Daily 9am–8pm or 10pm, depending on business.

10 FJAERLAND: ARTISTS & MOUNTAINEERS ★★

62km (38 miles) S of Olden

A town without road connections until 1986, Fjaerland lies along the banks of the Fjaer landsfjord, a scenic branch of the greater Sognefjord. Overpopulation is hardly a problem here. Back in the Viking age, some 300 hearty souls lived here. Amazingly, today's population is about the same number. Locals tell us that dozens of its stout-hearted citizens emigrated to America at the turn of the 19th century, heading for such places as the Dakotas or Minnesota. Looking around at the stunning beauty of the area makes us wonder why they left in the first place. The landscape, shaped by glaciers through various ice ages over the past 3 million years and by towering mountains, glacier rivers, and U-shaped valleys, has attracted landscape painters from all over the world.

Mountaineers find the terrain here some of the most challenging in Norway, as both the Supphelle Glacier and the Bøya Glacier come down to the floor of the valley in Fjaerland. Both of these glaciers are "pups," the term for chunks of ice that fall from a massive glacier—in this case, Jostedalsbreen, the largest on the European continent. The lower Supphelle, at an elevation of 60m (197 ft.), is the lowest-lying glacier in southern Norway.

The center of the Fjaerland is a section called Mundal, with a church, school, shops, and accommodations. Its population, incidentally, is the most well-read in Scandinavia, so it's not surprising that Fjaerland is called "the book town of Norway." Book lovers from all over the world come here to peruse its shops, especially its legendary second-hand-book shops.

ESSENTIALS

GETTING THERE From the resort of Balestrand (see "Balestrand: Center for Sognefjord," earlier in this chapter), ferries depart from Fjaerland at 8:15am daily. Several buses run daily between Fjaerland and the transportation hub at Sogndal, taking 45 minutes and costing NOK110 ($22/£11) one-way. Daily buses also run to and from Stryn (see below), taking 2 hours and costing NOK220 ($44/£22) one-way. Motorists from Olden can take E39, following the signposts to Skei, a village at the base of Lake Jølster. There the road goes under the glacier for more than 6km (3¾ miles) for the final lap into Fjaerland. The tunnel on the Skei road is free; however, if you're driving from Sogndal, you must pay a toll of NOK200 ($40/£20).

VISITOR INFORMATION The **Fjaerland Tourist Information Center** (© **57-69-32-33;** www.fjaerland.org) lies on the main road in Mundal and is open daily from 9am to 5pm June to August. It also doubles as a bookshop.

SEEING THE SIGHTS

This is great hiking country in summer, as parts of Fjaerland lie within the **Jostedalsbreen Nasjonalpark (Jostedalsbreen National Park) ★★★**, a landscape that ranges from mountains to glaciers, from fjords to low-lying valleys. Our favorite of the scenic routes is at the southern tier of the park, lying between Lunde and Fjaerland, and crossing Marabreen.

At the head of the fjord lies the **Bøyaøyri Estuary ★**, a protected nature reserve, 2km (1¼ miles) north of the village. In the spring and fall migrations, 90 species of birds can be spotted passing through the area. Some 50 species make their nests at Fjaerland, so birders from all over Scandinavia flock here.

The best trail for the average visitor in good physical condition is from the Supphelle Valley up to the mountain hut Flatbrehytta. The more adventurous go on from this mountain hut to explore the glaciers. The local sports association in Fjaerland has mapped out 10 other trails, ranging from a relatively easy 1-hour walk to more difficult treks of 5 to 6 hours. At visitor information, you can pick up a map, *Turkart Fjaerland,* for NOK80 ($16/£8), outlining all these walks in great detail.

It's possible to drive within 500m (1,640 ft.) of the Supphelle Glacier. You can stroll over and actually touch the ice, if you want to. During a period in summer from the first of July to August 10, you can take guided glacier trips on Supphelle, starting from the car park at the northeast of the Norsk Bremuseum (see below), 4km (2½ miles) off Rte. 5. Trips leave Monday to Saturday at 9am, and the jaunt includes a hike up the Kvanneholtnipa Mountain, at 1,640m (5,379 ft.).

In town, you can visit the **Norsk Bremuseum (Norwegian Glacier Museum;** © **57-69-32-88**), which is open June to August daily 9am to 7pm. In April and May, and again in September and October, it's open daily 10am to 4pm. Admission is NOK110 ($22/£11) for adults or NOK50 ($10/£5) for children, with a family ticket going for NOK240 ($48/£24). This is very much a hands-on museum. Exhibits inform you about how fjords are formed, and there is a multiscreen audiovisual show on the Jostedal Glacier. You can perform your own experiments with thousand-year-old glacier ice. You can also see a mammoth tusk from the largest mammal ever to live in Norway; it's some 30,000 years old. Exhibits also tell the story of Ötzi, "the man from the ice," whose 5,000-year-old body was found in a glacier in the European Alps in 1991.

Time permitting, you should also visit **Astruptunet ★**, lying across the southern shore of Lake Jølster and reached from the center of Fjaerland after a 10-minute drive. Celebrated for his landscapes, Nicolai Astrup (1880–1928) was one of the country's best-known and most-reproduced artists. You can visit the studio where he died and wander about a colony of little sod-roofed buildings. Some of his artwork is on view. Guides bring Astrup alive again with their colorful anecdotes. On-site is a cafe serving old-fashioned sour-cream porridge, tasty waffles, and coffee. The location is at Sandal i Jolster

(✆ **57-72-67-82**), and admission is NOK50 ($10/£5) for adults and NOK25 ($5/£2.50) for children. It's open daily May 23 to the end of August 11am to 4pm.

SHOPPING

Norway's book town offers some 20,000 books for sale in a dozen or so secondhand shops, which remain open from mid-May to the beginning of September from 10am to 6pm daily. Most of the titles are in Norwegian, but there are many English-language books, including some rare ones. Contact **Den norske bokbyen** at ✆ **57-69-22-10** for more information.

WHERE TO STAY & DINE

Hotel Mundal ★★ Although up-to-date, this hotel is one of the best examples of the fashionable architecture that characterized the hotels in Norway in the closing years of the 19th century, the era when Norwegians first started heading for scenic resorts for a vacation. Beloved of landscape painters and glacier hikers for decades, this hotel dates from 1891 and has been operated by the same family ever since. A bit quirky, with its wooden scrollwork, peaked roofs, cavernous dining room, and round tower, it would be the Addams family's hotel of choice if they were traveling the fjord country. In the center of Fjaerland, it lies 3km (1¾ miles) from the glacier museum. Although old-fashioned, it has kept abreast of the times with constant improvements. The helpful staff will offer bikes or rowboats and assist you in your mountain- and glacier-climbing plans.

Bedrooms come in a range of sizes and styles, but all are comfortably and traditionally furnished, with private bathrooms equipped with tub/shower combinations. Even if you're passing through for the day, consider stopping at the hotel's restaurant for a traditional Norwegian meal of regional specialties. A lavish four-course dinner goes for NOK540 ($108/£54).

N-6848 Fjaerland. ✆ **57-69-31-01.** Fax 57-69-31-79. www.fjordinfo.no/mundal. 35 units. NOK835–NOK1045 ($167–$209/£84–£105) per person double; NOK1,300 ($260/£130) per person suite. Rates include breakfast. DC, MC, V. Closed Oct–Apr. **Amenities:** Restaurant; cafe; bar; lounge; laundry service; library. *In room:* TV, beverage maker.

11 LOEN/OLDEN/STRYN & THE JOSTEDAL GLACIER

50km (31 miles) S of Hellesylt

For a close encounter with nature, little changed over the centuries, come to this incredible land created by the last Ice Age. Other Scandinavian countries, especially Denmark, but also Sweden, just can't compete with what Mother Nature has to show us here. Choose one of the cluster of hamlets and little resorts for your base and set out for trips through the Jostedalsbren National Park or other scenic wonders. It doesn't matter which village you choose as a base because they are all within easy reach of one another, essentially forming the same community.

The largest settlement, with a population of only 1,500, is **Stryn,** the capital of the upper Nordfjord district. **Olden** is one of the best centers for excursions to the Briksdal Glacier. Its population is 800. Even smaller is **Loen,** with only 400 residents. Loen lies at the mouth of the panoramic Lodalen valley and is used by many as the gateway into the national park. The village itself is touristy and of little interest, but it makes a good refueling stop for some of the most dramatic excursions in Norway.

ESSENTIALS

GETTING THERE Stryn is your gateway to the area, as it is linked by public transportation to major cities in Norway. **Nor-Way Buss Ekspress** (✆ **81-54-44-44;** www.nor-way.no) travels west from Oslo at the rate of three times daily, taking 8½ hours and costing NOK580 ($116/£58) one-way. There are also three to five buses daily from Bergen, taking 6 hours and costing NOK451 ($90/£45) one-way. The buses also stop at Olden and Loen.

Motorists leaving Geiranger (see below) can continue south to Stryn, taking the ferry across the Geirangerfjord to the town of Hellesylt, the trip taking less than an hour. From Hellesylt, take Rte. 60 into Stryn. Once at Stryn, you can drive immediately to the east to Loen or south to Olden. Distances are short—for example, Loan lies only 10km (6¼ miles) from Stryn.

VISITOR INFORMATION The **Stryn & Nordfjord Reisemål** (✆ **57-87-40-40;** www.nordfjord.no) is most helpful, dispensing information about touring the entire area, including hiking trips into the national park. It offers a free booklet, *Guide for Stryn,* outlining trips and cycling routes, and it also rents mountain bikes at the rate of NOK190 ($38/£19) per day, NOK120 ($24/£12) per half-day, NOK50 ($10/£5) per hour. In July, it's open daily 8:30am to 8pm; in June and August daily 8am to 6pm, and September to May Saturday and Sunday 9am to 4pm.

There is also **Olden Tourist Information** (✆ **57-87-31-26**) in the center of the village, open June 10 to August 15 from 10am to 6pm daily.

SEEING THE SIGHTS

In addition to the wonders of Norway's largest glacier, Jostedal, the little towns and villages of Olden, Loen, and Stryn are good bases for trips on the **Nordfjord** ★★★, which is the only fjord to rival the scenic wonders of Sognefjord. The panoramic Nordfjord, with its deep-blue waters, penetrates inland from the coast for 100km (62 miles) before it abruptly halts at the glacier itself. If you have a car, you can **drive the length of the north bank** ★★ along Rte. 15 almost to the head of the fjord at Loen. This is one of the grand motor trips of the fjord country. In the distance are snowcapped mountain peaks, and along the way are many grazing pastures, fjord farms, and rock-strewn promontories.

Jostedalsbreen National Park ★★★

Jostedalsbreen is an ice plateau, spreading across 487 sq. km (190 sq. miles) dominating the inner Nordfjord district and stretching out in the direction of Sognefjord and the majestic Jotunheimen mountains. Sprawling northeast from Rte. 5 to Rte. 15, it plunges a total of two dozen "arms" into the neighboring valleys.

In certain parts, the mammoth ice mountain is 400m (1,312 ft.) thick, reaching up to 1,950m (6,396 ft.) above sea level. Wildlife includes reed deer, elk, brown bear, and smaller creatures such as hares and elusive squirrels.

For years until the advent of modern engineering, the glacier formed an almost impenetrable barrier between the east and west of Norway.

Beginning in 1991, Norway placed the glacier under the protection of the Jostedalsbreen Nasjonalpark (Jostedalsbreen National Park).

Before setting out, visit the **Jostedalsbreen Nasjonalparksenter** at Oppstryn (**© 57-87-72-00**), lying 15km (9¼ miles) east of the town of Stryn. Exhibits tell you everything you ever wanted to know about glaciers—and a lot more. You're treated to a panoramic history of the glacier from "attacks" by meteorites to avalanches. We found a highlight to be wandering through the **Arctic Garden ★★**, with 325 species of endemic plant life. The center is open May to September daily 10am to 4pm (June 18–Aug 13 10am–6pm), charging NOK80 ($16/£8) for adults, NOK45 ($9/£4.50) for children.

Nigardsbreen ★

The Jostedal is noted for its glacial "arms," sometimes called "tongues," which shoot out into valleys, flowing from the plateau glacier. The most famous of these glacial tongues is **Nigardsbreen ★★**. This section is a remnant of the ice sheet that covered Norway 10,000 years ago.

The well-preserved moraine landscape looks much as it did centuries ago, or so scientists believe. Biochemical dating has also found that many moraines date from the "Little Ice Age" that culminated only about 250 years ago. At that time, a deterioration in climate made the Jostedal glacier grow, as its tongues surged forward, damaging farms and vegetation in the valley. The Nigard valley and the Nigard glacier are still studied by scientists every year who keep a watch on it.

Nigardsbreen is one of the most popular areas for climbing and walking, a virtual ice-blue wonderland of deep crevasses and oddly shaped pinnacles. From May until mid-September, walks are possible. During the other months, weather conditions are too harsh.

At Nigardsbreen you can visit the **Jostedal Breheimsenteret** at Jostedal (**© 57-68-32-50**), which is designed in the shape of twin ice peaks divided by a crevasse, nicknamed the "Glacier cathedral." In addition to a film on the glacier, you can see exhibits about the formation and continued movement of this awesome ice block here.

The center is open May to September daily from 10am to 7pm. Before June 21 and after August 20, hours are daily 10am to 5pm. Admission is NOK50 ($10/£5) for adults, NOK35 ($7/£3.50) for children 10 to 14.

In Jostedal, you can hook up with **Jostedalen Breførarlag** (**© 57-68-31-11**) for **guided glacier walks ★★**, including a short trip across the Nigardsvatnet and a hike along the glacier arm. This walk carries our most enthusiastic endorsement, and it's one of the most dramatic in terms of winter wonderland scenery in the fjord district. Tours take 1 hour, costing NOK200 ($40/£20). Three-hour walks on ice are also possible in summer, leaving at 12:15pm daily and costing NOK475 ($95/£48) per person. From June 30 to August 20, there is an additional afternoon departure leaving at 10:15am.

Briksdalsbreen (the Briksdal Glacier) ★★

One of the most dramatic natural sights of Norway, this glacier is reached from the large village of Olden by taking a signposted panoramic road for 24km (15 miles). The route winds its way to the double glacial "arms" of the Briksdalsbreen and Brenndalsbreen ice masses. The Briksdal glacier is not only the most accessible, but also the most stunning glacier. Nearby residents grew alarmed in the 1990s when it advanced by 300m (984 ft.), but it now seems to be retreating.

The water flowing from the glacier forms a trio of lakes in the valley, which have a dramatic emerald-green color. For a part of the jaunt up the glacier, you can take a two-wheeled cart pulled by a *stolkjerre,* one of those sturdy-footed fjord horses.

Along the way you'll pass by a thundering waterfall. At the end of the track, hikers may wander deeper into the glacier mass to a height of 1,700m (5,576 ft.), a distance of only 346m (1,135 ft.) above sea level. In summer, the glacier can be seen "pupping"—that is, giving birth to smaller chunks of ice that fall from the mother lode.

Rides are available from **Oldedalen Skysslag** (✆ **57-87-68-05**), costing NOK200 ($40/£20) for adults and NOK115 ($23/£12) for children, for the 15-minute jaunt.

The best **organized tours** ★★ are conducted by **Briksdal Breføring** (✆ **57-87-68-00**) at the Briksdalsbre Fjellstove at Briksdalsbre, a small hotel. A 3-hour hike on the ice costs NOK350 ($70/£35). In summer, there are five departures a day, beginning at 10am, with the last one setting out at 4pm.

Stryn

Stryn was put on the map by British fishermen coming to catch salmon in its waters back in the 1860s. Since then it has grown and developed into a major resort in the fjord district. The **Stryn Sommerskisenter (Summer Ski Center)** lies on the Tystigen branch of the Jostedalsbreen. This area offers the country's best summer skiing and is a popular setting for photographers capturing beauties skiing in their bikinis. Its longest run stretches 2,100m (6,888 ft.), with a drop of 518m (1,699 ft.). In addition, some 10km (6¼ miles) of cross-country ski tracks are offered. Lift tickets for 1 day cost NOK360 ($72/£36), and ski equipment is available for rent. For more information, call the center at ✆ **92-25-83-33.**

The road to the ski center, **Gamble Strynefjellsvegen** ★★, is one of the most dramatic in central Norway, with hairpin curves. It goes past waterfalls, glacier arms, or tongues, and opens onto panoramic vistas at an altitude of 1,139m (3,736 ft.).

Olden

This little resort makes a great launchpad for jaunts to the Briksdal glacier (see above). In town, you can visit **Singersamlinga** (✆ **57-87-31-06**), which displays the artwork of William Henry Singer of Pittsburgh, a famous American millionaire. Singer and his wife, Anna Spencer, spent summers in Olden from 1913 until the late 1930s. He was fond of painting landscapes of western Norway. The house can be visited by appointment by calling ✆ **57-87-31-06.** The cost is NOK40 ($8/£4) for adults, or NOK20 ($4/£2) for children.

Loen

A small fjord farming hamlet, this is a summer resort with many outdoor pursuits. It is also the site of some of the best accommodations in the area.

From Loen you can take one of the most scenic trips in the area to the beautiful **Kjenndal Glacier** ★, lying 17km (11 miles) along a glacial lake, the Lovatnet. This is the least visited of the glaciers.

You can take a boat, the *Kjenndal,* going up Lovatnet from Sande and costing NOK200 ($40/£20) per person, including a return bus from the Kjenndalstova Kafe (✆ **91-84-87-67**), a cafe-restaurant with some of the most panoramic views of the area. The cafe is close to the Kjenndal Glacier, so you can soak in the backdrop of cascading waterfalls as you enjoy your freshly caught trout. Closed October to April. From the cafe, it's a 2km (1¼-mile) hike to the glacier's face.

Boats depart Sande from June to August, leaving daily at 10:30am.

WHERE TO STAY & DINE

Alexandra ★★ English tourists used to dominate as the majority guests here. When the guests were allowed to select a name for the hotel, probably in 1892, they dubbed it Alexandra—a label that is still honored to this day. The most luxurious hotel in the area, the Alexandra dates from 1884 and has been run by the Grov family since it opened. The hotel is also the best equipped in the area, making it the town's only real resort hotel. The hotel received its last wholesale renovation before the millennium, but needed repairs have occurred every year since that time. All the bedrooms are different sizes, but all come with up-to-date furnishings. The location makes a good base for touring the attractions of the Nordfjord and the national park, including the Briksdal Glacier. The hotel for decades has been known for its cuisine, and the same high standards still prevail. The only difference is that the menu is no longer strictly Norwegian, but wanders the globe for inspiration. It's also a fine choice for dining for nonguests, serving a lavish buffet dinner costing NOK455 ($91/£46) per person. Or you can select one of its a la carte meals.

N-6789 Loen. ✆ **57-87-50-00.** Fax 57-87-50-51. www.alexandra.no. 189 units. NOK2,520–NOK2,920 ($504–$584/£252–£292) double. Children 4 and under stay free in parent's room. Rates include half-board. AE, DC, MC, V. Closed Dec 15–27 and Jan 1–25. **Amenities:** Restaurant; 3 bars; nightclub; outdoor pool; fitness center; Jacuzzi; spa; sauna; room service; babysitting; laundry service/dry cleaning; nonsmoking rooms; rooms for those w/limited mobility. *In room:* TV, minibar, hair dryer.

Briksdalbre Although primarily a restaurant, Briksdalbre is also a lodge offering you a rare chance to stay near the Briksdal Glacier. The original lodge was constructed in 1890, but it's been rebuilt many times, most recently in 1997. Bedrooms are simply furnished and have small bathrooms equipped with showers. Expect little in the way of amenities, as most of the staff is engaged in tending to the restaurant. However, they will advise on glacier walking and even arrange a trip in a horse and carriage. The lodge serves some of the best regional cuisine in the area and is particularly busy at lunchtime. The cuisine is very regional, with many different cod and salmon dishes caught in local waters (ever had deep-fried cod jaws?). Typically, you can order filet of reindeer in a well-flavored sauce, or sautéed trout. Dinners range from NOK150 to NOK220 ($30–$44/£15–£22) and are served daily from 8:30 to 9:30pm, with no reservations needed.

N-6792 Briksdalbre. ✆ **57-87-68-00.** Fax 57-87-68-01. www.briksdalsbre.no. 6 units. NOK750–NOK950 ($150–$190/£75–£95) double. Rates include continental breakfast. AE, DC, MC, V. Closed Nov–Apr. *In room:* TV, no phone.

Loen Pensjonat ★ (Kids) (Finds) Built in 1910 next to the Church of Loen, this B&B is so family-friendly that it's almost like staying in someone's home. We've found it among the most personally run of all the accommodations in the area, with the staff genuinely taking an interest in their guests' welfare. It lies on a sheep farm, but in summer the owners send the herd to the upper elevations for better grazing in the mountains. The little inn has a large garden with panoramic views of the fjords. The location is only 400m (1,312 ft.) from the center of Loen, in the middle of great hiking and fishing country, with many opportunities for glacier trekking. The carpeted bedrooms are small to medium in size, coming with doubles or twins. Five of the units have a bathroom with a shower; occupants of the other rooms share the adequate bathrooms in the corridors.

N-6789 Loen. ✆ **57-86-76-24.** Fax 57-87-76-78. www.loen-pensjonat.com. 14 units, 5 w/private bathroom. NOK450 ($90/£45) double w/shared bathroom; NOK550 ($110/£55) double w/private bathroom. Children stay free in parent's room. No credit cards. **Amenities:** Breakfast lounge; nonsmoking rooms. *In room:* No phone.

Olden Fjordhotel ★ Beautifully located in Nordfjord, with a backdrop of mountains, this first-class hotel is close to the Briksdal Glacier. You can relax here in comfort and do nothing, or else use the hotel as a base for glacier excursions and a center for summer skiing (you heard that right), horseback riding in the hills and along the fjord, or else plain old fishing for trout and salmon. Built in 1971, the hotel added a modern annex in 1996. It is one of the best-maintained hotels in this fjord and glacier country, with renovations every winter. There are two types of units, either standard or superior. The standard rooms are medium in size and are well furnished, offering good comfort. The superior rooms have more style, are larger, and are allergy-free, with a sitting area included. The superior rooms contain bathrooms with a tub and shower; the standard units come with a shower only. The hotel is one of the liveliest in the area at night, with live piano music. The on-site restaurant serves the best and largest buffet dinners in Olden for NOK370 ($74/£37).

N-6788 Olden. ✆ **57-87-04-00.** Fax 57-87-04-01. www.olden-hotel.no. 60 units. NOK1,440–NOK1,740 ($288–$348/£144–£174) double. Children 2 and under stay free in parent's room. Rates include continental breakfast. AE, DC, MC, V. Closed mid-Sept to May. **Amenities:** Restaurant; bar; babysitting. *In room:* TV, coffeemaker (some units), hair dryer.

Visnes Hotel & Villa Visnes ★ (Finds) If you are a devotee of inns with character and quirky architecture, but want comfort as well, check in here. On our first visit years ago, the smell of home-baked bread lured us inside, where we found a personal atmosphere and good Norwegian food.

Visnes Hotel was built first in 1850 by an ancestor of the present owners. Opening originally as both an inn and a farmhouse, it was later expanded and given a "typical Swiss style"—all the architectural rage in 19th-century Norway. A grand tower that was built for the restaurant is still in use today. Closed from 1957 to 1986, modern facilities were added, but the original style was kept. Most rooms open onto a private balcony with a view of the fjord. Units are spacious and still maintain much of their original style from 1937. Of the two classics, we like the Villa Visnes best because it is even more fanciful in its 1898 architecture, offering the same comfort on par with its older sister. Either hotel is a good base for climbing the Josteldalsglacier, and both are convenient for excursions to either Geiranger or the Sognefjord.

The on-site restaurant is the best in town, serving a three-course dinner for NOK450 ($90/£45), with both Norwegian and French specialties.

Prestegen 1, N-6781 Stryn. ✆ **57-87-10-87.** Fax 57-87-20-75. www.visnes.no. 15 units. NOK1,250–NOK1,750 ($250–$350/£125–£175) double; NOK1,950–NOK2,250 ($390–$450/£195–£225) suite. Rates include continental breakfast. AE, DC, MC, V. Closed Sept–May. **Amenities:** Restaurant; nonsmoking rooms. *In room:* No phone.

12 GEIRANGERFJORD: NORWAY'S MOST MAJESTIC FJORD ★★★

85km (53 miles) SW of Åndalsnes; 413km (256 miles) NE of Bergen; 455km (282 miles) NW of Oslo

Most Norwegians consider Geirangerfjord, a favorite body of water for cruises, their most majestic—and we agree. The fjord stretches out for 16km (10 miles) and is 292m (958 ft.) deep. The village of Geiranger, one of the most justifiably famous resorts in the fjord country, is set at the very head of this narrow fjord.

Perched on rocky ledges high above the fjord are a number of small farmsteads. Waterfalls, such as the celebrated **Seven Sisters** (Syr Søstre) ★★, the **Wooer,** and the **Bridal Veil,** send their shimmering veils cascading down the rock face.

Almost daily in summer, large cruising liners anchor in the Geirangerfjord, as they have done since 1869. Occasionally, some of the world's best-known vessels are moored here at the same time.

The fjord is so deep that the old behemoth *Queen Elizabeth 2* once sailed safely this far inland. Such depth was created by the Ice Age, when mammoth masses of ice widened and deepened existing valleys. When the ice melted, former valleys became fjords. The Geirangerfjord is hemmed in by mountain walls rising to a height of 1,600m (5,248 ft.).

ESSENTIALS

GETTING THERE Geiranger is linked by regular ferry service to the old Viking port of Hellesylt. The **Møre og Romsdal Fylkesbåtar ferry** ★★★ costs NOK120 ($24/£12) per passenger or NOK150 ($30/£15) per day, and is the most magnificent ferry route in all of Norway. Take the ride even if you don't need to get to the other side. Depending on the season, fjord ferries run from May 1 to September 25 at the rate of 4 to even 10 a day; the latter run only in the peak season of July. For information and schedules, call **✆ 71-21-95-00.**

From the first of April until the end of September, Hurtigruten **coastal steamers** also sail into Geiranger, but only when en route to the North Cape.

The most frequently used public transport is a daily **bus** in summer running from Åndalsnes (see below), which takes 3 hours and costs NOK170 ($34/£17). For the visitor wanting wild fjord scenery, the morning bus from Åndalsnes goes on from Geiranger to Langvatn, and on the way back to Geiranger takes a rather thrilling 10km (6¼-mile) ★★ jaunt just for visitors. The bus goes up to the summit of Dalsnibba at 1,500m (4,920 ft.), stopping at Flydalsjuvet (see below). The return fare is NOK140 ($28/£14) per person.

By **car,** it's also possible to reach Dalsnibba by toll road, costing NOK55 ($11/£5.50) per vehicle. From Stryn, take routes 15/63 into Geiranger. The mountain road, known as Strynefjellsveien, offers gleaming white snow and views of glacier "tongues" well into the summer months. The final stretch to Geiranger is called **Geirangervegen** ★★★, and it takes you through 38 bends, offering fantastic mountain and fjord views at every turn. The most dramatic routing is to drive the famous Trollstigvegen from Åndalsnes (see below), a 2-hour scenic drive along Rte. 63.

VISITOR INFORMATION In the post office complex adjacent to the quay, the **Geiranger Tourist Office** (**✆ 70-26-30-99**) is open only from mid-May to early September. Hours vary, so call ahead.

SEEING THE FJORD

Accurately acclaimed as "the most beautiful fjord in the world," **Geirangerfjord** ★★★ invites exploration. The best and least expensive way to see the majesty of the fjord is to take a regular ferry service between the port of Hellesylt (see above) and Geiranger, which sails daily from May to September. An organized tour, however, gives you a greater view, by going closer to the banks.

The best jaunts are run by **Geiranger Fjordservice** (**✆ 70-26-30-99**), offering 1½-hour sightseeing boat tours at a cost of NOK125 ($25/£13) per person. Bookings can be made at the tourist office. Departures are June to August at the rate of five times daily. From June 25 to the end of July, there is also a tour in the evening.

Geiranger is also blessed with having some of the finest excursions in the fjord country, notably to **Dalsnibba ★★★**, lying 21km (13 miles) to the south. Opened in 1889, this dramatic road goes through a valley hemmed in by tall mountains until it reaches a lookout point at 1,500m (4,920 ft.). There are many panoramic lookout points along the way, and you're rewarded with a dramatic view at the top. As one local told us, "This is the lookout point where Satan took Jesus to tempt him with the beauty of the world."

A second great excursion is the **Flydalsjuvet ★★**, lying 4km (2½ miles) south of Geiranger. This gigantic overhanging rock, opening onto the fjord, is the most photographed in Norway, especially by cruise-ship passengers. To reach it, take the signposted road to Stryn until you see the turnoff.

SHOPPING

E-Meroks Turisthandel (✆ **70-26-30-14**) has been selling gifts and souvenirs to visitors since 1928 from its location in the center of the village overlooking the fjord. Their specialty is Norwegian knitwear, including a fine selection from the prestigious manufacturer Dale of Norway. They also sell items in silver and gold, along with Norwegian enamel, pewter, and crystal, as well as souvenirs. In summer, they remain open daily from 9am to 10pm. **Audhild Vikens Vevstove** (✆ **70-26-32-12**) also has a large selection of gifts and souvenirs, as well as clothes, knitted goods, pewter, books, music, and other items.

WHERE TO STAY & DINE

Geiranger Hotel ★★ This hotel opened in 1860 in the center of the village, the year America was launched into Civil War. Despite its ups and downs over the years, it has remained a durable favorite, staying abreast of the times by installing modern facilities while retaining much of its 19th-century aura. It runs a close second to the Union Hotel (see below), offering attractively furnished bedrooms with views over the Geiranger Fjord that most often can be experienced from your own private balcony. Overcrowded with summer visitors, the hotel nonetheless manages to offer personalized service. The bedrooms are midsize and comfortably carpeted, some painted in the deep greens and blues of the fjord itself. Nonguests often stop in to patronize the 300-seat Restaurant Skageflå, serving regional specialties. A Norwegian buffet at NOK350 ($70/£35) is a special delight. The staff can arrange for you to rent rowboats to explore the fjord or advise on how to obtain a fishing license to fish that same body of water.

N-6216 Geiranger. ✆ **70-26-30-05.** Fax 70-26-31-70. www.hotel-geiranger.no. 151 units. NOK1,040–NOK1,360 ($208–$272/£104–£136) double. Children 3 and under stay free in parent's room. Rates include buffet breakfast. AE, DC, MC, V. Closed Oct–Apr. **Amenities:** Restaurant; bar; outdoor pool; nonsmoking rooms. *In room:* TV.

Grande Fjordhotel ★ This hotel doesn't carry the pedigree, historical baggage, and charm of the Union or the Geiranger, but for service, contemporary comfort, and staff efficiency, it rates high marks. This 1996 inn looks like a Norwegian country lodge with a wooden interior. Its magnet is its sixth-floor restaurant with a panoramic view of fjord waters and some of the world's greatest cruise ships coming and going. The bar/lounge on the sixth floor is the best place to begin or end an evening at Geiranger. Bedrooms are tastefully though rather simply furnished and are midsize and immaculately maintained. The carpeted rooms open onto views of the fjord, and 42 of them have a tub and shower; the rest come with a shower only. Many cruise-ship passengers can be found in the restaurant in the summer, enjoying the classical Norwegian buffet of regional specialties at a cost of NOK250 ($50/£25) per person. The staff can arrange boat rentals for tours of the fjord or book tours on sightseeing vessels.

N-6216 Geiranger. ✆ **70-26-30-90.** Fax 70-26-94-91. www.grandefjordhotel.com. 48 units. NOK980–NOK1,150 ($196–$230/£98–£115) double. Children 3 and under stay free in parent's room. Rates include continental breakfast. MC, V. Closed Oct–Apr. **Amenities:** Restaurant; bar; laundry service. *In room:* TV, coffeemaker, hair dryer.

Union Hotel ★★★ (Kids) Over the years, this hotel has entertained more kings, queens, and kaisers than any other in the area. Dating from 1891 and perched along fjord waters with scenic views, the hotel is not lavish or overly decorated, but imbued with a country feel with its "rosemaling" decorated wood furniture, a style very popular in Norway for both farmers and royalty. The bedrooms are beautifully furnished; all come with immaculately kept bathrooms with tub/shower combinations. Try to book into one of the rooms with a balcony or into the 50 or so accommodations with views of the fjords; the other units have mountain views. The hotel restaurant is the finest in the area, serving a classic Norwegian buffet for NOK350 ($70/£35), although you can dine a la carte as well. In summer, a live band entertains and there is dancing.

N-6216 Geiranger. ✆ **70-26-83-00.** Fax 70-26-83-50. www.union-hotel.no. 168 units. NOK1,430–NOK3,500 ($286–$700/£143–£350) double; NOK3,500–NOK5,000 ($700–$1,000/£350–£500) suite. Children 4 and under stay free in parent's room. Rates include continental breakfast. AE, DC, MC, V. Closed Dec 15–Feb 1. **Amenities:** 2 restaurants; bar; sauna; room service; babysitting; Turkish bath; nightclub. *In room:* TV, minibar, beverage maker, hair dryer.

13 ÅNDALSNES: LAUNCH PAD FOR TROLLSTIGVEIEN ★

127km (79 miles) E of Ålesund; 1,058km (656 miles) W of Oslo

Although situated in one of the most scenic regions in Norway, Åndalsnes itself is rather banal. That's because the invading Nazis in 1940 practically bombed it out of existence. The king and his family used Åndalsnes as their exit route in their dramatic escape from Norway, following the German invasion of their borders. The royals made it, but Åndalsnes was left to pay the price.

The industrial alpine town today is modern and all too ready to forget the period when it was used as a military base for the Nazis. Åndalsnes lies in one of the most beautiful parts of scenic Norway, with scenic grandeur in almost every direction.

This alpine village is the starting point for the grandest drive in Norway, the **Trollstigvegen** (see below). It is also the last stop on the rail line from Oslo and, as such, is the gateway to the fjord country. Hiking through the Romsdalen Alps with natural beauty like thundering waterfalls and boating the scenic Romsdalsfjord are also good reasons to use Åndalsnes as your base.

ESSENTIALS

GETTING THERE **Trains** run daily from Oslo to Åndalsnes, taking 6 to 8 hours. From June 15 through August 30, daily **buses** link Åndalsnes to Geiranger, taking 3 to 4 hours. Daily buses also run to Ålesund (trip time: 2½ hr.) and to Molde (trip time: 1½ hr.). **Motorists** take E6 northwest from Oslo toward Lillehammer. At Dombås, head west on the E9 to Åndalsnes.

VISITOR INFORMATION At the train station, the **Åndalsnes og Romsdal Reiselivslag Tourist Office** (✆ **71-22-16-22;** www.visitandalsnes.com) dispenses information. Open mid-June to mid-August Monday to Friday 9am to 6pm, Saturday and Sunday 11am to 6pm; the rest of the year, it's open Monday to Friday 8am to 3:30pm.

SEEING THE SIGHTS

Åndalsnes is the starting point for one of the great motor drives in Norway: the **Trollstigvegen** ★★★, a 2-hour drive along Rte. 63 south to Geiranger. The highway climbs to 620m (2,034 ft.) over a distance of 8km (5 miles). The Ørneveien, or "Eagle's Road," down to Geiranger was a marvel of Norwegian engineering upon its completion in 1952.

Along the way, you'll encounter 11 hairpin turns. The last hairpin curve is called **Ørnsvingen** ★★★, or "Eagle's Bend," offering the greatest views in the fjord country—that of the Geirangerfjord. The dramatic route will take you right into Geiranger. This road for daredevils has a 1:12 gradient. To make matters even more exciting, it's one lane for most of the hair-raising journey. Passing another car could be lethal unless you're careful.

If you're driving or even on a bus, vehicles stop in front of the thundering **Stigfossen Waterfall** ★, whose waters drop 180m (590 ft.).

Vegmuseum, Trollstigen (✆ **71-22-14-65**), is a little museum at the pass, with exhibitions relating the story of how this incredible road came to be. It's open late June to mid-August daily from 11am to 3:30pm, charging an admission of NOK20 ($4/£2).

Another grand highlight of the area is en route to **Dombås** (Rte. 9). Both road and train lines follow the Troll Wall or **Trollveggen** ★, a major challenge for mountaineers, rising 1,800m (5,904 ft.). A combined Norwegian and British team "conquered" it in 1965.

The visitor center (see above) distributes more than a dozen leaflets outlining the best hiking trails through the **Romsdalen Alps,** a string of mountains enveloping Åndalsnes. The most dramatic route—and our all-time favorite—is the full-day jaunt that begins 50m (164 ft.) north of Åndalsnes and climbs to the summit of **Nesaksla Mountain** ★★, rising 715m (2,345 ft.) over Åndalsnes. At the top, you're rewarded with another one of those awesome panoramas. On a clear day, you can see down to the Romsdalsfjord. From here, the climb continues to the summit of **Høgnosa,** at 991m (3,250 ft.), and on to **Åkesfjellet,** at 1,215m (3,985 ft.).

The **Romsdalsfjord** ★ is one of the most scenic in western Norway, cutting a deep gash into the earth and extending west of Åndalsnes. The tourist office can arrange 4-hour fishing tours of the fjord at a cost of NOK300 ($60/£30) per person. An annual local license can be obtained for NOK270 ($54/£27) from the tourist office.

If mountain climbing is your thing, you can drive 2km (a mile) south of the center of Åndalsnes, following E139 to reach **Norsk Tindemuseum** (Norwegian Mountain Museum; ✆ **71-22-12-74;** www.tindemuseet.no); it's signposted. Dedicated to mountain climbing, the museum was founded by Arne Randers Heen (1905–91), one of Norway's most famous mountaineers. He was the first to scale many of his beloved country's mountains. These included Romsdalshorn at 5,101 feet. He climbed that mountain an amazing total of 233 times, the last time when he was at the ripe old age of 85. Admission is NOK30 ($6/£3), and the museum is open mid-June to mid-August Tuesday to Sunday 1 to 5pm.

WHERE TO STAY & DINE

Grand Hotel Bellevue ★ Judging from the photographs in the lobby, staying at the original 1890 Grand might have been a hoot, at least architecturally. But along came Hermann Göring's Luftwaffe in 1940, firebombing the hotel in its blitz of Norway and its pursuit of the fleeing king. It wasn't until 1954 that the owners of this property got enough money to rebuild the hotel, which, as was typical of Norway in those reconstruction years, is not imaginative looking like its grandpa. Nonetheless, it's a bastion of comfort and hospitality, the finest in the area and your best base for exploring the fjord and mountain country around Åndalsnes. The bedrooms range from midsize to spacious, and the suites open onto balconies with views of the mountains and the fjord waters. The staff can arrange sightseeing, golf, and fishing for salmon in a nearby river or for cod in the ocean. The on-site restaurant is the best choice for dining in Åndalsnes, even if you're not a guest. The fresh salmon is a delight, and meals cost from NOK125 to NOK180 ($25–$36/£13–£18).

Andalgata 5, N-6301 Åndalsnes. ✆ **71-22-75-00.** Fax 71-22-60-38. www.grandhotel.no. 84 units. NOK950–NOK1,150 ($190–$230/£95–£115) double; NOK1,300 ($260/£130) suite. AE, DC, MC, V. **Amenities:** Restaurant; bar; nonsmoking rooms. *In room:* TV, minibar.

14 ÅLESUND: THE GREAT FISHING HARBOR ★★

127km (79 miles) W of Åndalsnes; 131km (81 miles)—plus 2 ferry rides—SW of Kristiansund N; 59km (37 miles)—plus 1 ferry ride—SW of Molde

In our humble opinion, this small town on a fishhook-shaped peninsula is even more beautiful than Bergen because it is smaller and more architecturally unified, and its builders had a romance with the past. Ålesund is at the top of the fjord country, spread over three islands in an archipelago, with the snowcapped Sunnmøre Alps in the background. After a fire destroyed the town in 1904, Ålesund was rebuilt in the style of the times, Art Nouveau. To help rebuild, Kaiser Wilhelm II ordered that ship after ship of building materials and provisions be sent north to his favorite vacationland. Towers, turrets, and medieval romantic facades are pure Art Nouveau, and the Ålesund version includes elements from Nordic mythology.

ESSENTIALS

GETTING THERE **By Plane** The easiest way to reach Ålesund is to fly from such cities as Oslo, Trondheim, and especially Bergen, arriving at the Ålesund/Vigra airport. There are also daily flights from Bodø, Kristiansand S, Røros, Stavanger, and Tromsø. Flights are on **SAS** (✆ **70-10-49-00;** www.sas.no). The airport is a 20-minute ride north of Ålesund on the island of Vigra. A 15km (9¼-mile) network of bridges and tunnels connects Ålesund with four inhabited offshore islands.

By Train Go to Åndalsnes and then take a bus from the rail station to Ålesund. A daily train arrives from Oslo.

By Bus More tourist buses run June 15 to the end of August. Good connections are possible from Åndalsnes, the nearest rail terminal. There are one to three buses daily from Åndalsnes, taking 2½ hours and costing NOK220 ($44/£22) one-way. One bus a day also arrives from Bergen, taking 11 hours. One or two buses a day arrive from Trondheim, taking 7½ hours.

By Coastal Steamer The coastal steamer departs Bergen daily at 10pm and arrives at Ålesund at noon the following day.

By Car Take the A69 west from Åndalsnes all the way to Ålesund. A car ferry operates between Åndalsnes and Ålesund.

VISITOR INFORMATION The **Ålesund Reiselivslag,** Rådhuset (© **70-15-76-00**), provides tourist information June to August Monday to Friday 8:30am to 7pm, on Saturday 9am to 3pm, and on Sunday noon to 5pm; the rest of the year, it's open Monday to Friday 8:30am to 4pm. Also visit www.virtualalesund.com for information.

SEEING THE SIGHTS

Even more fun than exploring Ålesund is escaping from it and checking out the other wonders of the islands and peninsulas. The mountain guardian of the area is **Aksla,** at 182m (597 ft.), a scenic sanctuary with a terrace restaurant, offering a view of fjord landscape, ancient Viking islands, and the Sunnmøre mountains. From the center you can take 418 steps up to Aksla to the lookout point, **Kniven (the Knife).** To reach the ascent point, go along Lihauggata, reached from the pedestrian shopping street **Kongens Gate ★★**—one of the best streets for viewing Art Nouveau–style architecture. Motorists can also reach Aksla by road by taking Røysegata east of the core and following the signposts for Fjellstua.

In the harbor nestles the flat island of **Giske,** believed to have been the birthplace of Rollo, 10th-century founder of the Duchy of Normandy and father of William the Conqueror. Giske is the site of a 12th-century marble church, many stretches of white-sand beaches, and the Makkevika bird sanctuary.

Once the only access to many of the surrounding areas was by ferryboat, whose services were sometimes cut off during stormy weather. In 1987, a 15km (9¼-mile) network of tunnels was built connecting Ålesund to four nearby islands, including Giske, the island of **Vigra** (site of the city's airport), and the inhabited islands of **Ellingsøy** and **Valderøy.**

If you have time for only one island, we suggest you make it Giske, which was the historic seat of the Arnungane, a famous Viking family whose feudal control lasted from 990 to 1582.

At Giske you can visit the 12th-century **Giske Kirke,** a marble Romanesque church (© **70-18-80-00**) that was restored in 1756. Admission is NOK20 ($4/£2), and hours are June 1 to August 20 Monday to Saturday 10am to 5pm and Sunday 1 to 7pm. Bus no. 64 runs from the center of Ålesund, taking half an hour and costing NOK55 ($11/£5.50) one-way.

Several tours that begin in Ålesund are designed for bird-watchers. The most popular and best of these head to the island of **Runde ★★**, 67km (42 miles) southwest of town. This is Norway's southernmost bird rock, where on jagged cliffs half a million seabirds, representing nearly 250 species, breed each year. They are protected from humans by strict government regulations and from natural enemies by the forbidding terrain.

You can see colonies of these birds beginning in May. They stick around until late in July before flying out. The migrating puffins are worth the trek alone, but you'll also see the razor-billed auk, guillemots, auks, storm petrels, kittiwakes, gannets, and other seabirds.

The best tour is a 2½-hour boat ride leaving May to August daily from Runde Quay at 11am, and 1 and 4pm. The cost is NOK170 ($34/£17) adults, NOK120 ($24/£12) children; call © **70-08-59-16** to make a reservation.

For more information, contact the summer-only **Runde Reiselivslag** (✆ **70-01-37-90**), which keeps irregular hours.

You can take a **bus and catamaran tour** from the Ålesund's Skateflukaien Quay, taking 2½ hours and costing NOK200 ($40/£20) one-way. Departures are from mid-June to mid-September. You'll leave Ålesund on a catamaran, going to the neighboring island of **Hareid,** where you'll then board a bus for **Fosnavåg,** which will take you into **Runde** for the boat tours (see above). You can go back to Ålesund by bus; the last one leaves at 5pm.

Ålesund Museum ★ The development of hunting and fishing methods, shipbuilding, and life in Ålesund before and after the big fire of 1904 are the subjects of this museum off Korsegata near the harbor. The museum's focal points include a large-scale model of Ålesund and one of the most famous boats of the Norwegian fjords, the *Brudeegget.* Originally built in 1904 in the difficult-to-capsize shape of an egg, it became the prototype of thousands of covered rescue boats. Its sturdy design has helped save hundreds of lives after mishaps during stormy weather in the Norwegian seas. You can even wander into an 1812 barn that was turned into an old-fashioned grocery store or see exhibits of the town's distinctive Art Nouveau architecture. Especially interesting are exhibits of the dreaded German occupation from 1940 to 1945.

Rasmus Rønnebergs Gate 16. ✆ **70-12-31-70.** Admission NOK35 ($7/£3.50) adults, NOK15 ($3/£1.50) children. Nov 1–Aug 13 Mon–Sat 11am–3pm; Aug 14–Oct 31 Mon–Sat 11am–3pm and Sun noon–3pm.

Atlanterhavsparken ★★ (Kids) At Norway's most awesome aquarium, and one of the largest in Europe, you'll meet the denizens of the deep, including some pretty strange marine mammals that you may never have seen before, even if you're an avid aquarium-goer. The 4-million-liter (over-1-million-gal.) aquarium is enormous, and the sea park contains exhibits of marine life found only in the deepest of the fjords. The sanctuary for orphaned seals is inspiring.

Many families spend the day here, going for hikes along marked trails nearby and even getting in the chilly waters for some sea bathing. Time your visit to see the 1pm daily feeding when sea divers feed some of the fish by hand. On-site is a cafeteria where you can eat or else secure the makings of a picnic. At the western extremity of the Ålesund peninsula, the aquarium lies at Tueneset, 3km (1¾ miles) west of Ålesund.

Tueneset. ✆ **70-10-70-60.** www.atlanterhavsparken.no. Admission NOK120 ($24/£12) adults, NOK60 ($12/£6) children. Sept 1–May 31 daily 11am–4pm; June 1–Aug 31 Sun–Fri 10am–7pm, Sat 10am–4pm. Bus: 18.

Sunnmøre Museum & Borgundkaupangen ★★ (Kids) The site of this settlement was the most important ecclesiastical center between Bergen and Trondheim from the end of the Viking period (around 1000) to 1500. The open-air museum contains some 50 original buildings dating from the late Middle Ages to around 1900. Outbuildings include a sawmill, a boat-builder's shed, a fishermen's inn, and a small 1743 boarding school. The boat halls feature 30 special boats—one of Norway's largest collections of fishing boats as well as an exact replica of the *Fjørtoft* boat from the Viking era. The Museum Quay is home to the *Heland,* a fishing boat built in 1937, and a "Shetland Bus" dating from World War II. The *Borgundknarren* is an exact replica of a Viking trading vessel from 1000. A replica of the *Kvalsund* (8th c.) drops anchor at the quay in summer. The main building focuses on the cultural history of Sunnmøre and also contains a cafe and a handicrafts shop. The Medieval Museum was built over the excavated remains of 12th-century buildings. The exhibit depicts daily life in a market town back then.

 Borgundgavlen. ✆ **70-17-40-00.** Admission NOK65 ($13/£6.50) adults, NOK15 ($3/£1.50) children. Sept 11–May 21 Mon–Tues and Fri 11am–3pm, Sun noon–4pm; May 22–June 25 Mon–Fri 11am–4pm, Sun noon–4pm; June 26–Aug 20 Mon–Sat 11am–5pm, Sun noon–5pm; Aug 21–Sept 10 Mon–Fri 11am–4pm, Sun noon–4pm. Lies 4km (2 1/2 miles) east of town center by bus 13, 14, 18, 23, or 24.

WHERE TO STAY

Clarion Collection Hotel Bryggen ★ Finds On a comfort level, most first-class hotels of Ålesund are on par with each other. But this steeply gabled six-story hotel has the most character, as it was originally constructed in 1906 as a fish-processing factory. It is now artfully decorated with some of the antique fishmonger's tools and artifacts. Taken over by the prestigious Clarion, the hotel is well run and inviting. In fact, it would be the best in town were it not for the stiff competition from the Radisson SAS Hotel (see below). The hotel contains a library with a working fireplace, and the interior decor incorporates the thick walls and massive beams of the original structure into an otherwise modern design. The bedrooms are contemporary and tastefully furnished, half of them opening onto views of the water.

Apotekergata 1–3, N-6004 Ålesund. ✆ **70-12-64-00.** Fax 70-12-11-80. www.choicehotels.no. 105 units. NOK1,090–NOK1,780 ($218–$356/£109–£178) double; NOK2,050 ($410/£205) suite. Children 11 and under stay free in parent's room. Rates include buffet breakfast and dinner. AE, DC, MC, V. Parking NOK90 ($18/£9). **Amenities:** Restaurant; bar; sauna; bike rentals; playground; babysitting; laundry service/dry cleaning; picnic area; nonsmoking rooms; rooms for those w/limited mobility. *In room:* TV, Wi-Fi, minibar, coffeemaker, hair dryer, iron, trouser press, safe.

Radisson SAS ★★ We respect this hotel for its decision to construct a 21st-century building in the Art Nouveau style of the city. Best in modern comfort and convenience, this hotel inhabits the most scenic area of Ålesund, the Skansekaia district (also known as the top of the fjord), with panoramic views over the sea and mountains.

Attracting business clients in winter and foreign visitors in summer, the hotel boasts an international restaurant and bar that serves a first-rate Norwegian and international cuisine with gorgeous views. Rooms are bright and spacious, and all guests enjoy a sumptuous breakfast buffet at Bulls Brygge, the pub/restaurant, which later in the day weds Norwegian seafood to Mediterranean flavors. The standard rooms are perfectly comfortable, but if you're willing to pay more for business class you'll have amenities such as better bathrobes, slippers, and newspapers delivered to your door. The very best places to stay in Ålesund are the luxuriously designed and furnished seven suites.

Sorenskriver Bullsgate 7, N-6002 Ålesund. ✆ **70-16-00-00.** Fax 70-16-00-01. www.alesund.radissonsas.com. 131 units. NOK1,380–NOK1,880 ($276–$376/£138–£188) double; year-round NOK3,700 ($740/£370) suite. Children 11 and under stay free in parent's room. Rates include buffet breakfast buffet. AE, DC, MC, V. Parking NOK90 ($18/£9). **Amenities:** Restaurant; bar; room service; laundry service/dry cleaning. *In room:* TV, Wi-Fi, minibar, coffeemaker (some units), hair dryer, trouser press.

Rica Hotel Scandinavie ★ This hotel has a lot going for it, mainly the friendly and efficient staff, who are perhaps the most helpful in town. Set on a gently sloping street in the town's historic core, this hotel was originally built in 1905 after the great fire destroyed its predecessor. Today it's one of the most authentic Art Nouveau buildings in Ålesund, offering midsize and tastefully furnished bedrooms with either antiques or reproductions. Bathrooms are freshly restored and immaculately kept, 30 of them coming with a tub and shower, the rest with a shower only. The staff arranges boat rides on the fjords or bird-watching at Runde. The on-site restaurant serves mainly Italian food. The hotel is entirely nonsmoking.

Lovenvoldgt 8, N-6002 Ålesund. ✆ **70-15-78-00.** Fax 70-15-78-01. www.rica.no. 70 units. NOK1,140–NOK1,640 ($228–$328/£114–£164) double; NOK1,995–NOK2,100 ($399–$420/£200–£210) suite. Children 4 and under stay free in parent's room. Rates include buffet breakfast. AE, DC, MC, V. Closed Dec 20–Jan 6. Parking NOK90 ($18/£9). **Amenities:** Bar; pub (with live music on weekends); room service; laundry service/dry cleaning; rooms for those w/limited mobility. *In room:* TV, Wi-Fi, minibar, hair dryer, trouser press (in some).

Rica Parken ★ At this 1981 hotel that is on par with the Thon (see below), we were won over by the sauna and some of the suites, which are on the uppermost (ninth) floor, offering panoramic views of the Art Nouveau town and the sea. A tasteful but slightly bland modern design prevails throughout, and each room is comfortable, with a small, immaculate private bathroom—half with tub and shower, the rest with shower. Depending on what you want to pay, you can rent a standard double or a business-class room, the latter with better amenities. The most luxurious way to stay here is in a series of suites that are designed to evoke an upscale private home. A little park in back of the hotel has a pathway leading into the mountains for a lovely hike on a summer day.

Storgata 16, N-6002 Ålesund. ✆ **70-13-23-00.** Fax 70-13-22-80. www.rica.no. 197 units. NOK1,645–NOK1,870 ($329–$374/£165–£187) double; from NOK2,400 ($480/£240) suite. Rates include continental breakfast. AE, DC, MC, V. Closed Dec 22–27. Free parking. **Amenities:** Restaurant; bar; sauna; laundry service; nonsmoking rooms, rooms for those w/limited mobility. *In room:* TV, Wi-Fi, minibar, hair dryer, safe.

Thon Hotel Ålesund ★ Not imbued with the same style and character of the previous, more glamorous recommendations, this member of the Thon chain is nonetheless one of the most desirable addresses in town. In spite of a post-millennium overhaul, it still lives on architecturally in 1954, the year of its creation. The location is certainly choice, on the main pedestrian shopping street, within a short distance of the airport shuttle bus and the coastal steamer dock by the bus station. The small-to-midsize bedrooms come with tasteful, comfortable furniture and wooden floors. The most desirable rooms open onto views of the water (these book first, of course). On-site is a well-run restaurant, Storm, specializing in a high-quality Scandinavian and international cuisine typical of Norway's first-class hotels.

Kongens Gate 27, N-6002 Ålesund. ✆ **70-12-29-38.** Fax 70-12-66-60. www.thonhotels.com. 110 units. NOK1,095–NOK1,495 ($219–$299/£110–£150) double. Children 10 and under stay free in parent's room. Rates include continental breakfast. AE, DC, MC, V. Closed Dec 22–Jan 3. Free parking. **Amenities:** Restaurant; 3 bars; nightclub; room service; nonsmoking rooms; rooms for those w/limited mobility. *In room:* TV, minibar, hair dryer.

WHERE TO DINE

Whether the food is good or bad, all of the restaurants in Ålesund share a common bond: The prices are high.

Brasserie Normandie ★ FRENCH/INTERNATIONAL/NORWEGIAN One of the top restaurants in town is known for its good food, romantic decor, wine selection, and service, attracting those who appreciate the delicacies of the sea. Authentic regional produce is harmoniously blended with international recipes. Recommended starters are the fish soup, the most savory in town, and the salmon, which comes marinated in gin with fresh herbs and is served with a mustard sauce. The fish platter is the town's finest, loaded with carefully prepared monkfish, catfish, salmon, mussels, scallops, and shrimp. Or you might choose to order an herb-flavored roasted filet of lamb, finishing your meal with one of the sundry pastries made fresh daily.

Storgata 16, in the Rica Parken Hotel. ✆ **70-12-50-50.** Reservations required. Main courses NOK290–NOK340 ($58–$68/£29–£34). AE, DC, MC, V. Mon–Sat 6–11pm. Closed Dec 22–27.

Fjellstua ★ NORWEGIAN The food at this cafeteria-style restaurant is good, but the view is the reason to come. This mountaintop restaurant opens onto one of the most panoramic vistas in the fjord country. The chef specializes in fish, including *bacalao* (cod), monkfish, and freshly caught fjord salmon. At lunch you might want to settle for sandwiches and burgers. At night, if you don't want fish, tender beef emerges perfectly cooked from the charcoal grill. Other savory meat choices include well-flavored lamb cutlets and pork schnitzels. You can drive to the restaurant's mountaintop location via a complicated system of roads or climb the 418 rock-hewn steps from a parking lot below.

Aksla Mountain. ✆ **70-10-74-00.** Reservations recommended. Main courses NOK210–NOK326 ($42–$65/£21–£33). AE, DC, MC, V. Daily 11am–8pm. Closed Nov–Mar 15.

Sjøbua Fiskerestaurant ★★ SEAFOOD The rustic walls of this former 1904 warehouse were retained in this restaurant, where parts of its foundation piers are sunk into the harbor. If there is a wait, the maritime-style bar is a good place for a drink. In the coldest months, a blazing fireplace may greet you. The chefs here are in top form, as proven by their tangy fish platter with three different types of whitefish, salmon, mussels, and shrimp. The pan-fried monkfish is especially recommendable, coming with a curry cream sauce. Lobster selected from the tank can be steamed or served grilled with a shellfish sauce. If you arrive in summer, you might prefer a seat in the Flottman's Bar next door, which is under the same management.

Brunholmgate 1. ✆ **70-12-71-00.** Reservations recommended. Main courses NOK280–NOK340 ($56–$68/£28–£34). AE, DC, MC, V. Mon–Sat 2–11pm.

ÅLESUND AFTER DARK

Hos Naboen Pub This small, traditional pub playing recorded music is one of the most popular in town, attracting patrons ranging in age from 20 to 60. It's a friendly, convivial place with the hard-core regulars showing up in winter, giving way to summer visitors from abroad. Typical pub grub is served. It's open Monday to Saturday 9:45am to 1am and Sunday 1pm to 1am. Thon Hotel Ålesund, Kongens Gate 27. ✆ **70-12-29-38.**

O This nightclub is the most popular in town, with an upstairs bar area and a downstairs bar with a dance floor. It draws the young people of Ålesund nightly, ranging in age from 21 to 35. These patrons dance to recorded music, and the DJ changes every month. Open Friday and Saturday 9pm to 2:30am. In the Thon Hotel Ålesund, Kongens Gate 27. ✆ **70-12-29-38.** Cover Sat NOK50–NOK100 ($10–$20/£5–£10).

15 MOLDE: CITY OF ROSES

59km (37 miles) N of Ålesund; 50km (31 miles) NW of Åndalsnes

Lacking the architectural excitement of Art Nouveau Ålesund, Molde is a bit dull in its architecture, yet it occupies one of the most scenic locations in the northern fjord country: the Romsdalfjord, in the More og Romsdal district. Lying on the Romsdal Peninsula, it is one of Norway's most dramatic coastlines. Molde is an ideal starting point for excursions along the coast and into the surrounding untamed area.

Norway's "town of jazz and roses" is famed for its view of 87 white-capped Romsdal Alps. When the Nazis attacked Norway during World War II, Molde briefly became, in effect, the country's capital, because the king and the gold reserves were here. King Haakon VII hid in a forest outside the town until he and his son, the future King Olav V, could board a boat for England. Three hundred houses were destroyed during the German bombings in 1940.

The name of Molde, from the Molde farm that occupied much of the area, has appeared in records since the Middle Ages. It was officially recognized as a trading place in 1614, and King Christian IV signed a royal decree declaring that Molde was a trading city in 1742. A modern, pleasant town, it boasts 18,000 citizens.

ESSENTIALS

GETTING THERE **By Plane** Årø Airport (✆ **71-21-47-80;** www.molde-airport.com), bordering the coast, lies 4km (2½ miles) east of the heart of Molde. **SAS** (✆ **71-21-97-00;** www.sas.no) offers three to five flights daily to and from Oslo. Once here, bus no. 252 goes from the airport into the center, taking 10 minutes and costing NOK35 ($7/£3.50).

By Train You can go from Oslo as far as Åndalsnes (see above) by train. From there, you must take a connecting bus to Molde. Call ✆ **71-22-48-78** for schedules.

By Bus Buses run between Ålesund and Molde daily, taking 2 hours and costing NOK131 ($26/£13) one-way. There is a ferry crossing at Vestnes. Call ✆ **71-58-78-00** for schedules.

By Car Driving should take about 1½ hours from Åndalsnes or Ålesund, 3 hours from Dombås, or 4 hours from Trondheim. From Trondheim, take the E6 south to Dombås, and then connect with the E69 west. From Ålesund, take the E69 east. From Molde, board the ferry to Vikebukt and then go east on the E69.

By Ferry Coming from either Ålesund or Åndalsnes, board the frequent car ferries at Vikebukt or at Vestnes for the crossing north to Molde. In July only, at the height of the tourist season, there is an express ferry called *Fjørtoft,* between Ålesund and Molde, sailing twice daily Monday to Friday, taking 2½ hours, and costing NOK185 ($37/£19) one-way.

By Coastal Steamer The coastal steamer *Hurtigruten* visits Molde on its way between Bergen and Hammerfest (both directions).

VISITOR INFORMATION The **Destination Molde,** Torget 4 (✆ **71-20-10-00;** www.visitmolde.com), will provide tourist information and assist in arranging excursions. From June 15 to August 15, it's open Monday to Friday 9am to 6pm, Saturday 9am to 4pm, and Sunday 10am to 3pm. In the off season, it's open Monday to Friday 8:30am to 3:30pm.

SPECIAL EVENTS The preeminent event on the Molde calendar is its international **Jazz Festival ★★★**, sponsored around the middle of July and attended by some 60,000 fans. The major open-air concerts are held near the Romsdalsmuseet, although many indoor venues are used as well, including the Idrettenshus or Sports Hall. For more information, contact the **Molde International Jazz Festival,** Sandvegen 1A (✆ **71-20-31-50;** www.moldejazz.no). Tickets cost from NOK150 to NOK700 ($30–$140/£15–£70) for seats.

SEEING THE SIGHTS

The view of the 87 peaks of the **Romsdal Alps ★★★** is worth the trip to Molde. The most scenic and most dramatic peaks are the **Romsdalshorn,** at 1,559m (5,114 ft.), and the **Troll Tinder,** at 1,905m (6,248 ft.). The best vantage point for all of this wonder is the **Belvedere Varden,** rising 396m (1,299 ft.) over Molde. Visitors can take a taxi up and ask the driver to wait for 20 minutes or so while you absorb the view. An alternative way for the more athletic is to walk up a marked trail from the center. We prefer this climb to a taxi, although you must allow about an hour of huffing and puffing to reach the top. Once here, you should be able to take in the island-studded Romsdalfjord as well as the peaks.

Molde Domkirke In the heart of town near Torget, Molde Cathedral, created by architect Finn Bryn in 1957, is the largest postwar cathedral in Norway and the third church to rise on this site. The old altarpiece, *Resurrection,* by Axel Ender, is from the church that the Nazis bombed in April 1940 when they learned that the king was escaping from Molde. As the bombs were falling, a local patriot ripped out the painting with a knife and managed to save it from the Nazi fire.

Kirkebaken 2. ✆ **71-11-14-60.** Admission NOK15 ($3/£1.50). Daily 10am–3:30pm.

Rådhuset (Town Hall) This 1966 Town Hall, near Torget, is a well-conceived municipal building of concrete and glass. *The Rose Maiden* fountain celebrates Molde as the "town of roses." Marble floors and stone walls blend harmoniously, and domes and skylights capture the northern lights. The roof terrace has a garden with 2,000 roses.

Rådhusplassen. ✆ **71-11-10-00.** Free admission. Mon–Fri 8am–4:30pm.

Romsdalmuseet (Romsdal Museum) ★★ Kids This is one of the better open-air museums in the fjord district, and its creators showed a certain cleverness. They not only designed Bygata, an early-20th-century street, but they also used remnants of wooden stave churches that were about to be scrapped to create a single, whole church, a neat feat of architectural design. Some "scavengers" went raiding the Romsdal region, searching for antique buildings, including a 16th-century *aarestue,* or log cabin. In all, they managed to save 50 buildings, which stand today. In summer, local children in regional costumes may sometimes perform folk dances. The open-air museum is a 10-minute walk northwest of the center.

Romsdal Park. ✆ **71-20-24-60.** Admission NOK70 ($14/£7) adults, NOK50 ($10/£5) children. Mid-June to June 30 Mon–Sat 11am–3pm, Sun noon–3pm; July Mon–Sat 11am–6pm, Sun noon–6pm; Aug 1–Aug 13 Mon–Sat 11am–3pm, Sun noon–3pm.

NEARBY ATTRACTIONS

Part of the previously explored Romsdal Museum, the **Fiskerimuseet (Fisheries Museum; ✆ 93-42-54-06)** lies on the island of Hjertøya. Its collection consists of more than two dozen buildings moved here from the western coast of Romsdal, including dwellings, boathouses, a mechanic's workshop, and other maritime buildings. There's a number of authentic old fishing boats and gear, and you can see how the Norwegian coastal fishermen, sealers, and whalers lived in olden times. A water taxi leaves from the marketplace, Torget, in the center of Molde during the museum's open hours. The round-trip fare is NOK60 ($12/£6) for adults and NOK40 ($8/£4) for children. Trip time is 10 minutes. The Fisheries Museum keeps the same hours as the Romsdal Museum (see above); your ticket to the major museum entitles you to visit this attraction as well.

Finds Memories of the Literati

Today the famous **Moldegård** house, Fannestrandveien 40, lying 1km (1/2 mile) east of Molde, is privately owned and can be viewed only from the outside. It was the main house of the original Molde farm, built in 1710 by Hans Nobel. Bjørnstjerne Bjørnson, who wrote Norway's national anthem, among other poems, often visited here, taking his last trip to Moldegård in 1907. The cottage's more famous association is with Henrik Ibsen, who lived here in 1885 and used this beautiful rococo building for the setting of one of his best-known plays, *Rosmersholm.*

Another attraction, **Trollkirka (Troll's Church)** ★, near Eide, is a natural wonder with seven underground caves and grottoes. There's also a 14m (46-ft.) waterfall. Going through these grottoes, with their subterranean streams, is a mystical experience. To reach the gateway to the cave, you have to walk up from the signposted main road, a distance of 2.5km (1 1/2 miles). Because it's a scenic walk, it's most pleasurable. Allow about 1 hour to make the trip and wear sturdy shoes. Bus no. 241 goes to the site two to seven times per day. The area is an open site and can be explored at any time.

To wander back into the past, you can visit **Vey Stone Church,** dating from the 11th century, on **Vey Island.** The little village of Kaupangen on the island was the center of Romsdal until the 14th century and has a rich Viking past. If you'd like to visit, make your request through the Molde tourist office, which will give you a key to the church. You're taken here by a boatman for a cost of NOK90 ($18/£9) per person, although each boat must have at least four people.

Finally, motorists, armed with a map and directions from the tourist office, can drive 2 hours up Langfjorden and along the lake Eikesdalsvatneet to the waterfalls at **Mardalsfossen** ★★. At one time, this was the highest waterfall in the world, a two-level cascade dropping 655m (2,148 ft.). Its greatest single drop is 297m (974 ft.). Mardalsfossen flows only between mid-June and mid-August. (How did Mardalsfossen lose its status among the top waterfalls of the world? Its power was extinguished by a hydroelectric project in the 1970s, which was constructed in spite of massive protests by Norwegian environmentalists.)

WHERE TO STAY

Expensive

Quality Hotel Alexandra Molde ★★ At the Molde Jazz Festival, you'll find us sitting in the Getz Bar, named after the famous saxophonist, drinking and talking to some of the world's leading jazz artists who like to stay here. This is the town's choicest traditional hotel, named for Princess Alexandra of Wales, who checked in here in the 1880s. After being destroyed and reconfigured over the years, it consists of three different structures from the '50s, '70s, and '80s, all facing a common grassy area. The hotel stands on the main street of town, overlooking the public gardens and the nearby fjord. The comfortable bedrooms are furnished in a sleek modern style. The hotel is one of the best equipped in town, and its restaurant, Varthusaet (reviewed separately below), and bar are popular with both locals and visitors.

 Storgaten 1–7, N-6413 Molde. ✆ **71-20-37-50.** Fax 71-20-37-87. www.choicehotels.no. 163 units. NOK1,195–NOK1,700 ($239–$340/£120–£170) double; from NOK1,800 ($360/£180) suite. Children 11 and under stay free in parent's room. Rates include buffet breakfast. AE, DC, MC, V. Parking NOK90 ($18/£9). Closed Dec 15–Jan 3. **Amenities:** 2 restaurants; bar; indoor heated pool; gym; sauna; babysitting; laundry service/dry cleaning; nonsmoking rooms. *In room:* TV, minibar, hair dryer, trouser press.

Rica Seilet Hotel Molde ★★ If you want tradition, hang out at the long-established Alexandra (above). But if you're seeking avant-garde architectural style and post-millennium amenities and comfort, head here. Jutting out into Romsdalsfjorden, the hotel was designed to evoke a boat. Rising 15 floors, this well-run "ship" is sleek and efficient, and often the venue for conferences. Of all the lodgings in Molde, the rooms here have the most spectacular views. The best way to enjoy the scenery is to treat yourself to one of several suites, with their own balcony. The most spacious suites have the best-designed interiors in Molde, providing real luxury in this provincial outpost. Some of the junior suites offer a round bed. The Alexandria can't match some of the dramatic features of this hotel, especially the Skybar, with its own terrace suspended 60m (197 ft.) above the water. There is also a lobby bar and a waterfront restaurant serving light fare in summer. The on-site a la carte restaurant features gourmet and international specialties.

Gideonvegen 2, N-6412 Molde. ✆ **71-11-40-00.** Fax 71-11-40-01. www.rica.no. 169 units. NOK1,600–NOK1,885 ($320–$377/£160–£189) double; NOK2,000–NOK3,500 ($400–$700/£200–£350) suite. Rates include buffet breakfast. AE, DC, MC, V. Free parking. **Amenities:** 2 restaurants; Sky Bar; fitness center; sauna; room service; laundry service/dry cleaning; nonsmoking rooms; rooms for those w/limited mobility. *In room:* TV, minibar, hair dryer.

Moderate

Comfort Hotel Nobel Originally built in 1920, this is one of the few buildings—and the only hotel in Molde—that was not destroyed by Nazi bombs in the '40s. Although the reception area retains some of its antique accessories, the hotel has been modernized and enlarged. Today it offers some of the best and the most up-to-date accommodations in Molde in the moderate price range. A few of the better rooms have views of the sea; these get booked up first, of course. The staff can arrange trips to the museums or to the mountains. Under separate management, Amalie, a restaurant, is on the same site.

AMTM Kroghsgata 5, N-6413 Molde. ✆ **71-25-15-55.** Fax 71-21-59-54. www.choicehotels.np. 49 units. NOK990–NOK1,390 ($198–$278/£99–£139) double. Children 11 and under stay free in parent's room. Rates include continental breakfast. AE, DC, MC, V. Closed Dec 22–Jan 3. Free parking. **Amenities:** Restaurant; nonsmoking rooms. *In room:* TV, Wi-Fi, minibar, iron.

Thon Hotel Moldefjord This is hardly the shining star of the Thon chain, but it is a long-standing favorite of more budget-minded travelers. Dating from the late 1940s, this building was converted into a hotel in 1998, and right away it became one of the town's most desirable places to stay. Opening onto harbor views, with the mountains in the backdrop, the hotel upholds the traditions of Thon, a leading Norwegian chain. Guests are comfortably housed in carpeted, midsize rooms with a choice of twins or a "honeymoon bed." Complimentary breakfast is served in your room daily.

Storgata 8, N-6400 Molde. ✆ **71-20-35-00.** Fax 71-20-35-01. www.thonhotels.com. 88 units. NOK1,095–NOK1,445 ($219–$289/£110–£145) double. Children 3 and under stay free in parent's room. Rates include continental breakfast. AE, DC, MC, V. Free parking. **Amenities:** Restaurant; lobby bar; nonsmoking rooms; 1 room for those w/limited mobility. *In room:* TV, Wi-Fi, minibar, hair dryer.

Inexpensive

Hotell Molde Value In an expensive town, this hotel still keeps its prices reasonable. In the commercial center near Torget, the market square, this hotel first opened its doors in 1910. Regrettably, the Nazis bombed it in World War II. Today, following renovations, it's one of the more up-to-date choices in town. Painted as gray as a Norwegian November afternoon, it is a privately owned and family-run establishment. Rooms are merely functional but well kept and comfortably furnished with wooden floors and small bathrooms (with showers). The on-site restaurant, the Red, is a more popular venue than the hotel itself (see below).

Storgata 19, N-6413 Molde. ✆ **71-21-58-88.** Fax 71-21-58-90. www.hotellmolde.no. 36 units. NOK845–NOK1,160 ($169–$232/£85–£116) double. Children 2 and under stay free in parent's room. Rates include continental breakfast. AE, DC, MC. Free parking. **Amenities:** Restaurant; bar; laundry service/dry cleaning. *In room:* TV, minibar.

WHERE TO DINE

Lubbenes ★ NORWEGIAN This 1860s alpinelike chalet, 2km ($1^1/_4$ miles) from the town center, is one of the town's best restaurants. Its chefs put a modern spin on classical Norwegian food. For a starter, we recommend the lobster soup, the town's finest, or the fish soup of the day. Scampi flavored with sautéed onions is another good appetizer. Generous main courses include plates of perfectly executed dishes such as sautéed filet of reindeer in a velvety smooth cream sauce, fried catfish in another savory sauce, or beef cooked in a tangy onion sauce.

Sanestrandsvn 117. ✆ **71-21-12-86.** Reservations recommended. Main courses NOK190–NOK310 ($38–$62/£19–£31). AE, DC, MC, V. Daily 4–9pm. Closed Jan.

The Red SOUTHWESTERN On the street level of the Hotell Molde (see above), this restaurant serves a medley of food that has won it many admirers locally and abroad. Many fjord dwellers like to come here for a change of pace from the usual offerings in the area. The chefs roam the world for inspiration, stopping off, perhaps, at Louisiana before heading on to Mexico. Tempting menu items include fish and scampi cooked in a wok with vegetables or else marinated salmon with a mustard vinaigrette. You can also order a big steak grilled and served with a pepper sauce. Dried codfish also comes with potatoes and olives in a spicy tomato sauce.

In the Hotell Molde, Storgata 19. ✆ **71-21-58-88.** Reservations recommended. Main courses NOK165–NOK295 ($33–$59/£17–£30). AE, DC, MC, V. Daily 11am–10pm.

Vartshusaet NORWEGIAN This is the busiest restaurant in town at the time of the jazz festival. The well-patronized restaurant, located in the Quality Hotel Alexandra Molde (see above), a short walk from Town Hall, has known various incarnations. It's decked out in Norwegian-tavern style with antiques and massive ceiling timbers. If you've traveled Norway the menu is all too familiar, but fine regional products are used even if the recipes are pretty much the same as many other establishments. The inevitable fish soup appears on the menu, and it's good-tasting and generous in proportion. For spicier fare, ask for the garlic shrimp as an appetizer. The marinated house salmon is the chef's specialty, and it's invariably good and fresh. That other favorite, cod, is prepared poached, fried, or baked with different sauces. Meat fanciers opt for the filet of reindeer with fresh vegetables.

In the Quality Hotel Alexandra Molde, Storgata 1–7. ✆ **71-20-37-50.** Reservations recommended. Main courses NOK180–NOK220 ($36–$44/£18–£22). AE, DC, MC, V. Daily noon–11pm.

13

Trondheim

Founded by the Viking king Olaf I Tryggvason in the 10th century, Trondheim is Norway's third-largest city and was the country's capital until the early 1200s. Scenic and pleasant, it's a bustling university center, with expansive avenues created after a fire razed most of the town in 1681. The city lies on the south bay of the Trondheim Fjord, at the mouth of the Nidelven River.

Noted for its timbered architecture, Trondheim retains much of its medieval past, notably the Gothic-style Nidaros Cathedral. Pilgrims came from all over Europe to worship at the shrine of Olaf, who was buried in the cathedral and canonized in 1031.

The city's fortunes declined during the Reformation. Under the Nazi occupation Trondheim became the base of German naval forces in northern Norway, with U-boats lurking deep in its fjord.

Today Trondheim is a progressive city with a rich cultural life, as well as a high-technology center for research and education. Its town center is compact and best explored on foot; most of the historic core of Trondheim lies on a small triangular island surrounded by water but linked via bridges.

Trondheim lies some 684km (424 miles) north of Bergen and 552km (342 miles) northwest of Oslo. Oslo and Bergen are more major destinations, but if you have a day or two to spare, make it to Trondheim. We often prefer it during "term time," when 25,000 students bring it to vibrant life, biking around town, drinking in the bars, hanging out in the cafes, and listening to the sounds of jazz, often imported from New Orleans.

If you're heading north from here, savor city life before journeying into the wilds, which are hardly tamed, except for Tromsø. If you're arriving in Trondheim from the north, you'll view it as a return to civilization and all those pleasures it brings.

1 ORIENTATION

ESSENTIALS

Arrival

BY PLANE Flights to Trondheim land at **Vaernes Airport** (**© 74-84-30-00**), lying 32km (20 miles) east of the city center. Most visitors fly here from either Bergen or Oslo. There are also daily connections to and from Copenhagen. Service is provided by **SAS** (**© 74-80-41-00;** www.sas.no).

After you arrive at the airport, you can take an airport bus, **Flybussen** (**© 73-82-25-00**), costing NOK90 ($18/£9) for a one-way trip into the center. The trip takes 40 minutes, ending at the rail depot. From the center of Trondheim, buses leave from Erling Skakkes gate daily from 5am to 9pm. Departures Monday to Friday are every 15 minutes, with curtailed departures on Saturday and Sunday. You can also take a taxi from the airport to the center, costing around NOK480 ($96/£48) for up to three people.

BY TRAIN Two trains a day arrive from Stockholm (trip time: 12 hr.) and three trains per day arrive from Oslo (trip time: 7 hr.) into **Trondheim Sentralstasjon.** A typical fare—say, from Oslo to Trondheim—costs NOK813 ($163/£81) one-way. Trondheim also has links to Bodø if you're heading for the Arctic Circle. This latter trip takes 10 hours, costing around NOK938 ($188/£94) one-way. For rail information, call ✆ **81-50-08-88** or visit www.nsb.no.

BY BUS Buses from various parts of Norway arrive at the **Rutebilstasjon,** or city bus terminal, adjoining Trondheim Sentralstasjon, where the trains pull in. Trondheim lies at the crossroads of bus travel in Norway, as it is a transportation hub between southern Norway, including Oslo and Bergen, and northern Norway, including the city of Bodø. The most frequented bus route is from Oslo, taking 9½ hours and costing NOK495 ($99/£50) one-way. The more difficult route from Bergen takes more than 10 hours, costing NOK751 ($150/£75) one-way. For information about long-distance buses, contact **Norway Buss Ekspress** (✆ **81-54-44-44;** www.nor-way.no).

BY BOAT The **Hurtigruten coastal steamer** (✆ **77-64-82-00**) stops in Trondheim. In addition, **Fosen Teraffikklag Kystekspressen boats** (✆ **73-89-07-00**) travel between Kristiansund N and Trondheim, taking 3½ hours and costing NOK560 ($112/£56). Departures are at Pirterminalen Quay in Trondheim.

BY CAR From Oslo, motorists can take the express highway E6 north, going via Lillehammer all the way into Trondheim.

Visitor Information

Contact the **Trondheim Tourist Office,** Munkegate 19 (✆ **73-80-76-60;** www.trondheim.no), near the marketplace. In peak season—from June 23 to August 10—it is open Monday to Friday 8:30am to 6pm, Saturday and Sunday 10am to 6pm; from June 2 to 22, it's open Monday to Friday 8:30am to 6pm, Saturday and Sunday 10am to 4pm. During other months, hours are Monday to Friday 9am to 4pm, Saturday 10am to 2pm.

Getting Around

You can travel all over Trondheim and to outlying areas on city buses operated by **Trondheim Trafikkselskap** (it's also referred to as Team Traffikk, or TT), Dronningens Gate (✆ **81-53-52-30**). Tickets for **single rides** are sold on buses for NOK30 ($6/£3) for adults, NOK15 ($3/£1.50) for children 4 to 16; children 3 and under travel free. If you don't have exact change and offer a bank note that's worth more than the bus fare, you'll receive a credit slip from the driver, which can be redeemed at the TT office or on a later trip. A **day card** for 24 hours of unlimited rides costs NOK70 ($14/£7) per person.

For a local **taxi,** TrønderTaxi maintains a special five-digit telephone number (✆ **07373**) that's in service 24 hours a day. The biggest taxi ranks are found at Torvet, the market square, and also at the central rail station. For local bus information serving the Greater Trondheim area, call ✆ **81-53-52-30.**

Trondheim is a city that's known for its allegiance to all things "green" (ecologically speaking). As such, it maintains a fleet of some 150 red-painted bicycles at bike racks scattered around the city. To secure one, head for the tourist office and pay a fee of NOK70 ($14/£7), plus a cash or credit card deposit of NOK500 ($100/£50), in exchange for which someone will give you a sort of credit card. After you insert it into a slot on the bike rack, it releases the bike, which you're then free to use for up to 5 days without additional charge. When you're through with the bike, bring it back undamaged and your deposit will be returned. The whole system will make you want to write an ode to the joys of a temporary visit to a civilized country.

City Layout

From the Trondheim train station, simply walk south across the bridge to the triangular-shaped island forming the city's central core. The center is called **Midtbyen.** In Norse sagas, it was referred to as Nidarneset or the Nidar headland. The best way to explore this area is on foot, and you can easily walk to all the major attractions, including Nidaros Cathedral and the Archbishop's Palace.

The very center of Trondheim is the **Torvet,** or market square. A major street, **Kongens Gate,** splits the island into two parts. The **Fish Market (Fisketorvet),** reached from Torvet by walking north along Munkegate, lies to the north.

At Nidareid, by the narrow isthmus between the river and the fjord, lies ancient **Skansen.** The remnants of the old city fortifications toward the west can still be seen here. Today this area is a green park with a panoramic view of the fjord.

The **Bakklandet** district is the most easily accessible from the rest of Trondheim via the "Old Town Bridge," an early-20th-century iron structure that is the most-often-photographed bridge in Trondheim. Noted for its slightly out-of-kilter antique wooden houses built for low-income canning-factory workers and fishermen, the area used to stink of rotting fish, and in the 1910s and 1920s it came very close to being demolished. But after the demise of the town's fishing industry and the end of the town's canning factories, a greater emphasis was placed on preserving the site as a historical record of days gone by. Today its most famous and most celebrated restaurant is **Bryggen,** and its most famous pub is **Den Gode Nabo ("The Good Neighbor").** The neighborhood also holds a number of students' pubs, one of which is the **Kaktus** (see "Trondheim After Dark," later in this chapter). The neighborhood is quite small—40 buildings or so—and easily toured on foot.

Fast Facts Trondheim

Automobile Association Driving in the wilds of central Norway in the vast open stretches around Trondheim might be hazardous if the weather turns bad. For directions or information about road conditions or even reroutings, call the **Norwegian Automobile Association** at ✆ **73-95-73-95.**

Consulates There is no U.S. consulate in Trondheim. The consulate for Great Britain is at Beddingen 8 (✆ **73-60-02-00**). For embassies and consulates in Norway, see "Fast Facts: Norway," in appendix A.

Dentists If you need emergency assistance, call ✆ **73-50-55-00.**

Emergencies For a fire dial ✆ **110,** for the police ✆ **112,** and for an ambulance ✆ **113.**

Hospitals For a non-emergency, your hotel can put you in contact with an English-speaking doctor. For a medical emergency, call ✆ **73-52-25-00.**

Internet Access Go to the Trondheim Public Library, Peter Egges Plass 1 (✆ **72-54-75-00**). From July 1 to August 12, it is open Monday, Tuesday, Thursday, and Friday 10am to 4pm; Wednesday 10am to 7pm; and Saturday 10am to 3pm. At other times, hours are Monday to Thursday 9am to 7pm, Friday 9am to 4pm, Saturday 10am to 3pm, and Sunday noon to 4pm.

Laundry If you don't use the services your hotel provides, you can go to **Elefanten Vaskeri,** Mellomveien 20 (✆ **73-51-29-89**), which is open Monday to Friday 10am to 6pm and Saturday 11am to 4pm. It's one of the most northerly laundromats in Norway.

Parking Garages The major garages are **Bakke P-hus,** Nedre Bakklandet 60 (✆ **72-54-65-33**), and **Midtbyen P-hus,** Sandgata 28 (no phone).

Pharmacies The most central pharmacy is Løveapoteket, Olav Tryggvasons Gate 28 (✆ **73-83-32-83**), which is a bustling and busy emporium of the health industry within the Behaven Shopping Complex in the heart of town. Hours are Monday to Friday 9am to 5pm, Saturday 10am to 3pm.

Police The police station is at Gryta 4 (✆ **73-89-90-90**). For emergencies, dial 112.

Post Office The main post office is at Dronningens Gate 10 (✆ **81-00-07-10**), open Monday to Friday 8am to 5pm, Saturday 9am to 2pm.

2 WHERE TO STAY

Many hotels offer special summer prices from mid-June to the end of August. The rest of the year, hotels feature weekend discounts if you stay 2 nights.

EXPENSIVE

Britannia Hotel ★★ Stay at the Grand Olav if you want a dramatic decor, at the Royal Garden if you want the latest in modern and the most facilities, but at the Britannia if you want old-world tradition. The grande dame of Trondheim hotels, built in 1897, with many subsequent renovations keeping the place up to high standards, this white-stucco structure is graced with a majestic slate-covered dome and tower evocative of the grand Victorian monuments of England. Conservative, stable, and dependable, but lacking a cutting-edge sense of glamour, the Britannia offers a physical plant that, frankly, would be more appealing if some badly conceived modernizations hadn't been made in the 1960s. The ornate Palm Garden (see p. 355), with its Art Nouveau winter garden, fountain, and piano, captures the grand spirit. The renovated guest rooms have wooden floors, and the most tranquil units front the courtyard but are also the smallest rooms. They are called "the economy rooms." In contrast, some of the double rooms are large enough to accommodate two additional guests. The 11 regal suites come in various sizes and decor, half of them duplexes. A unique feature that sets the Britannia apart from its competitors is a series of "Artists' Rooms," decorated with works from nationally famous artists. If you like boas and gilt-plated "ice," you can check into the Flettfrid Andresen Room (no. 724)—it's the campiest room in Norway.

Dronningens Gate 5, N-7001 Trondheim. ✆ **73-80-08-00.** Fax 73-80-08-01. www.britannia.no. 247 units. Mon–Thurs NOK1,882–NOK2,232 ($376–$446/£188–£223) double; Fri–Sun NOK1,229–NOK1,579 ($246–$316/£123–£158) double; NOK3,078–NOK6,310 ($616–$1,262/£308–£631) suite. Rates include buffet breakfast. AE, DC, MC, V. Parking NOK200 ($40/£20). Bus: 3, 4, 5, or 7. **Amenities:** 3 restaurants; 4 bars; indoor heated pool; fitness center; spa; sauna; room service; babysitting; laundry service/dry cleaning; nonsmoking rooms; rooms for those w/limited mobility. *In room:* TV, Wi-Fi, minibar, hair dryer.

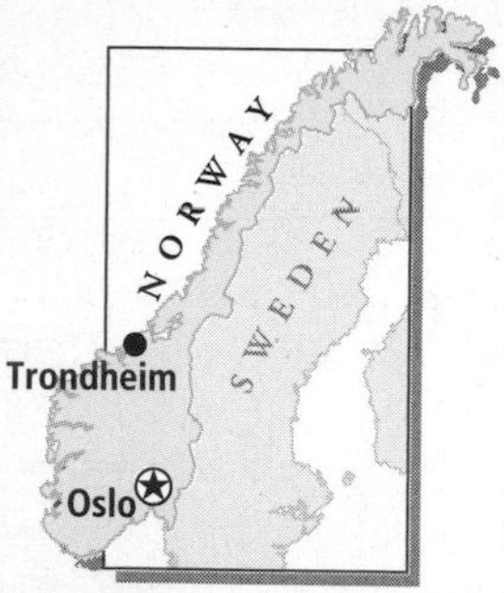

ACCOMMODATIONS ■

Best Western Chesterfield Hotel **4**
Britannia Hotel **15**
City Living Viking Hotel **11**
Clarion Collection Hotel Bakeriet **6**
Clarion Collection Hotel Grand Olav **7**
Comfort Hotel Park **17**
Nova Hotel **13**
Prinsen Hotel **1**
Radisson SAS Royal Garden Hotel **8**
Thon Hotel Gildevangen **5**
Thon Hotel Trondheim **16**

DINING ◆

Akropolis **3**
Chablis Brasserie & Bar **20**
Credo **9**
Fru Inger **2**
Grenaderen **21**
Havfruen (Mermaid) **18**
Jonathan's **15**
Kafe Choco Boco **19**
Kvilhaugen Gård (Rest Hill Farm) **14**
Palm Garden **15**
Prins Olavs Grill **8**
Restaurant Egon **12**
Sushi Bar **10**
Tavern på Sverresborg **21**

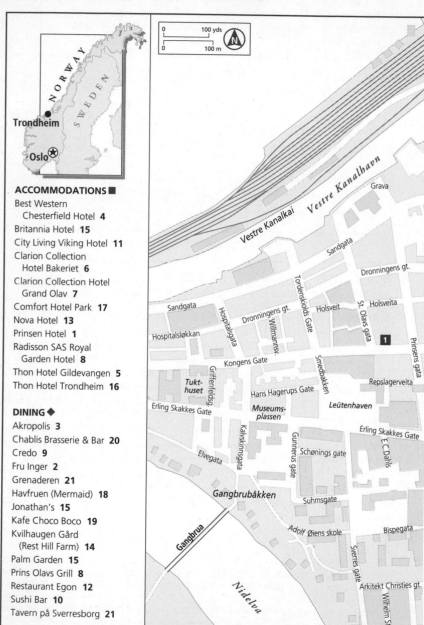

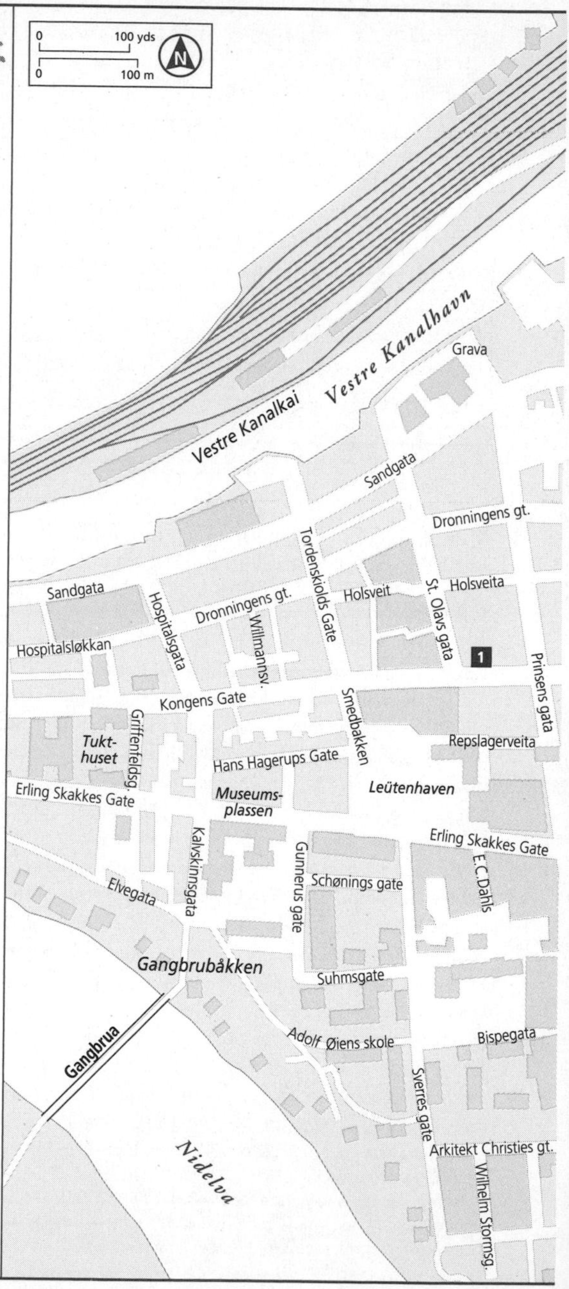

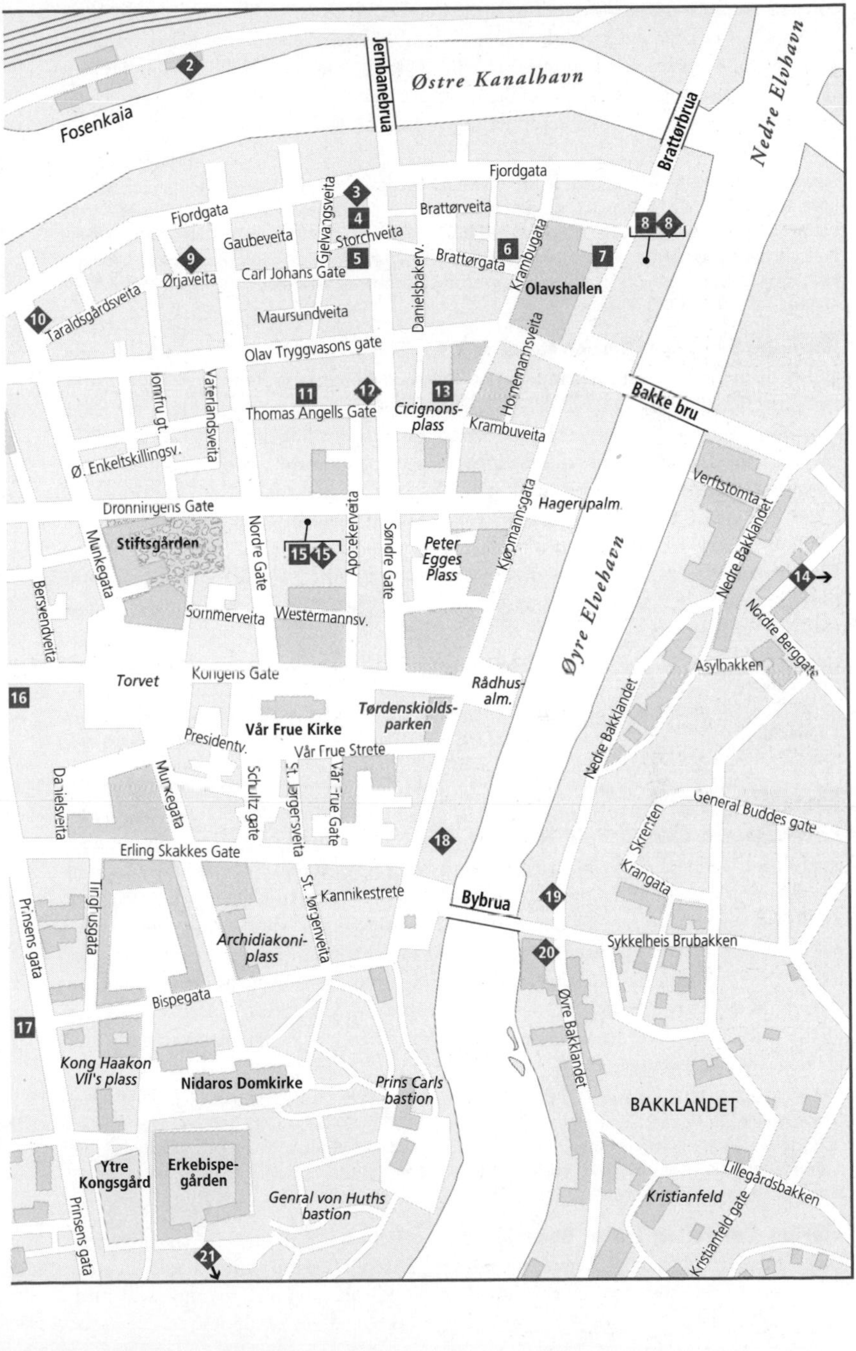
Østre Kanalhavn
Nedre Elvhavn
Fosenkaia
Jernbanebrua
Brattørbrua
Fjordgata
Brattørveita
Brattørgata
Gjelvangsveita
Storchveita
Gaubeveita
Carl Johans Gate
Ørjaveita
Taraldsgårdsveita
Maursundveita
Danielsbakerv.
Krambugata
Olavshallen
Olav Tryggvasons gate
Jomfru gt.
Vaterlandsveita
Thomas Angells Gate
Cicignons-plass
Hornemannsveita
Krambuveita
Bakke bru
Ø. Enkeltskillingsv.
Dronningens Gate
Kjøpmannsgata
Hagerupalm.
Verftstomta
Nedre Bakklandet
Nordre Berggate
Munkegata
Stiftsgården
Nordre Gate
Apotekerveita
Søndre Gate
Peter Egges Plass
Øvre Elvehavn
Asylbakken
Bersvendveita
Sommerveita
Westermannsv.
Torvet
Kongens Gate
Rådhus-alm.
Tordenskiolds-parken
Vår Frue Kirke
Presidentv.
Vår Frue Strete
Danielsveita
Munkegata
Schultz gate
St. Jørgensveita
Vår Frue Gate
General Buddes gate
Skrenten
Krangata
Erling Skakkes Gate
St. Jørgenveita
Kannikestrete
Bybrua
Sykkelheis Brubakken
Tinghusgata
Prinsens gata
Archidiakoni-plass
Bispegata
Øvre Bakklandet
Kong Haakon VII's plass
Nidaros Domkirke
Prins Carls bastion
BAKKLANDET
Ytre Kongsgård
Erkebispe-gården
Genral von Huths bastion
Lillegårdsbakken
Kristianfeld
Kristianfeld gate
Prinsens gata
2
3
4
5
6
7
8
9
10
11
12
13
14
15
16
17
18
19
20
21

Clarion Collection Hotel Grand Olav ★★ This six-story hotel was designed in 1989 by the architect of the nearby Radisson SAS Royal Garden Hotel, a close competitor, and radically renovated into a style the hotel refers to as "modernized rococo." The Grand Olav is a bit more stylish than its sibling, Hotel Bakeriet (see below), and we prefer it for its grace and character. The hotel is adjacent to a building complex that includes elegant boutiques and Trondheim's largest concert hall. The midsize-to-spacious bedrooms are tastefully and comfortably furnished, all with a certain flair. The hotel is entirely nonsmoking.

Kjøpmannsgata 48, N-7010 Trondheim. ✆ **73-80-80-80.** Fax 73-80-80-81. www.choicehotels.no. 106 units. Mon–Thurs NOK1,645–NOK1,945 ($329–$389/£165–£195) double; Fri–Sun NOK1,075–NOK1,245 ($215–$249/£108–£125) double; NOK1,500–NOK6,000 ($300–$1,200/£150–£600) suites. Rates include buffet breakfast and a light evening meal. AE, DC, MC, V. Parking NOK180 ($36/£18). Bus: 6 or 7. **Amenities:** Small lobby bar; laundry service/dry cleaning; rooms for those w/limited mobility. *In room:* A/C, TV, minibar, coffeemaker, hair dryer.

Radisson SAS Royal Garden Hotel ★★★ This glittering extravaganza on the see-and-be-seen circuit is Trondheim's largest and best hotel. It lacks the tradition of the Britannia but clearly outdistances the Clarions for pure luxury and amenities. This is the most architecturally dramatic and innovative hotel in Trondheim. Originally built in 1984 to replace a row of waterfront warehouses that had burned down in a fire, it rises on stilts—a glowing, glass-sided jewel-box—abruptly above the Nid River, so close to the water that you can catch salmon from your balcony if you're so inclined. Inside is an intriguing array of angled glass skylights, stone floors, soaring atriums, and plants. Rooms are comfortable and tastefully contemporary, outfitted in pale tones of gray, earth tones, and/or blue. The most elegant of the hotel's restaurants, the Prins Olavs Grill, is recommended separately in "Where to Dine," below.

Kjøpmannsgata 73, N-7010 Trondheim. ✆ **73-80-30-00.** Fax 73-80-30-50. www.radissonsas.com. 298 units. Mon–Thurs NOK1,595–NOK1,900 ($319–$380/£160–£190) double; Fri–Sun NOK1,195–NOK1,495 ($239–$299/£120–£150) double; NOK2,500 ($500/£250) suite. AE, DC, MC, V. Parking NOK185 ($37/£19). Bus: 1 or 4. **Amenities:** 2 restaurants; bar; indoor heated pool; health club and exercise center; Jacuzzi; sauna; boutiques; room service; laundry service/dry cleaning; solarium. *In room:* TV, Wi-Fi, minibar, hair dryer, safe.

MODERATE

Best Western Chesterfield Hotel ★ (Finds) This small, cozy, centrally located, English-inspired hotel has a lobby that resembles an English pub. (They sell drinks from the reception desk.) A collection of leather-upholstered Chesterfield sofas completes the Anglophile theme. Built in 1947, it originally functioned as a doctor's office and an office building, but in 1992 it was transformed into the charming seven-story hotel you see today. Only breakfast is served, but a light evening meal—usually featuring a stew pot of some kind of hearty, rib-sticking soup and fresh bread—is included, buffet-style, as part of the price. Bedrooms are medium size, high-ceilinged, and very pleasant, with full-grained wooden furniture.

Søndregate 26, N-7010 Trondheim. ✆ **800/780-7234** in the U.S., or 73-50-37-50. Fax 73-50-37-55. www.bestwestern.com. 43 units. Mon–Thurs NOK1,485–NOK1,800 ($297–$360/£149–£180) double; Fri–Sun NOK1,180 ($236/£118) double. Rates include buffet breakfast. AE, DC, MC, V. No on-site parking. Bus: 1 or 4. **Amenities:** Pub-style lobby bar; sauna; laundry service/dry cleaning; solarium; nonsmoking rooms; rooms for those w/limited mobility. *In room:* TV, hair dryer, trouser press.

Clarion Collection Hotel Bakeriet ★ (Finds) (Kids) Although its chain partner Grand Olav (see above) has a more cutting edge, Bakeriet is also a worthy choice in every way. One of the most atmospheric hotels in Trondheim occupies the mock-fortified, solid-looking premises of what functioned between 1863 and 1963 as the largest bakery in Norway. You might be reminded of a museum, thanks to a number of displays that showcase the ovens, cooling racks, and paraphernalia associated with the building during its early days. Kids should eat up these displays, including the elaborate 20th-century bakers costumes that decorate the upstairs hallways leading to the large and very comfortable bedrooms. Many of these have carefully finished half-paneling and easy chairs and settees.

Brattørgata 2, N-7010 Trondheim. ✆ **73-99-10-00.** Fax 73-99-10-01. www.choicehotels.no. 109 units. NOK995–NOK1,655 ($199–$331/£100–£166) double; year-round NOK2,200 ($440/£220) suite. Rates include breakfast and a light evening supper. AE, DC, MC, V. Parking NOK185 ($37/£19). Bus: 1 or 4. **Amenities:** Breakfast room and lounge; fitness room; Turkish bath; sauna; bicycle rental; babysitting; laundry service/dry cleaning; nonsmoking rooms; rooms for those w/limited mobility. *In room:* TV, Wi-Fi, minibar, hair dryer, trouser press.

Comfort Hotel Park In the center of Trondheim, near Nidaros Dome and the river, this well-run, redbrick chain hotel enjoys a prime location. Bedrooms are midsize, sleek, and streamlined, offering good though not grand comfort. What makes this hotel different from its competitors is its number of special features such as a top floor with a sauna and an outdoor hot tub. In the basement laundry facilities are made available to guests, and there is ironing equipment in the room. The best accommodations offer free Internet access, plus a kitchenette. In addition to the good Norwegian breakfast in the morning, freshly baked waffles are served to guests in the afternoon.

Prinsensgate 4A, N-7012. ✆ **73-83-39-00.** Fax 73-83-39-01. www.choicehotels.no. 116 units. NOK995–NOK1,895 ($199–$379/£100–£190) double, NOK1,295–NOK2,295 ($259–$459/£130–£230) suite. AE, DC, MC, V. Parking: NOK110 ($22/£11). Bus: 1 or 4. **Amenities:** Bar; sauna; laundry service/dry cleaning; Wi-Fi in lobby. *In room:* TV, minibar, iron (on request).

Prinsen Hotell This six-story building dating from the early 1960s is now one of Trondheim's better hotels. Set in the heart of the historic center, the hotel is a blend of pale pastel colors and solid, substantial furnishings. It caters mainly to business clients in the winter but is favored by non-Norwegian tourists in the summer. Most of the bedrooms are midsize and comfortably and tastefully furnished, often with wooden copies of Norwegian country furniture. Many of the rooms open onto a view of the fjord waters. On-site is the oldest pub in Trondheim, **Kieglekroa,** whose specialty is a locally famous steak (called the "Fairytale Steak"), served in the immediately adjacent Egon restaurant.

Kongens Gate 30, N-7012 Trondheim. ✆ **73-80-70-00.** Fax 73-80-70-10. www.prinsen-hotell.no. 81 units. NOK1,040–NOK1,390 ($208–$278/£104–£139) double. Children 11 and under stay free in parent's room. Rates include buffet breakfast. AE, DC, MC, V. Parking NOK100 ($20/£10). Bus: 1 or 4. **Amenities:** Restaurant; bar; pub; coffee shop; room service; laundry service/dry cleaning; nonsmoking rooms. *In room:* TV, Wi-Fi, minibar, hair dryer, iron.

Thon Hotel Gildevangen ★ Value One of Trondheim's most architecturally distinctive antique hotels, the Gildevangen sits behind a dramatic-looking facade of massive, carefully chiseled stone blocks. Originally built in 1910 as an office building and transformed into a hotel in 1930, it was restored in 2007 with a series of clean, upgraded, uncomplicated, and tranquil bedrooms. Breakfast is served here, and from Monday to Thursday a light evening meal is included in the overnight price. Each unit has big windows, generous dimensions, and a high ceiling.

Søndregate 22B, N-7010 Trondheim. ✆ **73-87-01-30.** Fax 73-52-38-98. www.thonhotels.no. 110 units. NOK1,490–NOK2,400 ($298–$480/£149–£240) double. Rates include buffet breakfast. AE, DC, MC, V. No on-site parking. Bus: 46. **Amenities:** Bar; laundry service/dry cleaning; nonsmoking rooms. *In room:* TV, minibar, hair dryer.

INEXPENSIVE

City Living Viking Hotel (Value) This serviceable though lackluster choice offers some of the most affordable rooms in town—and it's conveniently located in the town's commercial core. Built in the early 1990s and set behind a modern, angular facade that evokes a somewhat foreboding office building, this middle-bracket hotel has rooms that are comfortable and cozy, but without any frills. Accommodations are outfitted in neutral, monochromatic tones, each with hardwood floors and a meticulously tiled bathroom that's more up-to-date and appealing than that of other hotels of its caliber in Trondheim. Immediately adjacent to the hotel, but under separate management, is an unpretentious bar and grill, Graffi's, which serves burgers, steaks, pastas, seafood, and salads.

Thomas Engells Gate 12B, N-7011 Trondheim. ✆ **73-51-21-33.** Fax 73-51-43-14. www.cityliving.no. 35 units. NOK580–NOK845 ($116–$169/£58–£85) double. AE, DC, MC, V. Bus: 3 or 4. **Amenities:** Restaurant; bar; laundry service/dry cleaning; nonsmoking rooms. *In room:* TV, fridge, beverage maker, hair dryer.

Nova Hotell (Value) Situated in a public office building, this hotel lies close to the attractions at the historic center. An experienced staff runs a well-maintained and tastefully furnished place. Bedrooms are outfitted in a conservatively modern style and are quite cozy, with cushioned furniture and small bathrooms. Most have carpeted floors, and each has been renovated and upgraded. The doubles have tub/shower combinations, while singles come with showers only.

Cicignons Plass, N-7011 Trondheim. ✆ **73-80-63-00.** Fax 73-50-20-42. www.nova-hotell.no. 44 units. Mon–Thurs NOK1,195 ($239/£120) double; Fri–Sun NOK850 ($170/£85) double. Children 3 and under stay free in parent's room. Rates include continental breakfast. AE, DC, MC, V. Closed 2 weeks at Christmas and 1 week at Easter. No on-site parking. Bus: 1 or 4. **Amenities:** Restaurant; nonsmoking rooms; rooms for those w/limited mobility. *In room:* TV, Wi-Fi, hair dryer, iron.

Thon Hotel Trondheim This six-story hotel near the market square is a deliberately simple, relatively inexpensive B&B-style hotel with medium-size guest rooms and not a lot of supplemental flair and frills. Outfitted with sun-kissed color schemes, many of the rooms contain an extra foldaway bed. The beds are comfortable, and the bathrooms, though small, are equipped with tub/shower combinations. Constructed in 1913, the hotel was renovated and expanded in 1990, with additional small-scale renovations conducted ever since.

Kongens Gate 15, N-7013 Trondheim. ✆ **73-88-47-88.** Fax 73-51-60-58. www.thonhotels.no. 115 units. NOK895 ($179/£90) double. AE, DC, MC, V. Parking NOK120 ($24/£12). Bus from airport stops here. **Amenities:** Breakfast room; coin-operated laundry; nonsmoking rooms; rooms for those w/limited mobility. *In room:* TV, minibar, hair dryer.

3 WHERE TO DINE

Be sure to try the local specialty, ***vafler medøst* (waffle and cheese),** sold at most cafeterias and restaurants. Most restaurants will automatically add around a 15% service charge to your bill. If you like the service, it's customary to leave some extra small change as well.

EXPENSIVE

Chablis Brasserie & Bar ★ FRENCH This casual and informal dining spot serves excellent food. A polished choice, it is a combined brasserie and restaurant, where half the tables are covered with white napery and the other half are deliberately bare tabletops for an artfully rustic brown and white decor. Mix in elaborate place settings and lots of sparkling crystal for one of the most appealing dining venues in the neighborhood. In summer, many diners prefer an outside table to soak up the fair weather. The best dishes include wild salmon with asparagus, leek confit, potato purée, and a *beurre blanc* with caviar, or grilled turbot with fresh mushrooms, spinach, and a potato and truffle purée. Another specialty is reindeer with a ragout of Puy lentils and a puree of Jerusalem artichokes. Always check to see what the catch of the day is, as the fish served here is extremely fresh.

Øvre Bakklandet 66. ✆ **73-87-42-50.** Reservations required. Main courses NOK255–NOK295 ($51–$59/£26–£30); fixed-price 3-course menu NOK450 ($90/£45). AE, DC, MC, V. Daily 5–11pm. Bus: 4, 5, 7, or 52.

Credo ★★ CONTINENTAL This is the most urban-conscious and trendy restaurant in Trondheim, with a three-pronged allure that includes an upscale restaurant, an art gallery, and—one floor above street level—a jazz bar. It lies within a mostly contemporary setting of modern furniture and white walls that showcase a changing array of paintings (most of which are for sale) on loan from a nearby art gallery. The seasonal cuisine combines very fresh local meats, vegetables, and produce, with many cooking techniques inspired by France, Italy, and Spain. Menu items change with the inspiration of the chef but might include any of several variations of codfish; fresh Arctic char served with beurre blanc and herring caviar; or Norwegian lamb with red wine sauce, foie gras, and mushrooms. A changing array of macho game dishes features duck, elk, pheasant, venison, and grouse. The cellar boasts more than 1,700 kinds of wine, including a collection of German Rieslings that is among the most comprehensive in Scandinavia. For more about this place as a jazz bar, refer to "Trondheim After Dark."

Ørjaveita 4. ✆ **73-53-03-88.** Reservations recommended. Set-price menus NOK470–NOK600 ($94–$120/£47–£60). AE, DC, MC, V. Restaurant Mon–Sat 6–9:30pm (last order). Closed July and 1 week at Christmas and Easter. Bar Mon–Sat 4pm–3am. No annual closings. Bus: 3, 4, or 5.

Havfruen (Mermaid) ★★ SEAFOOD The freshness of the seafood served here never fails to impress us. Set amid a cluster of some of the oldest warehouses in town, along the Nidelven River, this is the best fish restaurant in Trondheim—and the most atmospheric. Built around 1800 on the site of a much older warehouse, it's studded with old beams and trusses and lots of authentic antique charm. Meals are prepared in the open-to-view kitchen and served by a staff with impeccable manners and technique. The menu changes each season, based on local fish migration patterns in the frigid waters surrounding Trondheim, and the staff enjoys evaluating and offering advice about the daily harvest. You might begin enticingly enough with the creamy fish chowder, the town's best, although other contenders include lobster bisque with lobster and fresh spinach ravioli; or poached filets of arctic char served with an apple-cider vinaigrette. For a main course, you are likely to be won over by the oven-baked halibut with *pommes dauphines* and a confit of shellfish, or perhaps the pan-fried Norwegian redfish with a tantalizing orange sauce.

Kjøpmannsgata 7. ✆ **73-87-40-70.** Reservations required. Main courses NOK265–NOK310 ($53–$62/£27–£31); fixed-price menus NOK460–NOK770 ($92–$154/£46–£77). AE, DC, MC, V. Mon–Sat 6pm–midnight. Closed Dec 23–Jan 7. Bus: 5, 6, 7, or 9.

Palm Garden ★★★ NORWEGIAN/INTERNATIONAL This is the most elegant restaurant in Trondheim, housed in the first-rate Britannia Hotel (p. 349. Illuminated with a Victorian-era skylight, it is ringed with exotic-looking columns inspired by the Corinthian/Moorish look. There is some of the atmosphere of the ambulatory of a medieval cloister here, as well as the Belle Epoque era. True to its namesake, the restaurant is filled with palms. Lunch is served as a sandwich-and-salad buffet, attracting many of the town's leading business clients. Dinner is grandly elaborate, with an array of top-quality dishes prepared with the finest of ingredients. Standards remain high here—the classic cuisine never has seemed to bog down on our repeated visits over the years. The service is also the most grandly formal in town. Begin, perhaps, with a marinated wild salmon in a fennel bouillon with apple salsa, or else a creamed curry mussel soup (the little ravioli in the soup are stuffed with mussels). For real Norwegian flavor, opt for the "top side of stag," with fresh mushrooms, creamed vegetables, and—just the right touch—red whortleberry chutney. You can also enjoy the loin filets of veal stuffed with Parma ham and fresh sage.

In the Britannia Hotel, Dronningens Gate 5. ✆ **73-80-08-00.** Reservations recommended. Lunch salads and sandwiches NOK85–NOK95 ($17–$19/£9–£10); fixed-price 3-course dinner NOK570 ($114/£57); dinner main courses NOK250–NOK310 ($50–$62/£25–£31). AE, DC, MC, V. Daily 11am–2pm and 6–11pm. Bus: 5, 6, 7, or 9.

Prins Olavs Grill ★★★ CONTINENTAL In a fierce neck-and-neck race for culinary supremacy over the Britannia, the chefs at this bastion of good food have created a whole new repertoire of dishes that are ultramodern and harmonious in their imaginative flavor combinations. Set on the lobby level of the also-recommended hotel, this restaurant is named after a once-majestic sailing ship, the *Alexandra,* which was commissioned early in the 20th century by the British Navy. It was purchased (and renamed the *Prins Olav*) by the Norwegian navy in the 1930s and then sunk by the Nazi air force in 1940. Today some of the ship's gilded architectural fretworks and embellishments, as well as a photographic history of the vessel, decorate the walls of a room that's noteworthy for its sense of comfort and well-being. Dishes that emerge from the busy, open-to-view kitchen include such appetizing starters as a carpaccio of beef with pine kernels and grated Parmesan; citrus-marinated salmon with Szechuan peppers and an endive-flavored cream sauce; roasted rack of lamb with a parsnip-and-garlic-flavored cream sauce; and oven-baked halibut with a nut crust and seasonal mushrooms and a sherry-flavored cream sauce.

In the Radisson SAS Royal Garden Hotel, Kjøpmannsgata 73. ✆ **73-80-30-00.** Reservations recommended. Main courses NOK240–NOK310 ($48–$62/£24–£31); fixed-price 5-course menu NOK625 ($125/£63). AE, DC, MC, V. Daily 5–11pm. Closed July. Bus: 1 or 4.

MODERATE

Fru Inger ★ SEAFOOD This is one of the two most popular seafood restaurants in Trondheim. It's not as chic, cutting-edge, and sophisticated as the also-recommended Havfruen (see above), but it serves an intelligent, imaginative cuisine at less expensive prices. Named after a 1950s-era cargo ship (*Fru Inger,* or "Miss Inger") now based in Mexico, it's housed in a glass-sided pavilion that overlooks the old and new fishing vessels moored beside a canal, a short walk from the railway station. Inside, a navy-blue color scheme, varnished mahogany, and pin lighting work to enhance the nautical decor. We recommend lime-and-chili-marinated scallops served on a salad bed of fresh tomato and sweet peppers as a starter. Drawn from the cold, deep waters of Norway, shark is delectably served with smoked salmon, a skewer of fresh vegetables, and risotto. The salt-baked filet of cod comes with a savory basil sauce. At Christmastime, a traditional favorite is *lutefiske,* the controversial and aromatic dish that many Norwegians remember, often with conflicting feelings, from their childhoods. If you're here on a summer day, opt for the rhubarb soup with cinnamon ice cream.

Fosenkaia. ✆ **73-51-60-71.** Reservations recommended. Main courses NOK220–NOK245 ($44–$49/£22–£25). AE, DC, MC, V. Mon–Sat 5pm–midnight. Bus: 1 or 4.

Grenaderen ★ Finds NORWEGIAN For rustic charm and an authentic taste-of-Norway dishes, this longtime favorite is hard to beat. The setting of this place is a much-gentrified update of what was built more than a century ago as a blacksmith shop. Today, amid flickering candles and a collection of 19th-century wood- and metal-working artifacts, you get a sense of rustic, old-fashioned Norway, much spiffed up from the dingy, smoke-filled days when the place would have been a lot less appealing. Menu items include some of the time-tested workhorses of the Norwegian culinary repertoire, including gin-marinated smoked salmon; cream of fish and shellfish soup; small-scale platters of fish roe, served with very fresh bread and Norwegian butter; a traditional air-dried fish specialty, lutefisk, that's notoriously difficult to make and, in this case, is served with bacon; several kinds of grilled beefsteaks, some accompanied with grilled shrimp; barbecued pork ribs; and a dessert specialty: wild-berry parfait with whisky sauce. One of the town's best values is the lunchtime buffet, served year-round; in autumn, it focuses on fresh game dishes from the surrounding tundras and forests. A more elaborate version of that same buffet is also served throughout the day on Sunday.

Kongsgårdsgata 1. ✆ **73-51-66-80.** Reservations recommended. Main courses NOK145–NOK310 ($29–$62/£15–£31); lunchtime buffet NOK150 ($30/£15); Sun buffet NOK195 ($39/£20). AE, DC, MC, V. Mon–Sat noon–midnight; Sun noon–9pm. Closed Mon Dec–Apr. Bus: 5, 6, 7, or 9.

Jonathan's ★ NORWEGIAN/FRENCH This restaurant, though fine in every way, is far less impressive than the elegant Palm Garden in the same hotel—but it's also far more affordable. Jonathan's is designed in the manner of a Mediterranean wine cellar, with antiques; a big, open fireplace; and waiters colorfully dressed as troubadours. The beautifully prepared food relies on high-quality ingredients. Launch yourself with such tantalizing starters as the classic smoked salmon or the "Trondheim caviar" (really fish roe). Smoked salmon is also grilled as a main course, especially tasty when garnished with shellfish and accompanied by fresh vegetables. The veal schnitzel is as good as anything this side of Vienna.

In the Britannia Hotel, Dronningens Gate 5. ✆ **73-80-08-00.** Reservations required. Main courses NOK230–NOK280 ($46–$56/£23–£28). AE, DC, MC, V. Mon–Sat 5–11pm; Sun 4–10pm. Bus: 5, 6, 7, or 9.

Kvilhaugen Gård (Rest Hill Farm) ★ Finds NORWEGIAN Go here not just for the good food, but also to experience Trondheim as it used to be. Surrounded by the trees and lawns of a prosperous residential suburb, about 4km (2½ miles) east of Trondheim's commercial core, this historic restaurant, convention center, and pub is contained in what used to be the barn of a manor from the early 19th century. The most convivial part of the compound today, however, is the red-sided barn *(fjøset),* originally built around 1820, which still retains signs indicating to diners and drinkers which area of the interior used to be reserved for cows, sheep, and pigs. Be careful not to bump your head against the massive antique ceiling beams as you enjoy either midafternoon snacks or full meals that might include melon with Parma ham; creamy fish soup; chicken salad; baked trout, arctic char, turbot, or salmon; and roasted filets of beef or reindeer. The food is good, wholesome, regional fare, made with well-chosen ingredients and cooked with local flavor.

 Blussuvollsbakken 40. ✆ **73-52-08-70.** Reservations recommended for meals, not necessary for tea, coffee, or snacks. Snacks NOK85–NOK135 ($17–$27/£9–£14); main courses NOK195–NOK269 ($39–$54/£20–£27). AE, DC, MC, V. Mon–Thurs 4pm–midnight; Fri–Sat 4pm–1am; Sun 2–8:30pm. Bus: 60.

Sushi Bar JAPANESE One of only two sushi restaurants in Trondheim, this is the superior choice. Set on the town's main street, dubbed Trondheim's "Champs-Elysées," it's outfitted in neutral tones of beige (which tend to showcase the refrigerated racks of very fresh fish), with large oil paintings and an open kitchen where a team of experts filet, roll, and prepare wooden and ceramic trays of artfully simple raw fish, many of which come ultrafresh from local waters. The best value is a sushi main-course platter, consisting of 10 pieces of sushi and six pieces of *makki* (fish filet rolled, with rice, into a roulade). Priced at NOK229 ($46/£23), it sells for less than what you'd have paid if you had assembled and paid for each of its components individually.

Munkegate 39. ✆ **73-52-10-20.** Main courses NOK185–NOK245 ($37–$49/£19–£25). AE, DC, MC, V. Daily 3–10:30pm. Bus: 5, 6, 7, or 9.

INEXPENSIVE

Akropolis GREEK As good as Norwegian food is, the foreign palate needs to take a break from time to time. This is the best of the Greek restaurants in Trondheim, and at least some of its business comes from Norwegians who remember their long-ago holidays in Greece with nostalgia. Set inside the cellar of a white-fronted masonry building across the river from the railway station, it has two dining rooms, each outfitted (in blue and white with lots of paneling) like a Greek tavern somewhere in the Peloponnesus. All the Greek favorites appear on the menu and are admirably prepared, including an especially tasty moussaka, curried shrimp, a meal-size portion of Greek salad, various kabobs, roasted lamb aromatically flavored with herbs, and, our favorite, pork souvlaki. All of these dishes might be preceded with a tantalizing assortment of *mezes* (small, bite-size dishes intended as starters).

Fjordgata 19. ✆ **73-51-67-51.** Reservations recommended. Main courses NOK149–NOK245 ($30–$49/£15–£25). AE, DC, MC, V. Sun–Thurs 4–11pm; Fri–Sat 4pm–midnight. Bus: 1 or 4.

Ramp VEGETARIAN A delectable vegetarian cuisine is served here at this restaurant, which is a popular hangout with young people, often students at the university. Norway traditionally has been a land of carnivores, and it's rare to encounter a vegetarian restaurant in the north. Here the cooks emphasize flavor and borrow freely from an international repertoire of meat-free dishes, including hummus or a tantalizing Greek salad with feta cheese and olives. A delectable Caesar salad is also served. Veggie burgers, even a fish burger, also emerge from the kitchen. Always count on an array of freshly made pastries.

Strandveien 25A. ✆ **73-51-80-20.** www.lamoramp.net. Main courses NOK75–NOK125 ($15–$25/£7.50–£13). MC, V. Mon–Wed 10am–midnight; Thurs–Fri 1am–1am; Sat noon–1am; Sun noon–midnight. Bus: 1 or 4.

Restaurant Egon AMERICAN This is one of the friendliest joints in Trondheim and a good place to hang out if you're young with a gleam in your eye. Nothing about this place even pretends to be gourmet or even upscale. It's set in the center of town in an early-20th-century stone building that was originally built as a bank. Within a labyrinth of dark, woodsy-looking pub areas and dining rooms, the restaurant serves the Norwegian equivalent of American-style diner food. There's a beery kind of sudsiness to the place, an appropriate foil for the pizzas that emerge from the open-to-view brick-lined ovens. In summer, the venue spills out onto the terrace outside.

Thomas Angellsgate 8 (entrance on Søndregate). ✆ **73-51-79-75.** Pizzas, burgers, salads, and platters NOK125–NOK222 ($25–$44/£13–£22). AE, DC, MC, V. Mon–Sat 11am–midnight; Sun noon–11pm. Bus: 1 or 4.

Tavern på Sverresborg ★ *Finds* NORWEGIAN No restaurant in town offers more authentic Norwegian cuisine than this historic eatery, 4.8km (3 miles) south of Trondheim's commercial center and immediately adjacent to the Trondelag Folk Museum. Built as a private merchant's house in 1739 and later transformed into a clapboard-sided tavern, it's one of the few wooden buildings of its age in this area. Cramped and cozy, it's the town's most vivid reminder of the past, with wide-plank flooring and antique rustic accessories. The most desirable and oft-requested table is directly in front of a fireplace in a side room, and as such it's usually reserved in advance. There's an emphasis on 18th- and 19th-century recipes. Try the *blandet spekemat,* served with flatbrød; it consists of thinly sliced smoked ham, diced meat, slices of salami, smoked mutton, and garnishes of lettuce and tomato. From the taste of Norway menu, you can also enjoy homemade fishcakes fried in butter or lightly cured herring with beets and onion rings. Another good-tasting dish is marinated chicken breast with a sour cream sauce laced with chervil and parsley.

Sverresborg Allé, at Trøndelag Folk Museum. ✆ **73-87-80-70.** Reservations recommended. Main courses NOK77–NOK330 ($15–$66/£7.70–£33). AE, DC, MC, V. Mon–Fri 4pm–midnight; Sat–Sun 2pm–midnight. Bus: 8.

THE LEADING CAFE

Kafe Choco Boco DRINKS/PASTRIES If you have a desire for "Death by Chocolate," patronize this cafe. There are several branch locations throughout town for this chocolate-obsessed cafe, but this is the hot address, attracting young people, most often university students, to its precincts. Once here, they devour not only *varm chocolade,* but also several other chocolate drinks, including one rather horrifyingly sweet concoction made with marshmallows. Mint and caramel also flavor these chocolate drinks. For the non–chocolate lover, there are plenty of other items on the menu, including sandwiches, freshly made salads ranging from Greek to Caesar, a fresh soup of the day, and bagels and freshly made cakes, muffins, and brownies. There is also an on-site art gallery, featuring revolving exhibitions of local talent.

Nedre Bakklandet 5. ✆ **73-50-43-35.** Reservations not necessary. Sandwiches NOK90–NOK120 ($18–$24/£9–£12); chocolate drinks NOK40–NOK55 ($8–$11/£4–£5.50); cakes NOK22–NOK50 ($4.40–$10/£2.20–£5). MC, V. Daily 11am–midnight. Bus: 1 or 4.

4 SEEING THE SIGHTS

Erkebispegården (Archbishop's Palace) ★★ Visit Scandinavia's oldest secular building in conjunction with Nidaros Cathedral (see below). It was once the center of the Norwegian archdiocese, comprising not only Norway but also the Faeroe and Shetland Islands, the Isle of Man, and even Greenland and Iceland. Today's museum, which was started in the second part of the 1100s, lies close to the cathedral precincts. Until the Reformation came in 1537 and the ruling archbishop got the boot, the palace was the home of every reigning ecclesiastical authority in Trondheim. Once the archbishops were gone, it became the official address for the Danish governors, and was later taken over by the Norwegian military. As you stand in the courtyard, you can see buildings that date

Trondheim Attractions

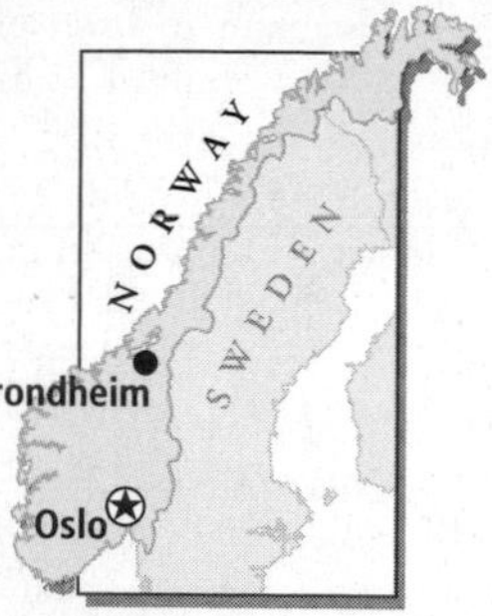

Erkebispegården (Archbishop's Palace) **8**

Kristiansen Festnung **9**

Nidaros Domkirke (Cathedral of Tronheim) **7**

Nordenfjeldske Kunstindustrimuseum **5**

Ringve Museum **2**

Stiftsgården **4**

Sverresborg Trøndelag Folk Museum **1**

Trondheim Kunstmuseum **6**

Trondhjems Sjøfartsmuseum (Maritime Museum) **3**

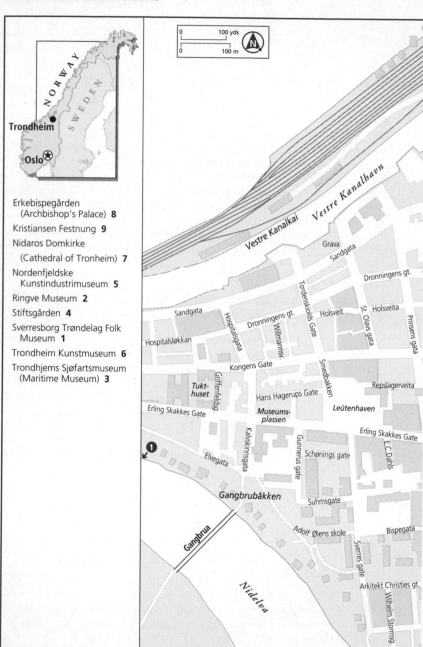

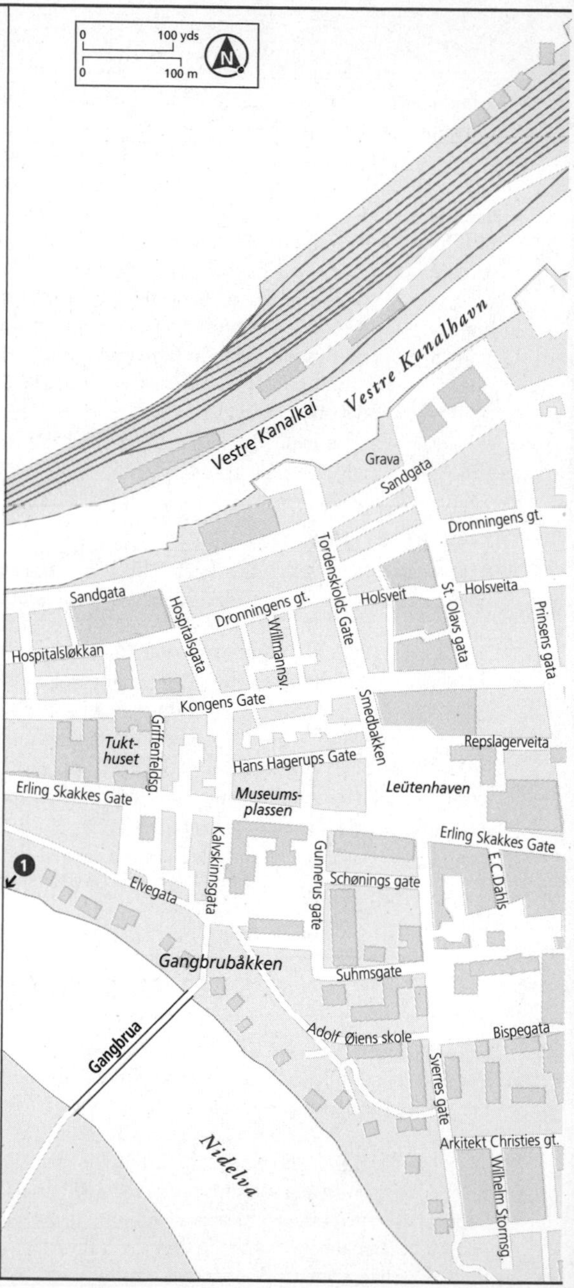

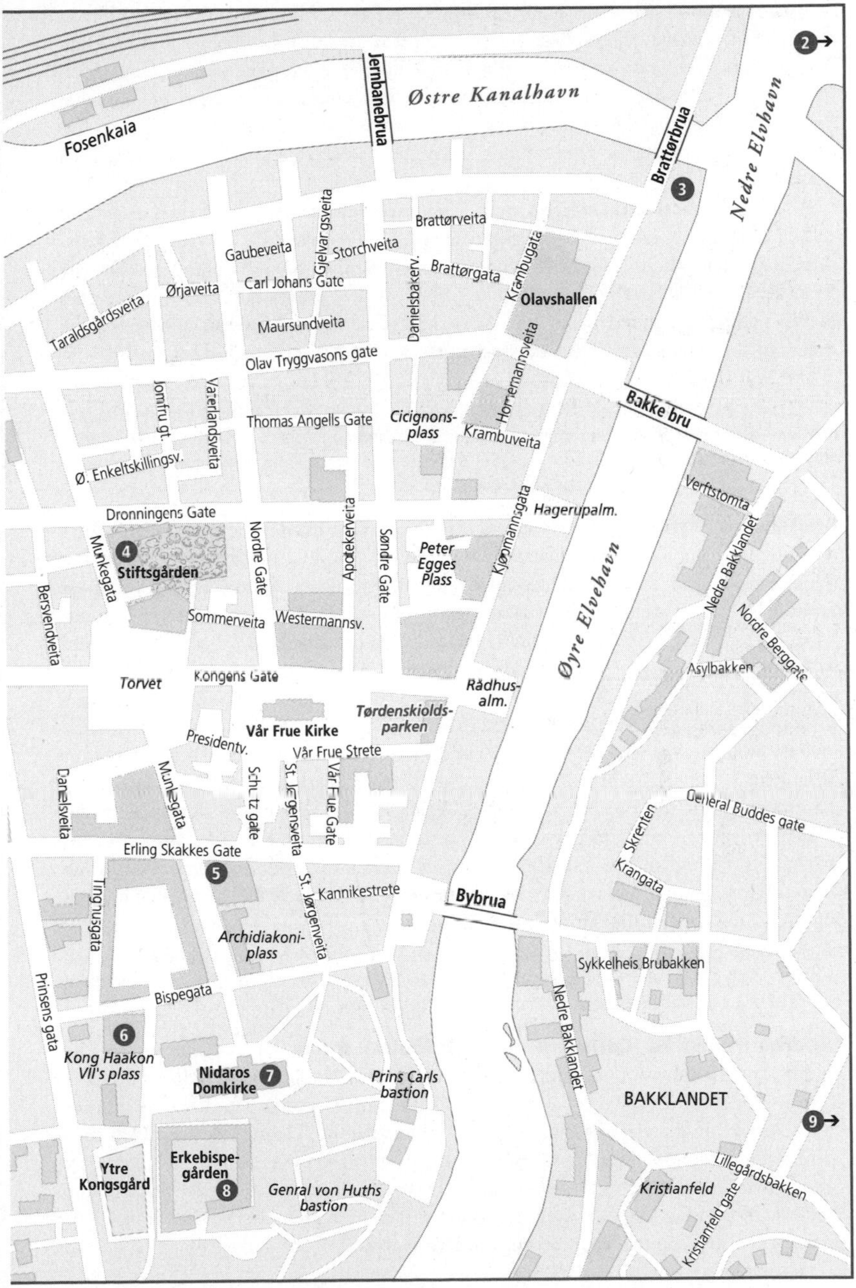

Østre Kanalhavn
Fosenkaia
Jernbanebrua
Brattørbrua
Nedre Elvhavn
Brattørveita
Gjelvargsveita
Storchveita
Gaubeveita
Carl Johans Gate
Brattørgata
Krambugata
Olavshallen
Ørjaveita
Taraldsgårdsveita
Danielsbakerv.
Maursundveita
Olav Tryggvasons gate
Hornemannsveita
Bakke bru
Jomfru gt.
Vaterlandsveita
Thomas Angells Gate
Cicignons-plass
Krambuveita
Ø. Enkeltskillingsv.
Verftstomta
Dronningens Gate
Kjøpmannsgata
Hagerupalm.
Munkegata
Stiftsgården
Nordre Gate
Apotekerveita
Søndre Gate
Peter Egges Plass
Nedre Bakklandet
Bersvendveita
Sommerveita
Westermannsv.
Øyre Elvehavn
Nordre Berggate
Torvet
Kongens Gate
Rådhus-alm.
Asylbakken
Tørdenskiolds-parken
Vår Frue Kirke
Presidenty.
Vår Frue Strete
Danielsveita
Munkegata
Schultz gate
St. Jørgensveita
Vår Frue Gate
General Buddes gate
Skrenten
Erling Skakkes Gate
Krangata
Tinghusgata
Kannikestrete
St. Jørgenveita
Bybrua
Archidiakoni-plass
Sykkelheis Brubakken
Prinsens gata
Bispegata
Nedre Bakklandet
Kong Haakon VII's plass
Nidaros Domkirke
Prins Carls bastion
BAKKLANDET
Ytre Kongsgård
Erkebispe-gården
Genral von Huths bastion
Lillegårdsbakken
Kristianfeld
Kristianfeld gate

from the 1160s to the 1990s. In summer, there are daily guided tours of the historic buildings.

If time is short, visit at least the **Archbishop's Palace Museum,** displaying artifacts discovered when two large storage buildings on this site burned to the ground in 1983. After 5 years of excavations, many artifacts were discovered, and the museum opened in 1997. More intriguing still are the **sculptures** ★★★ removed from Nidaros Cathedral for safekeeping; the gargoyles, mythological figures, and animals of the Middle Ages live on here. The cathedral and its famous sculptures are also depicted in an audiovisual presentation.

Also here is the **Rustkammeret med Hjemmefrontmuseet,** Trondheim's army and resistance museum, entered at Kongsgårdsgata (✆ **73-53-91-60**), charging no admission. It is open June to August Monday to Friday 9am to 3pm, Saturday and Sunday 11am to 4pm. It is closed otherwise. The history of the military is traced from the days of the Vikings. Of more recent vintage is the **Home Front Museum,** presenting the drama of the Norwegian Resistance during the horrendous occupation by the Nazis in World War II.

Kongsgårdsgata. ✆ **73-53-91-60.** Admission NOK50 ($10/£5) adults, NOK25 ($5/£2.50) children. May to mid-June Mon–Sat 9am–3pm, Sun noon–4pm; mid-June to mid-Aug Mon–Fri 9am–5pm, Sat 9am–3pm, Sun noon–5pm; mid-Aug to mid-Sept Mon–Sat 9am–3pm, Sun noon–5pm; mid-Sept to Apr Mon–Fri 11am–3pm, Sat 11am–2pm, Sun noon–2pm. Bus: 5, 6, 7, or 9.

Kristiansen Festnung This fortress is a bit grim for us, but the view from its precincts is reason enough to visit. Located about 2km (1¼ miles) east of the center of town, this is a stone-sided, thick-walled vestige of the military power of the army that occupied Trondheim during the 17th and 18th centuries. Built by the Danes between 1681 and 1682 as a defense against the Swedes during the reign of Christian IV, it alone is credited with repelling the attacks of the Swedish army in 1718, and thereby saving Trondheim from foreign occupation. It was constructed according to the most advanced military wisdom of its day, in a nine-sided design that might have been influenced by the French military architect Vauban. Between 1816 and 1901, it functioned as the headquarters of Trondheim's firefighting brigades. Under the Nazi occupation, the fort was used as a place of execution for members of the Norwegian Resistance; a plaque has been erected in their memory. On warm days, expect to see sunbathers and families with children playing on the verdant lawns that have replaced the muddy, pounded-earth floor of the historical fort. From its ramparts, you'll see the best **panorama** ★★ in town, encompassing fjords, towers, and the rest of Trondheim.

Rosenborg. No phone. Free admission. Year-round, gates to the compound open Mon–Tues when the Norwegian flag is flying above the fortress; Wed–Sun 8am–midnight. The interior of the compound can be visited btw. June and mid-Aug daily 11am–4pm, without charge. Bus: 63.

Nidaros Domkirke (Cathedral of Trondheim) ★★★ It was the goal of the medieval pilgrim to visit this grand cathedral, and it's still the goal of thousands of today's travelers. Usually the capital city of a country has the most spectacular cathedral, but not so in Norway. In grandeur, Nidaros dwarfs Oslo Cathedral. Dating from the 11th century, it's the most important, most historic, and most impressive ecclesiastical building in Scandinavia. It's located in the town center, near the Rådhus. The burial place of the medieval Norwegian kings, it was also the site of the coronation of Haakon VII in 1905, an event that marked the beginning of modern Norway.

Moments An Escapist's Retreat

The **Ringve Botaniske Hage (Ringve Botanical Gardens)** lie on Lade Allé 58 (✆ **73-59-22-69**) and form part of the University of Trondheim's Museum of Natural History and Archaeology. This is one of the finest places to be on a summer day in Norway. You can wander through a historic and Renaissance-style herb garden, enjoying the trees of the Northern Hemisphere. The entire park is laid out in the English garden style. Head for the nearest bench—and the day is yours. The admission-free park is open all year.

Construction actually began on the cathedral in 1070, and some of its oldest parts still remain, mainly from the middle of the 1100s. Following the battle of Stiklestad, King Olaf Haraldson was entombed under the high altar. In time, Olaf became Saint Olaf, and his remains were encased in a gem-studded shrine.

The cathedral has weathered several unfortunate events. It's been a victim of fires that swept over Trondheim. The church was reconstructed each time in its original Gothic style. (The section around the transept, however, is Romanesque.) During the Reformation, the cathedral was looted of precious relics. By 1585, Nidaros had been reduced to the status of a parish church. Around 1869 major reconstruction work was begun to return the gray sandstone building to its former glory.

The west facade is particularly impressive, with its carved figures of royalty and saints. It's especially appealing after dark, when the facade is floodlit (the lights usually stay on every evening till midnight—it's worth a stroll even if you have to make a detour to do it). The interior is a maze of mammoth pillars and columns with beautifully carved arches that divide the chancel from the nave. The grandest feature is the stunning **rose window** ★. The cathedral's **stained-glass windows** ★, when caught in the proper light, are reason enough to visit. Gustav Vigeland, the famous sculptor, carved the **gargoyles and grotesques** ★ for the head tower and northern transept. A small museum inside displays the **crown jewels** ★★ of Norway.

Bispegaten 5. ✆ **73-53-91-60.** Admission to cathedral and museum NOK50 ($10/£5) adults, NOK25 ($5/£2.50) children. Cathedral and museum May 1–June 10 Mon–Fri 9am–3pm, Sat 9am–2pm, Sun 1–4pm; June 11–Aug 19 Mon–Fri 9am–6pm, Sat 9am–2pm, Sun 1–4pm; Aug 20–Sept 14 Mon–Fri 9am–3pm, Sat 9am–2pm, Sun 1–4pm; Sept 15–Apr 30 Mon–Fri noon–2:30pm, Sat 11:30am–2pm, Sun 1–3pm. Bus: 5, 6, 7, or 9.

Nordenfjeldske Kunstindustrimuseum ★★★ This is the single greatest museum of central Norway, holding one of the most eclectic collections in the country. Dating from 1893, the museum is devoted to applied arts, placing special focus on the changing trends in world art, especially in modern design and handcrafts. You'll see both historical and modern collections of furniture, textiles, silver, and a lot more, along with temporary exhibitions.

Displayed on the lower floor, the historical exhibitions span the period from 1500 to 1990, specializing in furnishings from northern Europe, including Germany and England. The **Arts and Crafts collection** focuses on the creative breakthroughs of British craftsman and designer William Morris and his followers at the end of the 1800s and is rich in metal craft, avant-garde ceramics, and printed textiles. The **Art Nouveau collection** is heavy on French art; most of it was purchased at the 1900 World Exhibition in Paris. An entire salon on the lower floor is devoted to the contributions in Art Nouveau architecture by architect and designer Henri Van de Velde, a citizen of Belgium.

The **Contemporary Collection** concentrates on objects created in the postwar era—not only in Europe but also from as far away as Australia or even America. Scandinavian design gets the most focus, of course, and there is an interior entirely designed by Finn Juhl, the Danish architect, in 1952. Of special interest are 200 **wall hangings and tapestries by Hannah Ryggen ★**, clustered in one gallery. This Swedish artist, born in 1894, married Hans Ryggen, the Norwegian painter, and lived outside Trondheim until her death in 1970.

Other collections include a **Costume Exhibition,** with garments dating from the 17th century, the era of the 1920s and 1930s most heavily represented. Other exhibitions are devoted to some **300 pieces of jewelry** in modern design and a **Japanese collection** showcasing that country's creativity in metalwork, lacquer, textiles, and pottery.

Munkegate 3–7. ✆ **73-80-89-50.** www.nkim.museum.no. Admission NOK60 ($12/£6) adults, NOK30 ($6/£3) children, students, and seniors. June 1–Aug 20 Mon–Sat 10am–5pm, Sun noon–5pm; off season Tues–Sat 10am–3pm (Thurs until 5pm), Sun noon–4pm. Bus: 5 or 46.

Ringve Museum ★★ Finds This is the only Norwegian museum specializing in musical instruments from all over the world. Set on the Ringve Estate on the Lade Peninsula, the building originated in the 1740s as a prosperous manor house and farmstead. The mansion was the birthplace of Admiral Tordenskiold, the Norwegian sea hero. The museum today consists of two parts—the museum in the manor house and a permanent exhibition in the estate's former barn. In the barn you can hear the special sound of Norwegian folk music instruments; there's even a hands-on exhibition where you can discover the budding musician in yourself. At specified times, concerts are given on carefully preserved antique instruments, including an impressive collection of spinets, harpsichords, clavichords, pianofortes, and string and wind instruments. Also on the premises is an old *kro* (inn) that serves waffles, light refreshments, and coffee.

Lade Allé 60 (3.3km/2 miles east from the center of town at Ringve Manor). ✆ **73-87-02-80.** www.ringve.no. Admission NOK75 ($15/£7.50) adults, NOK25 ($5/£2.50) children 7–15, NOK50 ($10/£5) students, NOK150 ($30/£15) families. Mid-Apr to mid-May Mon–Fri and Sun 11am–4pm; mid-May to mid-June daily 11am–3pm; mid-June to Aug 5 daily 11am–5pm; Aug 6–Sept 9 daily 11am–3pm; Sept 10 to mid-Apr Sun 11am–4pm. During hours, multilingual guided tours depart at least once per hour, sometimes more frequently. Bus: 3 or 4.

Stiftsgården When the royal family visits Trondheim, they stay here—and they never run out of bedrooms. With 144 rooms, it is the largest wooden building in northern Europe, a massive pile in the late baroque style. This buttercup-yellow royal palace near the marketplace was built as a private home by a rich merchant's widow in the 1770s, when Trondheim began to regain its prosperity. The exterior walls were notched together, log-cabin style, then sheathed with wooden exterior panels. The unpretentious furnishings represent an amalgam of design styles.

Munkegate 23. ✆ **73-84-28-80.** Admission NOK60 ($12/£6) adults, NOK30 ($6/£3) children, NOK100 ($20/£10) family. Guided tours every hour on the hour. June 1–June 19 Mon–Sat 10am–3pm, Sun noon–5pm; June 20–Aug 20 Mon–Sat 10am–5pm, Sun noon–5pm. Closed Aug 21–May 31. Bus: 3, 4, 5, 46, 52.

Sverresborg Trøndelag Folk Museum ★★★ Kids This is the best folkloric museum in Norway, and it's filled with farmhouses, cottages, churches, and town buildings,

Fun Facts The First European to Discover America

Trondheimers have no doubt who first discovered America—or, put more politically correct, the first European to discover an already inhabited continent. Here is the official line as taught in local schools: "Leiv Eiriksson sailed to Nidaros in the year A.D. 999. The visit to Olaf Tryggvason's new royal farm must have been a success. Leiv Eiriksson became the king's man and stayed as a guest all winter. Spring came and he was a changed man. He had been baptized as a Christian. He launched his mighty boats at Skipakrok and sailed over the ocean to Greenland and further, far, far to the west. Leiv Eiriksson made the discovery of a lifetime—America."

To honor Leiv Eiriksson, there is an emigrant monument, **Leiv Eiriksson Statue,** at Pirsenheret, Brattøra (take any bus circulating through Trondheim's downtown to Pirterminalen). It was a gift from Americans of Scandinavian heritage to honor Trondheim's millennium celebration in 1997. The statue was erected and dedicated to emigrants who left Norway to seek a new life in America. The monument is an exact copy of the original, which stands in Seattle.

representing aspects of everyday life in the region over the past 3 centuries. Kids often find this attraction a kind of "Trondheim Disneyworld," but it's more real than Mickey Mouse land. It's both educational and fun to wander about, like a journey back to a living past. Standing 5km (3 miles) west of the center, the complex is composed of 60 historic, laboriously dismantled and reassembled buildings, all made from wood and stone, including the first all-brick building in Trondheim (ca. 1780). Among the compound's most intriguing buildings are the 200-year-old barns, many with sod roofs, many painted red, and most built of weathered natural wood. There's a cafe on the premises, but if you want a good meal, we recommend that you head next door to the celebrated restaurant **Tavern på Sverresborg** (see "Where to Dine," earlier in this chapter), which serves traditional Norwegian dishes. The proudest possession here is Norway's northernmost stave church.

On the grounds of the folk museum, within an antique building hauled in from some other part of the province, is an all-separate museum, the **Sverresborg Ski Museum.** Entrance to the ski museum is included in the price of admission to the Folk Museum, and hours are the same, too. Tracing the history of skiing in Norway, it contains antique skis from the 1600s to today, some carved in patterns inspired by the Vikings, and some with fur or sealskin cladding, which prevented them from sliding backwards during cross-country skiing. The museum is also surrounded by a nature park with animals.

Sverresborg Allé. ✆ **73-89-01-00.** www.sverresborg.no. Admission NOK80 ($16/£8) adults, NOK30 ($6/£3) children, NOK195 ($39/£20) family ticket, free for children 4 and under. June–Aug daily 11am–6pm; off season Mon–Fri 11am–3pm, Sat–Sun noon–4pm. Bus: 8.

Trondheim Kunstmuseum ★ We used to come here just to gaze upon the collection of lithographs by Edvard Munch, on loan from the Munch Museum in Oslo. In the wake of Munch thefts, the art was returned to Oslo due to security concerns. But there is an array

Finds Zealots, "Perverts" & the Ax Man

Munkholmen (Monk's Island), is a small, rocky, inhospitable, and richly historic island a short distance offshore from Trondheim's core. When the weather permits, daily ferries depart from a point at the northern terminus of Munkegate at hourly intervals between 10am and 7pm for the 10-minute jaunt offshore for picnicking, bird-watching, and beach excursions on the island. Round-trip passage requires less than 12 minutes each way and costs NOK55 ($11/£5.50) for adults, NOK30 ($6/£3) for children 14 and under. Advance bookings aren't necessary, and you can buy your ticket directly from the on-board driver. When the boats operate, departures from the landing stages at Trondheim are hourly, and the boats pick up whichever Munkholmen passenger is trying to reverse his or her direction.

But there's more to this sparse island than fun, games, and picnicking sites. For hundreds of years, beginning in 1658, the island functioned as a prison and an execution site, with a prominent hangman's scaffold, instruments of torture, and wooden blocks where ax men would lop off the heads of wretches condemned as criminals, "perverts," or enemies of the church or state. Before that, in the 11th century, the island was developed by Benedictine monks into one of the first two Christian monasteries in Scandinavia, housing zealots who shivered away the winters as winds and snows howled down the edges of the fjord. You can take a guided tour of the island's **historic fortress** for NOK30 ($6/£3) for adults and NOK20 ($4/£2) for children. There are many panoramic sites if you've opted to bring a picnic. You can buy supplies at the Ravnkloa fish market, a few steps from the landing piers. Otherwise, a cafe and snack bar are built into the much-restored fortifications.

Today Monk's Island is moderately popular as a destination for beachgoers, historians, and bird-watchers, even though the beach is small, gravelly, and relatively narrow, and the island is also very small. Some locals even insist the place is haunted. What you may come away with—at least, in our opinion—is a pervasive sense of melancholy and a profound new appreciation for the hardships and severity of life in medieval Norway. Most first-timers to Munkeholmen return to Trondheim and head immediately for the nearest bar for food, drink, and a replenishment of whatever good cheer they might have lost during their excursion.

Incidentally, **Munkegate,** the broad boulevard known ironically (facetiously?) as the "Champs-Elysées of Trondheim," was named after the medieval monks who lived here and who made frequent, sometimes daily, processionals between the landing pier at the avenue's base and Trondheim's cathedral, a 20-minute walk to the south.

of Norwegian painters to introduce yourself to here, and none is better known nationally than Christian Krohg (1852–1925). He is one of the leading figures in the transition from romanticism to naturalism. Other than Munch, he is our favorite Norwegian artist and is celebrated today for his pictures of prostitutes. But when he published a novel, *Albertine,* on this theme in 1886 he was arrested.

You'll also see works by Theodor Kittelsen (1857–1914), who bridges the gap between the neoromantic and naïve painting. He is known for his illustrations of fairy tales and legends, especially of trolls. Black-metal bands such as Burzum have used some of his pictures as album art, including illustrations from his book *Svartedauen (The Black Death).* No one painted Norwegian landscapes better than Hans Fredrik Gude (1825–1903), a romantic painter who celebrated nature. His work is displayed along with his friend's, Adolph Tidemand, another leading figure in Norwegian painting. Both artists drew inspiration from dramatic mountain scenery and idyllic, sunny landscapes.

In all, there are more than 2,750 paintings that go back as early as 1800. Most of the art is Norwegian, although there is a fairly good treasure trove of Danish art as well, along with a limited selection from international artists.

Bispegate. 7B. ✆ **73-53-81-80.** www.tkm.museum.no. Admission NOK50 ($10/£5) adults, NOK30 ($6/£3) children and students, NOK40 ($8/£4) seniors. June–Aug daily 10am–5pm; off season Tues–Sun 11am–4pm. Bus: 4.

Trondhjems Sjøfartsmuseum (Maritime Museum) An old penitentiary from 1725 was turned into this Norwegian maritime showcase that offers all the models of sailing ships, marine instruments, and figureheads any sea dog would want. Some unusual exhibitions include an 18th-century whaling ship and a harpoon gun. Nautical artifacts rescued from the frigate *The Pearl,* which sank off Norwegian waters in 1781, are on display. Daring divers rescued these artifacts in *Titanic*-cold waters.

Fjordgata 6A. ✆ **73-89-01-00.** Admission NOK25 ($5/£2.50) adults, NOK15 ($3/£1.50) children, students, and seniors. June–Aug daily 10am–4pm. Closed off season. Bus: 52.

ORGANIZED TOURS

At the tourist office (p. 347), you can purchase tickets for guided tours of the city, lasting 2 hours and taking in the highlights. Departure is from Torvet or Market Square daily at 11am between May 26 and August 24. Adults pay NOK195 ($39/£20), while children under 16 enter free if they're accompanied by an adult.

The tourist office publicizes a 1½-hour sea tour, going along the canal harbor and up the River Nidelven and out to the fjord. From June 18 to August 13, it leaves Tuesday to Sunday at noon and 2pm, costing NOK140 ($28/£14) for adults and NOK55 ($11/£5.50) for ages 3 to 14. From August 14 to September 17 tours are on Wednesday, Friday, and Sunday at 2:30pm.

The tourist office can also recommend an evening boat tour, lasting 1½ hours, departing every night between July 2 and August 13 at 6pm from the Ravnkloa market. The cost is NOK140 ($28/£14) for adults and NOK55 ($11/£5.50) for children ages 3 to 14. For this and the sea tour above, buy your tickets directly on the boat.

WALKING TOUR TRONDHEIM'S HISTORIC CENTER

START:	**Torvet at the junction of Munkegate and Kongens gate.**
FINISH:	**Torvet.**
TIME:	**2½ hours.**
BEST TIME:	**Mornings after 8:30am when the Fiskehaller is at its most active.**
WORST TIME:	**Any time in midwinter after 4pm when it's dark, or one of the typical rain-soggy days of Trondheim.**

Begin your tour at the:

❶ Torvet

Here is Trondheim's most prominent traffic circle, at the edge of which is the tourist office and in the middle of which rises the **Trondheim Torg,** a soaring granite column. At its top stands a statue of the world's most handsome Viking—in this case, an idealized portrait of Olaf Tryggvason, founder (in A.D. 997) of Trondheim. Markings on the pavement, tracking the seasonal direction of the sun, define the column on which he stands as the world's largest sundial.

From here, walk north along the Munkegate (the "Champs-Elysées of Trondheim"); its exceptional width was conceived as a firebreak during the rebuilding of Trondheim after a fire destroyed many of the city's wooden buildings in 1681. On your right side, within a 2-minute walk, is the wood-sided, rustic-looking exterior of Trondheim's most prestigious home, the low-slung 18th-century premises of the:

❷ Kongen Lige/Stiftsgården (Royal Residence)

Built in 1778 as the home of the (then-Danish) king, and with 140 rooms that cover almost 4,000 sq. m (43,056 sq. ft.) of floor space, it's the largest secular all-wooden building in northern Europe. Positioned (at least, in the opinion of modern-day security guards) alarmingly close to the street, it's the home of the Norwegian monarch and his/her associates whenever they're in Trondheim on official business. If you're interested in visiting its interior as part of the occasional 30-minute tours conducted only in midsummer, know in advance that its entrance is on the back side, near the building's functional and rather unimaginative garden.

Continue walking north along the Munkegate to the:

❸ Ravnkloa Fiskehaller

This glass-sided, very clean, and modern venue is one of the best places in Trondheim for a snack. You can opt for a bagful of fresh peeled (or unpeeled) shrimp or perhaps a salmon sandwich at this cornucopia of seafood and all things fresh. For more details on this place, refer to the box "Beauty from the Sea—On Ice," below.

Adjacent to the fish market is the ferryboat pier for the boats that travel to Munkeholmen (Monk's Island), a short distance offshore.

Fronting the piers is a contemporary-looking statue, erected in 1990 by artist Nils Aas and dedicated to *Den Siste Viking (The Last Viking).* Its somber caricature was inspired by a novel *(Den Siste Viking)* by Johan Bøjer, a former resident of Trondheim who honored the brave and tough fishermen of Norway for their bravery and fortitude.

From here, walk east along the Fjordgata, then right (south) onto the all-pedestrian Nordre Gate; its edges are lined with Trondheim's densest collection of shops. Within a few blocks, rising from the center of the street, you'll see an exuberant testimonial to young love, the:

❹ Statue to Student Life

This is a life-size male-female depiction of young people swept away in a frenzy of love, dancing ecstatically on a pile of granite books.

Continue walking south on Nordre Gate to the smaller of the town's two medieval churches:

❺ Vår Frue Kirke (Our Lady's Church)

Built in 1150 and enlarged in 1686 and again in 1739, this bulky, boxy, and dignified church (and its bell tower, tacked onto the existing structure in 1739) is almost as wide as the nave of the church itself. Regrettably, there were once 17 medieval churches in Trondheim. Now only two (this church and the cathedral, visited later as part of this walking tour) remain. Consider yourself lucky if you happen to arrive during its rare, regularly scheduled opening hours (Wed only, 11am–2pm).

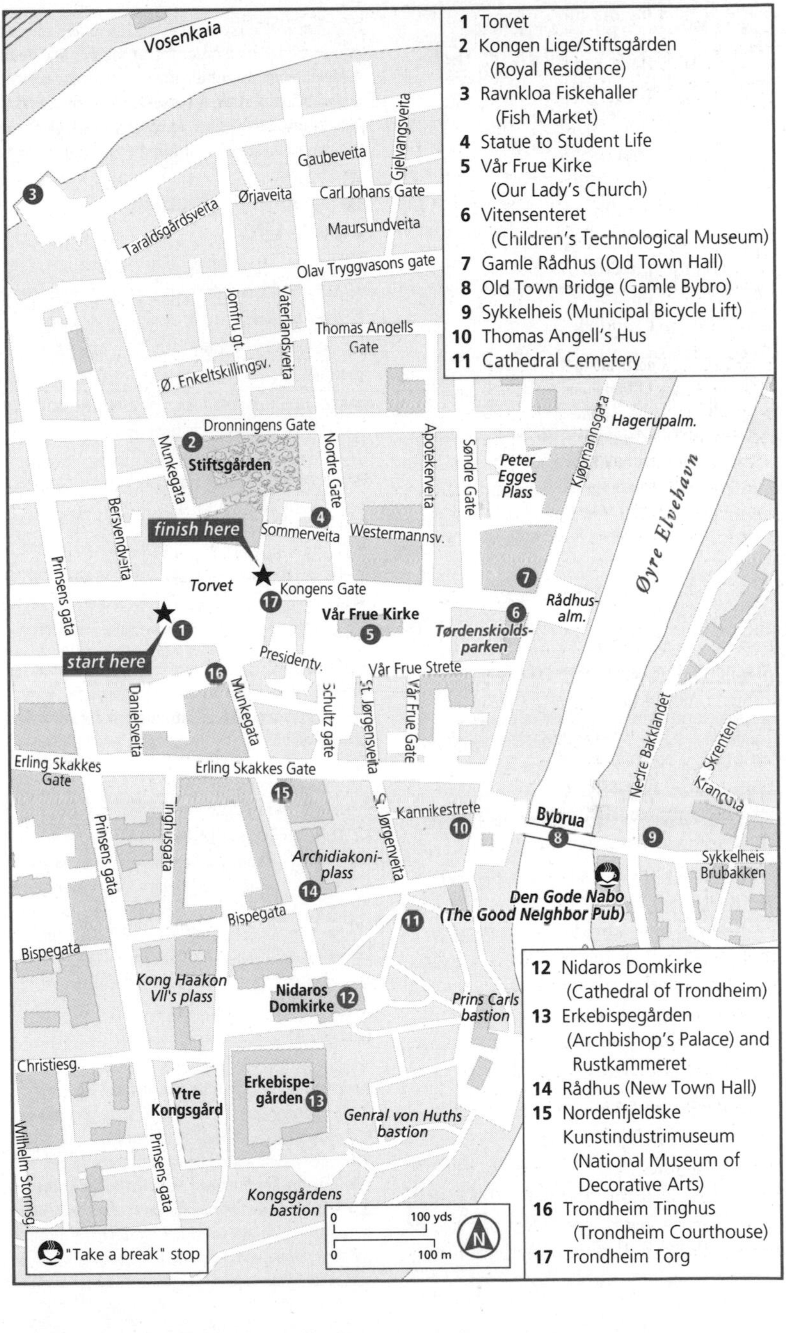
1 Torvet
2 Kongen Lige/Stiftsgården (Royal Residence)
3 Ravnkloa Fiskehaller (Fish Market)
4 Statue to Student Life
5 Vår Frue Kirke (Our Lady's Church)
6 Vitensenteret (Children's Technological Museum)
7 Gamle Rådhus (Old Town Hall)
8 Old Town Bridge (Gamle Bybro)
9 Sykkelheis (Municipal Bicycle Lift)
10 Thomas Angell's Hus
11 Cathedral Cemetery
12 Nidaros Domkirke (Cathedral of Trondheim)
13 Erkebispegården (Archbishop's Palace) and Rustkammeret
14 Rådhus (New Town Hall)
15 Nordenfjeldske Kunstindustrimuseum (National Museum of Decorative Arts)
16 Trondheim Tinghus (Trondheim Courthouse)
17 Trondheim Torg
Vosenkaia
Gaubeveita
Gjelvangsveita
Carl Johans Gate
Ørjaveita
Taraldsgårdsveita
Maursundveita
Olav Tryggvasons gate
Jomfru gt.
Vaterlandsveita
Thomas Angells Gate
Ø. Enkeltskillingsv.
Dronningens Gate
Munkegata
Stiftsgården
Nordre Gate
Apotekerveita
Søndre Gate
Peter Egges Plass
Kjøpmannsgata
Hagerupalm.
Øyre Elvehavn
Bersvendveita
finish here
Sommerveita
Westermannsv.
Prinsens gata
Torvet
Kongens Gate
Vår Frue Kirke
Tørdenskiolds-parken
Rådhus-alm.
start here
Presidentv.
Vår Frue Strete
Danielsveita
Schultz gate
St. Jørgensveita
Vår Frue Gate
Nedre Bakklandet
Skrenten
Krangata
Erling Skakkes Gate
Inghusgata
Kannikestrete
Bybrua
Sykkelheis Brubakken
Archidiakoni-plass
Bispegata
Den Gode Nabo (The Good Neighbor Pub)
Kong Haakon VII's plass
Nidaros Domkirke
Prins Carls bastion
Christiesg.
Ytre Kongsgård
Erkebispe-gården
Genral von Huths bastion
Wilhelm Stormsg.
Kongsgårdens bastion
0 100 yds
0 100 m
N
"Take a break" stop

From here, turn left onto Kongens Gate and walk east for about a block to Kongens Gate 1. Here, at the corner of the Kjøpmannsgata, behind an impressive-looking 19th-century redbrick facade, is the:

6 Vitensenteret (Children's Technological Museum)

Originally designed in 1833 as the Trondheim branch of the Bank of Norway, it was rebuilt in 1900 into the late-Victorian design you see today. Most visitors come here as part of school groups from the surrounding region, and unless you have small children in tow, we recommend you move on to other venues.

Directly across Kongens Gate, behind a Hanseatic-inspired facade that's adorned with an eight-pointed star-shaped window and the city's seal, is the:

7 Gamle Rådhus (Old Town Hall)

Originally built in the 1700s, this is now mostly a decorative monument, because most of Trondheim's day-to-day administrative duties are handled by a contemporary-looking new Town Hall positioned close to the cathedral and noted later as part of this walking tour.

Now turn right onto Kjøpmannsgata. In a short distance, on your left side, you'll see a row of the oldest warehouses in town, each individual building painted in a cheerful palette of colors. A short distance later, on your left, you'll arrive at the wood planks and iron girders of the:

8 Old Town Bridge (Gamle Bybro)

Originally built of wood in 1861 as a replacement for an all-wood predecessor in 1685, this is the most evocative, beloved, and frequently photographed bridge in Trondheim. Locals refer to it as the "Bridge of Happiness" and claim that your dreams will come true if you wish for them fervently as you walk across it. As you're articulating your dreams, note the neo-Gothic mass, atop the ridge on the distant horizon to your right, of the headquarters of Trondheim's University. Also look to your left from the bridge, noticing the dozens of carefully preserved 18th- and 19th-century warehouses rising on pilings above the river—proof of how extensive the maritime economy of Trondheim once was.

Continue walking straight across the cobble-covered intersection (Øvre Bakklandet on one side and Nedre Bakklandet on the other) after you cross the bridge, and walk uphill along the street identified as Sykkelheis. Within 27m (89 ft.), on the right side, you'll see the civic government's contribution to fresh air and exercise, the:

9 Sykkelheis (Municipal Bicycle Lift)

Designed to assist bike riders in their ascent of the steep hill, this mechanized conveyor belt (most of which is concealed underground beneath a metal-edged groove in the pavement) hauls bicycles, with their riders, up a steeply inclined stretch of a scenic bike path. The cost for 15 minutes of continuous operation is NOK100 ($20/£10), which you can pay by inserting coins into the machine's coin slot. Frankly, most individual riders either walk their bikes or cycle in low gear up the relatively short hill, but as a conversation piece, the Sykkelheis is worth a look.

From the Sykkelheis, retrace your steps downhill and turn left onto Øvre Bakklandet. Within a few steps, behind the vine-covered brown-plank facade of one of the first buildings on your right, you'll find an appropriate place to:

> **TAKE A BREAK**
> ***Den Gode Nabo* (The Good Neighbor),** Øvre Bakklandet 66 (✆ **73-87-42-40**), is our favorite pub in the city, where you can dine on delectable fish soup. For more about the pub, see "Trondheim After Dark," later in this chapter.

Now retrace your steps back across the Old Town Bridge. When you reach the other side, turn left onto Kjøpmannsgata and walk for about a minute. When you reach a clearing in the bank of trees on your left (the side toward the river), look in the far distance to a point across the river on the crest of a stony ridge, for a view of Trondheim's once-strategic 18th-century military stronghold, Kristiansen Festnung, which is separately described in "Seeing the Sights," earlier in

this chapter. During clement weather, a Norwegian flag proudly flies from its summit. When Kjøpmannsgata intersects with Bispegate, turn right and look on the Bispegate's right side for a view of Trondheim's most elaborate baroque building, the:

⑩ Thomas Angell's Hus

Originally built in 1770 and extensively restored according to its original design in 1903, this was conceived as a retirement home for indigent widows. Later its venue was expanded to allow widows to cohabit with well-recommended widowers outside the bounds of traditional marriages—a liberal 19th-century trend of which many Trondheimers seem appropriately proud. There's a pleasant garden in the building's interior courtyard, but hours of visitation are erratic, and the doors are very likely to be locked at the time of your visit.

Continue walking west along the Bispegate, detouring into the intensely evocative:

⑪ Cathedral Cemetery

Cemetery walks aren't for everyone, but this one is spiritually evocative and appropriately eerie. For centuries, grave sites here were reserved only for the town's more prominent citizens, and consequently, many of the grave markers are carefully planned sculptures in their own right. Note the location of this cemetery on your visit in the daylight hours; you may want to make a return visit, perhaps late at night and—preferably—when it's raining and the wind is howling. Its majestic trees and undulating walkways lead to the cemetery's centerpiece, the:

⑫ Nidaros Domkirke (Cathedral of Trondheim)

We think this is the single most amazing, stunning, and majestic building in Norway. Spend some quality time here and plan on a return sometime before you leave Trondheim for a second view of the cathedral's amazing rear (we define it as the most spectacular bas-relief in Europe). Plan your second visit after dark, when much of the cathedral's exterior is illuminated nightly until around midnight. For more about this cathedral, see "Seeing the Sights," earlier in this chapter. Through a medieval gatehouse that's accessible from the cathedral's back side, wander into the vast and interesting courtyard that was created by the juxtaposition of two rambling buildings:

⑬ The Erkebispegården (Archbishop's Palace) and the Rustkammeret (Hjemmefrontmuseet)

The architecture on this square takes you back to the dim, often unrecorded past of Norway in the Middle Ages. Erkebispegården is the oldest secular building in Scandinavia; work started on the structure in the second half of the 12th century. Rustkammeret, or the army museum, is one of the oldest structures in Norway.

From here, return to the cathedral's front side, and walk briskly north along the Munkgate. The first building you'll see on the Munkegate's right side (on the eastern corner of the Bispegate), is Trondheim's:

⑭ Rådhus (New Town Hall)

This is not to be confused with the Gamle Rådhus, visited earlier on this tour. This modern, fortresslike brick building is where most of the day-to-day administrative functions of city government are carried out, and it's not open to the public for casual visits.

Continue walking north along the Munkegate. At the corner of the Erling Skakkes Gate, on the street's eastern flank, you'll see Trondheim's homage to the contemporary decorative arts of Norway, the:

⑮ Nordenfjeldske Kunstindustrimuseum (National Museum of Decorative Arts)

Here exhibits celebrate Norway's contribution to the tenets of modern decor and designs in glass, wood, textiles, and metal.

Continue your northward progression along the Munkegate, admiring the occasional piece of public sculpture along its path. Our favorite is the life-size representation, in bronze, of a group of grazing deer. About a block farther along the same street, at Munkegate 20, behind a bas-relief sculpture from the 1940s, is the:

Moments Beauty from the Sea—On Ice

Some Norwegians believe that genuine beauty can be found in the fruits of the sea, and even if you don't agree, you should make a point to visit one of Norway's most appealing indoor fish markets, **Ravnkloa Fiskehalle** ★ (✆ **73-52-55-21**). Set at the northern terminus of the Munkegate, adjacent to the ferry piers servicing Munkeholmen Island, this is a glass-and-steel structure of impeccable cleanliness—with the kind of hard-surface interior that gets hosed down frequently as a means of taking away some of the fishiness. Inside, a series of independent vendors sell meat on one side and stunning-looking fish, laid out in ordered rows on beds of ice, on the other. The variety and freshness of the scenario are memorable, and even if you're not—as a traveler—prepared to actually cook your purchases, you still might be tempted by the salmon sandwiches, fish salads, and small platters designed as takeout food—perhaps the raw ingredients for a picnic on Munkeholmen Island or elsewhere. Consider buying a half-kilo of shrimp per person, along with fresh bread, butter, and mayonnaise (sold here in tubes that you squeeze like toothpaste). Purchase a glass of beer from the on-site beer tap, commandeer one of the indoor or outdoor tables, and dine like Neptune himself. Platters, which include such fare as pan-fried turbot with risotto, or warm fish cakes with salad, cost NOK55 to NOK80 ($11–$16/£5.50–£8) each; sandwiches cost NOK40 ($8/£4), and stuffed crab goes for NOK55 ($11/£5.50). The complex is open Monday to Friday 10am to 5pm, Saturday 10am to 4pm.

⑯ Trondheim Tinghus (Trondheim Courthouse)

The courthouse facade bears a post–World War II frieze with symbols and personalities important to the history of Trondheim. Its interior is not open for casual visits.

From here, a bit to the north, is the Torvet, site of the:

⑰ Trondheim Torg

You're now back at the point where you started this walking tour.

5 ACTIVITIES INDOORS & OUT

In summer the people of Trondheim take to their great outdoors. Summer is short, and they aim to make the best of it.

FISHING Fishing aficionados throughout Norway have heard about the waters below the Leirfossen Dam, 8.8km (5½ miles) south of Trondheim's center. When it was built, no provisions were made—much to the rage of ecologists—for the migration of salmon to spawning grounds upriver. Consequently, the waters at the dam's base have traditionally teemed with a rich variety of marine life, especially salmon. The largest salmon ever caught at the dam's base weighed 32 kilograms (71 lb.)—an awe-inspiring record. In addition, the River Nidelva is one of the best salmon and trout rivers in Norway. For more information about fishing licenses, contact **TOFA (Trondheim og Omland**

Jakt- og Fiskeadministrasjon), Leirfossvn 76 (✆ **73-96-55-80**), the authority controlling fishing in Trondheim and its surroundings.

GOLF Just a 5-minute drive from the Trondheim Airport at Vaernes, **Stjørdal Golfklubb** (✆ **74-84-01-50**) is the only 18-hole golf course between Rena in the south and Narvik in the north. For Norway, its season is long, lasting from May until the end of October. Another of the city's golf courses, **Trondheim Golfklubb,** lies at Sommerseter in Bymarka. This 9-hole course opens onto panoramic views of the city. The Midnight Golf Tournament takes place here in June. For play time, call ✆ **73-53-18-85.**

HIKING The greenbelt on the outskirts of Trondheim is called **Bymarka,** and locals use the woodland as a giant park. It offers 60km (37 miles) of gravel paths, plus 80km (50 miles) of ordinary paths. In winter, skiers find 80km (50 miles) of tracks, including six that are floodlit. In summer, our favorite hike is the **Ladestien (the Lode Trail)** ★, stretching for 14km (8.7 miles), going along the Lade Peninsula and opening onto panoramic views of Trondheimsfjord. A shorter and equally scenic trail, the Nidelvstien, runs along the banks of the Nidelva River, going from Tempe to the waterfalls at Leirfossene.

SKIING On the eastern flank of the Vassfjellet mountains, the **Vassfjellet Skisenter (ski center)** lies in a sheltered position with good snow conditions. The area begins 8km (5 miles) south of the city limits and offers six tow lifts, including one for kids, plus nine runs in all. The area boasts 4km (2½ miles) of the largest illuminated slopes in Norway. Ski buses run to the area. For more information, call ✆ **72-83-02-00.**

SWIMMING **Pirbadet & the 3-T Fitness Center,** Havnegate 12 (✆ **73-83-18-00**), lies in one of the most avant-garde buildings in Trondheim. Perched beside the sea and the town's commercial piers, and separated from the rest of the city by the sprawling bulk of the railway station, this futuristic-looking, mostly glass free-form structure houses one of the best-equipped gyms in Norway (the 3-T Fitness center) and Pirbadet, a collection of pools, water slides, Jacuzzis, and wave-making machines that's among the most up-to-date

Moments — A Midsummer Night's Dream: Warm-Weather Ski-Jumping in Trondheim

An offbeat adventure that might appeal to those with a high-adrenaline thirst for danger involves the brave athletes who stay well rehearsed in ski-jump techniques throughout the summer. The **Granåsen Ski Jump** in Trondheim (about 8km/5 miles south of the center), along with the slightly older and Olympic-famous ski jump in Lillehammer, are the only ski jumps in the world that prepare for summer by lining their downhill slopes with high-impact, very slippery plastic. The result is a bizarre, even surreal sport—warm-weather ski-jumping—that's televised throughout Norway, drawing fans from around the region. The schedule for these events is highly fluid (after all, they're rehearsals, not competitions), and events seem to crop up at erratic moments that sometimes (but not always) correspond to the arrival of cruise ships near the town's harbor. If you want to attend such an event, ask the tourist office for information on when the next rehearsals will be conducted. Entrance is free.

 of any indoor pool in the world. It's municipally funded, and clients tend to be office workers early in the morning, swim students at midday, and recreational swimmers later in the day. On weekends several thousand recreational swimmers cram into its sun-filtered interior. Entrance to the Pirbadet pool complex costs between NOK110 and NOK130 ($22–$26/£11–£13) for adults, depending on what time of day they arrive; entrance to the 3-T fitness center is NOK185 ($37/£19).

TENNIS Trondheim has several courts, both indoor and outdoor. For reservations at a court close to your hotel, call **Trondhjems Tennisklubb** (mobile) at ✆ **93-63-55-01.**

6 SHOPPING

Annes Keramik ★ Founded in 1797, this outlet is your best bet for ceramics based on 2-centuries-old Trøndelag-styled designs, mainly in green, yellow, and blue. A number of intriguing household wares are also sold at this small store. Open Monday, Wednesday, and Friday 9:30am to 5pm; Thursday 9:30am to 8pm; and Saturday 10am to 3pm. Kongesgt 27. ✆ **73-52-53-82.**

Arne Ronning This is the finest outlet for Norwegian knitwear, outfitting the whole family in sweaters and cardigans that can last for a generation or so. It also offers the largest selection of menswear in Trondheim. Open Monday, Wednesday, and Friday 9am to 5pm, Thursday 9am to 7pm, and Saturday 9am to 4pm. Nordregt 10. ✆ **73-53-13-30.**

Galleriet, Trondheim Berukunstforening At the Byrhaven Shopping Center, this is a small store on the ground floor of the mall. But it is choice, with an intriguing selection of glasswork, pottery, silver, jewelry, women's clothing, textiles, ceramics, and more. It's a showcase for applied arts from the Trøndelag district. Open Monday to Friday 10am to 8pm, Saturday 9am to 6pm. Olav Tryggvasonsgat 26. ✆ **73-53-51-10.**

Gift Shop at Sverresborg Trøndelag Folk Museum The gift shop in the museum's reception building stocks some of the most genuinely charming handmade objects in Trondheim, including hand-woven tablecloths and generally endearing hand-knit children's clothing. Open from June to August daily 11am to 6pm; off season Monday to Friday from 11am to 3pm, Saturday and Sunday noon to 4pm. Sverrsborg Allé. ✆ **73-89-01-00.**

Modern Art Gallery This is the city's largest art gallery. Local artists, including some of the best in the area, are represented at this store along with international artists. It carries paintings, watercolors (most often central Norway landscapes), prints, lithographs, and some sculptures. Open Monday to Wednesday and Friday 9:30am to 5pm, Thursday 9:30am to 6pm, and Saturday noon to 4pm. Olav Tryggvasonsgat 33. ✆ **73-87-36-80.**

7 TRONDHEIM AFTER DARK

If you're here in late July or early August at the time of the week-long **St. Olaf Festival,** Dronningensgt 1B (✆ **73-84-14-50**), you can enjoy organ concerts, outdoor concerts, and even opera at the Nidaros Cathedral. The internationally acclaimed **Trondheim Symphony Orchestra ★★★**, Olavskvartalet, Kjøpmannsgata 46 (✆ **73-99-40-50**), presents concerts weekly with some of Europe's most outstanding conductors and soloists. Depending on the event and the day of the week, tickets cost from NOK90 to NOK400 ($18–$80/£9–£40).

Bar Credo Set upstairs from one of Trondheim's most hip and charming restaurants (the also-recommended Credo, p. 355), this bar does a flourishing after-dark business in its own right. Come here for a view of the dozens of modern paintings hanging on the walls—the place doubles as an art gallery, and many of the works are for sale. Live music is presented virtually every night from young and ambitious jazz artists deriving from points throughout Norway and the rest of Europe. The space is divided into a trio of silver-toned rooms, with lots of flickering candles, making the scene even more intimate. Cocktails cost from around NOK75 ($15/£7.50) each, and the venue is cozy enough that you might make some new friends. Although it's associated with the restaurant of the same name, its separate entrance from the street below allows it to remain open when the restaurant is closed. Open Monday to Saturday 4pm to 3am. Ørjaveita 4. © **73-53-03-88.**

Bar 3B Sweaty, shadowy, and candlelit, this is the most extreme of the town's counterculture bars, loaded with clients in their 20s, 30s, and 40s who sometimes proclaim proudly how much they resist hanging out at more mainstream, "bourgeois" bars. Within an environment sheathed in colors of blue and black and the occasional mirror, expect a clientele of bikers, tattoo freaks, students, and the routinely disgruntled. Two bars lie on two different floors of this place, and if you manage to strike up some dialogues (and have a drink or two), you might actually have a lot of fun. It's open Monday to Saturday from 2pm to 2:30 or 3:30am, depending on business, and Sunday from 8pm to 2:30am. Brattørgate 3B. © **73-51-15-50.**

Den Gode Nabo ("The Good Neighbor") Pub ★ This is our favorite pub in Trondheim, occupying the cellar of a 250-year-old warehouse. You enter a low-ceilinged labyrinth of rough-hewn timbers and planking, eventually choosing a seat from any of dozens of slightly claustrophobic banquettes, being careful not to hit your head on the timber-built trusses. Before you get too comfortable, however, we advise that you continue walking as deep into the innards of this place as possible, for access to the woodsy-looking bar area, where up to 16 kinds of beer on tap cost from NOK62 to NOK99 ($12–$20/£6.20–£10) per half-liter. During clement weather, the seating options expand outside onto a wooden platform floating on pontoons in the swift-flowing river Nid, a romantic and soothing refuge from which you get a water-level view of the way Trondheim's antique warehouses were built on pilings sunk deep into the riverbed. The "pub food" will always include the establishment's best-known dish, the "Good Neighbor" fish plate. Priced at NOK125 ($25/£13), it contains heaping portions of vegetables, potatoes, and (usually grilled) fish of the day, accompanied by whatever sauce the chef has dreamed up. You can be a good neighbor at this place every day between 4pm and 1am. Øvre Bakklandet 66. © **40-61-88-09.**

Kaktus This is one of Trondheim's counterculture bars—the kind of place where bourgeois airs are either ridiculed or simply not tolerated, where the clients tend to be students in their early 20s, and where many of the patrons seem to have known one another throughout the duration of their university careers. Music by Billie Holiday or a Swedish punk rock band might be playing softly, avant-garde photographs are for sale, and the staff may or may not be acting weird almost as a matter of defiant public policy. We especially admired the bulky and thick-topped wooden tables, which were crafted in

 India. The place serves platters of food, some of them vegetarian, others inspired by the traditions of Italy or Mexico. Meals are priced at from NOK90 to NOK210 ($18–$42/£9–£21). It's open daily 3 to 11pm. Nedre Bakkland 6. © **73-51-43-03.**

8 SIDE TRIPS FROM TRONDHEIM

Unlike Oslo or Bergen, Trondheim isn't surrounded by a lot of "must-see" satellite attractions. But all true Norwegians, or Norwegian-Americans, head for Stiklestad.

STIKLESTAD Lying 90km (56 miles) northeast of Trondheim, Stiklestad is the most famous historic site in Norway. It was the site of an epic battle on July 29, 1030, between the forces of King Olaf Tryggvason and a better-equipped army of Viking chieftains. The battle marked the twilight of the Viking era and the inauguration of the Middle Ages, a transition that would greatly change the face of Norway.

Although Olaf lost the battle and was killed, in death he triumphed. Word of his death spread, and in time he was viewed as a martyr to Christianity. His followers made him a saint, and as the years went by, Saint Olaf became the very symbol of Norway itself. In the wake of his martyrdom, Christianity quickly spread across the land, and monasteries sprouted up all over the country. As his fame and popularity grew, Olaf's grave site at Nidaros Cathedral in Trondheim became the goal of nationwide pilgrimages. In time, his death would lead to the unification of Norway under one king.

Every year on the anniversary of his death, a pageant is staged at the open-air theater in Stiklestad, using 350 actors and drawing thousands in the audience. Launched in 1992, the **Stiklestad Nasjonale Kulturhus** (**© 74-04-42-00**) is like a virtual theme park, with exhibitions of the famous battle, plus a folk museum and a church from the 12th century. Some of the artifacts on display here were actually relics of the battle, which were discovered by archaeologists.

The open-air **Stiklestad Museum** is a living tableau of regional village life from the 17th century. In summer. there are demonstrations of farm life, and on-site is a carpenter's cottage, along with a water mill and an old-fashioned, 18th-century style sauna.

Stiklestad Kirke ★ is a Romanesque church from 1150 built over a former wooden church on the exact spot where it is believed that King Olaf was felled in battle. In 1500, the nave of the little church was extended, and some 9 centuries later a series of 16th-century frescoes that had been used to decorate the walls of the nave were uncovered. At one time a stone that was said to have been the rock on which Olaf leaned before he died was on display here. In medieval times it was said that the stone had miraculous healing powers, but in time it disappeared, never to resurface. A soapstone baptismal font from the 12th century is the only artifact remaining from ancient times. A series of paintings in the chancel, commissioned for the 900th anniversary of the battle, relates the events of that fateful day.

The center can be visited from June to mid-August daily from 9am to 8pm. In the off season, hours are daily 11am to 5:30pm. In summer, admission is NOK110 ($22/£11) for adults, NOK65 ($13/£6.50) for children. In the off season, the price is reduced to NOK75 ($15/£7.50) for adults, or NOK45 ($9/£4.50) for children. On-site is a restaurant with a museum cafe.

There is no train station at Stiklestad. The nearest depot is at Verdal, lying 6km (3³/₄ miles) away. The train from Trondheim to Verdal takes 1³/₄ hours, costing NOK138 ($28/£14). At Verdal you can take local bus no. 22; all go within 2km (1¹/₄ miles) of the site, costing NOK30 ($6/£3). The trip takes only 15 minutes. Motorists from Trondheim can reach the center by taking the E6 northeast.

14

Tromsø

Tromsø, the gateway to the Arctic, is a North Sea boomtown—both a trade and a financial center. The surrounding snow-topped mountain peaks reach 1,800m (5,904 ft.), and mountain plateaus have good fishing lakes and birch forests. Tromsø has been the jumping-off point for several Arctic expeditions, including one of the most famous. The great explorer Roald Amundsen took off in a plane from Tromsø to meet his death in 1928 on an Arctic ice cap. Visitors today come here to hike in the summer or go dog-sledding during winters in this Klondike country.

Tromsø is the administrative center of the county of Troms, a trade center and the site of one of Norway's four universities. It is the capital of northern Norway and the country's fourth-largest finance center. Tromsø is 1,744km (1,081 miles) north of Oslo, and 566km (351 miles) north of Bodø.

Lying 400km (248 miles) north of the Arctic Circle, Tromsø gets the midnight sun from May 14 to July 30—but not one ray comes through from November 25 to January 21. The climate has a heat record of 88°F (31°C) and a low of –4°F (–20°C).

The title of "Paris of the North" is a bit much, but Tromsø surprised even 19th-century visitors with its sophistication. A church was established here as early as the 1200s, and Tromsø was a thriving community in the Middle Ages. This trading station and fishing port attracted seamen who trafficked in polar bears, seals, and arctic foxes. Its city charter wasn't granted until 1794, however.

The city limits of Tromsø, the largest municipality in Norway, extend for 2,558 sq. km (998 sq. miles), though most of the area is not built up. Tromsø is home to some 63,000 residents, 9,000 of whom are students at the world's northernmost university.

If you should arrive in this polar town in summer, the time of the Midnight Sun, you'll find Tromsø rocking around the clock, with more pubs per capita than any other town in hard-drinking Norway.

1 ORIENTATION

ESSENTIALS

Arrival

BY PLANE Flights from Oslo, Bergen, and Trondheim arrive at Langnes Airport, 13km (8 miles) west of the center of Tromsø. Flights from Oslo take 1 hour, 40 minutes; flights from Bergen take 3 hours, 10 minutes. Tromsø also has air links with Trondheim in central Norway and such far-northern outposts as Alta, Hammerfest, Honningsvåg, and Kirkeness. Tromsø is served by such carriers as **SAS** (✆ **74-80-41-00;** www.sas.no), **Widerøe** (✆ **81-00-12-00;** www.wideroe.no), and Norwegian Air Shuttle (✆ **81-52-18-15;** www.norwegian.no). For general information, call the Tromsø Airport at ✆ **77-64-84-00.**

BY TRAIN There is no rail link in Tromsø. The nearest connection is via Narvik. (see "Narvik: World War II Battleground," in chapter 15). From Narvik, you'll have to go the rest of the way overland by bus (see below).

BY BUS **Nor-way Buss Ekspress** (✆ **77-85-21-00;** www.nor-way.no) runs daily express buses to Tromsø from Narvik (see "Narvik: World War II Battleground," in chapter 15), taking 4 hours and 15 minutes and costing around NOK370 ($74/£37) one-way or NOK740 ($148/£74) for a round-trip ticket. There are at least three daily buses Monday to Friday and at least two on Saturday and Sunday. The same company, in summer, also operates buses that run to the North Cape, although a transfer in Alta (see "Alta: City of Northern Lights," in chapter 15) is necessary. Details about this bus might change from week to week, so call in advance if you're contemplating such a journey.

BY CAR Take E6 from Oslo all the way north.

BY COASTAL STEAMER ***Hurtigruten*** (coastal steamer; ✆ **866/552-0371;** www.hurtigruten.us) connections link Tromsø with at least a dozen other cities along the Norwegian coast, including Narvik, Bergen, and Bodø.

Visitor Information

For information about Tromsø and the surrounding area, call the **Tromsø tourist office**—also known as Destination Tromsø—at Kirkegate 2 (✆ **77-61-00-00;** www.destinasjontromso.no). From June to August it's open Monday to Friday 9am to 7pm, Saturday and Sunday 10am to 5pm. During other months, it is open only Monday to Friday 9am to 4pm.

City Layout

The center of Tromsø lies on the eastern shore of the island of **Tromsøya.** It is divided by hills from the western shore and the airport at Langnes. A bridge and tunnel link the mainland of Norway to the island of Tromsøya. Coastal steamers pull into the piers at the foot of Kirkegata right in the town center.

The heart of town is small enough to make walking around it relatively easy. Running in a north/south axis, the main street is **Storgata**. At the center of this street is **Stortorget,** the main square of town opening onto the harbor. Stortorget is the site of a daily open-air market selling flowers and crafts. The most bustling and busiest part of town lies south of Storgata reaching the harbor. Some major streets include **Strandgata, Skippergata,** and **Skansegata.** This area is filled with shops, restaurants, bars, and cafes.

Local buses can take you to attractions outside the center.

Getting Around

If you arrive at the airport, **Flybussen** (✆ **98-23-02-30**) will take you into the center in about 15 minutes, costing NOK50 ($10/£5) for a one-way fare. A city bus also makes the run for NOK30 ($6/£3), and you can take a taxi for around NOK150 ($30/£15).

Local buses branch out from the center to serve Greater Tromsø. A one-way ride costs NOK30 ($6/£3). If you plan to use the buses a lot, you can purchase a 24-hour pass for NOK60 ($12/£6) at the tourist office.

The major **taxi stand** is at Strandveien 30 (✆ **77-60-30-00**), outside of Øldhallen.

In summer consider cycling around town. Bikes are rented at **Sportshuset,** Storgata 87 (✆ **77-66-11-00**), for between NOK70 to NOK100 ($14–$20/£7–£10) per day, depending on the model you rent. Our favorite bike ride is to head east of the city center in the direction of the Arctic Cathedral. You must cross the spindly Tromsø Bridge to the other side of the water, arriving in the suburb of Tromsdal. After a visit to the Arctic Cathedral (p. 386) here, you can ride for about 10 minutes to the cable car at Fjellheisen (p. 386). You can lock your bike at the bottom of the cable-car station and take the ride to the top for one of the most panoramic views in the north of Norway.

FAST FACTS: TROMSØ

The main **post office** is at Strandgata 41 (✆ **81-00-07-10**). If you patronize the **Amtmandens Datter Pub,** Grønnegata 81 (✆ **77-68-49-06**), you can get Internet access for NOK40 ($8/£4) per half-hour. The pub, named for the 1830s novel by Camille Collett, is open June to August Monday to Thursday noon to 1:30am, Friday to Saturday noon to 3am, and Sunday noon to midnight. In off-season months, hours are Monday to Saturday noon to 3am and Sunday 3pm to 3am. Keeping the same hours is **Dark Light,** Stortorget 1 (✆ **77-68-74-44**), where it costs NOK45 ($9/£4.50) per half-hour to use the computers or NOK60 ($12/£6) per hour. Coffee, mineral water, and sandwiches are served, but no alcohol.

2 WHERE TO STAY

EXPENSIVE

Clarion Collection Hotel With ★★ This is the best and most comfortable of the Clarion chain's two hotels in Tromsø. We prefer its waterfront location and views to any other hotel in town. Built in a six-story format in 1989, it was named after Richard With, a 19th-century sea captain who contributed to the development of Tromsø and northern Norway. This hotel is cozy, warm, and inviting. Set behind a modern twin-gabled facade immediately adjacent to the waterfront, it offers good-sized rooms, with hardwood floors; a woodsy, well-upholstered decor, sometimes with leather chairs; big weather-tight windows; and tiled bathrooms. A special feature is the skylit top-floor lounge, a nice place to spend a cold winter's night.

Sjøgata 35–37, N-9291 Tromsø. ✆ **77-66-42-00.** Fax 77-68-96-16. www.choicehotels.no. 76 units. Mon–Thurs NOK1,675 ($335/£168) double; Fri–Sun NOK1,090 ($218/£109) double. Rates include buffet breakfast and light evening supper (buffet 6–10pm). Parking NOK170 ($34/£17). AE, DC, MC, V. **Amenities:** Dining room; health club; sauna; room service; laundry service/dry cleaning; library; nonsmoking rooms; rooms for those w/limited mobility. *In room:* TV, minibar, hair dryer, trouser press.

Radisson SAS Hotel Tromsø ★★★ Reigning today as the grande dame hotel of Tromsø, this well-managed staple from 1965 is the oldest and best established of the town's large-scale hotels, rising 10 stories. The hotel was radically overhauled and expanded in 2008, making it the largest in northern Norway. Rooms come in two distinct styles, Arctic or Chili. Rooms in the Arctic style come with soothing white, orange, and green tones with lots of wood. Those in the Chili style are imbued with hot colors, including red tones, each with modern furnishings. It has a highly competent staff and boasts a larger and more diverse array of food and beverage facilities than any other hotel in town. Its most upscale restaurant (Aurora) and most famous of its bars (Rorbua) are each separately recommended within other sections of this chapter.

Sjøgata 7, N-9259 Tromsø. ✆ **77-60-00-00.** Fax 77-68-54-74. www.radissonsas.com. 269 units. Mon–Thurs NOK1,695–NOK1,995 ($339–$399/£170–£200) double; Fri–Sun year-round and daily mid-June to mid-Aug NOK1,230–NOK1,400 ($246–$280/£123–£140) double; year-round NOK2,500–NOK3,500 ($500–$700/£250–£350) suite. Rates include buffet breakfast. AE, DC, MC, V. Parking NOK185 ($37/£19). **Amenities:** 2 restaurants; 2 bars; health club/sauna on top floor; laundry service/dry cleaning. *In room:* TV, minibar, hair dryer, safe (in some), trouser press.

Rica Ishavshotel ★★ Although not as lavish or well equipped as the Radisson SAS, this 1995 hotel is the most dramatic-looking in the region, a conversation piece that evokes a metallic space-age yacht. It's also the town's most dramatic site, at the edge of the harbor, a few steps from the busiest quay in town. The lobby is cozy and warm, with a postmodern edge. Lots of business travelers stay here; because of that, about half of the rooms are designated as singles. Whether they're single or double, all rooms have a subdued decor, with tiled bathrooms and Nordic modern furniture. The more panoramic of the hotel's two bars is the Skipsbroen, set on the hotel's uppermost floor.

Fr. Langes Gate 2, N-9252 Tromsø. ✆ **77-66-64-00.** Fax 77-66-64-44. www.rica.no. 180 units. Mon–Thurs NOK2,095 ($419/£210) double; Fri–Sun NOK1,545 ($309/£155) double. AE, DC, MC, V. **Amenities:** 2 restaurants; 2 bars; business center; room service; babysitting; laundry service/dry cleaning; nonsmoking rooms; rooms for those w/limited mobility. *In room:* TV, minibar, hair dryer.

MODERATE

Amalie Hotell (Value) Set in a former office building almost immediately adjacent to the Radisson SAS Hotel, this hotel is known for its affordable rates and well-maintained, comfortable rooms. Bedrooms are simple and cheerful, evoking a dorm room from college, without frills but with sturdy, utilitarian wooden furniture.

Sjøgata 5B, N-9008 Tromsø. ✆ **77-66-48-00.** Fax 77-66-48-10. www.amalie-hotell.no. 48 units. Mon–Thurs NOK1,295 ($259/£130) double; Fri–Sun NOK1,195 ($239/£120) double. Rates include buffet breakfast. Light evening supper (served 6:30–9:30pm nightly) costs NOK75 ($15/£7.50) extra per person. AE, DC, MC, V. **Amenities:** Dining room; laundry service/dry cleaning. *In room:* TV, minibar, beverage maker, hair dryer, trouser press.

Clarion Hotel Bryggen Clarion is one of the best hotel chains in Norway, and their Tromsø entry is a serviceable and inviting hotel. Built in 2001, this is a large-scale hotel for Tromsø, with a harborfront position that's only a few steps from its main competitor, the Rica Ishavshotel. The hotel has a contemporary lobby, wide hallways, and big-windowed bedrooms that are comfortably laid out. Bathrooms are tiled, brightly lit, and very modern, and most of them have only showers, although 40 units feature tub/showers. Our favorite spot here is the outdoor hot tub that is sheltered on the rooftop terrace near the hotel's sauna, with panoramas over the frigid waters of Tromsø's harbor. There's a congenial bar (the Aquarius Bar) and a good restaurant (the Astro) on the lobby level, open daily for lunch and dinner.

Sjøgata 19–21, N-9291 Tromsø. ✆ **77-78-11-00.** Fax 77-78-11-01. www.choicehotels.no. 121 units. Mon–Thurs NOK1,550 ($310/£155) double; Fri–Sat NOK1,395 ($279/£140) double; NOK1,900–NOK3,900 ($380–$780/£190–£390) suite. AE, DC, MC, V. Parking NOK150 ($30/£15). **Amenities:** Restaurant; bar; rooftop sauna w/outdoor hot tub; laundry service/dry cleaning; nonsmoking rooms; rooms for those w/limited mobility. *In room:* TV, minibar, hair dryer.

Quality Hotel Saga (Kids) Not as architecturally exciting as the Rica Ishavshotel, and not as upscale or as plush as the Radisson SAS, this conservative, somewhat boxy and banal-looking hotel is near Tromsø's wood-sided cathedral. It was built in 1969, and most of its rooms were renovated during 2006. The best rooms are positioned on the uppermost (sixth) floor. Accommodations are warm and comfortable, each with contemporary, blond-toned wooden furniture, wooden floors, and off-white walls. Bigger rooms come

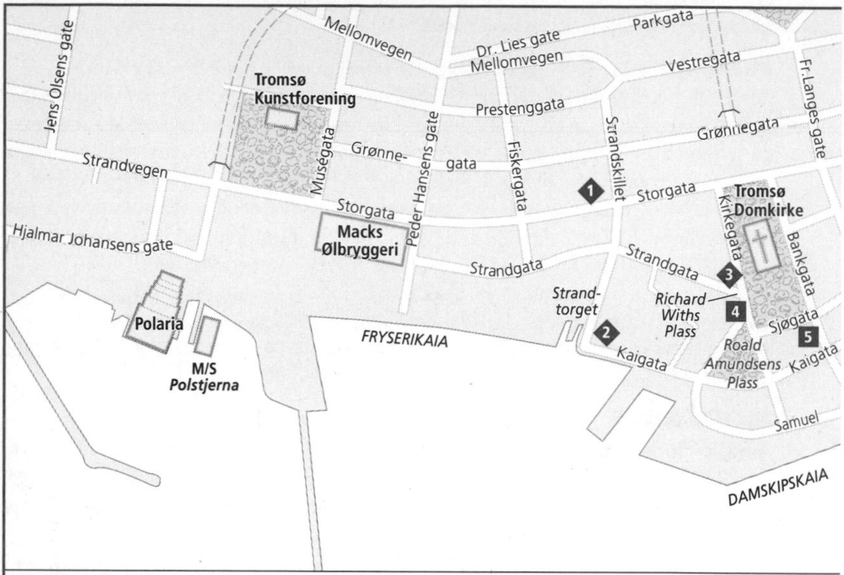

ACCOMMODATIONS ■
Amalie Hotell **5**
Clarion Hotel Bryggen **11**
Clarion Collection Hotel With **10**
Quality Hotel Saga **4**
Radisson SAS Hotel Tromsø **6**
Rica Ishavshotel **7**

DINING ◆
Arctandria **2**
Aunegården (O.L. Aune) **12**
Aurora **6**
Compagniet **9**
Emma's Drømmekjøkken (Emma's Dream Kitchen) **3**
Peppermølle **1**
Steakers **8**
Store Norske Fiskekompani **13**
Vertshuset Skarven A.S. **2**

with a sofa that can be converted to a bed, extra beds for children are available, children 7 and under stay free when sharing a room with their parents, and kids 8 to 12 get a 50% discount. The hotel is entirely nonsmoking.

Richard Withs Plass 2, N-9008 Tromsø. ✆ **77-60-70-00.** Fax 77-60-70-10. www.choicehotels.no. 67 units. Mon–Thurs NOK1,560 ($312/£156) double; Fri–Sun NOK1,070 ($214/£107) double; year-round NOK2,800 ($560/£280) suite. Rates include buffet breakfast. Light evening supper (buffet 6–9:30pm) costs NOK95 ($19/£9.50) per person. AE, DC, MC, V. Parking NOK110 ($22/£11). **Amenities:** Dining room; laundry service/dry cleaning; rooms for those w/limited mobility. *In room:* TV, alcohol-free minibar, beverage maker, hair dryer, safe, trouser press.

3 WHERE TO DINE

EXPENSIVE

Arctandria ★★ SEAFOOD A jewel among rhinestones, this best fish restaurant in town is patronized by many savvy locals who make their living from the sea and have high standards for seafood. It's set on the top floor of a sprawling antique warehouse

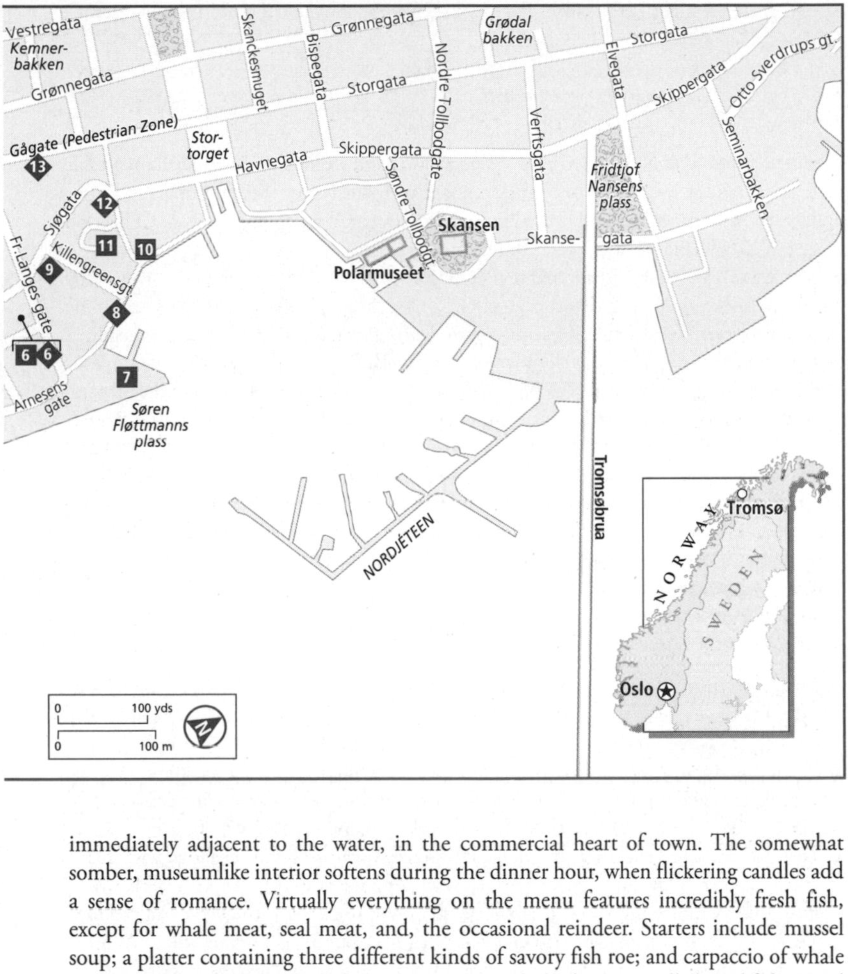

immediately adjacent to the water, in the commercial heart of town. The somewhat somber, museumlike interior softens during the dinner hour, when flickering candles add a sense of romance. Virtually everything on the menu features incredibly fresh fish, except for whale meat, seal meat, and, the occasional reindeer. Starters include mussel soup; a platter containing three different kinds of savory fish roe; and carpaccio of whale meat, a politically incorrect dish. Main courses include the tasty grilled stockfish served with roasted mushrooms and bacon. For an adventurous treat, try the arctic char with hazelnuts or grilled arctic shark meat with a pepper sauce.

Strandtorget 1. ✆ **77-60-07-28.** Reservations recommended. Main courses NOK190–NOK350 ($38–$70/£19–£35). AE, DC, MC, V. Mon–Sat 4–11pm.

Aurora ★ ARCTIC At the most upscale of the recommended restaurants within the town's hotels, this is one of the best places for well-established classics. The interior evokes the Northern Lights, with a minimalist Scandinavian decor. The charming staff members serve food that celebrates the culinary traditions and raw ingredients (shellfish, reindeer, and cold-water fish) of Norway's far northern tier. The best examples of the cuisine include six different preparations of mussels, including a version with curry. For a true taste of Norway, enjoy such palate-pleasing dishes as poached salt cod with an onion-and-tomato sauté, or else pan-fried filet of reindeer with a carrot-and-celery purée spiced with a juniper berry sauce. For dessert, we opt for the delicious lime cheesecake with a coulis of berries.

In the Radisson SAS Hotel Tromsø, Sjøgata 7. ✆ **77-60-00-00.** Reservations recommended. Fixed-price lunch buffet, available Mon–Fri 11:30am–2pm, NOK210 ($42/£21); main courses NOK190–NOK350 ($38–$70/£19–£35). AE, DC, MC, V. Mon–Sat 11:30am–11pm.

Compagniet ★★ NORWEGIAN The movers and shakers of Tromsø call for a table here, especially if they want to impress an out-of-town visitor. Set within an old-fashioned wood-sheathed building, directly across the street from the Clarion Collection Hotel With and the Clarion Hotel Bryggen, this restaurant is noted as the most charming in town. The cuisine is original and consists of only the freshest ingredients, usually local. All dishes are prepared with a finely honed technique, as exemplified by the arctic sea char flavored with fresh chives and a tantalizing fish roe. From Norwegian meadows comes a tender and flavorful rack of lamb served with raspberry sauce and a potato-and-fresh-vegetable tart, and from the far north, filet of reindeer in a blueberry sauce. Menu specialties vary with the arrival of fresh fish and game from the surrounding waters, tundra, and forests. Fresh fish, including turbot and wolfish, can be served breaded and fried, perhaps with either a beurre blanc (white butter) or a mustard sauce, or steamed en papillotte, according to your wishes and the whims of the chef. A particularly good game dish involves filets of both wild grouse and reindeer, both grilled and drizzled with blueberry sauce, on the same platter and served with root vegetables. The service is the best in Tromsø, and the wine cellar is wide ranging.

Sjøgata 12. ✆ **77-66-42-22.** Reservations required. Main courses NOK269–NOK340 ($54–$68/£30–£34). AE, DC, MC, V. Mon–Sat 6–11pm.

Emma's Drømmekjøkken (Emma's Dream Kitchen) ★★★ Finds NORWEGIAN If there's such a thing as a culinary personality in Tromsø, it is Emma (also known as Anne Brit), owner of this cozy restaurant across the street from Tromsø's cathedral. Her restaurant, which she runs with a partner named Lars, contains only 34 seats, so reservations are important. Before dinner you can descend into the wine cellar, site of an impressive inventory of bottles. If you order champagne, it will be dramatically uncorked by a saber-wielding sommelier. Appetizers feature grilled scallops with marinated asparagus, pine nuts, and parmesan; or pepper-roasted Arctic king crab. Main courses burst with freshness and originality, including stockfish with bacon and creamed cabbage or else breast of Norwegian duck with a raspberry Béarnaise sauce. Another specialty is grilled and marinated rib of lamb with couscous. The best dessert you are likely to encounter in town is the passion fruit cheesecake with raspberry coulis and a white chocolate mousse.

Kirkegata 8. ✆ **77-63-77-30.** Reservations required. Main courses NOK285–NOK325 ($57–$65/£29–£33); fixed-price menus NOK695–NOK850 ($139–$170/£70–£85). AE, DC, MC, V. Mon–Sat 6–10:30pm. Closed 1 week at Christmas.

Peppermølle ★ INTERNATIONAL Satisfying to both eye and palate, this is one of Tromsø's genuinely warm and appealing restaurants. "The Peppermill" is set one floor above the street level of a modern building along the town's main shopping thoroughfare. There are a total of three separate dining rooms, including the "green room" and "the middle room." But we prefer the "Amundsen Room," which is lined with photos of

Norway's polar explorers, many of whom used Tromsø as their base of operations before heading to points much farther north. Menu items are savory and well prepared, including a tartare of smoked salmon; broiled tenderloin with a tarragon-flavored mustard sauce; tenderloins stuffed with crayfish and served with crayfish sauce; and filet of monkfish fried with mushrooms, shrimp, and crème fraîche.

Storgata 54. ✆ **77-68-62-60.** Reservations recommended. Main courses NOK269–NOK299 ($54–$60/£27–£30). AE, DC, MC, V. Mon–Thurs 5:30–10pm; Fri–Sat 5:30–11pm.

Steakers (Kids) STEAKHOUSE This warm, candlelit steakhouse, the most popular in town, is adjacent to the wharves where the coastal steamers dock, midway between the Rica and Clarion hotels. From its oversize windows, you can watch the arrivals and departures of the fishing and cargo ships. Simple, grilled beefsteaks are on the petite side (150g/5 oz.), while boneless tenderloins weigh in at a knockout 400 grams (14 oz.). More elaborate meat dishes are stuffed, basted, or marinated, and might include a "Chicago gangster" (tenderloin marinated with garlic-flavored butter); a rack of barbecued ribs; and steaks marinated in—among other things—tequila and chili peppers. Other specialties include tenderloin of beef in garlic butter or rack of lamb with potatoes gratinée.

Frederik Langesgate 13. ✆ **77-61-33-30.** Reservations recommended. Main courses NOK167–NOK414 ($33–$83/£17–£41). AE, DC, MC, V. Mon–Sat 3–11pm; Sun 2–10pm.

Store Norske Fiskekompani ★ NORWEGIAN Not quite up to the high standards of Arctandria (see above), this is still a very good addition to Tromsø's dining scene. A visible monument in town, this place is on the town's main shopping street. The decor looks older than it is. Menu options, which change with the season, include such starters as extremely fresh seafood, including a tartare of salmon and scallops flavored with coriander and truffle oil, cream of lobster soup with pistachio oil and scallops, or salted redfish with sour cream and onions. Main courses include grilled whale steak with anchovy sauce and rösti-style potatoes; fried filet of sea char with spinach, fennel, and almonds; butterflied and batter-fried monkfish served with sun-dried tomatoes, asparagus, and parma ham; and a seafood bouillabaisse made only with fish that thrive in the Arctic waters offshore, served (incongruously) with a garlic-laced aioli inspired by the cuisine of Provence.

Storgata 73. ✆ **77-68-76-00.** Reservations recommended. NOK255–NOK335 ($51–$67/£26–£34). AE, DC, MC, V. Mon–Fri 11:30am–2pm and daily 4–10:30pm.

MODERATE

Aunegården (O. L. Aune) (Value) NORWEGIAN/CONTINENTAL Named after a 19th-century butcher shop (O. L. Aune) that stood here for many years, this restaurant is a culinary icon in a city loaded with worthy competitors. The setting includes a Victorian-era tearoom near its entrance and a darker, less prim series of dining rooms lined with slabs of volcanic rock in back. The main dining room is busy throughout the day, serving as a venue for salads, sandwiches, and light meals. Lunch brings tuna sandwiches on baguettes, salads, pastas, club sandwiches, and chicken cutlets; dinner offerings move into heartier territory with platters filled with filets of salmon and wolf fish with duchesse potatoes, marinated scampi, and catfish fried in curry.

Sjøgata 29. ✆ **77-65-12-34.** Reservations recommended. Main courses NOK120–NOK200 ($24–$40/£12–£20) dinner. AE, DC, MC, V. Mon–Thurs 10:30am–midnight; Fri–Sat 10:30am–12:30am; Sun 1–10pm.

Vertshuset Skarven A.S. (Value) NORWEGIAN Long a favorite of Tromsø's vast student population, this cafeteria is the cheapest of five different restaurants within a 19th-century warehouse adjacent to the waterfront. In the large and high-ceilinged room, you'll be surrounded by lots of nautical memorabilia, antique farm implements, models of 19th-century clipper ships, and an unusual collection of stuffed birds. Good-tasting dishes include hearty stews, baked filet of fish, pork cutlets, soups, and sandwiches—the kind of fare that might be served in the homes of the town's older residents. Overall, this is a cheap and highly atmospheric place for a drink, snack, or meal.

Strandtorget 1. ✆ **77-60-07-20.** Reservations not accepted. Sandwiches NOK45–NOK70 ($9–$14/£4.50–£7); platters NOK90–NOK95 ($18–$19/£9–£9.50). AE, DC, MC, V. Sun–Thurs 11:30am–12:30am; Fri–Sat 11:30am–1:30am.

4 SEEING THE SIGHTS

For the Midnight Sun or Northern Lights, the small-scale cable car **Fjellheisen** (✆ **77-61-00-00** for information) hauls sightseers in orange-and-red gondolas from a spot near the Arctic Cathedral in Tromsdal uphill to a small, not-very-exciting cafe and restaurant **(Fjellstua Restaurant),** 420m (1,378 ft.) above sea level. Your vertiginous trip is rewarded with a **panoramic view** ★★ from the restaurant that extends out over the surrounding countryside. The cable car operates in March Saturday and Sunday 10am to 5pm, April to September daily 10am to 5pm. Round-trip passage costs NOK95 ($19/£9.50) for adults, NOK45 ($9/£4.50) for children 6 to 16, and is free for children under 6. Round-trip transport of a bicycle (some bike and hiking trails originate near the cable car's upper station) costs NOK35 ($7/£3.50).

Full meals in the Fjellstua Restaurant cost around NOK250 ($50/£25) and include reindeer, dried cod, and fish. Although the tourist office tries to promote this as a big-deal kind of excursion, it's actually kind of tame. The cable car is a bit of a weak-lemonade replay of something the Swiss and Austrians do in ways that are flashier and higher.

The Arctic Cathedral (also known as Tromsdal Church and the Boathouse Church) ★★ North Norway's most distinctive-looking and controversial church rose from a location across the harbor from downtown Tromsø in 1965, requiring a transit of the town's longest bridge, completed in 1960, to reach it. Since then, its simple A-frame design has evolved into one of the town's most visible symbols and—thanks to the late-night concerts conducted here for cruise-ship passengers between June and mid-August—one of the most frequently visited sights in the area. Its theme, thanks to huge stained-glass windows set into the triangular-shaped front of the church, is a celebration of the light that filters through a grid work of thin glass strips, the effect of which has been described as mystical, especially during the brief moments of daylight that creep up to this far northern outpost during the middle of winter. Consistent with Norway's long-established custom of hanging replicas of sailing ships within Norwegian churches as a good luck charm for the vessels' occupants, the shape of the organ at the back of the church resembles the sails of a ship. Other references to the Arctic's climate and culture abound. Incidentally, when the pope paid an official visit to this remote place on June 11, 1989, it drew a small crowd of around 2,000 people.

Tromsdal. ✆ **77-75-34-50.** www.ishavskatedralen.no. Free admission during worship services; otherwise, NOK25 ($5/£2.50) adults, free for children 14 and under; admission to concerts NOK100 ($20/£10),

Moments Aurora Borealis ★★★: The Northern Lights

The Northern Lights are one of nature's most spectacular and mysterious phenomena. In the right conditions, they can be seen in the night sky north of the Arctic Circle in winter. The most practical place to view them in Norway is Tromsø. If seeing these lights is one of your goals, plan to be in Tromsø for at least 3 days in order to increase your odds of getting the right atmospheric conditions. Anytime in the period from November to March is good, but the end of December, with its 24 hours of darkness, is best.

no discounts available for children or students. Mid-Apr to May daily 4–6pm; June to mid-Aug daily 10am–8pm; mid-Aug to Sept daily 4–6pm. Otherwise, the church is closed except for Sun worship services. Concert times coincide with the arrival of cruise ships, but they're usually scheduled for around 10pm every night btw June and mid-Aug.

Macks Ølbryggeri (Mack's Brewery) Talk about cold beer. This is the northernmost microbrewery in the world. Launched in 1877, it's been going strong ever since. The brewery currently turns out nearly two dozen brews, including Haakon and Macks Pilsner. Tours are conducted of the brewery, and you're given a shot glass and a sample of beer as a souvenir. You can also sample the brew at the on-site Ølhallen Pub.

Storgata 5. ✆ **77-62-45-80.** Tours NOK120 ($24/£12). Oct–May Mon–Thurs 9am–6:30pm, Fri 9am–7pm, Sat 9am–3pm; guided tours at 1pm. June–Sept Mon–Thurs 9am–5:30pm, Fri 9am–6pm, Sat 9am–3pm. Guided tours Mon and Thurs at 1pm; otherwise, by special arrangement. Closed Sun.

Nordnorsk Kunstmuseum The Art Museum of North Norway traces art and applied art from 1838 to the present day, with special attention paid to northern Norwegian artists. It features non-Norwegian artists as well, along with sculpture and photography. Anything by Edvard Munch, Scandinavia's best known artist, attracts the most attention, even if it's a lesser work. Lesser-known artists such as Christian Krohg and Axel Revold are displayed, along with the romantic peasant scenes of Adolph Tidemand and the beautiful rugged Norwegian landscape paintings of Johan Dahl and Thomas Fearnley. The National Gallery in Oslo frequently sends up major works for temporary exhibitions.

Sjøgata 1. ✆ **77-68-00-90.** Free admission. Mon–Sat 11am–5pm.

Polaria ★ Kids Polaria is a Disney-esque scientific homage to the ecologies, climates, and technological potentialities of the Arctic. Viewed from any of the boats out on the harbor, its stainless-steel surfaces resemble a jagged ice floe pressed into fragile but irregular vertical alignments. Inaugurated in 1998, in a location beside the waterfront, immediately adjacent to the world headquarters of the Polar Institution of Norway (a deeply respected subdivision of the Norwegian Ministry of the Environment), it's one of the most frequently visited attractions in town. Its design resulted from a contest wherein 45 noted architects from North America and Europe competed. The result as viewed from the town evokes a weather-tight factory, industrial-looking in wood, glass, and stainless steel, that looks like it could survive the harshest Arctic winter.

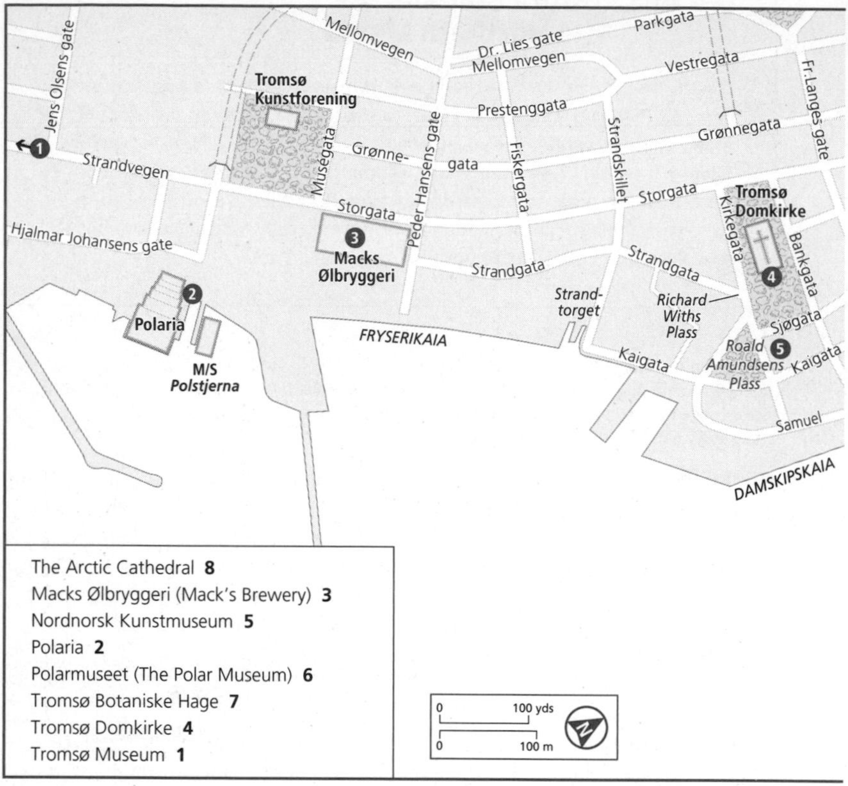

The dioramas and tableaux—some with artificially induced snow flurries behind thick sheets of Plexiglas, will leave you with a deeper understanding of the complex and delicate ecosystems of the Arctic. There's an IMAX-size movie theater where an 18-minute film, shot mostly on the Norwegian/Russian island of Svalbard, celebrates the beauty and biodiversity of the Arctic. There's also an aquarium holding what might be the ugliest fish anywhere. Where the signs indicate, you can reach out and touch some of the species—a favorite of children.

An indoor pool is for the care, shelter, and feeding of arctic seals, with regular feedings and seal gymnastics. And in the lobby, there's a genuinely wonderful gift shop—one of the best in town—selling souvenirs and some remarkably charming gift items, including hand-painted lacquered boxes hauled in from across Norway's frontiers with Russia.

Hjarmar Johansens gata. ✆ **77-75-01-00.** www.polaria.no. Admission NOK95 ($19/£9.50) adults, NOK80 ($16/£8) seniors; NOK65 ($13/£6.50) students, NOK45 ($9/£4.50) children 3–16. Mid-May to mid-Aug daily 10am–7pm; mid-Aug to mid-May daily noon–5pm.

Polarmuseet (The Polar Museum) ★ Not to be confused with Polaria, a space-age celebration of the Arctic's ecosystems (described separately above), the Polar Museum

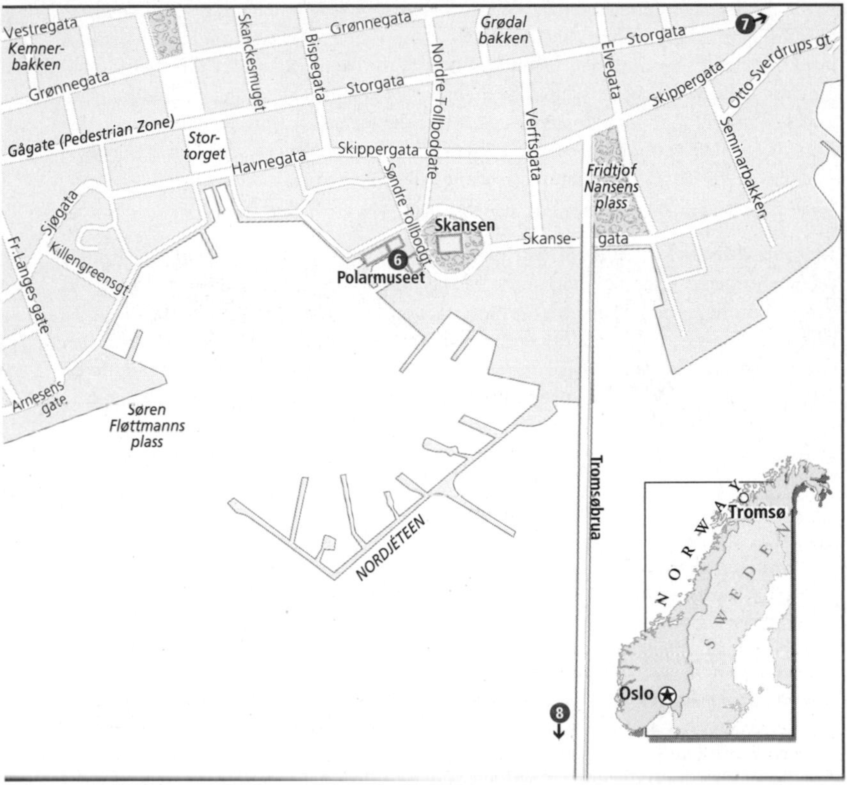

showcases the bravery and ingenuity of the 19th- and early-20th-century fishermen, hunters, whalers, trappers, and explorers who made the Arctic their home. The museum is set into an interconnected wood-sided complex of red-painted buildings adjacent to Tromsø's harbor. A bronze statue of explorer Roald Amundsen is positioned directly in front of the museum. Inside, in an antique warehouse whose stout timbers illustrate the construction techniques of the 19th century, you'll find gruesome photographs and dioramas showing how genuinely rough life in the frozen north could be, even as late as the 1960s. On display are antique versions of the hempen ropes, sealskins, sledges, and survival equipment that kept the fishing, hunting, and whaling industries alive. If you ask, a staff member will give you abbreviated pamphlets in English that superficially describe each of the exhibits.

Søndre Tollbugatell. ✆ **77-68-43-73.** www.polarmuseum.no. Admission NOK50 ($10/£5) adults, NOK40 ($8/£4) students and seniors, NOK10 ($2/£1) children 6–18, free for children 5 and under; NOK100 ($20/£10) family ticket, granting entrance to 2 adults plus any number of children 15 and under. July–Aug daily 10am–7pm; off season daily 11am–3pm.

Tromsø Botaniske Hage ★ (Finds On the grounds of the University of Tromsø, the world's northernmost botanic garden is one of the most unique we've ever encountered. Arctic tundra and alpine mountain botanicals converge here in a landscape where plants have a shortened growing season and very low temperatures. The season technically lasts from the end of May until mid-October, although the plants experience their real growth only when the Midnight Sun shines on them day and night. The setting is beautiful, with slopes, a stream, a pond, and terraces. Many of the plants are from the Arctic and Antarctic, as well as various alpine and Himalayan locations. You've seen better botanical gardens, we are certain, but not one growing rare specimens this far north.

Breivika. ✆ **77-64-40-00.** Free admission. May–Sept daily 24 hr.

Tromsø Domkirke One of Norway's largest wooden churches, this is a barnlike, yellow, "carpenter Gothic" monument in the heart of town that's difficult to heat in winter. It is the world's northernmost Protestant cathedral, lying 182m (597 ft.) from the harbor. Consecrated in 1861, it was the creation of architects D. J. Evjen and Heinrich Grosch. Seating 750 persons, the cathedral shows some classical and Swiss influences. The altarpiece, painted by Christian Brun, is a copy of one within Bragernes church in Drammen. Built by Claus Jensen in 1863, the organ was one of his largest works. In 1944, the church was at the center of history when it was used by evacuees during the Nazi-enforced evacuation of Finnmark and Northern Troms. In 1994, the church was restored and returned to its original colors.

Storgata 25. ✆ **77-66-25-80.** Free admission. Tues–Sat 10am–5pm; Sun 10am–2pm.

Tromsø Museum ★ (Kids Associated with the University of Tromsø, this museum's collections grew out of artifacts gathered by the oldest scientific institution in North Norway, which was established in 1872. It sprawls over three floors and addresses various aspects of natural science (including loads of information on the ecology, botany, geology, and zoology of Norway's far north). There are also exhibits about the Sami people and some exhibits about the cultural history of Norway's far north. Many of the exhibitions are kid-friendly, especially a life-size dinosaur that children can enter and explore. Our favorite exhibit contains Norwegian church art crafted between the Middle Ages and the 17th century—at least the little bits of it that remain, since so much of it was burned during the Norwegian Reformation. The church artworks that are on display in the museum escaped destruction during the Reformation because they were kept in church basements and outbuildings, considered less valuable than the works that were actually on display in churches. The museum also contains a device (one of only two in the world, they say) that emulates, planetarium-style, the Northern Lights for which the region is famous. There is also a dazzling video about the Northern Lights phenomenon. ***Note:*** The gift shop in the lobby contains copies of Viking jewelry that are a lot better than what's sold in some of the town's tourist shops.

Lars Thoringsvei 10. ✆ **77-64-50-00.** Admission NOK30 ($6/£3) adults, free students and children. Mid-Sept to mid-May Mon–Fri 9am–3:30pm, Sat–Sun 11am–5pm; mid-May to mid-June and mid-Aug to mid-Sept Mon–Fri 9am–6pm, Sat 11am–6pm; mid-June to mid-Aug daily 9am–8pm.

5 OUTDOOR ACTIVITIES

In the wilds of north Norway, walking and especially summer hiking are all the rage, by both locals and visitors. In the environs of Tromsø, there are more than 100km (62 miles) of trails cut across the mountains. The best hiking trail begins right at the upper station of the cable car, **Fjellheisen** (p. 386).

For more extensive hiking, including overnight trips, you need to contact **Troms Turlag-DNT** (✆ **77-68-51-75;** www.turistforeningen.no), which organizes tours through the wilderness areas around Tromsø, with stopovers in hotels or mountain shelters maintained by local municipalities and conservation groups. Accommodations are usually within bare-bones mountain cabins, staffed lodges, and self-service huts that come with army-ration-style provisions such as canned goods and freeze-dried staples.

One of the most spectacular trails meanders through the rugged peaks of the **Lyngen Alps** ★, forming the spine of the Lyngen Peninsula, with its glaciated terrain, lying to the east of Tromsø. Arm yourself with a good map from the tourist office before setting out, and don't embark at all unless you're an experienced hill climber. From the eastern banks of the Lyngenfjord, stretching for 150km (93 miles), you'll enjoy panoramic views in all directions. Mountaineers climb the highest peak, the Jiekkevarre, at 1,833m (6,012 ft.).

Tromsø Villmarkssenter (✆ **77-69-60-02**) lies 20km (12 miles) west of the center of Tromsø. This outfitter organizes the best tours in the area, giving you a real close-up experience with nature in the north. Glacier walking, mountain hiking, kayaking, and winter dog-sledding are just some of the activities available. The dog-sledding is pursued November to May, and costs NOK1,220 ($244/£122) per person per day, including pickup and drop-off at your hotel.

On one of the less strenuous jaunts, you can visit Tove and Tore, two of Norway's most experienced dog-sled racers. You can see their home and hang out with 130 *Call of the Wild*–esque huskies. The trip takes 2½ hours and is conducted during the summer, at a cost of NOK610 ($122/£61) per person, including transport.

Kayaking is one of the more popular summer sports here, allowing you to paddle along cold, racing waters against a mountain backdrop. Sometimes, if the weather is right, groups take time out to harvest sea mussels. Tours, each scheduled to last for a full day, leave daily May to October 9am to 4pm, costing NOK1,000 ($200/£100) per person, including transport and lunch.

Mountain hikers are taken to **Store Blåmann** ★, at 1,044m (3,424 ft.), the tallest mountain on Kvaløya outside Tromsø. This is not like climbing the Matterhorn, and the fairly athletic can handle the challenge. The season begins in June and lasts until the first snowfall. Escorted hill-climbing expeditions, each lasting a strenuous 9 hours, go for NOK850 ($170/£85) per person, including transportation to and from your hotel, as well as one meal.

In the unlikely event that you're in Tromsø for winter skiing, call the **Tromsø Alpine Ski Center** (✆ **77-60-66-80**), the region's best site for downhill skiing. There is also an array of cross-country skiing trails, some 70km (43 miles) in all. Because of the pitch blackness, nearly three dozen of these trails are floodlit.

Horseback riding across rugged terrain can be arranged by calling **Holmeslet Gård** at ✆ **77-61-99-74.**

6 SHOPPING

Bianco Footwear This shop is Tromsø's exclusive distributor for the footwear of the most hip and cutting-edge shoe manufacturer in Scandinavia, Denmark-based Bianco Footwear. When a bevy of blonde and buxom female beauties failed to promote consumer interest in the company's line of footwear, Bianco's art department opted for an all-male lineup of cross-dressing (and not particularly pretty) models, sassily sporting Bianco's women's line of shoes and clothing. Be reassured that if you happen to be male and not into cross-dressing, the company markets conventional men's clothing and shoes as well. The store owners call their campaign "extreme art based on solid commercial profits." The Norwegian marketplace seems to agree. Strandgate 26. ✆ **77-65-61-90.**

Hekle-Kroken Early in their childhoods, many residents of Norway's far north learn different ways to while away the long winter nights. Many of them turn to arts and crafts. If you're interested in seeing what's available in terms of quilting, embroidery supplies, and knitting patterns, head for this grandmotherly looking repository of all the ingredients you'll need to engage in some of the most popular hobbies in the region. The setting is a plank-sided antique building in the heart of town. Storgata 91. ✆ **77-68-17-87.**

Husfliden As we mentioned in the review of Hekle-Kroken above, winter nights in Tromsø are long, dark, and very cold, and many locals labor, from within their well-heated and weather-tight homes, at arts and crafts. If you're a knitter, a quilter, an embroiderer, or a leatherworker, this shop stocks your raw materials. There's also a small inventory of handmade sweaters knitted by people loosely affiliated with the store. The staff here tends to be elderly, kindhearted, grandmotherly aficionados of the arts-and-crafts scene. Sjøgata 4. ✆ **77-75-88-60.**

Intersport Sports Huset This is the biggest sporting-goods store in town, with subdivisions that focus on the equipment you'll need for every conceivable sport, in any season, that's practiced in this severe Arctic climate. Scattered over two separate floors of a showroom in the heart of town, the store stocks bicycles, hiking equipment, white-water rafting and kayaking equipment, all manner of skis, and a state-of-the-art collection of boots, backpacks, and severe-weather clothing. Sometimes the staff isn't always too well trained here, and some don't seem to have a clue as to what it is they're actually selling, but if you're motivated to figure out the inventories on your own, there are many worthwhile options. Storgata 39. ✆ **77-66-11-00.**

7 TROMSØ AFTER DARK

The bitter cold and an appetite-inducing position immediately adjacent to the blustery fjords of the North Sea seem to unite in a setting that's conducive to hard partying, hard living, and hard drinking in sybaritic Tromsø. This, coupled with a large student population and a passionate interest in all things sports-related, makes victory and defeat events whose joys or sorrows can easily be fueled or quaffed with drink.

Evocative of some Alaskan cities, nightlife here mainly consists of heavy drinking on a massive pub crawl. In Tromsø, the party goes on 24 hours a day, summer or winter: "In winter, you drink all night because of the darkness," said one local pub crawler. "In midsummer, we drink all night because the sun never sets."

Amtmandens Datter This pub was previously recommended as an Internet cafe. Smoky and mellow, it is also one of the most frequented pubs in party town Tromsø, drawing a mostly male crowd in their 20s to 50s. Patrons also come in here to read the newspapers and play board games. Believe it or not, there are even books to read. It's open Monday to Thursday noon to 1:30am, Friday and Saturday noon to 3am, and

Sunday noon to midnight. Food is also served until 7pm Monday to Saturday. The pub is part of an entertainment complex that includes yet another two pubs, the Victoria Fun Pub, attracting a broad age range, and Subsirkus, which sometimes features live bands, attracting a young crowd. Duck into either to see what might be happening at the time of your visit. Grønnegata 81. ✆ **77-75-74-77.**

Åpen Bar ★ This much-frequented nightspot is a modern bar that opens toward a view of Tromsø's major shopping street. It is decorated with art by some of North Norway's leading young artists. Some of the best tapas and other light fare are served here, with plates that cost from NOK150 ($30/£15). An under-30 crowd frequents the place, and there is often dancing to recorded music. A mug of beer costs NOK60 ($12/£6). It's open Tuesday to Thursday 3pm to midnight, and Friday and Saturday noon to 3am. Grønnegata 15. ✆ **77-68-46-00.**

Blå Rock Café You'll be greeted at the entrance to this battered but congenial pub with a sign that screams ROCK AND ROLL RULES, and if you opt to abide by that premise, you might find yourself having a perfectly marvelous, albeit a bit grungy, time. The setting is a blue-sided wooden house at the end of the town's main shopping street (Stortorget). The staff is friendly, the youthful clientele looks like it was just assigned *Catcher in the Rye* as a reading assignment, and the pub's visual and musical references invariably revolve around punk cultural icons from Britain and the U.S. They stock about 50 kinds of beer here, most of it priced at around NOK56 ($11/£5.60) for a foaming half-liter mugful. It's open Monday to Thursday 11:30am to 2am, Friday and Saturday from 11:30am to 3am, and Sunday 1pm to 2am. Strandveien 14. ✆ **77-61-00-20.** Cover NOK45 ($9/£4.50) Fri–Sat.

Compagniet Nightclub ★ On the premises of a previously recommended restaurant (see "Where to Dine," earlier in this chapter), this is one of the more legitimate nightclubs of Tromsø, as opposed to one of the hard-drinking taverns. It is both a nightclub and disco, drawing a 20s-to-40s crowd. Live acts might be featured, but only occasionally—and don't expect any big names this far north. Most often a DJ plays for your dancing pleasure. Entrance is free until after midnight; then there's a NOK50 ($10/£5) cover. It's open Thursday to Saturday 9pm to 1:30am or 3am, depending on business. Sjøgata 12. ✆ **77-66-42-22.**

Driv Café ★ Finds For virtually any activity in Tromsø that's aimed at, organized by, or attended by university students, this antique wood-sided warehouse, set directly adjacent to the harbor in the heart of town, will be involved in some way. It was originally built in 1902 as a warehouse for fish, and today its thick interior beams and aged planking evoke an age when hardworking, hard-drinking fishermen, hunters, trappers, and whalers made their sometimes precarious living from the sea. Today there's a simple cafe filling up the seaward side of the place, and a bigger and more battered-looking bar area where bulletin boards list virtually every cultural activity available within the region. The cafe is open Monday to Thursday from noon till 2am, and Friday and Saturday from noon to 3:30am. Some kind of concert is scheduled every Wednesday and Thursday night beginning around 9:30pm, and every Friday and Saturday the place becomes a disco and pickup bar between 10pm and 2am. Entrance fees to concerts range from NOK30 to NOK160 ($6–$32/£3–£16), depending on the artist, and admission to the disco costs NOK40 ($8/£4). Søndre Tollbodgate 3B. ✆ **77-60-07-76.**

G. In the center of town, this is both a modern cafe and bar that is especially popular from morning until late at night. As the night wears on, the patrons get younger, presumably because the over-40 crowd retires. Light food is served; platters cost around NOK70 to NOK100 ($14–$20/£7–£10), with mugs of beer going for NOK56 ($11/£5.50). Paintings by local artists are not only exhibited, but they're also for sale. It's open Monday to Thursday 10am to 1:30am, Friday and Saturday 10am to 3am, and Sunday noon to 2am. Storgata 49 ✆ **77-68-25-80.**

Kaffe å Lars This is another one of Tromsø's cozy cafes. During the day it serves lunch, mainly light fare such as sandwiches, until 6pm, costing NOK65 to NOK85 ($13–$17/£6.50–£8.50). Patrons in their 30s and 40s frequent the joint. In the evening, a younger crowd in their 20s and 30s flocks here, listening to recorded jazz and drinking lots of beer, costing NOK55 ($11/£5.50) a mug. It's open Monday to Thursday 7am to midnight, and Friday and Saturday 11am to 2am. Kirkegata 8. ✆ **77-63-77-30.**

Kulturscenen & Studenthuset Driv Lying on Tromsø's inner harbor in a grand building from 1902, this is a cafe, bar, and occasional venue for live concerts. In summer, there's outdoor dining and drinking, plus dancing on Friday and Saturday nights for a young university crowd. In the dining section, you can order main courses costing NOK110 to NOK190 ($22–$38/£11–£19). It's open Monday to Thursday 11am to 2am, Friday and Saturday 11am to 3:30am, and Sunday noon to 1:30am. Søndre Tollbodgate 3. ✆ **77-60-07-76.**

Le Mirage ★ The leather sofas at this cutting-edge bar are deep, plush, and comfortable, and the walls are painted in conversation-inducing shades of pale beige and lime. It exists as a hipster bar, with a striking-looking postmodern decor that's in deliberate contrast to the more rustic pubs that surround it on all sides. The 20-something clientele is hip enough to remain completely unfazed at the way this bar, somewhat confusingly, seems to have been repeatedly designated, often in newspaper articles in many different languages throughout Europe, as a gay bar. If you ask one of the barmaids about it, she'll politely maintain that the place is predominately straight, and we'd tend to agree. But despite that, we still suspect that this, more than any other bar, is the most gay-tolerant and accommodating in town. It's open Monday to Thursday noon to 2am, Friday and Saturday 11am to 3:30am, and Sunday 1pm to 2am. There is no cover charge. Storgata 42. ✆ **77-68-52-34.**

Meieriet This fully licensed cafe and pub is one of the most visited in town, with a welcoming atmosphere that draws patrons in a wide age range. Seating 100, it is large yet cozy, and vaguely evocative of a British pub. Its atmosphere changes throughout the day. During the day, visitors drop in for light meals such as hamburgers, baguettes, and freshly made salads. Different kinds of wok dishes are also featured, with prices of main courses ranging from NOK75 to NOK150 ($15–$30/£7.50–£15). Billiards, backgammon, and newspapers (some in English) occupy the patrons' time. Background music is played in the late afternoon, and on weekends a DJ directs the music. It's open Monday to Thursday 8am to 2am, Friday 11am to 3:30am, and Sunday noon to midnight. Grønnegate 37–39. ✆ **77-61-36-39.**

Rorbua Pub This is Norway's most famous pub, thanks to the fact that one of Norway's most popular weekly TV talk shows, *Du skal høre mye,* whose name roughly translates as "You've Heard a Lot," was broadcast from here until 2003. At its height of popularity, the show attracted a million viewers every Wednesday night. Despite the fact that the hotel that contains the pub was built in 1965, the thick timbers and rough-textured planking evoke a fisherman's cottage *(rorbu)* from the late 19th century. A hard-drinking crowd from their 20s to their 50s is attracted here nightly. There's live music in the pub every Wednesday to Sunday beginning around 8:30pm. In the cellar of the Radisson SAS Hotel Tromsø, Sjøgata 7. ✆ **77-75-90-05.**

15

The Route to the North Cape

Northern Norway. The name itself can give you a chill, conjuring up thoughts of polar bears, the summer midnight sun, and arctic winters of total darkness. It is an eerie and fascinating land of deep fjords, snowcapped mountains, vast open plains, dramatic island formations, and even fertile farmland (although the growing season is short).

Northern Norway is the land of the *Sami,* where you come face to face with nature under the foreboding sky of **Finnmark,** the name of the region. Rushing rivers and lakes are teeming with fish, and many tiny, weather-beaten fishing hamlets depend almost entirely on the sea for their livelihood.

For most visitors, the ultimate goal is the **Nordkapp** (North Cape), or "the end of the world," as the ancient Vikings called it.

Traveling in north Norway and meeting the *Nordlendinger* (northerners) is an adventure in travel. However, it may not be as cold as you think. Because of the warming influences of the Gulf Stream, Finnmark has the longest ice-free coast in the Arctic region. Finnmark shares the same latitudes as Siberia, Greenland, and Alaska.

Of course, flying is the fastest way to get here, but you can also drive toward the Arctic Circle from such cities as Bergen on one of Europe's most scenic drives. Don't, however, underestimate driving times. Allow at least 3 days to reach the Arctic Circle from Bergen or 5 days to reach the North Cape.

Coastal Steamer: The Way to Go

Coastal steamers ★★ are elegantly appointed ships that travel along the Norwegian coast from Bergen to Kirkenes, carrying passengers and cargo to 34 ports. A total of 11 ships make the journey year-round. Along the route, the ships sail through Norway's more obscure fjords, revealing breathtaking scenery and numerous opportunities for adventure. At points along the way, passengers have the opportunity to take sightseeing trips to the surrounding mountains and glaciers, and to go on excursions on smaller vessels.

The chief cruise operator is the **Hurtigruten,** 405 Park Ave., New York, NY 10022 (✆ **866/552-0371;** www.hurtigruten.us). Various packages are available. Tours may be booked heading north from Bergen, south from Kirkenes, or round-trip. The 15-day northbound journey from Bergen to Oslo costs $6,999 per person, including meals and taxes. The 13-day round-trip voyage from Oslo to Kirkenes and back to Bergen is $4,699 per person (days 7–16 include a round-trip cruise). For information on these and other trips, including air-cruise packages from the United States, contact Hurtigruten.

1 MO I RANA: ARCTIC CIRCLE CITY

450km (279 miles) N of Trondheim

It's not pretty, but "Mo on the Ranafjord" is your gateway to the Arctic Circle, which crosses its municipal boundaries from east to west. With a population of some 25,000 people, it is the third-largest city in the north of Norway.

Credit for the city's recent rapid population growth goes to the steel and iron industry. In fact, the buildings here are industrial, ugly boxes for the most part, though they are welcoming havens on cold and windy days.

We suggest that you use Mo i Rana only as a refueling stop and as a gateway to one of the largest wildernesses in Europe. You don't visit it for its grand architecture, but for the magnificent setting that it occupies, with adventure travel possible in all directions.

ESSENTIALS

GETTING THERE The quickest way to Mo i Rana is to fly in on a daily flight from Trondheim, arriving at the Røssvoll airport, lying 14km (8¾ miles) from the center.

Widerøe Airlines (© **81-00-12-00;** www.wideroe.no) flies here. You can also arrive by train at the **Mo i Rana Train Station** (© **75-15-01-77**). Two or three trains arrive daily from Trondheim, costing NOK758 ($152/£76) one-way and taking just under 7 hours. Check www.nsb.no for information. Bus service takes longer, is inconvenient, and saves you neither time nor money, so it's not recommended. Motorists can take the E6 north from Trondheim.

VISITOR INFORMATION Near the Sørlandsveien roundabout, **Rana Turistforening,** Ole Tobias Olsensgate 3 (© **75-13-92-00**), offers information about the area and is one of the most helpful tourist bureaus in Norway. From mid-June to early August, it is open Monday to Friday 9am to 8pm, Saturday 9am to 4pm, and Sunday 1 to 7pm. In the off season, it's open Monday to Friday 9am to 4pm.

SEEING THE SIGHTS

The town itself has some minor attractions, but if your time is severely limited, it would be better spent taking a tour of the wilderness.

The **Rana Museum of Natural History,** Moholmen 15 (© **75-11-01-40**), reveals the flora and fauna of the Arctic Circle, with a number of "touch-me-if-you-want" exhibits of particular appeal to families with young kids. The fascinating geology and ecology of this Arctic wilderness come alive here. Admission is NOK40 ($8/£4) or free for children 11 and under, for both this museum and the one below. It's open mid-June to mid-August Tuesday to Friday 10am to 3pm and also Thursday 7 to 9pm. In the off season, it's open Tuesday to Friday 9am to 3pm.

North of Mo (30km/19 miles) lies the grandest natural attraction in this part of Norway, the **Svartisen Glacier ★★★** (means "black ice" in Norwegian). Svartisen is second in size in the country only to the Jostedal Glacier. The ice plateau is 1,005m (3,296 ft.) above sea level, covering 370 sq. km (137 sq. miles) of high mountains and narrow fjords.

Svartisen (more accurately known as Engen Glacier) consists of two main glaciers, the Østisen (East Glacier) and Vestisen (West Glacier). One arm of the West Glacier is the lowest-lying glacier on the European mainland. The glacial arm continues all the way down to Engenbrevannet Lake. It continues to grow, advancing 40m (131 ft.) a year. Motorists driving along Rte. 17 by Holandsfjorden can see many arms of the glacier stretching down between mountain peaks.

The Vestisen ice cap is our favorite section to visit if your time is limited. The **Engen Skyssbåt** (© **94-86-55-16**) operates two ferries running across Holandsfjorden, taking 15 minutes and costing NOK50 ($10/£5) each way. From June to August, the ferries run 12 times daily Monday to Friday from 7:30am to 8pm, and 10 times on Saturday and Sunday 10am to 8pm. Ferries depart from the Holand and Brasetvik quays. Additional information about the glacier and the fjord-based ferryboats that access the climbing trails leading up to it are available from the **tourist office** at Meløy (© **75-75-48-88**).

You can also drive to the glacier by going north from Mo on the E6 for 12km (7½ miles), following the signs to the glacier for 23km (14 miles). At the end of the line, you'll find **Svartisbåten** boats (© **75-16-23-79**) crossing the lake and coming within 2.5km (1½ miles) of the Østerdal arm of the glacier. From the disembarkation point, it's still a rigorous 3km (1¾-mile) hike up to Austerdalsvatnet lake and the glacier.

If you happen to be in superb physical shape, and if you thrive on high-altitude adventures with just a whiff of primordial danger, there's a local tour operator that might appeal to your cravings: **Rana Special Sports, Ltd.** (✆ **75-12-70-88;** www.spesialsport.no). Its guides can take you on a full-day climbing excursion on the glacier, with all the equipment included (including pitons and special ice cleats for your hiking boots) for NOK750 ($150/£75) per person. We advocate this only for climbers who thrive on rough adventures in the savage outdoors.

The glacier is part of the **Saltfjellet-Svartisen Nasjonalpark ★★★**, stretching over a landmass of 2,015 sq. km (746 sq. miles). The park takes in the ice field of Svartisen, along with various moorlands that reach as far east as the Swedish border.

Information about hiking trails in the park can be obtained from the tourist office in Mo i Rana (see above). The trails can be approached from Rte. 77, which heads east off the E6 to the Swedish frontier.

Norway's best-known "show cave," **Gronligrøtta ★** (✆ **75-13-25-86**) lies in the hamlet of Grønli, 26km (16 miles) northwest of Mo. The only cave with electric lights in Scandinavia, it'll illuminate your way as you take the half-hour tour into the cave, which has an underground river. As a curiosity, you can see a mammoth granite block ripped off by a glacier and dumped into the cave by the sheer force of the onrushing waters. Visits cost NOK100 ($20/£10) for adults, NOK50 ($10/£5) for children 15 and under. The cave can be toured hourly and daily from mid-June to mid-August from 10am to 7pm.

EN ROUTE TO BODØ

North of Mo i Rana (80km/50 miles) toward the Arctic Circle, you'll come to the **Polarsirkelsenteret,** on E6. It offers a multiscreen show depicting the highlights of Norway. Many people send cards and letters from here with a special postmark from the Arctic Circle. There are also a cafeteria and gift shop on the grounds. The center is at N-8242 Polarsirkelen (✆ **75-12-96-96;** www.polarsirkelsenteret.no). It's open in May and June daily from 9am to 6pm, July to September daily 8am to 10pm; admission is NOK70 ($14/£7).

Continue north to Fauske and then follow Rte. 80 west along the Skjerstadfjord. Depending on weather conditions, you should reach Bodø in under an hour.

WHERE TO STAY

Comfort Hotel This is a sibling hotel of the Comfort chain member recommended below, and it uses the same reservation systems. Originally built in 1949, reconstructed in the late 1960s, and radically renovated in the late 1980s, this is a boxy-looking but comfortable haven, attracting business travelers and enjoying a reputation as the most stable and most central hotel in town. Rising three stories above a barren-looking neighborhood of waterfront commercial and efficiently weather-tight buildings, it opens into a bland but soothing decor of contemporary furniture. The in-house restaurant serves Norwegian and international food. All rooms are nonsmoking.

Thomas Von Westensgate 2, N-8624 Mo i Rana. ✆ **75-12-05-00.** Fax 75-12-05-01. www.choicehotels.no. 30 units. Mon–Thurs NOK995–NOK1,510 ($199–$302/£100–£151) double; Fri–Sun NOK895 ($179/£90) double; NOK1,350 ($270/£135) suite. Rates include buffet breakfast. AE, DC, MC, V. **Amenities:** Restaurant; lobby bar; sauna; laundry service/dry cleaning; rooms for those w/limited mobility. *In room:* TV, minibar.

Comfort Hotel Ole Tobias ★ *Finds* Built in 1993, this is the smallest and coziest hotel in town. The hotel was named after Ole Tobias (1827–1912), a local priest, inventor, and visionary whose well-publicized treks (on foot) between Trondheim and Bodø led to the construction of a railway for the transport of fish from the Arctic waters of the north to canning factories and consumers of the south. Reproductions of many of Ole Tobias's photographs hang, framed, throughout the hotel. If you come here, expect an aura that's akin to a well-mannered but extroverted private club. Its social headquarters lie within the hotel basement, site of a cozy bar and restaurant. Here you'll find a wide-screen TV and a light evening buffet (available nightly 6–10pm) that's included in the price of a room. The bedroom decor includes a use of deep-toned "farmer romantic" colors, thick pine furniture, and turn-of-the-20th-century nostalgia, with representations of trains woven into the carpets.

Thora Meyers Gate 2, N-8602 Mo i Rana. ✆ **75-12-05-00.** Fax 75-12-05-01. www.choicehotels.no. 30 units. NOK895–NOK1,710 ($179–$342/£90–£171) double. AE, DC, MC, V. **Amenities:** Bar; sauna; room service; nonsmoking rooms; rooms for those w/limited mobility. *In room:* TV, iron.

WHERE TO DINE

Babette's Gjestebud GREEK/TURKISH/MEDITERRANEAN It may not have great food, but, frankly, you're lucky just to get a warm meal in these chilly climes. Babette's is a cozy, candlelit tavern, with lots of exposed wood and warmth that's particularly welcome in this frigid climate. It was named after the Danish film *Babette's Feast,* in which closed and bitter psyches were released and healed through good food, good wine, and love. The chef focuses on grilled meats and fresh salads, some of them garnished with feta cheese and Mediterranean herbs. Don't expect a particular allegiance to the cuisines of either Greece or Turkey, because what is served is a simplified blend of them both. Expect a medley of grilled meats, salads garnished with ham slices and/or shrimp, pastas that include a savory version with curried chicken, and body-warming starters such as French onion soup with your choice of either garlic-butter or herb-butter bread.

Jernbanegata 22. ✆ **75-15-44-33.** Reservations recommended. Main courses NOK160–NOK280 ($32–$56/£16–£28). AE, DC, MC, V. Daily 11am–midnight.

MO I RANA AFTER DARK

Ramona, Fridtjof Nansensgate 28 (✆ **75-13-40-00**), in the Hotel Meyergården, is the only genuinely viable nightclub and dance club in town. Because of the lack of competitors and a floor space that sprawls over an area that's bigger than the ground floors of many of the region's department stores, it promotes itself as the largest nightclub in north Norway. The space, set within an ugly commercial building in the heart of town, is subdivided by banquettes and arrangements of seating areas, into three "regions," painted in tones of pink or yellow. There are bars scattered strategically throughout and a clientele whose age and priorities change according to whichever night of the week you happen to arrive. According to popular hipster wisdom, Thursday nights attract the student crowd, with a lot of 18-year-olds wearing various forms of punk-inspired clothing. Saturday is for an older, recently-divorced-and-somewhat-embittered-but-still-hoping-for-an-active-dating-and-sex-life crowd. Friday is the let-down-your-guard and be-sure-not-to-drive-your-own-car-home-because-you've-been-drinking crowd. The place is open every Tuesday to Saturday 10pm to 3am, charging an entrance fee of NOK85 ($17/£8.50) per person.

2 BODØ: GATEWAY TO THE NORTH ★

479km (297 miles) N of Trondheim; 1,430km (887 miles) N of Bergen; 1,305km (809 miles) N of Oslo

This is a great place to spend a day or two—not for the city itself, which is dull architecturally, but for the attractions of nature in the wilds that envelop the town. This seaport, the terminus of the Nordland railway, lies just north of the Arctic Circle. Visitors arrive here, the capital of Nordland, for a glimpse of the midnight sun, which shines from June 1 to July 13. But don't expect a clear view of it. What those tourist brochures don't tell you is that many nights are either rainy or hazy, cutting down considerably on your enjoyment of the spectacle. From December 19 to January 9, Bodø gets no sunlight at all.

Bodø is Nordland's largest city, with some 40,000 inhabitants living at the northern entrance to Salt Fjord. Although burned to the ground by the retreating Nazis at the end of World War II, the city dates back to 1816, when it was founded by merchants from Trondheim seeking a northern trading post. In time it became one of the leading fishing centers of Norway, specializing in the drying of cod, and it has also become known for its ship repair yards.

Bodø faces an archipelago rich in bird life, and no other town in the world boasts such a large concentration of sea eagles. From Bodø, you can take excursions in many directions to glaciers and bird islands; the most attractive are the Lofoten Islands (p. 410).

ESSENTIALS

GETTING THERE If you're not driving or traveling by coastal steamer, you can reach Bodø from major cities throughout Norway, usually with connections through either Trondheim or Oslo, on **SAS (✆ 74-80-41-00;** www.sas.no). The airport lies just over a kilometer (½ mile) southwest of the city center and is accessed by a bus (it's marked CENTRUMS BUSSEN) that departs at 20-minute intervals every Monday to Friday for NOK90 ($18/£9) each way. Passengers arriving on a Saturday or Sunday hire one of the many taxis waiting at the arrivals gate. Bodø is at the end of the Nordland rail line.

Two **trains** a day leave Trondheim for Bodø. The trip takes 10 hours, 20 minutes. Visit www.nsb.no for information.

For **bus** information, contact **Saltens Bilruter** in Bodø (**✆ 75-54-80-20**). Fauske is a transportation hub along the E6 highway to the north and Rte. 80 west to Bodø. From Fauske there are two buses a day to Bodø. The trip takes an hour and 10 minutes. If you take the train from Stockholm to Narvik (north of Bodø), you can make bus connections to Fauske and Bodø, a total trip of 5 hours. When asked about what and where Fauske was, an employee of the local bus company quipped, "All roads (in and out of Bodø) lead to Fauske." Know in advance that if you're taking public transportation, you are likely to pass through Fauske on your way to and from other parts of Norway's far north.

Motorists can continue north from Mo i Rana, our last stopover, until they come to the junction with Rte. 80 heading west to Bodø.

VISITOR INFORMATION The **tourist office, Destination Bodø,** is at Sjøgaten 3 (**✆ 75-54-80-00;** www.visitbodo.com), in the town center. It's open January 2 to May 31 and September 1 to December 19 Monday to Friday 9am to 4pm and Saturday 10am to 2pm; June 1 to August 31 Monday to Friday 9am to 8pm Saturday 10am to 6pm, Sunday noon to 8pm. It's closed December 20 to January 1. The town is relatively flat, and bikes can be rented here for NOK80 ($16/£8) for 3 hours and NOK180 ($36/£18) for 24 hours.

Atelier 88-Galleri Bodøgaard Lying 2.5km (1½ miles) from the heart of town, this museum exhibits the largest private ethnographical collection in north Norway. Boats, artifacts of daily life, and tools used in hunting and fishing are just some of the collection items on parade. The site encompasses the Russian prisoner of war camp at Bodøgaard.

Skeidalen 2. ✆ **75-56-32-41.** Admission NOK50 ($10/£5). Tues–Fri 9am–3pm; Sat–Sun noon–3pm (hours subject to change—check before coming here).

Bodin Kirke Sitting pretty in clover fields, this intriguing onion-domed church can be visited along with a trip to the Norwegian Aviation Museum (see below). It lies about 1km (½ mile) southeast of the museum. Dating from 1240, the church has seen many changes over the years. The addition of many 17th- and 18th-century baroque adornments jazzes up what was once a severe interior.

Gamle Riksvei 68. ✆ **75-56-54-20.** Free admission. June–Aug Mon–Fri 10am–2pm. Closed Sept–May. Bus: 23 from the station.

Bodø Domkirke As Norwegian cathedrals go, the Bodø Dom ranks low on the totem pole. But when the Nazis bombed their previous church on May 27, 1940, locals were eager to open a major place of worship even if they could find no Michelangelo—or money—to build it. What they came up with is fairly respectable. Completed in 1956, this is the most notable building constructed since those German bombers flew over. It features tufted rugs depicting ecclesiastical themes, wall hangings, and a stained-glass window that captures the Northern Lights. A memorial outside honors those killed in the war with the inscription NO ONE MENTIONED, NO ONE FORGOTTEN. There's also an outstanding spire that stands separate from the main building.

Torv Gate 12. ✆ **75-51-95-30.** Free admission. June–Aug daily 9:30am–11:30pm. Closed Sept–May.

Nordlandmuseet (Nordland Museum) In the town center, the main building of this museum is one of the oldest structures in Bodø. Here you'll find, among other exhibits, artifacts recalling the saga of local fishermen and artifacts from the Sami culture. There's also a "dry" aquarium, with stuffed fish, along with silver treasure dating from the Viking era. An open-air part of this museum contains more than a dozen historical buildings moved to the site, plus a collection of boats. Part of the exhibit includes *Anna Karoline of Hopen,* the only surviving Nordland cargo vessel.

Prinsengate 116. ✆ **75-52-16-40.** Admission NOK35 ($7/£3.50) adults, students/children free. May–Aug Mon–Fri 9am–4pm, Sat–Sun 11am–4pm; rest of year Mon–Fri 9am–3pm.

Norsk Luftfartsmuseum (Norwegian Aviation Museum) Kids So this is where that infamous U-2 spy plane ended up. In 1960, the ill-fated plane made headlines around the world when it was shot down over the Soviet Union, creating a major diplomatic incident. The spy plane was en route from Peshawar in Pakistan to Bodø. This museum, shaped like an airplane propeller, takes you on its own exciting "fly-over" of Norway's civil and military aviation history. Kids and adults alike should soar through the exhibits. You're allowed to have a close encounter with large and small aircraft such as the Spitfire and JU52. Hands-on demonstrations reveal to you the dynamics of flight. In addition to the exhibition of aircraft, the museum shows a collection of photographs about the largest predators in the Nordic countries, including lynx, bears, wolves, wolverines, and, more surprisingly, humans. The museum was built on the site of a German World War II airfield.

The museum lies 2km (1¼ miles) north of town. Olav V Gata. ✆ **75-50-78-50.** www.luftfart.museum.no. Admission NOK90 ($18/£9) adults, NOK40 ($8/£4) children 15 and under. June–Aug Sun–Fri 10am–7pm, Sat 10am–5pm; Sept–May Mon–Fri 10am–4pm, Sat–Sun 11am–5pm. Bus: 23 or marked CITY NORD.

ON THE OUTSKIRTS

Blodveimuseet ★ Finds On the southeastern outskirts of the city, at a distance of 5km (3 miles), you can visit this "Blood Road Museum." The museum re-creates those horrible POW days during 1942 to 1945 when the Nazis held an iron grip on northern Norway before burning it to the ground during their infamous retreat. Thousands of European prisoners of war labored to build a system of road and railroads in the area, and, of course, many lost their lives. In Saltdal alone there were 15 to 18 different prisoner-of-war camps, with nearly 10,000 Russian, Serbian, and Polish prisoners held captive.

The "Road of Blood" extended for 2km (1¼ miles) from Saltnes to Saksenvik from the center of Rognan. People still walk this horrible road today, noting the blood-colored cross a prisoner painted on a rock face.

At Saltnes, about 1km (½ mile) east of Rognan, the Blood Road Museum contains a collection of original rural buildings, the oldest dating from 1750. The original and horribly bleak German barracks are here as well, revealing the harsh life of the prisoners. The museum was opened in 1995 as part of Norway's 50th anniversary of its liberation from the Nazis.

Bygetunet, Saltnes, outside Rognan. ✆ **75-69-06-60.** Admission NOK35 ($7/£3.50), NOK10 ($2/£1) children 15 and under. June 20–Aug 20 Mon–Fri 10am–5pm; Sat 1–4pm; Sun 1–6pm. Closed rest of year.

ACTIVE SPORTS

If you'd like to go horseback riding under the midnight sun, **Bodø Hestecenter,** Soloya Gård (✆ **75-51-41-48**), about 14km (8¾ miles) southwest of Bodø, rents horses. Buses go there Monday to Friday mornings and evenings and on Saturday morning. For more information, ask at the Bodø Tourist Office (see "Visitor Information," above). The cost is NOK120 ($24/£12) for a 45-minute ride.

At the visitor center (see above), you can pick up maps detailing the best hiking in the area. The best area is through **Bodømarka (Bodø forest),** with its 35km (22 miles) of marked hiking and cross-country skiing trails. For detailed touring, including overnighting in the forest, contact **Bodø og Omegn Turist-forening,** the **Bodø Mountain Touring Association** (✆ **75-52-14-13**), which operates a dozen cabins in the forest.

The most up-to-date and well-recommended indoor swimming pool in the region is the **Mørkved Badet** (✆ **75-55-08-90**), in the hamlet of Mørkved, about 4km (2½ miles) north of Bodø's center. If you want to use it, know that it gives priority to local swim teams and school groups, so public hours are limited to Wednesday from 5 to 10pm, Friday 5 to 9pm, Saturday 9am to 3pm, and Sunday 9am to 4pm. Admission costs NOK60 ($12/£6) for adults, NOK40 ($8/£4) for persons 17 and under.

A popular man-made attraction, **Saltstraumen Opplevelsesenter,** or adventure center, lies at Saltstraumen, Rte. 17 (✆ **75-56-06-55**), and is fun for the whole family. The center gives an in-depth preview through exhibits and artifacts tracing the history of the area and its people from the Ice Age to the coming of the Vikings. An on-site aquarium includes a pond for seals and fish found in regional waters. Admission is NOK80 ($16/£8). From May to mid-June, it's open daily from 11am to 6pm; from mid- to late June and from mid- to late August, it's open daily 10am to 7pm; from July to mid-August, it's open daily 9am to 8pm; and in September, it's open Saturday and Sunday only 11am to 6pm.

THE MAELSTROM From Bodø, you can take a bus to the mighty maelstrom, the **Saltstraumen Eddy** ★, 33km (20 miles) south of the city. The variation between high- and low-tide levels pushes immense volumes of water through narrow fjords, creating huge whirlpools known as "kettles." When the eddies and the surrounding land vibrate, they produce an odd yelling sound. Saltstraumen is nearly 3.3km (2 miles) long and only about 167m (548 ft.) wide, with billions of gallons of water pressing through at speeds of about 10 knots. Buses from Bodø run five times a day Monday to Saturday, twice on Sunday. The cost is NOK75 ($15/£7.50) for adults round-trip, half-price for children 11 and under. A round-trip taxi excursion costs NOK550 ($110/£55) for two passengers.

VISITING A GLACIER One of Norway's major tourist attractions, **Svartisen Glacier** ★★★ was previewed under Mo i Rana (see earlier) but can also be visited south of Bodø. About 161km (100 miles) from Bodø, the glacier can be reached by car, although a boat crossing over the Svartisenfjord is more exciting to us. Tours to the glacier on the Helgeland Express, a combination bus-and-ferry excursion, are offered from Bodø several times in the summer (usually every second Sat July to Aug). The cost is NOK600 ($120/£60) for adults, NOK400 ($80/£40) for children 15 and under. The tours leave Bodø at 1pm and return around 8pm on the same day. You can go ashore to examine the Engaglacier and see the nearby visitor center (✆ **75-75-10-00**). The local tourist office can provide more information and make reservations. Depending on ice conditions, the visitor center may be able to arrange boat transportation across a narrow but icy channel so that you can have a closer look at the ice floe.

WHERE TO STAY

The **Bodø Tourist Office** (see "Visitor Information," above) can help you book a room in a hotel. It also maintains a list of local B&Bs and will book you a room for a fee of NOK18 to NOK27 ($3.60–$5.40/£1.80–£2.70).

Many locals within this maritime community, as well as the staff at the Bodø tourist office, will be alert to the schedule of high and low tides on the day of your arrival. The phenomenon occurs four times within any 24-hour period, twice for incoming tides, twice for outgoing tides, with a brief interlude between high and low tides when the waters are almost eerily still.

Expensive

Radisson SAS Royal Hotel ★★ By far the finest and most expensive hotel in the area, this glistening structure is an inviting waterfront oasis that opens onto panoramic views. The good-size guest rooms are furnished in sleek contemporary style and decorated in a number of motifs, including Japanese, Nordic, Chinese, and British. The Royal is located on the main street at the harborfront and offers some of the best drinking and dining facilities in Bodø, including the Sjøsiden Restaurant. Live music and dancing are offered every Saturday night in the Moloen Bar. But, in our view, the greatest place for a drink is the Top 13 Rooftop Bar. An original promotion for the hotel had a typo, which read that the bar "is a fantastic place to have a drunk and take in the view."

Storgata 2, N-8000 Bodø. ✆ **800/333-3333** in the U.S., or 75-51-90-00. Fax 75-51-90-02. www.radissonsas.com. 190 units. NOK1,650 ($330/£165) double; NOK1,950 ($390/£195) suite. Rates include buffet breakfast. AE, DC, MC, V. Free parking. **Amenities:** 2 restaurants; 2 bars; lounge; fitness center; sauna; room service; babysitting; laundry service/dry cleaning; nonsmoking rooms; rooms for those w/limited mobility. *In room:* TV, Wi-Fi, minibar, hair dryer, trouser press.

Rica Hotel ★ Located at the harbor and offering a view of Vestfjorden, this is one of Bodø's best hotels, built in 1986 and enlarged in 1990. It's no match for the Radisson SAS but is a full-service hotel and a bastion of comfort, even though its facade is as severe as the cold weather that often envelops it. Most of the somberly furnished rooms have large writing desks. Only moderate in size, rooms are comfortable and well maintained, with large, comfortable beds. The hotel has two popular restaurants (see "Where to Dine," below).

Sjøgata 23, N-8001 Bodø. ✆ **75-54-70-00.** Fax 75-54-70-55. www.rica.no. 113 units. NOK1,075–NOK1,810 ($215–$362/£108–£181) double; NOK1,350–NOK1,950 ($270–$390/£135–£195) junior suite. Rates include buffet breakfast. AE, DC, MC, V. Parking NOK80 ($16/£8). **Amenities:** 2 restaurants; bar; fitness center; sauna; room service; laundry service/dry cleaning; nonsmoking rooms; rooms for those w/limited mobility. *In room:* TV, minibar, hair dryer.

Moderate

Bodø Hotell (Value) Opened in 1987, this family-run hotel, located in the town center about 2½ blocks from the harbor, is known for its good value. The bedrooms are modern, and although the bathrooms are small, they are well maintained and equipped with shower units. The rooms, also a bit small, are quite cozy, with an attempt toward an intimate homelike feeling. Oriental carpeting, swag draperies, and art on the walls add up to a welcoming ambience.

Professor Schyttesgate 5, N-8001 Bodø. ✆ **75-54-77-00.** Fax 75 52 57 78. www.bodohotell.no. 31 units. Fri–Sat and June 20–Aug 15 daily NOK850 ($170/£85) double; Sun–Thurs NOK1,100 ($220/£110) double; year-round NOK950–NOK1,300 ($190–$260/£95–£130) suite. Rates include buffet breakfast. AE, DC, MC, V. Free parking. Closed Dec 22–Jan 3. **Amenities:** Lunch restaurant; bar; lounge; sauna; laundry service/dry cleaning; nonsmoking rooms; rooms for those w/limited mobility. *In room:* TV, Wi-Fi, hair dryer.

Skagen Hotel ★ (Finds) This discovery offers a lot of charm in a somewhat bleak landscape. The hotel is the best in this part of Norway for arranging memorable adventures, including wilderness camping and adventure weekends in some of the most magnificently varied landscape reachable from Bodø. Other adventures include deep-sea rafting, sea eagle feedings, fishing trips, canoeing, rock climbing, and glacier walks. Bedrooms are midsize and comfortably furnished, with well-maintained bathrooms with a shower and toilet. Rooms are individually decorated, often in attractive cherrywood. Thoughtful extras here include breakfast served at 6am or coffee and tea always available in the library. That's not all: A free buffet is served nightly from 7 to 10pm.

Nyholmsgata 11, N-8001 Bodø. ✆ **75-52-24-00.** Fax 75-52-59-30. www.skagen-hotel.no. 72 units. NOK1,100–NOK1,490 ($220–$298/£110–£149) double; NOK1,750–NOK2,100 ($350–$420/£175–£210) junior suite. AE, DC, MC, V. Free parking. **Amenities:** Bar; gym; sauna; nonsmoking rooms; rooms for those w/limited mobility. *In room:* TV, Wi-Fi, minibar, hair dryer, beverage maker.

Thon Hotel Nordlys This modern hotel rises six floors to overlook Bodø's harbor. Inside, a collection of valuable contemporary art is housed—and some of it is for sale. The guest rooms are contemporary, with yellow palates, wooden floors, plus tiled bathrooms with tub/shower combinations. Some of the rooms were specifically tailored to the "female business traveler," but the woman vacationing in the area would also be comfortable here. Egon, the hotel's restaurant, specializes in robust American and Norwegian fare.

Moloveien 14, N8001 Bodø. ✆ **75-53-19-00.** Fax 75-53-19-99. www.thonhotels.com. 152 units. Mon–Thurs NOK1,050–NOK1,450 ($210–$290/£105–£145) double; Fri–Sun NOK1,050 ($210/£105) double; NOK1,800 ($360/£180) junior suite. AE, DC, MC, V. Free parking. **Amenities:** Restaurant; laundry service/dry cleaning; rooms for those w/limited mobility; nonsmoking rooms. *In room:* TV, Wi-Fi, minibar.

WHERE TO DINE

China Garden CANTONESE Although it doesn't rank with Oslo's Chinese restaurants, this eatery run by emigrants from Hong Kong is a welcome change of pace this far north. Serving flavorful Chinese food, the restaurant's two finest dishes are sweet-and-sour prawns and sweet-and-sour pork laced with garlic and served with black beans. The cooks really go for that sweet-and-sour flavor, but they also prepare many other standard dishes competently.

Storgata 60. ✆ **75-52-71-25.** Reservations recommended. Main courses NOK150 ($30/£15). AE, MC, V. Sun and Tues–Sat 2–11pm.

Rica Hotel Restaurants NORWEGIAN/INTERNATIONAL You don't get palate-tantalizing excitement here, but the solid, reliable fare uses fresh ingredients whenever available this far north. Although the Rica is best known for its well-maintained accommodations, it also runs two restaurants (the Spisestuen and Blix) that serve some of the best food in town. Usually the Spisestuen serves lunch and the Blix covers dinner, but the arrangement changes depending on the number of bus tours and cruise ships expected. Wherever the meal is served, you're likely to be joined by local residents. Main courses include lasagna, steak, filet of reindeer, fish soup, and fresh local fish. The catch of the day is generally your best bet.

In the Rica Hotel, Sjøgata 23. ✆ **75-54-70-00.** Reservations recommended. Lunch main courses NOK150–NOK245 ($30–$49/£15–£25); luncheon buffet NOK250 ($50/£25); dinner main courses NOK250–NOK320 ($50–$64/£25–£32). AE, DC, MC, V. Spisestuen daily 11:30am–2pm. Blix Mon–Sat 3–11pm and Sun 2–9pm.

Svendgård NORWEGIAN/INTERNATIONAL Although this restaurant is managed and staffed by employees from Bodø's best-established hotel, the Radisson SAS (see above), it occupies a redbrick building that lies a short walk away from the hotel itself. Inside, within a cream-colored environment that's made cozier by a blazing open fireplace, you'll find touches of red, blue, and black; a well-trained staff; and a tempting combination of Norwegian and international cuisine. You might begin with a carpaccio of venison, or perhaps grilled scallops served with terrine of oxtail, or even fried scampi with a sweet-and-sour "Asian" sauce. Main courses focus on some of the freshest fish in Bodø, including codfish served with shredded beetroot; poached anglerfish in a peanut-based satay sauce; breast of duckling with an herb-based creamy risotto; or stockfish served with tarragon-flavored wine sauce and fresh root vegetables.

Dronningensgate 26. ✆ **75-52-52-50.** Reservations recommended. Main courses NOK255–NOK269 ($51–$54/£26–£27). AE, DC, MC, V. Daily 3–11pm.

BODØ AFTER DARK

The largest nightclub in Bodø is the **Rock Café und Nightclub,** Tollbugata 13B (✆ **75-50-46-33**), which can hold up to 550 patrons, most of them usually in their 20s and 30s. Live bands perform twice a month. The DJs here are some of the best in the north of Norway. It's open Friday and Saturday 9am to 3am and charges a cover of NOK50 to NOK70 ($10–$14/£5–£7).

Nordloenningen, Stogata 16 (✆ **75-52-06-00**), is a laid-back cellar pub often featuring live music, such as blues, country, or rock, to a crowd ranging in age from 20 to 50. They also serve pub grub, everything from burgers to omelets. Local artists' paintings dominate the decor. A cover charge is imposed only on Friday and Saturday nights, ranging from NOK80 to NOK100 ($16–$20/£8–£10). It's open Monday to Thursday 1pm to 1:30am, Friday and Saturday 1pm to 2:30am, and Sunday 2pm to 1:30am.

3 NARVIK: WORLD WAR II BATTLEGROUND

301km (187 miles) NE of Bodø; 1,647km (1,021 miles) NE of Bergen; 1,479km (917 miles) N of Oslo

This ice-free seaport on the Ofotfjord is in Nordland *fylke* (country), 403km (250 miles) north of the Arctic Circle. Narvik, founded in 1903 when the Ofoten (not to be confused with "Lofoten") railway line was completed, boasts Europe's most modern shipping harbor for iron ore. It's also the northernmost electrified railway line in the world. It covers a magnificent scenic route, through precipitous mountain terrain and tunnels, over ridges, and across tall stone embankments.

Only 11km (6¾ miles) from Narvik, Straumsnes station is the last permanent habitation you'll encounter as you go east. The last Norwegian station, Bjørnfjell, is well above the timberline and about 3 hours from Kiruna, Sweden, some 140km (87 miles) north of the Arctic Circle. You can catch a train at Kiruna to Stockholm. If you're driving from Kiruna to Narvik, take no. 98 heading northwest to E6 heading southwest toward Narvik.

Narvik looms large in World War II history books. On April 9, 1940, 10 Nazi destroyers entered Narvik waters to sink two Norwegian battleships. On April 10, a series of five British destroyers arrived to take the German boats on in combat. The tragic battle at sea resulted in the sinking of two destroyers on each side.

On April 12, the British sent planes to attack the Germans. Allied forces were successful in reclaiming Narvik by late May. However, the victory was only momentary. In early June, the Nazis came back to decimate Narvik. The port of Narvik became a graveyard not only of men, but also of ships from Germany, Britain, Norway, France, and the Netherlands. On June 8, 1940, Narvik surrendered to the invading Nazis, who stayed here until the Allies chased them out on May 8, 1945.

The rebuilt Narvik can be a bit of an eyesore. But its setting in the midst of panoramic forests, majestic fjords, and towering mountains makes it an appealing choice worth a visit. As an added plus, the Midnight Sun shines here from May 27 to July 19.

ESSENTIALS

GETTING THERE From the Lofoten Islands, catch the car-ferry to Skutvik, operating three times a day. Follow Rte. 81 northeast to the junction with E6, and then take E6 north to Bognes. Cross the Tysfjord by ferry and continue north on E6 to Narvik.

The train from Stockholm to Narvik takes 21 to 24 hours. From Stockholm to Narvik, the train costs NOK950 ($190/£95) one-way. There are also two buses a day from Fauske/Bodø (5 hr.). Check www.nsb.no or www.nor-way.no for information.

VISITOR INFORMATION The **Narvik Tourist Office** is at Kongensgate 26 (✆ **76-96-56-00;** www.narvikinfo.no). It's open Monday to Friday 9am to 4pm; June to August, it's also open on Saturday 9am to 2pm.

SEEING THE SIGHTS

To get a good look at Narvik, take the **Gondolbanen cable car** (✆ **76-96-04-94**), whose departure point is located directly behind the Norlandia Narvik Hotel, a 10-minute walk from the town center. The car operates from March to October, and the round-trip fare is NOK110 ($22/£11) for adults, NOK75 ($15/£7.50) for children 6 to 15 (free for 5 and under). In just 13 minutes, it takes you to an altitude of 640m (2,099 ft.), at the top of Fagernesfjell. Here you can soak in the impressive panorama of the town and its surroundings or visit the simple restaurant at the tip.

From the peak here, you can "hike till you drop," as a local advised us. Marked trails branch out in several directions, all equally impressive. A downhill mountain bike trail also starts near the cable car's final stop. From mid-February to mid-June and in August and September, the cable operates Monday to Friday from 1 to 9pm and every Saturday and Sunday from 10am to 5pm. From mid-June to the end of July, it operates daily from noon to 1am.

Nordland Røde Kors Krigsminnemuseum (War Museum) Near Torghallen in the town center, this museum re-creates the tragic events of the early 1940s, revisiting the epic struggle of the Narvik campaign of 1940 and the dreaded years of Nazi occupation from 1940 to 1945. Events from Narvik's destruction by the Germans, who occupied it until the end of the World War II, are the focus here. Exhibits detail Germany's battle for Narvik's iron ore and how Nazi forces fought troops from France, Poland, and Norway, and a considerable British flotilla at sea. Experiences of the civilian population and foreign POWs are also highlighted.

Kongensgate. ✆ **76-94-44-26.** www.warmuseum.no. Admission NOK60 ($12/£6) adults, NOK35 ($7/£3.50) children. Mar–June 7 and Aug 21–Sept daily 11am–3pm; June 8–Aug 20 Mon–Sat 10am–10pm, Sun 11am–5pm; Oct–Feb Thurs–Sat 11am–3pm.

Ofoten Museum The Ofoten Museum displays artifacts tracing the oldest human settlements in the area, going back to the Stone Age, which is revealed in rock carvings. Other exhibits (including a scraper for animal skins and a flint-and-tinder box) show how ancient people lived and worked in the area. Most of the displays are from the 20th century, beginning with the construction of the rail line.

Administrasjonsveien 3. ✆ **76-96-00-50.** www.ofoten.museum.no. Admission NOK40 ($8/£4) adults, free for children. June 21–Aug 17 Mon–Fri 10am–3pm, Sat–Sun noon–3pm; rest of year Mon–Fri 10am–3pm.

OUTDOOR ACTIVITIES

The Narvik tourist office (see "Visitor Information," above) has a wealth of information about outdoor activities in the city's hinterlands.

One of the great golf courses in north Norway is the **Narvik Golfklubb at Skomendalen** (✆ **76-95-12-01**), lying 18km (11 miles) south of Narvik. In a dramatic setting, surrounded by mountain peaks, this is the world's northernmost 18-hole golf course (par 72). A full round of golf costs NOK350 ($70/£35), with club rentals going for NOK130 ($26/£13). To reach the course from Narvik, follow the signs to Skjomdal to just before the Skjomen Bridge on E6.

Narvik has a long skiing season, lasting from November until early June. The cable car (see "Seeing the Sights," above) will deliver you up some 1,000m (3,280 ft.) where you'll find trail and off-piste skiing. For more information about conditions, call the **Narvik Ski Center** at ✆ **76-94-27-99.**

Divers from all over the world are attracted to Narvik waters, as it was the scene of a major World War II naval battle. More than 50 planes, both Nazi and Allied, were gunned down here, and three German destroyers are still underwater. **Narvik Dykk & Eventyr** (✆ **99-51-22-05**) can make arrangements for accredited divers for this incredible undersea adventure.

The mountainous landscape around Narvik attracts sports enthusiasts from around Norway and the rest of Europe, some of whom, if they're physically fit and equipped to handle such savage terrain, embark upon hiking excursions on the surrounding tundra. For information about all kinds of adventure sports within dramatically windswept regions around Narvik, including hill climbing, rock rappelling, fishing trips on the Ofotfjord, whale-sighting expeditions, and dog-sled safaris, contact the tour operator that works in very close conjunction with the local tourist office, **Destination Narvik,** Kongensgate 26 (✆ **76-96-56-00**). It maintains the same open hours as the tourist office (see "Visitor Information," above).

WHERE TO STAY

These hotels are located among the few buildings in Narvik that survived World War II.

Moderate

Quality Hotel Grand Royal ★ The monolithic exterior is a bit off-putting, but the Grand Royal is the largest and best-equipped lodging in Narvik. It opens onto the main street in the town center, between the train station and the harbor. Built in the 1920s, it has seen many enlargements since. It was originally named the Grand Royal because the late King Olav was a frequent visitor and his portraits adorn some of the public rooms. The comfortable, good-size rooms are tastefully and traditionally furnished, and all but a handful have been renovated and upgraded. The artfully contemporary lobby bar is one of the most alluring cocktail bars in northern Norway. The Royal Blue, the finest restaurant in town, is also here (see "Where to Dine," below).

Kongensgate 64, N-8501 Narvik. ✆ **76-97-70-00.** Fax 76-97-70-07. www.choicehotels.no. 119 units. NOK990–NOK1,495 ($198–$299/£99–£150) double. Rates include buffet breakfast. AE, DC, MC, V. Bus: 14, 15, 16, or 17. **Amenities:** 2 restaurants; 2 bars; sauna; babysitting; laundry service/dry cleaning; nonsmoking rooms; rooms for those w/limited mobility. *In room:* TV, Wi-Fi, minibar, hair dryer, safe.

Inexpensive

Nordstjernen Hotel Value In 1970, the present owner of this hotel opened its doors on the main street of Narvik to produce a viable alternative to the Grand Royal. Much improved over the years, it's still here, still going strong, and keeping its prices within an affordable range, at least for this part of the world. South of the bus station, the hotel has long been known as one of the best values in the area. Guest rooms are decorated in pastels to offset the winter gloom. Rooms vary in size, but all are comfortable and well maintained.

Kongensgate 26, N-8500 Narvik. ✆ **76-94-41-20.** Fax 76-94-75-06. www.nordstjernen.no. 24 units. NOK950 ($190/£95) double. Rates include buffet breakfast. DC, MC, V. Bus: 14 or 16. **Amenities:** Restaurant; lounge. *In room:* TV, hair dryer.

WHERE TO DINE

Pub und Kro INTERNATIONAL Less expensive and less formal than the Grand Royal's main dining room (see below), this cozy restaurant is one of the most popular venues for dining and drinking in town. The menu offers an array of fresh foodstuff with zesty flavors and spices—providing a change of pace from reindeer. For a main course, try the marinated steak prepared in a Tex-Mex style or traditionally with mushrooms or béarnaise sauce. The pizza and a creamy pasta carbonara are also good choices.

In the Quality Hotel Grand Royal, Kongensgate 64. ✆ **76-97-70-00.** Reservations recommended. Main courses NOK120–NOK270 ($24–$54/£12–£27). AE, DC, MC, V. Mon–Thurs 11am–12:30am; Fri–Sat 11am–1:30am; Sun noon–1am.

Royal Blue ★ NORWEGIAN The best restaurant in the region is decorated, appropriately, in strong royal blues. It's the preferred choice of visiting dignitaries, including the king. Service is polite and the food's delectable. Specialties include sauna-smoked ham with asparagus, cured salmon with crème fraîche, reindeer curry with Brussels sprouts and apricots, and large beefsteaks. Royal Blue is located on the lobby level of the Grand Royal (see above). The menu changes seasonally.

In the Quality Hotel Grand Royal, Kongensgate 64. ✆ **76-97-70-00.** Reservations recommended. Main courses NOK220–NOK430 ($44–$86/£22–£43). AE, DC, MC, V. Tues–Sat 5–10pm. Bus: 14, 15, 16, or 17.

NARVIK AFTER DARK

An animated (and sometimes hard-drinking and rowdy) pub that attracts lots of good-looking and accessible locals ages 25 to 50 is the wood- and stone-trimmed **Pub** within the Norlandia Narvik Hotel, Skistuaveien 8 (✆ **76-96-48-00**). They tend to offer live music, for which the schedule varies widely throughout the year.

Resepten, Industriveien 5 (✆ **76-94-26-38**), is a 50-seat cozy bar whose walls are adorned with artwork from Norwegian artists. Light background music is played most nights, giving way to rock on the weekends. Some of the beers on tap come from England's Newcastle-upon-Tyne. Most patrons here range in age from 30 to 50. It's open Monday to Thursday from 8pm to 1am, and Friday and Saturday 8pm to 3am.

4 THE LOFOTEN ISLANDS: THE SOUL OF NORWAY ★★★

Svolvær (southernmost point of the Lofoten): 280km (174 miles) N of Bodø; 1,425km (884 miles) NE of Bergen; 1,250km (775 miles) N of Oslo

The island kingdom of Lofoten, one of the most beautiful regions of Norway, lies 197km (122 miles) north of the Arctic Circle. Its population of 35,000 spreads over large and small islands. Many visitors come just to fish, but the area also offers abundant bird life and flora. The midnight sun shines from May 25 to July 7.

Hans Olsen, a local guide, told us, "If you are not already a poet by the time you come here, you will be by the time you leave." He was referring, of course, to the area's beauty, the remoteness of the archipelago, and the mystical Arctic light.

The Lofoten Islands stretch from Vågan in the east to Røst and Skomvaer in the southwest. The steep Lofoten mountain peaks—often called the Lofotwall—shelter farmland and deep fjords from the elements.

The major islands are **Austvågøy, Gimsøy, Vestvågøy, Flakstadøy, Moskenesøy, Vaerøy,** and **Røst.** The southernmost part of Norway's largest island, Hinnøy, is also in Lofoten. Vestfjorden separates the major islands from the mainland of Norway.

In winter, the Gulf Stream makes possible the world's largest cod-fishing event. Called **Lofotfisket,** it takes place between January and March, though it dwindled in importance in the latter half of the 20th century. Arctic sea cod spawn beyond Lofoten, especially in the Vestfjord, and huge harvesting operations are carried out between January and April.

The first inhabitants of the Lofoten Islands were nomads who hunted and fished, but excavations show that agriculture existed here at least 4,000 years ago. The Vikings pursued farming, fishing, and trading; examples of Viking housing sites can be seen on Vestbågøya, where more than 1,000 burial mounds have been found.

From the 14th century on, the people of Lofoten had to pay taxes to Bergen. This was the beginning of an economic dominance lasting for 6 centuries—first executed by the German Hansa tradesmen and then by their Norwegian heirs.

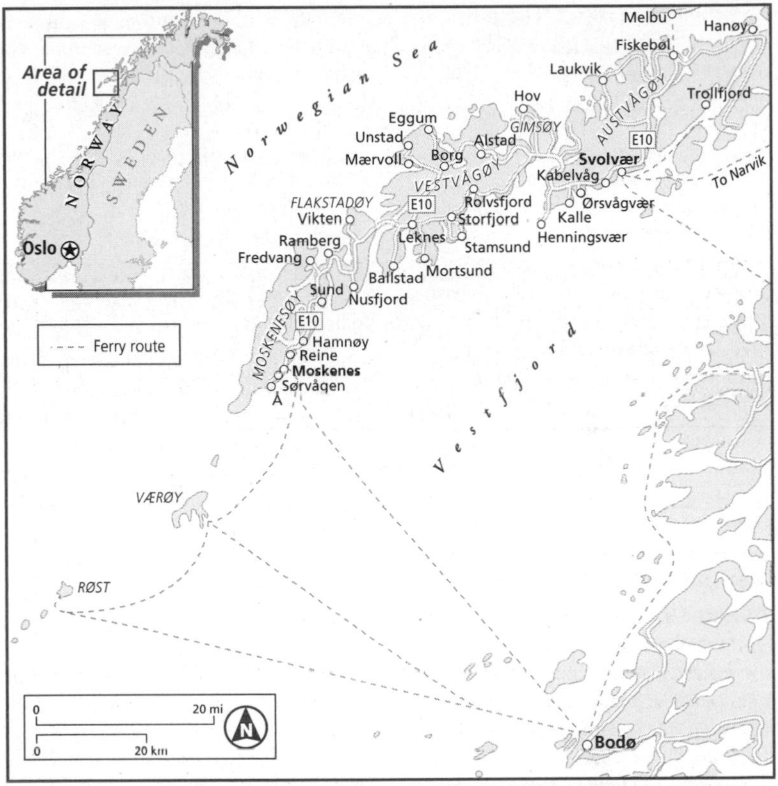

Harsh treatment of local residents by the Nazis during the World War II played a major part in the creation of the famous Norwegian resistance movement. Allied forces, which landed here to harass the German iron-ore boats sailing from Narvik, withdrew in June 1940. They evacuated as many Lofoten residents as they could to Scotland for the duration of the war.

Today the Lofotens have modern towns with shops, hotels, restaurants, and public transportation.

In addition to hotels, guesthouses, and campsites, the Lofoten Islands offer lodging in old traditional fishing cottages known as *rorbuer.* The larger (often two stories), usually more modern version, is a *sjøhus* (sea house). The traditional *rorbu* was built on the edge of the water, often on piles, with room for 10 bunks, a kitchen, and an entrance hall used as a work and storage room. Many *rorbuer* today are still simple and unpretentious, but some have electricity, a woodstove, a kitchenette with a sink, and running water. Others have been outfitted with separate bedrooms, private showers, and toilets. The best and most convenient booking agent is **Destination Lofoten** (see "Visitor Information," below).

GETTING THERE On the eastern coast of Austvågøy, **Svolvær** is the largest town on the archipelago's largest island. It lacks the charm of the island's other fishing communities, but nothing tops it as a refueling stop. The port is a bit dull, but its surroundings of craggy backdrops and sheltered bays form a dramatic Lofoten backdrop. From Bodø, drive east on Rte. 80 to Fauske. Take E6 north to Ulvsvåg and head southwest on Rte. 81 toward the town of Skutvik. From Skutvik, take the 2-hour ferry to Svolvær. For ferry information and reservations, contact **Hurtigruten** (✆ **81-00-30-30;** www.hurtigruten.com for reservations and information). Passengers without cars pay NOK76 ($15/£7.50) adults, NOK38 ($7.60/£3.80) children, each way for passage to Svolvær from Skutvik. One-way transport of a car with its driver costs NOK262 ($52/£26).

You can fly to Svolvær on **Widerøe Airline,** which has seven flights a day from Bodø. For information, call ✆ **75-51-35-00** in Bodø for reservations, or visit www.wideroe.no.

You can also travel the Lofotens by using a combination of rail, bus, and ferry. Many visitors take a train to Bodø and then transfer to a bus that crosses from Bodø to Svolvær on a ferry. Most bus departures from Bodø are timed to coincide with the arrival of trains from Oslo, Bergen, and other points. Buses also take passengers from elsewhere in Norway to Ulvsvåg, then on to Skutvik, where you can board a ferry to Svolvær. For information on train-bus-ferry connections, contact **Destination Bodø Office** (✆ **75-54-80-00**).

A coastal steamer, departing from Bodø at 3pm daily, also calls at Stamsund and Svolvær.

VISITOR INFORMATION Contact **Destination Lofoten,** Box 210, N-8301 Svolvær (✆ **76-06-98-00;** www.lofoten.info), on the harborfront in a big red building right in the middle of the town square. It's open January 1 to May 21 Monday to Friday 9am to 3:30pm; May 22 to June 11 Monday to Friday 9am to 4pm, Saturday 10am to 2pm; June 12 to June 24 Monday to Friday 9am to 7:30pm, Saturday 10am to 2pm, Sunday 4 to 7pm; June 25 to August 6 Monday to Friday 9am to 9:30pm, Saturday 9am to 8pm, Sunday 10am to 9:30pm; August 7 to August 27 Monday to Friday 9am to 7pm, Saturday 10am to 2pm; August 28 to December 31 Monday to Friday 9am to 3:30pm.

GETTING AROUND At the tourist office at Svolvær, you can pick up a free pamphlet, *Lofoten Info-Guide,* with information about all ferries and buses throughout the archipelago. All inhabited islands are linked by ferry, and buses service the four major islands, including Svolvær. Motorists can drive the E10 from Svolvær to the outer rim of Lofoten, a distance of 130km (81 miles). One of the **great drives ★★ in the north of Norway,** this route will give you a good overall look at the Lofotens.

Our preferred method of getting around the Lofotens is by bike. Cycles can be rented at most of the archipelago's little hotels.

Impressions

Mirages turn floating mountains topsy-turvy ahead of you and behind your back, while whales are at play and birds are a'shrieking.

—Poet Bjørnstjerne Bjørnson, 1869,
describing the Lofoten Islands

Moments These Boots Are Made for Walking

We recommend specific walks or hikes that we've found enjoyable in the following pages. But know that the entire archipelago of the Lofoten Islands was made for walking or hiking. In places, you'll make your way along lakes dark as peat and past fields of delectable yellow-orange Arctic cloudberries. Or you'll pass bilberries, while taking in fields of reindeer moss and sea eagles flying overhead. Perhaps you'll even come across the most characteristic animal of the north (other than reindeer)—the stately moose.

You can wander field, hill, and dale, even climb a mountain. Also rewarding are walks along the rugged coast, past dwarf willow trees and mountain ash. In some parts of the Lofotens, especially Moskenesøy, you'll discover the ruins of deserted villages. In these cases, the sea proved too harsh a place to make a living, and the inhabitants finally threw in the fishing net and moved on.

SUGGESTED ITINERARIES

IF YOU HAVE 1 DAY Arrive at the main port city of **Svolvær,** which will be your gateway to the Lofotens. We suggest you use this as a refueling stop and an arrival and exit port because of its superior transportation links.

Instead of spending the night here, you can head immediately to the south to the more attractive port of **Kabelvåg** for an overnight stopover. However, while still in Svolvær, you might want to take one of the most dramatic boat trips in the Lofotens to the famous **Trollfjord** (p. 414).

IF YOU HAVE 2 DAYS Based in the little port of Kabelvåg, you can pay morning visits to the Lofoten Museum (p. 417), which will give you a useful insight into the people of the islands. You might also visit the **Lofoten Aquarium** (p. 417). For some Lofoten thrills, try to sign up for an adventure trip for the afternoon. See "Seeing the Sights," under "Kabelvåg," below.

IF YOU HAVE 3 DAYS Head south to **Henningsvaer,** the largest and liveliest of the Lofoten fishing villages. You will find good hotels and restaurants here if you want to spend the night. We suggest a morning visit to the **Lofoten Hus Gallery** (p. 419) to see the largest and best collection of north Norway art. An even more exciting idea is to take one of the **mountain tours** or **Sea Eagle Safaris** offered in the area (p. 419). The Sea Eagle jaunt will take only an hour, allowing you time to do some mountain climbing even if it's getting late. If you arrive in midsummer, the sun never sets.

IF YOU HAVE 4 DAYS Continue south to explore **Vestvågøy,** the second-largest island. You can visit the hamlet of **Borg,** where the biggest Viking Age chieftain's homestead in Scandinavia has been excavated. A full-scale replica of the chieftain's house has been reconstructed. **Stramsund,** with its 1,500 inhabitants, makes a good base here, as it is one of the largest fishing villages in West Lofoten.

A mountainous region lies both north and south of Stamsund. You can spend most of the afternoon walking and exploring at random, perhaps climbing one of the steep mountains. For our favorite walk in the area, see the "Walking from Fishing Village to Fishing Village" box on p. 425.

IF YOU HAVE 5 DAYS Another day can be spent on the island of **Flakstadøy** visiting fishing hamlets such as **Ramberg,** which lies next to a lovely white beach facing the Arctic Ocean. Drop in at the **Flakstad Kirke,** built in 1780 of wood (p. 422). In 1 day you can visit our favorite island fishing ports, including **Sund,** with its fishing museum, Fiskerimuseum (p. 423), and also **Nusfjord,** which is justifiably the most famous of the little ports because of its agglomeration of fishermen's huts. These are used by fishermen in the winter and visitors in the summer.

IF YOU HAVE 6 DAYS While still based at Flakstadøy, perhaps in the village of Ramberg, you can explore the island to its immediate south: **Moskenesøy** (p. 424). For a true adventure and a chance to capture the spirit of the Lofoten Islands—and its people—we consider this the most evocative island. Sculptured by glaciers, the landscape is far more savage than what we'd visited so far.

The most dramatic experience you can enjoy here is a 5-hour tour over often-turbulent waters to the **Moskestraumen,** the treacherous strait separating Moskenesøy from the offshore island of Vaerøy to the south. These are called "the world's most dangerous waters" and could be the highlight of a trip to the Lofotens. They even inspired Edgar Allan Poe to write a nautical tale. Marine mammals and thousands of seabirds can be seen here.

We'd vote **Reine** as one of the most charming and typical of the Lofoten villages. You can even spend the night here, if you wish, in a rented fisherman's hut. What we recommend is to explore the Moskestraumen one day, then go on a Midnight Sun cruise the following day.

SVOLVÆR

This bustling modern port town lies on the island of **Austvågøy,** the northernmost in the archipelago. Most of the Lofoten cultural attractions are within an easy reach if you decide to base here. Svolvær attracts the most visitors and has some of the area's best hotels and restaurants. The most adventurous readers will view it merely as a place to pass through and stock up on supplies before heading out to some more remote destination.

Seeing the Sights

Lofoten Krigsminnemuseum, Fiskergata 12 (✆ **91-73-03-28**), is the finest museum in the north devoted to the tragic World War II era. There's a little-known collection of 1940s photographs, some of which document the 1941 commando raid on the islands. Also on display is a collection of military uniforms. Admission is NOK40 ($8/£4) for adults and NOK40 ($8/£4) for children. It's open only from mid-May to mid-August daily 11am to 4pm. The rest of the year it's open daily from 6 to 10pm.

Daredevils are lured to Svolvær in an attempt to conquer the most daring (and dangerous) climb in the Lofotens. They surmount the **Svolværgeita (Svolværur goat),** at 40m (131 ft.). This stone column is perched on a hill behind the port and is known for its two pinnacles, which locals have labeled the horn or the horns of a goat. There's a 1.5m (5-ft.) jump between the two "horns"; if you don't make it, you're as good as dead.

One of the most dramatic boat rides in the Lofotens is the short trip into the impossibly narrow **Trollfjord ★★**, stretching for 2km (1¼ miles). This is part of the channel that separates the Lofoten island of Austvågøy from the Vesterålen island of Hinnøya. Coastal steamers can barely navigate this narrow passage without scraping the rock walls on either side. One of the most visited sites in the Lofotens, this fjord cuts its way westward from the Straits of Raftsundet, opening onto an idyllic Lofoten landscape, famed as the subject of many paintings.

Trollfjord is the easternmost island in Lofoten and was the scene of the "Battle of the Trollfjord," as related by Johan Bojer in his novel *The Last Viking.* The battle, which took place more than a century ago between fishermen in small vessels and those in larger steamships, was first recorded on canvas by one of its witnesses, the artist Gunnar Berg (1863–93). His painting is on view at the Svolvær Town Hall. Ask at the tourist office (see "Visitor Information," above) about linking up with a boat tour of Trollfjord. Departures are from June 10 to August 20, costing NOK350 ($70/£35) per adult, NOK150 ($30/£15) children.

For the best and most scenic walks in the area, take the ferry ride over to the islet of **Skrova.** Here you can stroll around and leisurely take in the seascapes. Before heading over, pick up the makings of a picnic at one of the shops in Svolvær and prepare to enjoy it in splendid isolation. Ferries leave from Svolvær port every 2 hours, taking only half an hour to reach Skrova and costing NOK70 ($14/£7) per person.

Another good walk from Svolvær is to the north, heading to the Lille and Store Kongsvatn lakes, on whose banks you might want to have a picnic. You will know you've reached the end of the trail when you come to a power station. If you wish, you can take a path to **Kabelvåg** (p. 417), following the shoreline for most of the way. Or you can return to Svolvær on the same trail you came up on.

Shopping

Artists have long been drawn to the archipelago because of the particular quality of its Northern Lights. The leading gallery is **Nordnorsk Kunstnersentrum** ★ (✆ **76-06-67-70**), on the island of Svinøya, lying 1km (1/2 mile) from the center of Svolvær. This North Norwegian Artist's Center is run by the artists themselves, offering a wide range of paintings, plus handicrafts, posters, and other items. From June 19 to August 20, it is open daily 10am to 6pm. Off-season hours are Tuesday to Sunday 11am to 3pm. Entrance to the permanent museum collection costs NOK40 ($8/£4) for adults and NOK30 ($6/£3) for students and seniors. It's free for children 14 and under.

Where to Stay

Anker Brygge ★★ Kids On a tiny island in the middle of Svolvær harbor and connected with a bridge to the "mainland," this is one of the most atmospheric lodging choices in the area. The quay-side structure dates from 1880, when it was a fish-landing station with its own "saltery" and barrel factory. In 1996, it was converted into an inn. Guests can stay in individual red-painted cottages that are rustically adorned with timbers but also have all the modern conveniences. Cabins, called *rorbu* cabin suites, can sleep up to six guests, so they're ideal for families. Each *rorbu* cabin is distinctively furnished; you may feel as if you're staying at some remote lodge in the wilds of a far northern frontier post. *Rorbu* suites lie on the quay side or along the shore, with views of the harbor and the Lofoten mountains.

Lamholmen, N-8300 Svolvær. ✆ **76-06-64-80.** Fax 76-06-64-70. www.anker-brygge.no. 80 units. NOK1,300–NOK2,650 ($260–$530/£130–£265) cottages and suites for 2–4 people. Rates include continental breakfast. AE, DC, MC, V. **Amenities:** Restaurant (closed Jan–Feb); bar; sauna; laundry service/dry cleaning. *In room:* TV.

Norlandia Vestfjord Hotel This is a comfortable but unexceptional place. The building was a former warehouse that stored marine supplies and fish. After extensive remodeling, it reopened as this well-managed hotel. The guest rooms are all comfortable; but ask for one that overlooks the sea. Facilities include a lobby bar and a pleasant restaurant that specializes in fish and steaks. It serves sustaining fare—nothing remarkable.

 Fiskergt 46, N-8300 Svolvær. ✆ **76-07-08-70.** Fax 76-07-08-54. www.norlandia.no/vestfjord. 63 units. June–Aug Sun–Thurs NOK1,600 ($320/£160) double, Fri–Sat NOK1,100 ($220/£110) double; Sept–May Sun–Thurs NOK1,300 ($260/£130) double, Fri–Sat NOK850 ($170/£85) double; year-round NOK1,700 ($340/£170) suite. Rates include buffet breakfast. AE, DC, MC, V. **Amenities:** Restaurant; bar; room service; laundry service/dry cleaning; nonsmoking rooms; rooms for those w/limited mobility. *In room:* TV, minibar (in some), hair dryer.

Rica Hotel Svolvær ★ If you book into the right suite here, you can go fishing through a hole in the floor of your room. This is the sleekest, the best, and the most desirable of the chain hotels. Right next to the water, it was opened in 1995 and is renovated and kept in tiptop shape every year. The bedrooms are in separate *rorbu* cabins built of wood, opening onto your private harbor-view terrace. Each room is comfortably furnished, containing immaculate private bathrooms with shower. Norwegian specialties, especially salmon, are served in the first-class restaurant on-site. The restaurant is constructed in the shape of a boat, opening onto panoramic vistas of the ocean.

Lamholmen, N-8301 Svolvær. ✆ **76-07-22-22.** Fax 76-07-20-01. www.rica-lofoten.no. 147 units. Sun–Thurs NOK1,400–NOK1,850 ($280–$370/£140–£185) double. Rates include continental breakfast and evening buffet. AE, DC, MC, V. Closed Dec 20–Jan 3. **Amenities:** Restaurant; bar; laundry service/dry cleaning; nonsmoking rooms; rooms for those w/limited mobility. *In room:* TV.

Svinøya Rorbuer ★★ Finds Nothing is as authentic to the Lofoten experience as staying in one of these cottages across a bridge on the island of Svinøya, site of Svolvær's first settlement. You'll be welcomed at the reception area, which was once the general store for the community and was the first shop ever to open in Svolvær. Then you'll be shown to one of the historic restored cabins. The main building is from 1820, some of the cabins are from the 19th century, and others are modern but constructed in the old style. All of these fishermen's cabins are furnished to a high standard. Extra amenities include a well-equipped kitchen. The inn contains the town's best restaurant, the Børson Spiseri (see below).

Gunnar Bergs vei 2, N-8300 Svolvær. ✆ **76-06-99-30.** Fax 76-07-48-98. www.svinoya.no. 30 cabins. NOK1,350–NOK2,700 ($270–$540/£135–£270) double. Rates include continental breakfast. AE, DC, MC, V. **Amenities:** Restaurant; bar; Jacuzzi; laundry service/dry cleaning. *In room:* W-Fi, kitchen (in some). No phone.

Where to Dine

Børson Spiseri ★ SEAFOOD The town's best restaurant is housed in the previously recommended Svinøya Rorbuer (see above) across a bridge on the island of Svinøya. We'd come here for the atmosphere alone, but fortunately the food is first-rate. The restaurant has been installed in an old quay-side building from 1828, a setting for an "arctic menu" that features some of the freshest fish we've ever consumed in the north. The setting is old-fashioned, with antiques from 2 centuries ago, along with maritime artifacts such as fishing equipment and old boats. What chef can top their deep-fried cod tongue served as an appetizer with sour cream and a salad? The traditional dried cod for which the Lofoten is famous is served with bacon and potatoes. Other excellent dishes include filet of salmon fried in butter and accompanied by mussels or else grilled stockfish with a fennel risotto. A dessert specialty is citrus cheesecake with passion fruit sauce. In summer, you can opt for fresh fruit for dessert, or feast on crème brûlée the rest of the time.

Gunnar Bergs vei 2. ✆ **76-06-99-30.** Reservations recommended. Main courses NOK259–NOK289 ($52–$58/£26–£29). AE, DC, MC. Daily 5–10pm. Closed Jan and Mon in winter.

KABELVÅG

Much more romantically situated than Svolvær is the port of Kabelvåg, lying 5km (3 miles) to the south. This is also a much better introduction to the quaintness of the Lofotens than Svolvær. The port of wooden buildings encircles the shore of a narrow inlet. In its heyday it was the major village in the Viking era, a position it maintained until the early years of the 20th century. The first *rorbuer* (fishermen's cottages) were erected here in 1120.

One of the best walks in the area, giving you a flavor of the Lofotens, is the road between Svolvær and Kabelvåg. You go from the hustle and bustle of Svolvær, without all that much charm, to a little center of wooden houses hugging the shore of a knobby inlet. Along the way you're treated to seascapes of a certain majesty. Otherwise, frequent buses (every 20 min. in summer) run from Svolvær, taking 15 minutes and costing NOK50 ($10/£5) for a one-way fare.

Seeing the Sights

For NOK140 ($28/£14), you can purchase (at any of the sites) a combination ticket, granting admission to the Lofoten Museum, the Lofoten Aquarium, and the Galleri Espolin.

Lofoten Museum, Storvågan (✆ **76-06-97-90**), was constructed over the site of the first town built in the polar world. The regional museum depicts past life in the Lofoten, and excavations continue at the site of an old trading post. On the museum grounds, you can visit a boathouse with antique boats, *rorbu* cabins from the 18th and 19th centuries, and cultural artifacts dating from prehistoric and medieval times. Admission is NOK60 ($12/£6) for adults, NOK25 ($5/£2.50) for children. Open June to August daily 9am to 6pm; May and September Monday to Friday 9am to 3pm; closed Saturday, Sunday 11am to 3pm; October to December 20 and January 2 to April Monday to Friday 9am to 3pm.

For the adventurous is a **Killer Whale Safari** in inflatable boats. Day trips to spot whales—the largest group of killer whales in the world come to the Lofotens—are staged from November 1 to January 11. Trips take 4 hours and cost NOK940 ($188/£94) per passenger. Departures are daily at 9am and 1:30pm. To arrange a tour contact Tysfjord Turistsenter based in Storjord (✆ **75-77-53-70;** www.tysfjord-turistsenter.no).

Jann's Adventure Lofoten (✆ **76-07-89-10;** www.lofoten-aktiv.no) offers the best **sailing trips** around the Lofotens in boats built of wood. On these trips, boats cross open water to get from one island to the other. Three-hour trips cost NOK475 ($95/£48) for adults and NOK324 ($65/£33) for children 15 and under. Departures are daily on request.

This same outfitter also offers **cycling trips** around the archipelago. These leave at 3pm on Saturdays throughout the summer, as it doesn't get dark because of the midnight sun. The cost of a 1-day jaunt is NOK845 ($169/£85) per person. If you possess the necessary skills, you can also rent **kayaks** to test your luck in the waters of the Lofotens. A single kayak for the day rents for NOK420 ($84/£42). Fishing trips are also arranged, with no more than 12 fishermen aboard at one time. Trips last 4 hours and cost NOK350 ($70/£35). Departures are daily at 6pm in summer.

Close by and opening onto the sea, **Lofoten Aquarium,** Storvågan (✆ **76-07-86-65;** www.lofotakvariet.no), offers nearly two dozen aquariums of various sizes filled with fish and other marine animals, including mammals, from the Arctic world. Of special interest are the seal and otter ponds. There's also a salmon-farm exhibit, and much attention is given to the "noble" cod, which has sustained life in these parts for centuries. Admission is NOK80 ($16/£8) for adults, NOK40 ($8/£4) for children ages 5 to 15, and free for children 4 and under. Hours are February to May 31 Monday to Friday 11am to 3pm, June 1 to August 31 daily 10am to 7pm, and September to November daily 11am to 3pm.

The distinctive, contemporary **Galleri Espolin,** Storvågan (✆ **76-07-84-05;** www.galleri-espolin.no), is devoted to the works of artist Kaare Espolin Johnson (1907–94), one of Norway's best-known artists. Espolin was drawn to the archipelago and was fascinated by its life and that of its fishermen. Amazingly, this almost lyrical artist was practically blind for most of his life. He painted not only the fishermen, but also their wives, their boats, and the drama they faced at sea. From June 11 to August 8, the museum is open daily 10am to 7pm (closing earlier off season). Admission is NOK60 ($12/£6) for adults and NOK25 ($5/£2.50) for children.

On the eastern approach to town, along E10, stands **Vågan Kirke** (✆ **76-07-82-90**), a church from 1898 that is the second-largest wooden church in Norway, with a seating capacity of 1,200. It was constructed to house the seasonal population of fishermen who came mostly for the winter catches, swelling the population of little Kabelvåg. Admission is NOK20 ($4/£2), but the church keeps no regular hours (it's usually open during the day in summer).

Where to Stay

Kabelvåg Hotell In the center of Kabelvåg's little port, this hotel is a 1995 reconstruction of the original Art Deco villa that once stood here. It is also the site of the best restaurant in town (see "Where to Dine," below). Rising three floors, it's very much an antique wooden structure on the outside, but inside it is modern and completely up-to-date. The small to midsize bedrooms are rather simply but comfortably furnished, opening onto views of the ocean and mountains.

Kong Øysteinsgate 4, N-8310 Kabelvåg. ✆ **76-07-88-00.** Fax 76-07-80-03. 28 units. NOK1,000–NOK1,400 ($200–$280/£100–£140) double. Children 7 and under stay free in parent's room. Rates include buffet breakfast and dinner. AE, DC, MC, V. Closed Oct 1–May 15. **Amenities:** Restaurant; bar; laundry service/dry cleaning; nonsmoking rooms. *In room:* TV, hair dryer.

Nyvagar Rorbuhotell ★ Finds This contemporary *rorbu* cabin resort offers architecture based on those rustic cabins inhabited by fishermen who came in winter to harvest cod. But the surroundings here are far more comfortable and elegant than those men of the sea used to endure. The location is convenient, lying only a 3-minute stroll from the area's museums. Each of the well-furnished cabins contains two bedrooms and a kitchen, along with a small bathroom with a shower. Expect wood furnishings and wood walls. About half of the units open onto views of the harbor. This hotel also offers one of the most helpful staffs in the area, each of whom is skilled at arranging such adventures as deep-sea rafting or "eagle safaris," as well as fishing-boat jaunts. Even if you're not a guest, you might visit its lively quay-side pub with outdoor table service in summer. In the main building, the Lorchstua Restaurant serves an array of regional dishes from the north.

Storvåganveien 22, N-8310 Kabelvåg. ✆ **76-06-97-00.** Fax 76-06-97-01. www.dvgl.no. 30 units. NOK1,600 ($320/£160) cabin for 2–4 occupants. Rates include continental breakfast. AE, DC, MC, V. Closed Sept–Apr. **Amenities:** Restaurant; bar; sauna; laundry service/dry cleaning; nonsmoking rooms. *In room:* TV.

Where to Dine

Krambua SEAFOOD/NORWEGIAN In the rebuilt Art Deco villa, the previously recommended Kabelvåg Hotell, this restaurant is the best at the port. It has a mellow atmosphere, decorated with old books, antiques, and animal skin furnishings. It feels like you're in the far north if you dine here, especially when you're served whale carpaccio. Because many politically conscious readers will object to eating whale meat, an endangered species, you can choose the smoked salmon instead. Main courses include the island mainstay, cod, served here after a "soft" baking in the oven. It comes with a white-wine sauce and butter-boiled vegetables. Meat-eaters prefer the filet of reindeer with sautéed potatoes. In summer, wild berries from these Arctic climes will adorn your plate.

Kong Øysteinsgate 4. ✆ **76-07-88-00.** Reservations recommended. Main courses NOK180–NOK250 ($36–$50/£18–£25). AE, DC, MC, V. Mon–Sat 11am–11pm; Sun 2–8pm. Closed Oct 1–May 15.

HENNINGSVAER ★

The nickname of "Venice of the North" is a bit much, but that shouldn't obscure the fact that this is the liveliest and most artistic of Lofoten villages. Lying 20km (12 miles) southwest of Svolvær, this is the largest fishing village in the Lofoten. The village was built without any professional architects. Bus no. 510 runs here from Svolvær, taking 35 minutes and costing NOK60 ($12/£6) one-way.

Seeing the Sights

Based in Henningsvaer, the **North Norwegian School of Mountaineering (Nord Norsk Klatreskole; ✆ 76-07-49-11;** www.nordnorskklatreskole.no) conducts summer guided tours in the mountains of the Lofotens, following only the most scenic routes, such as to the top of Svolværgeita Peak. Climbing holidays, depending on the trip, cost from NOK3,800 to NOK4,800 ($760–$960/£380–£480) for a 3-day jaunt. It's always best to stop by to discuss your desires and have the options explained to you. Of course, you can call in advance and have a game plan mapped out before your arrival in town. In Henningsvaer, the mountaineering school also operates a Climber's Café and a store that rents mountaineering gear.

Also in Henningsvaer there are **Sea Eagle Safaris** conducted in summer by Lofoten Opplevelser (✆ **76-07-50-01;** www.lofoten-opplevelser.no). Call for information and details. Nordland is the land of the sea eagle, and in summer these safaris take you off the coast to see these birds of prey in their natural environment. Near Henningsvaer is the world's most compact flock of these majestic birds, which often have a wing span of some 2m ($6^1/_2$ ft.). Guides include John Stenersen, author of the book *The Birds of the Lofoten.* From June 20 to August 10, 1-hour safaris cost NOK370 ($74/£37).

At the **Lofoten Hus Gallery ★**, Henningsvær (✆ **76-07-15-73**), you can see Norway's largest collection of its north-country painters, dramatically installed in a former fish-canning house. The major focus centers on the paintings of the well-known artist Karl Erik Harr, plus other notable artists who came to the Lofoten at the end of the 19th century. Frank Jenssen presents a 20-minute slide show of Lofoten landscapes and its people, with rare photographs of the white-tailed eagle. It's open June 11 to August 12 10am to 9pm (closes earlier in winter). Admission is NOK70 ($14/£7) for adults or NOK35 ($7/£3.50) for children.

Henningsvaer Bryggehotel ★ This is a white-painted house idyllically placed on the quay by the harbor against a backdrop of mountains. Although the setting is old-fashioned and picture-postcardy, the interior design is contemporary and stylish. In all, it's a good choice as your base for exploring the northern Lofoten. Built in 1995, it rises three floors. For decor, it uses pictures of the Lofoten from the 1900s. Bedrooms are midsize and attractively and comfortably furnished. On-site is Bluefish, one of the best restaurants on the island (see "Where to Dine," below). The staff will help you arrange sea trips, including rafting and fishing.

Hjellskoeret, N-8312 Henningsvaer. ✆ **76-07-47-50.** Fax 76-07-47-30. www.dvgl.no. 31 units. NOK1,400 ($280/£140) double; NOK3,200 ($640/£320) suite. Children 11 and under stay free in parent's room. Rates include continental breakfast. AE, DC, MC, V. Closed Oct 1–Mar 1. **Amenities:** Restaurant; bar; sauna; room service; laundry service/dry cleaning. *In room:* TV.

Henningsvaer Rorbuer ★ Finds Lying just outside the center of the village, this is an atmospheric choice of *rorbuer,* or fishermen's cabins, standing at quay side against the backdrop of the "Lofoten Wall" (a string of mountains). You're housed in cabins that simulate a fisherman's cottage from long ago but that offer all the modern amenities. Rooms open onto panoramic views of the Vestfjorden and Mount Vågakallen. These quay-side buildings were converted from old fish-landing warehouses. Its special feature is a quay-side wood-fired sauna and a large wooden bathtub. In addition, the hotel's boat, *Kysten,* will take you for trips around the archipelago, and the staff will arrange deep-sea fishing trips in summer. You can also rent boats and ask to be hooked up with a deep-sea rafting trip. Cabins contain two or three bedrooms, a kitchenette, and a bathroom with shower. All rooms are nonsmoking.

Banhammaren 53, N-8312 Henningsvaer. ✆ **76-06-60-00.** Fax 76-06-60-01. www.henningsvar-rorbuer.no. 21 cabins. NOK930–NOK2,600 ($186–$520/£93–£260) double. MC, V. **Amenities:** Bar; sauna. *In room:* TV, kitchen.

Where to Dine

Bluefish Restaurant NORWEGIAN/SEAFOOD Attached to the previously recommended Henningsvaer Bryggehotel (see above), this is one of the island's best restaurants, often feeding 60 satisfied diners at a time. You'll sit at wooden tables enjoying views of the sea from the restaurant's windows. The chefs try to use whatever fresh ingredients are found in the Arctic so they don't have to import so much. Environmentalists may shun the smoked whale because that animal is an endangered species. Fresh salmon is aromatically baked with herbs and served with fresh vegetables. You can also order that food staple of the Lofoten, cod. It's most often fried and served with a lobster sauce or a white-wine sauce. Boiled halibut is another fine choice, appearing in a creamy butter sauce with cucumber salad and boiled potatoes.

In the Henningsvaer Bryggehotel, Hjellskoeret. ✆ **76-07-47-50.** Reservations recommended. Main courses NOK250–NOK450 ($50–$90/£25–£45). AE, DC, MC, V. Mon–Sat 3–10pm; Sun 3–6pm.

Fiskekrogen ★★ NORWEGIAN/SEAFOOD This quay-side restaurant located in a former fish factory is the town's finest, and chef/owner Otto Asheim is justifiably acclaimed in the area. It even enjoys patronage from Queen Sonja, who first discovered it during her backpacking days through the Lofoten and has returned several times since. The chef is skilled at serving fish almost any way you want it. He cooks with robust flavor and intelligent associations of ingredients, using regional produce whenever possible. His fare is based on the season and what's fresh and good at the market. He does

Tips: Your Own Private Boat for Fishing

As you make your way across the Lofotens, you don't need to make elaborate plans to go fishing. At almost any fisherman's shack or boathouse at the island ports, you can go right up and request a pram for rent for a morning or an afternoon of fishing. An outboard motor is often an optional choice.

wonders with the famed cod of the area and also serves his own "homemade" caviar. His sautéed salmon or catfish is always tempting. Your best bet might be to order Lofoten lamb with seaweed and a red wine sauce.

Dreyersgate 29. © **76-07-46-52.** Reservations necessary in summer. Main courses NOK255–NOK295 ($51–$59/£26–£30). AE, DC, MC, V. Summer daily 4–11pm. Closed in winter.

VESTVÅGØY

The second major island in the archipelago, and relatively flat, Vestvågøy is home to some 11,000 rugged island people who turn to the sea for their livelihood.

If you base here, we recommend you skip the air and bus transport home of **Leknes** and head inside the **Stramsund** to the immediate east, the best base along the southern coast, with numerous accommodations (see "Where to Stay & Dine," below). Stramsund is the island port where the coastal steamers from Bergen stop.

Buses from Leknes take only 30 minutes to reach Stramsund, costing NOK50 ($10/£5) one-way. Leknes can be reached by bus from Svolvær, taking 2 hours and costing NOK120 ($24/£12) one-way.

Seeing the Sights

In the hamlet of Borg, archaeologists dug out the biggest Viking Age building ★★ ever found. It's been turned into the **Viking Museum of Borg** (© **76-08-49-00**). The museum has been built up around this impressive full-scale reconstruction of a Viking chieftain's house, measuring 83m (272 ft.) in length. Also on display is the Viking ship *Lofotr,* reconstructed as a replication of the Gokstad ships. The ruins were discovered in 1981 when a farmer was plowing his fields.

The museum setting duplicates the aura of the Iron Age, with light flickering from the hearths or gleaming from cod-liver oil lamps, and the smell of tar wafting through the air. Demonstrations of handicrafts authentic to the Viking era are presented. Artifacts are on display as well, including gold foil fertility figures, Frankish pottery, and Rhineland glass. Outside you can see some domestic animals such as horses, sheep, and hens that would have been commonplace 1,000 years ago.

Admission is NOK100 ($20/£10) for adults, NOK90 ($18/£9) for seniors and students, and NOK50 ($10/£5) for children, including a guided tour. From May 8 to May 31, it's open daily 11am to 5pm; June 1 to August 24 daily 10am to 7pm; August 25 to September 14 daily 11am to 5pm; otherwise, it's open only Friday from 1 to 3pm. The Svolvær bus to Leknes passes by the entrance to the museum.

The best walk in the area begins at the road at the local youth hostel. Go for about 300m (984 ft.) and then take Ringveien for another 400m (1,312 ft.). Here a trail begins that will take about 3 hours to walk, passing the hamlet of Ørntuva and going up to the Heah, a big cairn with a panoramic view toward Henningsvaer. This is an easy trail to follow, about 380m (1,246 ft.) above sea level.

Skjaerbrygga Hotel ★ *Finds* These old fishermen's cabins have been renovated with modern comforts and are the most evocative place to stay on Vestvagøy. Located at the middle of the harbor in Stamsund, these cabins await you with two to six beds each, equipped with a private bathroom with shower, kitchen, and living room. An 1845 klipfish (dried cod) storehouse, the Skjaerbrygga, has been turned into a good restaurant. There are also a library and lounge with a fireplace.

N-8340 Stamsund. ✆ **76-05-46-00.** Fax 76-05-46-01. www.skjaerbrygga.no. 27 cabins. NOK1,000 ($200/£100) for 1–2 persons; NOK1,400 ($280/£140) 3–4 persons. AE, DC, MC, V. **Amenities:** Restaurant; cafe; pub. *In room:* TV.

Stamsund Lofoten Opened in 1974, this brightly painted hotel in the heart of town offers a view of the harbor. It's a decent place to sleep, and an affordable one, at that. The small guest rooms are simply furnished but have good beds. On the premises are a bar and a restaurant that serves standard Norwegian fare.

N-8340 Stamsund. ✆ **76-08-93-00.** Fax 76-08-97-26. www.stamsund.no. 28 units. NOK950–NOK1,400 ($190–$280/£95–£140) double. Rates include buffet breakfast. AE, DC, MC, V. **Amenities:** Restaurant; bar; lounge; nonsmoking rooms. *In room:* TV, minibar, hair dryer.

FLAKSTADØY

Having visited Austvågøy and Vestvagøy, E10 continues west to the next island of Flakstadøy, with most of the population of 1,600 hearty souls living along the northern tier, around the town of Ramberg (see below), which makes a good base for exploring the island.

Flakstadøy is serviced by buses running along the main route via Leknes to the end of the line, the curiously named hamlet of Å. If you're motoring, you can take a toll tunnel from Vestvagøy (our last stopover) to Flakstadøy for a cost of NOK100 ($20/£10) per vehicle.

Seeing the Sights

If you're touring the island, head for the secluded village of **Nusfjord** ★, on the south coast, a setting for some of the island's most dramatic scenery. Both the beauty and the bleakness of this remote village have drawn many artists to the area. The European Conservation List has added this 19th-century fishermen's village to its list of protected sites.

A favorite walk for us begins 300m (984 ft.) south of the old school in Nusfjord. Here you will see a cairned path leading to **Nesland,** a trek of about 4 hours round-trip. On this walk, you'll go about 200m (656 ft.) before you reach **Østre Nesland,** where you'll come across several big potholes near the shore. You'll also see the only remaining watermill in the Lofotens.

You'll find a colony of fishermen's huts, some still inhabited during the winter season or rented out to visitors in summer.

Ramberg, with its backdrop of snowcapped Arctic peaks, opens onto a beautiful white beach facing the Arctic Ocean. Just outside the village you can visit **Flakstad Kirke** at Flakstad (✆ **76-09-93-19**), built of wood in 1780 with a distinctive onion-shaped cupola. The altarpiece is older than the church, and the pulpit was painted by Godtfred Ezechiel, a master painter from Bergen. Charging an admission of NOK30 ($6/£3), the church is open in summer daily from 10am to 4pm; otherwise, it's open only during church services.

At Flakstad, another of our favorite walks begins first with a drive out to Fredvang, following the signpost to Yttersand. At this point, you can park your car and walk for about 30 to 40 minutes along the shore to **Mulstøa.** Along the way, you'll find an idyllic spot for a picnic.

The old fishing hamlet of **Sund** lies west of Ramberg along E10. It's visited mainly by those wishing to see **Sund Fiskerimuseum,** Sund (✆ **76-09-36-29;** www.sundfiskeri museum.no), near the bridge leading to the next island of Moskenesøy. A collection of fishing huts here contains all the paraphernalia needed to capture cod. The fisherman's cabin, or *rorbu,* is the oldest building in Sund, containing a wide range of domestic utensils, tools, and other artifacts used in fishermen's huts of old. On-site is a resident smithy known for his iron sculptures of cormorants. The museum is open June to mid-August daily from 10am to 6pm, charging NOK50 ($10/£5) for adult admission and NOK15 ($3/£1.50) for children. A final attraction is **Glasshytta** at Vikten (✆ **76-09-44-42**). This is the original Lofoten glass-blower's cabin, offering products of high quality and innovative design. It is also the home base of north Norway's first glass blower, Åsvar Tangrand, who designed Lofoten's seven-pronged logo, which evokes a longboat. The studio, charging an admission of NOK20 ($4/£2) for adults (free admission for children), is open from mid-June to mid-August daily 9am to 7pm (curtailed hours off season). You can purchase some very distinctive and charming pieces here at rather reasonable prices.

Where to Stay

Nusfjord Rorbuer ★ Finds These historic red-sided cabins are secluded and tranquil, offering the most authentic and atmospheric way to stay on the island of Flakstadøy. Many Norwegian families from the south come here for summer holidays, booking a cabin for a week or more, but you can also stay overnight. Outdoor activities such as fishing, boating, and hiking fill one's agenda during the day. Rowboats come with the price of the room, and the helpful staff will also rent you motorboats if you'd like to fish Lofoten waters. The original fishermen's cabins were built around 1900 but have since been modernized. They are constructed of timbers, and the wooden floors are original, the furnishings a mixture of antique and modern. In summer, there is also a restaurant (see below), serving mainly seafood. In winter, bookings are made by the Rica Hotel in Svolvær (✆ **76-07-22-22;** www.rica.no).

N-8380 Ramberg. ✆ **76-09-30-20.** Fax 76-09-37-49. www.rica.no. 34 cabins. NOK800–NOK1,200 ($160–$240/£80–£120) double. Rates include continental breakfast. AE, DC, MC, V. **Amenities:** Restaurant; laundry service/dry cleaning. *In room:* Kitchenette, no phone.

Where to Dine

Nusfjord Rorbuer Restaurant (Oriana Kro) SEAFOOD/NORWEGIAN Cozy, intimate, and much sought after as a dining enclave during its limited seasonal opening, this place seats only 30 diners at a time within a *rorbu* (fisherman's cottage) that reeks of character and rustic charm. The fish soup is a good choice, followed by the local seafood specialties of the day. As a dining oddity, you might opt to sample the deep-fried cod tongues, one of the islanders' favorite dishes. Meat-eaters can enjoy grilled beef kabobs and a few other dishes. For dessert? Try the old-fashioned apple pie with vanilla ice cream, like your good old mum used to bake.

In the Nusfjord Rorbuer, at the quay. ✆ **76-09-30-20.** Main courses NOK160–NOK220 ($32–$44/£16–£22). AE, DC, MC, V. June–Aug noon–3pm and 6–10pm.

MOSKENESØY ★

Continuing east on E10, you'll come to the final road link at the hamlet of Å. This glaciated island extends for 34km (21 miles). Nature has turned this landscape into one of the wildest and most fascinating in Norway. In Moskenesøy you'll reach the highest peak in the Western Lofoten at Hermannsdalstind, rising to 1,029m (3,375 ft.).

People live on the eastern side of the island, with its sheltered harbors for the fishing fleet. Even if you're not driving, the island maintains good ferry-bus links with Leknes, Stamsund, and Svolvær. Leknes, for example, lies 55km (34 miles) to the east.

Hurtigruten (✆ **76-96-76-00,** or reservations 81-03-00-00; www.hurtigruten.com) runs car ferries between Bodø and Moskenes, which take 3 hours and cost NOK561 ($112/£56) per vehicle and driver.

The village of Moskenes, with its ferry terminal, is a mere refueling stop. You can stop in for information and guidance at the **Fiskevaersferie Lofoten turistkontoret** (✆ **76-09-15-99**), at the harbor. Hours are from May 2 to June 22 and August 7 to August 25 Monday to Friday 10am to 5pm, June 23 to August 6 daily 10am to 7pm.

Seeing the Sights

Directly east of Moskenes lies the village of **Reine** ★, one of the most scenically located in the Lofoten, its little timber houses set against the panorama of seascapes. **Midnight Sun cruises** ★★ often set out from here in summer from late May to mid-July. Tours cost NOK725 ($145/£73) and last 6 hours. Ask about tickets at the Moskenes tourist office (see above).

There are many *rorbuer* colonies here, because these fishermen's cottages are rented out to summer visitors, many of whom book for a week or two.

Reine's tranquil lagoon, set against a backdrop of mountain pinnacles, has appeared on many a postcard. For the ultimate panorama, you can climb up to the summit of **Reinebringen** at 670m (2,198 ft.), one of our favorite walks in the area.

You can also ask at Moskenes about 5-hour tours, costing NOK600 ($120/£60) and leaving Reine twice daily Friday to Sunday in summer. They'll take you to the turbulent **Moskestraumen** ★★★, the strait that separates Moskenesøy from the offshore island of Vaerøy. First written about by Pytheas 2,000 years ago, these wicked straits also inspired nautical tales by Edgar Allan Poe and Jules Verne. Mariners claim that they are the "world's most dangerous waters," yet they attract marine mammals and thousands of seabirds, which can be observed on these organized boat tours.

Lying 3km (1¾ miles) from Reine is **Sakrisøy,** which is called the "Lilliput of Lofoten fishing villages." If you want to overnight on Moskenesøy, this would make the best base. In what used to be a barn filled with sheep and cows, you will find **Dagmars Dukke og Legetøy Museum** (✆ **76-09-21-43**), in the center of Sakrisøy. In this "journey back to childhood," a local woman has collected more than 2,500 dolls from all over, including antique teddy bears and some historic toys dating from 1860 and beyond. It's open June 16 to August 15 daily from 10am to 8pm; August 16 to 31 and June 1 to 15 daily 10am to 6pm; and in May and September, Saturday and Sunday noon to 5pm. Off season by appointment only. Admission is NOK50 ($10/£5) for adults and NOK30 ($6/£3) for children.

You'll reach the hamlet of Å at the end of E10, and from here the only road to take is back to Svolvær. The little fishing village of Å is the setting of the **Norsk Fiskevaermuseum** (✆ **76-09-14-88**), Lofoten's most intriguing fishing museum, founded in 1987. Nothing brings alive the role of a Lofoten fisherman like this museum, which covers a

Walking from Fishing Village to Fishing Village

If time allows, we suggest spending a day exploring some of north Norway's most charming little fishing villages. The landscape is characterized by sheer mountains and a narrow shoreline. The settlements are no longer on the western side of the island (the seas were too turbulent). The rugged inhabitants have moved to the eastern side of the island, where you can stroll along, taking in the fishing fleets, cargo vessels, and pleasure crafts. Along the way you'll find simple cafes for eating (fish, of course, what else?).

Begin in the north at little Hamnøy. In rapid order as you stroll south, you'll approach **Sakrisøy, Reine, Moskenes, Sørvågen,** and **Å.** Of course, the way to do it, if you have unlimited time, is to rent one of the fishermen's huts in one of these villages, settle in for the summer, and write a novel.

Once at Sørvågen, a 2-hour hike filled with dramatic scenery will lead you along a signposted and marked rambler's trail. Following along, you'll reach the Lofoten Tour Association's mountain rambler cabin. At Sørvågen you can also break up your trip by taking an hour's walk along beautiful lake Sørvagvannet. To extend the walk, you can take a detour into the scenic Studalen Valley.

boathouse, Norway's oldest cod-liver oil factory, the homes of fishermen, a *rorbu* cabin, and a 150-year-old bakery, plus exhibits on coastal farming in the Arctic. You can also visit a smithy who still makes cod-liver oil lamps. Admission is NOK55 ($11/£5.50) for adults and NOK30 ($6/£3) for children. Hours are late June to late August daily from 10:30am to 5:30pm, or Monday to Friday 10:30am to 3:30pm in the off season.

Close by is **Norsk Torrfiskmuseum** (✆ **76-09-12-11**), a museum devoted to stockfish, at which you'll learn more than you might ever want to know about Norway's oldest export commodity. You'll see what happens when cod is hauled in from the sea, going through the production processes including drying, grading, and sorting. Admission is NOK50 ($10/£5) for adults and NOK40 ($8/£4) for children. From June 16 to June 19, it is open Monday to Friday 11am to 4pm; June 20 to August 20 daily 10:30am to 5:30pm.

Where to Stay

Sakrisøy Rorbuer This collection of old-fashioned fishermen's cottages is the best place to stay on this island, as the other overnight possibilities consist of camping, caravan sites, hostels, and restored fishing huts. Opening onto the water, this is a series of genuine ocher-colored cottages that have been comfortably converted for guests. Under stone roofs, the cottages contain modern conveniences such as private bathrooms with showers. The buildings date from the 1880s but have been much altered and improved over the years.

Sakrisøy, N-8390 Reine. ✆ **76-09-21-43.** Fax 76-09-24-88. www.lofoten-info.no/sakrisoy. 11 cabins. NOK500–NOK1,500 ($100–$300/£50–£150) double. MC, V. **Amenities:** Laundry. *In room:* TV, kitchen, no phone.

VAERØY

Remote craggy Vaerøy, along with the even more remote island of Rost, lies to the far southwest of the Lofoten archipelago and is a bird-watcher's paradise. Vaerøy's **Mount**

Mostadfjell ★★ is the nesting place for more than 1.5 million seabirds, including sea eagles, auks, puffins, guillemots, kittiwakes, cormorants, arctic terns, eider petrels, gulls, and others that breed from May to August.

Vaerøy's population is only 775 hearty souls who live on an island of Lilliputian fishing villages; white-sand beaches open onto Arctic-chilled waters, towering ridges, and seabird rookeries.

Ferries from Bodø (✆ **76-96-76-00**) arrive here in 4½ hours and cost NOK514 ($103/£52) for a one-way passage with car. For passengers without a car, it's NOK143 ($29/£14) each way. There is also a ferry link from Moskenes taking less than 2 hours and costing NOK210 ($42/£21) one-way.

Seeing the Sights

The hamlet of **Sørland** lies to the east and south of the mountainous area on the island. At Nordland there is a large pebble beach, **Mollbakken,** right by the road from Sørland. Several burial sites from the Stone Age and also the Viking Age have been found here.

The mighty bird cliffs of Mount Mostadfjell can be found on the southwesterly side, facing the ocean. During the summer, trips to these cliffs are organized every day. Contact the tourist office (see above) for more information. If you don't like to join groups, you can explore on your own, as many hiking trails lead to the bigger of the seabird rookeries. One jaunt starts at the end of the route curving along the north of the island 6km (3¾ miles) from Sørland. This is our favorite walk in the remote southern islands because it not only has the best bird-watching in Norway, but it also leads rather eerily over the Isthmus of Eidet to the almost abandoned fishing village of **Mastad,** opening onto the rugged waters of the eastern shore. At one time, some 150 inhabitants lived here, catching puffins as a source of income, then curing the meat in salt. An unusual puffin dog, called the Mastad, was used to catch the puffins.

Stout-hearted men or women can make the steep climb from Mastad up to the **Måhornet peak,** at 435m (1,427 ft.). Allow 1 arduous hour each way.

The only man-made attraction at Vaerøy is the Vaerøy **Kirke,** a wooden church with an onion-shaped dome at Nordland. It was taken apart and moved from the village of Kabelvåg and reassembled at Vaerøy in 1799. This is the oldest church in Lofoten. The altarpiece, from around 1400, is a late medieval English alabaster relief, depicting the Annunciation, the three Magi (or wise men), the Resurrection, and the Ascension. The church is usually open to visitors in summer but keeps no regular hours.

Where to Stay

Gamle Prestegård (Old Vicarage) ★ **Finds** Built in 1898, this used to be the residence of a Lutheran priest. The hotel is run and owned by the charming Hege Sørli, who welcomes guests in style. Her rooms have been modernized and are tastefully and comfortably furnished. Five of the units contain a small bathroom with shower; guests in the other accommodations share the adequate public facilities. Sometimes it's possible to arrange to have dinner here. She doesn't keep a sign out, but it's the house to the left of the church.

N-8063 Vaerøy. ✆ **76-09-54-11.** Fax 76-09-54-84. www.prestegaarden.no. 11 units. NOK600 ($120/£60) double w/shared bathroom; NOK690 ($138/£69) double w/private bathroom. Rates include buffet breakfast. No credit cards.

Kornelius Kro Built in 1991, this is a series of cabins furnished to a high standard and offering a snug nest in this remote part of the world. The red-sided cabins are spacious, like a big hotel suite, and are comfortably inviting, with small bathrooms with showers. In summer, it becomes quite festive, and, amazingly, this place keeps going even in the midst of the harshest, darkest nights of winter. The cozy bar, one of only two bars in town, comes complete with a blazing fireplace. It is also known for a pair of wood-fired seawater hot tubs, the scene of the only parties in town. While enjoying the tub, you can be served drinks from the bar.

N-8063 Sørland, Vaerøy. ✆ **76-09-52-99.** Fax 76-09-57-99. 5 cabins. NOK1,350 ($270/£135) double for up to 4 people. Discounts available for 5 or more people. MC, V. **Amenities:** Restaurant; bar. *In room:* TV, kitchen, coffeemaker, hair dryer.

Where to Dine

Kornelius Kro Restaurant NORWEGIAN The most popular venue in town is this 110-seat restaurant, installed in a modern building at the Kornelius Kro hotel (see above). It is decorated with antique fish netting and nautical equipment. The lounge bar with its cozy fireplace is liked by both locals and visitors. You can eat dinner by firelight or candlelight. Everything is very informal here, and the place is always open in summer, but only for groups in winter. You might begin with a shrimp cocktail and then inquire as to what the cook has prepared for dinner that night. Most often it's fresh Norwegian salmon and the invariable cod prepared pretty much as you like it. Beefsteak with vegetables also appears on the menu.

Sørland. ✆ **76-09-52-99.** Meals NOK230–NOK350 ($46–$70/£23–£35). MC, V. Daily 5–10pm.

5 ALTA: CITY OF NORTHERN LIGHTS

809km (502 miles) N of Bodø; 329km (204 miles) N of Tromsø; 1,989km (1,233 miles) N of Oslo

At the dawn of the 21st century, Alta was renamed rather romantically Nordlysbyen Alta, or "Northern Lights City Alta." For years, this far-northern outpost of 18,000 inhabitants belonged to Finland and was inhabited almost solely by the Sami, who, until the end of the 1960s, held a famous fair here in spring and autumn. Because of fires and the Nazi destruction of the city at the close of World War II, almost everything looks new and rather dull. People come here for nature, not for town architecture.

Alta is the commercial and mercantile capital of Finnmark (as opposed to Finland, two names that some visitors confuse). The role of administrative capital of Finnmark goes to the city of Vadsø. The River Altaelva runs through the town. In its 19th-century heyday, Alta enjoyed patronage by British lords who came here to fish the Altafjord, known to have the best salmon waters in the world.

In one of the major environmental protests in Scandinavia, the Altadammen was constructed in the 1970s, rising 100m (328 ft.). A former salmon-spawning stream was diverted for hydroelectric power.

ESSENTIALS

GETTING THERE The airport at Alta lies 7km (4¼ miles) northeast of the center of Elvebakken. Three daily direct flights from Oslo take 3 hours. Most passengers transfer through Tromsø, which receives the most flights in north Norway. From Tromsø to Alta, there are four daily flights. There are no train lines here, but buses run between Tromsø and Alta, taking 7 hours and costing NOK484 ($97/£48) one-way. For schedules and information about this bus, call ✆ **177** from phones within Norway or the local tourist office (✆ **78-44-50-50**) for information about Alta or other towns and districts within Finnmark.

 VISITOR INFORMATION For information about the area, call or visit Via Alta Tours, Sentrums Parken #4, Alta Sentrum, N-9504 Alta (✆ **78-44-50-50;** www.altatours.no). From June to August, it's open Monday to Friday 10am to 4pm, Saturday and Sunday 11am to 5pm. The rest of the year (Sept–May), it's open Monday to Friday 8:30am to 4:30pm and Saturday 10am to 2pm.

SEEING THE SIGHTS

A series of prehistoric rock carvings at **Hjemmeluft ★★**, about 1km (1/2 mile) southwest of Alta, dates from 2,000 to 5,000 years ago and is the biggest collection of prehistoric rock carvings in the north of Europe. These pictographs, discovered in 1973 and now a UNESCO World Heritage Site, form part of the **Alta Museum** (✆ **78-45-63-30**). It is believed that the rock carvings were originally painted in red ocher. They have been repainted in the same color to make them stand out better. The rock carvings from both the Stone Age and the Iron Age are linked to the museum by a series of 3km (1 3/4 miles) of boardwalks, the best place for a walk in Alta. The carvings depict hunting scenes, with clear likenesses of moose, bears, and reindeer. One stunning carving shows an ancient boat carrying a crew of 32 hunters. The paintings aren't visible during snowfalls.

The museum itself shelters an array of exhibitions related to Finnmark and its history, going back 11,000 years. It is open June to August daily 8am to 9pm; May and September daily 9am to 6pm; and October to April Monday to Friday 9am to 3pm, Saturday and Sunday 11am to 4pm. Admission is NOK85 ($17/£8.50) for adults, NOK20 ($4/£2) for children 11 and under.

From Alta you can take a riverboat excursion along the Alta River up to the **Sautso-Alta Canyon ★★★**, which, at 400m (1,312 ft.), is the "Grand Canyon" not only of Scandinavia, but of northern Europe. Despite the protests of environmentalists, the canyon has been dammed, but it and the region around it still offer massive scenic beauty. (***Historical note:*** Some historians claim that the controversies that surrounded the dam's construction between 1979 and 1986 eventually led to some degree of government autonomy for the Sami people. At least in theory, they benefited from the many changes that the spotlighting of the dam and the region introduced.)

To hook up with a tour, contact **Alta Riverboat Service** (✆ **78-43-33-78**). From June 5 to September 5, 2 1/2-hour tours to the outer canyon cost NOK575 ($115/£58) for adults or NOK375 ($75/£38) for children 11 and under.

SHOPPING

Within Alta's town center, the best inventories of local handcrafts are located within the **Håndverkshuset,** Løkkeveien 55 (✆ **78-44-22-33**), where stacks and stacks of knitted sweaters, hats, gloves, scarves, as well as Sami (or Sami-inspired) carvings in wood or bone, jewelry, and gift items are presented in abundance. It's open Monday to Friday 10am to 5pm, and Saturday 10am to 4pm. During midsummer it remains open later, depending on the weather, business, and the mood of the shopkeepers.

A bit farther outside of town, an equivalent and perhaps even more esoteric collection of merchandise is for sale at **Manndalen Husflidslag** (✆ **77-71-62-73**), lying at Løkvoll in Manndalen and reached along the E6 15km (9 1/4 miles) west of Alta. The Sami often make marvelous weavings on their vertical looms, some of which are suitable as wall hangings. You can also purchase such clothing as knitwear. Open Wednesday to Saturday 10am to 3pm.

WHERE TO STAY

Nordlys Hotell Alta ★★ **Finds** Our favorite nest for an overnight stopover in the area is this well-run far-northern inn, lying just off the E6 heading north. It lies in Bossekop, a residential suburb about half a kilometer (1/4 mile) south of Alta's center. This is a comfortable hotel whose allure increased greatly after a renovation and upgrading. We now consider it the most appealing hotel in the area. Bedrooms are attractively and pleasantly furnished, without generating too much excitement. There is a computer with Internet access in the reception area. The hotel enjoys a well-deserved reputation in the area for its food, attracting many locals because its cuisine is based in part on raw materials from Finnmark—that means reindeer and fresh fish.

Bekkefaret 3, N-9512 Alta. ✆ **78-45-72-00.** Fax 78-45-72-01. www.nordlyshotell.no. 32 units. NOK1,045–NOK1,345 ($209–$269/£105–£135) double; NOK1,550–NOK1,745 ($310–$349/£155–£175) suite. MC, V. Closed Dec–Jan. **Amenities:** Restaurant; bar; sauna; whirlpool; nonsmoking rooms; rooms for those w/ limited mobility. *In room:* TV, minibar (in some), hair dryer.

Park Hotel Alta Sentrum Built in 1987, this is a cozy alternative to the more expensive and expansive Rica Hotel Alta nearby. It's what Norwegians call a Frokosthotellet, or "breakfast hotel." This is the only hotel in the north of Norway that has been given the European "Eco-label," meaning it was built with and maintains environmentally friendly standards. Just off the North Cape Road, it provides a suitable and comfortable overnight before pressing on the next day to the outposts in the north. Furnishings are modern, and the small to midsize bedrooms have wooden floors. Each has an immaculate bathroom; eight come with a bathtub and shower, the rest come with a shower only. Breakfast plus a light meal in the evening are served to guests daily.

E6, N-9501 Alta. ✆ **78-45-74-00.** Fax 78-45-74-01. www.parkhotell.no. 34 units. NOK1,075–NOK1,345 ($215–$269/£108–£135) double; NOK1,695–NOK2,200 ($339–$440/£170–£220) suite. Rates include buffet breakfast and light evening meal. AE, DC, MC, V. **Amenities:** Restaurant; lounge; sauna; laundry service; nonsmoking rooms. *In room:* TV, hair dryer.

Rica Hotel Alta ★ The city's biggest hotel was built in the 1980s in a very contemporary design. In an often gray and gloomy climate, the hotel stands out for its brightness, even using white furnishings to decorate its midsize bedrooms. Half of the units are carpeted, and the rest offer wooden floors. The Rica has the most dining, drinking, and entertainment facilities in town. Friday and Saturday nights are especially popular here from 10pm to 3am. Sometimes live bands are brought in, and the cover can run up to NOK20 ($4/£2), depending on the evening.

Løkkeveien 61, N-9150 Alta. ✆ **78-48-27-00.** Fax 78-48-27-77. www.rica.no. 155 units. NOK1,520–NOK1,770 ($304–$354/£152–£177) double. Children 14 and under stay free in parent's room. Rates include continental breakfast. AE, DC, MC, V. **Amenities:** 2 restaurants; bar; disco; sauna; laundry service/dry cleaning; rooms for those w/limited mobility. *In room:* TV, Wi-Fi, minibar.

Thon Hotel Vica **Value** Built right after World War II, this was a former farmhouse before its conversion to an affordable hotel in 1988. In a town of buildings with no architectural distinction, this timber-built structure has some atmosphere and style. Rooms are decorated in a homelike way and are tastefully furnished with warm colors and small bathrooms with showers. Many locals drop in for the traditional north Norway fare, a three-course meal in the evening going for NOK539 ($108/£54).

Fogdebakken 6 Bossekop, N-9500 Alta. ✆ **78-48-22-22.** Fax 78-43-42-99. www.thonhotels.com. 24 units. NOK1,100–NOK1,500 ($220–$300/£110–£150) double. Rates include buffet breakfast. AE, DC, MC,

 V. Closed Dec 22–Jan 5 and 1 week at Easter. **Amenities:** Restaurant; bar; sauna; room service; babysitting; laundry service; nonsmoking rooms; 1 room for those w/limited mobility. *In room:* TV, minibar (some units).

WHERE TO DINE

Han Steike (Beef House) ★★ STEAKS/GRILLS The most appealing and popular restaurant in Alta sits in the center of town, behind a relatively drab gray-painted facade that you'll imagine can withstand virtually any snowstorm. Inside you'll find a warm and cozy steakhouse that's accented with what locals refer to as "Norwegian stone" (gray flagstones) and dark wood paneling. Your waitstaff will ask you what size you prefer for your grilled beefsteak, veal, whale steak, lamb chops, spareribs, reindeer, salmon, or cod. Know in advance that the "average" appetite might go for the 150- or 200-gram size (about 5–7 oz.); a hungry diner might opt for the 300-gram size (about 10½ oz.); and someone who's been felling timber in the forest all day and who hasn't eaten since breakfast might conceivably gravitate toward the 400-gram portion (about 14 oz.). Anything you order comes with a choice of sauces that include mustard, horseradish, peppercorn, mushroom gravy, or hollandaise.

Løkkeveien 2. ✆ **78-44-08-88.** Reservations recommended. Main courses NOK170–NOK359 ($34–$72/£17–£36). AE, DC, MC, V. Tues–Sat 3pm–midnight; Sun 2–8pm.

ALTA AFTER DARK

The chief hot spot in town is **Alfa-Omega,** Markedsgata 16 (✆ **78-44-54-00**), attracting a crowd whose average age is from 30 to 40. There is no cover, and the place is definitely inspired by Cuba, with recorded salsa music, pictures of Havana, and Cuban cigars de rigueur. There are seats for 40, but often 70 to 80 patrons crowd in here. One section is a very laid-back bar; the other's a contemporary cafe. It's open Monday to Thursday 11am to midnight, and Friday and Saturday 11am to 2am. Its only drawback, according to some of the young and restless clients we met here, involves its lack of facilities for dancing.

If you want to go dancing, the town's only disco is **Panella,** which is situated on the lobby level of Alta's Rica Hotel, Løkkeveien 61 (✆ **78-48-27-00**). Sporting a color scheme of black, red, and blue, and describing itself as a grown-up place for adults (most of the clientele is over 30), it allows guests of the Rica Hotel to enter free but charges nonresidents between NOK50 and NOK150 ($10–$30/£5–£15) each, depending on the musical venue (live or recorded) on the night of your arrival. It's open nightly from 8pm to between midnight (Sun–Thurs) and 2am (Fri–Sat).

6 KARASJOK: CAPITAL OF THE SAMI

110km (68 miles) NE of Kautokeino; 11km (7 miles) W of Finnish border

This is the capital of the Sami, with a population of 2,900 inhabitants. Of these, some 90% are of Sami descent, making Karasjok, along with its neighboring town of Kautokeino, a seat of Sami culture.

Karasjok, whose Sami name translates as "river current," thrives in part on reindeer herding. With its many handicrafts and Sami institutions, Karasjok is both the cultural and social hub of Samiland.

The town is the best place to learn about these once nomadic people who lived on the roof of Europe. The Sami—historically called Lapps by non-Sami—have inhabited these inhospitable lands since ancient times. Sami settlements stretch along the entire Nordic region, including Finland, Sweden, and Norway. Some of the Sami maintain links to their ancient culture, whereas others have been assimilated.

The language of the Sami belongs to the Finno-Ugric group. A large part of Sami literature has been published in Northern Sami, which is spoken by approximately 75% of Sami. As with all Arctic societies, oral literature has always played a prominent role. Among Sami, this oral tradition takes the form of *yoikking,* a type of singing. (Once governments tried to suppress this, but now yoikking is enjoying a renaissance.) One of the classic works of Sami literature is Johan Turi's *Tale of the Lapps,* first published in 1910.

Handicrafts are important in the Sami economy. Several craft designers have developed new forms of decorative art, producing a revival in Sami handicraft tradition.

Many members of the Sami community feel that the term *Lapp* has negative connotations; it's gradually being replaced by the indigenous minority's own name for itself, *sábme,* or other dialect variations. Sami seems to be the most favored English translation, and the word is being used increasingly.

ESSENTIALS

GETTING THERE The town is reached by bus, with most visitors arriving from Hammerfest. This overland trip takes $4^1/_2$ hours and costs NOK360 ($72/£36) one-way. Motorists can continue east from Hammerfest along E6.

VISITOR INFORMATION At Porsangerveien 1, **Karasjok Opplevelser Tourist Office** (✆ **78-46-88-10;** www.karasjokinfo.no) dispenses information for the entire area. It is open June to mid-August daily 9am to 7pm. It's open Monday to Friday 9am to 4pm the rest of the year.

SEEING THE SIGHTS

Sami vourká dávvirat (Sami Museum) ★, Museumsgate 17 (✆ **78-46-99-50**), is an open-air museum devoted to the Sami people, their history, and their culture. There are other Sami exhibitions, but this venue is the only one to be called a national museum of Sami culture. Most intriguing is the exhibition of old dwellings and such artifacts as an old hunting trap for wild reindeer, showing how people earned their living. Of special interest are the examples of regional dress used in these subfreezing conditions. Also on display are works by local artists. Admission is NOK75 ($15/£7.50). From January 1 to June 4, open Monday to Friday 9am to 3pm, Saturday and Sunday 10am to 3pm; June 5 to August 20, hours are Monday to Friday 9am to 6pm, Saturday and Sunday 10am to 6pm. In the off season, hours are Monday to Friday 9am to 3pm, and Saturday and Sunday 10am to 3pm.

Since 2000, the **Sametinget (Sami Parliament),** Sámediggi (✆ **78-47-40-00**), has had its headquarters at this impressive piece of modern architecture encased in Siberian lark wood. To carry out this far-north theme, the interior is also filled with native woods such as pine and birch. Unique among parliament buildings, the assembly hall was constructed in the shape of a *gamma* (Sami tent). Tiny bulbs, evoking the Northern Lights, illuminate the 35,000-volume Sami library. Free tours are conducted Monday to Friday in summer from 8:30am to 2:30pm.

Samisk Kunstnersenter (Sami Artists Center), Jeagilvármádii 54 (✆ **75-46-99-40**), is an art gallery devoted to Sami painters, with new exhibitions every month. This is not just about folk art; many Sami painters are as modern as the 21st century. Sami art and handicrafts are also sold here. Admission is free, and it is open Monday to Wednesday and Friday 10am to 3pm, Thursday 10am to 7pm, and on Sunday from noon to 5pm. In summer, it is also open on Saturday from 10am to 3pm.

Finally, **Karasjok Opplevelser** (✆ **78-46-88-10**) organizes adventures in the area, including everything from visits to a Sami camp to gold-panning and riverboat trips. In winter, you can even go reindeer sledding like Santa Claus. If you're coming into the area, call in advance to see what type of adventure might be offered at the time of your visit.

Many visitors come from all over the world to hunt and fish in the area. If you'd like some fishing trips and wilderness adventure tours, the guide to call is **Nils Rolf Johnsen,** Svenskebakken 35 (✆ **78-46-63-02**), who makes arrangements for such outings. He can arrange for you to stay in *lavvu* (Sami tents) beside Finnmark's largest lake, Lesjavri, which is excellent for fishing.

SHOPPING Most visitors who make it this far north like to come back with some souvenirs, particularly handmade Sami knives, a craft and tradition going back four generations. The best selection of Sami crafts is available at **Samellandssenteret** (✆ **78-46-88-01**), a cooperative crafts store in the town center.

WHERE TO STAY

Engholm's Huskyi Lodge ★ Finds Next to the Karasjohka River, lying 6km (3¾ miles) outside Karasjok, this is a real frontier outpost that connects you with local life more than any other lodging in the area. You cannot only rent a cabin, but you can go on summer hikes with the huskies or, when the weather turns, join in a dog-sledding tour. Gold-panning, fishing trips, and wilderness tours are also part of the action here. Accommodations are in cozy log houses, each personalized and comfortable. Some of the cabins have private bathrooms; others are shared. Most cabins contain a kitchenette as well. In the *Barta,* a special turf-covered log house, guests gather around the open fire sitting on reindeer furs, enjoying good food and drink. Lunch costs NOK150 ($30/£15), with a dinner going for NOK250 ($50/£25).

N-9730 Karasjok. ✆ **78-46-71-66.** www.engholm.no. 5 cabins. NOK400 ($80/£40) double, plus NOK200 ($40/£20) per person. V. **Amenities:** Restaurant; bar. *In room:* TV, no phone.

Rica Hotel Karasjok ★ This frontier outpost is the best hotel in the area. And with its cozy bar and dining facilities, it's also the major social hub and entertainment venue for the district. The two-story wooden building looks like a ski lodge. It was built in 1983 but has been completely renovated to offer contemporary bedrooms, with comfortable furnishings resting on wooden floors. All accommodations have strong elements of Sami culture mixed into the interior design, colors, and materials. The bedrooms open onto views of the surrounding forests. The staff is most helpful in arranging tours regardless of the season—winter dog-sled rides and reindeer races or summer riverboat trips.

Porsangervn 1, N-9730 Karasjok. ✆ **78-46-88-60.** Fax 78-46-68-02. www.rica.no. 56 units. NOK1,095–NOK1,635 ($219–$327/£110–£164) double. Children 3 and under stay free in parent's room. Rates include continental breakfast. AE, DC, MC, V. **Amenities:** 2 restaurants; fitness center; sauna; nonsmoking rooms; rooms for those w/limited mobility. *In room:* TV.

WHERE TO DINE

Rica Hotel Karasjok Restaurant ★★ Finds NORWEGIAN For a unique, exotic experience, head for this restaurant, where you can sit on reindeer skins around the fire while you're served a cuisine based on Sami recipes dating back several centuries. Built of timber and turf, this is called the Storgammen section of the restaurant. You can also dine more elegantly in the regular a la carte restaurant, with formally laid tables and comfortable chairs. Adjacent to Sami Park, this restaurant is the best in the area. A ski lodge restaurant, it is built of timbers and decorated with native Sami costumes. For an appetizer, its smoked reindeer heart is even better than your mother made for you. This might be followed with such regional dishes as filet of reindeer in a game sauce with vegetables. If you've had enough reindeer, you can opt for the delectable grilled arctic char with white-wine sauce and vegetables. The gourmet's favorite summer dessert in Sami land is a bowl of fresh cloudberries.

In the Rica Hotel Karasjok, Porsangervn 1. ✆ **78-46-74-00.** Reservations recommended. Main courses NOK220–NOK340 ($44–$68/£22–£34). AE, DC, MC, V. Daily 11am–11pm.

KARASJOK AFTER DARK

Once again, the **Rica Hotel Karasjok,** Porsangervn 1 (✆ **78-46-74-00**), a cozy wood-paneled room, is the scene of the "action," whatever there is. Patrons who come here range in age from their 20s to 50s. There's no cover. Open Friday and Saturday 11am to 11pm.

7 HAMMERFEST: WORLD'S NORTHERNMOST TOWN

2,314km (1,435 miles) N of Bergen; 144km (89 miles) N of Alta; 2,195km (1,361 miles) N of Oslo

It's easy to poke fun at Hammerfest as author William Bryson did in *Neither Here Nor There.* He found Hammerfest an "agreeable enough town in a thank-you-God-for-not-making-me-live-here sort of way." Locals are quick to defend how civilized they are, pointing out that they were the first town in Europe to have electric street lighting while Paris and London were lit by gas.

That Hammerfest is here at all is a sort of miracle. The town was founded because of its natural harbor, something that is equally important today. A hurricane flattened it in 1856, and one of Norway's worst fires leveled it again in 1890, the year the town got that street lighting. Hitler ordered that "no building be left standing" during the infamous Nazi retreat of 1945. But Hammerfest bounced back and has been attracting visitors from all over the world who use it as a base for exploring the North Cape in summer. Arctic hunters enjoy their last few drinks in cozy bars here before setting off on expeditions into the wilderness. You just might encounter a polar bear wandering the streets as you stroll back to your hotel.

But it will be oil, not tourism, fueling the economy of Hammerfest, at least for the next 30 years. In 2006, the pumps started sucking oil from the offshore oil wells, which are estimated to possess 195 billion cubic meters of the black gold. At present, running for some 145km (90 miles), the world's longest undersea pipeline goes from the mammoth natural gas fields in the Barents Sea to the small island of Melkøya out in the bay off the coast of Hammerfest.

The Hammerfest area stretches from Måsøy, near the North Cape, to Loppa in the south, the wide region including the rugged coasts along the Arctic Sea. The city lies 70° 39' 48" north and achieved its town status on July 7, 1789, making it the oldest town in northern Norway. But is Hammerfest really the world's northernmost town, as often claimed? Other communities exist north of here but locals say that they are villages—not towns.

A **Meridianstøtta,** or meridian column, stands on the Fuglenes peninsula, across from the harbor. The monument commemorates the work of scientists from Norway, Sweden, and Russia who conducted surveys at Hammerfest between 1816 and 1852 to establish a meridian arc between Hammerfest and the Danube River at the Black Sea. This led to an accurate calculation of the size and shape of Earth.

Today Hammerfest is a modern town with an open and unique atmosphere, where the town's square and harbor are natural meeting places.

ESSENTIALS

GETTING THERE If you don't take the coastal steamer, you can drive, although it's a long trek. From Oslo, take E6 north until you reach the junction with Rte. 94 west. Hammerfest is at the end of Rte. 94. During the summer there are three buses a week from Oslo. Travel time is 29 hours. SAS has daily flights from Oslo and Bergen to Alta, where you can catch a bus to Hammerfest (Apr–Sept only). For bus information, call **Veolia Transport** (✆ **78-40-70-00**).

VISITOR INFORMATION The **Hammerfest Tourist Office,** Havnegate 3 (✆ **78-41-21-85;** www.hammerfest-turist.no), in the town center, is open in summer daily from 9am to 5pm, in winter daily 10am to 2pm. The tourist office also organizes boat trips in the area for those who want to go deep-sea fishing and bird-watching. Offerings can change from week to week, but these 3-hour outings require a minimum of eight people, costing NOK490 ($98/£49) per person.

SEEING THE SIGHTS

This is the world's northernmost town of significant size and a port of call for North Cape coastal steamers. Sami from nearby camps often come into town to shop. Count yourself lucky if they bring their reindeer.

The port is free of ice year-round, and shipping and exporting fish is a major industry. The sun doesn't set from May 12 to August 1, and it doesn't rise from November 21 to January 23.

For the best panoramic view of the town, take a zigzag walk up the 72m (236-ft.) **Salen** "mountain." Atop Salen is a 6m-tall (20-ft.) square tower, with walls built of gray and blue stones. The old tower was torn down during World War II but was restored in 1984. On a clear day, you can see the offshore islands.

There is also a Sami "turf hut" here, **Mikkelgammen,** which can be booked 2 days in advance if you'd like to have a Sami meal here. Guests gather around a campfire for a traditional three-course meal, or *bidos.* You'll get reindeer soup as well as reindeer meat for your main course, followed by Arctic cloudberries in whipped cream. The cost of the meal is NOK245 ($49/£25) per person. It is followed by a Sami program called *Joik,* including singing (more like chanting) and stories about life in the far north.

Why not take time to do as 150,000 others have and join the **Royal and Ancient Polar Bear Society** (✆ **78-41-31-00**) here? Apply in person while you're in Hammerfest. Membership costs NOK180 ($36/£18) annually, and the money is used to protect endangered Arctic animals through conservation programs. The society's building is filled with stuffed specimens of Arctic animals. The Society has moved into a new building next to the Coastal Voyager Docks on Havnegata 3. Entrance is 40NOK ($8/£4). There's a small museum devoted to the hunting heyday of Hammerfest, which lasted from 1910 to 1950, when eagles, arctic foxes, and polar bears were trapped by the English, and by German officers during World War II. It's in the basement of the Town Hall, on Rådhusplassen. The center is open only June to August Monday to Friday from 6am to 6pm.

Gjenreisningsmuseet, Söröygatan (✆ **78-42-26-40**), commemorates the cold, bleak years after World War II, when local residents, deprived of most of their buildings, livelihoods, and creature comforts, heroically rebuilt Finnmark and north Norway in the wake of Nazi devastation. Entrance is NOK50 ($10/£5) for adults, NOK30 ($6/£3) for students, free for children 15 and under. It is open June to September daily from 10am to 3pm; in the off season, it's open daily from 11am to 2pm.

Lying a 5-minute walk from the harbor, **Hammerfest Kirke (Church),** Kirkegate 33 (✆ **78-42-74-70**), was consecrated in 1961 and is known for its avant-garde architecture. Unusual for a church, this *kirke* doesn't have an altarpiece. Instead, you get a large and detailed stained-glass window that is quite beautiful. The altarpiece is found in a hall lying to the right of the main sanctuary. Local carver Knit Arnesen carved the friezes, depicting the history of Hammerfest. Note the chapel across from the church. Dating from 1933, it is the only structure in Hammerfest to survive the Nazi scorched earth retreat. Admission is free, and the church is open in summer from Monday to Friday 8am to 3pm, Saturday 11am to 3pm, and Sunday noon to 1pm.

WHERE TO STAY

Rica Hotel Hammerfest ★ A bit grim and foreboding—one of our readers likened its facade to a prison—the Rica actually offers more comfort than the Thon, although it doesn't have as much character. It, too, opens onto views of the harbor and arguably has a more efficient staff. If you're seeking the best appointed and most spacious accommodations in Hammerfest, ask for a junior suite here. The largest hotel in town was built in the mid-1970s on steeply sloping land and has been regularly spruced up since then. The standard, midsize guest rooms are decorated with Nordic-inspired pastels, but the look is strictly functional.

Sørøygata 15, N-9600 Hammerfest. ✆ **78-42-57-00.** Fax 78-42-57-01. www.rica.no. 80 units. NOK1,150–NOK1,900 ($230–$380/£115–£190) double; NOK1,550–NOK2,050 ($310–$410/£155–£205) junior suite. AE, DC, MC, V. **Amenities:** Restaurant; bar; disco; fitness center; sauna; babysitting; laundry service/dry cleaning; nonsmoking rooms. *In room:* TV, Wi-Fi, minibar, hair dryer.

Thon Hotel Hammerfest ★ Although playing second fiddle to the Rica Hotel (see above), the Thon opens onto views of the harbor, standing right on the Rådhusplassen (Town Hall Square). Built in 1964, it's been improved and kept up-to-date over the years, adding a newer wing that replicates a ship's cabin. The small to midsize bedrooms are tastefully and comfortably furnished, each with a small bathroom with a shower. If you can afford it, go for a suite here, as they not only open onto views of the harbor, but they also have more luxurious bathrooms with a tub *and* a shower. The staff can arrange such adventures as rides in a snowmobile or on horseback, and can advise about fishing in local waters. The on-site trio of bars is livelier than the watering hole at the Rica.

Strandgt. 2-4, N-9600 Hammerfest. ✆ **78-42-96-00.** Fax 78-42-96-60. www.thonhotels.com. 50 units. NOK1,745 ($349/£175) double; from NOK1,890 ($378/£189) minisuite. Rates include buffet breakfast. AE, DC, MC, V. Closed Dec 20–Jan 2. **Amenities:** Restaurant; 3 bars; sauna; room service; solarium; nonsmoking rooms; rooms for those w/limited mobility. *In room:* TV, Wi-Fi, minibar, hair dryer, iron.

Odd's Mat og Vinhus ★★ NORTHERN NORWEGIAN Following its opening in 1992, this rustic restaurant became famous in the late 1990s, thanks to a survey by a Trondheim radio station that voted it the best restaurant in Norway. It's adjacent to the town's largest pier, overlooking the harbor. Inside, every effort has been made to simulate the wild splendor of Finnmark (northern Norway), with the use of roughly textured wood, stone, and many yards of natural hemp knotted into ropes that form curtains. The kitchen opens to the dining room, adding to the cozy feel.

The recipes and ingredients are almost completely derived from northern Norway, with an emphasis on fish and game. You might try filet of carp, partially sun-dried, then boiled and served with mustard sauce and bacon fat; or freshly killed grouse prepared "like beef," with a game-laced cream sauce. To start, try the filet of reindeer, served raw and chopped, like a tartar, or smoked and thinly sliced, like a carpaccio.

Strandgata 24. ✆ **78-41-37-66.** Reservations recommended. Main courses NOK230–NOK320 ($46–$64/£23–£32). AE, DC, MC, V. Mon–Thurs 2:30–11pm; Fri 1–11pm; Sat 6–11pm.

Skansen Mat og Vinstue ★ NORWEGIAN/INTERNATIONAL This small, intimate restaurant has an open-to-view kitchen with a fireplace in the center. Because it's the north of Norway, you expect the chefs to specialize in filet of reindeer, and they do prepare the meat exceedingly well. But personally, we prefer to look for the daily specials based on the day's catch from the fjord. Pepper steak is another specialty here, and we found it tender, pink, and flavorful—the sauce has just the right amount of fire. The Rica Bar and Disco, also in the cellar of the hotel, is open Friday and Saturday from 10pm to 3am so you can dance and drink the night away. Admission is NOK75 ($15/£7.50). The minimum age is 20, and beer costs NOK45 to NOK55 ($9–$11/£4.50–£5.50) per half-liter.

In the Rica Hotel Hammerfest, Sørøygata 15. ✆ **78-41-13-33.** Main courses NOK200–NOK330 ($40–$66/£20–£33). AE, DC, MC, V. Daily 4–11pm.

HAMMERFEST AFTER DARK

Your best bet is **Banyean & Hans Highness,** Strandgt. 2–4 (✆ **78-42-96-00**), found in the previously recommended Thon Hotel Hammerfest. Banyean is a sailor's pub, whereas Hans Highness is more like a nightclub. In the pub, you can order plenty of mugs of beer or other drinks along with burgers and pastas. In the nightclub, live music is frequently featured, at which time a cover of NOK40 to NOK100 ($8–$20/£4–£10) is imposed. Sometimes the night is devoted to karaoke. Most patrons range in age from 25 to 45. Banyean is open daily from noon to 1am (until 2am Fri–Sat), and Hans Highness is open only on Friday and Saturday from midnight to 3am. If you'd like a cozy retreat from all this Nordic madness, you can head for a drink in the **hotel bar.**

8 HONNINGSVÅG & THE NORTH CAPE ★★

130km (81 miles) NE of Hammerfest; 2,444km (1,515 miles) NE of Bergen

You have to journey a long way to see **Nordkapp** (North Cape), the most celebrated attraction in Norway. Nearer the North Pole than Oslo, the mighty rock stands at a latitude of 71° 10' 21" N. The attraction is generally viewed from mid-May to the end of July, when the Midnight Sun does not drop below the horizon. Before you've come all this way, we'll let you in on a secret. Nordkapp is supposed to be the northernmost point of continental Europe, although it actually isn't. See our box, "Europe's Real Northernmost Point." To the Sami, the North Cape held great religious significance and was a site for sacrifices. The name of North Cape came from the British explorer, Richard Chancellor, who drifted here in 1553. Actually, he was looking for the Northeast Passage.

The world's northernmost village, the gateway to the North Cape, is a completely modern fishing harbor set in a land of forests, fjord waters, and crashing waterfalls, everything bathed in summer by the eerie light of the midnight sun. Only the chapel withstood the village's destruction by Germans in 1944. It's some 80km (50 miles) nearer to the North Pole than Hammerfest, on the Alta-Hammerfest bus route.

Honningsvåg is on the southern side of the island of Magerøy, connected to the North Cape by a 35km (22-mile) road.

ESSENTIALS

GETTING THERE If you don't take the coastal steamer (visit www.hurtigruten.us for information), you can reach Honningsvåg by car. From Oslo (a very long trip—about 30 hr. June–Sept), take E6 north to the junction with Rte. 95 north. That route leads to Honningsvåg, with one ferry crossing. SAS flies from Oslo or Bergen to Alta; there you can catch a bus to Hammerfest (Apr–Sept only), where you change to another bus to Honningsvåg. For bus information, call **Veolia Transport** (✆ **78-40-70-00**).

VISITOR INFORMATION The **North Cape Tourist Office,** in the Nordkapphuset (✆ **78-47-70-30;** www.nordkapp.no), can give you information on sightseeing boat trips, museums, walks, and deep-sea fishing. The office is open June to August Monday to Friday from 8:30am to 8pm, Saturday and Sunday noon to 8pm; September to May Monday to Friday 8:30am to 4pm.

A SPECIAL EVENT The **North Cape Festival,** held for 1 week in mid-June each year, presents a wide display of local culture. During the festival, participants in the **North Cape March** trek from Honningsvåg to the North Cape and back, a total of around 70km (43 miles).

SEEING THE SIGHTS

Check at the tourist office (see above) about organized tours of the area. In the summer, tours visit the splendid bird colony on the little island of **Gjesvaerstappan** ★★. All sorts of arctic seabirds, including kittiwakes, skuas, razorbills, gannets, puffins, and cormorants, can be seen on the cliffs, along with seals. The details of each tour will vary according to the molting and breeding seasons of the birds, so for further information about tours that might happen to be available at the time of your visit, contact the local tourist office (see above), and expect to pay around NOK500 ($100/£50) for a 6-hour excursion, by boat and Land Rover, to see the birds. Know in advance that tours are erratic and hastily arranged on an as-needed basis, so it's wise to remain as flexible as possible in your bird-watching aspirations.

Nordkapphallen This visitor center has a video presentation and museum exhibits. Downstairs you'll find an excellent videograph and a cave with a panoramic window facing the Arctic Ocean. On the way to the cave, you'll see several scenes from the history of the North Cape. A monument commemorates the visit of King Oscar (king of Norway and Sweden) to the Cape in 1873, and another exhibit commemorates the arrival of King Chulalongkorn of Siam (now Thailand) who came for a look at the Cape in 1907;

Chulalongkorn was the son of the king in the musical *The King and I.* There's also a monument marking the terminus of the "Midnight Sun Road." You might be dismayed at the steep entrance price, but the exhibits and the views from within manage to artfully and effectively evoke the meteorological and geological drama of the far North. Call before you visit; even in high season, open hours and days are subject to change without notice, and it's locked up like a drum between October and March.

Nordkapp. ✆ **78-47-68-60.** Admission NOK200 ($40/£20) adults, NOK80 ($16/£8) children, NOK380 ($76/£38) family. Apr 1–May 20 daily 2–5pm; May 21–June 16 daily noon–1am; June 17–Aug 4 daily 9am–2am; Aug 5–31 daily noon–midnight; Sept 1–Oct 5 daily noon–5pm. Closed Oct 6–Mar.

Nordkappmuseet This museum displays the cultural history of the North Cape, including fishery artifacts and an exhibit that details the effects of World War II on the North Cape. The museum lies at the harbor and town center, a 3-minute walk from the coastal steamer and the North Cape Hotel.

In the Nordkapphuset, Fiskeriveien 4. ✆ **78-47-28-33.** www.nordkappmuseet.no. Admission NOK30 ($6/£3) adults, NOK5 ($1/50p) children 6–16, free for children 5 and under. June 5–Aug 15 Mon–Sat 11am–8pm, Sun noon–7pm; Aug 16–June 4 Mon–Fri noon–3:30pm.

WHERE TO STAY

Honningsvåg Brygge ★ Finds This hotel in the center of town is the only one with any real character, and the views from its windows are the best along the pier. The family-run establishment was a fish factory until the 1970s, when the owners decided to convert it into a hotel. The conversion was a success, and discerning travelers to the North Cape have been making their way here ever since. The walls, ceiling, and floor are all wood, but the furnishings are contemporary. Bedrooms are small to midsize, each cozy and comfortably furnished.

Vagen 1A, N-9751 Honningsvåg. ✆ **78-47-64-64.** Fax 78-47-64-65. www.hvg-brygge.no. 26 units. NOK1,260 ($252/£126) double; NOK1,800 ($360/£180) suite. Children 11 and under stay free in parent's room. Rates include continental breakfast. AE, DC, MC, V. **Amenities:** Restaurant; bar; laundry service; nonsmoking rooms; rooms for those w/limited mobility. *In room:* No phone.

Rica Bryggen Hotel Opened in 1989, this portside hotel is filled with facilities and accommodations that lure members of the fishing industry in summer and international visitors in winter. It was closed for most of 2008 for massive renovations, with no set opening date, but should be up and running at the time of your visit. An enduring and reliable choice, the two-floor hotel offers midsize bedrooms, most of them with a view of the harbor. Each unit is carpeted and comfortably furnished; some of the suites contain a private sauna. The on-site restaurant is one of the best dining spots in town (see "Where to Dine," below).

Vagen 1, N-9750 Honningsvåg. ✆ **78-47-72-50.** Fax 78-47-72-51. www.rica.no. 42 units. NOK1,200–NOK1,500 ($240–$300/£120–£150) double. Children 11 and under stay free in parent's room. Rates include continental breakfast. AE, DC, MC, V. Closed Dec 21–Jan 2 and 2 weeks at Easter. **Amenities:** Restaurant; bar; sauna; nonsmoking rooms; 1 room for those w/limited mobility. *In room:* TV, minibar, beverage maker.

Rica Hotel Honningsvåg The North Cape's northernmost hotel is located in the central zone, near the quay. Advance reservations are strongly advised. This five-story, yellow-fronted building was enlarged and considerably upgraded in the 1990s. The guest rooms, which have views of the harbor, are functionally furnished with modern but plain pieces. The rooms and bathrooms are a bit small (each comes equipped with a shower), but the beds are comfortable. In this part of the world, you'll happily settle for a roof over your head. Restaurant Carolina (see "Where to Dine," below) is one of the best in town. The hotel also runs an unpretentious grill and offers disco action on Friday and Saturday nights, charging a cover of NOK20 to NOK25 ($4–$5/£2–£2.50). The hotel is entirely nonsmoking.

Storgata 4, N-9751 Honningsvåg. ✆ **78-47-72-20.** Fax 78-47-72-21. www.rica.no. 174 units. NOK1,630–NOK2,080 ($326–$416/£163–£208) double. Rates include buffet breakfast. AE, DC, MC, V. Closed in winter. **Amenities:** Restaurant; lounge; sauna; dry cleaning; rooms for those w/limited mobility. *In room:* TV.

WHERE TO DINE

Corner NORWEGIAN Ever had Arctic pizza? This is the place for it, along with an array of other regional dishes. A lot of fishermen as well as international visitors flock here for good, affordable food. The 1960s building and decor aren't all that much, but the chef will feed you well at a reasonable price. There are no appetizers to speak of, but the main courses are generous. Your best bet is the grilled and locally caught salmon, which comes with fresh vegetables and potatoes. You can also order locally caught grilled cod or halibut. Meat-eaters may find the veal schnitzel satisfying. No matter what main course you choose, finish your meal with a slice of apple pie and ice cream. A live band sometimes entertains in the adjoining bar.

Fiskerveien 2A. ✆ **78-47-63-40.** Main courses NOK130–NOK220 ($26–$44/£13–£22). AE, DC, MC, V. Summer daily 10am–10pm; rest of year Sun–Thurs 10am–8pm, Fri–Sat noon–10pm.

Restaurant at the Rica Bryggen Hotel ★ NORWEGIAN Looking onto a view of the port, this first-rate restaurant remains committed to opening at least 4 days a week (see hours below), and, if business warrants, it opens on weekends as well. Expect a cozy, weather-tight environment where views of the frigid Arctic night might even stimulate your appetite for standard Norwegian fare that typically includes delicacies from the Arctic Ocean and land-based specialties from the Finnmark plateau—whale or reindeer steaks, perhaps with juniper berry sauce; at least three types of fish (usually salmon, catfish, or halibut), depending on what arrived from lower latitudes that week; and tender and well flavored grilled beefsteaks. We suggest you arrive a bit early for a drink in the cozy, intimate lobby bar, where you can chat with fellow Arctic "explorers."

Vagen 1. ✆ **78-47-28-88.** Reservations not necessary. Main courses NOK180–NOK214 ($36–$43/£18–£21). AE, DC, MC, V. Mon–Thurs noon–2pm and 5–11pm.

Restaurant Carolina NORWEGIAN Located in the cellar of the Rica Hotel Honningsvåg, this place is at its most elegant in the winter, when the tour groups are gone. During the summer, the smorgasbord is in the dining room and a la carte dinners are served in the less formal bistro. The cuisine is competently prepared but never exciting; most of the ingredients are shipped in. In the evening, music begins at 8pm, and the place is very popular with locals. It's decorated with old-fashioned photographs of Honningsvåg.

In the Rica Hotel Honningsvåg, Nordkappgata 2–4. ✆ **78-47-23-33.** Reservations recommended. Buffet NOK210 ($42/£21). AE, DC, MC, V. Summer daily 6–10pm.

A TRIP TO THE NORTH CAPE

The **Nordkapp (North Cape)** symbolizes the "top of Europe." In prehistoric times, the North Cape Horn was a Sami place of sacrifice. The North Cape's name used to be Knyskanes, but, in 1553, it was renamed "North Cape" by the Lord Richard Chancellor

Finds Europe's Real Northernmost Point

It comes as a surprise to some visitors that the continent's actual northernmost point is not the North Cape, but **Knivskjelodden,** which is west of the cape. Europe's northernmost point is at 71° 11′08″. You can hike the trail, which is not too difficult if you're in good shape. Wear sturdy boots, of course. Figure on about 5 hours there and back. Once here, you'll have a **panoramic sweep** ★ of the North Cape Plateau. After you've walked the world's northernmost hiking trail, you can sign your name in the hiking association's minute book at Knivskjelodden.

To reach Knivskjelodden, head southwest from the North Cape for 6km (3¾ miles) until you reach a car park. Once at the car park, you still have 3km (2 miles) to go to the northernmost point from the beginning of the Knivskjelodden Track. In all, it's a round-trip of 18km (11 miles) from the North Cape.

of England, who was searching for a sea passage to China. The road to the North Cape is open to traffic from May 1 to October 20.

The first tour ships arrived in 1879. They anchored in Hornvika Bay, and the visitors had to climb 280m (918 ft.) up to the plateau. After the road from Honningsvåg opened in 1956, the flow of tourists turned into a flood. In summer, buses to the North Cape leave daily from outside the tourist office at Fergeveien 4 at Honningsvåg, stop briefly at the ferry terminal across from the Sifi Sommerhotell, and then continue to the visitor center at the North Cape. The one-way passage from Honningsvåg to the North Cape, a travel time of 45 minutes, is NOK120 ($24/£12) adults, NOK80 ($16/£8) children. For more information, call **Veolia Transport** (✆ **78-40-70-00**).

On the road to the Cape is a Sami encampment. It's a bit contrived, but visitors do have an opportunity to go inside one of the tents, and they come away with an idea of how nomadic Sami used to live.

HONNINGSVÅG AFTER DARK

The Irish pub, **Bryggerie,** Nordkappgate 1 (✆ **78-47-26-00**), attracts a varied crowd of patrons who drink endless mugs of beer or listen to recorded music when not conversing. This is one of the world's northernmost microbreweries, and you can sample the home-made brews: Oleanton and Oleanton Christmas. Pizzas and light snacks are available. It's open Monday to Thursday 10am to midnight, Friday and Saturday 10am to 2am, and Sunday 6pm to midnight (closed Sun in winter).

The competitor is **Norden Pub,** Larsfjorda 1 (✆ **78-47-27-11**), a maritime-styled pub and also the leading soccer pub in town. Patrons range in age from 25 to 50. Music, ranging from regional music to Elvis, is live 1 night a week during the summer. Pizza is the snack of choice here. It's open Monday to Thursday 6pm to midnight, Friday and Saturday noon to 2am, and Sunday noon to midnight (closed Mon in winter).

Appendix A: Fast Facts, Toll-Free Numbers & Websites

1 FAST FACTS: NORWAY

AMERICAN EXPRESS There is an office in Oslo. American Express Reisebyrå, Maribores Gate 13 (✆ **22-98-35-00**), is open Monday to Friday 9am to 6pm, Saturday 10am to 4pm.

AREA CODE The international country code for Norway is **47.** If you're calling from outside the country, the city code is **2** for Oslo and **5** for Bergen. When calling within Norway, no area or city codes are needed. Phone numbers have eight digits.

ATM NETWORKS See "Money & Costs," in chapter 3.

BABYSITTERS Hotels can often enlist the help of a housekeeper for "child-minding." Give at least a day's notice, two if you can. You can also contact one of the local tourist offices as well; they often keep a list of available sitters on file.

BUSINESS HOURS Most **banks** are open Monday to Friday from 8:15am to 3:30pm (on Thurs to 5pm), and are closed Saturday and Sunday. The bank at Gardermoen Airport in Oslo is open Monday to Saturday from 6:30am to 8pm and Sunday from 7am to 8pm. Most **businesses** are open Monday to Friday from 9am to 4pm. **Stores** are generally open Monday to Friday from 9am to 5pm (many stay open on Thurs until 6 or 7pm) and Saturday 9am to 1 or 2pm. Sunday closings are observed.

CAR RENTALS See "Toll-Free Numbers & Websites," below.

CASH POINTS See "Money & Costs," in chapter 3.

CURRENCY See "Money & Costs," in chapter 3.

DOCTORS Your embassy or consulate, as well as most hotels, keep a list of recommended English-speaking physicians. See "Embassies & Consulates," below.

DRINKING LAWS Most restaurants, pubs, and bars in Norway are licensed to serve liquor, wine, and beer. The drinking age is 18 for beer and wine and 20 for liquor.

DRIVING RULES See "Getting There and Getting Around," in chapter 3.

DRUGSTORES Drugstores, called *apotek,* are open during normal business hours.

ELECTRICITY Norway uses 220 volts, 30 to 50 cycles, AC, and standard Continental two-pin plugs. Transformers and adapters will be needed with Canadian and American equipment.

EMBASSIES & CONSULATES In case you lose your passport or have some other emergency, contact your embassy in Oslo. The embassy of the **United States** is at Henrik Ibsensgate 48, N-0244 Oslo (✆ **22-44-85-50;** http://norway.usembassy.gov);

United Kingdom, Thomas Heftyesgate 8, N-0244 Oslo (✆ **23-13-27-00;** http://ukinnorway.fco.gov.uk); and **Canada,** Wergelandsveien 7, N-0244 Oslo (✆ **22-99-53-00;** http://norway.gc.ca). The **Irish Embassy** is at Haakon VII's gate 1, N-0244 Oslo (✆ **22-01-72-00;** www.embassyofireland.no). The **Australian Embassy** is closed in Oslo; contact the Australian Consulate, Strandveien 20, N-1324 Lysaker (✆ **67-58-48-48**). The **New Zealand Embassy** is also closed in Oslo; contact the **New Zealand Consulate,** Strandveien 50, N1324 Lysaker (✆ **67-11-00-33**). There is a British consulate in Bergen at Carl Konowsgate 34 (✆ **55-36-78-10**).

EMERGENCIES Throughout Norway, call ✆ **112** for the **police,** ✆ **110** to report a **fire,** or ✆ **113** to request an **ambulance.**

GASOLINE (PETROL) See "Getting There & Getting Around," in chapter 3.

HOLIDAYS Norway celebrates the following public holidays: New Year's Day (Jan 1), Maundy Thursday, Good Friday, Easter, Labor Day (May 1), Ascension Day (mid-May), National Day (May 17), Whitmonday (late May), Christmas (Dec 25), and Boxing Day (Dec 26).

HOSPITALS Nearly all places throughout Norway contain hospitals with English-speaking doctors.

INSURANCE **Medical Insurance** For travel overseas, most U.S. health plans (including Medicare and Medicaid) do not provide coverage, and the ones that do often require you to pay for services up front and reimburse you only after you return home.

As a safety net, you may want to buy travel medical insurance, particularly if you're traveling to a remote or high-risk area where emergency evacuation might be necessary. If you require additional medical insurance, try **MEDEX Assistance** (✆ **410/453-6300;** www.medexassist.com) or **Travel Assistance International** (✆ **800/821-2828;** www.travelassistance.com; for general information on services, call the company's **Worldwide Assistance Services, Inc.** at ✆ **800/777-8710**).

Canadians should check with their provincial health plan offices or contact **Health Canada** (✆ **866/225-0709;** www.hc-sc.gc.ca) to find out the extent of their coverage and what documentation and receipts they must take home in case they are treated overseas.

Travelers from the U.K. should carry their European Health Insurance Card (EHIC), which replaced the E111 form as proof of entitlement to free/reduced cost medical treatment abroad (✆ **0845/606-2030;** www.ehic.org.uk). Note, however, that the EHIC only covers "necessary medical treatment." For repatriation costs, lost money, baggage, or cancellation, travel insurance from a reputable company should always be sought (www.travelinsuranceweb.com).

Travel Insurance The cost of travel insurance varies widely, depending on the destination, the cost and length of your trip, your age and health, and the type of trip you're taking, but expect to pay between 5% and 8% of the vacation itself. You can get estimates from various providers through **InsureMyTrip.com** (✆ **800/487-4722**). Enter your trip cost and dates, your age, and other information, for prices from more than a dozen companies.

U.K. citizens and their families who make more than one trip abroad per year may find an annual travel insurance policy works out cheaper. Check out **Moneysupermarket House** (✆ **0845/345-5708;** www.moneysupermarket.com), which compares prices across a wide range of providers for single- and multitrip policies.

Most big travel agencies offer their own insurance and will probably try to sell you their package when you book a holiday.

Think before you sign. **Britain's Consumers' Association** recommends that you insist on seeing the policy and reading the fine print before buying travel insurance. **The Association of British Insurers** (✆ **020/7600-3333;** www.abi.org.uk) gives advice by phone and publishes "Holiday Insurance," a free guide to policy provisions and prices. You might also shop around for better deals: Try **Columbus Direct** (✆ 0870/033-9988; www.columbusdirect.net).

Trip Cancellation Insurance Trip-cancellation insurance will help you retrieve your money if you have to back out of a trip before departing, if you have to end your trip abruptly, or if your travel supplier goes bankrupt. Trip cancellation traditionally covers such events as sickness, natural disasters, and State Department advisories. The latest news in trip-cancellation insurance is the availability of **expanded hurricane coverage** and the **"any-reason"** cancellation coverage—which costs more but covers cancellations made for any reason. You won't get back 100% of your prepaid trip cost, but you'll be refunded a substantial portion. **TravelSafe** (✆ 888/885-7233; www.travelsafe.com) offers both types of coverage. Expedia also offers any-reason cancellation coverage for its air-hotel packages. For details, contact one of the following recommended insurers: **Access America** (✆ 866/807-3982; www.accessamerica.com); **Travel Guard International** (✆ 800/826-4919; www.travelguard.com); **Travel Insured International** (✆ 800/243-3174; www.travelinsured.com); and **Travelex Insurance Services** (✆ 888/457-4602; www.travelex-insurance.com).

LANGUAGE Norwegians are taught English in grade school. There are two official versions of Norwegian itself, one called *Bokmail,* spoken by about 85% of the population, the lesser known called *Nynorsk.* Nynorsk is identified as "new Norwegian," but it actually isn't. The language is a form of older dialects spoken in rural parts of the country. In the north, the Sami or Lapps have their own language, which is a distant cousin of Finnish.

LAUNDRY & DRY CLEANING Most hotels provide these services. There are coin-operated launderettes and dry cleaners in most Norwegian cities.

LOST & FOUND Be sure to tell all of your credit card companies the minute you discover that your wallet has been lost or stolen, and then file a report at the nearest police precinct. Your credit card company or insurer may require a police report number or a police record of the loss. Most credit card companies have an emergency toll-free number to call if your card is lost or stolen; they may be able to wire you a cash advance immediately or deliver an emergency credit card in a day or two. **Visa's** emergency number outside the U.S. is ✆ **410/581-3836;** call collect. **American Express** cardholders should call collect ✆ **336/393-1111. MasterCard** holders should call collect ✆ **314/542-7111.** If you need emergency cash over the weekend when all banks and American Express offices are closed, you can have money wired to you via **Western Union** (✆ **800/325-6000;** www.westernunion.com).

MAIL Airmail letters or postcards to the United States and Canada cost NOK10.5 ($2.10/£1.10) for up to 20 grams (7/10 oz.). Airmail letters take 7 to 10 days to reach North America. The principal post office in Norway is the Oslo Central Post Office, at Dronningensgate 15, N-0101 Oslo. Mailboxes are vibrant red and are embossed with the trumpet symbol of the postal service. They're found on walls, at chest level, throughout cities and towns. Stamps can be purchased at the post office, at magazine kiosks, or at some stores.

MAPS See "Visitor Information," in chapter 3.

PASSPORTS The websites listed below provide downloadable passport applications as well as the current fees for processing applications. For an up-to-date, country-by-country listing of passport requirements around the world, go to the International Travel Web page of the U.S. Department of State at http://travel.state.gov (click on "International Travel for U.S. Citizens"). International visitors to the U.S. can obtain a visa application at the same website. ***Note:*** Children are required to present a passport when entering the United States at airports. More information on obtaining a passport for a minor can be found at http://travel.state.gov. Allow plenty of time before your trip to apply for a passport; processing normally takes 4 to 6 weeks (3 weeks for expedited service) but can take longer during busy periods (especially spring). And keep in mind that if you need a passport in a hurry, you'll pay a higher processing fee.

For Residents of Australia You can pick up an application from your local post office or any branch of Passports Australia, but you must schedule an interview at the passport office to present your application materials. Call the **Australian Passport Information Service** at ✆ **131-232,** or visit the government website at www.passports.gov.au.

For Residents of Canada Passport applications are available at travel agencies throughout Canada or from the central **Passport Office,** Department of Foreign Affairs and International Trade, Ottawa, ON K1A 0G3 (✆ **800/567-6868;** www.ppt.gc.ca). ***Note:*** Canadian children who travel must have their own passport.

For Residents of Ireland You can apply for a 10-year passport at the **Passport Office,** Setanta Centre, Molesworth Street, Dublin 2 (✆ **01/671-1633;** www.irlgov.ie/iveagh). Those under age 18 and over 65 must apply for a 3-year passport. You can also apply at 1A South Mall, Cork (✆ **21/494-4700**) or at most main post offices.

For Residents of New Zealand You can pick up a passport application at any New Zealand Passports Office or download it from their website. Contact the **Passports Office** at ✆ **0800/225-050** in New Zealand or 04/474-8100, or log on to www.passports.govt.nz.

For Residents of the United Kingdom To pick up an application for a standard 10-year passport (5-yr. passport for children under 16), visit your nearest passport office, major post office, or travel agency or contact the **United Kingdom Passport Service** at ✆ **0870/521-0410** or search its website at www.ukpa.gov.uk.

POLICE Dial ✆ **112** nationwide.

SAFETY See "Safety," in chapter 3.

SMOKING This progressive country bans smoking in public places. Under the law, Norwegians are allowed to smoke in private homes and outdoors. One of the main reasons for law is to protect employees in restaurants and bars, and other places, from secondhand smoke.

TAXES Norway imposes a 19.4% value-added tax (VAT) on most goods and services, which is figured into your final bill. If you buy goods in any store bearing the TAX-FREE sign, you're entitled to a cash refund of up to 18.5% on purchases costing over NOK315 ($63/£32). Ask the shop assistant for a tax-free shopping check. You may not use the articles purchased before leaving Norway, and they must be taken out of the country within 3 months of purchase. Complete the information requested on the back of the check you're given at the store; at your point of departure, report to an area marked by the TAX-FREE sign, not at Customs. Your refund check will be exchanged there in kroner for the amount due you. Refunds are available at airports, ferry and cruise-ship terminals, borders, and train stations.

TELEPHONES The country code for Norway is **47,** but there are no area codes inside Norway. Phone numbers have eight digits. In every case, you dial all eight digits. Toll-free numbers begin with the prefix 800 or 810. If a number has a prefix of 815, it is not toll free, and you must pay NOK1 (20¢/10p) per call. Also, phone numbers that start with the prefix of **82** cost extra.

Norway is the land of the cellular phone. It is estimated that some 90% of all Norwegians carry these phones. If the number you're calling starts with a 4 or a 9, chances are good that you're calling a mobile phone number. It is more expensive to call a mobile phone than it is to call a regular phone.

For information in Norway, dial 1881, or else call 1882 for international phone numbers. Dial **115** if you want to call collect or need help from an operator. Outside of Norway, call **117** for collect or operator assisted calls.

If you wish to place an international call, you can dial directly using the access code of **0,** then the country code and the number: **1** for the United States and Canada; **61** for Australia; **44** for Great Britain, and **64** for New Zealand. Access codes are as follows: **AT&T Direct** (✆ 800/CALL-ATT); **MCI WorldPhone** (✆ 800/19912), and **Sprint International Access** (✆ 800/19877).

To use public phones in Norway, you can purchase a *Tellerskritt* or phone card at most shops and kiosks. These costs NOK40 ($8/£4) to NOK140 ($28/£14). About 50% of the public phones in Norway also take major credit cards.

Some public phones are called "Green Card" phones, and these will only accept phone cards, *Tellerskritt* (see above), or a major credit card.

Others are push-button phones, taking coins of NOK1 (20¢/10p), NOK5 ($1/50p), or NOK10 ($2/£1). Some of these phones will also accept NOK20 ($4/£2) coins. Lift the receiver and listen for the dial tone, then insert the coins and dial the number. Local calls from a pay phone cost NOK3 to NOK5 (60¢–$1/30p–50p).

TIME Norway operates on Central European Time—1 hour ahead of Greenwich Mean Time and 6 hours ahead of Eastern Standard Time. (At noon Eastern Standard Time—say, in New York City—it's 6pm in Norway.) Norway goes on summer time—1 hour earlier—from the end of March until around the end of September.

TIPPING Hotels add a 10% to 15% service charge to your bill, which is sufficient unless someone has performed a special service. Most bellhops get at least 10NOK ($2/£1) per suitcase. Nearly all restaurants add a service charge of up to 15% to your bill. Barbers and hairdressers usually aren't tipped, but toilet attendants expect at least 4NOK (80¢/40p). Taxi drivers throughout Norway don't expect tips unless they handle heavy luggage.

TOILETS All terminals, big-city squares, and the like have public lavatories. In small towns and villages, head for the marketplace. Hygiene standards are usually adequate. If you patronize the toilets in a privately run establishment (such as a cafe), it's polite to buy something, such as a small pastry or coffee.

USEFUL PHONE NUMBERS U.S. Dept. of State Travel Advisory ✆ 202/647-5225 (24 hrs.); **U.S. Passport Agency** ✆ 202/647-0518; **U.S. Centers for Disease Control International Traveler's Hotline** ✆ 404/332-4559.

WATER Tap water is generally safe to drink throughout Norway. Never drink from a mountain stream, fjord, or river, regardless of how clean it might appear.

WEATHER See the temperature chart in section 3, "When to Go," in chapter 3.

2 TOLL-FREE NUMBERS & WEBSITES

MAJOR U.S. AIRLINES

(*flies internationally as well)

American Airlines*
✆ 800/433-7300 (in U.S. and Canada)
✆ 020/7365-0777 (in U.K.)
www.aa.com

Continental Airlines*
✆ 800/523-3273 (in U.S. and Canada)
✆ 084/5607-6760 (in U.K.)
www.continental.com

Delta Air Lines*
✆ 800/221-1212 (in U.S. and Canada)
✆ 084/5600-0950 (in U.K.)
www.delta.com

Northwest Airlines
✆ 800/225-2525 (in U.S. and Canada)
✆ 870/0507-4074 (in U.K.)
www.nwa.com

United Airlines*
✆ 800/864-8331 (in U.S. and Canada)
✆ 084/5844-4777 (in U.K.)
www.united.com

US Airways*
✆ 800/428-4322 (in U.S. and Canada)
✆ 084/5600-3300 (in U.K.)
www.usairways.com

Virgin America*
✆ 877/359-8474
www.virginamerica.com

MAJOR INTERNATIONAL AIRLINES

Air France
✆ 800/237-2747 (in U.S.)
✆ 800/375-8723 (U.S. and Canada)
✆ 087/0142-4343 (in U.K.)
www.airfrance.com

Air New Zealand
✆ 800/262-1234 (in U.S.)
✆ 800/663-5494 (in Canada)
✆ 0800/028-4149 (in U.K.)
www.airnewzealand.com

Alitalia
✆ 800/223-5730 (in U.S.)
✆ 800/361-8336 (in Canada)
✆ 087/0608-6003 (in U.K.)
www.alitalia.com

British Airways
✆ 800/247-9297 (in U.S. and Canada)
✆ 087/0850-9850 (in U.K.)
www.british-airways.com

British Midland
✆ 800/788-0555 (in U.S.)
✆ 877/660-1354 (in Canada)
✆ 0870/6070-555 (in U.K.)
www.flybmi.com

Finnair
✆ 800/950-5000 (in U.S. and Canada)
✆ 087/0241-4411 (in U.K.)
www.finnair.com

Iberia Airlines
✆ 800/722-4642 (in U.S. and Canada)
✆ 087/0609-0500 (in U.K.)
www.iberia.com

Lufthansa
✆ 800/399-5838 (in U.S.)
✆ 800/563-5954 (in Canada)
✆ 087/0837-7747 (in U.K.)
www.lufthansa.com

SAS Scandinavian Airlines
✆ 800/221-2350 (in U.S. and Canada)
✆ 0871/521-2772 (in U.K.)
www.flysas.com

Swiss Air
✆ 877/359-7947 (in U.S. and Canada)
✆ 0845/601-0956 (in U.K.)
www.swiss.com

Virgin Atlantic Airways
✆ 800/821-5438 (in U.S. and Canada)
✆ 087/0574-7747 (in U.K.)
www.virgin-atlantic.com

BUDGET AIRLINES

bmibaby
✆ 870/126-6726 (in U.S. and Canada)
✆ 087/1224-0224 (in U.K.)
www.bmibaby.com

easyJet
✆ 870/600-0000 (in U.S. and Canada)
✆ 090/5560-7777 (in U.K.)
www.easyjet.com

Ryanair
✆ 353/01-249-7791 (in U.S. and Canada)
✆ 081/830-3030 (in Ireland)
✆ 087/1246-000 (in U.K.)
www.ryanair.com

SAS Scandinavian Airlines Norge
✆ +47/91-50-54-00
www.sas.no

Widerøe
✆ +47/81-00-12-00
www.wideroe.no

CAR RENTAL AGENCIES

Alamo
✆ 800/GO-ALAMO [462-5266] (in U.S. and Canada)
www.alamo.com

Auto Europe
✆ 888/223-5555 (in U.S. and Canada)
✆ 0800/2235-5555 (in U.K.)
www.autoeurope.com

Avis
✆ 800/331-1212 (in U.S. and Canada)
✆ 084/4581-8181 (in U.K.)
www.avis.com

Budget
✆ 800/527-0700 (in U.S.)
✆ 800/268-8900 (in Canada)
✆ 087/0156-5656 (in U.K.)
www.budget.com

Hertz
✆ 800/654-3001 (in U.S. and Canada)
✆ 087/0844-8844 (in U.K.)
www.hertz.com

Kemwel
✆ 877/820-0668
www.kemwel.com

National
✆ 800/CAR-RENT (227-7368)
www.nationalcar.com

Best Western International
✆ 800/780-7234 (in U.S. and Canada)
✆ 0800/393-130 (in U.K.)
www.bestwestern.com

Clarion Collection by Choice Hotels
✆ 877/424-6423 (in U.S. and Canada)
✆ 0800/444-444 (in U.K.)
www.choicehotels.com

Clarion Hotels
✆ 877/424-6423 (in U.S. and Canada)
✆ 0800/444-444 (in U.K.)
www.choicehotels.com

Comfort Hotels
✆ 877/424-6423 (in U.S. and Canada)
✆ 0800/444-444 (in U.K.)
www.choicehotels.com

First Hotels
✆ +47/23-11-60-80
www.firsthotels.com

Quality Hotels and Resorts
✆ 877/424-6423 (in U.S. and Canada)
✆ 0800/444-444 (in U.K.)
www.choicehotels.com

Radisson Hotels & Resorts
✆ 888/201-1718 (in U.S. and Canada)
✆ 0800/374-411 (in U.K.)
www.radisson.com

Rica Hotels
✆ +47/66-85-45-60
www.rica-hotels.com

Scandic Hotels
✆ +46/085-175-1720
www.scandichotels.com

Sheraton Hotels & Resorts
✆ 800/325-3535 (in U.S.)
✆ 800/543-4300 (in Canada)
✆ 0800/3253-5353 (in U.K.)
www.starwoodhotels.com

Thon Hotels
✆ +47/23-08-02-00
www.thonhotels.com

Appendix B: Useful Terms & Phrases

When traveling, it always helps to know a few basic phrases. Here's a list of some Norwegian phrases for expressing your needs.

1 BASIC NORWEGIAN VOCABULARY & PHRASES

English	Norwegian	Pronunciation
Yes	Ja	yaa
No	Nei	næi
Thank you	Takk	tahk
Thank you very much	Mange takk	*mahn*-ger tahk
You're welcome	Inger årsak	*in*-gern *aw*-shaak
Please	Vær så snill	vær saw snil
Excuse me	Unnskyld meg	ewnshewl mæi
Hello	Hallo	hah *loo*
Goodbye	Adjø	ah-*dyur*
Good morning	God morgen	goo-*maw*-ern
Good afternoon	God dag	goo-*daag*
Good night	God natt	goo-*naht*
I do not understand	Jeg forstår ikke	yæi fo-*shtwr*-ikker
Does anyone here speak English?	Er det noen her som snakker engelsk?	ær del *noo*-ern hær som *snah*-kerr *ehng*-erlsk
Do you speak English?	Snakker du engelsk?	*snah*-kerr dew *ehng*-erlsk
How do you pronounce this?	Hvordan uttaler du?	*voo*-rdahn *ew*-tah-lerr dette *deh*-ter
I'm lost	Jeg hat gått meg bort	yær haa got mæi boot
How are you?	Hvordan star det til?	*voo*-rdahn *stawr deh* til
Can you tell me	Kan du si meg	kahn dew see mæi
Which bus goes to	Hvilken buss går til	*Vil*-kern bewss gawr til
I	Jeg	yær
We	Vi	vee
He	Han	hahn
She	Hun	hun

English	Norwegian	Pronunciation
It	Den	den
They	De	duh
You (plural)	Dere	dare
Good	Bra	braa
Bad	Dårlig	*daw*-rli
Wife	Kone	*koo*-ner
Husband	Mann	mahn
Daughter	Datter	*dah*-terr
Son	Sønn	surn
Mother	Mor	moor
Father	Far	faar
Friend	Venn	vehn
Open	Åpen	*aw*-per
Shut	Stengt	stehngt
My name is	Mitt navn er	mit nshvn ær
Pleased to meet you	Hyggelig å treffes	*hew*-gerli aw *treh*-ferss
Where are the toilets?	Hvor er toilette?	voor ær tooah-*leh*-ter

2 RESTAURANT TERMS

English	Norwegian	Pronunciation
Tea/coffee shop	Konditori	koondittoo-*ree*
Restaurant	Restaurant	reh-stewr-*ahng*
Breakfast	Frokost	*froo*-kost
Bacon and eggs	Egg og bacon	ehg og *bae*-ikern
Bread	Brød	brur
Butter	Smør	smurr
Cereal	Frokostblandi	*froo*-kost-blahn-ing
Cheese	Ost	oost
Coffee	Kaffe	*kah*-fer
Grapefruit	Grapefrukt	*grayp*-frewkt
Juice	Juice	yewss
Lemon	Sitron	si-*troon*
Milk	Melk	mehlk
Orange juice	Appelsinjuice	ah-perl-*seen*-yewss
Pepper	Pepper	*peh*-per
Salt	Salt	sahlt
Sausage	Pølse	*purl*-ser
Soft drink	Leskedrikk	*lehs*-ker-dirk
Tea	Te	tay
Omelet	Omelett	oo-mer-*leht*

English	Norwegian	Pronunciation
Lunch	Lunsj	lurnsh
Dinner	Middag	*mid*-dahg
Open sandwiches	Smørbrød	*smurr*-brur
Soup	Supper	sew-per
Fish	Fisk	fisk
Fish soup	Fiskesuppe	*fis*-ker-sew-per
Salad	Salater	sah-*laa*-ter
Mixed salad	Blandet salat	*blahn*-ert sah-*laat*
Shellfish (seafood)	Skalldyr	*skahl*-dewr
Beef	Oksekjøtt	*ook*-ser-khurt
Chicken	Kylling	*khew*-ling
Lamb	Lammekjøtt	*lah*-mer-khurt
Pork	Svinekjøtt	*svee*-ner-khurt
Reindeer	Reinsdyr	*racins*-dewr
Veal	Kalvekjøtt	*kahl*-ver-khurt
Boiled	Kokt	kokt
Beaded	Panert	pah-*nayrt*
Fried	Sekt	stehkt
Grilled	Grillet	*grill*-ert
Poached	Pochert	poo-*shayrt*
Smoked	Røkt	rurkt
Beef stew	Lapskaus	lahps kouss
Hamburgers with onions	Kjøttkaker med løk	*khurt*-kaa-kerr mehd lurk
Lamb and cabbage stew	Fårikål	*fawr*-ikawl
Noodles	Nudler	*newd*-lerr
Apple	Eple	*ehp*-ler
Asparagus	Asparges	ah-*spahr*-ggers
Banana	Banan	bah-*naan*
Beans	Bønner	*bur*-nerr
Beetroot	Rødbeter	*rur*-beh-terr
Cabbage	Kål	kawl
Carrots	Gulrøtter	*gewl*-rur-terr
Cauliflower	Blomkål	*blom*-kawl
Cucumber	Agurk	ah-*gewrk*
Corn	Mais	maayss
Grapes	Druer	*drew*-err
Lettuce	Hodesalat	*hoo*-der-sah-laat
Melon	Melon	meh-*loon*
Onions	Løk	lurk
Orange	Appelsin	ahper-*lseen*

English	Norwegian	Pronunciation
Peach	Fersken	*faesh*-kern
Pear	Pære	*pae*-rer
Peas	Erter	*aer*-terr
Pineapple	Ananas	*ah*-nah-nahss
Potato	Potet	poo-*tay*-t
Baked potato	Bakt potet	bahkt poo-*tay*-t
Boiled potato	Kokte potet	*kook*-ter poo-*tay*-t
French fries	Pommes frites	pom frit
Red cabbage	Rødkål	*rur*-kawl
Spinach	Spinat	spi-*nnaat*
Strawberries	Jordbæ	*yoor*-bær
Tomatoes	Tomater	too-*maa*-terr
Watermelon	Vannmelon	*vahn*-meh-loon
Beer	Øl	url
Wine	Vin	veen
Bill, please	Regningen takk	*raei*-nin-gern tahk
Can I pay with this credit card?	Kan jeg betale med dette kredittkorter?	kahn yæi ber-*taa*-ler mehd *deh*-ter kreh-*dit*-kor-ter

INDEX

See also Accommodations and Restaurant indexes, below.

General Index

ACCOMMODATIONS

Restaurants

Frommer's® Complete Travel Guides

Alaska
Amalfi Coast
American Southwest
Amsterdam
Argentina
Arizona
Atlanta
Australia
Austria
Bahamas
Barcelona
Beijing
Belgium, Holland & Luxembourg
Belize
Bermuda
Boston
Brazil
British Columbia & the Canadian Rockies
Brussels & Bruges
Budapest & the Best of Hungary
Buenos Aires
Calgary
California
Canada
Cancún, Cozumel & the Yucatán
Cape Cod, Nantucket & Martha's Vineyard
Caribbean
Caribbean Ports of Call
Carolinas & Georgia
Chicago
Chile & Easter Island
China
Colorado
Costa Rica
Croatia
Cuba
Denmark
Denver, Boulder & Colorado Springs
Eastern Europe
Ecuador & the Galapagos Islands
Edinburgh & Glasgow
England
Europe
Europe by Rail
Florence, Tuscany & Umbria
Florida
France
Germany
Greece
Greek Islands
Guatemala
Hawaii
Hong Kong
Honolulu, Waikiki & Oahu
India
Ireland
Israel
Italy
Jamaica
Japan
Kauai
Las Vegas
London
Los Angeles
Los Cabos & Baja
Madrid
Maine Coast
Maryland & Delaware
Maui
Mexico
Montana & Wyoming
Montréal & Québec City
Morocco
Moscow & St. Petersburg
Munich & the Bavarian Alps
Nashville & Memphis
New England
Newfoundland & Labrador
New Mexico
New Orleans
New York City
New York State
New Zealand
Northern Italy
Norway
Nova Scotia, New Brunswick & Prince Edward Island
Oregon
Paris
Peru
Philadelphia & the Amish Country
Portugal
Prague & the Best of the Czech Republic
Provence & the Riviera
Puerto Rico
Rome
San Antonio & Austin
San Diego
San Francisco
Santa Fe, Taos & Albuquerque
Scandinavia
Scotland
Seattle
Seville, Granada & the Best of Andalusia
Shanghai
Sicily
Singapore & Malaysia
South Africa
South America
South Florida
South Korea
South Pacific
Southeast Asia
Spain
Sweden
Switzerland
Tahiti & French Polynesia
Texas
Thailand
Tokyo
Toronto
Turkey
USA
Utah
Vancouver & Victoria
Vermont, New Hampshire & Maine
Vienna & the Danube Valley
Vietnam
Virgin Islands
Virginia
Walt Disney World® & Orlando
Washington, D.C.
Washington State

Frommer's® Day by Day Guides

Amsterdam
Barcelona
Beijing
Boston
Cancun & the Yucatan
Chicago
Florence & Tuscany
Hong Kong
Honolulu & Oahu
London
Maui
Montréal
Napa & Sonoma
New York City
Paris
Provence & the Riviera
Rome
San Francisco
Venice
Washington D.C.

Pauline Frommer's Guides: See More. Spend Less.

Alaska
Hawaii
Italy
Las Vegas
London
New York City
Paris
Walt Disney World®
Washington D.C.

Frommer's® Portable Guides

Acapulco, Ixtapa & Zihuatanejo
Amsterdam
Aruba, Bonaire & Curacao
Australia's Great Barrier Reef
Bahamas
Big Island of Hawaii
Boston
California Wine Country
Cancún
Cayman Islands
Charleston
Chicago
Dominican Republic
Florence
Las Vegas
Las Vegas for Non-Gamblers
London
Maui
Nantucket & Martha's Vineyard
New Orleans
New York City
Paris
Portland
Puerto Rico
Puerto Vallarta, Manzanillo & Guadalajara
Rio de Janeiro
San Diego
San Francisco
Savannah
St. Martin, Sint Maarten, Anguila & St. Bart's
Turks & Caicos
Vancouver
Venice
Virgin Islands
Washington, D.C.
Whistler

Frommer's® Cruise Guides

Alaska Cruises & Ports of Call
Cruises & Ports of Call
European Cruises & Ports of Call

Frommer's® National Park Guides

Algonquin Provincial Park
Banff & Jasper
Grand Canyon
National Parks of the American West
Rocky Mountain
Yellowstone & Grand Teton
Yosemite and Sequoia & Kings Canyon
Zion & Bryce Canyon

Frommer's® With Kids Guides

Chicago
Hawaii
Las Vegas
London
National Parks
New York City
San Francisco
Toronto
Walt Disney World® & Orlando
Washington, D.C.

Frommer's® PhraseFinder Dictionary Guides

Chinese
French
German
Italian
Japanese
Spanish

Suzy Gershman's Born to Shop Guides

France
Hong Kong, Shanghai & Beijing
Italy
London
New York
Paris
San Francisco
Where to Buy the Best of Everything.

Frommer's® Best-Loved Driving Tours

Britain
California
France
Germany
Ireland
Italy
New England
Northern Italy
Scotland
Spain
Tuscany & Umbria

The Unofficial Guides®

Adventure Travel in Alaska
Beyond Disney
California with Kids
Central Italy
Chicago
Cruises
Disneyland®
England
Hawaii
Ireland
Las Vegas
London
Maui
Mexico's Best Beach Resorts
Mini Mickey
New Orleans
New York City
Paris
San Francisco
South Florida including Miami & the Keys
Walt Disney World®
Walt Disney World® for Grown-ups
Walt Disney World® with Kids
Washington, D.C.

Special-Interest Titles

Athens Past & Present
Best Places to Raise Your Family
Cities Ranked & Rated
500 Places to Take Your Kids Before They Grow Up
Frommer's Best Day Trips from London
Frommer's Best RV & Tent Campgrounds in the U.S.A.
Frommer's Exploring America by RV
Frommer's NYC Free & Dirt Cheap
Frommer's Road Atlas Europe
Frommer's Road Atlas Ireland
Retirement Places Rated